*Kamwaldeep Phoolka
Student Paralegal*

SMALL CLAIMS COURT
Procedure and Practice
SECOND EDITION

S. Patricia Knight

emp

2010
Emond Montgomery Publications Limited
Toronto, Canada

Emond Montgomery Publications Limited
60 Shaftesbury Avenue
Toronto ON M4T 1A3
http://www.emp.ca

Printed in Canada.

Reprinted November 2012.

We acknowledge the financial support of the Government of Canada through the Canada Book Fund for our publishing activities.

The events and characters depicted in this book are fictitious. Any similarity to actual persons, living or dead, is purely coincidental.

Acquisitions and development editor: Bernard Sandler

Marketing director: Christine Davidson

Indexer: Paula Pike

Proofreader: David Handelsman

Production and copy editor: Cindy Fujimoto

Text designer: Tara Wells

Cover designer: John Vegter

Library and Archives Canada Cataloguing in Publication

Knight, S. Patricia
    Small claims court : procedure and practice / S. Patricia Knight. — 2nd ed.

Includes index.
ISBN 978-1-55239-392-5

    1. Small claims courts—Ontario.   2. Civil procedure—Ontario.   3. Actions and defenses—Canada.   I. Title.

KEO1090.K55 2010   347.713'04   C2010-904997-7
KF8769.K55 2010

This book is dedicated to Jean Higgins,
Dr. Sheila Cheeseman, and Dr. Michael Cheeseman.

Acknowledgments

I would like to thank Cindy Fujimoto and David Handelsman for their patience and painstaking editing as this book went through many changes.

Contents

CHAPTER TWO
You and Your Client

CHAPTER THREE
Acting for the Plaintiff: Preliminary Considerations

CHAPTER FOUR
Acting for the Plaintiff: Commencing the Action

CHAPTER FIVE
Acting for the Plaintiff: Default Proceedings

CHAPTER SIX
Acting for the Defendant

CHAPTER SEVEN
Motions

CHAPTER TEN

Motions for New Trial and Appeals

CHAPTER ELEVEN

Enforcing Small Claims Court Judgments

Introduction to Small Claims Court

LEARNING OBJECTIVES

After reading this chapter, you will understand:

- What type of action is heard in Small Claims Court
- What the *Courts of Justice Act* is and what it does
- Small Claims Court monetary jurisdiction
- Who may hear and decide Small Claims Court matters
- The purpose of Small Claims Court
- Who may represent a party in Small Claims Court
- Orders for payment of money and costs in Small Claims Court
- Appeals of Small Claims Court trial decisions
- How to read the *Small Claims Court Rules*

WHAT IS SMALL CLAIMS COURT?

Small Claims Court is a civil trial court. In Ontario, Small Claims Court is a division of the Superior Court of Justice.

Unlike the Ontario Court of Justice and the Trial Division of the Superior Court of Justice, Small Claims Court has no criminal or quasi-criminal jurisdiction. **Jurisdiction** is a court's area of legal authority. Small Claims Court hears civil actions only—that is, actions in which one party sues another party for some form of private relief. In Small Claims Court, the relief sought is usually money. Small Claims Court also has jurisdiction to make orders for the return of property.

For legal purposes, an **action** is a proceeding brought in a court. The persons involved in the action or proceeding are called the **parties** to the action. Parties to a civil action are also known as **litigants** because they are engaged in civil litigation.

> ## BOX 1.1
>
> ### Who May Litigate?
>
> When we think of the word "person," most of us think of an individual human being. However, for legal purposes, a corporation is a person, and may be named as a party to an action along with individuals.
>
> Other business entities, such as sole proprietorships, partnerships, and unincorporated organizations, may also be named as parties in an action.
>
> In civil actions, the parties to the proceeding usually take the stand as witnesses at the trial of the matter (if it goes all the way to trial). A sole proprietorship, partnership, or corporation cannot take the stand, so the owners, senior officers, or directors will give evidence on its behalf.

The party who commences the action is called the **plaintiff**. The party who defends the action is called the **defendant**. There may be multiple plaintiffs, or co-plaintiffs, in an action, so long as the relief they are seeking from the defendant is based on a common set of facts or issues. There may be multiple defendants, or co-defendants, in an action, if the plaintiff has reason to believe that one or more persons may be liable for the relief sought.

> ## BOX 1.2
>
> ### Naming Multiple Plaintiffs or Defendants
>
> On the plaintiff's claim (Form 7A) there is space on the first page for the name, address, and telephone number of one plaintiff and his legal representative, and one defendant and his legal representative. What do you do if there are two plaintiffs, or more than one defendant? This may happen in a debt collection proceeding—for example, where a credit card company is suing a husband and wife who both use the same credit card and are both liable for the unpaid balance on the account.
>
> When this happens, tick off the box marked "Additional plaintiff(s) listed on attached Form 1A" or "Additional defendant(s) listed on attached Form 1A." Then fill in the information about the additional parties on Form 1A—Additional Parties, or a Form 1A.1—Additional Debtors, and insert it in Form 7A after page 1. See figures 1.1, 1.2, and 1.3 below. See also Small Claims Court Rule 1.06(3)—Additional Parties.

A Small Claims Court plaintiff may also be called a **claimant**. A claimant is a person who commences a claim. In Small Claims Court, claimants are charged filing fees according to the frequency of their court use.

An **infrequent claimant** is anyone who files fewer than 10 Small Claims Court claims in a Small Claims Court office on or after January 1 in any calendar year. Infrequent claimants are charged $75.00 to file a claim.

A **frequent claimant** is anyone who files 10 or more claims in a Small Claims Court office on or after January 1 in any calendar year. A frequent claimant is charged $145.00 per claim.

FIGURE 1.1 Plaintiff's Claim (Form 7A)

ONTARIO

Superior Court of Justice
Cour supérieure de justice

Plaintiff's Claim
Demande du demandeur
Form / *Formule* 7A Ont. Reg. No. / *Régl. de l'Ont.* : 258/98

Small Claims Court / *Cour des petites créances de*   Claim No. / *N° de la demande*

Seal / *Sceau*

Address / *Adresse*

Phone number / *Numéro de téléphone*

Plaintiff No. 1 / *Demandeur n° 1*   ☐ Additional plaintiff(s) listed on attached Form 1A.
Le ou les demandeurs additionnels sont mentionnés sur la formule 1A ci-jointe.   ☐ Under 18 years of age. *Moins de 18 ans.*

Last name, or name of company / *Nom de famille ou nom de la compagnie*		
First name / *Premier prénom*	Second name / *Deuxième prénom*	Also known as / *Également connu(e) sous le nom de*
Address (street number, apt., unit) / *Adresse (numéro et rue, app., unité)*		
City/Town / *Cité/ville*	Province	Phone no. / *N° de téléphone*
Postal code / *Code postal*		Fax no. / *N° de télécopieur*
Representative / *Représentant(e)*		LSUC # / *N° du BHC*
Address (street number, apt., unit) / *Adresse (numéro et rue, app., unité)*		
City/Town / *Cité/ville*	Province	Phone no. / *N° de téléphone*
Postal code / *Code postal*		Fax no. / *N° de télécopieur*

Defendant No. 1 / *Défendeur n° 1*   ☐ Additional defendant(s) listed on attached Form 1A.
Le ou les défendeurs additionnels sont mentionnés sur la formule 1A ci-jointe.   ☐ Under 18 years of age. *Moins de 18 ans.*

Last name, or name of company / *Nom de famille ou nom de la compagnie*		
First name / *Premier prénom*	Second name / *Deuxième prénom*	Also known as / *Également connu(e) sous le nom de*
Address (street number, apt., unit) / *Adresse (numéro et rue, app., unité)*		
City/Town / *Cité/ville*	Province	Phone no. / *N° de téléphone*
Postal code / *Code postal*		Fax no. / *N° de télécopieur*
Representative / *Représentant(e)*		LSUC # / *N° du BHC*
Address (street number, apt., unit) / *Adresse (numéro et rue, app., unité)*		
City/Town / *Cité/ville*	Province	Phone no. / *N° de téléphone*

FIGURE 1.2   Additional Parties (Form 1A)

ONTARIO
Superior Court of Justice   PAGE 1A   **Additional Parties**
Cour supérieure de justice   *Parties additionnelles*
Form / *Formule* 1A Ont. Reg. No. / *Règl. de l'Ont.* : 258/98

Claim No. / *N° de la demande*

☐ **Plaintiff No. /** *Demandeur n°*   ☐ **Defendant No. /** *Défendeur n°*

Last name, or name of company / *Nom de famille ou nom de la compagnie*		
First name / *Premier prénom*	Second name / *Deuxième prénom*	Also known as / *Également connu(e) sous le nom de*
Address (street number, apt., unit) / *Adresse (numéro et rue, app., unité)*		
City/Town / *Cité/ville* Province		Phone no. / *N° de téléphone*
Postal code / *Code postal*		Fax no. / *N° de télécopieur*
Representative / *Représentant(e)*		LSUC # / *N° du BHC*
Address (street number, apt., unit) / *Adresse (numéro et rue, app., unité)*		
City/Town / *Cité/ville* Province		Phone no. / *N° de téléphone*
Postal code / *Code postal*		Fax no. / *N° de télécopieur*

☐ **Plaintiff No. /** *Demandeur n°*   ☐ **Defendant No. /** *Défendeur n°*

Last name, or name of company / *Nom de famille ou nom de la compagnie*		
First name / *Premier prénom*	Second name / *Deuxième prénom*	Also known as / *Également connu(e) sous le nom de*
Address (street number, apt., unit) / *Adresse (numéro et rue, app., unité)*		

FIGURE 1.3   Additional Debtors (Form 1A.1)

ONTARIO
Superior Court of Justice   **Additional Debtors**
Cour supérieure de justice   *Débiteurs additionnels*
Form / *Formule* 1A.1 Ont. Reg. No. / *Règl. de l'Ont.* : 258/98

Claim No. / *N° de la demande*

If a debtor has "also known as names", list each also known as name in a separate set of boxes below. / *Si un débiteur a d'autres noms sous lesquels il est également connu, indiquez chacun de ces noms ci-dessous dans un ensemble séparé de cases.*

Last name of debtor, or name of company / *Nom de famille du débiteur/de la débitrice ou nom de la compagnie*		
First name / *Premier prénom*	Second name / *Deuxième prénom*	Third name / *Troisième prénom*

Last name of debtor, or name of company / *Nom de famille du débiteur/de la débitrice ou nom de la compagnie*		
First name / *Premier prénom*	Second name / *Deuxième prénom*	Third name / *Troisième prénom*

Last name of debtor, or name of company / *Nom de famille du débiteur/de la débitrice ou nom de la compagnie*		
First name / *Premier prénom*	Second name / *Deuxième prénom*	Third name / *Troisième prénom*

ACCESS TO JUSTICE

Litigation can be an expensive and time-consuming method of resolving a dispute. In the civil courts, the parties themselves bear the costs of litigating. They must pay for legal representation and all other expenses connected with advancing the matter through the court. A civil proceeding in the Superior Court of Justice is governed by complex procedural rules and requirements. This makes it very difficult to advance or defend an action in the Superior Court of Justice without a lawyer's assistance. In other words, your access to justice depends on whether or not you can afford a lawyer. At the same time, the complicated rules and procedures drive the cost of legal representation up. A plaintiff who is suing for $100,000.00 does not want to have to pay a lawyer $75,000.00 to recover that amount, but that can happen in a lengthy proceeding that is fiercely contested.

Small Claims Court is intended to improve the public's access to justice by providing a forum for proceedings where the parties are likely to be self-represented and the amount being claimed is comparatively modest—that is, proceedings where it is not cost-effective for the parties to hire a lawyer to represent them. Small Claims rules and procedures have been simplified with a view to resolving these matters expeditiously. The court's simplified procedures are also intended to be easily understood by self-represented parties.

Keep in mind that "simple" is a relative term. Something that is simple for a person with some legal background and experience can be very confusing and intimidating for a person without that knowledge. Completing a plaintiff's claim can be extremely difficult for someone who has no experience with legal drafting or whose first language is not English. Issuing the claim and complying with the rules for proper service are almost impossible for such a plaintiff.

Another thing to consider is the time commitment required by any legal proceeding. Often a self-represented party who is working full time at a day job cannot take three hours off to attend on a motion for set aside or a pretrial—let alone take a whole day off to attend at trial.

It is arguable that, in spite of the best intentions of legislators and the Civil Rules Committee, many people who appear in Small Claims Court would prefer to have legal representation if they had the resources to pay for it and if it were cost-effective to do so. Section 26 of the *Courts of Justice Act* states that a party may be represented in a proceeding in Small Claims Court by a person authorized by the *Law Society Act* to represent the party—that is, a licensee who is a lawyer or a paralegal, or a student-at-law working under the supervision of a lawyer. Small Claims Court presents excellent opportunities for paralegals, who can provide legal services that are often more affordable than those of a lawyer. For litigants who are self-represented, either because they cannot afford legal representation or for other reasons, Small Claims Court provides a comparatively inexpensive and user-friendly forum.

Fee Waiver

Parties who cannot afford to pay court fees may apply for a fee waiver. The fee waiver forms can be found at http://www.attorneygeneral.jus.gov.on.ca, the Attorney General's website, or can be obtained from the Small Claims Court office. To find the forms at the Attorney General's website, select the "Court Services" link. In the "Court Fees" section, select "A Guide to Fee Waiver Requests." See figure 1.4 below.

FIGURE 1.4   **Requesting a Fee Waiver**

Jury Duty

- <u>General Information about the Jury System in Ontario</u>
- <u>Frequently Asked Questions about Jury Duty</u>
- <u>General Information about the Jury Questionnaire</u>
- <u>Frequently Asked Questions about the Jury Questionnaire</u>

Policies and Procedures

- <u>Directives to Court Staff on Access to Documents</u>

Court Fees

- <u>A Guide to Fee Waiver Requests</u>
- <u>Superior Court of Justice and Court of Appeal Fees</u>
  - <u>Estate Matters</u>
  - <u>Action under the *Construction Lien Act*</u>
  - <u>Repair and Storage Liens Act</u>
  - <u>Official Examiner</u>
- <u>Prejudgment and postjudgment interest rates pursuant to section 127 of the *Courts of Justice Act*, R.S.O 1990, c. C. 43</u>
- <u>Superior Court of Justice - Sheriff's Fees</u>
- <u>Small Claims Court Fees and Allowances</u>
- <u>Superior Court of Justice - Family Court Fees</u>
- <u>Ontario Court of Justice - Fees</u>

HOME | CONTACT | ACCESSIBILITY | WEB HELP
FRANÇAIS | ONTARIO.CA

THE COURTS OF JUSTICE ACT

The *Courts of Justice Act* is the statute that sets out the court system in Ontario. It governs all courts from the Ontario Court of Justice to the Court of Appeal for Ontario. The procedural rules for Ontario courts, as well as other matters such as the salaries of provincial court judges and the monetary jurisdiction of Small Claims Court, are contained in the regulations to the *Courts of Justice Act*.

The general principles governing Small Claims Court are set out at ss. 22 to 33.1 of the *Courts of Justice Act*. Anyone who practises in Small Claims Court should be thoroughly familiar with these principles.

BOX 1.3

What Is the Courts of Justice Act?

The *Courts of Justice Act* is a statute. Statutes are laws that are put in place by the federal Parliament in Ottawa, or by the legislatures of the provinces and territories.

Federal statutes apply to all of Canada. Provincial or territorial statutes apply only to the province or territory in which they were passed. The *Courts of Justice Act* is a provincial statute that applies only to the court system in Ontario. Other provinces have similar legislation. Because the court system in each province is set up by that province's legislature, the courts in each province often have different names and different (though similar) procedural rules. For example, in Brit-ish Columbia, the superior trial court is called the British Columbia Supreme Court. In Alberta, the superior trial court is called the Alberta Court of Queen's Bench.

In Ontario, the superior trial court is called the Ontario Superior Court of Justice. The Small Claims Court is a branch of the Ontario Superior Court of Justice.

When reading statutes, you will often come across the Latin word "Idem." See, for example, the heading for s. 22(2) of the *Courts of Justice Act*. "Idem" means "the same as something previously mentioned." In other words, the content of subsection 22(2) deals with the same subject matter as subsection 22(1).

MONETARY JURISDICTION OF SMALL CLAIMS COURT

General

Monetary jurisdiction is the amount of money that the court may order one party to pay another, not including interest and costs. Interest, and how it is calculated, will be discussed in later chapters.

Costs are amounts that the court orders one party to pay to the other party. Costs are awarded in addition to any other relief, monetary or otherwise, that may be ordered. The general rule is that costs (legal fees and disbursements) are awarded to the successful party, to reimburse the successful party for expenses incurred in the course of litigation.

Legal fees are what you are charged by a lawyer or paralegal for legal representation and advice.

Disbursements are the out-of-pocket expenses of a legal proceeding. Disbursements include court filing fees, charges for service of documents, photocopying charges, postage, courier charges, etc.

In Small Claims Court, court filing fees tend to be modest, in comparison to other civil trial courts. For example, it costs $75.00 for an infrequent claimant (someone who files fewer than 10 claims per calendar year in a Small Claims Court office) to file a plaintiff's claim in Small Claims Court. By contrast, it costs $181.00 to file a statement of claim or notice of action in the Superior Court of Justice. It costs $157.00 to file an application for divorce in Family Court, and $280.00 to place the application for divorce on the list for hearing (trial).

Small Claims Court fees and allowances can be found in the regulations to the *Administration of Justice Act*. Links to these regulations can also be found at the At-torney General's website under "Court Fees" on the Court Services page (see figure 1.4 above), and at the e-Laws website (see figure 1.5 below). You will find a sched-ule of Small Claims Court fees at appendix 1.1 to this chapter.

FIGURE 1.5   Finding Court Fees and Allowances in e-Laws

Current Consolidated Law (HTML)	Download	Legislative History
⊕ Absconding Debtors Act, R.S.O. 1990, c. A.2	📄	H
⊕ Absentees Act, R.S.O. 1990, c. A.3	📄	H
⊕ Accessibility for Ontarians with Disabilities Act, 2005, S.O. 2005, c. 11	📄	H
⊕ Accumulations Act, R.S.O. 1990, c. A.5	📄	H
⊕ Adams Mine Lake Act, 2004, S.O. 2004, c. 6	📄	H
⊕ Adjudicative Tribunals Accountability, Governance and Appointments Act, 2009, S.O. 2009, c. 33, Sched. 5	📄	H
⊖ Administration of Justice Act, R.S.O. 1990, c. A.6	📄	H
O. Reg. 587/91 COURT REPORTERS AND COURT MONITORS	📄	H
O. Reg. 2/05 FEE WAIVER	📄	H
R.R.O. 1990, Reg. 6 FEES AND EXPENSES - SHERIFF'S OFFICERS, PROCESS SERVERS, ESCORTS AND MUNICIPAL POLICE FORCES	📄	H
R.R.O. 1990, Reg. 4 FEES AND EXPENSES OF JURORS AND CROWN WITNESSES	📄	H
R.R.O. 1990, Reg. 10 INVESTIGATION FEE - OFFICIAL GUARDIAN	📄	H
R.R.O. 1990, Reg. 11 KILOMETRE ALLOWANCES	📄	H
O. Reg. 451/98 MEDIATORS' FEES (RULE 24.1, RULES OF CIVIL PROCEDURE)	📄	H
O. Reg. 43/05 MEDIATORS' FEES (RULE 75.1, RULES OF CIVIL PROCEDURE)	📄	H
O. Reg. 210/07 ONTARIO COURT OF JUSTICE - FEES	📄	H
O. Reg. 294/92 SHERIFFS - FEES		H
O. Reg. 432/93 SMALL CLAIMS COURT - FEES AND ALLOWANCES	📄	H
O. Reg. 417/95 SUPERIOR COURT OF JUSTICE - FAMILY COURT - FEES	📄	H
O. Reg. 293/92 SUPERIOR COURT OF JUSTICE AND COURT OF APPEAL - FEES	📄	H
⊕ Age of Majority and Accountability Act R.S.O. 1990, c. A.7	📄	H

Maximum Recoverable Amount

The monetary jurisdiction of Small Claims Court in Ontario is the maximum amount of money a party may recover in a Small Claims action in Ontario, exclusive of interest and costs. It is established by s. 23(1) of the *Courts of Justice Act*, and by regulations published pursuant to ss. 23 and 53. Effective January 1, 2010, the monetary jurisdiction of Small Claims Court throughout Ontario, as set out in O. Reg. 626/00, is $25,000.00, exclusive of interest and costs. "Exclusive of interest and costs" means that interest on the money recovered, plus the successful party's costs, will be awarded in addition to the amount of money ordered to be paid. If the action is for the recovery of possession of personal property, the value of that personal property cannot exceed $25,000.00.

The Small Claims Court monetary jurisdiction changes from time to time. In 1970, it was $1,000.00. In 1979, this amount was increased to $3,000.00 for Small

Claims Court (then known as the Ontario Court (Civil Division)) in Metropolitan Toronto only. In 1993, the Small Claims Court monetary jurisdiction was increased to $6,000.00 throughout Ontario. In 2001, that amount was increased to $10,000.00, and effective January 1, 2010 the amount recoverable was increased to $25,000.00.

Every time the monetary jurisdiction of Small Claims Court increases, there will be actions pending in the Superior Court of Justice (the higher court) that will then fall within the Small Claims Court jurisdiction. Section 23(2) of the *Courts of Justice Act* provides that an action that is commenced in the Superior Court of Justice for a money payment or return of property with a value that falls within Small Claims Court jurisdiction may be transferred to Small Claims Court at any time before trial if all the parties consent. If all parties do not consent, the party seeking the transfer must make a motion to a Superior Court judge for an order authorizing the transfer.

Note that, at present, paralegals are not allowed to appear in the Superior Court of Justice.

Transfer to Small Claims—Consent

If all parties to an action in the Superior Court of Justice consent to a transfer to Small Claims Court at any time before trial, the party requesting the transfer must obtain written, signed consents from all other parties. The party requesting the transfer then fills out a requisition (Form 4E of the *Rules of Civil Procedure*, RRO 1990, Reg. 194) and files it, along with the written consent of all other parties, at the court office of the Superior Court of Justice. The party requesting the transfer must pay a court fee of $75.00 to transfer the file. The Registrar will then arrange the transfer.

You will find a sample Form 4E at figure 1.6.

Transfer to Small Claims—No Consent

Absent consent, at any time before trial a party wishing to transfer an action from the Superior Court of Justice to Small Claims Court may bring a motion in the Superior Court of Justice for permission to do so. The party requesting the transfer must contact the court office of the Superior Court of Justice where the action was commenced, and obtain a hearing date after January 1, 2010 that is convenient for all parties or their representatives. If the action was brought under the Rule 76 Simplified Procedure, the motion will be made using the simplified procedure motion form (Form 76B). If the action was brought in the ordinary procedure, the motion will be made under Rule 37 using a notice of motion (Form 37A) supported by affidavit evidence. The motion may be made in writing. See Rule 37.12.1(4) of the *Rules of Civil Procedure*, which permits opposed motions to be made in writing where the issues of fact and law are not complex.

FIGURE 1.6   Form 4E Requisition—Rules of Civil Procedure

FORM 4E

Courts of Justice Act

REQUISITION

(General heading)

REQUISITION

TO THE LOCAL REGISTRAR at *(place)*

I REQUIRE *(Set out a concise statement of what is sought and include all particulars necessary for the registrar to act. Where what is sought is authorized by an order, refer to the order in the requisition and attach a copy of the entered order. Where an affidavit or other document must be filed with the requisition, refer to it in the requisition and attach it.)*

(Date)   *(Name, address and telephone number of lawyer or other person filing requisition)*

(The following are examples of different kinds of requisition.)

(Simple requisition)

I REQUIRE a certified copy of the *(identify document by nature and date)*.

(Order attached)

I REQUIRE, in accordance with the order dated *(date)*, a copy of which is attached, a commission authorizing the taking of evidence before the commissioner named in the order and a letter of request.

I REQUIRE, in accordance with the order dated *(date)*, a copy of which is attached, a certificate of pending litigation in respect of the land described in the statement of claim.

(Affidavit attached)

I REQUIRE an order to continue this action with *(name)* as plaintiff and *(name)* as defendants. An affidavit stating that the defendant *(name)* has reached the age of majority is attached.

RCP-E 4E (July 1, 2007)

WHO MAY HEAR AND DETERMINE A SMALL CLAIMS COURT PROCEEDING?

Section 22(1) of the *Courts of Justice Act* establishes Small Claims Court as a branch of the Superior Court of Justice. Pursuant to ss. 22(2) and (3), justices of the Superior Court of Justice may also preside as judges in Small Claims Court matters. A **justice** is the same thing as a judge.

Section 24(2) provides that, in addition to judges of the Superior Court of Justice, provincial judges and deputy judges may hear and determine Small Claims Court matters.

Superior Court judges are appointed federally, by the governor general. Provincial judges are appointed provincially, by the lieutenant governor. An appointment to the bench is a lifetime appointment, which ends only when a judge retires, is dismissed for serious wrongdoing, becomes incapacitated, or dies.

Deputy judges are found only in Small Claims Court. Unlike other judges in the Superior Court of Justice and the Ontario Court of Justice, deputy judges are not granted lifetime appointments. They are lawyers who are appointed for a term of three years by a regional senior judge of the Superior Court of Justice, with the approval of the attorney general. A deputy judge's appointment is renewable for one or more terms.

Section 24(3) of the *Courts of Justice Act* gives deputy judges unrestricted authorization to hear and determine any Small Claims Court matter.

GENERAL MANDATE OF SMALL CLAIMS COURT

The general mandate of Small Claims Court, as set out in s. 25 of the *Courts of Justice Act*, is "to hear and determine in a summary way all questions of law and fact and ... make such order as is considered just and agreeable to good conscience." In other words, the parties to a Small Claims Court action are entitled to have the matter resolved and enforce their judgment, if any, without being hindered or prejudiced by complex, expensive, and time-consuming procedures.

Like all procedural rules for Ontario courts, the *Rules of the Small Claims Court* (also known as the *Small Claims Court Rules*) are published as a regulation to the *Courts of Justice Act*. The Rules implement the mandate set out in s. 25 by establishing a simplified (or summary) procedure that is designed to be user-friendly for self-represented or unsophisticated users, while preserving and protecting the rights of the parties. The basic steps in a Small Claims Court proceeding are the same as those in the Superior Court of Justice (Civil Division), but at every stage, the Small Claims Court forms and procedures have been simplified and streamlined.

To understand how streamlined the Small Claims Court procedure is, compare the "Summary of Contents" for the *Rules of Civil Procedure*, which govern proceedings in the Superior Court of Justice, with the "Summary of Contents" for the *Rules of the Small Claims Court*. In the Superior Court of Justice, 58 rules are required to cover procedure from commencement of a claim through discoveries, pretrial, and

BOX 1.4

What Are Questions of Law and Questions of Fact?

A **question of law** is an issue that requires the application or interpretation of a law or legal principle. In both jury and non-jury trials, questions of law are determined by judges.

A **question of fact** is a factual dispute. All actions involve factual disputes. The plaintiff makes a series of assertions, or **allegations**, that tell his version of the story. The defendant then makes a series of allegations that tell her version of the story. Both parties and their witnesses give evidence at trial, and, based on that evidence, the finder of fact decides which allegations to accept as facts, on a balance of probabilities, and which allegations to reject as untrue.

In jury trials, the finder of fact is the jury. Being a court of summary procedure, Small Claims Court does not have jury trials. The judge determines all questions of fact and law.

trial, to assessment of costs. Additional rules govern enforcement of orders and particular proceedings such as mortgage actions, administration of estates, applications for judicial review, and the simplified procedure.

By contrast, the *Rules of the Small Claims Court* consist of 21 rules. Rules 1 to 20 govern all aspects of procedure from commencement of an action to enforcement of orders. Rule 21 sets out the role of referees in Small Claims Court matters.

For the basic steps in an undefended Small Claims Court proceeding, see figures 5.2 and 5.4 in chapter 5. For the basic steps in a defended proceeding, see figures 6.2 and 6.3 in chapter 6.

WHO MAY REPRESENT A PARTY IN SMALL CLAIMS COURT?

Section 26 of the *Courts of Justice Act* provides that a party may be represented in a proceeding by a person authorized under the *Law Society Act* to represent the party. However, if the person is not licensed under the *Law Society Act*, the court may exclude that person from appearing on behalf of a party if the court finds that the unlicensed person is not competent to properly represent the party, or does not understand and comply with the duties and responsibilities of an advocate.

Examples of licensed persons are **lawyers** and **paralegals**. Lawyers are persons who have been called to the Bar of Ontario and are licensed to practise law in Ontario. Paralegals are non-lawyer agents who are licensed to provide legal services to clients for a fee in Ontario.

Non-licensees may provide legal services to the public if they fall within any of the exemptions set out in By-law 4, s. 30. The exemptions are reviewed and amended from time to time. Some examples of non-licensees who might appear in Small Claims Court as of this writing are:

1. An individual who is employed by a single employer that is not a licensee or a licensee firm, who provides legal services only for and on behalf of the employer, and who does not provide any legal services to any person other than the employer.

2. A law student who volunteers in or is completing a clinical education course at a student legal aid services society, provides legal services through the clinic to that clinic's designated community only, and acts under the direct supervision of a lawyer.

3. Any individual whose profession or occupation does not include the provision of legal services or the practice of law; who provides legal services only occasionally for or on behalf of a related person, a friend, or a neighbour; and who does not ask for and does not receive any form of compensation or benefit for providing those legal services.

EVIDENCE

The general rule with respect to **hearsay** evidence is that a witness is not allowed to repeat in court what they were told by a third party, if the reason for presenting the evidence is to prove the truth of the contents of the third-party statement. It does not matter how relevant the contents of the statement are—its use is inadmissible if the person who made the statement is not there to give evidence to the court as to what she said.

Section 27 of the *Courts of Justice Act* states that at a hearing, a Small Claims Court judge may admit and act on any oral testimony, document, or other thing so long as it is relevant and not unduly repetitious, regardless of whether that evidence would be admissible in any other court. Any statutory rules with respect to evidence (as set out in the Ontario *Evidence Act*, for example) must be complied with (ss. 27(3) and 27(4)). In other words, in Small Claims Court, hearsay evidence is admissible. The judge hearing the matter must decide how much weight, or credibility, to give the hearsay evidence.

Section 27(5) provides that a copy of a document or other thing may be admitted if the trial judge is satisfied as to its authenticity.

This relaxed approach to evidence is in keeping with the general mandate of Small Claims Court to provide a forum where parties may have their proceedings resolved in a just, speedy, inexpensive, and simple manner. Where comparatively modest sums of money are involved, unsophisticated or self-represented parties should be able to present their case without being obliged to master complex rules of evidence.

OTHER PROCEDURAL MATTERS

Payment Terms

Section 28 of the *Courts of Justice Act* permits a judge to impose terms when making an order with respect to payment of money. A Small Claims Court order may provide for a **lump sum payment**—that is, the entire amount owing is to be paid in a single payment. Or the court may order **installment (or partial) payments**, stating the amount of each partial payment and the date on which it is to be paid.

Costs (Rule 19)

GENERAL

The general rule is that costs are awarded to the successful party in order to reimburse the successful party for legal fees and expenses incurred in the course of litigation. A successful party who is self-represented is entitled, at a minimum, to an order for costs for disbursements and expenses, and may also be entitled to additional costs as set out in the *Rules of the Small Claims Court*.

Section 29 of the *Courts of Justice Act* provides that, in a Small Claims Court proceeding, a costs award cannot exceed 15% of the amount claimed or the value of the property to be recovered, excluding disbursements. Rule 19.02 also sets out

BOX 1.5

Reminder: Costs and Disbursements

Costs are money amounts that the court orders one party to pay to another party. Costs are awarded in addition to any other relief, for money or return of property, that may be ordered.

Legal fees are what you are charged by a lawyer or paralegal for legal representation and advice.

Disbursements are the out-of-pocket expenses of a legal proceeding. These include court filing fees, charges for service of documents, photocopying charges, postage, courier charges, and witness fees.

Ordinarily, a costs award does not reimburse the successful party for all of her legal fees and expenses connected with the litigation. In Small Claims Court, the costs that may be awarded by the court to a successful party are subject to the *Courts of Justice Act* and the *Rules of the Small Claims Court*. See the discussion below.

this restriction. Fifteen percent of the current Small Claims Court maximum monetary jurisdiction of $25,000.00 is $3,750.00.

COMPENSATION FOR INCONVENIENCE AND EXPENSE (RULE 19.05) AND PENALTY COSTS (RULE 19.06)

Section 29 of the *Courts of Justice Act* also provides that if the court considers it necessary in the interests of justice to do so, it may award costs in excess of the 15% limit to penalize a party or the party's representative for unreasonable behaviour in the proceeding.

Rules 19.05 and 19.06 set out modified versions of the s. 29 exception to the 15% rule.

Rule 19.05 gives the court the discretion to award a penalty not exceeding $500.00 in costs against an unsuccessful party for inconvenience and expense if (1) the successful party is unrepresented, and (2) the amount claimed exceeds $500.00 excluding interest and costs.

Rule 19.06 has a much broader application. It states that if the court is satisfied that any party (self-represented or represented, successful or unsuccessful) has unduly complicated or prolonged an action or has otherwise acted unreasonably, the court may order the party to pay compensation to another party (self-represented or represented, successful or unsuccessful). Rule 19.06 applies to any party who abuses the court's process, regardless of the amount claimed.

OTHER EXCEPTIONS TO SECTION 29

Section 29 sets no restrictions, other than the 15% limit, on the amount of costs that may be awarded for the services of a representative. However, the rules establish some limits on the amount of costs that may be ordered. Rule 19.03 provides that the maximum amount that the court may award a successful party for preparation and filing of pleadings is $50.00. Remember that, in addition to any amount awarded under Rule 19.03, the successful party is also entitled to recover the court fee for filing the claim ($75.00 for infrequent claimants; $145.00 for frequent claimants).

Rule 19.04(1) states that, in cases where the amount claimed is more than $500.00 (exclusive of interest and costs) and the successful party is represented by a lawyer, paralegal, or student-at-law, the court may award a reasonable representation fee at trial or at an assessment hearing. However, if the successful party is represented by a student-at-law or paralegal, the representation fee cannot exceed half of the maximum costs award under s. 29 of the *Courts of Justice Act*—or $1,875.00 (half of $3,750.00), under the current monetary jurisdiction of $25,000.00.

Appeals

Section 31 provides that, in an action for payment of money in excess of $500.00 or recovery of property with a value in excess of $500.00, excluding interest and costs, a final order may be appealed to a single judge of the Divisional Court. Note that whether or not a party may appeal depends on how much they claimed originally, not how much they were awarded at trial.

The Divisional Court is the appellate branch of the Superior Court of Justice. Appeals to the Divisional Court are governed by Rule 61 of the *Rules of Civil Procedure*.

Paralegals are not allowed to appear in the Superior Court of Justice at present. The parties to an appeal may be self-represented or represented by a lawyer.

THE RULES OF THE SMALL CLAIMS COURT

What Are They?

As was discussed above, in Ontario, the *Courts of Justice Act* sets up the court structure for all courts in the province. The rules of the various courts are published as regulations to the *Courts of Justice Act*. See figure 1.7 for the e-Laws link to the *Rules of the Small Claims Court*.

The rules of any court establish its procedural requirements. You must be thoroughly familiar with the processes of the courts and tribunals you appear before, because failure to comply with procedural requirements may result in prejudice to your client.

How to Use the Rules

No matter how familiar you may think you are with a court's process, it is difficult to remember everything. If you are not sure about a procedure, do not guess. Check the applicable Rules. Read them carefully.

Whenever you are appearing for a client in Small Claims Court, you should have a copy of the Rules with you, so that you can refer to them if the need arises. You should never appear before any court or tribunal without having a copy of the rules of that court or tribunal handy.

FIGURE 1.7   Finding the Rules of the Small Claims Court on e-Laws

⊖ Courts of Justice Act, R.S.O. 1990, c. C.43		📄	H
O. Reg. 53/01	BILINGUAL PROCEEDINGS	📄	H
O. Reg. 535/96	CASE MANAGEMENT MASTERS - QUALIFICATIONS	📄	H
R.R.O. 1990, Reg. 186	DESIGNATION OF REGIONS	📄	H
R.R.O. 1990, Reg. 188	DUTIES OF CLERKS AND BAILIFFS OF THE SMALL CLAIMS COURT	📄	H
O. Reg. 114/99	FAMILY LAW RULES	📄	H
O. Reg. 407/93	FRAMEWORK AGREEMENT ON JUDGES' REMUNERATION	📄	H
R.R.O. 1990, Reg. 190	MONEY PAID INTO COURT	📄	H
O. Reg. 502/99	NUMBER OF JUDGES	📄	H
O. Reg. 339/07	PUBLICATION OF POSTJUDGMENT AND PREJUDGMENT INTEREST RATES	📄	H
O. Reg. 161/08	REMUNERATION OF DEPUTY JUDGES	📄	H
R.R.O. 1990, Reg. 194	RULES OF CIVIL PROCEDURE	📄	H
O. Reg. 721/94	RULES OF THE COURT OF APPEAL IN APPEALS UNDER THE PROVINCIAL OFFENCES ACT	📄	H
R.R.O. 1990, Reg. 200	RULES OF THE ONTARIO COURT (PROVINCIAL DIVISION) IN PROVINCIAL OFFENCES PROCEEDINGS	📄	H
O. Reg. 723/94	RULES OF THE ONTARIO COURT (GENERAL DIVISION) AND THE ONTARIO COURT (PROVINCIAL DIVISION) IN APPEALS UNDER SECTION 116 OF THE PROVINCIAL OFFENCES ACT	📄	H
O. Reg. 722/94	RULES OF THE ONTARIO COURT (PROVINCIAL DIVISION) IN APPEALS UNDER SECTION 135 OF THE PROVINCIAL OFFENCES ACT		H
O. Reg. 258/98	RULES OF THE SMALL CLAIMS COURT	📄	H
O. Reg. 68/92	SALARIES AND BENEFITS OF MASTERS	📄	H
O. Reg. 67/92	SALARIES AND BENEFITS OF PROVINCIAL JUDGES	📄	H
O. Reg. 626/00	SMALL CLAIMS COURT JURISDICTION	📄	H
⊕ Credit Unions and Caisses Populaires Act, 1994, S.O. 1994, c. 11		📄	H
⊕ Creditors' Relief Act, R.S.O. 1990, c. C.45		📄	H

Rule 1—General

Rule 1 deals with general matters that are not specifically covered by other rules.

DEFINITIONS (RULE 1.02)

Rule 1.02 contains a list of definitions to be used when interpreting and applying other rules. For example, in order to understand Rule 4—Parties Under Disability— you must know what "disability" means in the Small Claims Court context. You will find the definition of "disability" in Rule 1.02.

Whenever you take a procedural step in a Small Claims Court matter, you are required to give the other parties **notice**—serving documents on other parties to make them aware that a procedural step is about to take place. The **notice period** is the minimum amount of time you have to serve the documents, as prescribed by the Rules. Rule 3.01 of the *Small Claims Court Rules* provides that when calculating a notice period, you exclude the first day and include the last day of the period. If the last day of the notice period falls on a holiday, the periods ends on the next day that is not a holiday. If you are not sure whether a day is a holiday for purposes of cal-culating a notice period, you should consult the definition of "holiday" in Rule 1.02.

Although Rule 3.01 of the *Small Claims Court Rules* is silent on this point, it is prudent, when calculating notice periods, to apply the formula set out in Rule 3.01

BOX 1.6

Failing to Meet Procedural Deadlines

You are acting for the defendant in a Small Claims Court action for recovery of an unpaid debt of $3,500.00, plus interest and costs. Your client was served with the plaintiff's claim on September 1, 20—. Your client came to see you to discuss the claim on September 6.

September is a busy month for you. You put the copy of the plaintiff's claim into your inbox, where it slowly gets buried under a stack of paper.

Early in October, your client phones you to say that he just received a default judgment against him in the mail. He wants to know what is going on. At this point, you dig the plaintiff's claim out of your inbox, and pick up your copy of the *Small Claims Court Rules*. This is what you discover.

According to Small Claims Court Rule 9.01(1), a defendant must file a defence with the court within 20 days of being served with the plaintiff's claim. When you missed the 20-day deadline, the plaintiff filed proof of service of the claim with the court, and had your client noted in default (Rule 11.01). Because this was an action for a debt, the plaintiff was also entitled to have default judgment signed by the clerk against your client (Rule 11.02(1)). The default judgment can be enforced against your client under Rule 20.

Being noted in default means that your client is not permitted to take any further steps in the proceeding, except to bring a motion for an order setting aside the noting in default and the default judgment (Rule 11.05). Rule 11.05 permits you to correct your error, but in order to do so, you must draft additional documents, pay a $40.00 filing fee on the motion, serve the other side, and make an additional court appearance. Even if you are successful on the motion, the court may award costs against your client.

This error could have been prevented by having a proper tickler system in place for notifying you of approaching procedural deadlines on your files. As it is, your mistake may result in additional procedural delay and possible prejudice to your client by way of a costs award.

A tickler system is a list of tasks with deadlines for their completion. The deadline for a task may be a statutory limitation period or a procedural deadline set by the rules of a tribunal. A tickler system also contains tickler or bring-forward dates notifying you that a deadline is approaching, and that you should start working on a task in order to get it completed before the deadline.

of the *Rules of Civil Procedure*. When a notice period is seven days or less, you do not count holidays when calculating the end date of the notice period. When a notice period is more than seven days, holidays are included when you calculate the end date of the notice period. If a notice period ends on a holiday, you move the end date over to the next business day.

In Small Claims Court, "order" means an order or a judgment. A self-represented person is someone who is representing herself—that is, she does not have a lawyer, paralegal, or student-at-law assisting her.

INTERPRETATION OF THE RULES (RULE 1.03)

Rule 1.03(1) provides that the rules shall be **liberally construed** with a view to obtaining a just (fair), expeditious (speedy), and inexpensive resolution of every proceeding on its merits. Rule 1.03(1) makes specific reference to s. 25 of the *Courts of Justice Act*, which was discussed above.

"Liberally construed" means that the Rules will be interpreted in such a way as to bring about a just and fair conclusion, without undue emphasis on strict compliance with all procedural requirements and technicalities, so long as the rights of all parties are protected. In other words, the court may apply the Rules in a way that

BOX 1.7

How to Read the Rules

When taking any procedural step, you must be careful to look at all the relevant rules. This may seem a bit confusing at first, but it gets easier as you become more familiar with Small Claims Court procedures. Continuing with the example from box 1.6, let's look at some rules and subrules that would be relevant when making arrangements for the set aside motion.

As you already know, Rule 11.05 permits you to bring the motion. Since you missed the deadline for filing a defence, one of the things you will have to ask the court for on the motion is an order extending the time for filing a defence. Rule 3.02(1) authorizes the court to make this kind of order.

If you are not sure what forms to use on the motion, you will need to consult Rule 15, which governs motions. You will find the name and number of the form to use at Rule 15.01(1).

Rule 15.01(2) tells you that you must obtain a hearing date for the motion before serving the notice of motion on the other party. Rule 15.01(3) tells you the minimum number of days before the hearing date that the motion must be served on the other party. If you are not sure how to calculate the notice period, you must read Rule 15.01(3) together with Rule 3.01 (Time—Computation) of the *Small Claims Court Rules* and Rule 3.01 (Time—Computation) of the *Rules of Civil Procedure*. You may also wish to clarify the definition of "holiday" in the list of definitions at Rule 1.02 of the *Small Claims Court Rules*. Finally, you must check Rule 8 (Service) to find out how a motion may be served on another party, and what document you use to prove service.

Rule 15.02 tells you about methods of hearing a motion (in person, by telephone or video conference, and so on). If you want the motion to be heard by telephone or video conference, you must make a request to the court under Rules 1.07 and 15.02(1)(b).

How many rules and subrules did you count?

is not strictly provided for in the language on the page, but which is in keeping with the court's mandate under s. 25 to hear and decide matters without needless procedural delay, with a view to bringing about a fair and just resolution within a reasonable time.

Rule 1.03(2) provides further direction with respect to interpreting the Rules in a situation that the Rules do not cover adequately. In this kind of situation, the court may look at the Rules themselves, and may also look outside the Rules, at the *Courts of Justice Act*, the statute governing the action (if there is one), and, if appropriate, the *Rules of Civil Procedure*, for guidance in arriving at a decision. This is called "deciding by analogy."

ORDERS ON TERMS (RULE 1.04)

Rule 1.04 authorizes the court to impose terms and give directions when making an order, so long as the terms and directions are just.

TELEPHONE AND VIDEO CONFERENCES (RULE 1.07)

If a court has facilities for telephone or video conferencing, a settlement conference, a motion, or all or part of an examination of a debtor or other person under Rule 20.10 may be heard or conducted by telephone or video conference (Rules 1.07(1) and 1.07(1.1)).

To schedule a telephone or video conference, a party must file a request in Form 1B with the court, giving reasons for the request (Rule 1.07(2)). Before granting the request, the judge must consider whether the **balance of convenience** favours the party requesting the telephone or video conference, or that of any party opposing it; plus any other relevant matter (Rule 1.07(3)). A court applying the bal-

BOX 1.8

What Does "Liberally Construe" Really Mean?

No matter how carefully procedural rules are drafted, they cannot cover every possible situation that arises. Sometimes there is a "gap" in the rules—that is, there is no language that deals directly with a particular issue. Sometimes the existing language is ambiguous—that is, it can be read as having more than one meaning.

To **construe** the language of a rule (or, for that matter, a statute or a legal document such as a will or contract) means to interpret it—to read it and decide what it means. Construe is the verb. Construction is the noun.

Strict construction (also known as narrow construction) means that the language of the rule is read and applied using its exact, technical meaning. An example of strict construction would be the definition of "holiday" in Rule 1.02. If the rule says that, in a Small Claims Court proceeding, certain days are holidays, then they are holidays. It does not matter whether you, as a defendant, have to work on Saturdays and Sundays, New Year's Day, Good Friday, and Easter Monday—they are still holidays as far as the *Small Claims Court Rules* are concerned.

Liberal construction (also known as equitable construction) means that, when applying the Rules, the court goes beyond the exact meaning of the language in order to implement the principles behind the Rules, as stated in s. 25 of the *Courts of Justice Act* and Rules 1.03(1) and 1.03(2).

Let's consider service of a plaintiff's claim, which is governed by Rules 8.01(1), 8.02, 8.03, and 8.04. The rules of service are complex, and can be very confusing for the self-represented. When interpreting these rules, the court may not insist on strict technical compliance, so long as it is clear that the plaintiff has made good-faith efforts to deliver the claim to the defendant, and the defendant has received the claim.

What if the way the plaintiff serves the claim is in strict technical compliance with the Rules, but the defendant never receives it? Let's say that the plaintiff uses an alternative to personal service, Rule 8.03(2)—Service at Place of Residence. The plaintiff leaves the claim in a sealed envelope addressed to the defendant with an apparent adult member of the household, and mails a copy to the defendant on the same day. This is proper service under the Rules. However, for one reason or another, the defendant does not receive the claim. After the 20-day period for filing a defence set out in Rule 9.01(1) has passed, the plaintiff notes the defendant in default. When served with the default judgment, the defendant brings a motion to set aside the noting of default.

At the hearing of the motion, can the plaintiff rely on technical compliance with the letter of the law as set out in Rules 8.03(2) and 9.01(1) to argue that the defendant's motion should be dismissed?

The plaintiff may make the argument, but the court is unlikely to deny the defendant her right to be heard, based on a narrow, technical argument of this nature. Instead, the court will look at what is fair in all of the circumstances when coming to its decision. If appropriate, the court may compensate the plaintiff for any inconvenience, delay, and expense caused by the defendant's conduct with an order that the defendant pay the plaintiff some costs.

Procedure in the civil courts tends to be forgiving, in that it makes allowances for errors by parties or their legal representatives. Legal representatives should not use this as an excuse for carelessness. Know your rules and stay on top of your deadlines. If you are too busy to give a client's case the attention it needs, refer the matter to another paralegal with expertise in the area, or to a lawyer.

ance of convenience test will balance the prejudice to one party of denying the relief asked for, against the prejudice to an opposing party if the relief is granted.

If the balance of convenience favours the party requesting a telephone or video conference, the request will be granted, and the court will make the necessary arrangements and notify the parties (Rule 1.07(4)).

On motion by a party opposing a telephone or video conference, an order granting a telephone or video conference may be set aside or varied by a judge presiding over the proceeding or over a step in the proceeding (Rule 1.07(5)).

Rule 2—Non-Compliance with the Rules

Rule 2 complements Rule 1.03 (liberal construction of the Rules). Rule 2.01 states that a failure to comply with the rules is an irregularity—a mistake that can be corrected. If you make a mistake, it does not mean that a particular procedural step, document, or order has no legal force and effect. Instead, the court has discretion to grant amendments or other relief, with a view to obtaining a just resolution of the real issues that are in dispute. The court must exercise this discretion on such terms as are just to both or all parties. In other words, the party that made the mistake requiring correction may have to pay some costs to other parties; or the order may contain other terms intended to minimize potential prejudice to other parties.

Rule 2.02 provides that the court may dispense with compliance with any rule at any time, if it is just to do so.

Rule 3—Time

When calculating a period of time for taking a certain procedural step, you exclude the first day and include the last day of the period. If the last day of the period falls on a holiday as defined in Rule 1.02, then it ends on the next business day (Rule 3.01).

The court has discretion to lengthen or shorten the time prescribed by the Rules for doing anything, on such terms as are just (Rule 3.02(1)).

The time prescribed by the Rules for serving or filing a document may be lengthened or shortened by filing the consent of the parties (Rule 3.02(2)).

Closing Comment

You need to know the *Rules of the Small Claims Court* well, if you propose to practise in this area, or if you are working under the supervision of someone who practises in this area (for example, in debt collection). But the most important thing to remember is—when in doubt, do not guess. Read your Rules.

CHAPTER SUMMARY

Small Claims Court is a division of the Ontario Superior Court of Justice. It is a civil trial court that hears actions for money in amounts up to $25,000.00, excluding interest and costs, or for recovery of property with a value of $25,000.00 or less.

Small Claims Court is intended to improve the public's access to justice by providing a forum with simplified rules and procedures where claimants may have their matters resolved in a just, speedy, inexpensive, and simple manner.

The *Courts of Justice Act* sets up the court system in Ontario. Sections 22 to 31 of the *Courts of Justice Act* set out the general principles governing Small Claims Court, including who may be a judge of Small Claims Court (s. 24); monetary jurisdiction (s. 23 and O. Reg. 626/00); the general mandate or purpose of Small Claims Court (s. 25); legal representation (s. 26); evidence (s. 27); installment orders for payment of money (s. 28); costs (s. 29); and appeals (s. 31).

The *Rules of the Small Claims Court* are published as a regulation to the *Courts of Justice Act*. The Rules implement the mandate set out in s. 25 of the *Courts of Justice Act* by establishing a summary procedure that is designed to be user-friendly for self-represented or unsophisticated parties, while preserving and protecting the rights of all parties.

Anyone practising in Small Claims Court should be familiar with its procedural rules. This does not mean that you must have them memorized; but you should know them well enough so that, when you are not sure about a procedural point, you know where to look in the Rules to find the answer.

KEY TERMS

action	infrequent claimant	monetary jurisdiction
allegations	installment (or partial) payments	notice
balance of convenience	jurisdiction	notice period
claimant	justice	paralegal
construe	lawyer	parties
costs	legal fees	plaintiff
defendant	liberal construction	question of fact
disbursements	liberally construed	question of law
frequent claimant	litigants	strict construction
hearsay	lump sum payment	

REFERENCES

Administration of Justice Act, RSO 1990, c. A.6.

Courts of Justice Act, RRO 1990, Reg. 194, as amended.

Courts of Justice Act, RSO 1990, c. C.43.

Evidence Act, RSO 1990, c. E.23, as amended.

Law Society Act, RSO 1990, c. L.8.

Law Society of Upper Canada (LSUC), By-laws (Toronto: LSUC, 2005, as amended); available online at http://www.lsuc.on.ca.

Rules of Civil Procedure, RRO 1990, Reg. 194.

Rules of the Small Claims Court, O. Reg. 258/98.

REVIEW QUESTIONS

1. What is jurisdiction?

2. What is an action? What types of actions does Small Claims Court hear?

3. What is a frequent claimant? What is an infrequent claimant? Why is the distinction important?

4. What is the *Courts of Justice Act*? What is its purpose?

5. What is the monetary jurisdiction of Small Claims Court? Does the maximum amount that can be claimed include interest and costs?

6. What is the difference between costs, legal fees, and disbursements?

7. What is a deputy judge? What is the difference between deputy judges and other judges in Small Claims Court?

8. What is the general mandate of Small Claims Court? Please provide the statutory authority.

9. Who may appear as a legal representative in Small Claims Court? Please provide the statutory authority.

10. a. What is hearsay evidence?

    b. What is the general rule with respect to hearsay evidence?

    c. What is the general rule with respect to hearsay evidence in Small Claims Court? Please provide the statutory authority.

11. What are the *Small Claims Court Rules* and what is their purpose?

12. What is the general principle governing interpretation of the *Small Claims Court Rules*? Please provide the number of any rule(s) you are relying upon in support of your answer.

13. What is the general rule with respect to orders for payment of costs in Small Claims Court? Please provide the statutory authority.

14. If a party wants to appeal a final order of the Small Claims Court, what court do they appeal to? What procedural rule or rules govern the appeal?

APPENDIX 1.1   Schedule of Small Claims Court Fees and Allowances

Clerk's Fees

1. Filing of a claim by an infrequent claimant — $75.00
2. Filing of a claim by a frequent claimant — $145.00
3. Filing of a defendant's claim — $75.00
4. Filing a notice of motion served on another party, a notice of motion without notice or a notice of motion for a consent order (except a notice of motion under the *Wages Act*) — $40.00
5. Filing a defence — $40.00
6. Issuing a summons to a witness — $19.00
7. Receiving for enforcement a process from the Ontario Court (Provincial Division) or an order or judgment as provided by statute — $25.00
8. Issuing a certificate of judgment — $19.00
9. Issuing a writ of delivery, a writ of seizure and sale, or a notice of examination — $35.00
10. Issuing a notice of garnishment — $100.00
11. Preparing and filing a consolidation order — $75.00
12. Forwarding a court file to Divisional Court for appeal — $20.00
13. Issuing a certified copy of a judgment or other document, per page — $3.50
14. Transmitting a document other than by mail — cost of transmission
15. For the inspection of a court file,
    i. by a solicitor or party in the proceeding — no charge
    ii. by a person who has entered into an agreement with the attorney general for the bulk inspection of court files, per file — $1.00
    iii. by any other person, per file — $10.00
16. Making a photocopy of a document not requiring certification, per page — $1.00
17. Revoked
18. In an application under the *Repair and Storage Liens Act*,
    i. on the filing of,
       A. an application — $100.00
       B. a notice of objection — $35.00
       C. a waiver of further claim and a receipt — no charge

APPENDIX 1.1   Concluded

ii. on the issuing of,

    A. an initial certificate $35.00

    B. a final certificate $35.00

    C. a writ of seizure $35.00

19. Fixing of a date for trial or an assessment hearing by an infrequent claimant $100.00

20. Fixing of a date for trial or an assessment hearing by a frequent claimant $130.00

21. Entering of a default judgment by an infrequent claimant $35.00

22. Entering of a default judgment by a frequent claimant $50.00

Bailiff's Fees

1. Revoked.

2. For each attempt, whether successful or not, to enforce a writ of delivery $36.00

3. For each attempt, whether successful or not, to enforce a writ of seizure and sale of personal property,

    i. where no sale is necessary $36.00

    ii. where a sale is necessary $60.00

4. For each attempt, whether successful or not, to enforce a writ of seizure under the *Repair and Storage Liens Act* $36.00

5. Enforcing a writ of delivery or a writ of seizure and sale of personal property, removing property seized, advertising the sale of personal property, including obtaining assistance in seizing, securing, or retaining property

    [Fee:] Reasonable disbursements necessarily incurred, including appraisers' fees

Fees and Allowances to Witnesses

1. For attendance in court, unless item 2 applies, per day $6.00

2. For attendance in court by a barrister, solicitor, physician, surgeon, engineer, or veterinary surgeon who is not a party to the action, to give evidence of a professional service rendered or to give a professional opinion, per day $15.00

3. For travel to court

    [Fee:] Reasonable travelling expenses actually incurred, but not exceeding the kilometre allowance set out in Regulation 11 of the Revised Regulations of Ontario, 1990

You and Your Client

LEARNING OBJECTIVES

After reading this chapter, you will understand:

- The duty of competence

- The duty of honesty and candour

- The purpose and scope of the duty of confidentiality

- Permitted disclosure

- The duty to avoid conflicts of interest

- Compliance with client identification and verification (By-law 7.1, Part III)

- The basic concepts of effective communication

- The purpose of the engagement letter or retainer agreement

- How to handle the money retainer

- The purpose of the reporting letter

- Management of client files

INTRODUCTION

Many of a paralegal's duties and obligations to a client arise out of the fiduciary relationship between the paralegal and the client. A **fiduciary relationship** is a relationship of absolute trust and confidence between two persons, in which one person (the **fiduciary**) is required to act with scrupulous good faith, honesty, and candour for the benefit of the other person (the beneficiary). In the paralegal–client relationship, the paralegal is the fiduciary and the client is the beneficiary. The paralegal must put the client's interests ahead of her own in all dealings with the client. The client is entitled to place absolute confidence, reliance, and trust in the paralegal.

In this chapter, we will discuss the following duties owed by the paralegal to the client:

- the duty to be competent (Rule 3.01);

- the duty to be honest and candid with the client (Rule 3.02);

- the duty to hold client information in strict confidence (Rule 3.03); and

- the duty to avoid conflicts of interest (Rule 3.04).

The importance of effective communication with the client will also be considered.

In the following discussion, the *Paralegal Rules of Conduct* are referred to as the Paralegal Rules, and the *Paralegal Professional Conduct Guidelines* are referred to as the Guidelines.

COMPETENCE (PARALEGAL RULE 3.01; GUIDELINE 6)

Like all professionals, paralegals are required to be knowledgeable about the areas in which they provide services to the public. A client hires a paralegal because the paralegal has knowledge and skills the client does not have. A paralegal who holds herself out as having certain kinds of expertise must ensure that she does in fact possess that expertise and can apply it for the benefit of her clients.

Paralegals who fail to meet standards of professional competence when providing legal services to the public may cause harm to their clients, and to their business partners and associates. They may also bring the paralegal profession and the justice system into disrepute.

The Competent Paralegal (Paralegal Rules 3.01(1), (2), and (3))

Paralegal Rule 3.01(1) imposes a general obligation to perform any legal services undertaken on a client's behalf to the standard of a competent paralegal. A **competent paralegal** is a paralegal who has and applies the relevant skills, attributes, and values appropriate to each matter undertaken on behalf of a client, including but not limited to (1) knowledge; (2) client service and communication; and (3) skills and judgment.

You shall not undertake to represent a client in a matter unless you are familiar with the legal principles and procedures governing the applicable area of law, or are confident that you can become familiar with those legal principles and procedures in a timely and cost-effective manner (Paralegal Rule 3.01(2)).

If at any stage of the matter you discover that you are not competent to complete the tasks for which you were retained, you shall (Paralegal Rule 3.01(3)):

1. decline to act; or

2. obtain the client's consent to retain, consult, or collaborate with another licensee who is competent to perform the task and is licensed to do so.

When you are first approached by a client about a particular matter, you shall carefully consider whether you are competent to provide the legal services required. When assessing your own competence, keep in mind that a lack of competence on your part may do the client a disservice, bring discredit to the paralegal profession, and bring the administration of justice into disrepute. The best time to turn your mind to this is before accepting the retainer, at which time you may decline to act if you are not satisfied that you possess the required knowledge and skills. If you decline to act, you should consider referring the client to another paralegal or a lawyer with the required expertise. You should also consider sending a **non-engagement letter** to the client confirming that you have not accepted the retainer and stating your reasons. A non-engagement letter is a letter confirming that the paralegal has declined to accept the retainer, or that the client has declined to retain the paralegal.

BOX 2.1

What Is a Retainer?

In a legal services context, the word "retainer" may be used to mean several different things.

The **paralegal–client retainer** is the contractual relationship between the client and the paralegal. The terms of the paralegal–client retainer should be discussed with the client at the initial consultation.

The **retainer agreement** is the written contract between the paralegal and the client. It sets out the important terms of the paralegal–client retainer, including the scope of the legal services to be provided, the likely cost of those services, expected outcomes, billing practices, and events of termination of the retainer, among other things. It is called an agreement because it is signed back to the paralegal by the client. An **engagement letter** may be used for the same purpose. An engagement letter confirms the terms of the paralegal–client retainer, but is not signed back by the client.

A **money retainer** is money paid by the client to the paralegal for future legal services. A money retainer for future legal services belongs to the client, and must be held in trust for the client until legal services have been provided and billed to the client.

Sometimes a matter takes a direction that could not be anticipated when you accepted the retainer. If you are no longer competent to act for a client because of unforeseen developments in an ongoing matter, you may consider withdrawing from representation. Lack of competence is a ground for mandatory withdrawal of legal representation (Paralegal Rule 3.08(5)(e)).

If you have already agreed to the retainer, you may continue to represent the client if (1) you advise the client that you are not competent to perform a particular task, and (2) you obtain the client's consent to obtain expert advice or assistance from another licensee who is competent and licensed to perform the task.

Regardless of expertise, no paralegal licensee should provide legal services to a client in an unauthorized area of law (Paralegal Rule 3.02(2)). Clients with such matters should be directed to the Lawyer Referral Service (1-800-268-8326 or 416-947-3330 (within the GTA)) or referred to a lawyer with expertise in that area. There is no charge for the Lawyer Referral Service.

HONESTY AND CANDOUR (PARALEGAL RULE 3.02(1); GUIDELINE 7)

A paralegal must be honest and candid when advising a client. This is true whether the client is seeking to retain you in a matter or is a casual client seeking quick advice.

In this context, being **candid** means being forthright and sincere, and looking at both sides of each issue without bias. You must advise the client honestly and candidly of the applicable law, the client's options, possible outcomes, and possible risks. Your advice should enable the client to make informed decisions and give appropriate instructions in the matter.

You should always ensure that clients, including prospective clients, understand that you are a paralegal, not a lawyer.

You must never undertake or provide advice regarding a matter that is outside the scope of permissible practice for paralegals.

When advising a client, you must never knowingly assist in or encourage any dishonesty, fraud, crime, or illegal conduct. You must not instruct a client on how to violate the law and avoid punishment.

Bad News

Clients like to hear good news. If they intend to sue someone in Small Claims Court for an unpaid debt, they want to hear that they have a good case and will get their money back. If they are trying to evict a tenant from rental housing, they want to hear that they will get an eviction order. If they are fighting a speeding ticket, they want to hear that the case will be thrown out due to a deficiency on the face of the charging document.

Your duty to be honest and candid applies when the news is good and when it is bad. The downside of being honest and candid about bad news is that, if the client is not happy with what he hears, he may seek legal assistance elsewhere. In a competitive market, it can be difficult to let any client walk out the door, however unreasonable his expectations. Nonetheless, your professional duty requires you to give honest, candid advice as to the merits of the matter and whether the client's objectives are achievable.

In situations where you decline to accept a retainer or a client declines to retain you after the initial consultation, you should send the client a non-engagement letter, confirming that you will not be acting in the matter. The non-engagement letter should advise the client of any limitation periods, and recommend that the client seek other legal representation.

THE DUTY OF CONFIDENTIALITY (PARALEGAL RULE 3.02; GUIDELINE 8)

General

You have a professional and ethical duty to hold in strict confidence anything you learn at any stage of your professional relationship with the client about any aspect of the client's affairs. In other words, you must not share client information (including client information that other people may already know) with anyone, unless authorized by your client or required by law to do so (Paralegal Rule 3.03).

The duty of confidentiality is grounded in the principle that effective legal representation requires full and unreserved communication between the legal representative and the client. The client must be confident that anything discussed with or disclosed to you will not be disclosed to others, unless she authorizes that disclosure or the nature of the matter requires it. The duty applies whether your client is an individual or a business entity such as a corporation.

Scope of the Duty of Confidentiality

The duty of confidentiality applies to all information of any kind that you acquire from a client or on behalf of a client during the professional relationship. This includes:

1. The identity of the client and the fact that the client has consulted or retained you;

2. Information about the client that is not relevant to the specific matter on which you have been retained; and

3. Information that others may have knowledge of. For example, others may know your client's home address and telephone number. That does not release you from your obligation not to disclose that information, except with your client's consent or as required by law.

The duty to keep information confidential applies to you, your associates, and anyone in your employment or acting under your supervision, including students.

In the office, client information should not be left in places where it is visible to others. If you are meeting a client in your office, your desk should be clear of other client files and any other documents that might serve as client identifiers. Computer monitors should be situated so that their screens are not visible to the public. If screens are visible to the public, they should be filtered.

When Does the Duty of Confidentiality Arise, and When Does It End?

The duty of confidentiality arises when you enter into a professional relationship with a client. It applies to **casual** or **prospective clients** as well as to regular **clients**.

BOX 2.2

Gossip: What Not to Do

You are representing Rosemary Lawson, the plaintiff in a personal injury action. Over time, you have come to distrust your client. You think she is lying about the circumstances in which the injury (a sprained wrist) took place, and that she has unreasonable expectations about how much money she can expect to get. The defendant has made what you think is a reasonable settlement offer. You have been urging Ms. Lawson to accept it, but she refuses.

One evening after work you meet your husband for dinner at a restaurant near your office. The restaurant is crowded and noisy. You have told your husband about several incidents when Rosemary Lawson was particularly difficult. She has become a kind of joke between you. When you have ordered, your husband says, "So, how'd it go today? How's Rosemary?" While the waiter serves your drinks, you tell your husband the latest "Rosemary anecdote." It is an entertaining story, and makes your husband laugh. You and your husband have a pleasant dinner.

Comment: You should not discuss a client with your spouse or any other member of your family. You should not discuss a client in a public place like a restaurant, where wait staff and other diners can overhear what you are saying.

You should never discuss a client or anything connected with a client file with anyone who is not entitled to hear the information. Nor should you talk about these things in circumstances where third parties may overhear what you are saying. Your friends and relatives have no obligation to keep the information confidential, nor do third parties who may overhear your conversation. If they repeat the information to others, your client could be prejudiced. Even if no prejudice to your client results, you have breached the duty to hold all client information in strict confidence.

Even if you do not mention the client's name and remove other identifiers, you breach the duty of confidentiality when you share client information with someone who has no right to hear it and owes the client no duty to hold it in confidence.

A casual client is a client who consults with you about a legal issue, but then decides not to proceed, or not to hire you to act as his legal representative. A prospective client is a person who consults you about a legal issue but has not yet retained you. A client is a person who consults with you and hires you to represent her in a matter or a number of matters. The professional relationship with casual clients, prospective clients, and clients who retain you as their legal representative begins when they first approach you for legal advice. The duty of confidentiality arises at that point.

The duty of confidentiality continues indefinitely. It continues after the professional relationship has ended. It continues regardless of how the professional relationship ended. A client may fire you. You still owe that client the duty to hold his information in strict confidence. A client may die. You must continue to hold his information in strict confidence. Your associates, employees, and students must do the same.

Your duty to hold client information in strict confidence does not end when your association with a particular paralegal practice or law firm ends. It continues indefinitely. You may never use confidential information for your own benefit, whether personal or financial, even if doing so would not harm your client. You may never use confidential information for the personal or financial benefit of a third party. You may never use confidential information to the disadvantage of a client, including a former client.

When May You Disclose Confidential Information?

You may disclose confidential information to others if you have the client's **express consent** or **implied consent** to do so.

Express (or explicit) consent means that the client has given you written authorization to disclose particular information to specified third parties. For example, you must obtain a written authorization from your client before releasing medical records or reports from the client's treating physician to other parties.

Written authorizations should clearly state any restrictions on disclosure, and should specify who you may disclose the information to, and for what period of time, if that is appropriate. You will find a sample authorization at appendix 2.10 to this chapter.

Implied consent is not written down—it is implied by the professional relationship. Unless the client directs otherwise, you have implied consent to disclose confidential information to colleagues, employees, and students who are working on the client file. However, anyone to whom confidential information is disclosed must be aware of and comply with their duty to hold the information in strict confidence.

You also have implied consent to reveal a certain amount of client information because the matter requires it. For example, in court proceedings, client information that would otherwise be confidential may be disclosed in pleadings and other documents filed with the court. The contents of court files are open to the public unless legislation prohibits public access or the court imposes a publication ban.

THE DUTY TO AVOID CONFLICTS OF INTEREST (PARALEGAL RULES 3.04(1), (2), AND (3)) AND CONFLICTS OF INTEREST (PARALEGAL RULE 3.04; GUIDELINE 9)

General

A **conflict of interest** is any circumstance that may negatively affect a paralegal's ability to act in the client's best interests. Conflicts of interest may arise at any time in a client matter, as the matter evolves, new parties are added, and new circumstances or information comes to light.

Paralegal Rule 3.04(1) defines "conflict of interest" or "conflicting interest" as an interest, financial or otherwise,

(a) that would be likely to have an adverse effect on a paralegal's judgment on behalf of, or loyalty to, a client or prospective client; or

(b) that a paralegal might be prompted to give preference to over the interests of a client or a prospective client.

A paralegal shall not advise or represent more than one side in a dispute (Paralegal Rule 3.04(2)). A **dispute** is an argument or disagreement between two or more sides in which the interest of one side is in direct opposition to the interest of another side. A paralegal cannot act for persons with adverse interests in a dispute, because to do so would influence the paralegal's judgment and loyalty to the adverse persons.

Because conflicts of interest may result in harm to the client, paralegals have an obligation to prospective clients, current clients, and former clients to avoid conflicts of interest and potential conflicts of interest.

CONFLICT-CHECKING SYSTEM

How do you find out whether or not there may be a conflict of interest in a particular client matter? To assist in complying with the duty of avoidance of conflicts of interest, paralegals should consider maintaining a searchable database of information about prospective, current, and former clients, as well as information about related persons and conflicting or adverse parties. The database should include fields for the following information (the list is not exhaustive):

- client's name, and aliases and former names, if applicable;

- client contact information;

- date the file was opened;

- client file name and active file code;

- subject matter of the file;

- date the file was closed, and closed file code; and

- names and contact information of related persons, and of conflicting or adverse parties (if available), cross-referenced to the client file.

The database may be maintained in a paper or electronic format. Some legal software applications automatically enter client and other data into a conflicts databank as new electronic files are opened.

As part of your conflict-checking system, you should have standard office procedures in place for conducting conflict searches at critical points in the paralegal–client relationship. Your first search should take place after the initial contact with a prospective client. You should search for conflicts again when you have more information about the client, and related or adverse parties. If a retainer is entered into, you should conduct a conflict search any time a new party is added in a proceeding. If a conflict arises after you are retained, you may be required to withdraw from representing the client.

BOX 2.3

Conflicts of Interest—Who Is the Client?

Any person who is a client of the paralegal firm of which you are a partner or an employee is a client, regardless of whether you actually handle that person's work (Paralegal Rule 1.02). In a busy firm with many clients and/or a high client turnover, you may have no knowledge of a client's existence or that your firm ever represented him. Nevertheless, a paralegal–client relationship exists between you and that client and entails various duties, including the duty of confidentiality and the duty to avoid conflicts of interest.

Since every client of a paralegal firm is also the client of every other paralegal in the firm, if one paralegal has a conflict of interest in a matter, then all paralegals in the firm have a conflict of interest in that matter (Guideline 9).

This means that when you check for conflicts, you must review the names of all current and former clients of the firm, not just the clients you personally represented.

CLIENT CONSENT

The existence of a conflict or potential conflict does not always mean that you cannot represent the client. Paralegal Rule 3.04(3) permits you to act or continue to act if the client consents to your doing so.

Consent—Prospective Client

If practicable, whenever a prospective client contacts your firm, certain information (such as the client's name, including any aliases, and contact information) should be obtained from the client and entered immediately into your conflict-checking system. A conflict search should be carried out before there is any further contact with the prospective client. The results of the search should be reviewed by the paralegal.

If the search reveals a conflict or potential conflict, you must consider whether you should accept the retainer or decline to represent the prospective client. Paralegal Rule 3.04(3) permits you to accept the retainer if the prospective client consents. To comply, you must first disclose the conflict or potential conflict to the client. You must provide sufficient detail about the conflict to enable the client to make an informed decision about whether retaining you is in her best interests in the circumstances. This is called **informed consent**. Guideline 9 recommends that you give the prospective client some time to consider the disclosure and ask for further clarification.

If there are other persons who are involved in or connected with the client matter, you may have a duty to avoid conflicts of interest with respect to those persons as well. Examples of such individuals are members of the client's family, the client's spouse, and the client's business associates or employees. You must obtain informed consent from those persons as well (Paralegal Rule 3.04(4)).

If, having reviewed the information provided, the prospective client consents to your representation, you may accept the client retainer. The prospective client's consent, and the consents of any client associates, should be in writing.

Conflict of Interest—Client Declines Retainer. If, having reviewed the information provided, the prospective client declines to retain you, you should confirm the client's decision in a non-engagement letter. The non-engagement letter must recommend that the client obtain independent legal representation from a competent paralegal or lawyer with no personal interest in the matter.

Conflict of Interest—Paralegal Declines Retainer. There may be situations where you cannot provide full disclosure about the conflict of interest without revealing confidential information about another client or clients. When that happens, you must advise the prospective client that there is a conflict of interest and that you cannot accept the retainer (Guideline 9). You should confirm your decision in writing in a non-engagement letter. The non-engagement letter must recommend that the client obtain independent legal representation from a competent paralegal or lawyer with no personal interest in the matter.

Guideline 9 recommends that you consider whether to accept or decline a prospective client's retainer any time you become aware of a conflict or potential conflict. You should do this even if you have the client's consent and if, in your opinion, the retainer would not breach the Paralegal Rules. When considering whether to accept the client matter, you should take into account the delay, expense, and inconvenience that will arise for the client and/or for you, should you be required to withdraw at a later stage in the proceeding.

Guideline 9 also notes that, in some cases, even though the client has indicated that he wants to retain you, the only way to deal with the conflict is to decline the retainer. If you decide to decline the retainer, you should confirm your decision in writing in a non-engagement letter. The non-engagement letter must recommend that the client obtain independent legal representation from a competent paralegal or lawyer with no personal interest in the matter.

You will find examples of non-engagement letters at appendixes 2.1 and 2.2.

Consent—Existing Client

Existing client matters should be checked for conflicts at critical points throughout the paralegal–client retainer. You should conduct a conflict search any time a new party is added in a proceeding or new information about the client matter comes to light. If a conflict arises after you are retained, you may be required to withdraw from representing the client.

If a conflict search reveals a conflict or potential conflict in an existing client matter, you must consider whether or not to continue to act in the matter. Paralegal Rule 3.04(3) permits you to continue to act if the client gives you informed consent based on disclosure of all information regarding the conflict that the client requires to make a decision. The client should be given some time to consider the disclosure and ask for further clarification.

If there are other persons who are involved in or connected with the client matter, you may have a duty to avoid conflicts of interest with respect to those persons as well. You must obtain informed consent from those persons as well.

If, having reviewed the information provided, the client and any client associates consent to your continuing representation, you may continue to act in the client matter. The client's consent, and the consents of any client associates, should be in writing.

Conflict of Interest—Client Terminates Retainer. If, having reviewed the information provided, the client decides to terminate the retainer, you should confirm the termination of the retainer in writing. If the client requests that the matter be transferred to another paralegal or a lawyer, you should obtain a direction, in writing and signed by the client, for release of the client's file to the successor licensee. If the client collects the file herself, you should obtain an acknowledgment in writing and signed by the client confirming that she has received the file.

Conflict of Interest—Paralegal Declines Retainer. There may be situations where you cannot provide full disclosure about a conflict of interest without revealing confidential information about another client or clients. When that happens, you must advise the client that there is a conflict of interest and that you must refuse the retainer or, in the case of an ongoing matter, withdraw from representation. You should confirm your decision in writing to the client.

Any time you become aware of a conflict or potential conflict, you should consider whether or not to continue to act in the client matter. You should do this even if you have the client's consent to continue to act and are satisfied that your continued involvement would not put you in breach of the Paralegal Rules. When coming to a decision about whether to continue to act in the matter, you should take into account the delay, expense, and inconvenience that will arise for the client and/or for you, should you be required to withdraw at a later stage in the proceeding.

Sometimes the only way to deal with the conflict in an ongoing client matter is to withdraw from representation, even though the client may want you to continue to act in the matter. When withdrawing your services, you must comply with Paralegal Rule 3.08. You shall not withdraw from representation unless you are satisfied that there is good cause. You must give the client notice that is appropriate in the circumstances; try to minimize expense and avoid prejudice to the client; and do all that reasonably can be done to facilitate the orderly transfer of the client matter to a successor licensee.

CLIENT IDENTIFICATION AND VERIFICATION (BY-LAW 7.1)

Amendments to By-law 7.1 with respect to client identification and verification came into effect in Ontario on December 31, 2008. They are part of a Canada-wide initiative by provincial law societies to fight fraud and money laundering.

By-law 7.1, Part III applies to retainers in matters for new or existing clients entered into on or after December 31, 2008 (s. 21).

Unless otherwise noted, all references to section numbers in the following discussion refer to By-law 7.1, Part III.

Compliance with the By-law 7.1 Client Identification and Verification Requirements

Section 22(1) requires a licensee to comply with the client identification and verification requirements set out in s. 23 whenever he is retained to provide legal services to a new or existing client on or after December 31, 2008.

You do not have to identify or verify clients on matters that were in existence prior to December 31, 2008. However, if you are retained in a new or related matter for any of those clients on or after December 31, 2008, you must comply with the client identification and verification requirements in Part III.

LICENSEES WHO ARE EXEMPT FROM THE SECTION 23 CLIENT IDENTIFICATION AND VERIFICATION REQUIREMENTS

You are not required to comply with the s. 23 client identification and verification requirements if (s. 22(2)):

(a) you provide legal services to your employer (for example, as an in-house paralegal);

(b) you are acting as an agent for another licensee or paralegal who has already identified the client;

(c) you are acting for a client who was referred to you by another paralegal or a lawyer who has already identified the client; or

(d) you are acting as duty counsel or providing summary legal services under the *Legal Aid Services Act* or providing legal services through a duty counsel program of a non-profit organization, unless a financial transaction is involved.

With respect to (b) and (c) above, you should require the paralegal or lawyer for whom you are acting as an agent, or the paralegal or lawyer who made the referral, to confirm that they have already identified the client in compliance with the requirements of the by-law.

WHAT IS THE DIFFERENCE BETWEEN CLIENT IDENTIFICATION AND CLIENT VERIFICATION?

Client identification refers to information you obtain from the client regarding who the client is and what the client does. **Client verification** refers to information you must obtain in order to confirm that the client is who he says he is.

Licensees must obtain and record client identification information in accordance with the criteria set out in s. 23(1) for the client in every new client matter opened on or after December 31, 2008. This includes existing clients who retain you in new or related matters on or after December 31, 2008.

If you engage in or give instructions for the receiving, paying, or transferring of funds, then you must obtain the additional client identification information set out in s. 23(2) and you must comply with the client verification requirements set out in s. 23(4) (s. 22(1)(b)).

Funds include cash, currency, securities, negotiable instruments, or other financial instruments that indicate a person's title or interest in them (s. 20). A **negotiable instrument** is an unconditional order or promise to pay an amount of money, which can be transferred—for example, cheques or banknotes (paper money).

EXEMPTIONS FOR CERTAIN TYPES OF FUNDS (S. 22(3))

You do not have to comply with the s. 23(2) client identification requirements and the s. 23(4) client verification requirements if the funds you are handling fall within one of the following exemptions (the list is not exhaustive) (s. 22(3)):

(a) funds paid to or received from a financial institution such as a bank, credit union, trust company, and so on; a public body such as a government ministry or a municipality; or a reporting issuer (public company) or subsidiary of a reporting issuer;

(b) funds received from the trust account of another paralegal or a lawyer;

(c) funds received from a peace officer, law enforcement agency, or other public official acting in an official capacity;

(d) funds paid or received pursuant to a court order;

(e) funds paid for a fine or penalty;

(f) funds paid or received in settlement of legal or administrative proceedings;

(g) funds paid or received for professional fees, disbursements, expenses, or bail;

(h) funds paid, received, or transferred by electronic funds transfer.

CLIENTS WHO ARE EXEMPT FROM CLIENT IDENTIFICATION AND VERIFICATION

You are not required to comply with the Part III client identification and verification requirements if your client is (s. 22(4)):

1. a financial institution as defined at By-law 7.1, s. 20,

2. a public body as defined at By-law 7.1, s. 20, or

3. a reporting issuer as defined at By-law 7.1, s. 20.

BOX 2.4

Reminder

A **public company** (referred to as a "reporting issuer" in By-law 7.1, Part III) is a corporation whose shares are for sale to the general public. Public companies are subject to rigorous disclosure requirements under securities legislation.

A **private corporation** (also called a closely held corporation) is a corporation whose shares are not publicly traded. Its incorporating documents (1) restrict the right to sell shares, (2) limit the number of its shareholders (excluding employees) to 50, and (3) prohibit public trading of its shares or securities.

THE CRITERIA FOR CLIENT IDENTIFICATION AND VERIFICATION

The criteria for identifying and verifying clients are set out in table 2.1. Verification of identity forms for individuals, organizations, third-party beneficiaries, and principals are available at the Law Society of Upper Canada website. You will find samples, adapted for use in paralegal firms, at appendixes 2.3 and 2.4.

CLIENT VERIFICATION, NOT FACE TO FACE (S. 23(8))

You may use this form of client verification if you engage in or give instructions for the receiving, paying, or transferring of non-exempt funds on behalf of an individual client who is elsewhere in Canada, so that you are unable to receive instructions

TABLE 2.1   Criteria for Client Identification and Verification

Client identification requirements, exempt funds (ss. 22(1)(a), 22(3), 23(1))	
Individual	Organization (Private company, partnership, fund, trust, co-operative, or unincorporated association)
Full name	Full name
Business address and business telephone number, if applicable	Business address and business telephone number
Home address and home telephone number	The organization's incorporation or business identification number, if applicable The place of issue of its incorporation or business identification number, if applicable
Occupation(s)—does not have to be employment. If the client refuses to provide this information, you must inform the client that you will be in breach of By-law 7.1 if you do not obtain this information, and will be obliged to decline the retainer.	The general nature of the business or activity engaged in by the client. **This requirement does not apply** if the client organization is a financial institution, public body, or public company.
	The name, position, and contact information for the person(s) authorized to provide instructions in the matter
Whether the client is an individual or an organization, if the client is acting for or representing another person, you must obtain the same client identification information for that person as you would if that person were your client.	
Additional client identification requirements when handling non-exempt funds (ss. 22(1)(b)(i), 23(2))	
None	■ The name and occupation(s) of each director of the organization (other than an organization that is a securities dealer) ■ The name, address, and occupation(s) of each person who owns 25% or more of the organization or of the shares of the organization. You must make reasonable efforts to obtain the above information. Asking your client may be sufficient; or you may consult the corporate minute books if they are available, or an online corporate registry service.

from the client face to face (s. 23(8)). To comply with the s. 23(4) verification requirements, you must obtain an attestation from a commissioner of oaths or a guarantor certifying that he has verified the client's identity by looking at the appropriate independent source documents (s. 23(8)). Section 23(9) provides a list of professionals who may be used as guarantors, including dentists, lawyers, physicians, and accountants. You must exercise due diligence in confirming that the attestor is a member of one of these professions. **Due diligence** means exercising the prudence and vigilance that a reasonable and prudent paralegal would exercise in similar circumstances.

The attestation must be printed on a legible photocopy of the document. It must include the name, occupation, address, and signature of the attestor, and the type and number of the document seen by the attestor (s. 23(10)). A sample attestation form for use by paralegal firms is available at the Law Society website. You will find the text of a sample attestation at appendix 2.5.

TABLE 2.1   (Concluded)

Client verification requirements when handling non-exempt funds (s. 22(1)(b)(ii), 23(4))	
Individual	Organization (Private company, partnership, fund, trust, co-operative, or unincorporated association)
Verification must take place immediately after you first engage in or give instructions for the receiving, paying, or transferring of funds (s. 23(5))	Verification must take place by not later than 60 days after you first engage in or give instructions for the receiving, paying, or transferring of funds (s. 23(6))
You shall take reasonable steps to verify the identity of the client using what the licensee reasonably considers to be reliable, independent source documents, data, or information. You should take reasonable steps to comply with the verification requirement as early as possible in the retainer. Whether the client is an individual or an organization, if the client is acting for or representing another person, you shall take the same steps to verify the identity of that person as you would if that person were your client. You shall complete and sign a verification of identity form for each individual, organization, third-party beneficiary, or principal, with photocopies of the documentation relied upon attached.	
Examples of independent source documents (s. 23(7))	
An original government-issued identification that is valid and has not expired, and that you reasonably believe to be independent and reliable: ■ Driver's licence ■ Birth certificate ■ Passport ■ Provincial or territorial health card (if such use is not prohibited by law)	If the client is a private company or society created under legislative authority: ■ A certificate of corporate status ■ An annual filing ■ A similar record confirming the organization's existence If the client is a trust: ■ A trust agreement ■ Other documents establishing or amending the trust ■ Documents identifying the trustees If the client is a partnership: ■ The partnership agreement

CLIENT VERIFICATION, USE OF AGENT (S. 23(11))

You may use this form of client verification if you engage in or give instructions for the receiving, paying, or transferring of non-exempt funds on behalf of a client who is outside of Canada, or as an alternative to the s. 23(8) procedure for verifying the identity of an individual client who is elsewhere in Canada. Section 23(11) permits you to enter into a written agreement with an agent specifying the steps that the agent will be taking on your behalf to comply with the verification requirements and to provide you with the information. If the agent acting on your behalf is not an employee of your firm or a paralegal who provides legal services through your firm, you shall enter into a written agreement with the agent specifying the steps that the agent will be taking on your behalf to comply with the verification requirements (s. 23(11)). The agent may provide the information to you in the form of an attestation. See appendix 2.5 for a sample attestation.

PREVIOUS CLIENT VERIFICATION (S. 23(12))

For an individual client, a licensee complies with the s. 23(4) verification requirement if she has already verified the individual client's identity and recognizes the individual (s. 23(12)(a)).

For a client that is an organization, a licensee complies with the s. 23(2) identification requirements and the s. 23(4) verification requirements if she has already complied with those requirements with respect to the organization (s. 23(12)(b)).

DOCUMENTATION (SS. 23(13), (14))

You must obtain copies of every document used to verify the identity of a client, a third-party beneficiary, or a principal, including copies of documents used by agents for client verification under s. 23(11) (s. 23(13)).

You must keep records of all information obtained for purposes of client identification and verification, including copies of supporting documents, attestations, and so on, for the longer of (s. 23(14)):

(a) the duration of the paralegal–client relationship, and for as long as is necessary to provide service to the client; and

(b) at least six years following completion of the work for which you were retained.

CRIMINAL ACTIVITY (S. 24)

In the course of complying with the s. 23 client identification and verification requirements, you may begin to reasonably suspect that you are or will be assisting the client in dishonesty, fraud, crime, or illegal conduct. If that happens, you shall immediately cease to engage in any activities that would assist the client in dishonesty, fraud, crime, or illegal conduct (s. 24(a)), and, if necessary, withdraw from providing legal services to the client (s. 24(b)).

COMMUNICATING WITH THE CLIENT

General

Competent paralegals communicate effectively with their clients. This does not mean spending hours chatting on the phone with them. It means providing clients with the information they need as efficiently as possible.

Effective communication means advising the client during your initial contact with him that you are a paralegal, and explaining what that means; interviewing the client to find out what he wants; providing the client with honest advice as to the merits of his case and likely outcomes; keeping the client posted on next steps; obtaining and confirming client instructions when necessary; and generally keeping the client informed on the progress of the matter as things occur.

Advising Clients That You Are a Paralegal

Paralegals shall not hold themselves out as lawyers (Paralegal Rules 3.02(1) and 8.02(2)(a)) or undertake or provide advice with respect to a matter outside the permissible scope of paralegal practice (Paralegal Rule 3.02(2)).

When meeting a client for the first time, you should advise the client that you are a paralegal, not a lawyer, and you should explain the difference. You should inform the client that the legal services you provide are restricted to permissible areas of paralegal practice; and that if the client's problem falls outside these areas, the client should seek the services of a lawyer.

Small Claims Court is a permissible area of practice for paralegals (*Courts of Justice Act*, s. 26; By-law 4, s. 6).

The Initial Client Consultation

Although it does not have to take place in person, the initial client consultation is often the first time you meet a new client face to face. This is when the client gathers the information about you and your firm that he needs to decide whether he wants to hire you. This is also when you find out what the client's problem is and what the client's goals are; gather the information about the client's case that you need to decide whether he has a valid claim or defence; and determine what additional information or documents, if any, you need to go forward in the matter.

Prior to the consultation, you or your staff should perform a conflict check, and you should review the results. If there is a conflict or a potential conflict, you should comply with Paralegal Rule 3.04 and Guideline 9, discussed above.

You should take careful notes of what is said at the consultation. If the client gives you instructions to proceed, you should go over the notes with him before he leaves, to make sure that you have all the relevant details, correct any errors, and fill in any gaps. You should also make a list of any relevant documents. If he has not brought them with him to the interview, you should advise him to give them to you as soon as possible. You should discuss next steps with the client, and answer any questions he may have.

Your notes of the initial consultation should be dated and filed in the client file. You will need them to draft the retainer agreement or engagement letter, as well as the claim or defence. You should have a consistent practice with respect to where they are filed, so that you can always find them when you need them. For instance, you may wish to have a subfile in every client file that is dedicated to notes of interviews and telephone conversations, plus copies of emails.

If the client retains you, you must comply with the client identification and verification requirements set out in By-law 7.1, Part III.

Interviewing Strategies

Your interviewing strategy at the initial consultation will depend on whether you are talking to a plaintiff or a defendant. With a plaintiff, it is best to begin with open-ended questions, which let the plaintiff tell her story. When you have a sense of what she is there for, and what the likely legal issues are, you can start asking for details (such as dates, amounts owed or paid, and documentation), plus any other information you need to shape the plaintiff's story into a persuasive legal narrative.

When you are meeting with a defendant, one of the first questions you should ask her is when she was served with the claim, so that you know whether you are likely to be dealing with a noting of default. You will then want to review the claim itself. Your interview questions will be structured by the allegations in the claim. It is a good idea to go through the allegations one by one, and find out whether the defendant admits them, denies them, or has an alternative version of what happened. This will help you to develop a theory of what the defence should be. You can then ask additional questions to find out if there is any evidence to support that theory.

If the defendant wishes to make a defendant's claim, your questions should be open-ended until you have a sense of what the story is; then, as in a plaintiff interview, you can start asking more specific questions with a view to "shaping" the narrative.

When you are interviewing clients, you will find that they tell you a lot of things that may or may not be relevant to their matter. During the interview, and afterward, when you are going over your notes, keep the following questions in mind: What does the client want? What do I need to say to support the client's case? Which client statements support the client's case? Which client statements do not support the client's case? Which client statements are completely irrelevant to any issue that I am aware of in the client's case at this stage of the action?

When you have decided what the relevant facts are, you have to turn them into a persuasive narrative, which is carefully organized for maximum clarity. Sometimes, as in the case of a simple debt collection, this will be easy to do. In other cases, the narrative will be more complex, and will require careful thought, editing, and rewriting.

You cannot decide which facts are relevant unless you are familiar with the law applicable to a client matter. If you need a refresher in the applicable law, do some legal research at no cost to the client. If you are completely unfamiliar with the applicable legal principles, remember that Paralegal Rule 3.01(2) requires that you shall not undertake to represent a client in a matter unless you are familiar with the legal principles and procedures governing the applicable area of law, or are confident that you can become familiar with those legal principles and procedures in a timely and cost-effective manner.

Confirming the Retainer

PARALEGAL–CLIENT RETAINER

At the outset of the paralegal–client relationship, you should establish the scope of the paralegal–client retainer—that is, the terms of the contractual relationship between you and your client. You should discuss some or all of the following terms with the client at the initial consultation:

- specific client goals;
- if the client is an organization, the individual(s) in the organization authorized to give you instructions in the matter;
- the scope of the retainer (that is, the nature and extent of the legal services to be provided to achieve those goals);
- an estimate of the time it will take to complete key steps, if appropriate;
- an estimate of the likely cost of those services, along with any assumptions upon which your estimate is based;
- the fee structure (hourly rate, flat or fixed rate, fees by stages, or contingency fee);
- if an hourly rate is charged, your hourly rates and those of any associates who may be working on the file;
- standard disbursements and expenses for this type of matter;
- when and how often money retainers will be required, with confirmation that the money will be held in trust until the client is invoiced;
- your billing policies, and the consequences of late payment, including the interest charged on accounts that have been outstanding for more than 30 days;
- how settlement funds are to be handled;
- events of termination of the retainer; and
- a stipulation that any changes to the agreement are to be made in writing.

The agreed-upon terms should be confirmed in writing in a retainer agreement or engagement letter.

Whether you use an engagement letter or a retainer agreement to confirm the retainer, the document should advise the client that you are a licensed paralegal; that there are restrictions on the legal services you may provide; and that the client's matter falls within areas of practice authorized for paralegals.

You will find examples of an engagement letter and a retainer agreement at appendixes 2.6 and 2.7.

MONEY RETAINER

A **money retainer** is money paid to you by the client on account of future legal services and/or disbursements to be incurred. It is a deposit that secures your legal services. The money retainer belongs to the client until legal services have been provided and the client has been invoiced for those legal services.

Your paralegal practice should have, at the minimum, two bank accounts: a general account and a mixed trust account.

The **general account** is your operating account. You use the general account to pay ongoing business expenses, such as salaries, rent, insurance premiums, professional fees, client disbursements and expenses, and so on.

The **mixed trust account** is used for client money. It is called a mixed trust account because it holds money for many different clients.

You should never deposit a money retainer to your general account. You should never transfer money out of the mixed trust account to your general account to pay yourself for legal services without first providing the client with an invoice for those services.

It is permissible to reimburse yourself from the mixed trust account for proper disbursements and expenses that were paid from your general account for items like court filing fees, courier expenses, and so on in a client matter without invoicing the client. Proper books and records of the transaction must be kept.

PAYING YOURSELF OUT OF SETTLEMENT FUNDS PAYABLE TO THE CLIENT

Settlement funds that are payable to the client belong to the client. You should include a term in the retainer agreement or engagement letter stating that any settlement funds payable to the client are to be paid to you in trust, and that, upon delivery of an invoice, any outstanding fees and disbursements may be paid in full from the settlement funds, with the balance to be paid out to the client.

If the client matter settles (that is, it is resolved without a trial) on terms that another party is to pay your client money, the settlement agreement should state that the funds are to be paid to your firm in trust. If the other party is self-represented, the funds should be paid by certified cheque. The settlement funds will be deposited to your mixed trust account. When full and final releases have been signed by all parties, you may send the client your final report, along with your final invoice, which will be paid from the settlement funds held in trust. Any balance remaining in trust will be paid by trust cheque to your client.

When Should I Ask My Client for Instructions?

Clients hire you because you have professional knowledge and competence that they do not, and they pay you for that knowledge and competence.

For example, if you are representing a plaintiff in a Small Claims Court proceeding, you are expected to apply your knowledge and skills to advance the matter through the various procedural stages without seeking the client's instructions at every stage. However, you should keep the client informed of the progress of the matter. Often, this can be done by means of an **interim reporting letter**, which is delivered to the client, along with an **interim invoice**, before the client matter is concluded. An interim reporting letter reports the steps taken in the client matter to that point, the results obtained, and the likely next steps. An interim invoice is a bill delivered to the client before the client matter is concluded, in accordance with your billing policy.

If anything unusual occurs in a client matter, or if a procedure will result in significant additional cost to the client, you should advise the client and seek instructions. You should also seek client instructions before agreeing to an adjournment, or accepting or rejecting an offer of settlement.

If the other party makes an offer to settle, you should inform your client of the terms of the offer. Keeping in mind your duty to promote compromise and settlement (Paralegal Rule 3.02(5)), you should advise him whether you think the offer is reasonable or unreasonable, and why. Depending on the circumstances, you may wish to advise your client to make a counter-offer.

The final decision about accepting the offer, rejecting the offer, or making a counter-offer must be the client's, unless you have a written agreement or written instructions to the contrary. You cannot accept or reject the offer, or make a counter-offer, without first obtaining the client's instructions to do so.

Any time you talk to a client about his file, whether it is a casual telephone conversation or a scheduled meeting, you should keep a written record. This rule applies whether you are using paper files or file management software. Your notes should be identified by client name and dated. They should specify the nature of the contact, and describe what was discussed in a reasonable amount of detail. Any client instructions should be carefully and thoroughly noted. Your notes should be filed in a subfile in the client file. Depending on the circumstances, it may be advisable to confirm client instructions in writing to the client.

A **final reporting letter**, along with your final invoice for fees and disbursements incurred since the last interim invoice, should be sent to the client at the conclusion of the client matter. A final reporting letter provides a summary of the client's problem, steps taken, and results achieved in the client matter. If you are returning unused trust funds to the client, your trust cheque for the funds will be enclosed with the final reporting letter. You will find a sample of a final reporting letter at appendix 2.11.

CLIENT FILE MANAGEMENT

General

You do not need file management software to run an efficient practice. Whether you use file management software or set up your client files manually, the same principles of effective file management apply. File management software, if used properly, makes file management fast and easy by doing most of the organizing for you; but if you have proper procedures in place, you can provide timely, effective client service whatever your level of technology.

If you have office staff, they should understand the importance of setting up client files properly and maintaining orderly office systems. New staff should be trained in proper file management procedures. You should consider setting up and maintaining an office procedures manual for staff use.

You should also consider developing a database of precedent documents for use by paralegal employees and staff. The database should include routine correspondence, forms, standard retainer agreements and retainer letters, simple pleadings, etc. The contents of the database should be reviewed and updated on a regular basis.

The office procedures manual and database of precedents are intended to assist staff and paralegal employees to perform their duties efficiently. However, keep in mind that you shall assume complete professional responsibility for all business entrusted to you; and you shall directly supervise staff and assistants to whom particular tasks and functions are delegated. See Paralegal Rule 8.01 and By-law 7.1.

Setting Up a File System

THE CLIENT FILE

The client file is a file that is created either manually (that is, using paper) or electronically (using file management software) to contain all information pertaining to a particular client matter. Even if you do not use file management software, keep in mind that many of the documents in your client files will be assembled electronically. Electronic documents should be filed in an orderly fashion in folders cross-referenced to their client matters by **client matter number**. You should consider establishing a firm protocol for filing electronic documents and paper documents.

A separate client file with a unique matter number should be opened for each client matter. File management software will do this for you automatically. If you are handling several different matters for the same client, you should open a separate file with a unique matter number for each matter. The client matter number is used to track all transactions in a particular client matter, including time spent on the client matter, money held in trust to the credit of the client matter, billings, payments, and so on.

All correspondence, notes, pleadings and other documents connected with a particular client matter should be kept in appropriate subfiles in the client file folder. All subfiles should be cross-referenced to the client matter using the client matter number.

The client matter number is not the same as the claim number. The client matter number is a unique number assigned by the paralegal firm (or the file management software) to a particular client matter in order to identify that matter for filing, docketing, and billing purposes. The claim number is a unique number assigned to a particular proceeding by the Small Claims Court clerk for purposes of filing pleadings and other documents, identifying the matter on court dockets, monitoring the progress of the matter, and so on.

The client matter name that appears on file labels, correspondence, and so on should state, at a minimum, the client name and the client matter number.

CLIENT INFORMATION

The client file should contain complete client contact information, including the client's name, address, telephone and cell phone numbers, and email address. If the client is an institution or business entity of some kind, the name and other essential information of the person providing you with instructions should also be recorded in the client file.

There should be a record of the name (and address, if known) of the other party, and the name and other contact information for the other party's legal representative, if any. This information should be readily accessible, so that anyone opening the client file has it at their fingertips.

For a paper file, it should be standard procedure when opening a new file to complete a file information sheet containing a record of the above information. The file information sheet should be stapled to the inside front cover of the client file or kept in some other readily accessible place in the client file. See the sample file information sheet at appendix 2.8.

CHECKING FOR CONFLICTS

If practicable, whenever a prospective client contacts your firm, certain information (such as the client's name, including any aliases, and contact information) should be obtained from the client and entered into your conflict-checking system. A conflict search should be carried out before there is any further contact with the prospective client. The search results should be reviewed by the paralegal. The paralegal's decision should be noted on the file, and the search should be filed in the client file.

If the search reveals a conflict or potential conflict, you must advise the prospective client. The client may then decide to decline to retain you. The client's decision should be confirmed in a non-engagement letter.

Paralegal Rule 3.04(3) permits you to accept the retainer in certain circumstances, if the client consents. To comply with Paralegal Rule 3.04(3), you must disclose the conflict or potential conflict to the client in sufficient detail to enable the client to make an informed decision about whether retaining you is in his best interests. This is called informed consent. Guideline 9 recommends that you give the prospective client some time to consider the disclosure and ask for further clarification.

If you cannot provide sufficient detail about the conflict without breaching your duty of confidentiality to other persons, you must decline the retainer and recommend that the client seek other legal representation. You should confirm this in a non-engagement letter.

Even if the client consents and you are satisfied that you are not in breach of the *Paralegal Rules of Conduct*, you should still carefully consider whether it is advisable to decline the retainer in all of the circumstances, including potential delay, expense, and inconvenience to the client if you are obliged to terminate the retainer at a later stage in the proceeding due to the conflict. You should confirm your decision to decline the retainer and recommend that the client seek other legal representation in a non-engagement letter.

THE CHECKLIST AND TICKLER SYSTEM

For each client file you open, you should have a file-specific tickler and checklist, setting out tasks to be performed along with deadlines for their completion.

You should also have a general tickler system. For a small firm, this could be a calendar or desk diary. In the general tickler, all important dates and deadlines for all active client matters should be recorded, along with bring-forward reminders.

A tickler or bring-forward reminder (also called "diarizing") is a reminder to yourself that a particular matter will require attention in the near future. This gives you advance notice of work to be completed, along with the deadline for doing so. For example, if you have a Small Claims Court trial coming up, you should give yourself bring-forward reminders on a weekly basis starting at least two months before the scheduled court date, so that you can obtain and serve any documents, written statements, or audio or visual records that you intend to use as evidence on all parties (Rule 18.02(1)); summon witnesses; review the file and any relevant case law, etc.; and prepare your witnesses.

How much advance notice you give yourself for preparation depends on the applicable procedural rules, the complexity of the task to be completed, how much reliable support you have, and how busy your practice is.

You should also diarize for deadlines to be met by the other party, if the next steps on your file will depend on what action the other party takes. For example, if you are acting for the plaintiff in a Small Claims Court proceeding, you should always note the deadline for the defendant to deliver a defence (this will vary, depending on how service was effected). If the defendant fails to deliver a defence within that time, you must take steps to have the defendant noted in default, and, if appropriate, default judgment signed.

As tasks on the checklist are completed, they are initialled by the person who completed them and the date of completion is noted. This procedure allows you to pick up the file, look at the checklist, and know exactly where the file is at procedurally.

A sample checklist/tickler can be found at appendix 2.9.

Limitation Periods

A limitation period is a deadline prescribed by statute for commencing a court proceeding or otherwise protecting your legal rights. In Ontario, the *Limitations Act, 2002*, establishes a general limitation period for commencement of claims of no later than two years from the day on which the basis for the claim was discovered by the plaintiff. Limitation periods should be noted on your checklist/tickler in the client file. Serious prejudice to your client will result if you miss a limitation period. Limitation periods are dealt with in more detail in chapter 3.

Other Deadlines

The rules governing courts and tribunals provide deadlines for procedural steps in matters before the court or tribunal to which they apply. These procedural deadlines should also be noted on your checklist/tickler and diarized for follow-up.

It is extremely important to check for and note down any procedural deadlines when opening a new client file. Usually, missing a procedural deadline in a court proceeding does not result in permanent prejudice to your client, because courts have discretion to extend procedural deadlines. However, you must apply to the court for an order extending the deadline. This means an extra expense for your client. If the other party has been inconvenienced or prejudiced in any way, the court will likely order that your client pay them some costs.

If the missed deadline was your error, you should not bill the client for whatever action you must take to correct the error. If costs are awarded against your client because of your error, the amount of those costs should be deducted from your fee.

ORGANIZATION OF FILE CONTENTS

The contents of the client file should be organized into subfiles. Subfiles are separate, labelled folders that are kept in the client file. In an electronic file, they would be subfolders.

As with client documents, each subfile should be clearly labelled. The label on each subfile should state its contents, the client name, and the client matter number. This system of cross-referencing to the client file ensures that any subfiles that are pulled from the client file can be easily put back into the correct client file.

The number and type of subfiles you open for a particular client file will vary, depending on the nature of the proceeding. Client files may contain the following subfiles:

- Correspondence: All correspondence related to the file should be filed in this subfile. Notes of telephone conversations may also be kept in this file, along with hard copies of email correspondence. Every document should have a date on it. The contents of this subfile should be arranged in reverse chronological order, with the most recent communication on top.

- Pleadings: All court documents (plaintiff's claim, defence, other pleadings if any, affidavits or certificates of service, motions, etc.) are kept in this subfile.

- Documents: The originals of any documentary evidence upon which you intend to rely at the hearing of the matter should be kept in this subfile.

- Retainer agreement and billing information.

- Relevant case law and legal research.

You may not need all of the above subfiles in every case. Decide what is efficient for your practice. However, at a minimum, client files should have subfiles for correspondence, pleadings, and documents.

STORAGE OF FILES

When in use, active client files, such as file boxes, files, diskettes, CDs, etc., should not be left out in any area to which the public has access. This includes your office, if that is where you meet clients.

Staff who work in public areas should not be assigned to work on client files unless their work area is set up in such a way as to protect client confidentiality.

If your client files are electronic, computer monitors should be turned so that they are not visible to the public. Monitors that are visible to the public should be filtered. All electronic data of a personal nature should be password-protected or encrypted.

When not in use, all documentation connected with an active client file should be properly stored in the correct client file. The client file should be properly filed in the correct place in your filing system. That filing system should be in a secure place. For example, if you use filing cabinets, the filing cabinets should be in a separate area to which access is restricted.

Active client files should not be stored with closed files. Closed files should be pulled from the active client file system and stored separately, also in a secure place.

Closing Out Client Files

Client files may be closed when all services connected to the file have been completed, and the client has received a final account and reporting letter. The client is also entitled to receive her original documents back (after the appeal period of 30 days from the date of trial has elapsed), as well as any other documents that were not provided to her in the course of the retainer. You should have the client sign and return an acknowledgment of receipt of these documents.

When closing out client files, staff should check to ensure that appropriate data about the file have been entered into the conflict-checking database.

Closed files should be coded as closed. They should be stored in a secure place, separate from active client files. Closed electronic files should be stored in a format that will be retrievable by future technology.

CHAPTER SUMMARY

A competent paralegal is a paralegal who has and applies the relevant skills, attributes, and values appropriate to each matter undertaken on behalf of a client, including but not limited to (1) knowledge; (2) client service and communication; and (3) skills and judgment. You shall not undertake to represent a client in a matter unless you are familiar with the legal principles and procedures governing the applicable area of law, or are confident that you can become familiar with those legal principles and procedures in a timely and cost-effective manner (Paralegal Rule 3.01(2)).

A conflict of interest is any circumstance that may negatively affect a paralegal's ability to represent the client's best interests. Conflicts of interest may arise at any time in a client matter, as the matter evolves, new parties are added, and new circumstances or information come to light.

Because conflicts of interest may result in harm to the client, paralegals have an obligation to prospective clients, current clients, and former clients to avoid conflicts of interest and potential conflicts of interest.

Before agreeing to act for a client, you should check for conflicts of interest. You should maintain a database of all clients, their matters, and the opposing parties for this purpose.

By-law 7.1, section 22(1) requires a licensee to comply with the client identification and verification requirements set out in s. 23 whenever she is retained to provide legal services to a new or existing client on or after December 31, 2008. You do not have to identify or verify clients on matters that were in existence prior to December 31, 2008. However, if you are retained in a new or related matter for any of those clients on or after December 31, 2008, you must comply with the client identification and verification requirements in Part III of By-law 7.1.

The duty of confidentiality obliges you and your associates and employees to hold in strict confidence any information concerning any aspect of a client's affairs from the moment the professional relationship begins, unless disclosure is authorized by your client or required by law. The duty of confidentiality applies to clients who contact you but do not retain you, and to clients who retain you, sometimes on several client matters.

The duty of confidentiality applies to all information of any kind that you acquire from a client or on behalf of a client during the professional relationship, including information that is not specific to the matter in which you have been retained and information of which others may have knowledge.

The duty of confidentiality continues indefinitely.

You must never use confidential information for your own benefit, personal or financial, even if doing so does not harm the client.

You may disclose confidential client information to others only if you have written authority from the client to do so (express consent) or the nature of the matter requires it (implied consent).

In order to maintain good relations with the client, you must be an effective communicator. This includes advising the client during your initial contact with him that you are a paralegal, and explaining what that means; interviewing the client to find out what he wants; advising the client honestly and candidly as to the merits of his case and likely outcomes; obtaining and confirming client instructions when appropriate; and generally keeping the client informed on the progress of the matter as things occur.

When a client hires you, you should confirm the terms upon which you were hired in writing, using a retainer agreement or engagement letter. You should consider making it a term of the retainer that a money retainer will be required at the outset of the retainer, and that further money retainers will be required as the matter progresses and interim invoices are delivered to the client. The money retainer belongs to the client and should be deposited to your mixed trust account.

Money held in trust may not be transferred to your general account unless the client has received an invoice for legal fees and disbursements to that date, along with an interim reporting letter advising the client of the status of the matter. A final reporting letter will be sent out with your final account.

Whether you are using file management software or paper, a separate client file should be opened for each client. If you are handling several different matters for the same client, you should open a separate file for each matter. Each client file should be assigned its own client matter number, which will be used for file management purposes and for accounting and billing purposes. All correspondence, notes, and other documents and things connected with a particular matter should be filed in appropriate subfiles in the client file for that matter when not in use.

For each client file you open, you should have a file-specific tickler and checklist that sets out tasks to be performed along with deadlines for their completion. You should also maintain a general tickler system, setting out all important dates and deadlines on all active files, along with bring-forward reminders.

KEY TERMS

candid	funds
casual clients	general account
client	implied consent
client identification	informed consent
client matter number	interim invoice
client verification	interim reporting letter
competent paralegal	mixed trust account
conflict of interest	money retainer
dispute	negotiable instrument
due diligence	non-engagement letter
engagement letter	paralegal–client retainer
express consent	private corporation
fiduciary	prospective client
fiduciary relationship	public company
final reporting letter	retainer agreement

REFERENCES

Courts of Justice Act, RSO 1990, c. C-43, as amended.

Law Society of Upper Canada (LSUC), By-laws (Toronto: LSUC, 2005, as amended); available online at http://www.lsuc.on.ca.

Law Society of Upper Canada (LSUC), *Paralegal Professional Conduct Guidelines* (Toronto: LSUC, 2008, as amended) ("the Guidelines"); available online at http://www.lsuc.on.ca/paralegals/a/paralegal-professional-conduct-guidelines.

Law Society of Upper Canada (LSUC), *Paralegal Rules of Conduct* (Toronto: LSUC, 2007, as amended) ("the Paralegal Rules"); available online at http://www.lsuc.on.ca/paralegals/a/paralegal-rules-of-conduct.

Law Society of Upper Canada (LSUC), *Practice Management Guidelines* (Toronto: LSUC, 2008); available online at http://rc.lsuc.on.ca/pdf/pmg/pmg.pdf.

Legal Aid Services Act, 1998, SO 1998, c. 26.

Limitations Act, 2002, SO 2002, c. 24, sched. B, as amended.

Rules of the Small Claims Court, O. Reg. 258/98.

REVIEW QUESTIONS

1. What is a competent paralegal?

2. What should you do if you do not think you are competent to represent a client?

3. a. What is a conflict of interest?

   b. How can a paralegal prevent conflicts of interest?

4. a. What is the duty of confidentiality?

   b. What kinds of information does it apply to?

   c. Who does it apply to?

   d. When does the duty arise and when does it end?

5. When is it permissible to disclose confidential information about a client?

6. What are the essentials of effective client communication?

7. What should you do whenever you talk to a client about her file?

8. What should you do when interviewing a client for the first time? Assume that there are no conflict issues.

9. What is a retainer agreement? What is the difference between a retainer agreement and an engagement letter?

10. What is a money retainer?

11. When may you transfer client money from the mixed trust account to the general account?

12. What are the basic principles for setting up a client file?

APPENDIX 2.1   Non-Engagement Letter (Conflict of Interest— Client Declines Retainer)

[Date]

[File number]

[Client name and address]

Dear [Client name]:

Re: [Matter name]

As we discussed during our [telephone conversation/meeting/initial consultation] on [date], a preliminary search revealed that [paralegal firm name] has a conflict of interest in this matter. We provided you with details of the conflict and asked you to decide whether you wished to consent to the retainer based on this disclosure. You have now advised that you do not wish to retain us.

Please be aware that whatever claim you have may be barred by the passage of time. Since time limitations may be critical to your case, we recommend that you immediately contact another paralegal or a lawyer for assistance regarding your matter. If you do not have another paralegal or a lawyer in mind to represent you, the Law Society maintains a directory of paralegals and lawyers who may be available to assist you at its website (http://www.lsuc.on.ca), or you may wish to call the Lawyer Referral Service at 1-800-268-8326. There is no charge for the Lawyer Referral Service.

We confirm that we do not have any documents belonging to you. All documents were returned to you at the end of the initial meeting.

Although we were not able to assist you in this matter, we hope that you will consider [paralegal firm name] in the event that you require legal services in the future.

Thank you again for your interest in this firm.

Yours truly,

[PARALEGAL FIRM NAME]

[Signature]

[Signatory name]
Paralegal

[Adapted from the Law Society of British Columbia website (http://www.lawsociety.bc.ca) and the Law Society of Upper Canada website (http://www.lsuc.on.ca).]

APPENDIX 2.2   Non-Engagement Letter (Conflict of Interest—Paralegal Firm Declines Retainer)

[Date]

[File number]

[Client name and address]

Dear [Client name]:

Re: [Matter name]

As we discussed during our [telephone conversation/meeting/initial consultation] on [date], before [paralegal firm name] could agree to represent you in this matter, we had to investigate whether this representation could adversely affect existing or former clients' interests or whether there might be some other reason that we would be unable to adequately represent your interests.

On [date], we performed a conflict of interest check and found that our firm does indeed have a conflict of interest in this case. Unfortunately, we therefore cannot represent you and we must decline to do so in this matter.

Please be aware that whatever claim you have may be barred by the passage of time. Since time limitations may be critical to your case, we recommend that you immediately contact another paralegal or a lawyer for assistance regarding your matter. If you do not have another paralegal or a lawyer in mind to represent you, the Law Society maintains a directory of paralegals and lawyers who may be available to assist you at its website (http://www.lsuc.on.ca), or you may wish to call the Lawyer Referral Service at 1-800-268-8326. There is no charge for the Lawyer Referral Service.

We confirm that we do not have any documents belonging to you. All documents were returned to you at the end of the initial meeting.

Although we were not able to assist you in this matter, we hope that you will consider [paralegal firm name] in the event that you require legal services in the future.

Thank you again for your interest in this firm.

Yours truly,

[PARALEGAL FIRM NAME]

[Signature]

[Signatory name]
Paralegal

[Adapted from the Law Society of British Columbia website (http://www.lawsociety.bc.ca) and the Law Society of Upper Canada website (http://www.lsuc.on.ca).]

APPENDIX 2.3   Verification of Identity (Individual)

[PARALEGAL FIRM NAME]

Paralegals

VERIFICATION OF IDENTITY

(For use where the client or third party is an individual)

Name: _____

Address (home): _____

Telephone number (home): _____

Address (business): _____

Telephone number (business): _____

Occupation(s): _____

Original Document Reviewed—Copy Attached

_____ Driver's Licence

_____ Birth Certificate

_____ Passport

_____ Other (specify type): _____

Meeting date identity verified: _____

Identity verified by: _____

Date file reviewed by paralegal: _____

Name of paralegal: _____

APPENDIX 2.4   Verification of Identity (Organization)

[PARALEGAL FIRM NAME]

Paralegals

VERIFICATION OF IDENTITY

(For use where the client or third party is an organization)

Name: _____

Address (business): _____

Telephone number (business): _____

Incorporation or Business Identification Number: _____

Place of issue of number: _____

Type of business or activity: _____

Person Authorized to Instruct

Name: _____

Position: _____

Telephone number: _____

Original Document Reviewed—Copy Attached

_____ Driver's Licence

_____ Birth Certificate

_____ Passport

_____ Other (specify type): _____

APPENDIX 2.4   Concluded

Names and occupation(s) of directors:

[List]

Names, addresses and occupation(s) of owners or shareholders owning a 25% interest or more of the organization or shares in the organization:

[List]

Original Document Reviewed—Copy Attached

_____   Certificate of Corporate Status

_____   Annual Filings of the Organization (specify type): _____

_____   Partnership Agreement

_____   Trust Agreement

_____   Articles of Association

_____   Other (specify type): _____

Meeting date identity verified: _____

Identity verified by: _____

Date file reviewed by paralegal: _____

Name of paralegal: _____

APPENDIX 2.5   Attestation for Verification of Identity When the Client or Third Party Is Present in Canada and Is Not Instructing the Paralegal Face to Face

INSTRUCTIONS

The Attestor should photocopy the identity document being used to verify identity and ensure that it is legible, unexpired, and shows the name of the person whose identity is being verified, the number of the document, the name of the issuing authority, the date of issue, and a photograph of the person.

The Attestor will *print* the following attestation on the photocopy and date and sign the attestation.

> I, the Attestor named below, hereby certify to **[name of paralegal receiving the attestation]** that I met with **[name of person]** on **[date]** and verified this person's identity by examining the original of this person's identity document, of which a photocopy is contained on this page. The photograph in the identity document is a true likeness of the said person, and to the best of my knowledge and belief the identity document that I examined is valid and unexpired.
>
> Attested to by me at _____, on _____ ____, 20____.

Signature of Attestor: _____

Printed Name of Attestor: _____

Title or Profession of Attestor: _____

Address of Attestor for Service: _____

_____

Telephone Number of Attestor: _____

APPENDIX 2.6   Engagement Letter

[LETTERHEAD]

Client matter no. 632

June 14, 20—

Mrs. Maxine Chong
67 Harmony Avenue
Toronto, ON M4J 1J3

Dear Mrs. Chong:

Re: LeeAnn Kingman
Small Claims Court action

Further to our meeting on June 12, 20—, this will confirm that you have retained us to act in the above matter. By a tenancy agreement dated January 13, 20—, Ms. Kingman rented your basement apartment from February 1, 20— until April 17, 20—. The monthly rent was $775.00 including water, heat and hydro. Ms. Kingman did not pay a last month's rent deposit, and during her tenancy Ms. Kingman paid no rent. As well, she harassed you and interfered with your reasonable enjoyment of the premises, causing damage to your health. Ms. Kingman vacated the premises on April 17, 20—.

You have instructed us to commence an action immediately in Small Claims Court for $25,000.00 for unpaid rent, damage to property, and pain and suffering, plus interest and costs. You have agreed to waive any amounts you might recover over and above $25,000.00 in order to bring the matter within Small Claims Court jurisdiction.

We also wish to confirm our agreement as to fees and payment. We charge $85.00 per hour for legal services. You will also be billed for any out-of-pocket expenses (also known as disbursements) that may be incurred, such as court filing fees, etc.

We will bill you approximately monthly, depending on the amount of work that is completed on your file during that period of time. The amount of time and expenses that will be required to represent you in this matter cannot be predicted at this time. However, as we discussed, the fee will not be less than $3,000.00 excluding disbursements. We will advise you before undertaking any procedures that will substantially increase the amount of your fees, and will obtain your instructions to proceed.

This will confirm that you have provided us with a money retainer of $1,000.00. This money has been placed in our trust account and will be applied to payment of invoices when delivered. You may be asked to provide further money retainers from time to time as the matter goes forward.

APPENDIX 2.6 Concluded

Chong v. Kingman
Client matter no. 632
Page 2 of 2

As we discussed at our meeting, will you please forward copies of the tenancy agreement and the Notice of Early Termination to us as soon as possible. We will also require copies of your medical records and bills for the period after Ms. Kingman's tenancy commenced. These documents will be returned to you when the matter is concluded.

We will make every effort to reach a settlement with Ms. Kingman in accordance with your instructions. However, we cannot guarantee success or that we will be able to reach a negotiated settlement. This will confirm that you have agreed that, if the matter does settle in your favour, the settlement funds are to be paid to us in trust and any outstanding fees or disbursements may be paid from those funds. We will then pay any unused portion to you.

As I advised you, we are a paralegal firm. We are not lawyers. Paralegals are restricted to providing legal services in permissible areas of law only. You have indicated that you wish to proceed in Small Claims Court. Small Claims Court is an authorized area of practice for paralegals.

I trust that the foregoing is satisfactory. If you have any questions or concerns, please contact me. I will try to respond to your phone calls and emails as quickly as possible. If a matter is urgent, I will make every effort to respond to you on an urgent basis.

Yours very truly,

Prior Mustafa LLP

Joseph Mustafa
Paralegal

[Adapted from the Lawyers' Professional Indemnity Company website (http://www.practicepro.ca/practice/financesbookletprecedents.asp)]

APPENDIX 2.7   Sample Retainer Agreement

[LETTERHEAD]

Retainer Agreement

General

[Date]

[Client name and address]

Dear **[Name of client]**:

Re: [Description of matter]

1. Description of Services

You have asked us, and we have agreed, to act for you in the matter described below. On **[date]**, we **[met/spoke]** to discuss the scope of our firm's intended representation. We covered this subject in some detail and considered the nature of our fee arrangement. The purpose of this letter is to summarize and confirm the terms of your engagement of us.

You retain us to represent you in connection with **[description of matter]**. We anticipate that our representation will involve taking the following steps on your behalf:

   (a) **[Describe]**

   (b) **[Describe]**

   (c) **[Describe]**

[Optional] At this time we have not been retained to represent you generally or in connection with any other matter. We will not be performing the following services:

   (d) **[Describe]**

   (e) **[Describe]**

   (f) **[Describe]**

Your desired outcome and time frame for resolution of this matter is as follows:

   [Describe]

We will work with you toward your desired outcome. However, all legal actions are subject to many possible variables. Accordingly, we cannot guarantee that your desired result will in fact be achieved. For us to work toward your desired outcome, it will be necessary for you to abide by the terms described in this letter.

2. Paralegals

As I advised you, we are a paralegal firm. We are not lawyers. Paralegals are restricted to providing legal services in permissible areas of law only. We are satisfied that your matter falls within an authorized area of practice for paralegals.

We expect that most of the work will be performed or supervised by myself (a partner in this firm), assisted by **[name]**, an **[associate/student]** in this firm. However, we reserve the right to assign other paralegals in our firm to perform legal services if in our judgment that becomes necessary or desirable.

APPENDIX 2.7   Continued

3. Fees

(a) Our fee will be based principally on the time spent by us on your behalf. Records of all time spent will be kept and accounts will then be prepared and sent to you periodically.

Our hourly rates range from $[**amount**] for students to $[**amount**] for my associate to $[**amount**] for me.

While we expect that our fee will be calculated on the basis of our regular hourly rates, we reserve the right to charge more in appropriate cases, such as pressing circumstances, the requirement for work outside normal business hours, exceptionally successful or efficient representation, or special demands on us.

You will be charged GST/HST on fees and GST/HST on some disbursements.

[Option 1]

(b) The amount of time and expenses that will be required to represent you in this matter cannot be predicted at this time. However, as we discussed, the fee will be not less than $[**amount**] excluding disbursements. We will advise you before undertaking any procedures that will substantially increase the amount of your fees, and will obtain your instructions to proceed.

[Option 2]

(b) Based on our consideration of the materials and information you have provided to us, and assuming that there are no further developments or information that would cause us to vary our preliminary opinion and that nothing out of the ordinary is encountered in the course of completing this matter, we estimate that our fee, excluding disbursements, will be $[**amount**]. We are not guaranteeing that we can accomplish the work for that sum, but are representing to you that in our judgment that amount appears reasonable under the circumstances. We will advise you before undertaking any procedures that will substantially increase the amount of your fees, and will obtain your instructions to proceed.

4. Expenses and Allocated Charges (also called disbursements)

You will be responsible for reimbursing us for expenses (also called disbursements) we incur on your behalf and for office charges allocated to your file. These include long distance calls, faxes, postage, deliveries, travel expenses, photocopying, and government filing and search charges; the fees of agents who conduct investigations, searches, and registrations; and all other reasonable out-of-pocket expenses and office charges. We do not charge for staff overtime on evenings or weekends in order to meet time deadlines.

5. Interest

Payment is due on all of our accounts when rendered. If any account is not paid within 30 days, interest will be charged on the outstanding balance at a rate of [**rate**]% per annum from the date of the account, until paid.

6. Retainer

Before we begin work on your behalf, we require a retainer in the amount of $[**amount**]. The retainer will be placed in our trust account and will serve as a source of payment for all or part of our account or accounts when rendered. You will be asked to replenish the retainer from time to time. Any unused portion will be returned to you upon the completion or termination of our services.

APPENDIX 2.7   Concluded

[Optional]

7. Settlement funds

We have discussed and you have agreed that, if this matter settles in your favour, the settlement funds are to be paid to us in trust and any outstanding fees or disbursements may be paid from those funds. We will then pay any unused portion to you.

8. Termination of Legal Services

You have the right to terminate our services to you upon written notice to us.

Subject to our obligations to you to maintain proper standards of professional conduct, we reserve the right to terminate our services to you for good reasons, which include but are not limited to:

    (a)   if you fail to cooperate with us in any reasonable request;

    (b)   if our continuing to act would be unethical or impractical;

    (c)   if our retainer has not been paid; or

    (d)   if you fail to pay our accounts when rendered.

If you terminate our services or we withdraw, you will be responsible only for our fees and expenses up until the time we stop acting for you.

If you terminate our services or we withdraw, the following documents and information will be returned to you:

[List documents and information]

9. Agreement

You may want to have this agreement reviewed by another paralegal or a lawyer.

If you want us to proceed on the terms described above, please sign the enclosed copy of this letter in the space provided and return it to us, together with a retainer in the sum of $**[amount]**, in the enclosed self-addressed envelope. If you decide that you do not want us to proceed on your behalf in this matter, please inform us promptly.

Yours truly,

[PARALEGAL FIRM NAME]

[Signature]

[Signatory name]
Paralegal

I have read and understand the retainer agreement, and agree to its terms.

_____   _____

             Client's signature   Date

[Adapted from the Lawyers' Professional Indemnity Company website (http://www.practicepro.ca/practice/financesbookletprecedents.asp)]

APPENDIX 2.8   Sample File Information Sheet: Chong v. Kingman

FILE INFORMATION SHEET

Court file number: 5678
Court: Toronto Small Claims
Short title of matter: Chong v. Kingman
Client matter number: 632   File opened: June 13, 20—

OUR CLIENT: Plaintiff		OTHER PARTY: Defendant/~~debtor~~	
Full name:	Maxine Chong (Mrs.)	Full name:	LeeAnn Kingman
Address:	67 Harmony Avenue Toronto, Ontario M4J 1J3	Address:	48 Brimley Road, Apt. 1306 Toronto, Ontario M2L 3T6
Our contact:			
Telephone:	416 222 3333	Telephone:	
Fax number:		Fax number:	
Email:		Email:	

PARALEGAL ASSIGNED TO FILE: REPRESENTATIVE:

Joseph Mustafa
                                     Address:

ADDITIONAL NOTES:

APPENDIX 2.9   Checklist/Tickler: Chong v. Kingman

CHECKLIST

Title of matter:	Maxine Chong v. LeeAnn Kingman
Type of matter:	Small Claims
Client matter number:	632
Court file number:	5678
Court address:	Toronto Small Claims Court 47 Sheppard Avenue East, 3rd floor Toronto, Ontario M2N 5X5
Telephone number:	416 326 3554
Fax number:	
Email:	

CHECKLIST/TICKLER

Task	Deadline	Bring forward	Date completed	By
Open file	asap	asap	June 14, 20—	P.A.
Draft claim	Limitations Act 2 years from Feb. 1, 20—	asap	June 21, 20—	J.M.
Issue claim	asap	asap	June 24, 20—	P.A.
Service claim	Dec. 24, 20—	asap	July 12, 20—	C.I.
Deadline defence	Aug. 2, 20—	Aug. 3, 20—		Other side
Note in default		Aug. 3, 20—		

APPENDIX 2.10   Express Consent to Disclose Confidential Information

AUTHORIZATION

I, **[name of client]**, do hereby authorize **[name of legal representative]** of **[name of firm]** to release to **[name or names of authorized recipients]** or their legal representatives of record the following documents and other information: **[particulars of permitted disclosure]**

I have been advised of and understand the purpose and consequences of this disclosure.

Date: _____   Signature: _____

Client name

Date: _____   Witness: _____

Witness name

APPENDIX 2.11   Sample Final Reporting Letter

[LETTERHEAD]

Client matter no. 576

January 16, 20—

Mr. Henry Stamp
489 Champagne Avenue, Unit 22
Mississauga, ON L2M 4Z2

Dear Mr. Stamp:

Re: Stamp v. Champion
Small Claims Court debt collection

You retained us to act for you in an action for recovery of money owing for a painting sold to Gerald Champion at the Downtown Toronto Art Fair in July 20—. Mr. Champion paid $2,100.00 to you for the painting by personal cheque. The cheque was later returned to you for insufficient funds. Mr. Champion did not respond to demands for payment, and we commenced a Small Claims Court action in October 20—. The matter has now settled. The settlement funds of $2,100.00 plus costs of $130.00 were paid by certified cheque into our trust account on January 10, 20—.

This will end our involvement in the matter, and we are forwarding our final invoice #543 for $1,034.35, which has been paid in full out of the settlement funds in accordance with the terms of the retainer agreement. Our trust cheque payable to you for the balance of $1,195.65 is also enclosed, along with a duplicate original of the settlement agreement dated January 5, 20— and full and final releases signed by you and Mr. Champion.

We are very pleased with this prompt resolution of the matter. If we can be of any assistance in the future, please contact us. I look forward to seeing your new work at the next Downtown Toronto Art Fair.

Yours very truly,

[PARALEGAL FIRM NAME]

[Name of paralegal signatory]
Paralegal

Enclosures: Invoice #543
Trust cheque #177
Settlement agreement dated January 5, 20— and signed releases

Acting for the Plaintiff: Preliminary Considerations

LEARNING OBJECTIVES

After reading this chapter, you will understand:

- What to consider when deciding whether to bring a Small Claims Court action

- The types of cases that Small Claims Court may or may not hear

- What a limitation period is, and the consequences of missing a limitation period

- The monetary jurisdiction of Small Claims Court

- Liquidated and unliquidated claims

- The basic principles for determining damages

- Waiver or abandonment of the excess, and its consequences

- What territorial jurisdiction is, and how it is determined

INTRODUCTION

A paralegal must be honest and candid when advising a client (Paralegal Rule 3.02(1)). This is true whether the client is seeking to retain you in a matter, or is a casual client seeking quick advice.

In this context, being **candid** means being forthright and sincere, and looking at both sides of each issue without bias. You must advise the client honestly and candidly of the applicable law, the client's options, possible outcomes, and possible risks. Your advice should enable the client to make informed decisions and give appropriate instructions in the matter.

When a client comes to you for advice about commencing a court proceeding, the first thing you have to determine is whether their case has any legal merit. Remember, a client's sense of personal grievance does not necessarily translate into a **cause of action**—that is, valid legal grounds for commencing a court action.

Legal merit is not the only issue to be considered when advising a client whether or not to litigate. Even if you are satisfied that your client's case has legal merit, you need to ask yourself other questions as well. If you fail to ask yourself these questions, and to answer them honestly for your client's benefit, you may end up giving your client bad advice.

- Is it cost-effective to litigate, given the amount in dispute? A party with legal representation should consider the cost of paying for that legal representation as well as court fees and other disbursements, and balance those expenses against the amount to be recovered. A self-represented party should consider the cost of filing fees, as well as the hidden "costs" of litigation, such as stress and time lost from work to attend at court, and balance those "costs" against the amount being litigated.

- Is it cost-effective to litigate against a particular defendant? Does the defendant have any ability to pay a judgment, if one is obtained? A court judgment is just a worthless piece of paper if the judgment debtor has no income or assets against which the judgment may be enforced. When asking yourself this question, consider the effect on your client's rights if a limitation period expires, keeping in mind that a debtor's circumstances may change. A judgment that is not presently enforceable may become enforceable later on, when the debtor obtains employment or acquires assets against which the judgment can be enforced.

- Even if litigation is a valid option, is there another way of resolving the matter? You have a professional obligation to advise and encourage a client to compromise or settle a dispute whenever it is possible to do so on a reasonable basis (Paralegal Rule 3.02(5)). If a letter or a telephone call may settle things, you should try them first, before commencing a court proceeding. Where your client's interests are better served by litigation, you should continue to encourage settlement of the matter throughout the proceeding, if it can be achieved on reasonable terms.

Is It Worthwhile to Sue This Particular Defendant?

When advising a client who is contemplating litigation, you must consider whether the defendant has the ability to pay a judgment, if one is obtained. Remember, a court judgment is just a worthless piece of paper if the **judgment debtor** cannot be found, or is **judgment-proof**—that is, has no income or assets against which the judgment may be enforced. A judgment debtor is any person who owes money to another person pursuant to a court order.

You must also advise the client of the effect upon her rights if she chooses not to commence a proceeding and the limitation period for doing so expires. See the discussion of limitation periods at page 74.

There are a number of searches that may assist you in determining a defendant's financial status. The following list is not exhaustive. Searches will be discussed in more detail in chapter 11.

When deciding which searches to conduct and what you require before conducting those searches, you should consider the *Personal Information Protection and Electronic Documents Act* (PIPEDA). PIPEDA is federal legislation that applies to personal information collected, used, or disclosed by private sector organizations in the course of commercial activities. An exception is made for organizations operating in provinces with substantially similar provincial legislation. Because Ontario does not have substantially similar legislation, PIPEDA applies in Ontario.

PIPEDA sets up procedures for the collection, use, and disclosure of personal information. These procedures are intended to give individuals control over how their personal information is handled in the private sector. An organization is responsible for the protection of personal information and the fair handling of it at all times, both within the organization and in dealings with third parties.

Paralegal firms are engaged in commercial activity in Ontario; therefore, PIPEDA applies to the provision of legal services. You must implement a privacy policy and procedures for any personal information you gather in the course of your business (including information about debtors) in compliance with PIPEDA requirements.

This means you must:

- obtain the consent of people whose personal information you collect, use, or disclose, except in a few specific and limited circumstances;

- use or disclose people's personal information only for the purpose for which they gave consent;

- even with consent, limit collection, use, and disclosure of personal information to purposes that a reasonable person would consider appropriate under the circumstances;

- permit individuals to see the personal information that your business holds about them, and to correct any inaccuracies; and

- advise people whose personal information you collect of procedures to follow if they believe their rights have been violated.

Note, however, that under provincial legislation there are a limited number of situations in which consumer information may be collected without an individual's permission. Section 8 of the Ontario *Consumer Reporting Act* states:

To whom reports may be given

8(1) No consumer reporting agency and no officer or employee thereof shall knowingly furnish any information from the files of the consumer reporting agency except,

(a) in response to the order of a court having jurisdiction to issue such an order;

(b) in accordance with the written instructions of the consumer to whom the information relates;

(c) in response to an order or direction made under this Act; or

(d) in a consumer report given to a person who it has reason to believe,

(i) intends to use the information in connection with the extension of credit to or the purchase or collection of a debt of the consumer to whom the information pertains,

(ii) intends to use the information in connection with the entering into or renewal of a tenancy agreement,

(iii) intends to use the information for employment purposes,

(iv) intends to use the information in connection with the underwriting of insurance involving the consumer,

(v) intends to use the information to determine the consumer's eligibility for any matter under a statute or regulation where the information is relevant to the requirement prescribed by law,

(vi) otherwise has a direct business need for the information in connection with a business or credit transaction involving the consumer, or

(vii) intends to use the information for the purpose of up-dating the information in a consumer report previously given to the person for one of the reasons referred to in subclauses (i) to (vi).

Idem

(2) No person shall knowingly obtain any information from the files of a consumer reporting agency respecting a consumer except for the purposes referred to in subsection (1).

Obtaining consumer credit reports on individuals from credit bureaus as part of your litigation preparation does not appear to fall within these exceptions. The Privacy Commissioner of Canada has found that complaints made by individuals against law firms collecting their credit information without their consent in the normal course of the law firms' commercial activity were well-founded. There was no general exclusion for the activities of law firms undertaken on behalf of their clients. The same principles would apply to paralegal firms who investigate individuals without their consent.

CREDIT BUREAU SEARCH

If you are a member of a credit bureau such as Equifax, you can do an online search of the defendant's credit status, subject to compliance with PIPEDA, discussed above. A standard credit bureau report will give you a record of the defendant's credit history, including loans, defaults, etc., and will rank the defendant with respect to her creditworthiness. A poor credit rating is a reliable indicator that it may be difficult to enforce a judgment against the defendant.

EXECUTION SEARCH

Outstanding judgments from other proceedings against the defendant may be registered as writs of seizure and sale with the Sheriff's Office in the district or county where the defendant lives or carries on business. An execution search will provide information about outstanding writs and the creditors who filed them. Execution searches can be conducted online through websites such as Cyberbahn. They may be conducted on a county-specific basis, or province-wide.

If your execution search turns up outstanding executions against a person who you are satisfied is your defendant, this will tell you that there are other creditors out there. The proceeds of an enforcement against the defendant's income or assets, if any, may have to be shared with these creditors. Your client should be advised of this.

PERSONAL PROPERTY SECURITY ACT SEARCH

Property is either **real property**—that is, immovable (land, houses, etc.)—or **personal property**—that is, movable (vehicles, home entertainment centres, computers, books, stocks and bonds, business inventory, etc.). An outstanding loan against personal property such as a motor vehicle is called a **chattel mortgage**. The **chattel mortgagee** (the holder of the loan) may secure its interest by registering the chattel mortgage under the *Personal Property Security Act* (PPSA). Registration of the chattel mortgagee's interest under the PPSA means that, if the debtor defaults on the loan, the chattel mortgagee has the right to seize and sell the property to satisfy the balance owing. The chattel mortgagee's secured interest ranks ahead of that of other creditors.

If you are aware that the defendant owns personal property, such as a motor vehicle, a PPSA search will tell you if there are any **encumbrances** (that is, outstanding loans) secured against that vehicle. If there is a secured creditor with a registered interest in the vehicle, your client's chances of recovering some part or all of his judgment by seizing and selling the vehicle are slim to nil.

BANKRUPTCY SEARCH

A person who has assigned or been petitioned into bankruptcy turns over all her rights to deal with her property, real or personal, to the trustee in bankruptcy, who deals with the bankrupt's estate. Secured creditors may realize their interest in the property against which their interest has been secured (by way of a mortgage against land or a PPSA registration) outside of the bankruptcy. If there is money left after they have realized on their security, they must turn the surplus over to the trustee. If there is a deficiency—that is, there is still money owing after they have seized and sold the secured property—they may file a claim as ordinary creditors in the bankruptcy.

A bankruptcy search may be done by mail, by telephone, or online using websites such as Cyberbahn. If the search reveals that your defendant has assigned or been petitioned by other creditors into bankruptcy, you should consider advising your client not to proceed with litigation. Even if the litigation is permitted to go forward, judgment creditors rank with ordinary creditors in a bankruptcy.

DOES SMALL CLAIMS COURT HAVE JURISDICTION?

Jurisdiction is the lawful authority of a court. In Ontario, jurisdiction is established by the *Courts of Justice Act* and by the common law.

Before commencing an action in Small Claims Court, you must determine whether it falls within the jurisdiction of the court. In this discussion, jurisdiction will be broken down into three categories: legal, monetary, and territorial.

Legal Jurisdiction

GENERAL

Legal jurisdiction is the lawful authority of the court to deal with a particular type of matter. As a civil trial court, Small Claims Court has legal jurisdiction in a wide range of matters, so long as these matters also fall within its monetary jurisdiction.

Examples of cases that Small Claims Court may hear are:

- actions for money loaned and not repaid;

- actions for services rendered and not paid for;

- actions for goods sold and received and not paid for;

- actions for damage suffered in tort—for example, damage to property or personal injury;

- actions for unpaid rent for residential premises, where the defaulting tenant has vacated the premises at the time the action is commenced; and

- actions for recovery of property with a value of $25,000.00 or less.

Pursuant to s. 96(3) of the *Courts of Justice Act*, Small Claims Court has no jurisdiction to grant **equitable relief**. Simply put, equitable relief involves certain remedies other than money damages. Small Claims Court cannot make an order compelling a person to do something (specific performance), or to stop doing something (injunction). Similarly, Small Claims Court has no jurisdiction to adjudicate where a statute or the procedural rules grant jurisdiction to another court. See, for example, s. 1 of the *Construction Lien Act* (definition of "court") and Rule 1(2) of the *Family Law Rules* (application of *Family Law Rules*).

LIMITATION PERIODS

A limitation period is a deadline prescribed by statute for commencing a proceeding or doing some other thing, such as preserving and perfecting a lien against property under the *Construction Lien Act*. In Ontario, sched. B, s. 4 of the *Limitations Act, 2002* establishes a general limitation period for starting a claim of not later than two years from the day on which the claim was discovered. If your client discovers that someone has done him an actionable harm, but waits more than two years from the date of discovering the harm before starting a claim, he is barred by

BOX 3.1

Small Claims Court Jurisdiction

EXAMPLE 1

The plaintiff sues the defendant, a well-known national newspaper, for libel in Small Claims Court. The plaintiff alleges that a story published by the defendant is false and has injured the plaintiff's reputation. At trial, the judge finds in favour of the plaintiff (that is, the plaintiff wins). The judge awards the plaintiff $3,000.00 in damages for libel, plus costs. The judge also orders that the defendant publish a full apology and retraction (withdrawal) of the libel within 60 days of the date of the judgment if requested by the plaintiff to do so. The defendant pays the damages and costs, but appeals the part of the order compelling the defendant to publish an apology and retraction. On appeal, the defendant argues that Small Claims Court has no legal jurisdiction to make an order compelling performance of a specific act. The defendant relies on s. 96(3) of the *Courts of Justice Act*. The appeal is allowed (that is, the defendant's appeal is successful).

(Adapted from *Moore v. Canadian Newspapers Co.*)

EXAMPLE 2

Your neighbour decides to build a fence between her backyard and yours. The posts are being driven when you check your lot survey. You realize that the proposed fence line is six inches inside your property line. You need to stop your neighbour quickly. Can Small Claims Court make an order that she stop building the fence?

No. What you are asking for is an injunction—that is, an order stopping (enjoining) someone from doing something that harms another person. Pursuant to s. 96(3) of the *Courts of Justice Act*, Small Claims Court has no jurisdiction to make such an order.

EXAMPLE 3

While you are away from home on a three-week vacation, your neighbour decides to build a fence between her backyard and yours. By the time you get home, the fence is completed. You think the fence looks ugly and cheap, and you are angry because your neighbour did not consult you before putting it up. When you check your lot survey, you realize that the fence line is six inches inside your property's boundary line. You want the fence to be torn down. Can Small Claims Court make an order compelling your neighbour to tear down the fence?

No. What you are asking for is specific performance—that is, an order compelling someone to do a specific thing for the benefit of another. Pursuant to s. 96(3) of the *Courts of Justice Act*, Small Claims Court has no jurisdiction to make such an order. See example 1.

s. 4 of the *Limitations Act, 2002* from doing so. In other words, after the limitation period has expired, he is statute-barred from bringing the action. To be **statute-barred** means that a person is prevented by the governing statute from asserting his legal rights.

Note that the limitation period begins to run from the time the harm is discovered, not from the time the harm is done.

Table 3.1 sets out some limitation periods that would be relevant in a Small Claims Court context.

TABLE 3.1   Sample Limitation Periods

Legal issue	Limitation period	Legislation
Torts (civil wrongs)	2 years	*Limitations Act, 2002*, s. 4
Breach of contract	2 years	*Limitations Act, 2002*, s. 4
Provincial Crown	60-day notice of claim; notice served within 10 days for control of property matters	*Proceedings Against the Crown Act*, s. 5 and s. 7
Defamation	Notice within 6 weeks; action within 3 months	*Libel and Slander Act*, s. 5 and s. 7
Highway traffic accidents	2 years	*Limitations Act, 2002*, s. 4

BOX 3.2

Reminder: Limitation Periods

The *Limitations Act, 2002*, s. 4 provides that the two-year limitation period begins to run from the date that the claim is discovered—that is, from the date that the legal wrong which is the basis for the action is discovered by the injured party, not from the date the wrong is actually committed.

Other statutes governing limitation periods may provide differently. For example, where a claimant suffers damage as a result of failure to repair a provincial highway, s. 33(4) of the *Public Transportation and Highway Improvement Act* provides that no action for damages shall be brought unless notice in writing is given to the minister within 10 days from the date of the injury. However, the statute provides that if the 10 days' notice is not given or is given late, a judge may permit the action to proceed if satisfied that the claimant has a reasonable excuse and that the Crown is not prejudiced by the claimant's failure to comply.

Always remember to check all of the relevant legislation with respect to limitation periods before advising a client.

Monetary Jurisdiction

As was discussed in chapter 1, s. 23 of the *Courts of Justice Act* and O. Reg. 629/00 set the maximum amount that may be claimed in a Small Claims Court action at $25,000.00, not including interest on the amount owing and the legal costs of the proceeding.

QUANTIFYING DAMAGES

When advising a client about commencing a Small Claims Court proceeding, you must determine whether the claim falls within the court's monetary jurisdiction. This means that you must assess how much money is owing to your client, based on the facts as you know them, and the applicable law.

Quantifying damages means determining all of the different kinds of damage or harm your client has suffered because of another's alleged wrongdoing, and assigning a money value to that damage. At trial, the money value assigned must be supported by the evidence.

In a claim for **liquidated damages** (also known as a liquidated claim), the amount owing is a specific amount of money that may be established by unpaid invoices, or other documentation proving a debt or fixed amount. The amount of a liquidated claim is easily determined based upon documentary evidence, and does not require valuation by a court, so long as the plaintiff produces documents that prove the amount claimed.

Determining whether a liquidated claim falls within the Small Claims Court monetary jurisdiction is straightforward. You look at the document establishing

BOX 3.3

Quantifying Damages in an Unliquidated Claim

THE FACT SITUATION

The plaintiff was injured when she slipped and fell down icy steps as she was leaving a friend's house after a party. She broke her right wrist and suffered extensive bruising, especially to her lower back. As a result of the fall, she experiences recurrent back pain.

The plaintiff is a self-employed bicycle courier, who works year-round in downtown Toronto. Her annual income is $30,000.00. As a result of her injuries, she was unable to work for three months. She had to pay for prescriptions for painkillers for the pain from the fall and, later, for the recurrent pain in her back. To date, these prescriptions have cost her $286.47. She has kept the receipts.

During the time that she was off work, she was wholly dependent on her partner for support. Physiotherapy cost her $1,500.00. Her partner loaned her money to pay that amount.

She has now been back at work for three months. She has worked hard to get back into shape and get her income back up to where it was before her injuries, but for the first month she made only $1,500.00, and for the last two months she made only $1,800.00. Her wrist is still weak and her back still causes her pain. She is not sure that she can continue to work as a bicycle courier.

QUANTIFYING THE DAMAGES

The plaintiff may claim damages based on pain and suffering, loss of income, and other expenses that are a result of the slip and fall.

1. Loss of income before return to work: the plaintiff lost three months of income at a monthly rate of $2,500.00, for a total of $7,500.00 owing.

2. Loss of income after return to work: As a consequence of her time off work because of the injury, the plaintiff's monthly income was reduced by $1,000.00 (first month back at work) and $1,400.00 (second and third months back at work), for a total of $2,400.00 owing. Given the nature of her injuries, it appears that these losses may continue.

3. Medical expenses: The plaintiff may claim her prescription costs ($286.47) and the costs of physiotherapy ($1,500.00), for a total of $1,786.47.

The plaintiff's total damages on the above grounds are $11,686.47. Her claim for pain and suffering must be quantified based on medical and other evidence. If she wants to bring the claim in Small Claims Court, her total claim will be capped at $25,000.00. Because the claim for pain and suffering cannot easily be valued at this point, she should consider bringing her action in the Superior Court of Justice.

The plaintiff's partner may have grounds for a dependant's claim under part V of the *Family Law Act*. He should consider retaining separate legal representation.

the debt to determine whether the principal amount owing is $25,000.00 or less, exclusive of interest and costs.

In a claim for **unliquidated damages** (also known as an unliquidated claim), the amount owing is not fixed and must be determined based on all of the evidence. Some examples of unliquidated claims are actions for personal injury, libel, or wrongful dismissal. Some actions for breach of contract may also fall within this category. When advising a client about an unliquidated claim, you must be careful to ascertain the different types of damage your client has suffered as a result of the alleged wrongdoing, with a view to assigning reasonable values to that damage. If it appears that the client should bring the action in another court, based on the extent of the damage suffered, you should so advise them. You should consider sending the client a non-engagement letter confirming your reasons for declining the retainer, advising of any approaching limitation periods, and urging them to seek the assistance of a lawyer.

WHAT IF THE AMOUNT OWING IS MORE THAN $25,000.00?

Small Claims Court provides a summary, expeditious, and inexpensive forum for the recovery of comparatively modest sums of money. But what if you are trying to recover $26,000.00 from a debtor? Or $28,500.00? Must the plaintiff pay a lawyer to commence an action in the Superior Court of Justice because the amount she is owed is two or three thousand dollars over the Small Claims Court monetary jurisdiction?

In this situation, the plaintiff has two options. She may consider commencing the action under the Rule 76—Simplified Procedure in the Superior Court of Justice, in which case she must hire a lawyer if she prefers to have legal representation. Or she may waive the right to claim any amount owing over and above the monetary jurisdiction of Small Claims Court, in order to bring the action in Small Claims Court.

Superior Court of Justice Rule 76—Simplified Procedure

Rule 76—Simplified Procedure of the *Rules of Civil Procedure* governs actions for recovery of money amounts of $100,000.00 or less, exclusive of interest and costs, or recovery of property valued at $100,000.00 or less. The purpose of Rule 76 is similar to that of Small Claims Court—to provide a simple, fast, inexpensive way of obtaining judgments in matters within the court's jurisdiction.

Paralegals are not allowed to appear in the Superior Court of Justice, except for Small Claims Court. Parties to proceedings in the Superior Court of Justice may represent themselves, or be represented by a lawyer. A litigant who is not comfortable with Superior Court of Justice forms and procedures will require the assistance of a lawyer.

Table 3.2 provides a comparison of the filing fees for common steps in an action and enforcement in Small Claims Court and the Superior Court of Justice.

Waiving or Abandoning the Excess

In some cases, litigants with claims that fall outside the Small Claims Court monetary jurisdiction may wish to proceed in Small Claims Court anyway. They may prefer to represent themselves. They may be more comfortable with Small Claims

TABLE 3.2   Court Fees in the Small Claims Court and the Superior Court of Justice

Step in the proceeding	Small Claims Court	Superior Court of Justice
Claim	$75.00 (infrequent claimant) $145.00 (frequent claimant)	$181.00
Defence	$40.00	$144.00
Defendant's claim	$75.00	n/a
Statement of defence and counterclaim adding a party	n/a	$181.00
Default judgment	$35.00 (infrequent claimant) $50.00 (frequent claimant)	$127.00
Notice of motion	$40.00	$127.00
Notice of return of motion	n/a	$127.00
Fixing date for trial	$100.00 (infrequent claimant) $130.00 (frequent claimant)	n/a
Trial record (first time only)	n/a	$337.00
Summons to witness	$19.00	$22.00
Witness fees and allowances (non-professionals)	$6.00 per attendance plus mileage	$50.00 per attendance plus mileage
Writ of delivery, writ of seizure and sale, or notice of examination	$35.00	n/a
Writ of execution	n/a	$55.00
Notice of garnishment	$100.00	$115.00 (includes filing with sheriff)

Court procedures. In other cases, they may be able to afford legal representation, but decide that a Small Claims Court proceeding is quicker and less expensive, even with representation.

Plaintiffs who commence Small Claims Court actions for amounts that exceed the court's monetary jurisdiction must waive (or abandon) the excess in their claim. **Waiving the excess** means that they give up their right to claim any money owing above the $25,000.00 Small Claims Court limit, in order to bring the matter within Small Claims Court monetary jurisdiction—that is, to preserve their right to bring the action in Small Claims Court.

If a plaintiff is suing someone who owes him more than $25,000.00, and he chooses to waive the excess in order to bring the matter within the Small Claims Court monetary jurisdiction, he loses the right to claim the waived amount forever. He cannot abandon the excess in one proceeding, and then, after that proceeding has been resolved (whether by settlement or by adjudication), try to claim the waived amount in a subsequent proceeding. By his waiver, he has permanently abandoned any legal right to the excess.

BOX 3.4

Waiver of Excess

Background: The defendant owes the plaintiff $27,500.00, on account of a personal loan the plaintiff made to the defendant. The plaintiff makes several demands for payment, by email and by leaving messages on the defendant's voicemail. The defendant fails to make any payments on the loan. The plaintiff sues the defendant in Small Claims Court, waiving any amounts owing over $25,000.00 to bring the matter within the Small Claims Court jurisdiction. The defendant (who is out of province) fails to deliver a defence, and the plaintiff obtains a default judgment for $25,000.00 plus interest and costs.

The plaintiff waits a few months, and then commences a second action, this time for the $2,500.00 she waived in the first proceeding. Again, the defendant (who is still out of province) fails to deliver a defence. The plaintiff obtains a second default judgment for $2,500.00 plus interest and costs. Is the second judgment enforceable against the defendant?

Discussion: No. The plaintiff has no legal entitlement to money to which she has waived her rights, and the court has no authority to enter judgment with respect to an amount outside its monetary jurisdiction. The second judgment has no force and effect and if the defendant, on his return to Ontario, makes a motion to have it set aside, he will succeed. Any steps taken to enforce the second judgment will also be set aside, and the plaintiff will be ordered to return those moneys to the defendant. The defendant may also be awarded costs.

The defendant remains liable to pay the judgment of $25,000.00 plus interest and costs awarded to the plaintiff in the first proceeding, unless he has valid defences that he can raise, in which case he should obtain a court order setting aside that judgment as well.

The client's consent to the waiver must be informed. Depending on the amount being waived, you may wish to consider recommending that the client obtain independent legal advice from a lawyer regarding the advantages and potential cost of proceeding in the Superior Court of Justice. The client's instructions to waive the excess and proceed in Small Claims Court should be confirmed in writing by the client.

A sample plaintiff's claim containing the language of waiver can be found in appendix 3.1 to this chapter.

Multiple Actions

Rule 6.02 of the *Rules of the Small Claims Court* states that an action cannot be divided into two or more actions in order to bring it within Small Claims Court monetary jurisdiction. In other words, you cannot use **action splitting** to circumvent the court's monetary jurisdiction.

Action splitting is sometimes attempted where the defendant owes money on a **running account**. A running account is an account where the defendant is a regular customer who charges purchases against a standard account number on an ongoing basis. The defendant makes payments against the account from time to time (usually on a monthly basis), as invoices are received. A common consumer example would be a credit card account; but many other commercial relationships also involve running accounts (for example, suppliers and wholesalers or retailers).

Where a plaintiff engages in action splitting in order to circumvent the Small Claims Court monetary jurisdiction, a defendant may make a motion to the court for an order **quashing** the actions. An action that has been quashed is null and void, and cannot proceed any further. The order quashing the actions will be without prejudice to the plaintiff's right to bring the action in the proper court, or to

---

BOX 3.5

What Not to Do—Action Splitting

Your client, P Inc., is owed $30,000.00 on account of supplies and services provided to D Ltd. over the past five months. P Inc. bills D Ltd. on a monthly basis. The following invoices have not been paid:

Invoice number	Date	Amount
01234-1	January 1, 20—	$9,005.00
01234-2	February 1, 20—	$8,065.00
01234-3	March 1, 20—	$4,345.00
01234-4	April 1, 20—	$3,555.00
01234-5	May 1, 20—	$5,030.00

P Inc. does not want to pay a lawyer to collect the amount owing in the Superior Court of Justice. P Inc. commences two different actions in Small Claims Court to collect the amount owing. In Claim No. 2005, P Inc. seeks recovery of $17,070.00 on account of invoices 01234-1 and 01234-2. In Claim No. 2006, P Inc. seeks recovery of $12,930.00 on account of invoices 01234-3, 01234-4, and 01234-5.

D Ltd. is unrepresented, and raises no objection.

The two matters go to trial, and P Inc. is awarded judgment in both matters by a deputy judge. The deputy judge states his jurisdictional concerns in his reason for judgment.

D Ltd. appeals the two decisions. At the hearing of the appeal, P Inc. argues that action splitting is a mere procedural irregularity, which should be allowed pursuant to Rules 1.03 and 2.01 of the *Rules of the Small Claims Court*. Rule 1.03 provides for a liberal interpretation of the *Rules of the Small Claims Court* in the interest of securing a just, expeditious, and inexpensive determination in every proceeding. Rule 2.01 permits a court to waive technical compliance with the rules, including Rule 6.02, in the interests of justice.

The appeal judge does not accept these arguments. He observes that Rules 1.03 and 2.01 cannot be interpreted to permit the court to give itself jurisdiction it does not have. He allows D Ltd.'s appeal and sets aside the judgments in Claim No. 2005 and Claim No. 2006 without prejudice to P Inc.'s right to bring an action for the amount owing in the Superior Court of Justice. He orders P Inc. to pay D Ltd.'s costs of the appeal fixed at $2,000.00.

(Adapted from *Traditional Air Systems Inc. v. Custom Gas Heating Ltd.*)

waive the excess and bring the action in Small Claims Court. The defendant should have her costs of the motion. Rule 15.07 states that the costs of a motion, excluding disbursements, shall not exceed $100.00 unless the court orders otherwise because there are special circumstances. If bad faith can be shown on the part of the plaintiff by a defendant on a motion to quash based on action splitting contrary to Rule 6.02, the defendant should request costs in excess of $100.00 on grounds that the plaintiff's bad faith constitutes special circumstances justifying a higher costs award.

Bringing a Motion to a Judge to Have the Action Transferred from Small Claims Court to the Superior Court of Justice Pursuant to the Courts of Justice Act, s. 110

Where a proceeding or a step in a proceeding is brought or taken in the wrong court, it may be transferred to the proper court, and shall be continued as if it had been commenced in that court (*Courts of Justice Act*, s. 110). This procedure is intended to be used where a party has, due to inadvertence, brought a proceeding in the wrong court.

Section 110(1) states that a proceeding or a step in a proceeding brought before the wrong court *may* be transferred or adjourned to the proper court. In other words, the transfer is **discretionary**, not **mandatory**. Where an action is discretionary, the court *may* make up its own mind about a particular matter, giving due regard to all relevant factors. Where an action is mandatory, the court *must* do something if certain preconditions exist.

A s. 110 ruling on a transfer of a matter from Small Claims Court to the Superior Court of Justice must be obtained on a motion to a judge of the Superior Court of Justice. A judge sitting in Small Claims Court has no jurisdiction to make an order under s. 110, even if the parties consent to the order. Their consent cannot confer jurisdiction upon a Small Claims Court judge (see *Maple Lodge Farms Ltd. v. Penny Lane Fruit Market Inc.*).

The factors the court must consider in exercising its discretion under s. 110(1) are the merits of the matter, whether the other party will suffer undue prejudice, and whether the moving party has acted expeditiously to correct its error (*Dunnington v. 656956 Ontario Ltd.*, paras. 2 to 4). Where the court hearing the motion is satisfied that the matter to be transferred has no merit, the court may refuse to order that it be transferred to the proper court and order costs to the opposing party (*Dunnington v. 656956 Ontario Ltd.*, paras. 5 and 6).

In cases where the Superior Court of Justice lacks statutory jurisdiction under s. 110, it may exercise its **inherent jurisdiction** to control its own process when transferring a matter improperly brought in Small Claims Court to the Superior Court of Justice. Inherent jurisdiction refers to intrinsic judicial powers possessed by the court that are essential for the administration of justice. When invoking inherent jurisdiction, a court will pay due regard to the paramount consideration of doing justice while ensuring the most expeditious and least expensive resolution of every case on its merits (*Maple Lodge Farms*, para. 23).

Territorial Jurisdiction

Territorial jurisdiction is the geographical area where a court is authorized to conduct hearings and make orders that are binding on litigants. Territorial jurisdiction is governed by Rule 6.01 of the *Rules of the Small Claims Court*.

Rule 6.01(1) deals with where the action shall be commenced.

- The plaintiff may commence the action in the territorial jurisdiction where the cause of action arose—that is, where the event or wrongdoing giving rise to the action occurred (Rule 6.01(1)(i)); or

- The plaintiff may commence the action in the territorial jurisdiction where the defendant resides (lives) or carries on business (Rule 6.01(1)(a)(ii)); or

- If there are several defendants, the plaintiff may commence the action in the territorial jurisdiction where one of them lives or carries on business (Rule 6.01(1)(a)(ii)); or

- The plaintiff may commence the action at the court's place of sitting that is nearest to the place where the defendant lives or resides (Rule 6.01(b)); or

- If there are several defendants, the plaintiff may commence the action at the court's place of sitting that is nearest to the place where the defendant lives or resides (Rule 6.01(b)).

DETERMINING WHERE THE CAUSE OF ACTION AROSE

In some cases, it will be easy to decide where the event giving rise to the action occurred. For example, let's say that you operate a yard care service in Milton. A Milton resident asks you to maintain her lawn and garden for three months while she is away on a business trip. You quote her a price of $2,100.00. She pays you a $500.00 deposit. When she returns to Milton, she refuses to pay the balance, alleging various deficiencies.

In this case, you carry on business in Milton. The defendant lives in Milton. The contract was entered into in Milton, and the breach of contract (refusal to pay) took place in Milton. If you decide to sue, the court with territorial jurisdiction is the Milton Small Claims Court.

Similarly, if someone causes damage to property, the cause of action arises where the property is located, and the action may be commenced in the Small Claims Court with territorial jurisdiction for that geographical area.

In some cases, it will not be perfectly clear where the cause of action arose. This is often the case with breach of contract, particularly with distance contracts that are entered into by telephone or Internet, because it is not clear where the contract was made. If you are unsure about where the cause of action arose, you should commence the action in the Small Claims Court with territorial jurisdiction in the geographical area where the defendant resides or carries on business; or, if there are multiple defendants, where one of them resides or carries on business.

BALANCE OF CONVENIENCE (RULE 6.01(2))

The general rule is that a matter shall be tried in the place where it is commenced. However, if the court is satisfied that the balance of convenience substantially favours holding the trial at some place other than those described in Rule 6.01(1), the court may make an order to that effect.

Note that this rule applies to the trial of the matter only. A party seeking to have the **venue** (or place) of the trial moved to another territorial division under Rule 6.01(2) would do so by bringing a motion pursuant to Rule 15. Procedures on a motion are discussed in chapter 7.

The balance of convenience is a common law test. A court hearing a Rule 6.01(2) motion will look at the following factors when determining whether the balance of convenience favours changing the trial's venue: the number of witnesses to be called by each party, the distance those witnesses and the parties must travel to get to the place of the trial, and the expenses connected with that attendance. The court must balance the prejudice to one party of allowing the trial to proceed at the chosen venue, against the prejudice to the other party if the trial is moved to a new venue. The Supreme Court of Canada has stated that "a party whose case has a real and substantial connection with a forum has a legitimate claim to the advantages that that forum provides" (see *Amchem Products Inc. v. British Columbia (Workers' Compensation Board)*, at 920-921).

RULE 6.01(3) ORDER

If an action is called for a trial or a settlement conference, and the judge finds that the place where the action was commenced is not the proper place of trial, the court may make an order that the action be tried in any other place with jurisdiction under Rule 6.01.

It appears that the judge appearing on the settlement conference or at trial may raise the issue herself, based on her reading of the file, or it may be raised by one of the parties during discussion at the settlement conference or as an informal pre-trial motion.

Note that the order is discretionary. Even if the judge is satisfied that the action was brought in the wrong jurisdiction, she is not compelled to make an order changing the place of the trial. For example, if the judge raises the issue herself at a settlement conference, and the parties agree that the trial should take place in the court where the action was commenced, the judge may endorse the file to this effect.

FINDING YOUR COURT

Court addresses may be searched at the Ministry of the Attorney General website (http://www.attorneygeneral.jus.gov.on.ca).

CHAPTER SUMMARY

You should advise clients honestly and candidly about the merits of their case. If the defendant appears to be judgment-proof, the client should be advised of this before litigation is commenced. Carefully consider the effect on your client's rights if a limitation period expires, and keep in mind that a debtor's circumstances may change.

The client's matter must fall within Small Claims Court jurisdiction. At present, Small Claims Court has jurisdiction to hear civil actions for money in a maximum amount of $25,000.00 or recovery of property with a maximum value of $25,000.00, exclusive of interest and costs. Small Claims Court has no jurisdiction to grant equitable relief—that is, an order stopping someone from doing something that causes another harm (injunction) or an order compelling someone to do something for the benefit of another (specific performance). Small Claims Court has no jurisdiction to hear a matter where a statute or regulation designates another court as the court with jurisdiction.

A claim for more than $25,000.00 exclusive of interest and costs may be brought in Small Claims Court, so long as the claimant waives, or abandons, the excess. A claimant who is seeking damages of more than $25,000.00 may not split her claim into two or more actions in order to fall within the Small Claims Court monetary jurisdiction.

Quantifying damages means determining all of the different kinds of damage or harm your client has suffered because of another's alleged wrongdoing, and assigning a money value to that damage. At trial, the money value assigned must be supported by the evidence.

In a claim for liquidated damages (also known as a liquidated claim), the amount owing is a specific amount of money that may be established by unpaid invoices or other documentation proving a debt or fixed amount. The amount of a liquidated claim is easily determined based upon documentary evidence, and does not require valuation by a court, so long as the plaintiff produces documents that prove the amount claimed.

In a claim for unliquidated damages (also known as an unliquidated claim), the amount owing is not fixed and must be determined based on all of the evidence. When advising a client about an unliquidated claim, you must be careful to ascertain the different types of damage your client has suffered as a result of the alleged wrongdoing, with a view to assigning reasonable values to that damage. If it appears that the client should bring the action in another court, based on the extent of the damage suffered, you should so advise them. You should consider sending the client a non-engagement letter confirming your reasons for declining the retainer, advising of any approaching limitation periods, and urging them to seek the assistance of a lawyer.

A Small Claims Court action must be commenced in the territorial division where the cause of action arose, or where a defendant lives or carries on business, or at the court's place of sitting that is closest to where a defendant lives or carries on business. An action shall be tried in the place where it is commenced, unless the court is satisfied that the balance of convenience substantially favours holding the trial in another place, in which case the court may order that the action be tried at that other place.

KEY TERMS

action splitting	inherent jurisdiction	real property
candid	judgment debtor	running account
cause of action	judgment-proof	statute-barred
chattel mortgage	liquidated damages	unliquidated damages
chattel mortgagee	mandatory	venue
discretionary	personal property	waiving the excess
encumbrances	quantifying damages	
equitable relief	quashing	

REFERENCES

Amchem Products Inc. v. British Columbia (Workers' Compensation Board), [1993] 1 SCR 897, at 920.

Collection Agencies Act, RSO 1990, c. C.14.

Construction Lien Act, RSO 1990, c. C.30.

Consumer Reporting Act, RSO 1990, c. C.33.

Courts of Justice Act, RSO 1990, c. C.43.

Dunnington v. 656956 Ontario Ltd. (1991), 6 CPC (3d) 298, 89 DLR (4th) 607, 9 OR (3d) 124, 54 OAC 345, 1991 CarswellOnt 464 (Div. Ct.).

Family Law Act, RSO 1990, c. F.3.

Family Law Rules, O. Reg. 114/99.

Law Society of Upper Canada (LSUC), *Paralegal Rules of Conduct* (Toronto: LSUC, 2007, as amended); available online at http://www.lsuc.on.ca.

Limitations Act, 2002, SO 2002, c. 24, sched. B.

Maple Lodge Farms Ltd. v. Penny Lane Fruit Market Inc., 1997 CarswellOnt 4306, [1997] OJ no. 4401 (QL), at paras. 18 and 19 (Gen. Div.).

Moore v. Canadian Newspapers Co. (1989), 69 OR (2d) 262, [1989] OJ no. 948 (QL) (Div. Ct.).

Office of the Privacy Commissioner of Canada, Commissioner's Findings under the *Personal Information Protection and Electronic Documents Act* (PIPEDA), PIPEDA Case Summary #2006-340, *Law firms collected credit reports without consent*. http://www.priv.gc.ca/cf-dc/2006/340_20060502_e.cfm.

Personal Information Protection and Electronic Documents Act, SC 2000, c. 5.

Personal Property Security Act, RSO 1990, c. P.10.

Public Transportation and Highway Improvement Act, RSO 1990, c. P.50.

Rules of Civil Procedure, RRO 1990, Reg. 194.

Rules of the Small Claims Court, O. Reg. 258/98.

Traditional Air Systems Inc. v. Custom Gas Heating Ltd. (1995), 86 OAC 72, 1995 CarswellOnt 1793 (Div. Ct.).

REVIEW QUESTIONS

1. What is a judgment-proof defendant?

2. What steps must you take before collecting personal information about individuals in the course of your paralegal practice?

3. Briefly describe the following searches and the information they provide.

   a. Credit bureau search

   b. Execution search

   c. *Personal Property Security Act* search

   d. Bankruptcy search

4. a. You decide to build a wooden privacy fence between your neighbour's backyard and yours, so that you will no longer have to look at his collection of 42 brightly painted garden gnomes. You check the local by-law to ensure that your fence complies with height restrictions and so on. The posts are being driven when Mr. Gnomemeister approaches you. "I don't want you to build a fence. It's not neighbourly," he says. You reply that you have done everything according to local by-laws. "Oh yeah?" says Mr. Gnomemeister. "Well, I don't care what the by-laws say. I'm going to get a Small Claims Court order to stop you."

      Can Small Claims Court order you to stop building the fence? Give reasons for your answer.

   b. The day after the episode described above, your neighbour, Mr. Gnomemeister, goes away for a two-week vacation. He sends you a postcard from Tuscany: "Weather beautiful, food delicious, landscape sublime. See you in court when I get back." While he is away, you finish building your fence.

      When Mr. Gnomemeister gets home, the fence is finished. One evening while you are sitting in your backyard enjoying your privacy, he climbs up on a concrete toadstool and yells at you over the top of the fence, "This fence is ugly and cheap looking. It's an eyesore. I'm going to get a Small Claims Court order making you tear it down!"

      Can Small Claims Court make an order compelling you to tear down the fence? Give reasons for your answer.

5. a. What is a limitation period? What is the general rule in Ontario concerning limitation periods?

   b. What happens if you wait until after the limitation period has expired to start an action?

6. a. What is a liquidated claim? Give an example.

   b. What is an unliquidated claim? Give an example.

7. Plaintiff wishes to collect $31,500.00 from Defendant for unpaid invoices on a running account.

   a. Plaintiff wants to keep her costs down by collecting the amount owing in Small Claims Court. Is the claim within the Small Claims Court monetary jurisdiction?

   b. What must Plaintiff do to bring the claim in Small Claims Court?

   c. What steps should you as her paralegal adviser take?

8. Plaintiff lives and carries on business out of her home in Brampton. Defendant lives in Toronto and works in Markham. The contract between Plaintiff and Defendant was signed in Toronto; and the breach of contract occurred in Toronto. Where should the plaintiff commence her action? Give reasons for your answer, referring to the *Rules of the Small Claims Court*.

APPENDIX 3.1   Parrish v. Thurston: Plaintiff's Claim with Waiver of Excess

ONTARIO

Superior Court of Justice
Cour supérieure de justice

Plaintiff's Claim
Demande du demandeur
Form / *Formule* 7A Ont. Reg. No. / *Règl. de l'Ont.* : 258/98

Seal / *Sceau*

Brampton
Small Claims Court / *Cour des petites créances de*
7755 Hurontario Street
Brampton, Ontario
L6W 4T6
Address / *Adresse*

905 456 4700
Phone number / *Numéro de téléphone*

4567
Claim No. / *N° de la demande*

Plaintiff No. 1 / *Demandeur n° 1*

☐ Additional plaintiff(s) listed on attached Form 1A.
*Le ou les demandeurs additionnels sont mentionnés
sur la formule 1A ci-jointe.*

☐ Under 18 years of age.
Moins de 18 ans.

Last name, or name of company / *Nom de famille ou nom de la compagnie*		
Parrish		
First name / *Premier prénom* **Maxwell**	Second name / *Deuxième prénom*	Also known as / *Également connu(e) sous le nom de*
Address (street number, apt., unit) / *Adresse (numéro et rue, app., unité)* **c/o Prior Mustafa LLP**		
City/Town / *Cité/ville*	Province	Phone no. / *N° de téléphone*
Postal code / *Code postal*		Fax no. / *N° de télécopieur*
Representative / *Représentant(e)* **Prior Mustafa LLP Attn: Marie Prior**		LSUC # / *N° du BHC*
Address (street number, apt., unit) / *Adresse (numéro et rue, app., unité)* **22 County Court Boulevard**		
City/Town / *Cité/ville* **Brampton**	Province **ON**	Phone no. / *N° de téléphone* **905 111 2222**
Postal code / *Code postal* **A1A 2B3**		Fax no. / *N° de télécopieur* **905 111 2233**

Defendant No. 1 / *Défendeur n° 1*

☐ Additional defendant(s) listed on attached Form 1A.
*Le ou les défendeurs additionnels sont mentionnés
sur la formule 1A ci-jointe.*

☐ Under 18 years of age.
Moins de 18 ans.

Last name, or name of company / *Nom de famille ou nom de la compagnie*		
Thurston		
First name / *Premier prénom* **Frank**	Second name / *Deuxième prénom*	Also known as / *Également connu(e) sous le nom de*
Address (street number, apt., unit) / *Adresse (numéro et rue, app., unité)* **45 Labrador Court, Suite 103**		
City/Town / *Cité/ville* **Toronto**	Province **ON**	Phone no. / *N° de téléphone* **416 333 4444**
Postal code / *Code postal* **M3C 4D5**		Fax no. / *N° de télécopieur*
Representative / *Représentant(e)*		LSUC # / *N° du BHC*
Address (street number, apt., unit) / *Adresse (numéro et rue, app., unité)*		
City/Town / *Cité/ville*	Province	Phone no. / *N° de téléphone*
Postal code / *Code postal*		Fax no. / *N° de télécopieur*

SCR 7.01-7A (June 1, 2009 / *1er juin 2009*) CSD

APPENDIX 3.1   Continued

FORM / *FORMULE* 7A   PAGE 2   <u>4567</u>

Claim No. / *N° de la demande*

REASONS FOR CLAIM AND DETAILS / *MOTIFS DE LA DEMANDE ET PRÉCISIONS*

Explain what happened, including where and when. Then explain how much money you are claiming or what goods you want returned.
Expliquez ce qui s'est passé, en précisant où et quand. Ensuite indiquez la somme d'argent que vous demandez ou les biens dont vous demandez la restitution, explication à l'appui.

If you are relying on any documents, you **MUST** attach copies to the claim. If evidence is lost or unavailable, you **MUST** explain why it is not attached.
*Si vous vous appuyez sur des documents, vous **DEVEZ** en annexer des copies à la demande. Si une preuve est perdue ou n'est pas disponible, vous **DEVEZ** expliquer pourquoi elle n'est pas annexée.*

What happened?   **See Schedule A attached**
Where?
When?

Que s'est-il
passé?
Où?
Quand?

SCR 7.01-7A (June 1, 2009 / *1ᵉʳ juin 2009*) CSD   **Continued on next page /** *Suite à la page suivante*

APPENDIX 3.1   Continued

FORM / *FORMULE* 7A   PAGE 3   4567
Claim No. / *N° de la demande*

How much? $ _____ 25,000.00
Combien?   (Principal amount claimed / *Somme demandée*) $

☐   ADDITIONAL PAGES ARE ATTACHED BECAUSE MORE ROOM WAS NEEDED.
DES FEUILLES SUPPLÉMENTAIRES SONT ANNEXÉES EN RAISON DU MANQUE D'ESPACE.

The plaintiff also claims pre-judgment interest from 12% _____   under:
Le demandeur demande aussi des intérêts   (Date)   *conformément à :*
antérieurs au jugement de

(Check only   ☐ the *Courts of Justice Act*
one box /   *la* Loi sur les tribunaux judiciaires
Cochez une
seule case)   ☒ an agreement at the rate of 12 _____ % per year
                    un accord au taux de   % par an

and post-judgment interest, and court costs.
et des intérêts postérieurs au jugement, ainsi que les dépens.

Prepared on: November 1 _____ , 20 -- _____
Fait le :   (Signature of plaintiff or representative / *Signature du*
                                                    demandeur/de la demanderesse ou du/de la représentant(e))

Issued on: _____ , 20 ____ _____
Délivré le :   (Signature of clerk / *Signature du greffier*)

CAUTION TO DEFENDANT:	IF YOU DO NOT FILE A DEFENCE (Form 9A) with the court within twenty (20) calendar days after you have been served with this Plaintiff's Claim, judgment may be obtained without notice and enforced against you. Forms and self-help materials are available at the Small Claims Court and on the following website: www.ontariocourtforms.on.ca.
AVERTISSEMENT AU DÉFENDEUR :	*SI VOUS NE DÉPOSEZ PAS DE DÉFENSE (formule 9A) auprès du tribunal au plus tard vingt (20) jours civils après avoir reçu signification de la présente demande du demandeur, un jugement peut être obtenu sans préavis et être exécuté contre vous. Vous pouvez obtenir les formules et la documentation à l'usage du client à la Cour des petites créances et sur le site Web suivant : www.ontariocourtforms.on.ca.*

SCR 7.01-7A (June 1, 2009 / *1er juin 2009*) CSD

APPENDIX 3.1   Continued

Schedule A

1. The plaintiff claims:

    (a) $25,000.00;

    (b)   Pre- and post-judgment interest on the amount owing at a rate of 12% per annum commencing September 1, 20— until such time as all amounts owing are paid in full, in accordance with a promissory note dated March 1, 20— signed by Frank Thurston;

    (c)   In the alternative, pre- and post-judgment interest in accordance with the *Courts of Justice Act*;

    (d)   His costs of this action; and

    (e)   Such further and other relief as this Honourable Court deems just.

2. The plaintiff at all material times resided in the City of Brampton in the Province of Ontario.

3. The defendant at all material times resided in the City of Brampton in the Province of Ontario. On or about October 1, 20—, the defendant moved to 45 Labrador Court, Suite 103, in the City of Toronto in the Province of Ontario.

4. Pursuant to a promissory note dated March 1, 20—, the plaintiff loaned to the defendant the sum of $27,000.00.

5. Particulars of the note are as follows:

    By his signature hereto, the undersigned FRANK THURSTON acknowledges receipt of the sum of TWENTY-SEVEN THOUSAND DOLLARS ($27,000.00), paid by Maxwell Parrish to Frank Thurston on today's date. The entire principal amount shall be due and payable in full on September 1, 20—. In the event of default by Frank Thurston, interest shall accrue at a rate of 12% per annum until such time as all amounts owing are paid in full or judgment is obtained, and post-judgment interest shall accrue on the judgment amount at a rate of 12% per annum until such time as the judgment is paid in full.

APPENDIX 3.1　Concluded

6. The defendant failed to pay the amount owing pursuant to the note on the due date of September 1, 20—.

7. In spite of repeated requests for payment, the defendant failed to make any payment whatsoever on account of the amount owing.

8. The plaintiff waives his right to claim any amounts owing over and above $25,000.00 to bring this action within the jurisdiction of this Honourable Court.

[**Note:** In a real proceeding, photocopies of any documents upon which the plaintiff intends to rely, including the promissory note dated March 1, 20— and any demand letters sent to the defendant, would be attached to the claim.]

Acting for the Plaintiff: Commencing the Action

LEARNING OBJECTIVES

After reading this chapter, you will understand:

- Special and general damages
- Pre- and post-judgment interest
- Naming other parties
- Joint and several liability
- Parties under disability
- Ethical advocacy
- Drafting a plaintiff's claim
- Service of a plaintiff's claim and other documents
- Amending a pleading

INTRODUCTION

When you have satisfied yourself that your client has good grounds to litigate, and that Small Claims Court is the proper court in which to commence the action, the next step is to draft the plaintiff's claim. The **plaintiff's claim** is the document that sets out the names of the parties and their addresses for service, the amount of the claim, any other relief being sought, and the allegations of fact in support of the claim. It is essential that the information in the claim be complete and accurate. Parties must be properly named, and their addresses should be correct to the best of your knowledge. The amount owing should be properly calculated. The allegations in support of the claim should be set out in an organized narrative that includes all the facts the plaintiff relies on in support of the claim. These allegations of fact (also known as particulars) should be sufficient to allow the defendant to know the case that she has to respond to.

The proceeding is commenced when the plaintiff's claim, together with a copy for each named defendant, is taken to the office of the Small Claims Court with territorial jurisdiction, and issued by the clerk. The claim is issued when the clerk dates, signs, and seals it, and assigns a court file number ("Claim No." on the Form 7A). The court file number assigned by the clerk is the unique identifier for that court proceeding. It must appear on all documents filed in the proceeding. The plaintiff has six months from the date of issuing the claim to serve the other parties. In appropriate circumstances, the court may extend the time for service.

CALCULATING DAMAGES

Quantifying, or calculating, damages was discussed in chapter 3, in the context of deciding whether your client's case falls within the Small Claims Court monetary jurisdiction. When calculating damages, you must determine all of the different kinds of damage or harm that the plaintiff has suffered because of the defendant's alleged wrongdoing, and assign money values to the various categories of harm. The money values assigned must be supported by the allegations of fact in the plaintiff's claim, by the documentary evidence attached to the plaintiff's claim or disclosed later on in the proceeding to other parties, and by the evidence at trial.

Calculating Damages in a Liquidated Claim

In a claim for a debt or fixed amount (also known as a **liquidated claim**), the amount owing is a fixed debt that may be proven by documents such as unpaid invoices, NSF cheques, a credit card agreement, or a promissory note. A **promissory note** is a promise to pay that is signed and dated by the debtor. It should contain, at a minimum, the following terms: the names of the payor and the debtor; the amount advanced to the debtor and the date on which it was advanced; and the terms of the loan, including payment terms, interest rates, penalties on default, and so on.

So long as there is documentary evidence supporting the amount claimed, liquidated damages do not require valuation by a court.

Calculating Damages in an Unliquidated Claim

In a claim for **unliquidated damages** (also known as an **unliquidated claim**), the amount owing is not fixed. Instead, it must be determined based on all of the evidence. Examples of unliquidated claims are actions for personal injury, libel, wrongful dismissal, and some cases of breach of contract. When dealing with a plaintiff in an unliquidated claim, you must be careful to ascertain all of the different types of damage the plaintiff has suffered as a result of the alleged wrongdoing, with a view to assigning to that damage reasonable values that are supported by the evidence.

UNLIQUIDATED CLAIMS—TYPES OF DAMAGES

The law of damages is complex. The two main types of damages that you are likely to encounter in a Small Claims Court proceeding are **special damages** and **general damages**.

BOX 4.1

Dante v. Herrero: Calculating Liquidated Damages

You work for Prior Mustafa LLP, 22 County Court Boulevard, Brampton, Ontario A1A 2B3 TEL: 905 111 2222 FAX: 905 111 2233.

Your client is Francesca Dante. Ms. Dante lives at 98 Calendar Court, Mississauga, Ontario X2X 3Y4 TEL: 905 222 3333.

On December 1, 20—, Ms. Dante loaned $4,000.00 to her best friend, Suzanne Herrero. Ms. Herrero lives at 105 Morton Avenue, Mississauga, Ontario L2X 4Y5. The loan is secured by a promissory note dated December 1, 20— signed by Ms. Herrero. The terms of the note are as follows:

> By her signature hereto, the undersigned SUZANNE HERRERO acknowledges receipt of the sum of FOUR THOUSAND DOLLARS ($4,000.00), paid by Francesca Dante to Suzanne Herrero on today's date. Interest shall be payable on said sum at a rate of 12% per annum, commencing December 1, 20—. The entire principal amount plus interest thereon shall be due and payable in full on March 1, 20—. In the event of default by Suzanne Herrero, interest shall continue to accrue at a rate of 12% per annum until such time as all amounts owing are paid in full

or judgment is obtained, and post-judgment interest shall accrue on the judgment amount, including costs, at a rate of 12% per annum until such time as the amount owing is paid in full.

On March 1, 20—, Ms. Herrero gave Ms. Dante a cheque in the amount of $4,120.00, on account of the principal owing of $4,000.00 plus three months' interest of $120.00. The cheque was returned due to insufficient funds.

Ms. Dante comes to see you on March 27, 20—. She has phoned and emailed Ms. Herrero several times to demand payment, but has received no response. She wants to sue Ms. Herrero for the amount owing.

CALCULATING DAMAGES

This is a straightforward case of an unpaid loan of money. Fortunately, Ms. Dante had the good sense to write down the terms of the loan in the promissory note signed by Ms. Herrero. When calculating the amount owing, all you have to do is refer to the terms of the note.

Special Damages

Special damages are specific damages that compensate the plaintiff for specific losses, including out-of-pocket expenses connected with the injury or harm.

Examples of special damages would be loss of current and projected income, medical expenses including prescriptions, and travel costs connected with the injury. All of these types of expenses, if claimed, should be supported by documentary evidence, such as pay stubs, bills for prescriptions and other medical expenses, and income tax returns. Current and projected special damages, if proven, can be calculated fairly precisely, based on the documentary evidence.

In a Small Claims Court proceeding, the plaintiff's claim will be drafted and issued long before the matter actually gets to trial. You should plead all special damages as of the date of issuing the plaintiff's claim, and support the claim for special damages with photocopies of the documentary evidence attached to the claim form. The original documents should be filed in the documents subfile of the client file.

As the matter progresses, the plaintiff may become entitled to additional special damages. You should advise the other side and provide ongoing documentary disclosure in support of additional special damages claimed. If the matter goes to trial, all written statements, documents, and records upon which you intend to rely at trial must be served on the other parties no later than 30 days before the trial date in the notice of trial (Rule 18.02(1) of the *Rules of the Small Claims Court*).

General Damages

General damages are damages that compensate the plaintiff for injuries suffered (such as pain, suffering, disfigurement, physical impairment, loss of enjoyment of life, and so on) or breach of contract where no precise dollar amount flowing from the breach can be calculated. General damages tend to be speculative in nature. To the extent that it is possible, they must be calculated, itemized, and explained based on accepted criteria.

BOX 4.2

Chong v. Kingman: Calculating Damages

You work for Prior Mustafa LLP, 22 County Court Boulevard, Brampton, Ontario A1A 2B3 TEL: 905 111 2222 FAX: 905 111 2233. Your client is Mrs. Maxine Chong. Mrs. Chong is a 62-year-old widow who lives alone. Her children are both married. They live in Alberta and British Columbia. She has a legal basement apartment in her house at 67 Harmony Avenue, Toronto, Ontario M4J 1J3. After her last tenant left, she did not rent out the apartment for almost a year; but when she received a notice of property tax increase from the municipality, she decided she needed the income to supplement her existing income.

Pursuant to a residential tenancy agreement (apartment lease) dated January 13, 20—, Mrs. Chong agreed to lease the basement apartment to LeeAnn Kingman, for a tenancy commencing February 1, 20— at a monthly rent of $775.00, including water, heat, and hydro. Ms. Kingman did not pay a last month's rent deposit. She told Mrs. Chong she had just found a new job after several months of unemployment and was trying to put her life back together. She seemed like a nice person and Mrs. Chong felt sorry for her. Mrs. Chong accepted Ms. Kingman's personal cheque for the first month's rent, and told her to pay the last month's rent when she had the money.

Ms. Kingman's rent cheque for February 1 was returned for insufficient funds. When Mrs. Chong asked her for a replacement cheque, Ms. Kingman became extremely abusive. She screamed and shouted and ended up slamming the apartment door in Mrs. Chong's face. That evening, she played music very loud until one o'clock in the morning. Mrs. Chong could not sleep. She was afraid the neighbours would complain to the police. When she pounded on the floor to get the music to stop, Ms. Kingman pounded back, screaming abuse and obscenities. Eventually, she turned the music off,

but for the rest of the night there were sounds of banging and crashing from the basement. Mrs. Chong was terrified. "She had access to my washer, my dryer, my furnace, the fuse box, everything, down there," she tells you. "I thought she would set the house on fire."

Ms. Kingman never paid the February rent. When Mrs. Chong tried to approach her about it, she became extremely abusive. On several occasions, she came upstairs and stood outside Mrs. Chong's kitchen door, which opened onto the side entrance that Ms. Kingman used. She would pound on the door and scream. She would threaten to report Mrs. Chong to the Ontario Human Rights Tribunal for abuse and discrimination.

Ms. Kingman did not pay the rent for March. Mrs. Chong did nothing because she was afraid of how Ms. Kingman might react. She felt as if she did not own her house any more. There was always loud music, banging, and shouting from the basement, especially from around midnight until two or three o'clock in the morning.

Mrs. Chong began keeping the kitchen door locked. She could not sleep and she lost her appetite. She suffered from headaches and anxiety attacks. If she went out, she dreaded going home. Her physician prescribed diazepam and Prozac.

When Ms. Kingman did not pay the April rent, Mrs. Chong called her daughter, Alice, in Penticton. When Alice heard about the situation, she said, "I'm catching the next plane to Toronto."

Alice arrived late on April 15. On April 16, she got in touch with your office. You drafted and served a Form N4—Notice to End a Tenancy Early for Non-Payment of Rent on Ms. Kingman. On April 17, Ms. Kingman vacated the apartment, taking the keys to the side entrance and the basement apartment with her. She left the basement apartment in a filthy state. It cost Mrs. Chong $1,059.00 to have a contractor come in to clean it, replace the carpet, repair the damage, and repaint. She had to pay a locksmith $125.00 to rekey the locks.

Alice stayed long enough to find Mrs. Chong a reliable, quiet tenant for the basement apartment. The new tenant moved in on June 1. There have been no more problems. Mrs. Chong has stopped taking Prozac, but she continues to have anxiety attacks, and she still needs diazepam to sleep. "I've suffered so much," she says. "It's too much for a woman of my age to put up with someone like that."

On her tenancy application, Ms. Kingman stated that she is employed by a local non-governmental organization at a salary of $36,500.00 per year. You have confirmed that she is still employed by this organization. You have advised Mrs. Chong of this. She has instructed you to commence a Small Claims Court action against Ms. Kingman.

CALCULATING DAMAGES—SPECIAL DAMAGES

Mrs. Chong's special damages for all losses and out-of-pocket expenses connected to Ms. Kingman's wrongdoing are set out in the table below. Photocopies of documentation supporting these amounts should be attached to the plaintiff's claim.

If Mrs. Chong continues to incur special damages (such as additional prescription costs) as the matter progresses, you must advise the other side and produce documentary evidence in support of the additional special damages claimed as early as possible in the proceeding, and no later than 30 days before the trial date in the notice of trial (Rule 18.02(1)). If her claim includes future special damages (such as prescription costs) that will be incurred after the trial date, you must disclose this to the other side as well.

CALCULATING DAMAGES—GENERAL DAMAGES

Mrs. Chong's claim for general damages is intended to compensate her for current and future pain, suffering, and loss of enjoyment of life connected with Ms. Kingman's tenancy. Because of the speculative nature of general damages, you should ask for total damages (including the amount owing for special damages as of the date of issuing the claim) in the amount of $25,000.00. This will give the court some room to award Mrs. Chong general damages for pain, suffering, and loss of enjoyment of life, as well as current and future special damages, if proven.

Mrs. Chong's claim must contain specific allegations of fact in support of her claim for general damages, supported by evidence, written or oral, from her treating physician. In a Small Claims Court context, her physician's evidence will probably be in the form of a written statement. This written statement should be served at least 30 days before the original date set for trial. The written statement should include a written summary of the physician's qualifications.

Category of special damages	Amount owing	Supporting documentation
Loss of income—unpaid rent	Three months of unpaid rent at $775.00 per month = $2,325.00	Residential tenancy agreement dated January 13, 20— Form N4—Notice to End a Tenancy Early for Non-Payment of Rent
Cost of prescriptions for diazepam and Prozac	$183.47	Prescriptions, invoices
Cost of repairs	$1,059.00	Invoice from contractor, marked Paid
Rekeying locks	$125.00	Invoice from locksmith, marked Paid
Cost of drafting and serving N4	$300.00	Invoice from Prior Mustafa LLP
Total as of date of issuing plaintiff's claim	$3,992.47	

Pre- and Post-judgment Interest

Pre-judgment interest accrues on the amount claimed commencing on the date of default and ending on the date of judgment or final settlement. **Post-judgment interest** accrues on the judgment amount—that is, the amount, including costs, awarded to a successful party by a court or agreed to be owing by the parties—until such time as all amounts owing have been paid in full.

The **date of default** is the date the cause of action arose. The **cause of action** is the factual and legal grounds for seeking a remedy from a court. In an action for recovery of a debt, the date of default will be the date that the defendant failed to make a payment of money.

Page 3 of the plaintiff's claim (Form 7A) (shown in figure 4.1) requests pre-judgment interest from the date of default in accordance with the *Courts of Justice Act* or an agreement. If there is no written agreement, or if the written agreement is silent as to the rate of interest that applies in the event of a default, then pre- and post-judgment interest will be claimed at the rates set out in s. 127(1) of the *Courts of Justice Act*. If you are asking for pre-judgment interest in accordance with a written agreement (such as a credit card agreement or a promissory note), you must check that box and state the contractual interest rate.

WHAT IF THE DATE THE CAUSE OF ACTION AROSE CANNOT EASILY BE DETERMINED?

In liquidated claims, such as an action for recovery of a debt, the date of default is usually easy to determine, because the event that triggers the cause of action is failure to pay by the defendant. In unliquidated claims, the acts of wrongdoing giving rise to the cause of action may accrue over a period of time. For example, in *Chong v. Kingman* (the details of which are set out in box 4.2 above), the defendant, Ms. Kingman, defaulted on the rent over a period of three months. The defendant's other wrongful acts took place at intervals during the period of her tenancy. Because these wrongful acts took place over time, the amount and types of damage allegedly suffered by Mrs. Chong changed.

When dealing with this type of situation, you should consider using the date of the first wrongful act by the defendant as the date when pre-judgment interest commences for purposes of filling out page 3 of the plaintiff's claim.

NAMING PARTIES TO THE PROCEEDING

Introduction

When completing the plaintiff's claim, you must name all other parties to the proceeding. If there is more than one plaintiff, any additional plaintiffs must be listed on the additional parties form (Form 1A). If there is more than one defendant, any additional defendants must be listed on the additional parties form. When naming a party, you must use the party's correct name, properly spelled, and the party's correct address for service.

FIGURE 4.1   Plaintiff's Claim: Pre- and Post-judgment Interest (Form 7A)

FORM / *FORMULE* 7A   PAGE 3

Claim No. / *N° de la demande*

How much? $ ....
Combien?   (Principal amount claimed / *Somme demandée*) $

☐   **ADDITIONAL PAGES ARE ATTACHED BECAUSE MORE ROOM WAS NEEDED.**
      DES FEUILLES SUPPLÉMENTAIRES SONT ANNEXÉES EN RAISON DU MANQUE D'ESPACE.

The plaintiff also claims pre-judgment interest from _____ **under:**
Le demandeur demande aussi des intérêts   (Date)   *conformément à :*
antérieurs au jugement de

(Check only   ☐ **the *Courts of Justice Act***
one box /   *la* **Loi sur les tribunaux judiciaires**
Cochez une
seule case)   ☐ **an agreement at the rate of** _____ **% per year**
                      un accord au taux de   **% par an**

and post-judgment interest, and court costs.
et des intérêts postérieurs au jugement, ainsi que les dépens.

Prepared on: _____ , 20 _____   _____
Fait le :   (Signature of plaintiff or representative / *Signature du*
                                                            demandeur/de la demanderesse ou du/de la représentant(e))

Issued on: _____ , 20 _____   _____
Délivré le :   (Signature of clerk / *Signature du greffier*)

Naming Individual Defendants

The complete legal names of individual defendants must be stated on the claim, spelled in their correct form. Never use an initial instead of a proper name. For example, Brian Green should be named as Brian Green, not as B. Green. If you misspell a party's name, or provide an incorrect name, you have named the wrong person, and you will have to take steps to correct the error by amending the claim under Rule 12.

If an individual defendant uses more than one name, you should include all of them on the plaintiff's claim. The Form 7A contains an "Also known as" field for this purpose. All names used by the defendant must be spelled correctly. There must be evidence in the plaintiff's claim proving the defendant's use of different names.

You must make best efforts to ensure that correct, current addresses for all defendants are stated on the plaintiff's claim. There are various search engines and other online resources available for carrying out searches on an individual or a business.

You can search by name for a person or a business using Canada 411 (http://www.canada411.ca). You can also do a reverse search by phone number to obtain a person's name and address, plus a locator map.

Yahoo Canada Directory contains a list of Canadian search websites (including Canada 411), along with a multitude of international search sites. Web addresses change all the time, so try googling "Yahoo people search Canada."

If you are a law enforcement officer, a lawyer, a process server, or a registered debt collection agency, and you have the defendant's driver's licence number, you can search for a defendant's address using a provincial driver's licence search. You must have a pre-approved account to do this search.

Identifying Business Defendants

The three types of business entities you will most commonly encounter in Small Claims Court are sole proprietorships, partnerships, and corporations. They must be properly identified on the plaintiff's claim.

Note that the rules for correctly naming a business defendant also apply to business plaintiffs.

SOLE PROPRIETORSHIPS (RULE 5.06)

A **sole proprietorship** is a business owned and run by one person. There is no legal separation between the owner and the business—the business has no separate legal existence. This means that the business cannot sue or be sued, nor can it enter into contracts. It is the owner who enters into contracts and assumes all liability for the business. The owner is personally responsible for paying the debts of the business.

If the plaintiff is a sole proprietorship operating under a business name, you may sue using the plaintiff's business name (Rule 5.06(1)).

If you are acting for the plaintiff, and the defendant is a sole proprietorship operating under a business name, you may name the defendant using the owner's name, and name the business as an additional party.

Business names must be registered under the Ontario *Business Names Act*. To ensure that you have the correct business name for a sole proprietorship, you should search the name at the Ontario government website. Because site names change constantly, try googling "business name search Ontario." A fee is charged for the search. Another option is to use a commercial online search service such as Cyberbahn.

PARTNERSHIPS (RULE 5)

General

A **partnership** is a business that is owned by two or more persons. Like a sole proprietorship, a partnership has no separate legal existence from its owners, the partners. In a general partnership, the partners are jointly and severally liable for all debts, obligations, and liabilities of the partnership. **Joint and several liability** means that each partner in a general partnership is personally liable to the full extent of any debt, obligation, or liability incurred by other partners or partnership employees or agents acting in the ordinary course of the partnership business.

Partners may allocate liability among themselves and specify other terms and conditions of the general partnership by means of a **partnership agreement**. However, the partnership agreement is binding only on the partners themselves as parties to the agreement. If Rule 5.03 (discussed below) is complied with, a successful plaintiff may enforce her judgment against the assets of any or all of the partners, plus any assets of the partnership firm.

Different rules apply to a limited partnership formed under the *Limited Partnerships Act*. In a limited partnership, some partners are general partners, and some partners are limited partners. A limited partner is not liable for the obligations of the limited partnership except in respect of the value of money and other property the limited partner contributes to the limited partnership.

Commencing an Action Against a Partnership

A partnership who is a plaintiff may commence a proceeding using the firm name of the partnership (Rule 5.01).

A proceeding against a defendant who is a partnership may be commenced using the firm name of the partnership (Rule 5.01). As with sole proprietorships, if you are acting for the plaintiff, it is advisable to search the firm name online, to ensure that you have the correct business name for the partnership.

In a proceeding where the firm name is used to name the defendant partnership, any court order will be made using the firm name, and is enforceable against the firm's property only—that is, the assets of the firm, as opposed to those of the individual partners (Rule 5.05(1)). However, if the plaintiff serves the persons who are partners with copies of the plaintiff's claim, along with notices to alleged partners (Form 5A), she may then enforce any judgment against the assets of the partnership firm and the assets of all partners so served (Rules 5.03 and 5.05(2)).

How does the plaintiff find out the names of all the partners in the partnership? In a proceeding commenced by or against a partnership using the firm name, any other party may serve a notice requiring the partners to disclose immediately in writing the names and addresses of all partners belonging to the partnership at the time specified in the notice (Rule 5.04(1)).

A person who has been served with a notice to alleged partner is deemed to have been a partner at the material time unless the person delivers a defence separately from the defence of the partnership firm, denying having been a partner at the material time (Rule 5.03(2)).

You will find a sample Form 5A—Notice to Alleged Partner at appendix 4.1.

CORPORATIONS

General

A corporation is a separate legal entity from its owners, the shareholders. This arrangement is intended to protect the corporation's shareholders from risks, obligations, and liabilities incurred by the corporation. Because the personal assets of the shareholders are not available to satisfy debts, obligations, and liabilities incurred by the corporation, a court order obtained against the corporation must be enforced against the assets of the corporation.

Corporations may be private or public. The shares of a private corporation (also known as a closely held corporation) are held by a small group of people who usually know each other, such as family members. The shares of private corporations are not traded on public stock exchanges.

Public corporations offer their shares for sale to the public on stock exchanges. Generally speaking, their purpose is the same as that of privately held companies—that is, to run a business or businesses for profit.

Governmental organizations may also form corporations. For example, municipalities are usually incorporated.

Words such as "Inc.," "Incorporated," "Corporation," "Ltd.," or "Limited" indicate a corporate entity.

Whether they are governmental, public, or private, corporations are legal persons who can sue and be sued. Like any other party to a proceeding, corporations must be identified by their correct name on the plaintiff's claim.

Background Searches

Before commencing an action against a corporation, you should conduct a business name search to ensure that you are suing the correct corporate entity. The corporate owner of a business may be a numbered company—that is, the corporate owner uses the number it was assigned upon incorporation, but carries on business under a different name. Sometimes the corporate owner of a business uses one business name, and another business name for the business it owns. You need to ensure that you are naming the corporate defendant by its correct legal name. Words like "Inc.," "Incorporated," "Ltd.," or "Limited" must be spelled the way they appear in the registered name.

When a corporation is incorporated, it is assigned a six-digit registration number. Sometimes a corporation uses its registration number as its business name—for example, 123456 Ontario Limited. A company that uses its registration number as its business name is called a **numbered company**.

Sometimes the corporation's name is different from the business name. A corporation called Efficient Furnaces and Stoves Inc. may be the owner of a business called Efficient Heating Systems. A search of the registered business name "Efficient Heating Systems" will tell you that the name of the corporate owner is Efficient Furnaces and Stoves Inc. You must name "Efficient Furnaces and Stoves Inc." as the defendant.

When you have confirmed the corporate defendant's name by means of the business name search, you may use corporate searches to find out additional information, if required. For example, if you need to know whether the corporation is still in existence or has been dissolved, you may request a certificate of status. A corporation profile report will give you the address of the corporation, a list of all active directors and officers, and some historical information, including a name history.

Corporate searches and business name searches can be done online, either at the Ontario government website or using an online commercial search service such as Cyberbahn.

BOX 4.3

Who Should You Sue?

EXAMPLE 1

Nekea Marshall and Vladimir Oblomov are the sole owners and shareholders of a private, numbered company, 334445 Ontario Inc. 334445 Ontario Inc. owns a pet grooming and boarding facility, whose business name is Camp Happy Puppy. Ms. Marshall and Mr. Oblomov run Camp Happy Puppy.

Plaintiff boards her English sheepdog, Gerald, at Camp Happy Puppy for two weeks while she is away in Europe on business. When she gets back from Europe and goes to pick up Gerald, she finds him cowering in his cage. He seems depressed and nervous. When she gets him home, he refuses to eat, and she notices that he is limping. The next day, she takes Gerald to the vet. The vet examines Gerald, and tells Plaintiff that he appears to have been in at least one fight, which caused the injury to his leg. There are also other bites that are still healing. "They're hard to see because of all the hair," the vet says. "But some of them are infected. We'll put him on antibiotics, and keep him here for a couple of days, under observation."

In the end, some surgery is required. The vet's services cost Plaintiff $1,155.00.

Plaintiff wants to sue Camp Happy Puppy for the cost of the vet bill and for recovery of the boarding costs, on the grounds that Gerald did not receive the safe, healthy environment that Camp Happy Puppy advertised. Who should you sue?

Camp Happy Puppy is the business name of a business owned by 334445 Ontario Inc. As owner, 334445 Ontario Inc. is liable for any wrongdoing or negligence on the part of Camp Happy Puppy and its agents or employees.

Although they own the numbered company, Nekea Marshall and Vladimir Oblomov cannot be added as co-defendants, because they are not co-owners of the business itself. 334445 Ontario Inc. is the owner of Camp Happy Puppy, and will be the only defendant named in the lawsuit.

EXAMPLE 2

Plaintiff loans $8,000.00 to 445556 Ontario Inc., a corporation whose president and sole shareholder is Plaintiff's cousin, Ahmed Kabir. The money is intended to help Cousin Ahmed out with some cash-flow problems he has been having with his restaurant, Avocado Bistro. Before she advances the money to 445556 Ontario Inc., Plaintiff requires Cousin Ahmed to sign a personal guarantee for the loan.

The numbered company fails to make any payments on account of the loan, in spite of Plaintiff's repeated demands. Plaintiff wants to commence a Small Claims Court proceeding to recover the amount owing. Who should you sue?

The first step is to perform a business name search to confirm that 445556 Ontario Inc. is, in fact, the corporate owner of the restaurant. Having confirmed ownership and the correct spelling of the numbered company's name, you will name the numbered company as the defendant. The address will be that of the restaurant, as that is where the numbered company carries on business.

Because Cousin Ahmed is a guarantor for the loan, he will be named as a co-defendant on the additional parties form (Form 1A). His address for service will be either the restaurant (because he works there) or his home address.

The plaintiff's claim must state your grounds for adding Cousin Ahmed as a co-defendant, and a photocopy of the guarantee should be attached to the claim.

PARTY UNDER DISABILITY (RULE 4)

What Is a Party Under Disability?

The definition of "disability" is found at Rule 1.02(1). A person or party will be deemed to be under disability if:

1. the person is a minor—that is, under the age of majority;

2. the person is mentally incapable—that is, he is not able to understand information that is relevant to making decisions, or is not able to appreciate the reasonably foreseeable consequences of a decision or lack of a decision; or

3. the person is an absentee within the meaning of the *Absentees Act*—that is, a former resident of Ontario who has disappeared, whose whereabouts are unknown, and about whom there is no knowledge whether he or she is alive or dead.

Parties under disability are not necessarily physically or psychologically disabled (although they may be both). The disability is legal. Persons under disability are considered to lack legal capability to perform certain acts—for example, to understand legal advice and give instructions based on that understanding. For this reason, a person under disability, whether a plaintiff or a defendant, must have a **litigation guardian** to act on their behalf.

The Role of a Litigation Guardian

A litigation guardian is a competent person who undertakes to commence or continue a legal proceeding on behalf of a person under disability. A litigation guardian is not a legal representative for the person under disability; rather, the litigation guardian is advised by and provides instructions to the legal representative for the person under disability.

There is one exception to the general rule that a person under disability must have a litigation guardian. Rule 4.01(2) provides that a minor may sue for any sum not exceeding $500.00 as if he or she were of full age.

Any person who is not under disability may be a litigation guardian for a plaintiff or defendant (Rule 4.03(1)). The duties of a litigation guardian are to attend diligently to the interests of the person under disability and take all reasonably necessary steps to protect those interests, including commencing and conducting a defendant's claim if necessary (Rule 4.04(1)).

Rule 4.03(2) sets out the following guidelines for determining who may be a litigation guardian.

If the person under disability is a minor suing or being sued for a sum exceeding $500.00, (1) the litigation guardian shall be the minor's parent or legal guardian or any other suitable person; or (2) if no such person is available to act, the Children's Lawyer shall be the litigation guardian.

If the person under disability is mentally incapable and

1. has a guardian with authority to act as litigation guardian in the proceeding, then the guardian shall be the litigation guardian; or

2. does not have a guardian as set out in (1) above, but has a power of attorney with authority to act as litigation guardian in the proceeding, then the attorney shall be the litigation guardian.

A **power of attorney** is a document authorizing an individual to act on another person's behalf in a legal or business matter. The person authorized to act pursuant to the power of attorney is called the **attorney**. If neither (1) nor (2) apply, then the litigation guardian for the incapable person may be

3. a suitable person who does not have an interest contrary to that of the incapable person; or, if no such person is available and willing to act,

4. the Public Guardian and Trustee.

BOX 4.4

What Is the Children's Lawyer? What Is the Public Guardian?

The Office of the Children's Lawyer and the Office of the Public Guardian and Trustee are divisions of the Ministry of the Attorney General.

The Office of the Children's Lawyer provides legal representation for children under the age of 18 in various matters, including custody and access disputes, child protection matters, estate matters, and civil litigation.

The Office of the Public Guardian and Trustee performs a wide range of activities. Among other things, it safeguards the legal, personal, and financial interests of incapable people who have no one else who is authorized to do so. The Public Guardian may act as a litigation guardian or legal representative for individuals involved in lawsuits who lack sufficient capacity to give proper instructions to a lawyer or to make informed decisions.

More information about the services provided by the Office of the Public Guardian and Trustee and the Office of the Children's Lawyer is available at the Attorney General's website (http://www.attorneygeneral.gov.on.ca).

Litigation Guardians—Procedural Matters

ACTING FOR THE PLAINTIFF

Where a proceeding is commenced by a litigation guardian acting on behalf of a plaintiff under disability, the plaintiff should be named as follows:

[name of person under disability], a person under disability, by [his/her] litigation guardian, [name of litigation guardian].

For example, if Collette Desbarais is a minor whose mother, Antoinette Desbarais, is acting as her litigation guardian, the plaintiff would be named on the plaintiff's claim as follows:

Collette Desbarais, a person under disability, by her litigation guardian, Antoinette Desbarais.

The box beside "Under 18 years of age" should be ticked.

At the time of filing the claim or as soon as possible afterward, Antoinette Desbarais as litigation guardian for Collette Desbarais must file a consent in Form 4A in accordance with Rule 4.01(3). See appendix 4.2 to this chapter for a precedent Form 4A—Consent to Act as Litigation Guardian.

Where the Children's Lawyer or the Public Guardian acts as litigation guardian for a plaintiff under disability, no consent is required.

The contents of Form 4A are set out at Rule 4.01(3). Among other things, the litigation guardian must confirm that she has no interest in the proceeding contrary to that of the plaintiff (Rule 4.01(3)(d)). A person with a contrary interest—that is, an interest that is adverse to or conflicts with that of the plaintiff under disability—may not act as litigation guardian, because the contrary interest will prevent her from fulfilling her duty to diligently attend to the plaintiff's interests and take all reasonable steps to protect those interests.

The Form 4A must also contain an acknowledgment that the litigation guardian is aware that she is personally liable to pay any costs awarded against her, or against the plaintiff under disability. As the person commencing and conducting the action, the litigation guardian must take responsibility for the decisions she makes. She cannot pass on the consequences of her own procedural or other errors, in the form of costs awards, to the plaintiff under disability.

ACTING FOR THE DEFENDANT

A proceeding against a person under disability shall be defended by a defendant's litigation guardian (Rule 4.02(1)). If it appears to the court that a defendant who does not have a litigation guardian is a person under disability, the court may appoint any person who has no interest in the proceeding contrary to that of the defendant as the defendant's litigation guardian. Before making such an appointment, the court must give the proposed litigation guardian notice (Rule 4.02(3)).

The defendant's litigation guardian must file a consent in Form 4A with the defence. The terms of the consent are stated in Rule 4.02(2).

Where the Children's Lawyer or the Public Guardian acts as litigation guardian for a defendant under disability, no consent is required.

Where an action is commenced against a defendant under disability, and the defendant fails to defend, it is usually because (1) the defendant under disability does not have a litigation guardian, and does not understand the nature of the action and the consequences of failing to respond; or (2) the defendant under disability has a litigation guardian who has failed to take proper steps.

The general rule is that a defendant who fails to file a defence may be noted in default and, in the case of a liquidated claim, have default judgment signed against him. A default judgment may be enforced against the defendant's assets using any of the procedures set out in Rule 20.

Allowing enforcement of a default judgment against a defendant under disability who has failed to defend a proceeding could result in serious injustice. Rule 4.06 states that the court may set aside a noting in default or default judgment against a person under disability on such terms as are just. The court may also set aside any steps taken to enforce the judgment. To **set aside** an order or other procedural step means to declare the order or procedural step of no force and effect.

Default proceedings are discussed in chapter 5.

OTHER PROCEDURAL ISSUES

Removing or Replacing a Litigation Guardian

The duties of a litigation guardian are to attend diligently to the interests of the person under disability and take all reasonably necessary steps to protect those interests (Rule 4.04(1)).

The court may remove or replace a litigation guardian at any time (Rule 4.05).

Approval of Settlement

The court must approve any settlement of a claim by or against a person under disability (Rule 4.07). If the court has not approved the settlement, it is not binding on the person under disability.

Although the rule does not contain explicit language to this effect, it is arguable that Rule 4.07 applies to a settlement of a claim by or against a person under disability, regardless of whether a court proceeding has actually been commenced, so long as the settlement amount falls within the Small Claims Court legal and monetary jurisdiction. See Rule 7.08(1) of the *Rules of Civil Procedure*, which states that "[n]o settlement of a claim made by or against a person under disability, whether or not a proceeding has been commenced in respect of the claim, is binding on the person without the approval of a judge."

Rule 7.08(3) of the *Rules of Civil Procedure* states that "[w]here an agreement for the settlement of a claim made by or against a person under disability is reached before a proceeding is commenced in respect of the claim, approval of a judge shall be obtained on an application." Applications are not available under the *Rules of the Small Claims Court*. However, if settlement is reached in a matter where a party to the settlement is a person under disability and a Small Claims Court proceeding has not yet been commenced, you should consider seeking direction from a judge of the Small Claims Court as to whether judicial review and approval of the settlement is required.

Money Paid into Court

Any money payable to a person under disability pursuant to a court order or a settlement must be paid into court, unless the court orders otherwise (Rule 4.08(1)). If the money is paid into court, a judge may order the terms on which it shall be paid out.

Payment into court means that the money is paid to the clerk, who then arranges for the money to be deposited to the court bank account. When paying money into court on behalf of a client, you must complete a Form 9B—Request to Clerk providing details about the payment. You will receive a receipt for payment, which you should keep in the client file.

The money will be held in court until an order is made that it be paid out, and to whom. This is called **payment out of court**.

If the court orders that the money be paid directly to the person under disability, the payor is discharged of liability to the extent of the amount paid (Rule 4.08(2)).

ETHICAL ADVOCACY

When representing a client in a Small Claims Court proceeding, you must comply with the *Paralegal Rules of Conduct* and the *Paralegal Professional Conduct Guidelines*.

Paralegal Rule 4, which governs advocacy, applies to all appearances and proceedings before the Small Claims Court.

Duty to Clients, Tribunals, and Others (Paralegal Rules 4.01(1) to (4) and (7))

The paralegal advocate must balance a number of duties.

When acting as an advocate, you shall represent your client honourably and resolutely within the limits of the law. At the same time, you shall treat other licensees and the tribunal before which you are appearing with candour, fairness, courtesy, and respect (Paralegal Rule 4.01(1)), and you shall encourage public respect for, and try to improve, the administration of justice (Paralegal Rule 6.01(1)).

You have a duty to represent your client fearlessly and resolutely. Paralegal Rule 4 does not require you to assist an opposing party or raise matters that are harmful to your client's case, unless the Paralegal Rules state otherwise. Paralegal Rule 4 does place limits on how you may conduct yourself when acting as advocate in a Small Claims Court proceeding. Your professional obligations to other parties, other licensees, the court, and the administration of justice are paramount.

Paralegal Rule 4.01(4) sets out the following requirements for paralegal advocates:

(a) The paralegal shall raise fearlessly every issue, advance every argument, and ask every question, however distasteful, that the paralegal thinks will help the client's case.

(b) The paralegal shall try to obtain for the client the benefit of every remedy and defence authorized by law. A **remedy** is a method of enforcing a right, or preventing or compensating for a wrong.

(c) A paralegal shall never give up or abandon a client's legal rights without the client's informed consent. This Paralegal Rule applies to the client's legal rights generally, and refers specifically to an available defence under a statute of limitations. A statutory limitation period is a period of time established by a statute for commencing a proceeding. When the statutory limitation period has expired, any proceeding against your client is statute-barred—that is, it is stopped by the expiry of the statutory limitation period. Limitation periods were discussed in chapter 3.

  Informed consent is consent based on information that is sufficient to allow the client to assess the situation and make an informed decision.

(d) A paralegal shall avoid and discourage the client from:

  • Resorting to frivolous and vexatious objections. An **objection** is an argument by a party that a particular piece of evidence, line of questioning, or other matter is improper or illegal and should not be allowed by the court. A **frivolous and vexatious objection** is an objection that has no legal merit and is made to annoy, harass, or embarrass the other side.

- Trying to gain advantage from mistakes or oversights by the other side that do not go to the **merits of the case**. The merits of the case are the legal principles upon which a party's assertion of rights is based. A mistake or oversight that does not go to the merits of the case does not affect a party's legal rights.

- Using tactics designed merely to delay or harass the other side.

Regarding Paralegal Rule 4.01(4)(d), Guideline 12 recommends that a paralegal should not engage in rude or disruptive conduct before a tribunal, or ill-mannered correspondence, language, or behaviour toward opposing parties or their advocates. See also Paralegal Rule 7.01(3), which states that when providing legal services, a paralegal shall not communicate, in writing or otherwise, with a client, another licensee, or any other person in a manner that is abusive, offensive, or otherwise inconsistent with the proper tone of a professional communication from a paralegal.

BOX 4.5

Abuse of Tribunal Process

SCENARIO

A prospective client wishes to commence a Small Claims Court proceeding. Based on what she tells you and the documents she produces, you do not think she is entitled to what she says she wants. Throughout the consultation, she speaks of the person against whom she wishes to commence the proceeding in disparaging terms, with contempt and anger.

Question: Should you accept the retainer?

Discussion: A paralegal must be honest and candid when advising a client (Paralegal Rule 3.02). You must look at both sides of each issue without bias. You must advise the client honestly and candidly of the applicable law, the client's options, possible outcomes, and possible risks. Your advice should enable the client to make informed decisions and give appropriate instructions in the matter.

You should advise the client that, in your opinion, the proceeding has no legal merit, giving her your reasons. If she disregards your advice and insists on going forward, consider whether she is motivated solely by malice.

If you are satisfied that she is motivated solely by malice, you should decline the retainer. You should send her a non-engagement letter, confirming that you have decided to decline the retainer. You should also confirm that any documents in your possession have been returned to her.

Question: What are the consequences of going forward with the proceeding?

Discussion: You will be in breach of Paralegal Rule 4.01(5)(a), which prohibits paralegals from starting or continuing actions that have no merit and are brought solely to harm the other party. In this case, you have concluded that the proceeding has no merit, and you believe that the client's motives are malicious. Unmeritorious proceedings waste the time of the tribunal and its officers, and do not further the cause of justice.

The Paralegal and the Tribunal Process (Paralegal Rule 4.01(5))

ABUSE OF TRIBUNAL PROCESS

Malicious Proceedings (Paralegal Rule 4.01(5)(a))

A paralegal shall not abuse the process of the tribunal by commencing or continuing to act in proceedings that, although legal, are clearly motivated by malice on the part of the client and are brought solely for the purpose of injuring the other party (Paralegal Rule 4.01(5)(a)). Proceedings that have no merit waste the time of the tribunal and its officers, and do not further the cause of justice (Guideline 12).

MISLEADING THE TRIBUNAL (PARALEGAL RULES 4.01(5)(C), (D), AND (H))

A paralegal must ensure that neither the paralegal nor the client misleads the tribunal. To arrive at an appropriate decision, the tribunal must receive everything that is relevant to the issues to be decided in a matter (Guideline 12). If the tribunal is mistaken about or misunderstands some aspect of the facts or the law in a case, the paralegal should do what is necessary to correct the mistake or misunderstanding.

A paralegal shall not knowingly attempt to deceive a tribunal or influence the course of justice by (Paralegal Rule 4.01(5)(c)):

- offering false evidence,

- misstating facts or law,

- presenting or relying upon a false or deceptive affidavit,

- suppressing something that should be disclosed, or

- otherwise assisting in any deception, crime, or illegal conduct.

BOX 4.6

What Is an Affidavit?

An **affidavit** is a written statement of facts that is confirmed under oath or by affirmation by the person making the affidavit. The person making the affidavit is called the **deponent**.

The content of an affidavit is evidence. Swearing or affirming a false or deceptive affidavit or assisting another person to do so with intent to mislead is an offence contrary to s. 131 of the *Criminal Code*.

You must represent your client fearlessly and resolutely, but you shall not knowingly engage in dishonest conduct that misleads the tribunal and others in order to protect your client or gain an advantage for your client.

A paralegal shall not deliberately refrain from informing the tribunal of any binding authority that the paralegal considers to be directly on point and that has not been mentioned by an opponent (Paralegal Rule 4.01(5)(d)). **Binding authority** (also known as binding precedent) is a judicial decision by a higher court that must be followed by lower courts.

A paralegal shall not knowingly misstate the contents of a document, the testimony of a witness, the substance of an argument, or the provisions of a statute or similar authority (Paralegal Rule 4.01(5)(h)). The tribunal must be able to rely upon correct information when reviewing a case and arriving at a decision.

BOX 4.7

Binding Authority (Paralegal Rule 4.01(5)(d))

SCENARIO

You represent the defendant in a Small Claims Court proceeding. During some last-minute online research before the trial, you find a very recent appellate decision that is unfavourable to your client and favourable to the plaintiff. The decision is binding on the Small Claims Court. There are some minor legal and factual differences between the matter dealt with in the appellate decision and the matter before the court.

To your surprise, during submissions, the licensee representing the plaintiff does not refer to the decision.

Are you required to inform the court of a binding authority that is unfavourable to your client's case?

DISCUSSION

You are required to represent your client resolutely and honourably within the limits of the law, while treating the tribunal and other licensees with candour, fairness, courtesy, and respect, and upholding the high ethical standards of the paralegal profession (Paralegal Rule 4.01(1)). You are not required to assist an adversary or advance matters that may harm your client's case, unless the Paralegal Rules provide otherwise (Paralegal Rule 4.01(3)).

You must balance your duty to your client with your duty to treat the tribunal and other licensees with candour and fairness. Your opponent has not mentioned the appellate decision. You may not deliberately refrain from informing the tribunal of the appellate decision if you think the principles stated in the decision are relevant and applicable to this case, regardless of the minor legal and factual differences. You must consider whether the court is likely to arrive at an inappropriate decision if it does not know about the case.

IMPROPERLY INFLUENCING THE TRIBUNAL (PARALEGAL RULES 4.01(5)(E) AND (G))

Judges and deputy judges must be fair, impartial, independent, and neutral. A judge's decision-making must not be influenced by private or partisan interests, which may give rise to actual bias or to an appearance of bias in favour of a particular person.

A paralegal shall not appear before a judge if the paralegal, the paralegal's partner, a paralegal employed by the paralegal's firm, or the paralegal's client has a business or personal relationship with the adjudicator that either affects the judge's impartiality or may reasonably appear to affect the judge's impartiality (Paralegal Rule 4.01(5)(e)).

A paralegal shall not attempt or allow anyone else to attempt, directly or indirectly, to influence the decision or action of a tribunal or its officers in any case or matter except by open persuasion as an advocate (Paralegal Rule 4.01(5)(g)).

BOX 4.8

Offering False Evidence

SCENARIO

You are acting for the plaintiff in an unliquidated action in Small Claims Court. The defendant failed to file a defence within the prescribed time, and has been noted in default. You have prepared a motion in writing for an assessment of damages, and a supporting affidavit.

When the client reviews the supporting affidavit, she objects to several statements because they are harmful to her case. "If the judge reads this, I'll get less money," she says. "Why should I say anything that's going to take money out of my pocket? I never would have told you that stuff if I'd known you were going to use it against me. I want you to leave it out completely, or change it to say something that will get me what I'm asking for."

The client provided the material to you during a telephone conversation just after the defendant was noted in default. You phoned her because you wanted to clarify some issues before you got started on the supporting affidavit. You took detailed notes of what she said, and went over them with her before ending the call. The statements in the affidavit accurately reflect your notes of the conversation. The statements contain information that is relevant to issues in the matter.

The client is correct that the material is harmful to her case. You did not obtain her consent to disclose the harmful information.

Question: Is the harmful material confidential?

Discussion: You have a duty to hold all client information in strict confidence, unless disclosure is expressly or impliedly authorized by the client or required by law (Paralegal Rule 3.03(1)). You have neither implied nor express consent to disclose this information.

Question: Is disclosure required by law?

Discussion: Unless otherwise provided by the Paralegal Rules, you are not required to assist an adversary or advance matters that harm your client's case (Paralegal Rule 4.01(3)).

In this case, there is no adversary. The defendant has been noted in default, and is not entitled to notice of the motion for an assessment of damages. However, the court file is public, and its contents, including the affidavit supporting the motion for an assessment of damages, are available to the defendant, should he decide at some point to come forward and dispute the matter. If the harmful material is included in the affidavit, it may come to the attention of the defendant.

In cases where you are dealing with a self-represented party and the matter is uncontested, you should consider taking particular care to ensure that the tribunal has all the information necessary to come to an appropriate conclusion.

The client is not disputing the truth of the harmful statements, and you have taken careful steps to confirm their accuracy. Her concern is the harmful effect that their disclosure may have on her case.

The only material that the judge will have before her on the motion is the material that you file with the court. The harmful material is accurate, and relevant to issues in the case. If the material is deleted from the affidavit, you are knowingly attempting to deceive a tribunal and influence the course of justice by relying upon a deceptive affidavit and suppressing information that ought to be disclosed, contrary to Paralegal Rule 4.01(5)(c). You are knowingly deceiving the tribunal because you are not providing all the information that the judge will need to properly review the matter and arrive at an appropriate decision. You are knowingly attempting to influence the course of justice because you are suppressing relevant material in order to obtain a more favourable result for your client.

You are knowingly assisting or permitting the client to do something that is dishonest and dishonourable, contrary to Paralegal Rule 4.01(5)(b).

You must carefully weigh your duties of confidentiality and loyalty to the client against your duty to the tribunal and the administration of justice, keeping in mind your obligations under Paralegal Rules 4.01(4) and (5).

Question: Should you alter the harmful material so that it is favourable to your client's case?

Discussion: If you change the material to make it favourable to your client, the supporting affidavit will contain false statements. If you alter evidence you know to be true in order to gain an advantage for your client, you are knowingly attempting to deceive the tribunal and influence the course of justice by offering false evidence, relying upon a false or deceptive affidavit, and assisting in a crime, contrary to Paralegal Rule 4.01(5)(c). You are knowingly deceiving the tribunal because you are knowingly relying upon false evidence in support of the motion. You are knowingly attempting to influence the course of justice, because you are offering evidence you know to be false in order to obtain a more favourable result for your client.

You are knowingly assisting or permitting the client to do something that is dishonest and dishonourable, contrary to Paralegal Rule 4.01(5)(b).

Giving false evidence (spoken or written) under oath with intent to mislead is an offence contrary to s. 131 of the *Criminal Code*.

Question: What next?

Discussion: You should advise the client that you have a duty to provide the tribunal with everything it needs to arrive at an effective, appropriate decision. You cannot suppress or alter relevant evidence to obtain a more favourable result for her, nor can you assist her in swearing an affidavit you know to be false. You should advise her that swearing a false affidavit with intent to mislead is an offence. If she persists in her instructions, you may be required to withdraw from representation pursuant to Paralegal Rule 3.08.

Guideline 12 states that the only appropriate way to influence the decision of a court or other tribunal is by appearing before the court in the presence of, or on notice to, other parties, offering appropriate evidence in support of your client's case, and making persuasive submissions based upon applicable legal principles, unless a rule of the Small Claims Court permits or requires otherwise.

You should never communicate directly with a judge or deputy judge in the absence of other parties, unless a rule of the Small Claims Court permits you to do so (Guideline 12).

DISHONEST CONDUCT (PARALEGAL RULES 4.01(5)(B), (C), AND (F))

A paralegal shall not knowingly assist or permit the client to do anything that the paralegal considers to be dishonest or dishonourable (Paralegal Rule 4.01(5)(b)).

A paralegal shall not knowingly attempt to deceive a tribunal or influence the course of justice by offering false evidence (including false or deceptive affidavits), misstating facts or law, suppressing relevant information, or otherwise assisting in any deception, crime, or illegal conduct (Paralegal Rule 4.01(5)(c)).

A paralegal shall not knowingly assert a fact to be true when its truth cannot reasonably be supported by the evidence, or as a matter of which notice may be taken by the tribunal (Paralegal Rule 4.01(5)(f)).

BOX 4.9

Judicial Notice

What is meant by "a matter of which notice may be taken by the tribunal" (Paralegal Rule 4.01(5)(f))? This is known in the courts as **judicial notice**. Judges may notice, or accept as true, certain notorious facts (that is, matters of common knowledge) without hearing evidence and without inquiry. Other lesser-known facts (for example, matters that can be checked in a standard reference work and are not easily disputed) may be judicially noticed after inquiry.

DISCLOSURE OF DOCUMENTS (PARALEGAL RULE 4.01(6))

Where the rules of a court or other tribunal require the parties to produce documents, a paralegal advocate:

(a) shall explain to the client the necessity of making full disclosure of all documents relating to any matter in issue, and the duty to answer any proper question relating to any issue in the action to the best of his knowledge, information, or belief;

(b) shall assist the client in fulfilling his obligation to make full disclosure; and

(c) shall not make frivolous requests for production of documents or frivolous demands for information.

Timely, complete, and accurate disclosure lets the parties know the case they have to meet. It promotes settlement because it allows each party to assess the strengths and weaknesses of her own case and those of opposing parties. It also makes the hearing process more efficient and fair (Guideline 12).

The *Rules of the Small Claims Court* require early and ongoing disclosure by all parties. This should be explained to the client at the initial consultation, and confirmed in the retainer agreement or engagement letter.

DRAFTING THE PLAINTIFF'S CLAIM

What Are Pleadings?

Pleadings are the documents filed at the commencement of a proceeding in which the parties state the allegations of fact on which they rely in support of their claim or defence. In a Small Claims Court proceeding, the documents that make up the pleadings are the plaintiff's claim, the defence, the defendant's claim, and the defence to the defendant's claim. These are the documents in which the parties plead, or present, their case—thus the name pleadings.

It is important to remember that a pleading is made up of allegations of fact—that is, a series of assertions that have not yet been proven. In a Small Claims Court proceeding, an allegation of fact that is in dispute—that is, an allegation that one party says is true and the other party says is not true—does not become a fact, or the "truth," until the following process has been completed. The party making the allegation produces evidence in support of the allegation at trial. The opposing party leads evidence intended to prove that the allegation is not true. The Small Claims Court judge, who is the finder of fact, accepts one party's evidence over that of the other party, on a balance of probabilities. The allegation of fact that is accepted, based on the evidence, then becomes a fact, or the "truth," for legal purposes.

A pleading is a piece of advocacy. When drafting a pleading you must make the strongest possible case for your client. This does not mean that you should misrepresent the facts as you know them, based on what your client has told you. You must ensure that there is some evidentiary basis for the allegations you are making. Instead, it means emphasizing the strengths of your client's case, without making false statements or misrepresentations. It is up to your opponent to expose the weaknesses in your client's case—you have no obligation to assist him or her.

When you are interviewing a client, you will find that they tell you a lot of things that may or may not be relevant to their case. Relevant statements are allegations that go toward establishing a legal basis for the relief your client is claiming. When going over your notes of the client interview, keep the following questions in mind:

- What does the client want?

- What do I need to say to support the client's case?

- Which client statements support the client's case?

- Which client statements do not support the client's case?

- Which client statements are completely irrelevant to any issue that I am aware of in the client's case at this stage of the proceeding?

BOX 4.10

Drafting a Plaintiff's Claim: What Is Relevant?

You work for Prior Mustafa LLP, 22 County Court Boulevard, Brampton, Ontario A1A 2B3 TEL: 905 111 2222 FAX: 905 111 2233.

Your client is Juliette Greco. Ms. Greco is an attractive woman in her late thirties who works as a buyer for a large department store. She is very well dressed, and does not wear a wedding ring. She lives at 126 George Court, Brampton, Ontario L1X 2V4 TEL: 905 791 2234. In April 20—, she loaned $5,000.00 to her neighbour, James Hardwick, who lives at 128 George Court, Brampton, Ontario L1X 2V4 TEL: 905 791 3333. She has come to see you because he failed to pay the money back.

She has been neighbours with the Hardwick family for five years, since she moved into her house at 126 George Court. Until recently, she considered them her friends. She allowed the Hardwick boys (James and Charles) to swim in her pool in the summers, and occasionally she had the entire family (James, Pamela, and the two boys) over for a barbecue. She also attended a few parties at the Hardwick house. She felt sorry for James and Pamela. James is "kind of dumb," to use Juliette's own words, and Pamela has a big mouth and a bad temper.

From conversations with Pamela, Juliette knew the Hardwicks were having financial problems last spring. So when James came to her and asked her for a loan of $5,000.00, she agreed, but took the precaution of having him sign a promissory note, dated April 1, 20—. Under the terms of the note, he was supposed to pay the entire amount back on or before August 2, 20—. Juliette has a duplicate original of the promissory note.

When James failed to pay the money back, Juliette phoned him a couple of times. Pamela answered, and was extremely rude on the phone, so after that Juliette sent a couple of letters, asking for the money to be repaid. The letters are dated August 15, 20— and September 15, 20—. She sent the letters by registered mail. She has copies of the letters and the registration slips.

Juliette seems to be quite upset by what has happened. She says that she used to sit out by the pool on summer evenings when she got home from work; but whenever Pamela is in her own backyard and sees Juliette next door, Pamela makes loud, rude remarks about her. Now she is reluctant to use her backyard or her pool. Finally, she recently found dog feces on her driveway. She believes the Hardwick boys put them there.

Juliette wants to sue James for the unpaid $5,000.00 plus interest as provided in the promissory note.

What is the nature of Ms. Greco's claim? In other words, what does Ms. Greco want?

According to the last paragraph in the fact situation, Ms. Greco wants the money owing plus interest pursuant to the promissory note signed by James Hardwick on April 1, 20—. In other words, this is a debt collection.

What are the relevant facts? In other words, what facts need to be stated in the plaintiff's claim to support Ms. Greco's case?

This is a debt collection. Only those facts that relate to the debt are relevant. Relevant facts would include the amount of the loan, the terms of the loan agreement (if there is one), the circumstances of default, whether there have been any demands for payment, and whether there have been any payments on account of the balance owing.

The fact situation has been duplicated below, with the relevant facts emphasized in bold type. A brief explanation of why the facts are relevant follows each paragraph.

Your client is Juliette Greco. Ms. Greco is an attractive woman in her late thirties who works as a buyer for a large department store. She is very well dressed, and does not wear a wedding ring. **She lives at 126 George Court, Brampton, Ontario L1X 2V4 TEL: 905 791 2234. In April 20—, she loaned $5,000.00 to her neighbour, James Hardwick, who lives at 128 George Court, Brampton, Ontario L1X 2V4 TEL: 905 791 3333. She has come to see you because he failed to pay the money back.**

You need the correct names and addresses of the parties in order to correctly fill out the plaintiff's claim. You need the correct name and address of the defendant, James Hardwick, because this establishes Small Claims Court territorial jurisdiction under Rule 6. As well, you will need this information when enforcing the judgment. The information about the amount of the loan, the date the money was advanced, and the default in payment goes to establishing the basis for the claim.

She has been neighbours with the Hardwick family for five years, since she moved into her house at 126 George Court. Until recently, she considered them her friends. She allowed the Hardwick boys (James and Charles) to swim in her pool in the summers, and occasionally she had the entire family (James, Pamela, and the two boys) over for a barbecue. She also attended a few parties at the Hardwick house. She felt sorry for James and Pamela. James is "kind of dumb," to use Juliette's own words, and Pamela has a big mouth and a bad temper.

Nothing in this paragraph is relevant in the context of a debt collection.

From conversations with Pamela, Juliette knew the Hardwicks were having financial problems last spring. **So when James came to her and asked her for a loan of $5,000.00, she agreed, but took the precaution of having him sign a promissory note, dated April 1, 20—. Under the terms of the note, he was supposed to pay the entire amount back on or before August 2, 20—. Juliette has a duplicate original of the promissory note.**

Ms. Greco's motives for advancing the money are irrelevant to any legal issue in the case. The existence of the promissory note, and the fact that Ms. Greco has a duplicate original, are relevant because the note provides documentary evidence of the loan and its terms.

When James failed to pay the money back, Juliette phoned him a couple of times. Pamela answered, and was extremely rude on the phone, so after that Juliette sent a couple of letters, asking for the money to be repaid. The letters are dated August 15, 20— and September 15, 20—. She sent the letters by registered mail. She has copies of the letters and the registration slips.

This information is relevant because it establishes that Ms. Greco has made demands, both spoken and written, for payment of the debt. Also, she has documentary evidence to back this up.

Juliette seems to be quite upset by what has happened. She says that she used to sit out by the pool on summer evenings when she got home from work; but whenever Pamela is in her own backyard and sees Juliette next door, Pamela makes loud, rude remarks about her. Now she is reluctant to use her backyard or her pool. Finally, she recently found dog feces on her driveway. She believes the Hardwick boys put them there.

Nothing in this paragraph is relevant in the context of a debt collection.

Juliette wants to sue James for the unpaid $5,000.00 plus interest as provided in the promissory note.

This information is relevant because it tells you what your client wants.

When you have decided what the relevant facts are, you have to turn them into a persuasive narrative, which is carefully organized for maximum clarity. Sometimes, as in the case of a simple debt collection, this will be easy to do. In other cases, the narrative will be more complex, and will require careful thought, editing, and rewriting.

Small Claims Court Rules 7.01(2)(ii), 9.02(1), and 10.01(4) require that the grounds for a claim or defence be stated in concise and non-technical language with a reasonable amount of detail. Use plain, everyday language and simple sentence structures with active verbs whenever possible.

Consider using precedents. **Precedent documents** are legal documents that are used as guides for drafting subsequent documents with a similar purpose. The sample letters at appendixes 2.1, 2.2, 2.6, and 2.7 of chapter 2 are examples of precedent documents. They can be used as guides for writing certain types of correspondence, but you must adapt the language to different client situations. Similarly, the claim at appendix 3.1 of chapter 3 can be used as a guide if you are drafting a claim for a plaintiff in a similar situation.

You should develop a databank of precedent documents for use when providing legal services, keeping in mind your duty of confidentiality under Paralegal Rule 3.03. The databank should be updated on a regular basis.

Rules of Pleading

Small Claims Court Rule 7.01 sets out the requirements for a plaintiff's claim. Some of these requirements have been incorporated into the Form 7A. These include: the full names of the parties and the capacity in which they sue or are sued (see discussion above about parties under disability); the name, address, telephone number, fax number, and Law Society of Upper Canada registration number of the licensee representing the plaintiff, or, if the plaintiff is self-represented, the name, address, telephone number, and fax number of the plaintiff; and the address where the plaintiff believes the defendant may be served. Rule 7.01(2) states that the plaintiff's claim must also set out, in concise and non-technical language, the nature of the claim, with reasonable certainty and detail, including the date, place, and nature of the occurrences on which the claim is based; and the amount of the claim and the relief requested. There is space for these particulars at pages 2 and 3 of Form 7A.

Although it is not required by the *Small Claims Court Rules*, licensees should consider setting out the particulars of the client's claim in a separate Schedule A attached to the plaintiff's claim. The Schedule A should be formatted in accordance with the requirements of Rule 4 of the *Rules of Civil Procedure*. The text should be 10 point or 12 point size (12 point is preferable), and it should be double-spaced, with a left-hand margin of at least 1½ inches (40 millimetres).

The Schedule A should contain a separate first paragraph containing a formal **prayer or request for relief**—that is, a paragraph stating the particulars of the damages, interest, and other relief that the plaintiff thinks she is entitled to. It should then set out, in consecutively numbered paragraphs, the allegations of fact on which the claim is based. Use plain, everyday language and simple sentence structures with active verbs whenever possible.

See appendix 4.3 to this chapter for a sample plaintiff's claim, based on the fact situation in *Greco v. Hardwick* above. Refer also to the precedent plaintiff's claim in appendix 3.1 to chapter 3. In both cases, the claim is based on a promissory note.

See appendix 4.4 for a sample plaintiff's claim based on the fact situation in *Chong v. Kingman* at box 4.2 above.

Documentary Disclosure

The plaintiff must disclose any documents on which she is relying in support of her claim by attaching photocopies of the documents to each copy of the claim (Rule 7.01(2)2). Early disclosure serves two purposes: (1) it gives the defendant notice of the case he has to meet, and (2) it promotes negotiation and settlement.

ISSUING THE PLAINTIFF'S CLAIM

The official start of the court proceeding occurs when the plaintiff's claim is taken to the office of the Small Claims Court with territorial jurisdiction, and issued. Under Rule 7.03, the plaintiff's claim is issued when the clerk dates, signs, and seals it, and assigns a court file number. On the forms, the court file number is described as the "Claim No."

When a court file number has been assigned to a proceeding, all subsequent court documents filed in that proceeding must bear the same court file number.

The original plaintiff's claim (with photocopies of any documentary evidence attached) is sealed, dated, and filed in the court file opened for that particular proceeding. The plaintiff is required to provide a copy of the claim for each defendant. Any copies must be officially sealed also. This eliminates the possibility of procedural irregularity.

BOX 4.11

Reminder: Court Fees

An infrequent claimant is anyone who files fewer than 10 Small Claims Court claims in a Small Claims Court office on or after January 1 in any calendar year. Infrequent claimants are charged $75.00 to file a plaintiff's claim.

A frequent claimant is anyone who files 10 or more claims in a Small Claims Court office on or after January 1 in any calendar year. A frequent claimant is charged $145.00 per claim.

A plaintiff may file 10 or more Small Claims Court claims in any calendar year without losing infrequent claimant status, so long as fewer than 10 claims are filed in any one particular court office. For example, let us say that in 20— the plaintiff files 6 claims in Brampton Small Claims Court, 8 claims in Newmarket Small Claims Court, and 5 claims in Cambridge Small Claims Court, for a total of 19 claims filed in that year. The plaintiff still qualifies for infrequent claimant status in those court offices, because fewer than 10 claims were filed in each one.

The plaintiff is responsible for serving the sealed and dated plaintiff's claim, along with attached documentary disclosure, on the defendant or defendants (Rule 7.03(2)).

SERVICE OF THE PLAINTIFF'S CLAIM

Service means delivery of a legal document to another party in the proceeding. Service of the plaintiff's claim must take place within six months of the date it is issued (Rule 8.01(2)). The time may be extended by court order, either before or after the six-month period has expired, on a motion to the court by the plaintiff.

The claim may be served personally (Rules 8.01(1) and 8.02) or by an alternative to personal service (Rule 8.03). **Personal service** means that a copy of the issued claim is personally delivered to the defendant by the plaintiff herself or by a person authorized by the plaintiff to do so (such as a process server) in accordance with the procedures set out in Rule 8.02. The requirements for proper personal service vary, depending on who the defendant is.

Alternatives to personal service may be used where the defendant has a lawyer who has been instructed to accept service, or where personal service has been attempted but has been unsuccessful, for one reason or another (for example, where the defendant is avoiding service).

Personal Service (Rule 8.02)

For proper personal service to take place, a copy of the plaintiff's claim (or any other document required by the Rules to be personally served) must be handed over to the defendant (if the defendant is an individual) or to the defendant's designated representative (such as the defendant's litigation guardian, if the defendant is a party under disability).

The requirements for valid personal service vary, depending on who is being served. Valid personal service on an individual is different from valid personal service on a municipality, a corporation, or a partnership. You should review Rule 8.02 before attempting personal service yourself or giving instructions to an employee or agent to do so.

PERSONAL SERVICE ON AN INDIVIDUAL

Rule 8.02(a) provides that personal service of a document on an individual other than a person under disability is made by leaving a copy of the document with the individual.

The Affidavit of Service

For any document required to be served in accordance with Rule 8, an affidavit of service must be completed and sworn by the person who effected (carried out) service. The affidavit of service is proof that a document has, in fact, been properly served. The deponent in the affidavit of service is the person who carried out the service, and thus has personal knowledge of how service was effected. The affidavit

BOX 4.12

Personal Service on an Individual (Rule 8.02(a))

Refer to the fact situation in *Greco v. Hardwick* in box 4.10 above at pages 118-119. Claire Ivory is a process server employed by Prior Mustafa LLP, the paralegals for the plaintiff, Juliette Greco. Claire has been asked to serve the plaintiff's claim on the defendant, James Hardwick. On the evening of November 8, 20—, she goes to the Hardwick residence at 128 George Court, Brampton, Ontario L1X 2V4. She knocks on the door. James Hardwick answers the door. Claire asks him if he is James Hardwick. He says yes. Claire says, "I am serving a plaintiff's claim on you in *Greco v. Hardwick*." She hands him the claim, and he takes it. This takes place at 7:30 p.m.

As Claire turns to go back to her car, James Hardwick glances at the front page of the claim. He swears, flings the claim down on the front step, goes in the house, and slams the door.

Issue: Has valid personal service of the plaintiff's claim taken place?

Discussion: Yes. Claire obtained confirmation that the person who answered the door was the named defendant, James Hardwick. She identified the document being served, and left a copy with him. The fact that James then lost his temper and threw the claim on the ground without reading it does not invalidate service.

BOX 4.13

Affidavit of Service—Personal Service on an Individual

In the *Greco v. Hardwick* fact situation discussed above, Claire Ivory is the person who **effected**, or carried out, service of the plaintiff's claim on the defendant, James Hardwick. She will be the deponent in the affidavit of service of the plaintiff's claim, which will now be completed, sworn, and filed with the court.

A Small Claims Court defendant has 20 days from the date of service of the plaintiff's claim to deliver a defence (Rule 9.01(1)), failing which there may be adverse procedural consequences for the defendant. The affidavit of service of Claire Ivory, when filed with the court, is proof that personal service took place, and is also proof about when the 20-day period for James Hardwick to file a defence began to run.

See appendix 4.5 to this chapter for a sample affidavit of service of the plaintiff's claim, based on the fact situation in *Greco v. Hardwick* above.

of service will be sworn by the deponent in the presence of a commissioner of oaths. The original of the affidavit of service is filed with the court; and a copy goes into your pleadings subfile.

TABLE 4.1   Personal Service (Rule 8.02)

Who is being served?	Whom may the document be left with?	Where is personal service effected?
Individual (Rule 8.02(a))	■ The named individual	■ Not specified
Municipality (Rule 8.02(b))	■ The chair, mayor, warden, reeve, clerk, or deputy clerk of the municipality ■ A lawyer for the municipality if the lawyer has instructions to accept service	■ Not specified
Corporation (Rule 8.02(c))	■ An officer, director, or agent of the corporation ■ A person who appears to be in control or management of a place of business of the corporation	■ Not specified ■ Any place of business of the corporation
Board or commission (Rule 8.02(d))	■ A member or officer of the board or commission	■ Not specified
Person outside Ontario carrying on business in Ontario (Rule 8.02(e))	■ Anyone carrying on business in Ontario for the person	■ Not specified
Federal Crown (Rule 8.02(f))	■ The Deputy Attorney General of Canada ■ The chief executive officer of the agency in whose name the proceedings are taken	■ Not specified ■ Not specified
Provincial Crown (Rule 8.02(g))	■ A solicitor in the Crown Law Office (Civil Law) of the Ministry of the Attorney General	■ The Crown Law Office (Civil Law) of the Ministry of the Attorney General
Absentee (Rule 8.02(h))	■ The absentee's committee, if one has been appointed ■ If not, with the Public Guardian and Trustee	■ Not specified ■ The Office of the Public Guardian and Trustee
Minor (Rule 8.02(i))	■ The minor **and** ■ If the minor lives with a parent or other person having care and lawful custody, the parent or lawful guardian	■ Not specified
Mentally incapable person (Rule 8.02(j))	In order of preference ■ A guardian or attorney acting under validated power of attorney for personal care with authority to act in the proceeding ■ If the above does not apply, the mentally incapable person **and** an attorney under a power of attorney with authority to act in the proceeding ■ If the above does not apply, the mentally incapable person **and** the Public Guardian and Trustee	■ Not specified ■ Not specified ■ Not specified

TABLE 4.1   Concluded

Who is being served?	Whom may the document be left with?	Where is personal service effected?
Partnership (Rule 8.02(k)) NOTE: If any one or more of the partners is a corporation, refer to Rule 8.02(c)	■ Any one or more of the partners (see Rule 5) ■ A person who appears to be in control or management of the principal place of business of the partnership	■ Not specified ■ At the principal place of business of the partnership
Sole proprietorship (Rule 8.02(l))	■ The sole proprietor ■ A person who appears to be in control or management of the principal place of business of the sole proprietorship	■ Not specified ■ At the principal place of business of the sole proprietorship

PERSONAL SERVICE ON OTHER PERSONS

Rule 8.02 also sets out the requirements for valid personal service on legal persons such as parties under disability, municipalities, corporations, the federal and provincial Crowns, etc. See table 4.1 for details of personal service on various entities. The most important thing to remember about service is that its rules are complex, and no one can remember them all. If you cannot remember, do not guess. Read Rule 8.

Alternatives to Personal Service (Rule 8.03)

Alternative methods of service may be used when the party being served has a lawyer with instructions to accept service of documents, or when personal service has been attempted and has failed for various reasons. The defendant may have moved without the plaintiff's knowledge. In the case of a corporation, the address of the head office or principal place of business on record with the Ministry of Government Services may be out of date. In other cases, a defendant may actively be avoiding service. In such cases, the plaintiff's claim may be served by an alternative to personal service.

ALTERNATIVE TO PERSONAL SERVICE—ACCEPTANCE OF SERVICE BY LAWYER (RULES 8.03(5) AND (6))

Where a party has a lawyer of record, a document that would otherwise need to be served personally on that party in accordance with Rule 8.02 may instead be served on the lawyer of record or an employee in the lawyer's office. For service to be valid, the lawyer must have instructions to accept service, and the lawyer or employee accepting service must endorse the document or a copy of the document with acceptance of service and the date of the acceptance. By so doing, the lawyer or an employee in the lawyer's office is deemed to represent to the court that he or she has the client's instructions to accept service (Rule 8.03(6)).

If you are serving the lawyer of record under Rule 8.03(5), you must give your process server two copies of the document being served. One will be left with the lawyer or the lawyer's employee. The other will be stamped with an acceptance of service. When the lawyer or the lawyer's employee accepts service of the document,

BOX 4.14

Service on an Apparent Adult at an Individual's Place of Residence (Rule 8.03(2)(a))

When using this method of service, you should first ask for the defendant by name. If possible, you should obtain the name of the individual who answers the door and confirm that she or he is a member of the defendant's household before leaving the sealed envelope with the individual. However, keep in mind that in situations where the defendant is avoiding service, members of her household may be reluctant to provide any information. So long as the person to whom you hand the sealed envelope appears to be 19 years of age or older and appears to be a member of the defendant's household, proper service has been carried out.

they shall complete and sign the acceptance of service. The acceptance of service proves service in the same way that an affidavit of service does. A copy of the endorsement should be put in your pleadings subfile, and the original should be filed with the court office with the affidavit of service.

ALTERNATIVE TO PERSONAL SERVICE—SERVICE AT PLACE OF RESIDENCE (RULES 8.03(2) AND (4))

Where a party has already tried to serve personally a document at an individual's place of residence and for any reason personal service cannot be effected, the document may be served by leaving a sealed copy addressed to the individual at the place of residence with anyone who appears to be an adult member of the same household. On the same day or the following day, another copy of the document must be mailed or sent by courier to the individual at that address.

Service under Rule 8.03(2) is effective the fifth day after the day the document is mailed or the day the courier verifies delivery (Rule 8.03(4)). Applying Rule 1.03(2) of the *Small Claims Court Rules* and Rule 3.01(1)(b) of the *Rules of Civil Procedure*, when computing a notice period of seven days or less, holidays should not be counted. Refer to the definition of "holiday" in Rule 1.02(1) of the *Small Claims Court Rules*.

The 20-day period (including holidays) for delivering a defence begins to run after the 5-day period has elapsed.

ALTERNATIVE TO PERSONAL SERVICE—SERVICE ON A CORPORATION (RULES 8.03(3) AND (4))

All corporations incorporated under the Ontario *Business Corporations Act* are required to register their particulars, including officers, shareholders, and addresses of the head office and/or principal places of business, with the Companies and Personal Property Security Branch (Companies Branch) of the Ministry of Government Services.

Corporations incorporated under the *Canada Business Corporations Act* or under the laws of other countries, provinces, or territories are required to record the name and address of their lawyer for service in Ontario with the Ministry of Government Services.

Where these records are out of date, service of a document on an Ontario corporation may be made by mailing or sending by courier a copy of the document to the last-known address for service of the corporation recorded with the Ministry of Government Services, and by mailing or sending by courier a copy of the document to each director of the corporation as recorded at the Ministry of Government Services, at the director's last-known address recorded with the Ministry.

In the case of an extra-provincial corporation, where the attorney for service in Ontario cannot be found at the last address recorded with the Ministry, service may be made on the corporation by mailing or sending by courier a copy of the document to the attorney for service in Ontario at the last-known address, and by mailing or sending by courier a copy of the document to each director of the corporation as recorded at the Ministry of Government Services, at the director's last-known address recorded with the Ministry.

Service is effective on the fifth day after the day the document is mailed or the day the courier verifies delivery (Rule 8.03(4)). The 20-day period (including holidays) for delivering a defence begins to run after the 5-day period has elapsed.

ALTERNATIVE TO PERSONAL SERVICE—SERVICE OF CLAIM BY REGISTERED MAIL OR COURIER TO INDIVIDUAL AT THE INDIVIDUAL'S PLACE OF RESIDENCE (RULES 8.03(7), (8), AND (9))

This rule is restricted to service of a plaintiff's claim or defendant's claim on an individual against whom the claim is made. Where personal service of a claim cannot be effected because an individual cannot be located or is actively avoiding service, the claim may be served by registered mail or by courier at the individual's place of residence, but service is valid only if the individual's signature verifying receipt of the document is obtained (Rule 8.03(7)). Service under Rule 8.03(7) is effective on the date on which the individual verifies receipt of the copy of the claim by signature, evidenced by a delivery confirmation provided by Canada Post or the commercial courier, as the case may be (Rule 8.03(8)).

Substituted Service (Rule 8.04)

Sometimes prompt service of a claim personally or by an alternative to personal service cannot be carried out because the other party cannot be located or is actively avoiding service, or for other reasons. In these circumstances, the plaintiff may make a motion to the court for an **order for substituted service**—that is, an order permitting the plaintiff to serve the claim in a manner that is not set out in the Rules.

Before granting an order for substituted service, the court must be satisfied that all reasonable steps have been taken to serve the other party personally or by an alternative to personal service, without success. There should be some evidence put before the court as to what would be an appropriate form of substituted service in the circumstances.

If the order is granted, it will specify what steps the plaintiff must take to comply with the requirements for substituted service. Unless the court orders otherwise, the plaintiff must serve a copy of the order for substituted service along with the claim.

Service Outside Ontario (Rule 8.05)

If the defendant is outside Ontario, the plaintiff may incur extra expense trying to effect service of the claim. In a costs award to the plaintiff, the court may include any reasonable costs incurred by the plaintiff in effecting service on an out-of-province defendant.

Service of Other Documents

Table 4.2 lists the documents that must be served personally or by an alternative to personal service.

The court clerk shall serve the following documents:

- A defence (including a defence to a defendant's claim), by mail or by fax (Rule 8.01(3))

- A default judgment, by mail or by fax (Rule 8.01(4))

- An assessment order made on a motion in writing for an assessment of damages, by mail if the moving party provides a stamped, self-addressed envelope with the notice of motion (Rule 8.01(5))

- A settlement conference order by mail or by fax to all parties that did not attend the settlement conference (Rule 8.01(6))

The following documents shall be served personally, by an alternative to personal service, by mail, or by courier:

- Notice of garnishment and affidavit for enforcement request, on the debtor (Rule 8.01(8)(a))

- Notice of garnishment and garnishee's statement, on the garnishee (Rule 8.01(8)(b))

- Notice of garnishment hearing (Rule 8.01(9))

- Notice of examination (Rule 8.01(10))

- Financial statement (Rule 8.01(11))

Any document that is not referred to above or in table 4.2 may be served by mail, by courier, by fax, personally, or by an alternative to personal service, unless the court orders otherwise (Rule 8.01(14)).

SERVICE BY MAIL (RULE 8.07)

A document that may be served by mail may be sent by regular letter mail or registered mail to the last address of the person or the person's lawyer or paralegal that is known to the sender (Rule 8.07(1)(b)). If the court clerk is serving a document by mail, the document may be mailed to the last address on file with the court (Rule 8.07(1)(a)).

Service by mail becomes effective five days from the date of mailing (Rule 8.07(2)). Because this period is seven days or less, Rules 1.03(2) of the *Small Claims Court Rules* and 3.01(1)(b) of the *Rules of Civil Procedure* apply. When you are cal-

TABLE 4.2 Documents That Must Be Served Personally (Rule 8.01) or by an Alternative to Personal Service

Document	Who serves	Manner of service	Time for service
Plaintiff's claim (Form 7A)	Party or legal representative	– Personal (Rule 8.01(1)) – Alternative to personal service (Rule 8.03(1)) – Substituted service (with leave of court) (Rule 8.04)	Six months from date of issuance, unless court order extends the time (Rule 8.01(2))
Defendant's claim (Form 10A)	Party or legal representative	– Personal (Rule 8.01(1)) – Alternative to personal service (Rule 8.03(1)) – Substituted service (with leave of court) (Rule 8.04)	Six months from date of issuance, unless court order extends the time (Rule 8.01(2))
Summons to witness (Form 18A)	Party or legal representative	– Personal (Rule 8.01(7))	10 days before the hearing date
Notice of contempt hearing (Form 20I)	Creditor or legal representative	– Personal (Rule 8.01(13))	Affidavit of service filed at least 7 days before the date of hearing

The above documents must be served personally or by an alternative to personal service. All other Small Claims Court documents may be served personally, by an alternative to personal service, or by any other method of service permitted by Rule 8.

culating the earliest effective date for service, you must exclude weekends and holidays from the calculation, and the period must end on a business day.

Rule 8.07(2) does not apply when a claim is served by mail under Rule 8.03(7)—Service of Claim on an individual by mail or courier at the individual's place of residence (Rule 8.07(3)).

SERVICE BY COURIER (RULE 8.07.1)

Service of a document by courier must be sent by means of a commercial courier to the last address of the person or the person's lawyer or paralegal that is on file with the court or known to the sender.

Service takes effect five days after the date that the courier confirms delivery of the document (Rule 8.07.1(2)). The five-day period excludes holidays and must end on a business day.

Rule 8.07.1(2) does not apply when a claim is served by courier under Rule 8.03(7)—Service of Claim on an individual by mail or courier at the individual's place of residence (Rule 8.07.1(3)).

SERVICE BY FAX (RULE 8.08)

Service by fax is deemed to be effective on the date of the faxing, if faxing took place before 5:00 p.m. on a business day (Rule 8.08(1)(a)). In any other case, service by fax becomes effective on the next business day (Rule 8.08(1)(b)). In other words, if you serve the other party by fax at or after 5:00 p.m. on a business day, service is effective on the next business day. If you serve the other party by fax on a holiday (as defined in Rule 1.02), service is effective on the next business day.

The original of the fax transmission sheet, confirming the fax number of the recipient and the date and time that service took place, should be attached to the affidavit of service filed with the court. Your file copy of the affidavit of service by fax should have a copy of the fax transmission sheet attached.

If the document that you are serving contains 16 or more pages, including the cover page, it must be faxed outside regular business hours unless you have the other party's consent to fax it between 8:00 a.m. and 5:00 p.m. (Rule 8.08(2)).

NOTICE OF CHANGE OF ADDRESS (RULE 8.09)

Rule 8.09 requires that a party whose address for service has changed shall serve notice of the change on the court and other parties within seven days after the change takes place.

There is no form for a notice of change of address. However, best practice requires that it should be in writing and it should be sent to all other parties and filed with the clerk. The court may order that proof of service be filed by way of an affidavit of service (Rule 8.09(2)).

FAILURE TO RECEIVE DOCUMENT (RULE 8.10)

Sometimes a document is served in accordance with Rule 8 or a court order for substituted service, but the person on whom it was deemed to be served does not receive it, or receives it later than the time when service became effective. A person who fails to receive a document in the above circumstances may make a motion to set aside the consequences of default, for an extension of time, or in support of a request for an adjournment, raising failure to receive the document or late receipt of the document, as the case may be, as a ground for granting the relief sought.

AMENDMENT OF PLEADING (RULE 12)

General

If you make a mistake on a pleading, you are permitted to correct it by Rule 12.01(1), which provides that a plaintiff's or defendant's claim, or a defence to a plaintiff's or defendant's claim, may be **amended** (that is, changed or corrected or otherwise improved). Any changes or additions must be underlined on the pleading, and deletions or other changes should be identified. The amended pleading must be marked "Amended," filed with the clerk, and served on all parties, including parties in default (Rules 12.01(1) and (2)). An amended pleading may be served personally, by an alternative to personal service, by mail, by courier, or by fax (Rule 8.01(14)).

An amended pleading may be filed and served at any time up until at least 30 days before the original trial date, unless the court on motion allows a shorter notice period (Rule 12.01(3)(a)), or a request for clerk's order on consent under Rule 11.2.01(1) allowing a shorter notice period is obtained.

Where a person is added as a party at trial, the court may order that service of the claim be dispensed with (Rule 12.01(4)).

A party who is served with an amended pleading is not required to amend their own claim or defence, as the case may be (Rule 12.01(5)).

Motion to Strike Out or Amend a Document (Rule 12.02)

On a motion by a party, the court may strike out (delete) or amend (revise) all or part of a document if either or both of the following apply.

1. Part or all of the document should be struck out or amended because it discloses no reasonable cause of action or defence (Rule 12.02(1)(a)). A plaintiff's or defendant's claim must contain allegations of fact that support some lawful ground for requesting relief. For example, if your neighbour has a noisy party every weekend that keeps you awake until three o'clock in the morning, it may be irritating and disruptive and a reason for calling the police. However, your neighbour's parties become grounds for commencing a civil action for damages only if your neighbour or her guests cause damage to your property, and/or their behaviour negatively affects your psychological or physical health or that of your family in a way that can be documented by medical evidence, and/or your neighbour's conduct or that of her guests causes some other actionable damage.

   A defence must contain allegations of fact that support some lawful ground for denying the relief requested in the claim. If someone sues you for money, it is not a defence to say that you owe the money, but you need time to pay. That is an admission.

2. Part or all of the document should be struck out or amended because it may delay or make it difficult to have a fair trial, or is inflammatory, a waste of time, a nuisance, or an abuse of the court's process (Rules 12.02(1)(b) and (c)). These rules apply to claims or defences that contain allegations that are difficult to prove, unfair, insulting, or defamatory to other parties, and that cannot be supported by the evidence. The court may amend the allegations if there are any grounds for doing so.

On a motion where any or all of Rules 12.02(1)(a), (b), and (c) apply, the court may make an order for the following under Rule 12.02(2):

1. In the case of a claim, order that an action be stayed (stopped) or dismissed (as having no legal merit);

2. In the case of a defence, order that the defence be struck (dismissed as having no legal merit) and grant judgment for the other party; and/or

3. Impose such terms as are just (for example, costs to the successful party).

In an action where the parties are self-represented and/or unsophisticated, Rule 12.02(2) should be applied with caution. A claim should be dismissed or a defence struck only if it is perfectly clear that the flaws in pleading are deliberate, and not the result of a lack of familiarity with legal principles. If the material in support of the motion demonstrates this, then a Rule 12.02(2) order may be appropriate. Otherwise, the parties should have their day in court.

CHAPTER SUMMARY

When you have satisfied yourself that Small Claims Court has jurisdiction to try your client's matter, you must set about commencing the action. The first step is to identify and quantify your client's damages. In a liquidated claim, you will use the contract between the parties, unpaid invoices, and so on, to prove the amount owing. In an unliquidated claim, you must ascertain all of the different types of damage the plaintiff has suffered as a result of the alleged wrongdoing, with a view to assigning reasonable monetary values, which are supported by the evidence, to that damage. Special damages compensate the plaintiff for losses such as loss of current and projected income, medical expenses including prescriptions, and travel costs connected with the injury. General damages are more speculative in nature. They compensate the plaintiff for past and future pain and suffering caused by the injury or harm.

On the plaintiff's claim, other parties to the action must be properly named, in accordance with the applicable rules. If the plaintiff does not have complete or accurate information, you should take appropriate steps to ensure that you have the correct names and addresses for both individual and business defendants.

The plaintiff's claim should set out all of the factual allegations in support of the relief the plaintiff is claiming in an orderly narrative using concise, non-technical language and the dates, places, and nature of the occurrences on which the claim is based.

Copies of any documents upon which you intend to rely should be attached to the plaintiff's claim.

A proceeding is commenced when the plaintiff's claim, together with a copy for each defendant, is taken to the office of the Small Claims Court with territorial jurisdiction, and issued by the clerk. The claim is issued when the clerk dates, signs, and seals it, and assigns a court file number. The plaintiff's claim should be served personally (Rule 8.02) or by an alternative to personal service (Rule 8.03) on all defendants within six months after the date of issue. The court may extend the time for service in appropriate circumstances.

If prompt service of the claim personally or by an alternative to personal service is impractical, the court may make an order for substituted service (Rule 8.04).

A plaintiff's or defendant's claim or a defence may be amended by filing a copy marked "Amended" with the clerk and by serving copies on all other parties, including parties in default.

On a motion by a party, the court may strike out or amend a claim or a defence if it discloses no reasonable cause of action or defence, may delay or make it difficult to have a fair trial, or is inflammatory, a waste of time, a nuisance, or an abuse of the court's process (Rule 12.02).

KEY TERMS

affidavit	litigation guardian	power of attorney
alternatives to personal service	merits of the case	prayer or request for relief
amended	numbered company	precedent documents
attorney	objection	pre-judgment interest
binding authority	order for substituted service	promissory note
cause of action	partnership	remedy
date of default	partnership agreement	service
deponent	party under disability	set aside
effect service	payment into court	sole proprietorship
frivolous and vexatious objection	payment out of court	special damages
general damages	personal service	unliquidated claim
joint and several liability	plaintiff's claim	unliquidated damages
judicial notice	pleadings	
liquidated claim	post-judgment interest	

REFERENCES

Absentees Act, RSO 1990, c. A.3.

Business Corporations Act, RSO 1990, c. B.16.

Business Names Act, RSO 1990, c. B.17.

Canada Business Corporations Act, RSC 1985, c. C-44.

Courts of Justice Act, RSO 1990, c. C.43.

Criminal Code, RSC 1985, c. C-46.

Law Society of Upper Canada (LSUC), *Paralegal Professional Conduct Guidelines* (Toronto: LSUC, 2008, as amended); available online at http://www.lsuc.on.ca.

Law Society of Upper Canada (LSUC), *Paralegal Rules of Conduct* (Toronto: LSUC, 2007, as amended); available online at http://www.lsuc.on.ca.

Limited Partnerships Act, RSO 1990, c. L.16.

Rules of Civil Procedure, RRO 1990, Reg. 194.

Rules of the Small Claims Court, O. Reg. 258/98.

DRAFTING EXERCISE:
Dante v. Herrero—Drafting a Claim Using Precedent Documents

Review the fact situation in *Dante v. Herrero* in box 4.1 at page 97. Referring to the precedents for a claim for money owed pursuant to an unpaid promissory note in appendix 3.1 (*Parrish v. Thurston*) and appendix 4.3 (*Greco v. Hardwick*), draft a plaintiff's claim (Form 7A). The claim will be prepared on April 3, 20—, and issued on the same date. Do not fill in the date of issuing on the Form 7A—the court clerk will do that when the claim is issued. The court file number (claim number) is 6638.

The claim is served personally on Ms. Herrero at her home address on April 5, 20— by Martin Bruni of Brampton, Ontario. Complete an affidavit of service (Form 8A). The affidavit of service will be sworn on April 7, 20—.

REVIEW QUESTIONS

When answering the following questions, please refer to any rules or statutory authority upon which you are relying.

1. What are special damages?

2. What are general damages?

3. On a plaintiff's claim, how do you name each of the following?

    a. An individual defendant

    b. An individual defendant who uses more than one name

    c. A corporate defendant

    d. A sole proprietorship

    e. A partnership

4. What is joint and several liability?

5. What is a person under disability?

6. What is a litigation guardian?

7. What are pleadings?

8. What are the rules for service of a claim?

9. You draft a plaintiff's claim, naming one defendant. After the claim has been issued and personally served on the defendant, you discover that you spelled the defendant's name wrong, and that you need to add a second defendant. What must you do?

APPENDIX 4.1   Notice to Alleged Partner (Form 5A)

ONTARIO
Superior Court of Justice
Cour supérieure de justice

Notice to Alleged Partner
Avis au prétendu associé
Form / *Formule* 5A Ont. Reg. No. / *Règl. de l'Ont.* : 258/98

Brampton
Small Claims Court / *Cour des petites créances de*

4586
Claim No. / *N° de la demande*

7755 Hurontario Street
Brampton, Ontario
L6W 4T6
Address / *Adresse*

905 456 4700
Phone number / *Numéro de téléphone*

BETWEEN / *ENTRE*

Amrita Chakravarty

Plaintiff(s) / *Demandeur(s)/demanderesse(s)*

and / *et*

Complete Home Renovations

Defendant(s) / *Défendeur(s)/défenderesse(s)*

TO:
DESTINATAIRE :

Name of alleged partner / *Nom du (de la) prétendu(e) associé(e)*
Franklin Butler

Street and number / *Numéro et rue*
455 Lonsdale Court

City, province, postal code / *Ville, province, code postal*
Mississauga, Ontario X2X 3Y4

YOU ARE ALLEGED TO HAVE BEEN A PARTNER on _____, 20 ___
IL EST ALLÉGUÉ QUE VOUS ÉTIEZ UN(E) ASSOCIÉ(E) *le*

(or during the period) **June 1** _____, 20 -- to **October 31** _____, 20 --
(ou pendant la période du)   *au*

in the partnership/business of **Complete Home Renovations**   ,
de la société en nom collectif/l'entreprise de   (Firm name / *Raison sociale*)

a party named in this proceeding.
désignée comme partie à l'instance.

IF YOU WISH TO DENY THAT YOU WERE A PARTNER at any material time, you must defend this proceeding separately from the partnership, denying that you were a partner at the material time. If you fail to do so, you will be deemed to have been a partner on the date (or during the period) set out above.
SI VOUS SOUHAITEZ NIER QUE VOUS ÉTIEZ UN(E) ASSOCIÉ(E) *à l'époque en cause, vous devez présenter dans l'instance une défense distincte de celle de la société en nom collectif, selon laquelle vous niez avoir été un(e) associé(e) à cette époque. À défaut de ce faire, vous serez réputé(e) avoir été une(e) associé(e) à la date (ou pendant la période) susmentionnée.*

CAUTION:

AVERTISSEMENT :

AN ORDER AGAINST THE PARTNERSHIP MAY BE ENFORCED AGAINST YOU PERSONALLY if you are deemed to have been a partner, if you admit that you were, or if the court finds that you were at the material time.
UNE ORDONNANCE CONTRE LA SOCIÉTÉ EN NOM COLLECTIF PEUT ÊTRE EXÉCUTÉE CONTRE VOUS PERSONNELLEMENT *si vous êtes réputé(e) avoir été un(e) associé(e), si vous admettez ce fait ou si le tribunal conclut que vous étiez un(e) associé(e) à l'époque en cause.*

_____, 20 ___

(Signature of plaintiff or representative / *Signature du demandeur/de la demanderesse ou du/de la représentant(e)*)

SCR 5.03-5A (June 1, 2009 / *1er juin 2009*) CSD

APPENDIX 4.2   Consent to Act as Plaintiff's Litigation Guardian (Form 4A)

ONTARIO

Superior Court of Justice
Cour supérieure de justice

Consent to Act as Litigation Guardian
Consentement pour agir en qualité de tuteur à l'instance

Form / *Formule* 4A Ont. Reg. No. / *Règl. de l'Ont.* : 258/98

Brampton

Small Claims Court / *Cour des petites créances de*

7755 Hurontario Street
Brampton, Ontario
L6W 4T6

Address / *Adresse*

905 456 4700

Phone number / *Numéro de téléphone*

5311

Claim No. / *N° de la demande*

BETWEEN / *ENTRE*

Collette Desbarais

Plaintiff(s) / *Demandeur(s)/demanderesse(s)*

and / *et*

Emma Good

Defendant(s) / *Défendeur(s)/défenderesse(s)*

My name is *Je m'appelle*	Name / *Nom* **Antoinette France Desbarais**
And I live at *et j'habite à*	Street and number / *Numéro et rue* **15 Tranquillity Court**
	City, province, postal code / *Ville, province, code postal* **Brampton, Ontario A1B 2C3**
	Phone number and fax number / *Numéro de téléphone et numéro de télécopieur* **905 333 5555**

1. I consent to act as litigation guardian in this action for the
   Je consens à agir à titre de tuteur à l'instance dans la présente action au nom du

   ☒ plaintiff, named **Collette Desbarais**
   demandeur suivant :   (Name of plaintiff / *Nom du demandeur/de la demanderesse*)

   (Check one box only. / Cochez une seule case.)

   and I acknowledge that I may be personally responsible for any costs awarded against me or against this person.
   et je reconnais que je peux être tenu(e) personnellement responsable des dépens auxquels moi-même ou cette personne pourrions être condamné(e)s.

   ☐ defendant, named _____ .
   défendeur suivant :   (Name of defendant / *Nom du défendeur/de la défenderesse*)

2. The above-named person is under the following disability:
   La personne susmentionnée est incapable parce qu'elle est :

   ☒ a minor whose birth date is **December 12, 1999**   .
   un mineur dont la date de naissance est le   (State date of birth of minor / *Indiquez la date de naissance du mineur*)

   (Check appropriate box(es). / Cochez la ou les cases appropriées.)

   ☐ mentally incapable within the meaning of Section 6 or Section 45 of the *Substitute Decisions Act, 1992* in respect of an issue in a proceeding.
   mentalement incapable au sens de l'article 6 ou 45 de la Loi de 1992 sur la prise de décisions au nom d'autrui à l'égard d'une question dans une instance.

   ☐ an absentee within the meaning of the *Absentees Act*.
   une personne absente au sens de la Loi sur les absents.

APPENDIX 4.2   Concluded

FORM / *FORMULE* 4A	PAGE 2	5311

Claim No. / *N° de la demande*

3. My relationship to the person under disability is:
Mon lien de parenté avec l'incapable est le suivant :
(State your relationship to the person under disability. / Indiquez votre lien de parenté avec l'incapable.*)*
mother

4. I have no interest in this action contrary to that of the person under disability.
Je n'ai dans la présente action aucun intérêt opposé à celui de l'incapable.

5. I am
Je

(Check one box only. / Cochez une seule case.)

☒ represented and have given written authority to **Joseph Mustafa**
suis représenté(e) et j'ai autorisé par écrit :
(Name of lawyer/agent with authority to act in this proceeding / *Nom de l'avocat/du mandataire autorisé à agir dans la présente instance)*

of **Prior Mustafa LLP, 22 County Court Boulevard, Brampton, Ontario A1A 2B3**
de (Address for service / *Adresse aux fins de signification)*

TEL: 905 111 2222 FAX: 905 111 2233
(Phone number and fax number / *Numéro de téléphone et numéro de télécopieur)*

to act in this proceeding.
à agir dans la présente instance.

☐ not represented by a lawyer/agent.
ne suis pas représenté(e) par un avocat/un mandataire.

_____, 20 _____

(Signature of litigation guardian consenting / *Signature du tuteur à l'instance qui consent)*

_____

(Signature of witness / *Signature du témoin)*

Joseph Mustafa

(Name of witness / *Nom du témoin)*

NOTE:	Within seven (7) calendar days of changing your address for service, notify the court and all other parties in writing.
REMARQUE :	*Dans les sept (7) jours civils qui suivent tout changement de votre adresse aux fins de signification, veuillez en aviser par écrit le tribunal et les autres parties.*

SCR 4.01-4.02-4A (June 1, 2009 / *1er juin 2009*) CSD

APPENDIX 4.3   Greco v. Hardwick: Plaintiff's Claim for Liquidated Damages (Form 7A)

ONTARIO

Superior Court of Justice
Cour supérieure de justice

Plaintiff's Claim
Demande du demandeur
Form / *Formule* 7A Ont. Reg. No. / *Régl. de l'Ont.* : 258/98

Seal / *Sceau*

Brampton
Small Claims Court / *Cour des petites créances de*
7755 Hurontario Street
Brampton, Ontario
L6W 4T6
Address / *Adresse*

905 456 4700
Phone number / *Numéro de téléphone*

7891
Claim No. / *N° de la demande*

Plaintiff No. 1 / *Demandeur n° 1*

☐ Additional plaintiff(s) listed on attached Form 1A.
Le ou les demandeurs additionnels sont mentionnés sur la formule 1A ci-jointe.

☐ Under 18 years of age.
Moins de 18 ans.

Last name, or name of company / *Nom de famille ou nom de la compagnie*		
Greco		

First name / *Premier prénom*	Second name / *Deuxième prénom*	Also known as / *Également connu(e) sous le nom de*
Juliette		

Address (street number, apt., unit) / *Adresse (numéro et rue, app., unité)*		
c/o Prior Mustafa LLP		

City/Town / *Cité/ville*	Province	Phone no. / *N° de téléphone*

Postal code / *Code postal*		Fax no. / *N° de télécopieur*

Representative / *Représentant(e)*	LSUC # / *N° du BHC*
Prior Mustafa LLP Attention: Paralegal name	**######**

Address (street number, apt., unit) / *Adresse (numéro et rue, app., unité)*		
22 County Court Boulevard		

City/Town / *Cité/ville*	Province	Phone no. / *N° de téléphone*
Brampton	**Ontario**	**905 111 2222**

Postal code / *Code postal*		Fax no. / *N° de télécopieur*
A1A 2B3		**905 111 2233**

Defendant No. 1 / *Défendeur n° 1*

☐ Additional defendant(s) listed on attached Form 1A.
Le ou les défendeurs additionnels sont mentionnés sur la formule 1A ci-jointe.

☐ Under 18 years of age.
Moins de 18 ans.

Last name, or name of company / *Nom de famille ou nom de la compagnie*		
Hardwick		

First name / *Premier prénom*	Second name / *Deuxième prénom*	Also known as / *Également connu(e) sous le nom de*
James		

Address (street number, apt., unit) / *Adresse (numéro et rue, app., unité)*		
128 George Court		

City/Town / *Cité/ville*	Province	Phone no. / *N° de téléphone*
Brampton	**Ontario**	**905 791 3333**

Postal code / *Code postal*		Fax no. / *N° de télécopieur*
L1X 2V4		

Representative / *Représentant(e)*	LSUC # / *N° du BHC*

Address (street number, apt., unit) / *Adresse (numéro et rue, app., unité)*		

City/Town / *Cité/ville*	Province	Phone no. / *N° de téléphone*

Postal code / *Code postal*		Fax no. / *N° de télécopieur*

APPENDIX 4.3 Continued

FORM / *FORMULE* 7A PAGE 2 7891

Claim No. / *N° de la demande*

REASONS FOR CLAIM AND DETAILS / *MOTIFS DE LA DEMANDE ET PRÉCISIONS*

Explain what happened, including where and when. Then explain how much money you are claiming or what goods you want returned.
Expliquez ce qui s'est passé, en précisant où et quand. Ensuite indiquez la somme d'argent que vous demandez ou les biens dont vous demandez la restitution, explication à l'appui.

If you are relying on any documents, you **MUST** attach copies to the claim. If evidence is lost or unavailable, you **MUST** explain why it is not attached.
*Si vous vous appuyez sur des documents, vous **DEVEZ** en annexer des copies à la demande. Si une preuve est perdue ou n'est pas disponible, vous **DEVEZ** expliquer pourquoi elle n'est pas annexée.*

What happened? See Schedule A attached
Where?
When?

Que s'est-il
passé?
Où?
Quand?

SCR 7.01-7A (June 1, 2009 / *1er juin 2009*) CSD **Continued on next page / *Suite à la page suivante***

APPENDIX 4.3   Continued

How much? $ 5,000.00
Combien?   (Principal amount claimed / *Somme demandée*) $

☒   ADDITIONAL PAGES ARE ATTACHED BECAUSE MORE ROOM WAS NEEDED.
DES FEUILLES SUPPLÉMENTAIRES SONT ANNEXÉES EN RAISON DU MANQUE D'ESPACE.

The plaintiff also claims pre-judgment interest from   August 2, 20--   under:
Le demandeur demande aussi des intérêts   (Date)   *conformément à :*
antérieurs au jugement de

(Check only   ☐ the *Courts of Justice Act*
one box /   *la* Loi sur les tribunaux judiciaires
Cochez une
seule case)   ☒ an agreement at the rate of 10   % per year
                         un accord au taux de   % par an

and post-judgment interest, and court costs.
et des intérêts postérieurs au jugement, ainsi que les dépens.

Prepared on: November 2   , 20 --   _____
Fait le :   (Signature of plaintiff or representative / *Signature du*
                                                          demandeur/de la demanderesse ou du/de la représentant(e))

Issued on: ...., 20 ....   _____
Délivré le :   (Signature of clerk / *Signature du greffier*)

| CAUTION TO DEFENDANT: | **IF YOU DO NOT FILE A DEFENCE** (Form 9A) with the court within twenty (20) calendar days after you have been served with this Plaintiff's Claim, judgment may be obtained without notice and enforced against you. Forms and self-help materials are available at the Small Claims Court and on the following website: www.ontariocourtforms.on.ca. |
| *AVERTISSEMENT AU DÉFENDEUR :* | *SI VOUS NE DÉPOSEZ PAS DE DÉFENSE (formule 9A) auprès du tribunal au plus tard vingt (20) jours civils après avoir reçu signification de la présente demande du demandeur, un jugement peut être obtenu sans préavis et être exécuté contre vous. Vous pouvez obtenir les formules et la documentation à l'usage du client à la Cour des petites créances et sur le site Web suivant : www.ontariocourtforms.on.ca.* |

APPENDIX 4.3   Concluded

Schedule A

1. The plaintiff claims:

    (a)   Liquidated damages of $5,000.00;

    (b)   Pre- and post-judgment interest at a rate of 10% per annum from the date of default until such time as any amounts owing are paid in full in accordance with the terms of the promissory note dated April 1, 20—;

    (c)   In the alternative, pre- and post-judgment interest in accordance with the *Courts of Justice Act*;

    (d)   Her costs of this action; and

    (e)   Such further and other relief as this Honourable Court deems just.

2. The plaintiff is an individual residing in the City of Brampton in the Province of Ontario.

3. The defendant is an individual residing at 128 George Court in the City of Brampton in the Province of Ontario.

4. Pursuant to a promissory note dated April 1, 20—, the plaintiff loaned the defendant the sum of $5,000.00. According to the terms of the note, the entire sum was to be repaid in full by the defendant on or before August 2, 20—. In the event of default, interest became due and owing on the balance owing at a rate of 10% per annum from the date of default until such time as all amounts owing were paid in full.

5. The defendant failed to pay the amount owing on or before August 2, 20—.

6. In spite of repeated demands for payment, both spoken and written, the defendant has failed to pay anything whatsoever on account of the amount owing to the plaintiff.

Attached documents:

Promissory note signed by James Hardwick dated April 1, 20—

Letter dated August 15, 20— from Juliette Greco to James Hardwick and registration slip

Letter dated September 15, 20— from Juliette Greco to James Hardwick and registration slip

APPENDIX 4.4   Chong v. Kingman: Plaintiff's Claim for Unliquidated Damages (Form 7A)

ONTARIO

Superior Court of Justice
Cour supérieure de justice

Plaintiff's Claim
Demande du demandeur

Form / *Formule* 7A Ont. Reg. No. / *Règl. de l'Ont.* : 258/98

Toronto

Small Claims Court / *Cour des petites créances de*
47 Sheppard Avenue East
Toronto, Ontario

Seal / *Sceau*   **M2N 5X5**

5678

Claim No. / *N° de la demande*

Address / *Adresse*

416 326 3554

Phone number / *Numéro de téléphone*

Plaintiff No. 1 / *Demandeur n° 1*

☐ Additional plaintiff(s) listed on attached Form 1A.
Le ou les demandeurs additionnels sont mentionnés sur la formule 1A ci-jointe.

☐ Under 18 years of age.
Moins de 18 ans.

Last name, or name of company / *Nom de famille ou nom de la compagnie*		
Chong		
First name / *Premier prénom*	Second name / *Deuxième prénom*	Also known as / *Également connu(e) sous le nom de*
Maxine		
Address (street number, apt., unit) / *Adresse (numéro et rue, app., unité)*		
c/o Prior Mustafa LLP		
City/Town / *Cité/ville*	Province	Phone no. / *N° de téléphone*
Postal code / *Code postal*		Fax no. / *N° de télécopieur*
Representative / *Représentant(e)*		LSUC # / *N° du BHC*
Prior Mustafa LLP Attention: Paralegal name		**######**
Address (street number, apt., unit) / *Adresse (numéro et rue, app., unité)*		
22 County Court Boulevard		
City/Town / *Cité/ville*	Province	Phone no. / *N° de téléphone*
Brampton	**Ontario**	**905 111 2222**
Postal code / *Code postal*		Fax no. / *N° de télécopieur*
A1A 2B3		**905 111 2233**

Defendant No. 1 / *Défendeur n° 1*

☐ Additional defendant(s) listed on attached Form 1A.
Le ou les défendeurs additionnels sont mentionnés sur la formule 1A ci-jointe.

☐ Under 18 years of age.
Moins de 18 ans.

Last name, or name of company / *Nom de famille ou nom de la compagnie*		
Kingman		
First name / *Premier prénom*	Second name / *Deuxième prénom*	Also known as / *Également connu(e) sous le nom de*
LeeAnn		
Address (street number, apt., unit) / *Adresse (numéro et rue, app., unité)*		
48 Brimley Road, Apt. 1306		
City/Town / *Cité/ville*	Province	Phone no. / *N° de téléphone*
Toronto	**Ontario**	**416 444 5555**
Postal code / *Code postal*		Fax no. / *N° de télécopieur*
L2L 3T6		
Representative / *Représentant(e)*		LSUC # / *N° du BHC*
Address (street number, apt., unit) / *Adresse (numéro et rue, app., unité)*		
City/Town / *Cité/ville*	Province	Phone no. / *N° de téléphone*
Postal code / *Code postal*		Fax no. / *N° de télécopieur*

SCR 7.01-7A (June 1, 2009 / *1er juin 2009*) CSD

APPENDIX 4.4   Continued

FORM / *FORMULE* 7A   PAGE 2   5678

Claim No. / *N° de la demande*

REASONS FOR CLAIM AND DETAILS / *MOTIFS DE LA DEMANDE ET PRÉCISIONS*

Explain what happened, including where and when. Then explain how much money you are claiming or what goods you want returned.

Expliquez ce qui s'est passé, en précisant où et quand. Ensuite indiquez la somme d'argent que vous demandez ou les biens dont vous demandez la restitution, explication à l'appui.

If you are relying on any documents, you **MUST** attach copies to the claim. If evidence is lost or unavailable, you **MUST** explain why it is not attached.

*Si vous vous appuyez sur des documents, vous **DEVEZ** en annexer des copies à la demande. Si une preuve est perdue ou n'est pas disponible, vous **DEVEZ** expliquer pourquoi elle n'est pas annexée.*

What happened?   See Schedule A attached
Where?
When?

Que s'est-il
passé?
Où?
Quand?

SCR 7.01-7A (June 1, 2009 / *1er juin 2009*) CSD   Continued on next page / *Suite à la page suivante*

APPENDIX 4.4   Continued

FORM / *FORMULE* 7A   **PAGE 3**   **5678**

Claim No. / *N° de la demande*

How much? $ 25,000.00

Combien?   (Principal amount claimed / *Somme demandée*) $

⊠   **ADDITIONAL PAGES ARE ATTACHED BECAUSE MORE ROOM WAS NEEDED.**
     DES FEUILLES SUPPLÉMENTAIRES SONT ANNEXÉES EN RAISON DU MANQUE D'ESPACE.

The plaintiff also claims pre-judgment interest from February 1, 20--   under:
Le demandeur demande aussi des intérêts   (Date)   *conformément à :*
antérieurs au jugement de

(Check only   ⊠   **the *Courts of Justice Act***
one box /   *la* **Loi sur les tribunaux judiciaires**
Cochez une
seule case)   ☐   **an agreement at the rate of** .... **% per year**
                       un accord au taux de   **% par an**

and post-judgment interest, and court costs.
et des intérêts postérieurs au jugement, ainsi que les dépens.

Prepared on: June 24   , 20 --   _____
Fait le :   (Signature of plaintiff or representative / *Signature du*
                                                     demandeur/de la demanderesse ou du/de la représentant(e))

Issued on: _____ , 20   _____
Délivré le :   (Signature of clerk / *Signature du greffier*)

CAUTION TO DEFENDANT:	**IF YOU DO NOT FILE A DEFENCE** (Form 9A) with the court within twenty (20) calendar days after you have been served with this Plaintiff's Claim, judgment may be obtained without notice and enforced against you. Forms and self-help materials are available at the Small Claims Court and on the following website: www.ontariocourtforms.on.ca.
AVERTISSEMENT AU DÉFENDEUR :	***SI VOUS NE DÉPOSEZ PAS DE DÉFENSE*** (formule 9A) *auprès du tribunal au plus tard vingt (20) jours civils après avoir reçu signification de la présente demande du demandeur, un jugement peut être obtenu sans préavis et être exécuté contre vous. Vous pouvez obtenir les formules et la documentation à l'usage du client à la Cour des petites créances et sur le site Web suivant :* www.ontariocourtforms.on.ca.

APPENDIX 4.4   Continued

Schedule A

1. The plaintiff claims:

    (a) $25,000.00;

    (b)   Pre- and post-judgment interest in accordance with the *Courts of Justice Act*;

    (c)   Her costs of this action; and

    (d)   Such further and other relief as this Honourable Court deems just.

2. The plaintiff resides in the City of Toronto in the Province of Ontario.

3. At all material times the defendant resided in Toronto, Ontario. She currently resides at 48 Brimley Road, Apt. 1306, Toronto, Ontario L2L 3T6.

4. Pursuant to a residential tenancy agreement dated January 13, 20—, the plaintiff agreed to rent the basement apartment in the plaintiff's home at 67 Harmony Avenue, Toronto, Ontario to the defendant. The tenancy commenced February 1, 20— at a monthly rent of $775.00, including water, heat, and hydro. The defendant did not pay a last month's rent deposit.

5. The basement apartment at 67 Harmony Avenue is a legal basement apartment with a separate entrance. The plaintiff, who is an elderly widow, occupies the main floor.

6. The defendant's personal cheque for the February, 20— rent was returned due to insufficient funds. When the plaintiff asked the defendant for a replacement cheque, the defendant became extremely abusive. The February rent was never paid. The defendant also failed to pay the rent for March and April, 20—.

7. The plaintiff made repeated requests for payment of the rent owing. Whenever the plaintiff approached the defendant about collecting the rent, the defendant became extremely abusive. She screamed and shouted. She slammed doors, and played loud music until late in the night.

APPENDIX 4.4   Continued

8. On several occasions, the defendant stood outside the plaintiff's kitchen door, which opens onto the side entrance for the basement apartment. She pounded on the door and screamed obscenities and threats.

9. The defendant kept the plaintiff awake at night, playing loud music and making banging and crashing sounds in the basement. This behaviour would start around midnight and continue until two or three o'clock in the morning. The plaintiff was afraid the neighbours would complain to the police.

10. The defendant's behaviour terrified the plaintiff. The defendant had access to the plaintiff's washer, dryer, furnace, and fuse box, all of which were also in the basement. The plaintiff feared that the defendant would cause damage or start a fire.

11. The plaintiff began to keep the kitchen door locked. She could not sleep and she lost her appetite. She suffered from headaches and anxiety attacks. If she went out, she dreaded going home. Her physician prescribed diazepam and Prozac.

12. When the defendant failed to pay the April rent, the plaintiff phoned her daughter in British Columbia and told her about the situation. The plaintiff's daughter flew to Toronto, arriving on April 15. On April 16, the plaintiff and her daughter sought legal assistance. A notice of early termination for non-payment of rent was served on the defendant on April 16.

13. The defendant vacated the apartment on April 17. She took the keys with her, and left the basement apartment in a filthy state.

14. It cost the plaintiff $1,059.00 to have a contractor come in to clean the apartment, replace the carpet, repair the damage, and repaint. The plaintiff had to pay a locksmith $125.00 to rekey the locks.

15. On June 1, 20— the apartment was rented to a new tenant. There have been no problems with the current tenant.

APPENDIX 4.4   Concluded

16. The plaintiff was in excellent health before the events described above. She has now stopped taking Prozac, but she continues to have anxiety attacks and suffer from loss of appetite. She needs diazepam to get to sleep.

17. As of the date of preparing this claim, the plaintiff is claiming special damages of $3,992.47, calculated as follows:

Loss of income — unpaid rent

3 months × $775.00	$2,325.00
Medication	183.47
Cost of repairs	1,059.00
Rekey locks	125.00
Invoice for consultation, drafting and serving N4	300.00
Total as of June 15, 20—	$3,992.47

18. The balance of the claim is for general damages for pain, suffering, and mental distress suffered by the plaintiff as a direct result of the defendant's conduct.

Attached documents:

Tenancy agreement dated January 13, 20—

Prescriptions and invoices for payment to the date of the plaintiff's claim

Invoice from contractor for repairs

Invoice from locksmith

Invoice from Prior Mustafa LLP for residential tenancy services

APPENDIX 4.5   Greco v. Hardwick: Affidavit of Service (Form 8A)

ONTARIO

Superior Court of Justice
Cour supérieure de justice

Affidavit of Service
Affidavit de signification

Form / *Formule* 8A Ont. Reg. No. / *Règl. de l'Ont.* : 258/98

Brampton

Small Claims Court / *Cour des petites créances de*
7755 Hurontario Street
Brampton, Ontario
L6W 4T6

Address / *Adresse*

905 456 4700

Phone number / *Numéro de téléphone*

7891

Claim No. / *N° de la demande*

BETWEEN / *ENTRE*

Juliette Greco

Plaintiff(s) / *Demandeur(s)/demanderesse(s)*

and / *et*

James Hardwick

Defendant(s) / *Défendeur(s)/défenderesse(s)*

My name is Claire Ivory
Je m'appelle   (Full name / *Nom et prénoms*)

I live in Brampton, Ontario
J'habite à   (Municipality & province / *Municipalité et province*)

and I swear/affirm that the following is true:
et je déclare sous serment/j'affirme solennellement que les renseignements suivants sont véridiques :

1. **I served** James Hardwick   , **on November 8**   , 20 -- ,
   J'ai signifié à   (Full name of person/corporation served / *Nom et prénoms* , *le*   (Date)
                       de la personne/nom au complet de la personne morale
                       qui a reçu la signification)

   at **123 George Court, Brampton, Ontario L1X 2V4**
   au   (Address (street and number, unit, municipality, province) / *Adresse (numéro et rue, unité, municipalité, province)*)

   which is   ☒ the address of the person's home
   soit   *l'adresse du domicile de la personne*

   ☐ the address of the corporation's place of business
      l'adresse du lieu de travail de l'établissement de la personne morale

   ☐ the address of the person's or corporation's representative on record with the court
      *l'adresse du/de la représentant(e) de la personne ou de la personne morale figurant au
      dossier du tribunal*

   ☐ the address on the document most recently filed in court by the party
      l'adresse figurant sur le document déposé le plus récemment au tribunal par la partie

   ☐ the address of the corporation's attorney for service in Ontario
      l'adresse du fondé de pouvoir de la personne morale aux fins de signification en Ontario

   ☐ other address: _____
      autre adresse :   (Specify. / *Précisez.*)

   with   the plaintiff's claim
   ce qui suit :   (Name(s) of document(s) served / *Titre(s) du ou des documents signifiés*)

SCR 8.06-8A (November 1, 2009 / *1er novembre 2009*) CSD

APPENDIX 4.5   Continued

FORM / *FORMULE* 8A   **PAGE 2**   7891

Claim No. / *N° de la demande*

2. I served the document(s) referred to in paragraph one by the following method:
J'ai signifié le ou les documents mentionnés au numéro un de la façon suivante :
(Tell how service took place by checking appropriate box(es).)
(Indiquez la façon dont la signification a été effectuée en cochant la ou les cases appropriées.)

Personal service / *Signification à personne*

☒ leaving a copy with the person.
en laissant une copie à la personne.

☐ leaving a copy with the _____ of the corporation.
en laissant une copie au/à la   (Office or position / *Charge ou poste*)   *de la personne morale.*

☐ leaving a copy with: _____
en laissant une copie à :   (Specify person's name and office or position. / *Indiquez le nom de la personne ainsi que sa charge ou son poste.*)

Service at place of residence / *Signification au domicile*

☐ leaving a copy in a sealed envelope addressed to the person at the person's place of residence with a person who appeared to be an adult member of the same household, and sending another copy of the same document(s) to the person's place of residence on the same day or the following day by:
en laissant une copie au domicile de la personne, dans une enveloppe scellée adressée à celle-ci, auprès d'une personne habitant sous le même toit qui semblait majeure et en envoyant une autre copie du ou des mêmes documents au domicile de la personne le même jour ou le jour suivant :

   ☐ regular lettermail.
   par courrier ordinaire.

   ☐ registered mail.
   par courrier recommandé.

   ☐ courier.
   par messagerie.

Service by registered mail / *Signification par courrier recommandé*

☐ registered mail.
par courrier recommandé.
(If a copy of a plaintiff's claim or defendant's claim was served by registered mail, attach a copy of the Canada Post delivery confirmation showing the signature of the person being served to this affidavit.)
(Si une copie de la demande du demandeur ou de la demande du défendeur a été signifiée par courrier recommandé, annexez au présent affidavit une copie de la confirmation de livraison remise par Postes Canada sur laquelle figure la signature du destinataire de la signification.)

Service by courier / *Signification par messagerie*

☐ courier.
par messagerie.
(If a copy of a plaintiff's claim or defendant's claim was served by courier, attach a copy of the courier's delivery confirmation showing the signature of the person being served to this affidavit.)
(Si une copie de la demande du demandeur ou de la demande du défendeur a été signifiée par messagerie, annexez au présent affidavit une copie de la confirmation de livraison remise par le service de messagerie sur laquelle figure la signature du destinataire de la signification.)

Service on lawyer / *Signification à l'avocat*

☐ leaving a copy with a lawyer who accepted service on the person's behalf.
en laissant une copie avec l'avocat qui a accepté la signification au nom de la personne.
(Attach a copy of the document endorsed with the lawyer's acceptance of service.)
(Annexez une copie du document, sur lequel l'avocat a inscrit qu'il a accepté la signification.)

Service by regular lettermail / *Signification par courrier ordinaire*

☐ regular lettermail.
par courrier ordinaire.

SCR 8.06-8A (November 1, 2009 / *1er novembre 2009*) CSD   **Continued on next page / *Suite à la page suivante***

APPENDIX 4.5   Concluded

FORM / *FORMULE* 8A	PAGE 3	7891

Claim No. / *N° de la demande*

Service by fax /
Signification par télécopie

☐ fax sent at _____ at the following fax number: _____
par télécopie (Time / *heure*) *au numéro de télécopieur suivant :* (Fax number / *numéro de télécopieur*)
envoyée à

Service to last known address of corporation or attorney for service, and to the directors /
Signification à la dernière adresse connue de la personne morale ou de son fondé de pouvoir aux fins de signification et aux administrateurs

☐ mail/courier to corporation or attorney for service at last known address recorded with the Ministry of Government Services, and
d'une part, par la poste/par messagerie à la personne morale ou à son fondé de pouvoir aux fins de signification, à la dernière adresse connue figurant dans les dossiers du ministère des Services gouvernementaux;

☐ mail/courier to each director, as recorded with the Ministry of Government Services, as set out below:
d'autre part, par la poste/par messagerie à chaque administrateur mentionné dans les dossiers du ministère des Services gouvernementaux et dont le nom et l'adresse sont indiqués ci-dessous :

Name of director / *Nom de l'administrateur*	Director's address as recorded with the Ministry of Government Services (street & number, unit, municipality, province) / *Adresse de l'administrateur figurant dans les dossiers du ministère des Services gouvernementaux (numéro et rue, unité, municipalité, province)*

(Attach separate sheet for additional names if necessary. /
Joignez au besoin une feuille séparée s'il y a d'autres noms à ajouter.)

Substituted service /
Signification indirecte

☐ substituted service as ordered by the court on _____ , 20 _____ ,
par signification indirecte ordonnée par le tribunal le (Date)

☐ as follows: (Give details.)
comme suit : (*Précisez.*)

Sworn/Affirmed before me at **Brampton**
Déclaré sous serment/Affirmé solennellement devant moi à (Municipality / *municipalité*)

in **Ontario**
en/à/au (Province, state, or country / *province, État ou pays*)

on **November 10** , 20 --
le

Commissioner for taking affidavits
Commissaire aux affidavits
(Type or print name below if signature is illegible.)
(*Dactylographiez le nom ou écrivez-le en caractères d'imprimerie ci-dessous si la signature est illisible.*)

Signature
(This form is to be signed in front of a lawyer, justice of the peace, notary public or commissioner for taking affidavits.)
(*La présente formule doit être signée en présence d'un avocat, d'un juge de paix, d'un notaire ou d'un commissaire aux affidavits.*)

SCR 8.06-8A (November 1, 2009 / *1er novembre 2009*) CSD

Acting for the Plaintiff: Default Proceedings

LEARNING OBJECTIVES

After reading this chapter, you will understand:

- The time for delivering a defence
- Noting in default and default judgment
- The consequences of being noted in default
- When to file an affidavit for jurisdiction
- Obtaining a default judgment in a liquidated claim
- Calculating pre-judgment interest
- Motion in writing for an assessment of damages
- Motion for set aside of a noting in default
- Dismissal of an action as abandoned
- Discontinuance of an undefended action

INTRODUCTION

A Small Claims Court proceeding is commenced when the plaintiff's claim is issued by the clerk. The claim is issued when the clerk dates, signs, and seals it, and assigns a court file number. You have six months from the date of starting the action to serve the plaintiff's claim on the defendant. Best practice requires that the defendant be served with the plaintiff's claim as soon as possible after the action is started.

When the defendant or any other party has been served with the plaintiff's claim, the details of service (including date, time, place, and manner of service) should be noted on the client file, and an affidavit of service should be prepared. The affidavit of service must be sworn by the person who served the document.

A defendant who has been served with the plaintiff's claim has 20 days from the date that service becomes effective to file a defence with the court office. The plaintiff's paralegal should note the deadline for filing a defence on the checklist/tickler in the client file. If no defence is filed with the court by the deadline, the defendant should be noted in default. To note a defendant in default, the plaintiff's paralegal files the affidavit of service with the court office, along with a request to the clerk to note the defendant in default (Form 9B). A defendant who has been noted in default cannot file a defence or take any other procedural steps, except to bring a motion to set aside the noting in default.

In a liquidated claim, the plaintiff's paralegal may also request that the clerk sign a default judgment (Form 11B). In an unliquidated claim, where all defendants have been noted in default, you may make a motion for an assessment of damages based on affidavit evidence proving the amount of the claim, or request an assessment hearing to determine the amount owing to the plaintiff.

A default judgment may be enforced against a defendant under Rule 20.

REVIEW: LIQUIDATED AND UNLIQUIDATED CLAIMS

In a claim for an unpaid debt or liquidated amount (also known as a liquidated claim), the amount owing is a specific amount of money that may be established by unpaid invoices, a loan agreement, or other documentation proving a debt or fixed amount.

Determining the amount of a liquidated claim is straightforward. You look at the document or other evidence to determine how much money the defendant owes the plaintiff. Interest may be determined based on the interest rate stated in the document; or, if no interest rate was agreed on, interest may be determined using the rates set out in ss. 128 and 129 of the *Courts of Justice Act*. A table of these interest rates can be found at the Attorney General's website. Calculating interest is discussed below at pages 158-160 and 162-165.

Liquidated damages do not require valuation by a court, so long as there is documentation in support of the amount claimed, including interest.

In a claim for an unliquidated amount (also known as an unliquidated claim), the amount owing is not fixed. Instead, it must be determined by the court based on all of the evidence. Some examples of unliquidated claims are actions for personal injury or wrongful dismissal. Some actions for breach of contract will also involve a claim for an unliquidated amount.

NOTING A DEFENDANT IN DEFAULT

Time for Filing a Defence

GENERAL

The time for filing a defence with the court varies, depending on how the defendant was served with the claim.

You should diarize the deadline for the defendant to file a defence on every plaintiff's file you open. File management software should automatically calculate procedural and other deadlines on electronic client files and notify you as dead-lines approach. If you do not use file management software, you should note approaching deadlines and tickler reminders on your desk calendar and on the checklist/tickler in the client file.

The day after the deadline for the defendant to file a defence expires, you should contact the court office to find out whether a defence has been filed. If no defence has been filed, the affidavit of service should be filed along with a request to clerk (Form 9B) asking the clerk to note the defendant in default. If the claim is for a debt or liquidated amount, you may also arrange for the clerk to sign a default judgment (Form 11B). These procedures are discussed in more detail below.

PERSONAL SERVICE ON THE DEFENDANT (RULE 8.01)

A defendant who has been personally served with a plaintiff's claim has 20 days from the date of service to file a defence with the court office (Small Claims Court Rule 8.01(1)). Holidays and weekends are included when counting the 20 days, but if the period ends on a holiday or weekend, then the last day for filing the defence is the next business day. (Note that under the *Rules of the Small Claims Court*, the definition of "holiday" includes any Saturday or Sunday.)

ALTERNATIVES TO PERSONAL SERVICE (RULE 8.03)

If the defendant is served with the plaintiff's claim by an alternative to personal service, the time for delivering a defence varies, depending on the manner of service. See table 5.1 below.

BOX 5.1

Calculating Time for Delivery of a Defence

Refer to table 5.1 when reading the following examples.

EXAMPLE ONE: PERSONAL SERVICE

Ahmed B. is personally served with a plaintiff's claim at his home at 7:35 p.m. on Tuesday, July 4, 20—. The deadline for filing a defence is 20 days from July 4, including holidays and weekends. Ahmed B. must file the defence on or before July 24, 20—, or, if July 24 falls on a holiday, on the next business day thereafter.

EXAMPLE TWO: Alternative to Personal Service—Service at Individual's Place of Residence (Rule 8.03(2))

Ellen F. is the defendant. The plaintiff's claim is left with an adult member of Ellen F.'s household at 2:35 p.m. on Wednesday, September 6, 20—. On Thursday, September 7, 20—, the document is given to Commercial Couriers. Commercial Couriers verifies delivery of the document at Ellen's place of residence at 3:00 p.m. on Friday, September 8, 20—.

Service by courier takes effect five days after verification of delivery. Because the time period is less than seven days, holidays are excluded—so we cannot count Saturday, September 9 or Sunday, September 10. We begin counting off the five-day period on Monday, September 11. It ends on Friday, September 15. September 15 is the day that service takes effect.

Next, we have to determine the deadline for filing the defence. This time, we include holidays and weekends, because the period is longer than seven days. The 20-day period ends on Thursday, October 5. That is the deadline for Ellen F. to file her defence with the clerk.

EXAMPLE THREE: Alternative to Personal Service—Service by Registered Mail or by Courier at Individual's Place of Residence (Rule 8.03(7))

Gaetan F. is the defendant. The plaintiff's claim is served on Gaetan by registered mail at his place of residence.

Service by this method takes effect when Gaetan F. verifies receipt of the copy of the claim on the Canada Post delivery confirmation. The deadline for filing a defence is 20 days after the date of verification.

If Gaetan F. does not sign the delivery confirmation, this method of service is not valid.

EXAMPLE FOUR: Substituted Service (Rule 8.04)

If a party satisfies the court that it is not practical to effect prompt service of a claim personally or by an alternative to personal service, the court may make an order for substituted service.

Substituted service takes effect as stated in the court order.

Default Proceedings (Rule 11)

WHAT IS NOTING IN DEFAULT?

When a party who is required by the Rules to file a defence within a stated time fails to do so, an opposing party may file an affidavit of service proving that service took place with the court and request that the clerk note the party in default (Rule 11.01). The notation is made on the court file.

WHAT ARE THE CONSEQUENCES OF BEING NOTED IN DEFAULT?

A defendant who has been noted in default cannot file a defence or take any other procedural step without the plaintiff's consent or a court order (Rule 11.05(1)). The only exception is a motion for set aside of the noting in default under Rules 11.06 and 15. Motions for set aside will be discussed in more detail later in this chapter.

Other parties may take any step in the proceeding without the consent of a defendant who has been noted in default (Rule 11.05(2)).

A defendant noted in default is not entitled to notice of any step taken by other parties in the proceeding and does not have to be served with any document except the following:

1. default judgment (Rules 11.02(3) and 8.01(4));

2. amendment of claim or defence (Rule 12.01);

3. motion after judgment is signed (Rule 15.01(6)); and

4. documents in enforcement proceedings against a debtor under Rule 20.

A defendant who has been noted in default is at a serious procedural disadvantage. If you have a client who has been noted in default, you should take immediate steps to have the noting in default set aside, either on consent or by a motion under Rule 11.06.

TABLE 5.1   Time for Delivering a Defence to a Plaintiff's Claim or Defendant's Claim

Type of service	Rule	Method of service	Time for delivering defence	Rule
Personal service	8.01(1), 8.02	Personal service	20 days from date of service (including holidays and ending on a business day)	9.01(1)
Alternative to personal service: service on person's lawyer	8.03(5)	Leaving a copy with the lawyer or an employee in the lawyer's office (acceptance of service must be endorsed on a copy of the document)	20 days from date of service (including holidays and ending on a business day)	
Alternative to personal service: service at individual's place of residence	8.03(2)	(a) Handing document in sealed envelope addressed to individual to apparently adult member of same household; and (b) On the same day or following day, serving the document by mail or by courier	5 days after date of mailing or date that delivery by courier is verified (excluding holidays and ending on a business day) *plus* 20 days (including holidays and ending on a business day)	8.03(4) 9.01(1)
Alternative to personal service: Ontario corporation	8.03(3)	(a) Service by mail or courier to address of head office or principal place of business; and (b) Service by mail or courier to each director at that director's address on record with Ministry of Government Services	5 days after date of mailing or date that delivery by courier is verified (excluding holidays and ending on a business day) *plus* 20 days (including holidays and ending on a business day)	8.03(4) 9.01(1)
Alternative to personal service: corporation outside Ontario	8.03(3)	(a) Service by mail or courier to the attorney for service in Ontario; and (b) Service by mail or courier to each director at that director's address on record with Ministry of Government Services	5 days after date of mailing or date that delivery by courier is verified (excluding holidays and ending on a business day) *plus* 20 days (including holidays and ending on a business day)	8.03(4) 9.01(1)
Alternative to personal service: service by registered mail or courier to individual at individual's place of residence	8.03(7)	Sending a copy by registered mail or by courier to the individual's place of residence	The day the individual verifies receipt of the claim by signature, as shown in delivery confirmation provided by Canada Post or the commercial courier *plus* 20 days (including holidays and ending on a business day)	8.03(8) 9.01(1)
Substituted service	8.04	Awarded by court order where it is impractical to carry out service personally or by an alternative to personal service	By court order	

WHO MAY BE NOTED IN DEFAULT?

General Rule (Rule 11.01(1))

Any defendant in a plaintiff's claim who fails to file a defence within the time prescribed by the Rules may be noted in default.

Any defendant in a defendant's claim who fails to file a defence to the defendant's claim within the time prescribed by the Rules may be noted in default.

Person Under Disability (Rules 11.01(2) and 4.06)

A person under disability who fails to deliver a defence within the time prescribed by the Rules may not be noted in default, except with **leave of the court** (Rule 11.01(2)). Leave of the court means permission of the court to do (or not do) something. Leave of the court is usually obtained on motion by the party seeking leave. A party who wishes to note a person under disability in default must make a motion to the court for an order permitting them to do so.

In some cases the clerk may be unaware that a party in default is a person under disability. If the person under disability is noted in default and/or default judgment is signed against her in error, the court may set aside the noting in default, the default judgment if one has been signed, and any step that has been taken to enforce the judgment, on **such terms as are just** (Rule 4.06).

BOX 5.2

Such Terms as Are Just

Rule 4.06 states that a noting in default and default judgment signed against a person under disability, as well as any steps to enforce the judgment, may be set aside on such terms as are just. This means that the court examines the conduct of the parties, any prejudice to a party as a result of the order for set aside, and any prejudice to the defendant caused by the noting in default (and default judgment, if any), and imposes conditions and/or awards costs accordingly.

A party who is aware or who suspects that an opposing party is a person under disability should not take any steps under Rule 11 without a court order permitting that party to do so.

Defendants Who Have Been Served Outside the Court's Territorial Jurisdiction

Territorial jurisdiction was discussed in chapter 3. It is the geographical area where a court is authorized to conduct hearings and make orders that are binding on litigants. Territorial jurisdiction is governed by Small Claims Court Rule 6.01.

A plaintiff may commence an action

- in the territorial division where the cause of action arose—that is, where the event giving rise to the action occurred (Rule 6.01(1)(a)(i));

- in the territorial division where the defendant lives (Rule 6.01(1)(a)(ii));

- in the territorial division where the defendant carries on business (Rule 6.01(1)(a)(ii)); or

- if there are several defendants, in the territorial jurisdiction where one of them lives or carries on business (Rule 6.01(1)(b)).

Where all the defendants have been served outside the territorial jurisdiction of the court in which the action was commenced, the clerk will not note any defendant in default until the plaintiff provides the clerk with an affidavit for jurisdiction (Form 11A), or provides evidence to a judge that the action has been properly brought in that territorial division (Rule 11.01(3)).

Rule 11.01(3) means that, if there is only one defendant in the proceeding, and that defendant has been served outside the court's territorial jurisdiction, you must file an affidavit for jurisdiction with the court when requesting that the defendant be noted in default.

If the clerk is not satisfied that the action was properly brought in a territorial division, the matter may be referred to a judge for determination. The plaintiff would be required to make a motion to a judge for an order that the defendant(s) be noted in default. The supporting affidavit must contain sufficient evidence to satisfy the judge that (1) the plaintiff has a case against the defendant; (2) the proceeding was properly commenced in that territorial jurisdiction; and (3) the defendant was properly served in another territorial jurisdiction.

Liquidated Claims (Rule 11.02)

GENERAL

Where a defendant has failed to file a defence within the time prescribed by the Rules and the claim is for a debt or liquidated amount, the clerk may note the defendant in default and sign a default judgment, including interest if claimed, against the defendant, so long as there are no issues of territorial jurisdiction pursuant to Rule 11.01(3).

BOX 5.3

Reminder: Joint and Several Liability

Joint and several liability means that two or more persons are liable for the full amount of a debt or other amount of money owed.

Examples include co-holders of a credit card, co-signers on a debt, the mortgagor(s) and guarantor(s) on a mortgage, and co-owners of property where a person suffers injury.

When you are acting for a plaintiff, you must ensure that you name as defendants everyone who is potentially liable for the amount owing. This protects the plaintiff, because if successful, he has a range of persons against whom he can enforce the judgment (that is, from whom he can collect his money). If one defendant has no ability to pay or is otherwise judgment-proof, the plaintiff can enforce the judgment against the income and assets of any other defendant(s) who are jointly and severally liable.

An agreement among co-defendants allocating liability for a debt is enforceable only among the co-defendants themselves. It is not binding on the plaintiff as creditor.

The fact that default judgment has been signed against one defendant in a claim for a debt or liquidated amount does not affect the plaintiff's right to proceed against any other defendant for the full amount of the claim (Rule 11.02(2)).

Where part of the claim against the defaulting defendant is for a liquidated amount and part is for an unliquidated amount, the clerk may note the defendant in default and sign a default judgment against the defendant for the liquidated part of the claim. The plaintiff may proceed against the defendant and any co-defendants for the full amount of the unliquidated portion of the claim (Rule 11.02(2)).

PROCEDURE FOR OBTAINING DEFAULT JUDGMENT IN A LIQUIDATED CLAIM

To obtain default judgment in a liquidated claim, you must complete and file the following forms:

1. Affidavits of service (Form 8A) for all other parties, if they have not already been filed;

2. A request to clerk (Form 9B) naming all of the defendants whom you wish to have noted in default;

3. If all the defendants were served outside the court's territorial division, an affidavit for jurisdiction (Form 11A) for each defendant who is in default; and

4. A default judgment (Form 11B) naming all of the defendants against whom you are seeking a default judgment.

As of this writing, the fee for entering a default judgment for an infrequent claimant is $35.00. The fee for a frequent claimant is $50.00. Definitions of "infrequent claimant" and "frequent claimant" can be found at O. Reg. 432/93 to the *Administration of Justice Act*, and in the glossary to this book.

Calculating Interest Owing

PRE- AND POST-JUDGMENT INTEREST

There are two types of interest available to a successful party in a Small Claims Court proceeding—pre-judgment interest and post-judgment interest. **Pre-judgment interest** accrues on the amount determined to be owing commencing with the date of default and ending with the date of judgment. **Post-judgment interest** runs on the judgment amount, including costs, or on any outstanding balance, until such time as all amounts owing have been paid in full. Post-judgment interest will be discussed in more detail in chapter 11.

If there is a written agreement of some kind (such as a credit card agreement or a promissory note), you should calculate the interest owing using the interest rate set out in the agreement. If there is no agreement setting out the rate of interest that applies in the event of a default, then pre- and post-judgment interest rates must be determined in accordance with ss. 127 to 130 of the *Courts of Justice Act*, using the rates published pursuant to O. Reg. 339/07. Current tables of post-judgment and pre-judgment interest rates can be found at the Ministry of the Attorney General's website.

At page 2 of the default judgment (Form 11B), you are asked to fill in the amount the plaintiff is claiming, plus pre-judgment interest owing on that amount from the date that interest begins to accrue on the amount owing, to the present date. In the case of a draft judgment, this would be the date the draft default judgment is prepared. See figure 5.1.

Where there is a written agreement outlining the terms of the debt, the date that interest begins to accrue on the amount owing will depend on the terms of the agreement.

Where there is nothing in writing about the terms of the debt, the date that interest begins to accrue on the amount owing will be the date the cause of action arose—that is, the date that the defendant defaulted by failing to pay back part or all of the amount owing.

FIGURE 5.1   Default Judgment (Form 11B)

DEFAULT JUDGMENT IS GIVEN against the following defendant(s):
UN JUGEMENT PAR DÉFAUT EST RENDU contre le ou les défendeurs suivants :

Last name, or name of company / *Nom de famille ou nom de la compagnie*		
First name / *Premier prénom*	Second name / *Deuxième prénom*	Also known as / *Également connu(e) sous le nom de*

Last name, or name of company / *Nom de famille ou nom de la compagnie*		
First name / *Premier prénom*	Second name / *Deuxième prénom*	Also known as / *Également connu(e) sous le nom de*

Last name, or name of company / *Nom de famille ou nom de la compagnie*		
First name / *Premier prénom*	Second name / *Deuxième prénom*	Also known as / *Également connu(e) sous le nom de*

☐ Additional defendant(s) listed on attached page (*list in same format*).
Défendeur(s) additionnel(s) mentionné(s) sur une feuille annexée (énumérez-les en suivant le même format).

THE DEFENDANT(S) MUST PAY to the plaintiff(s) the following sums:
LE OU LES DÉFENDEURS DOIVENT VERSER au(x) demandeur(s) les sommes suivantes :

(A) **DEBT** (principal amount claimed minus any payments received since the plaintiff's claim was issued) $ _____
  LA CRÉANCE (somme demandée moins tout paiement reçu depuis la délivrance $
  de la demande du demandeur)

(B) **PRE-JUDGMENT INTEREST** calculated
  LES INTÉRÊTS ANTÉRIEURS AU JUGEMENT calculés

  on the sum of $ _____ at the rate of _____ %
  sur la somme de   *$ au taux de*   *pour cent*

  per annum from _____ , 20 _____ , to _____ , 20 _____ ,
  par an du   *au*

  being _____ days. $ _____
  soit   *jours.* $

The end date will be the date the draft default judgment is prepared.

When calculating the number of days during which pre-judgment interest accrues, remember to exclude the first day of the period and include the last day of the period. This happens automatically if you use a table of days to calculate the number of days in a time period. You will find a table of days at table 5.2.

TABLE 5.2   The Number of Each Day in the Year, for Calculating Pre- and Post-judgment Interest

Day of month	Jan	Feb	Mar	Apr	May	June	July	Aug	Sept	Oct	Nov	Dec	Day of month
1	1	32	60	91	121	152	182	213	244	274	305	335	1
2	2	33	61	92	122	153	183	214	245	275	306	336	2
3	3	34	62	93	123	154	184	215	246	276	307	337	3
4	4	35	63	94	124	155	185	216	247	277	308	338	4
5	5	36	64	95	125	156	186	217	248	278	309	339	5
6	6	37	65	96	126	157	187	218	249	279	310	340	6
7	7	38	66	97	127	158	188	219	250	280	311	341	7
8	8	39	67	98	128	159	189	220	251	281	312	342	8
9	9	40	68	99	129	160	190	221	252	282	313	343	9
10	10	41	69	100	130	161	191	222	253	283	314	344	10
11	11	42	70	101	131	162	192	223	254	284	315	345	11
12	12	43	71	102	132	163	193	224	255	285	316	346	12
13	13	44	72	103	133	164	194	225	256	286	317	347	13
14	14	45	73	104	134	165	195	226	257	287	318	348	14
15	15	46	74	105	135	166	196	227	258	288	319	349	15
16	16	47	75	106	136	167	197	228	259	289	320	350	16
17	17	48	76	107	137	168	198	229	260	290	321	351	17
18	18	49	77	108	138	169	199	230	261	291	322	352	18
19	19	50	78	109	139	170	200	231	262	292	323	353	19
20	20	51	79	110	140	171	201	232	263	293	324	354	20
21	21	52	80	111	141	172	202	233	264	294	325	355	21
22	22	53	81	112	142	173	203	234	265	295	326	356	22
23	23	54	82	113	143	174	204	235	266	296	327	357	23
24	24	55	83	114	144	175	205	236	267	297	328	358	24
25	25	56	84	115	145	176	206	237	268	298	329	359	25
26	26	57	85	116	146	177	207	238	269	299	330	360	26
27	27	58	86	117	147	178	208	239	270	300	331	361	27
28	28	59	87	118	148	179	209	240	271	301	332	362	28
29	29		88	119	149	180	210	241	272	302	333	363	29
30	30		89	120	150	181	211	242	273	303	334	364	30
31	31		90		151		212	243		304		365	31

For leap years, February 29 becomes day 60, and the numbers in the table are increased by 1 for all following days.

FIGURE 5.2   Undefended Action: Claim for Debt or Liquidated Amount

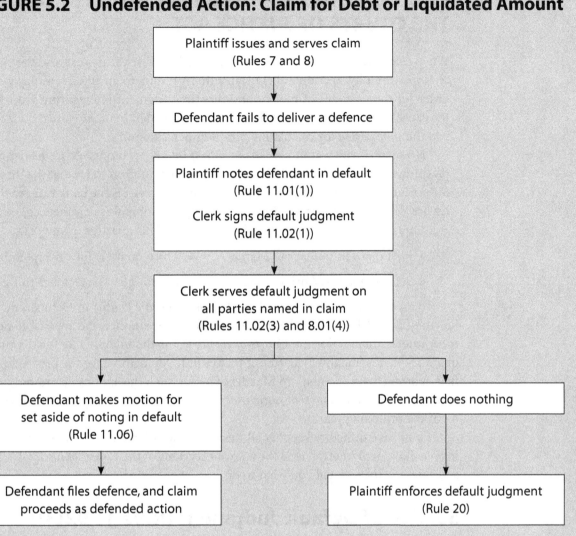

CALCULATING PRE-JUDGMENT INTEREST UNDER THE COURTS OF JUSTICE ACT

When calculating interest under the *Courts of Justice Act*, you must read the applicable sections carefully. Section 128(1) states that pre-judgment interest is payable on an order for the payment of money, and that pre-judgment interest runs from the date the cause of action arose to the date of the court order. In other words, s. 128(1) gives you the *time period* for calculating pre-judgment interest.

However, if you want to know the *rate of interest*, you must go to the definition of pre-judgment interest in s. 127(1). The s. 127(1) definition states that the interest rate for pre-judgment interest under the *Courts of Justice Act* is the bank rate for the quarter preceding the quarter in which the court proceeding was commenced.

A quarter is a three-month period. There are four quarters in any year:

- First quarter: January to March
- Second quarter: April to June
- Third quarter: July to September
- Fourth quarter: October to December.

If you commence the proceeding (that is, issue the claim) in October, during the fourth quarter (that is, October to December) of a year, then the applicable pre-judgment interest rate under the *Courts of Justice Act* is the interest rate for the preceding quarter—that is, the third quarter of that year. If you commence the proceeding in the first quarter (that is, January to March) of a year, then the applicable pre-judgment interest rate under the *Courts of Justice Act* is the interest rate for the fourth, or last, quarter of the preceding year.

If you have difficulty keeping all these dates and formulas in mind when calculating pre-judgment interest, read the relevant sections of the *Courts of Justice Act*. Statutes and rules are there to tell you what to do.

Service of Default Judgment (Rule 11.02(3))

The clerk is responsible for serving the default judgment on all parties named in the claim (Rule 11.02(3)). Service is by mail or fax (Rule 8.01(4)) to the address or fax number on file with the court. See also Rules 8.07 and 8.08.

Exception to Rule 11.02

A **defendant's claim** is a claim made by a defendant against any party named in the plaintiff's claim, including the plaintiff or a co-defendant, or against a third party not named in the plaintiff's claim. Defendant's claims will be discussed in more detail in chapter 6.

A party who wishes to dispute the defendant's claim may do so by filing a defence with the clerk, with enough copies for all parties or persons against whom the defendant's claim is made (Rule 10.03(1)). The deadline for doing so is 20 days after service of the plaintiff's claim (see table 5.1 above).

If a party to a defendant's claim fails to deliver a defence within the time set out in the Rules, they may be noted in default (Rule 11.01(1)). However, judgment against a defaulting party to a defendant's claim for a liquidated amount can be obtained only on a motion or at trial (Rule 11.04). The clerk cannot sign a default judgment against a defaulting party to a defendant's claim.

BOX 5.4

Calculating Pre-judgment Interest Using the Courts of Justice Act

You represent a plaintiff in an action for recovery of $4,000.00 loaned by the plaintiff to the defendant. The defendant agreed to repay the money in full on August 1, 2009. The defendant failed to make the payment. There is no written agreement as to the terms of the loan. However, the plaintiff has a written receipt signed by the defendant acknowledging receipt of the money.

The claim is commenced on September 3, 2009.

CALCULATING PRE-JUDGMENT INTEREST

Because there is no written loan agreement, the plaintiff must use the pre-judgment interest rate set out in the *Courts of Justice Act*.

Pursuant to s. 127(1) of the *Courts of Justice Act*, the pre-judgment interest rate is the bank rate for the quarter preceding the quarter in which the claim is commenced. In this case, the claim is commenced in September—that is, the third quarter of 2009. So the pre-judgment interest rate will be the bank rate for the second quarter of 2009—that is, 1.3%.

The defendant is served with the claim on September 7, 2009. The defendant fails to file a defence within the time prescribed by the Rules. The defendant is noted in default. The draft default judgment is prepared on September 30.

Pursuant to s. 128(1), pre-judgment interest is calculated from the date the cause of action arose, if that date can be determined. In the fact situation above, the date the cause of action arose is the date that the defendant failed to pay the money owing—that is, August 1, 2009. The end date for pre-judgment interest will be the date the draft default judgment is prepared—that is, September 30, 2009.

Step One: Calculate the per diem interest.

Per diem means per day. **Per diem interest** is the amount of interest that accrues on a daily basis. To calculate per diem interest, you must first convert the interest rate from a percentage out of 100 to a decimal.

You calculate per diem interest using the following steps.

- ▶ Convert the interest rate to a decimal. To do this, you divide the interest rate by 100.
- ▶ Multiply the amount owing by the interest rate expressed as a decimal.
- ▶ Divide the result by the number of days in a year—that is, 365.

In this case, the pre-judgment interest rate under the *Courts of Justice Act* is 1.3%. Following the above steps:

- ▶ Convert 1.3% to a decimal: $1.3 \div 100 = 0.013$
- ▶ Multiply the amount owing by the interest rate expressed as a decimal: $0.013 \times \$4,000 = \$52.00$
- ▶ Divide the result by the number of days in a year: $\$52.00 \div 365 = \$0.14$ per day in interest.

Step Two: Calculate the number of days that have elapsed since interest began to run.

The default in payment occurred on August 1, 2009. August 1 is the date that the cause of action arose, so August 1 is the start date for pre-judgment interest. The end date is the date the draft default judgment is prepared—that is, September 30. Use table 5.2 to calculate the number of days that elapsed between the start date for pre-judgment interest and the end date for pre-judgment interest.

Find the number (from 1 to 365) for the start date (in this case, the date of default, August 1), and subtract that number from the number for the end date (in this case, September 30, the date when the draft default judgment is prepared).

The end date for pre-judgment interest, September 30, is the 273rd day of the year. The start date for pre-judgment interest, August 1, is the 213th day of the year:

- ▶ $273 - 213 = 60$ days

Step Three: Calculate the amount of interest that has accrued from August 1, 2009 to September 30, 2009.

The interest that accrues from August 1, 2009 to September 30, 2009 = 60 days $\times$ $0.14 per day = $8.40.

BOX 5.5

Liquidated Claim: Noting Defendant in Default

Review the plaintiff's claim in *Parrish v. Thurston* at appendix 3.1 in chapter 3. The plaintiff's claim is prepared and issued on November 1, 20—. On November 3, 20—, the claim is served by leaving a copy with an apparent adult at the defendant's place of residence. Judy Cordero of Brampton, Ontario effects service.

What is the deadline for filing a defence?

The defendant was served pursuant to Rule 8.03(2). Service becomes effective 5 days from verification of service by the courier (Rule 8.03(4))—that is, on November 8. The defendant has 20 days from November 8 to file a defence.

Assume that November 28 does not fall on a holiday. The defendant, Frank Thurston, fails to file a defence on or before November 28. On December 1, the plaintiff's paralegal, Marie Prior, prepares the documents for noting the defendant in default and obtaining default judgment.

What documents must be filed with the court?

The defendant was served in Toronto, where he now lives. The action was commenced in Brampton. Ms. Prior must prepare and file

- an affidavit for jurisdiction (Form 11A);
- an affidavit of service (Form 8A);
- a request to clerk (Form 9B) to note the defendant in default and sign default judgment; and
- a draft default judgment (Form 11B).

The default judgment is referred to as a "draft" because it has not yet been entered—that is, signed, dated, and sealed by the clerk. In this case, because this is a liquidated claim, the clerk may also sign default judgment against the defendant.

The plaintiff is an infrequent claimant, so the fee for entering the default judgment will be $35.00.

Calculating Interest in Accordance with the Terms of the Promissory Note

Note that, because the monetary jurisdiction of Small Claims Court is $25,000.00, you are entitled to calculate pre-judgment interest on that amount only, even though the principal amount owing pursuant to the promissory note is $27,000.00.

When the plaintiff agrees to waive the excess in the plaintiff's claim, that waiver includes any interest owing on the excess.

Step One: Calculate the per diem interest.

Remember the steps for per diem interest.

- Convert the interest rate from a percentage to a decimal. To do this, you divide the interest rate by 100.
- Multiply the amount owing by the interest rate expressed as a decimal.
- Divide the result by the number of days in a year—that is, 365.

The interest rate set out in the promissory note is 12% per year.

- Convert 12% to a decimal: $12 \div 100 = 0.12$
- Multiply the amount owing by the interest rate expressed as a decimal: $0.12 \times \$25,000 = \$3,000$
- Divide the result by the number of days in a year: $\$3,000 \div 365 = \$8.219$ per day in interest.

Step Two: Calculate the number of days that have elapsed since interest began to run.

In this case, both the rate and the start date for pre-judgment interest are governed by the terms of the promissory note. The note states that the entire principal amount is payable in full on September 1, 20—, failing which pre-judgment interest at a rate of 12% starts to accrue. The defendant failed to pay the amount owing on September 1, so September 1 is the start date for pre-judgment interest of 12% per year.

The end date is the date the draft default judgment is prepared—that is, December 1, 20—.

Using the table of days, find the number (from 1 to 365) for the start date (in this case, the date of default, September 1), and subtract that number from the number for the end date (in this case, December 1, the date when the draft default judgment is prepared).

The start date, September 1, is the 244th day of the year. The end date, December 1, is the 335th day of the year.

- $335 - 244 = 91$ days

Note that subtraction automatically excludes the first day and includes the last day, so you do not have to worry about that.

Step Three: Calculate the amount of pre-judgment interest that has accrued from September 1, 20— to December 1, 20—.

Using the contractual rate of interest of 12%, the pre-judgment interest that accrues from September 1, 20— to December 1, 20— is:

▸ 91 days × $8.219 per day = $747.93

Costs: Rule 19.01(1) states that a successful party is entitled to have the party's reasonable disbursements, including costs of effecting service and expenses for travel, accommodation, photocopying, and experts' reports, paid by the unsuccessful party unless the court orders otherwise. Rules 19.01(1) and (2) permit the clerk to assess disbursements, including an amount for effecting service not exceeding $20.00 unless the court orders a greater amount.

At page 3 of the default judgment, you are required to state an amount for costs to the date of the default judgment. You should consider Rule 19.01 when calculating your costs.

In this case, the plaintiff is an infrequent claimant. Disbursements and expenses in the matter to the date of the default judgment are as follows:

▸ Issue claim $75.00
▸ Service of claim (Rule 19.01(3))   20.00
▸ Enter default judgment   35.00
▸ Photocopies   15.00

The plaintiff should claim costs of $145.00.

May the plaintiff claim an amount for legal fees paid to his paralegal on the default judgment? The answer appears to be "no." The language of Rule 19 speaks of the court awarding reasonable representation fees at trial or on an assessment hearing only. There is no provision for an award of representation fees on a default judgment signed by the clerk.

See appendix 5.1 to this chapter for the completed forms.

Unliquidated Claims (Rule 11.03)

A defendant who fails to deliver a defence to a plaintiff's or defendant's claim for an unliquidated amount may be noted in default pursuant to Rule 11.01(1). However, the plaintiff may obtain a default judgment only if all defendants have been noted in default (Rule 11.03(1)). If there is only one defendant in an unliquidated claim, and that defendant has been noted in default, then Rule 11.03 applies and the plaintiff may obtain a default judgment. If there are two or more defendants in an unliquidated claim, and one or more defendants have filed defences, then Rule 11.03(1) does not apply, and the matter must go forward to a settlement conference and, if necessary, a trial (Rule 11.03(7)).

OBTAINING DEFAULT JUDGMENT IN AN UNLIQUIDATED CLAIM

In an action for an unliquidated amount where all defendants in the proceeding have been noted in default, a plaintiff may obtain default judgment by (Rule 11.03(2)):

(a) filing a notice of motion and supporting affidavit (Form 15A) requesting a motion in writing for an assessment of damages, setting out the reasons why the motion should be granted, and attaching any relevant documents; or

(b) filing a request to clerk (Form 9B) requesting that an assessment hearing be arranged.

BOX 5.6

When Does Rule 11.03 Apply?

EXAMPLE ONE

Plaintiff sues Defendant 1, Defendant 2, and Defendant 3 for an unliquidated amount. All three defendants were served outside the court's territorial division.

Defendants 1 and 2 file defences within the time permitted by the Rules. Defendant 3 does not.

Can Plaintiff note Defendant 3 in default?

Yes, Plaintiff can note Defendant 3 in default (Rule 11.01(1)). Plaintiff must file a request to clerk (Form 9B) to note Defendant 3 in default. Plaintiff must also file the affidavit of service (Form 8A) proving service on Defendant 3, if it has not already been filed. Plaintiff must also file an affidavit for jurisdiction (Form 11A) because all three defendants were served outside the court's territorial division (Rule 11.01(3)).

Can Plaintiff obtain a default judgment against Defendant 3, using the procedures set out in Rule 11.03?

No, Plaintiff cannot use the procedures in Rule 11.03 to obtain a default judgment against Defendant 3. This is an unliquidated claim. Plaintiff can obtain a default judgment against Defendant 3 only if all the defendants in the action have been noted in default. In this case, Defendants 1 and 2 have filed defences in accordance with the Rules.

Therefore, all defendants in the action have not been noted in default, and Rule 11.03 does not apply.

Plaintiff will proceed to a settlement conference under Rule 13 and, if necessary, to trial under Rule 17 (Rule 11.03(7)).

EXAMPLE TWO

Plaintiff sues Defendant for an unliquidated amount. Defendant fails to deliver a defence within the time permitted by the Rules.

Can Plaintiff note Defendant in default?

Yes, Plaintiff can note Defendant in default (Rule 11.01(1)). Plaintiff must file a request to clerk (Form 9B) to note Defendant in default. Plaintiff must also file the affidavit of service (Form 8A) proving service on Defendant, if it has not already been filed with the court office.

Can Plaintiff obtain a default judgment against Defendant?

Yes, Plaintiff can obtain a default judgment against Defendant in these circumstances. This is an unliquidated claim. There is only one defendant, and that defendant has been noted in default. Therefore, all the defendants have been noted in default, and Plaintiff may obtain a default judgment pursuant to Rule 11.03(1).

Motion in Writing for an Assessment of Damages (Rule 11.03(2)(a))

A **motion** is an application to a judge to obtain an order directing that some kind of relief be granted to the party making the motion. The party who makes a motion is called the **moving party**. Other parties are called **responding parties**, because they respond to the moving party's motion. The moving party may be a plaintiff or a defendant. Motions may be made at any time in a proceeding, if a court order is required to resolve an issue. Small Claims Court motions are governed by Rule 15. The form used on a motion is a notice of motion and supporting affidavit (Form 15A).

The notice of motion sets out the relief requested. In part B at page 3 of Form 15A there is a separate section for a motion in writing for an assessment of damages.

An **assessment of damages** is a calculation of the money damages owed to the plaintiff by the defaulting defendant(s). The evidence in support of a motion in writing for an assessment of damages is presented in the supporting affidavit. On a motion in writing for an assessment of damages or at an assessment hearing, the plaintiff is not required to prove liability against a defendant noted in default. A defendant who has failed to respond to a claim is assumed to admit the truth of what is claimed. However, the plaintiff is required to prove the amount of the claim (Rule 11.03(5)).

An affidavit is written evidence that must be sworn by the **deponent** in the presence of a commissioner of oaths. The deponent is the person who makes the affidavit. The affidavit consists of a series of allegations of fact proving the amount of the claim, written in the first person singular (I, me, my), set out in separate paragraphs. If a document is relied upon in support of the motion, a photocopy of the document will be attached to the affidavit as an exhibit. The truth of its contents will be attested to in the body of the affidavit. Exhibits are stamped, dated, and signed by the commissioner of oaths at the time the affidavit is sworn.

There must be adequate evidence before the judge reading the motion and affidavit to satisfy her that the plaintiff is entitled to the damages claimed. If the judge is not satisfied with the written evidence in support of the motion, she may order that (1) a further affidavit be provided, or (2) the assessment of damages be determined at an assessment hearing (Rule 11.03(3)).

Because the motion is in writing, attendance in person by the plaintiff or the plaintiff's representative on a motion in writing for an assessment of damages is not required. However, you must confirm a hearing date for the motion to be scheduled before a judge with the court clerk. The judge will make her decision based on the written material filed, so long as that material is adequate to prove the damages claimed.

The judge's order will be served by the clerk on the moving party or the moving party's paralegal or lawyer if a stamped, self-addressed envelope is provided with the motion materials (Rules 11.03(6) and 8.01(5)).

BOX 5.7

Motion for an Assessment of Damages: (Rule 11.03(2)(a))

Review the fact situation in *Chong v. Kingman* set out in chapter 4 in box 4.2, as well as the sample plaintiff's claim in appendix 4.4.

The plaintiff's claim in *Chong v. Kingman* was issued on June 24, 20—. The claim was personally served on the defendant by Claire Ivory of Mississauga, Ontario on June 24, 20—.

The defendant, Ms. Kingman, fails to file a defence within the prescribed time.

This is an unliquidated claim. Mrs. Chong's paralegal, Joseph Mustafa, must note the defendant in default and request an assessment of damages by a motion in writing. The following documents must be prepared and filed:

▸ the affidavit of service (Form 8A)

▸ the request to clerk (Form 9B)

▸ the notice of motion and supporting affidavit (Form 15A).

Mr. Mustafa must confirm a hearing date for the motion to be scheduled before a judge with the court clerk. Mr. Mustafa will also provide a stamped, self-addressed envelope so that the clerk can mail the default judgment to him. The court fee for filing a motion is $40.00.

See appendix 5.2 at the end of this chapter for examples of the documents to be filed on the motion in writing for an assessment of damages in *Chong v. Kingman*.

Assessment Hearing (Rule 11.03(2)(b))

If a plaintiff in an undefended claim for an unliquidated amount wishes to have an assessment hearing, he may file a request to clerk (Form 9B) to have the hearing scheduled (Rule 11.03(1)(b)). See figure 5.3. All defendants must be noted in default before an assessment hearing can be requested (Rule 11.03(1)). If one or more defendants have filed a defence, the plaintiff must proceed to a settlement conference and, if necessary, to trial (Rule 11.03(7)).

FIGURE 5.3   Request to Clerk for an Assessment Hearing (Form 9B)

ONTARIO

Superior Court of Justice   **Request to Clerk**
Cour supérieure de justice   *Demande au greffier*

Form / *Formule* 9B Ont. Reg. No. / *Règl. de l'Ont.* : 258/98

Ottawa   **9888**

Small Claims Court / *Cour des petites créances de*   Claim No. / *N° de la demande*

161 Elgin Street, 2nd Floor
Ottawa, Ontario
K2P 2K1

Address / *Adresse*

613 239 1560

Phone number / *Numéro de téléphone*

BETWEEN / *ENTRE*

Sidney Carton

Plaintiff(s) / *Demandeur(s)/demanderesse(s)*

and / *et*

Max Robespierre

Defendant(s) / *Défendeur(s)/défenderesse(s)*

TO THE CLERK OF THE Ottawa   **SMALL CLAIMS COURT:**
AU GREFFIER DE LA COUR   (Name of Small Claims Court location / *Emplacement de la*
DES PETITES CRÉANCES DE   *Cour des petites créances*) :

My name is Sidney Carton   **and I request that the clerk of the court:**
Je m'appelle   (Name of party/representative / *Nom de la partie ou du/de la*   *et je demande au greffier du tribunal*
                                représentant(e))   *de faire ce qui suit :*

(Check appropriate box(es). / Cochez la ou les cases appropriées.)

☒   note defendant(s) **Max Robespierre**
     constater le ou les défendeurs   (Name of defendant(s) / *Nom du/de la/des défendeur(s)/défenderesse(s)*)

in default for failing to file a Defence (Form 9A) within the prescribed time period [R. 11.01(1)].
en défaut pour n'avoir pas déposé de défense (formule 9A) dans le délai prescrit [par. 11.01 (1)].

☒   schedule an assessment hearing (all defendants have been noted in default) [R. 11.03(2)(b)].

The fee for fixing a date for an assessment hearing is $100.00 for an infrequent claimant, and $130.00 for a frequent claimant.

The clerk will fix a date for the hearing and send a notice of hearing to the plaintiff (Rule 11.03(4)).

An assessment hearing proceeds like a trial (Rule 11.03(4)), except that the defendant is not present, and the only issue before the court is how much money the defendant owes the plaintiff (Rule 11.03(5)), because a defendant who has failed to respond to a claim is assumed to admit the truth of what is claimed. You do have to put forward all relevant evidence, including documentary evidence, which will assist the judge to assign a monetary value to the damage suffered.

Motion to Set Aside Noting in Default (Rule 11.06)

The court may set aside a noting in default or default judgment against a party, and any steps that have been taken to enforce a default judgment, if the party makes a motion to set aside. The court must be satisfied that

- the moving party has a meritorious defence;

- the moving party has a reasonable explanation for the default; and

- the motion is made as soon as is reasonably possible in all of the circumstances.

A defendant's motion for set aside is made on notice to the plaintiff. The plaintiff must be served with a copy of the motion and supporting affidavit, and any other material on which the defendant intends to rely at the hearing of the motion. The plaintiff or plaintiff's paralegal or lawyer may appear at the motion and make submissions as to why the order for set aside should not be granted, with reference to the conditions set out at Rule 11.06.

An order setting aside a noting in default or default judgment shall be made on such terms as are just. When making the order, the judge must consider the conduct of the parties, the legal issues (including the merits, if any, of the defence), and any prejudice to a party (such as delay or additional expense) as a result of the order, and may impose conditions and/or award costs accordingly.

In appropriate circumstances, a **responding party** should consider consenting to the set aside. If all parties consent, a party may then file with the court a request for clerk's order on consent (Form 11.2A) setting aside the noting in default or default judgment. Note that there is a provision for an award of costs to be paid by one party to another party or other parties on the Form 11.2A. However, there is no provision on the Form 11.2A or in Rule 11.2.01, which governs a request for clerk's order on consent, for other terms of the consent, such as an agreed-upon deadline for a defence to be filed with the court. If the parties agree to a deadline for filing of a defence as a condition of the consent, the deadline should be reasonable, and it should be confirmed in writing.

FIGURE 5.4   Undefended Action: Claim for Unliquidated Amount

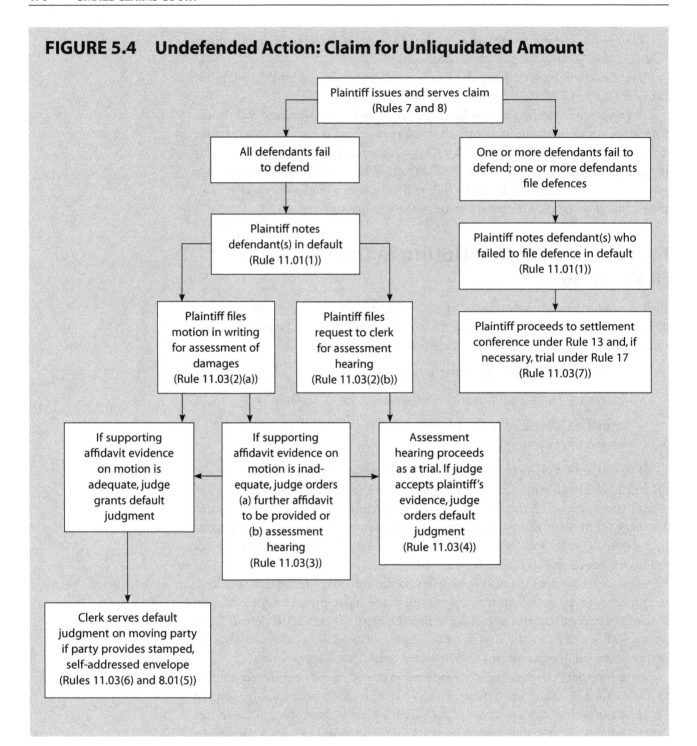

FIGURE 5.5   Request for Clerk's Order on Consent (Form 11.2A)

FORM / *FORMULE* 11.2A   PAGE 2   9888
                                                                                                    Claim No. / *N° de la demande*

TO THE PARTIES:
AUX PARTIES :

THIS REQUEST IS FILED BY: Max Robespierre
LA PRÉSENTE DEMANDE EST DÉPOSÉE PAR :   (Name of party / *Nom de la partie*)

I state that:
Je déclare que :

☒ Each party has received a copy of this form.
   Chaque partie a reçu une copie de la présente formule.

☒ No party that would be affected by the order is under disability.
   Aucune partie sur laquelle l'ordonnance aurait une incidence n'est incapable.

☒ This form has been signed and consented to by all parties, including any parties to be added, deleted or substituted.
   Toutes les parties, y compris celles qui doivent être jointes, radiées ou substituées, ont signé la présente formule et y ont consenti.

I request that the clerk make the following order(s) on the consent of all parties:
Je demande au greffier de rendre l'ordonnance ou les ordonnances suivantes sur consentement de toutes les parties :
(Check appropriate boxes. / *Cochez les cases appropriées.*)

☒ set aside the noting in default of **Max Robespierre**
   l'annulation de la constatation du défaut de   (Name of defendant(s) / *Nom du/de la/des défendeur(s)/défenderesse(s)*)

☐ set aside Default Judgment against
   l'annulation du jugement par défaut prononcé contre   (Name of defendant(s) / *Nom du/de la/des défendeur(s)/défenderesse(s)*)

☐ restore to the list the following matter that was dismissed under Rule 11.1: (Specify.)
   la réinscription au rôle de l'affaire suivante qui a été rejetée aux termes de la règle 11.1 :   (*Précisez.*)

☐ cancel the examination hearing regarding
   l'annulation de l'interrogatoire concernant   (Name of person to be examined / *Nom de la personne qui doit être interrogée*)

☐ with respect to the following step(s) taken to enforce the default judgment that are not yet completed:
   à l'égard de la ou des mesures suivantes qui ont été prises pour exécuter le jugement par défaut et qui ne sont pas encore menées à terme :

ABANDONMENT (RULE 11.1)

Where no steps are taken to advance a matter, the clerk is authorized by Rule 11.1 to make an order dismissing the action as abandoned.

In a proceeding where no defence has been filed, the clerk shall make an order dismissing the action as abandoned if all of the following conditions apply, unless the court orders otherwise (Rule 11.1.01(1)):

1. More than 180 days have passed since the date the claim was issued or the date of an order extending the time for service of the claim.

2. No defence has been filed.

3. The action has not been disposed of by order and has not been set down for trial.

4. The clerk has given 45 days' notice to the plaintiff that the action will be dismissed as abandoned.

In a defended proceeding, the clerk shall make an order dismissing the action as abandoned if all of the following conditions apply, unless the court orders otherwise (Rule 11.1.01(2)):

1. More than 150 days have passed since the date the first defence was filed.

2. The action has not been disposed of by order and has not been set down for trial.

3. The clerk has given 45 days' notice to all parties to the action that the action will be dismissed as abandoned.

The above conditions apply to proceedings commenced after July 1, 2006. Rules 11.1.01(3) and (4) set out transitional provisions for actions commenced before July 1, 2006.

If terms of settlement in Form 14D signed by all parties have been filed, the action will not be dismissed as abandoned by the clerk (Rule 11.1.01(5)). If the defence contains an admission of liability and proposal of terms of payment, the action will not be dismissed as abandoned by the clerk (Rule 11.1.01(6)).

The clerk shall serve a copy of an order made under Rules 11.1.01(1) and (4)(a) on the plaintiff, and a copy of an order made under Rules 11.1.01(2) and (4)(b) on all parties to the action.

DISCONTINUANCE (RULE 11.3)

A plaintiff may discontinue a claim against a defendant who fails to file a defence to all or part of the claim within the time prescribed by the Rules. To discontinue an undefended claim, the plaintiff shall (Rule 11.3.01(1))

(a) serve a notice of discontinued claim (Form 11.3A) on all defendants who were served with the claim; and

(b) file the notice with proof of service.

A notice of discontinued claim may be served personally, by an alternative to personal service, by mail, by courier, or by fax (Rule 8.01(14)).

The discontinuance of a claim is not a defence to a subsequent action on the matter, unless an order granting leave to discontinue the claim states otherwise (Rule 11.3.02).

A claim may not be discontinued by or against a person under disability except with permission from the court (Rule 11.3.01(2)).

CHAPTER SUMMARY

A defendant who has been personally served with a plaintiff's claim has 20 days from the date that service becomes effective to file a defence with the court office. The date that service becomes effective varies, depending on the manner of service.

If a defendant fails to deliver a defence within the time prescribed for doing so, the plaintiff may request that the clerk note the defendant in default. If the action is for a liquidated amount, the plaintiff may also request that the clerk sign default judgment against the defendant. A default judgment may be enforced by the plaintiff under Rule 20.

In an unliquidated claim, the plaintiff may note a defendant in default if the defendant fails to file a defence within the prescribed time. If all defendants have been noted in default, the plaintiff may then elect to make a motion in writing for an assessment of damages, or to have an assessment hearing.

A defendant who has been noted in default cannot file a defence or take any other procedural step without the plaintiff's consent or a court order (Rule 11.05(1)). The only exception is a motion for set aside of the noting in default and default judgment under Rules 11.06 and 15.

Other parties may take any step in the proceeding without the consent of a defendant who has been noted in default (Rule 11.05(2)).

A defendant noted in default is not entitled to notice of any step taken by other parties in the proceeding and does not have to be served with any document except the following:

1. default judgment (Rules 11.02(3) and 8.01(4))

2. amendment of claim or defence (Rule 12.01)

3. motion after judgment (Rule 15.01(6))

4. documents in enforcement proceedings against a debtor under Rule 20.

A defendant who has a good defence and a reasonable explanation for the default may make a set-aside motion under Rule 11.06 for an order setting aside the noting in default and default judgment, if one has been entered, as well as other relief. A motion for set aside is made on notice to the plaintiff. The plaintiff must be served with a copy of the notice of motion and supporting affidavit, as well as any other materials on which the defendant intends to rely at the hearing of the motion. On a contested motion for set aside, the plaintiff or plaintiff's paralegal or lawyer shall appear at the motion and make submissions as to why the order for set aside should not be granted.

In appropriate circumstances, a responding party should consider consenting to the set aside. If all parties consent, a party may then file with the court a request for clerk's order on consent (Form 11.2A) setting aside the noting in default or default judgment.

KEY TERMS

assessment of damages	per diem
defendant's claim	per diem interest
deponent	post-judgment interest
leave of the court	pre-judgment interest
motion	responding party
moving party	such terms as are just

REFERENCES

Administration of Justice Act, RSO 1990, c. A.6.

Courts of Justice Act, RSO 1990, c. C.43.

Law Society of Upper Canada (LSUC), *Paralegal Rules of Conduct* (Toronto: LSUC, 2007, as amended); available online at http://www.lsuc.on.ca.

Rules of the Small Claims Court, O. Reg. 258/98.

DRAFTING EXERCISE: Dante v. Herrero—Noting Defendant in Default

This is a continuation of the drafting exercise in chapter 4.

Review the fact situation in *Dante v. Herrero* in box 4.1 at page 97 and the drafting exercise at page 134 of chapter 4. The plaintiff's claim was prepared and issued on April 3, 20—. The claim number is 6638. The amount claimed was $4,000.00 plus pre-judgment interest commencing December 1, 20— at a rate of 12% per year, in accordance with the promissory note signed by Ms. Herrero.

The claim was personally served on the defendant on April 5, 20—. Assume that the affidavit of service has been filed with the court.

The deadline for filing a defence is 20 days from the date of service—in other words, April 25, 20—. The defendant fails to file a defence on or before that date.

Please draft a request to clerk (Form 9B) dated April 27, 20— to have the defendant noted in default, and default judgment signed (Form 11B). The Form 11B default judgment will also be dated April 27, 20—. Calculate pre-judgment interest owing from December 1, 20— to that date.

Calculate your costs. Your costs to the date of default judgment are the fee for issuing the claim and the fee for entering default judgment against the defendant. You are also entitled to request $20.00 for service of the claim pursuant to Rule 19.01(3). You will find a Small Claims Court fee schedule at the Attorney General's website (http://www.attorneygeneral.jus.gov.on.ca).

The post-judgment interest rate is 12% per year, in accordance with the promissory note.

REVIEW QUESTIONS

When answering the following questions, please refer to any rules or statutory authority upon which you are relying.

1. Calculate the deadline for delivering a defence in each of the following situations. Refer to table 5.1 and Rule 8 for assistance.

   a. The defendant is personally served with the plaintiff's claim on November 1, 20—.

   b. The defendant is served with the plaintiff's claim at her place of residence on November 1, 20—. The document is handed to an apparently adult member of her household, and couriered to her the next day. The courier company verifies delivery on November 2, 20—.

   c. The defendant is an individual who is served with the plaintiff's claim by registered mail to his last-known address on August 1, 20—. There is no verification of receipt.

2. What is noting in default?

3. Who may be noted in default?

4. What are the consequences of being noted in default?

5. When may a person under disability be noted in default?

6. When should an affidavit for jurisdiction be filed?

7. How do you obtain a default judgment in a claim for a debt or liquidated amount?

8. How do you obtain default judgment in a claim for an unliquidated amount?

9. When may a defendant make a motion for set aside of the noting in default and default judgment (if any)?

APPENDIX 5.1   Parrish v. Thurston: Default Judgment (Liquidated Amount) Affidavit of Service (Form 8A)

ONTARIO

Superior Court of Justice
Cour supérieure de justice

Affidavit of Service
Affidavit de signification

Form / *Formule* 8A Ont. Reg. No. / *Règl. de l'Ont.* : 258/98

Brampton

Small Claims Court / *Cour des petites créances de*

7755 Hurontario Street
Brampton, Ontario
L6W 4T6

Address / *Adresse*

905 456 4700

Phone number / *Numéro de téléphone*

4567

Claim No. / *N° de la demande*

BETWEEN / *ENTRE*

Maxwell Parrish

Plaintiff(s) / *Demandeur(s)/demanderesse(s)*

and / *et*

Frank Thurston

Defendant(s) / *Défendeur(s)/défenderesse(s)*

My name is Judy Cordero
Je m'appelle   (Full name / *Nom et prénoms*)

I live in Brampton, Ontario
J'habite à   (Municipality & province / *Municipalité et province*)

and I swear/affirm that the following is true:
et je déclare sous serment/j'affirme solennellement que les renseignements suivants sont véridiques :

1. **I served** Frank Thurston   , on **November 3**   , 20 -- ,
   J'ai signifié à   (Full name of person/corporation served / *Nom et prénoms*   , *le*   (Date)
                          de la personne/nom au complet de la personne morale
                          qui a reçu la signification)

   at   **45 Labrador Court, Suite 103, Toronto, Ontario M3C 4D5**
   au   (Address (street and number, unit, municipality, province) / *Adresse (numéro et rue, unité, municipalité, province)*)

   which is   ☒ the address of the person's home
   soit   *l'adresse du domicile de la personne*

                   ☐ the address of the corporation's place of business
                       l'adresse du lieu de travail de l'établissement de la personne morale

                   ☐ the address of the person's or corporation's representative on record with the court
                       l'adresse du/de la représentant(e) de la personne ou de la personne morale figurant au
                       dossier du tribunal

                   ☐ the address on the document most recently filed in court by the party
                       l'adresse figurant sur le document déposé le plus récemment au tribunal par la partie

                   ☐ the address of the corporation's attorney for service in Ontario
                       l'adresse du fondé de pouvoir de la personne morale aux fins de signification en Ontario

                   ☐ other address:
                       autre adresse :   (Specify. / *Précisez.*)

   with   the plaintiff's claim
   ce qui suit :   (Name(s) of document(s) served / *Titre(s) du ou des documents signifiés*)

APPENDIX 5.1   Form 8A Continued

FORM / *FORMULE* 8A   **PAGE 2**   4567
....
                                                                Claim No. / *N° de la demande*

2. **I served the document(s) referred to in paragraph one by the following method:**
    J'ai signifié le ou les documents mentionnés au numéro un de la façon suivante :
    (Tell how service took place by checking appropriate box(es).)
    (Indiquez la façon dont la signification a été effectuée en cochant la ou les cases appropriées.)

Personal   ☐ leaving a copy with the person.
service /   *en laissant une copie à la personne.*
Significa-
tion à   ☐ leaving a copy with the .... of the corporation.
personne   *en laissant une copie au/à la*   (Office or position / *Charge ou poste*)   *de la personne morale.*

               ☐ leaving a copy with: ....
                  en laissant une copie à :   (Specify person's name and office or position. / *Indiquez le nom de la personne ainsi que*
                                                                                  sa charge ou son poste.)

Service at   ☒ leaving a copy in a sealed envelope addressed to the person at the person's place of residence with
place of   a person who appeared to be an adult member of the same household, and sending another copy of
residence /   the same document(s) to the person's place of residence on the same day or the following day by:
Significa-   *en laissant une copie au domicile de la personne, dans une enveloppe scellée adressée à celle-ci,*
tion au   *auprès d'une personne habitant sous le même toit qui semblait majeure et en envoyant une autre*
domicile   *copie du ou des mêmes documents au domicile de la personne le même jour ou le jour suivant :*

                     ☐ regular lettermail.
                        par courrier ordinaire.

                     ☐ registered mail.
                        par courrier recommandé.

                     ☒ courier.
                        par messagerie.

Service by   ☐ registered mail.
registered   *par courrier recommandé.*
mail /
Significa-   *(If a copy of a plaintiff's claim or defendant's claim was served by registered mail, attach a copy of the Canada Post*
tion par   *delivery confirmation showing the signature of the person being served to this affidavit.)*
courrier   *(Si une copie de la demande du demandeur ou de la demande du défendeur a été signifiée par courrier recommandé,*
recom-   *annexez au présent affidavit une copie de la confirmation de livraison remise par Postes Canada sur laquelle figure la*
mandé   *signature du destinataire de la signification.)*

Service by   ☐ courier.
courier /   *par messagerie.*
Significa-
tion par   *(If a copy of a plaintiff's claim or defendant's claim was served by courier, attach a copy of the courier's delivery confirmation*
messa-   *showing the signature of the person being served to this affidavit.)*
gerie   *(Si une copie de la demande du demandeur ou de la demande du défendeur a été signifiée par messagerie, annexez au*
                   présent affidavit une copie de la confirmation de livraison remise par le service de messagerie sur laquelle figure la signature
                   du destinataire de la signification.)

Service on   ☐ leaving a copy with a lawyer who accepted service on the person's behalf.
lawyer /   *en laissant une copie avec l'avocat qui a accepté la signification au nom de la personne.*
Significa-
tion à   *(Attach a copy of the document endorsed with the lawyer's acceptance of service.)*
l'avocat   *(Annexez une copie du document, sur lequel l'avocat a inscrit qu'il a accepté la signification.)*

Service by   ☐ regular lettermail.
regular   *par courrier ordinaire.*
lettermail /
Significa-
tion par
courrier
ordinaire

SCR 8.06-8A (November 1, 2009 / *1ᵉʳ novembre 2009*) CSD   **Continued on next page /** *Suite à la page suivante*

APPENDIX 5.1   Form 8A Concluded

FORM / *FORMULE* 8A   **PAGE 3**   **4567**

Claim No. / *N° de la demande*

Service by fax / *Signification par télécopie*	☐ fax sent at _____ *par télécopie* (Time / *heure*) *envoyée à*	at the following fax number: *au numéro de télécopieur suivant :* _____ (Fax number / *numéro de télécopieur*)

Service to last known address of corporation or attorney for service, and to the directors / *Signification à la dernière adresse connue de la personne morale ou de son fondé de pouvoir aux fins de signification et aux administra- teurs ‹fr›*

☐ mail/courier to corporation or attorney for service at last known address recorded with the Ministry of Government Services, and
d'une part, par la poste/par messagerie à la personne morale ou à son fondé de pouvoir aux fins de signification, à la dernière adresse connue figurant dans les dossiers du ministère des Services gouvernementaux;

mail/courier to each director, as recorded with the Ministry of Government Services, as set out below:
d'autre part, par la poste/par messagerie à chaque administrateur mentionné dans les dossiers du ministère des Services gouvernementaux et dont le nom et l'adresse sont indiqués ci-dessous :

Name of director / *Nom de l'administrateur*	Director's address as recorded with the Ministry of Government Services (street & number, unit, municipality, province) / *Adresse de l'administrateur figurant dans les dossiers du ministère des Services gouvernementaux (numéro et rue, unité, municipalité, province)*

(Attach separate sheet for additional names if necessary. /
Joignez au besoin une feuille séparée s'il y a d'autres noms à ajouter.)

Substituted service / *Signification indirecte*	☐ substituted service as ordered by the court on _____ , 20 _____ , *par signification indirecte ordonnée par le tribunal le* (Date) as follows: (Give details.) *comme suit :* (*Précisez.*)

Sworn/Affirmed before me at **Brampton**
Déclaré sous serment/Affirmé   (Municipality / *municipalité*)
solennellement devant moi à

in **Ontario**
en/à/au   (Province, state, or country / *province, État ou pays*)

on **November 10**   , 20 **--**   _____
le   Commissioner for taking affidavits
                    Commissaire aux affidavits
                    (Type or print name below if signature is illegible.)
                    (*Dactylographiez le nom ou écrivez-le en caractères d'imprimerie ci-dessous si la signature est illisible.*)

_____
Signature
(This form is to be signed in front of a lawyer, justice of the peace, notary public or commissioner for taking affidavits.)
(*La présente formule doit être signée en présence d'un avocat, d'un juge de paix, d'un notaire ou d'un commissaire aux affidavits.*)

SCR 8.06-8A (November 1, 2009 / *1er novembre 2009*) CSD

APPENDIX 5.1   Affidavit for Jurisdiction (Form 11A)

ONTARIO

Superior Court of Justice
Cour supérieure de justice

Affidavit for Jurisdiction
Affidavit établissant la compétence
Form / *Formule* 11A Ont. Reg. No. / *Règl. de l'Ont.* : 258/98

Brampton
Small Claims Court / *Cour des petites créances de*

4567
Claim No. / *N° de la demande*

7755 Hurontario Street

Brampton, Ontario

L6W 4T6
Address / *Adresse*

905 456 4700
Phone number / *Numéro de téléphone*

BETWEEN / *ENTRE*

Maxwell Parrish

Plaintiff(s) / *Demandeur(s)/demanderesse(s)*

and / *et*

Frank Thurston

Defendant(s) / *Défendeur(s)/défenderesse(s)*

My name is   **Marie Prior**
Je m'appelle   (Full name / *Nom et prénoms*)

I live in   **Brampton, Ontario**
J'habite à   (Municipality & province / *Municipalité et province*)

and I swear/affirm that the following is true:
et je déclare sous serment/j'affirme solennellement que les renseignements suivants sont véridiques :

1. In this action, I am the
   Dans la présente action, je suis le/la

   ☐ plaintiff
       demandeur/demanderesse

   ☒ representative of the plaintiff(s)   **Maxwell Parrish**
       représentant(e) du/de la/des   (Name of plaintiff(s) / *Nom du/de la/des demandeur(s)/demanderesse(s)*)
       demandeur(s)/demanderesse(s)

2. I make this affidavit in support of the plaintiff's request to note the defendant(s) in default, where all the defendants have been or will be served outside the court's territorial division [R. 11.01 (3)].
   Je fais le présent affidavit à l'appui de la demande du demandeur de faire constater le ou les défendeurs en défaut étant donné que tous les défendeurs ont reçu ou recevront la signification en dehors de la division territoriale du tribunal [par. 11.01 (3)].

APPENDIX 5.1   Form 11A Concluded

FORM / *FORMULE* 11A   **PAGE 2**   **4567**

Claim No. / *N° de la demande*

3. The plaintiff is entitled to proceed with this action in this territorial division because this is:
Le demandeur a le droit de poursuivre cette action dans cette division territoriale parce que :

☒   where the event (cause of action) took place.
l'événement (cause d'action) a eu lieu dans cette division territoriale.

☐   where the defendant lives or carries on business.
le défendeur réside dans cette division territoriale ou y exploite une entreprise.

☐   the court nearest to the place where the defendant lives or carries on business [R. 6.01].
c'est dans cette division territoriale que se trouve le greffe du tribunal qui est le plus près de l'endroit où le défendeur réside ou exploite une entreprise. [règle 6.01].

Sworn/Affirmed before me at **Brampton**
Déclaré sous serment/Affirmé   (Municipality / *municipalité*)
solennellement devant moi à

in **Ontario**
en/à/au   (Province, state or country / *province, État ou pays*)

on **December 1**   , 20 **--**
le   Commissioner for taking affidavits
                                   Commissaire aux affidavits
                                   (Type or print name below if signature is illegible.)
                                   (Dactylographiez le nom ou écrivez-le en caractères d'imprimerie ci-dessous si la signature est illisible.)

Signature
(This form is to be signed in front of a lawyer, justice of the peace, notary public or commissioner for taking affidavits.)
(La présente formule doit être signée en présence d'un avocat, d'un juge de paix, d'un notaire ou d'un commissaire aux affidavits.)

WARNING:	IT IS AN OFFENCE UNDER THE *CRIMINAL CODE* TO KNOWINGLY SWEAR OR AFFIRM A FALSE AFFIDAVIT.
AVERTISSEMENT :	*FAIRE SCIEMMENT UN FAUX AFFIDAVIT CONSTITUE UNE INFRACTION AU CODE CRIMINEL.*

SCR 11.01-11A (June 1, 2009 / *1er juin 2009*) CSD

APPENDIX 5.1   Request to Clerk (Form 9B)

ONTARIO

Superior Court of Justice
Cour supérieure de justice

Request to Clerk
Demande au greffier

Form / *Formule* 9B Ont. Reg. No. / *Règl. de l'Ont.* : 258/98

Brampton

Small Claims Court / *Cour des petites créances de*
7755 Hurontario Street
Brampton, Ontario
L6W 4T6

Address / *Adresse*

4567

Claim No. / *N° de la demande*

905 456 4700

Phone number / *Numéro de téléphone*

BETWEEN / *ENTRE*

Maxwell Parrish

Plaintiff(s) / *Demandeur(s)/demanderesse(s)*

and / *et*

Frank Thurston

Defendant(s) / *Défendeur(s)/défenderesse(s)*

TO THE CLERK OF THE Brampton

AU GREFFIER DE LA COUR
DES PETITES CRÉANCES DE

(Name of Small Claims Court location / *Emplacement de la Cour des petites créances*) :

SMALL CLAIMS COURT:

My name is **Marie Prior**
Je m'appelle   (Name of party/representative / *Nom de la partie ou du/de la représentant(e)*)

and I request that the clerk of the court:
et je demande au greffier du tribunal de faire ce qui suit :

(Check appropriate box(es). / Cochez la ou les cases appropriées.*)*

☒ note defendant(s) **Frank Thurston**
constater le ou les défendeurs   (Name of defendant(s) / *Nom du/de la/des défendeur(s)/défenderesse(s)*)

in default for failing to file a Defence (Form 9A) within the prescribed time period [R. 11.01(1)].
en défaut pour n'avoir pas déposé de défense (formule 9A) dans le délai prescrit [par. 11.01 (1)].

☐ schedule an assessment hearing (all defendants have been noted in default) [R. 11.03(2)(b)].
fixer la date d'une audience d'évaluation (tous les défendeurs ont été constatés en défaut) [alinéa 11.03 (2) b)].

☐ schedule a terms of payment hearing because I dispute the defendant's proposed terms of payment contained in the Defence (Form 9A) [R. 9.03(3)].
fixer la date d'une audience relative aux modalités de paiement parce que je conteste les modalités de paiement proposées par le défendeur dans la défense (formule 9A) [par. 9.03 (3)].

☐ schedule a trial [R. 16.01(1)(b)].
fixer une date de procès [alinéa 16.01 (1) b)].

APPENDIX 5.1   Form 9B Concluded

FORM / *FORMULE* 9B   **PAGE 2**   **4567**

Claim No. / *N° de la demande*

☐ accept payment in the amount of $ _____ into court
   accepter que le paiement de   (Amount / *montant*)   *$ soit consigné au tribunal,*

    ☐ according to an order of the court, dated _____ , 20 _____ .
       conformément à une ordonnance du tribunal datée du

    ☐ for a person under disability according to an order or settlement dated
       au nom d'un incapable, conformément à une ordonnance ou à une transaction datée du

       _____ , 20 _____ [R. 4.08(1)].
                           [par. 4.08 (1)].

    ☐ pursuant to the attached written offer to settle, dated _____ , 20 _____ [R. 14.05(2)].
       aux termes de l'offre de transaction écrite ci-jointe datée du   *[par. 14.05 (2)].*

    ☐ according to the following legislation:
       conformément à la disposition législative suivante :

       _____ .

             (Name of statute or regulation and section / *Titre de la loi ou du règlement et mention de l'article*)

☒ Other: (Specify.)
   Autre : (*Précisez.*)

      Enter default judgment against Frank Thurston

December 1 _____ , 20 -- _____   _____

                                   (Signature of party or representative / *Signature de la partie ou du/de la*
                                       représentant(e)))

CAUTION:	To obtain an assessment of damages, all defendants must be noted in default. If one or more defendants has filed a defence, the matter must proceed to a settlement conference. To bring a motion in writing for an assessment of damages, file a Notice of Motion and Supporting Affidavit (Form 15A). You can get forms at court offices or online at www.ontariocourtforms.on.ca.
AVERTISSEMENT :	*Pour obtenir une évaluation des dommages-intérêts, tous les défendeurs doivent être constatés en défaut. Si un ou plusieurs défendeurs ont déposé une défense, l'affaire doit passer à l'étape de la conférence en vue d'une transaction. Pour présenter une motion par écrit en vue d'une évaluation des dommages-intérêts, déposez un avis de motion et affidavit à l'appui (formule 15A). Vous pouvez obtenir les formules aux greffes des tribunaux ou en ligne à l'adresse www.ontariocourtforms.on.ca.*

SCR 4-9-11-14-16-9B (June 1, 2009 / *1er juin 2009*) CSD

APPENDIX 5.1   Default Judgment (Form 11B)

ONTARIO

Su⬜erior Court of Justice
Cour supérieure de justice

Default Judgment
Jugement par défaut
Form / *Formule* 11B Ont. Reg. No. / *Règl. de l'Ont.* : 258/98

Seal / *Sceau*

Brampton
Small Claims Court / *Cour des petites créances de*
7755 Hurontario Street
Brampton, Ontario
L6W 4T6
Address / *Adresse*

905 456 4700
Phone number / *Numéro de téléphone*

4567
Claim No. / *N° de la demande*

Plaintiff No. 1 / *Demandeur n° 1*   ☐ Additional plaintiff(s) listed on attached Form 1A.
Le ou les demandeurs additionnels sont mentionnés sur la formule 1A ci-jointe.

Last name, or name of company / *Nom de famille ou nom de la compagnie* **Parrish**		
First name / *Premier prénom* **Maxwell**	Second name / *Deuxième prénom*	Also known as / *Également connu(e) sous le nom de*
Address (street number, apt., unit) / *Adresse (numéro et rue, app., unité)* **c/o Prior Mustafa LLP**		
City/Town / *Cité/ville*	Province	Phone no. / *N° de téléphone*
Postal code / *Code postal*		Fax no. / *N° de télécopieur*
Representative / *Représentant(e)* **Prior Mustafa LLP Attention: Marie Prior**		LSUC # / *N° du BHC* **######**
Address (street number, apt., unit) / *Adresse (numéro et rue, app., unité)* **22 County Court Boulevard**		
City/Town / *Cité/ville* **Brampton**	Province **Ontario**	Phone no. / *N° de téléphone* **905 111 2222**
Postal code / *Code postal* **A1A 2B3**		Fax no. / *N° de télécopieur* **905 111 2233**

Defendant No. 1 / *Défendeur n° 1*   ☐ Additional defendant(s) listed on attached Form 1A.
Le ou les défendeurs additionnels sont mentionnés sur la formule 1A ci-jointe.

Last name, or name of company / *Nom de famille ou nom de la compagnie* **Thurston**		
First name / *Premier prénom* **Frank**	Second name / *Deuxième prénom*	Also known as / *Également connu(e) sous le nom de*
Address (street number, apt., unit) / *Adresse (numéro et rue, app., unité)* **45 Labrador Court, Suite 103**		
City/Town / *Cité/ville* **Toronto**	Province **Ontario**	Phone no. / *N° de téléphone* **416 333 4444**
Postal code / *Code postal* **M3C 4D5**		Fax no. / *N° de télécopieur*
Representative / *Représentant(e)*		LSUC # / *N° du BHC*
Address (street number, apt., unit) / *Adresse (numéro et rue, app., unité)*		
City/Town / *Cité/ville*	Province	Phone no. / *N° de téléphone*
Postal code / *Code postal*		Fax no. / *N° de télécopieur*

APPENDIX 5.1   Form 11B Continued

FORM / *FORMULE* 11B   PAGE 2   <u>4567</u>

Claim No. / *N° de la demande*

NOTICE TO THE DEFENDANT(S):
AVIS AU(X) DÉFENDEUR(S) :
(*Check one box only. /* Cochez une seule case.)

☒ You have been noted in default according to Rule 11.01.
vous avez été constaté(e) en défaut aux termes de la règle 11.01.

☐ You have defaulted in your payment according to Rule 9.03(2)(b), pursuant to
vous n'avez pas effectué vos paiements aux termes de l'alinéa 9.03 (2) b), conformément à/au

_____   dated _____ , 20 _____ ,
(Name of document / *Titre du document*)   *daté(e) du*

and 15 days have passed since you were served with a Notice of Default of Payment (Form 20L).
et 15 jours se sont écoulés depuis qu'un avis de défaut de paiement vous a été signifié (formule 20L).

DEFAULT JUDGMENT IS GIVEN against the following defendant(s):
UN JUGEMENT PAR DÉFAUT EST RENDU contre le ou les défendeurs suivants :

Last name, or name of company / *Nom de famille ou nom de la compagnie*		
Thurston		
First name / *Premier prénom*	Second name / *Deuxième prénom*	Also known as / *Également connu(e) sous le nom de*
Frank		

Last name, or name of company / *Nom de famille ou nom de la compagnie*		
First name / *Premier prénom*	Second name / *Deuxième prénom*	Also known as / *Également connu(e) sous le nom de*

Last name, or name of company / *Nom de famille ou nom de la compagnie*		
First name / *Premier prénom*	Second name / *Deuxième prénom*	Also known as / *Également connu(e) sous le nom de*

☐ Additional defendant(s) listed on attached page (*list in same format*).
Défendeur(s) additionnel(s) mentionné(s) sur une feuille annexée (énumérez-les en suivant le même format).

THE DEFENDANT(S) MUST PAY to the plaintiff(s) the following sums:
LE OU LES DÉFENDEURS DOIVENT VERSER au(x) demandeur(s) les sommes suivantes :

(A) **DEBT** (principal amount claimed minus any payments received since the plaintiff's
claim was issued) $ 25,000.00
LA CRÉANCE (somme demandée moins tout paiement reçu depuis la délivrance $
de la demande du demandeur)

(B) **PRE-JUDGMENT INTEREST** calculated
LES INTÉRÊTS ANTÉRIEURS AU JUGEMENT calculés

on the sum of $ 25,000.00 at the rate of **12**   %
sur la somme de   *$ au taux de*   *pour cent*

per annum from **September 1**   , 20 **--** , to **December 1**   , 20 **--** ,
par an du   *au*

being **91**   days. $ 747.93
soit   *jours.* $

                    Continued on next page / *Suite à la page suivante*

APPENDIX 5.1   Form 11B Concluded

FORM / *FORMULE* **11B**   **PAGE 3**   4567

Claim No. / N° de la demande

(C)   **COSTS** to date $ 145.00
      LES DÉPENS *à ce jour* $

                                                      TOTAL $ 25,892.93

                                                           $

This judgment bears post-judgment interest at   **12**   % per annum commencing this date.
Le présent jugement porte des intérêts postérieurs   *pour cent à partir de la date du présent jugement.*
au jugement calculés au taux annuel de

December 1   , 20 --

(Signature of clerk / Signature du greffier)

CAUTION TO DEFENDANT:	**YOU MUST PAY THE AMOUNT OF THIS JUDGMENT DIRECTLY TO THE PLAINTIFF(S) IMMEDIATELY.** Failure to do so may result in additional post-judgment interest and enforcement costs.
AVERTISSEMENT AU DÉFENDEUR :	***VOUS DEVEZ VERSER DIRECTEMENT AU(X) DEMANDEUR(S) LE MONTANT DÛ AUX TERMES DU PRÉSENT JUGEMENT IMMÉDIATEMENT,*** *à défaut de quoi d'autres intérêts postérieurs au jugement et dépens de l'exécution forcée pourront vous être imputés.*

APPENDIX 5.2 Chong v. Kingman: Motion for an Assessment of Damages (Unliquidated Amount) Affidavit of Service (Form 8A)

ONTARIO

Superior Court of Justice
Cour supérieure de justice

Affidavit of Service
Affidavit de signification

Form / *Formule* 8A Ont. Reg. No. / *Règl. de l'Ont.* : 258/98

Toronto

Small Claims Court / *Cour des petites créances de*
45 Sheppard Avenue East
Toronto, Ontario
M2N 5X5

Address / *Adresse*

416 326 3554

Phone number / *Numéro de téléphone*

5678

Claim No. / *N° de la demande*

BETWEEN / *ENTRE*

Maxine Chong

Plaintiff(s) / *Demandeur(s)/demanderesse(s)*

and / *et*

LeeAnn Kingman

Defendant(s) / *Défendeur(s)/défenderesse(s)*

My name is Claire Ivory
Je m'appelle

(Full name / *Nom et prénoms*)

I live in Mississauga, Ontario
J'habite à

(Municipality & province / *Municipalité et province*)

and I swear/affirm that the following is true:
et je déclare sous serment/j'affirme solennellement que les renseignements suivants sont véridiques :

1. **I served** LeeAnn Kingman , on June 24 , 20 -- ,
   J'ai signifié à (Full name of person/corporation served / *Nom et prénoms* , *le* (Date)
   de la personne/nom au complet de la personne morale qui a reçu la signification)

   at 48 Brimley Road, Apt. 1306, Toronto, Ontario M2L 3T6
   au (Address (street and number, unit, municipality, province) / *Adresse (numéro et rue, unité, municipalité, province)*)

   which is ☒ the address of the person's home
   soit *l'adresse du domicile de la personne*

   ☐ the address of the corporation's place of business
   l'adresse du lieu de travail de l'établissement de la personne morale

   ☐ the address of the person's or corporation's representative on record with the court
   l'adresse du/de la représentant(e) de la personne ou de la personne morale figurant au dossier du tribunal

   ☐ the address on the document most recently filed in court by the party
   l'adresse figurant sur le document déposé le plus récemment au tribunal par la partie

   ☐ the address of the corporation's attorney for service in Ontario
   l'adresse du fondé de pouvoir de la personne morale aux fins de signification en Ontario

   ☐ other address:
   autre adresse : (Specify. / *Précisez.*)

   with the plaintiff's claim
   ce qui suit : (Name(s) of document(s) served / *Titre(s) du ou des documents signifiés*)

SCR 8.06-8A (November 1, 2009 / *1er novembre 2009*) CSD

APPENDIX 5.2   Form 8A Continued

FORM / *FORMULE* 8A	PAGE 2	5678

2. **I served the document(s) referred to in paragraph one by the following method:**
   J'ai signifié le ou les documents mentionnés au numéro un de la façon suivante :
   (Tell how service took place by checking appropriate box(es).)
   (Indiquez la façon dont la signification a été effectuée en cochant la ou les cases appropriées.)

Personal service /
Signification à personne

☒ leaving a copy with the person.
   en laissant une copie à la personne.

☐ leaving a copy with the _____ of the corporation.
   en laissant une copie au/à la   (Office or position / *Charge ou poste*)   *de la personne morale.*

☐ leaving a copy with: _____
   en laissant une copie à :   (Specify person's name and office or position. / *Indiquez le nom de la personne ainsi que sa charge ou son poste.*)

Service at place of residence /
Signification au domicile

☐ leaving a copy in a sealed envelope addressed to the person at the person's place of residence with a person who appeared to be an adult member of the same household, and sending another copy of the same document(s) to the person's place of residence on the same day or the following day by:
   en laissant une copie au domicile de la personne, dans une enveloppe scellée adressée à celle-ci, auprès d'une personne habitant sous le même toit qui semblait majeure et en envoyant une autre copie du ou des mêmes documents au domicile de la personne le même jour ou le jour suivant :

   ☐ regular lettermail.
      par courrier ordinaire.

   ☐ registered mail.
      par courrier recommandé.

   ☐ courier.
      par messagerie.

Service by registered mail /
Signification par courrier recommandé

☐ registered mail.
   par courrier recommandé.
   (If a copy of a plaintiff's claim or defendant's claim was served by registered mail, attach a copy of the Canada Post delivery confirmation showing the signature of the person being served to this affidavit.)
   (Si une copie de la demande du demandeur ou de la demande du défendeur a été signifiée par courrier recommandé, annexez au présent affidavit une copie de la confirmation de livraison remise par Postes Canada sur laquelle figure la signature du destinataire de la signification.)

Service by courier /
Signification par messagerie

☐ courier.
   par messagerie.
   (If a copy of a plaintiff's claim or defendant's claim was served by courier, attach a copy of the courier's delivery confirmation showing the signature of the person being served to this affidavit.)
   (Si une copie de la demande du demandeur ou de la demande du défendeur a été signifiée par messagerie, annexez au présent affidavit une copie de la confirmation de livraison remise par le service de messagerie sur laquelle figure la signature du destinataire de la signification.)

Service on lawyer /
Signification à l'avocat

☐ leaving a copy with a lawyer who accepted service on the person's behalf.
   en laissant une copie avec l'avocat qui a accepté la signification au nom de la personne.
   (Attach a copy of the document endorsed with the lawyer's acceptance of service.)
   (Annexez une copie du document, sur lequel l'avocat a inscrit qu'il a accepté la signification.)

Service by regular lettermail /
Signification par courrier ordinaire

☐ regular lettermail.
   par courrier ordinaire.

APPENDIX 5.2   Form 8A Concluded

FORM / *FORMULE* 8A	PAGE 3	5678
		Claim No. / *N° de la demande*

Service by fax / *Signification par télécopie*

☐ fax sent at _____ at the following fax number:
par télécopie   (Time / *heure*)   *au numéro de télécopieur*   (Fax number / *numéro de*
envoyée à   *suivant :*   *télécopieur*)

Service to last known address of corporation or attorney for service, and to the directors / *Signification à la dernière adresse connue de la personne morale ou de son fondé de pouvoir aux fins de signification et aux administrateurs <fr>*

☐ mail/courier to corporation or attorney for service at last known address recorded with the Ministry of Government Services, and
d'une part, par la poste/par messagerie à la personne morale ou à son fondé de pouvoir aux fins de signification, à la dernière adresse connue figurant dans les dossiers du ministère des Services gouvernementaux;

mail/courier to each director, as recorded with the Ministry of Government Services, as set out below:
d'autre part, par la poste/par messagerie à chaque administrateur mentionné dans les dossiers du ministère des Services gouvernementaux et dont le nom et l'adresse sont indiqués ci-dessous :

Name of director / *Nom de l'administrateur*	Director's address as recorded with the Ministry of Government Services (street & number, unit, municipality, province) / *Adresse de l'administrateur figurant dans les dossiers du ministère des Services gouvernementaux (numéro et rue, unité, municipalité, province)*

(Attach separate sheet for additional names if necessary. /
Joignez au besoin une feuille séparée s'il y a d'autres noms à ajouter.)

Substituted service / *Signification indirecte*

☐ substituted service as ordered by the court on _____ , 20 _____ ,
par signification indirecte ordonnée par le tribunal le   (Date)

as follows: (Give details.)
comme suit :   *(Précisez.)*

Sworn/Affirmed before me at   **Brampton**
Déclaré sous serment/Affirmé   (Municipality / *municipalité*)
solennellement devant moi à

in **Ontario**
en/à/au   (Province, state, or country / *province, État ou pays*)

on **July 15** _____ , 20 **--** _____
le   Commissioner for taking affidavits
                                        Commissaire aux affidavits
                                        (Type or print name below if signature is illegible.)
                                        (Dactylographiez le nom ou écrivez-le en caractères d'imprimerie ci-dessous si la signature est illisible.)

Signature
(This form is to be signed in front of a lawyer, justice of the peace, notary public or commissioner for taking affidavits.)
(La présente formule doit être signée en présence d'un avocat, d'un juge de paix, d'un notaire ou d'un commissaire aux affidavits.)

SCR 8.06-8A (November 1, 2009 / *1er novembre 2009*) CSD

APPENDIX 5.2   Request to Clerk (Form 9B)

ONTARIO

Superior Court of Justice
Cour supérieure de justice

Request to Clerk
Demande au greffier

Form / *Formule* 9B Ont. Reg. No. / *Règl. de l'Ont.* : 258/98

Toronto

Small Claims Court / *Cour des petites créances de*

45 Sheppard Avenue
Toronto, Ontario
M2N 5X5

Address / *Adresse*

416 326 3554

Phone number / *Numéro de téléphone*

5678

Claim No. / *N° de la demande*

BETWEEN / *ENTRE*

Maxine Chong

Plaintiff(s) / *Demandeur(s)/demanderesse(s)*

and / *et*

LeeAnn Kingman

Defendant(s) / *Défendeur(s)/défenderesse(s)*

TO THE CLERK OF THE Toronto   **SMALL CLAIMS COURT:**
AU GREFFIER DE LA COUR
DES PETITES CRÉANCES DE

(Name of Small Claims Court location / *Emplacement de la Cour des petites créances*) :

My name is   Marie Prior
Je m'appelle   (Name of party/representative / *Nom de la partie ou du/de la représentant(e)*)

and I request that the clerk of the court:
et je demande au greffier du tribunal de faire ce qui suit :

(Check appropriate box(es). / Cochez la ou les cases appropriées.)

☒   note defendant(s)   **LeeAnn Kingman**
    constater le ou les défendeurs   (Name of defendant(s) / *Nom du/de la/des défendeur(s)/défenderesse(s)*)

    in default for failing to file a Defence (Form 9A) within the prescribed time period [R. 11.01(1)].
    en défaut pour n'avoir pas déposé de défense (formule 9A) dans le délai prescrit [par. 11.01 (1)].

☐   schedule an assessment hearing (all defendants have been noted in default) [R. 11.03(2)(b)].
    fixer la date d'une audience d'évaluation (tous les défendeurs ont été constatés en défaut) [alinéa 11.03 (2) b)].

☐   schedule a terms of payment hearing because I dispute the defendant's proposed terms of payment contained in the Defence (Form 9A) [R. 9.03(3)].
    fixer la date d'une audience relative aux modalités de paiement parce que je conteste les modalités de paiement proposées par le défendeur dans la défense (formule 9A) [par. 9.03 (3)].

☐   schedule a trial [R. 16.01(1)(b)].
    fixer une date de procès [alinéa 16.01 (1) b)].

SCR 4-9-11-14-16-9B (June 1, 2009 / *1er juin 2009*) CSD

APPENDIX 5.2   Form 9B Concluded

FORM / *FORMULE* 9B   **PAGE 2**   <u>5678</u>

Claim No. / *N° de la demande*

☐   accept payment in the amount of $ _____ into court
   accepter que le paiement de   (Amount / *montant*)   *$ soit consigné au tribunal,*

☐   according to an order of the court, dated _____ , 20 _____ .
      conformément à une ordonnance du tribunal datée du

☐   for a person under disability according to an order or settlement dated
      au nom d'un incapable, conformément à une ordonnance ou à une transaction datée du

      _____ , 20 _____   [R. 4.08(1)].
                                 [par. 4.08 (1)].

☐   pursuant to the attached written offer to settle, dated _____ , 20 _____ [R. 14.05(2)].
      aux termes de l'offre de transaction écrite ci-jointe datée du   *[par. 14.05 (2)].*

☐   according to the following legislation:
      conformément à la disposition législative suivante :

      _____ .

      (Name of statute or regulation and section / *Titre de la loi ou du règlement et mention de l'article*)

☐   Other: (Specify.)
   Autre :   *(Précisez.)*

<u>July 15</u> _____ , 20 -- _____

(Signature of party or representative / *Signature de la partie ou du/de la représentant(e)*)

CAUTION:	To obtain an assessment of damages, all defendants must be noted in default. If one or more defendants has filed a defence, the matter must proceed to a settlement conference. To bring a motion in writing for an assessment of damages, file a Notice of Motion and Supporting Affidavit (Form 15A). You can get forms at court offices or online at <u>www.ontariocourtforms.on.ca</u>.
AVERTISSEMENT :	*Pour obtenir une évaluation des dommages-intérêts, tous les défendeurs doivent être constatés en défaut. Si un ou plusieurs défendeurs ont déposé une défense, l'affaire doit passer à l'étape de la conférence en vue d'une transaction. Pour présenter une motion par écrit en vue d'une évaluation des dommages-intérêts, déposez un avis de motion et affidavit à l'appui (formule 15A). Vous pouvez obtenir les formules aux greffes des tribunaux ou en ligne à l'adresse <u>www.ontariocourtforms.on.ca</u>.*

SCR 4-9-11-14-16-9B (June 1, 2009 / *1er juin 2009*) CSD

APPENDIX 5.2   Notice of Motion and Supporting Affidavit (Form 15A)

ONTARIO

Superior Court of Justice
Cour supérieure de justice

Notice of Motion and Supporting Affidavit
Avis de motion et affidavit à l'appui
Form / *Formule* 15A Ont. Reg. No. / *Règl. de l'Ont.* : 258/98

Toronto
Small Claims Court / *Cour des petites créances de*
45 Sheppard Avenue East
Toronto, Ontario
M2N 5X5
Address / *Adresse*

416 326 3554
Phone number / *Numéro de téléphone*

5678
Claim No. / *N° de la demande*

Plaintiff No. 1 / *Demandeur n° 1* ☐ Additional plaintiff(s) listed on attached Form 1A.
Le ou les demandeurs additionnels sont mentionnés sur la formule 1A ci-jointe.

Last name, or name of company / *Nom de famille ou nom de la compagnie* **Chong**		
First name / *Premier prénom* **Maxine**	Second name / *Deuxième prénom*	Also known as / *Également connu(e) sous le nom de*
Address (street number, apt., unit) / *Adresse (numéro et rue, app., unité)* **c/o Prior Mustafa LLP**		
City/Town / *Cité/ville*	Province	Phone no. / *N° de téléphone*
Postal code / *Code postal*		Fax no. / *N° de télécopieur*
Representative / *Représentant(e)* **Prior Mustafa LLP Attention: Marie Prior**		LSUC # / *N° du BHC* **######**
Address (street number, apt., unit) / *Adresse (numéro et rue, app., unité)* **22 County Court Boulevard**		
City/Town / *Cité/ville* **Brampton**	Province **Ontario**	Phone no. / *N° de téléphone* **905 111 2222**
Postal code / *Code postal* **A1A 2B3**		Fax no. / *N° de télécopieur* **905 111 2233**

Defendant No. 1 / *Défendeur n° 1* ☐ Additional defendant(s) listed on attached Form 1A.
Le ou les défendeurs additionnels sont mentionnés sur la formule 1A ci-jointe.

Last name, or name of company / *Nom de famille ou nom de la compagnie* **Kingman**		
First name / *Premier prénom* **LeeAnn**	Second name / *Deuxième prénom*	Also known as / *Également connu(e) sous le nom de*
Address (street number, apt., unit) / *Adresse (numéro et rue, app., unité)* **48 Brimley Road, Apt. 1306**		
City/Town / *Cité/ville* **Toronto**	Province **Ontario**	Phone no. / *N° de téléphone* **416 444 5555**
Postal code / *Code postal* **L2L 3T6**		Fax no. / *N° de télécopieur*
Representative / *Représentant(e)*		LSUC # / *N° du BHC*
Address (street number, apt., unit) / *Adresse (numéro et rue, app., unité)*		
City/Town / *Cité/ville*	Province	Phone no. / *N° de téléphone*
Postal code / *Code postal*		Fax no. / *N° de télécopieur*

APPENDIX 5.2 Form 15A Continued

FORM / *FORMULE* 15A PAGE 2 5678

Claim No. / N° de la demande

THIS COURT WILL HEAR A MOTION on August 1 , 20 -- , at 9:30 a.m. ,
LE TRIBUNAL PRÉCITÉ ENTENDRA UNE MOTION le , *à* (Time / *heure*)

or as soon as possible after that time, at 45 Sheppard Avenue East, Toronto, Ontario M2N 5X5
ou dès que possible par la suite à/au (Address of court location and courtroom number / *Adresse du tribunal et numéro de la salle d'audience*)

Complete Part A <u>or</u> Part B below, then complete the affidavit in support of motion on page 3. / *Remplissez la partie A <u>ou</u> la partie B ci-dessous. Remplissez ensuite l'affidavit à l'appui de la motion à la page 3.*

A. This motion will be made in person
by ,
La motion sera présentée en personne par : (Name of party / *Nom de la partie*)

for the following order : / *en vue d'obtenir l'ordonnance suivante :*

- ☐ the court's permission to extend time to (Specify)
  l'autorisation du tribunal de proroger le délai pour (*Précisez*)
  .

- ☐ set aside default judgment and noting in default.
  l'annulation du jugement par défaut et la constatation du défaut.

- ☐ set aside noting in default.
  l'annulation de la constatation du défaut.

- ☐ permission to file a Defence.
  l'autorisation de déposer une défense.

- ☐ permission to file a Defendant's Claim.
  l'autorisation de déposer une demande du défendeur.

- ☐ terminate garnishment and/or withdraw writ(s).
  la mainlevée de la saisie-arrêt ou le retrait d'un ou de plusieurs brefs, ou les deux.

- ☐ Other:
  Autre :

☒ **ADDITIONAL PAGES ARE ATTACHED BECAUSE MORE ROOM WAS NEEDED.**
DES FEUILLES SUPPLÉMENTAIRES SONT ANNEXÉES EN RAISON DU MANQUE D'ESPACE.

☒ **DOCUMENTS ARE ATTACHED.**
PIÈCES JOINTES.

NOTE: **IF YOU FAIL TO ATTEND AN IN-PERSON MOTION,** an order may be made against you, with costs, in your absence. If you want to attend the motion by telephone or video conference, complete and file a Request for Telephone or Video Conference (Form 1B). If the court permits it, the clerk will make the necessary arrangements and notify the parties [R. 1.07(5)].

REMARQUE : *SI VOUS NE VOUS PRÉSENTEZ PAS EN PERSONNE À L'AUDITION DE LA MOTION, une ordonnance peut être rendue contre vous en votre absence, avec dépens. Si vous voulez assister à l'audition de la motion par conférence téléphonique ou vidéoconférence, remplissez et déposez la Demande de conférence téléphonique ou vidéoconférence (formule 1B). Si le tribunal l'autorise, le greffier prendra les dispositions nécessaires et en avisera les parties [par. 1.07 (5)].*

SCR 15.01-15A (June 1, 2009 / *1er juin 2009*) CSD **Continued on next page** / *Suite à la page suivante*

APPENDIX 5.2   Form 15A Continued

FORM / *FORMULE* 15A   PAGE 3   5678

....
Claim No. / *N° de la demande*

B.   This motion in writing for an assessment of damages is made by
La présente motion par écrit en vue d'une évaluation des dommages-intérêts est présentée par

Maxine Chong   ,
....
(Name of plaintiff / *Nom du demandeur/de la demanderesse*)

who asks the court for an order assessing damages against
qui demande au tribunal de rendre une ordonnance d'évaluation des dommages-intérêts contre

LeeAnn Kingman
....
(Name of defendant(s) / *Nom du/de la/des défendeur(s)/défenderesse(s)*)

who have/has been noted in default.
qui a/ont été constaté(e)(s) en défaut.

AFFIDAVIT IN SUPPORT OF MOTION / *AFFIDAVIT À L'APPUI DE LA MOTION*

My name is Maxine Chong
Je m'appelle   (Full name / *Nom et prénoms*)

I live in Toronto, Ontario
J'habite à   (Municipality & province / *Municipalité et province*)

I swear/affirm that the following is true:
Je déclare sous serment/j'affirme solennellement que les renseignements suivants sont véridiques :

Set out the facts in numbered paragraphs. If you learned a fact from someone else, you must give that person's name and state that you believe that fact to be true.
Indiquez les faits sous forme de dispositions numérotées. Si vous avez pris connaissance d'un fait par l'entremise d'une autre personne, vous devez indiquer le nom de cette personne et déclarer que vous croyez que ce fait est véridique.

See Schedule A attached

APPENDIX 5.2   Form 15A Continued

AFFIDAVIT IN SUPPORT OF MOTION, continued / *AFFIDAVIT À L'APPUI DE LA MOTION, suite*
See Schedule A attached

If more space is required, attach and initial extra pages. / Si vous avez besoin de plus d'espace, annexez une ou des feuilles supplémentaires et paraphez-les.

Sworn/Affirmed before me at **Brampton**
Déclaré sous serment/Affirmé
solennellement devant moi à   (Municipality / *municipalité*)

in **Ontario**
en/à/au   (Province, state or country / *province, État ou pays*)

on **July 15**   , 20 **--**
le   Commissioner for taking affidavits
                                             Commissaire aux affidavits
                                  (Type or print name below if signature is illegible.)
                                  (Dactylographiez le nom ou écrivez-le en
                                  caractères d'imprimerie ci-dessous si la
                                  signature est illisible.)

                                             Signature
                                  (This form is to be signed in front of a
                                  lawyer, justice of the peace, notary public
                                  or commissioner for taking affidavits.)
                                  (La présente formule doit être signée en
                                  présence d'un avocat, d'un juge de paix,
                                  d'un notaire ou d'un commissaire aux
                                  affidavits.)

WARNING: **IT IS AN OFFENCE UNDER THE** *CRIMINAL CODE* **TO KNOWINGLY SWEAR OR**
                    AFFIRM A FALSE AFFIDAVIT.
AVERTISSEMENT :   *FAIRE SCIEMMENT UN FAUX AFFIDAVIT CONSTITUE UNE INFRACTION AU CODE*
                    CRIMINEL.

SCR 15.01-15A (June 1, 2009 / *1er juin 2009*) CSD

APPENDIX 5.2 Form 15A Continued

Schedule A

1. I, Maxine Chong, am the plaintiff in this action and have personal knowledge of the following.

2. Pursuant to a tenancy agreement dated January 13, 20—, I agreed to rent the basement apartment at 67 Harmony Avenue, Toronto, Ontario to the defendant. A true copy of the agreement is attached as Exhibit A.

3. The tenancy commenced February 1, 20— at a monthly rent of $775.00, including water, heat, and hydro.

4. The defendant did not pay a last month's rent deposit. She told me she had just found a new job after several months of unemployment and was trying to put her life back together. I told her to pay the last month's rent when she had the money.

5. The basement apartment at 67 Harmony Avenue is a legal basement apartment with a separate entrance. I occupy the main floor. The washer, dryer, furnace, and fuse box are in the basement, accessible from the basement apartment. The door to my kitchen opens onto the side entrance to the house and the stairs down to the basement apartment.

6. The defendant's rent cheque for February 1 was returned for insufficient funds. A true copy of the notice of NSF cheque is attached as Exhibit B.

7. When I asked her for a replacement cheque, the defendant became extremely abusive. She screamed and shouted and ended up slamming the apartment door in my face. That evening, she played music very loud until one o'clock in the morning. I could not sleep. I was afraid the neighbours would complain to the police. When I pounded on the floor to get the music to stop, the defendant pounded back, screaming abuse and obscenities. Eventually, the defendant turned the music off, but for the rest of the night there were sounds of banging and crashing from the basement. I was terrified. The defendant had access to my washer, dryer, furnace, and the fuse box. I feared that she would cause damage or set the house on fire.

8. The defendant never paid the February rent. When I tried to approach her about it, she became extremely abusive. On several occasions, she came upstairs and stood outside my kitchen door,

APPENDIX 5.2   Form 15A Continued

which opened onto the side entrance that the defendant used. She would pound on the door and scream. She would threaten to report me to the Ontario Human Rights Tribunal for abuse and discrimination.

9.   The defendant did not pay the rent for March. I did nothing because I was afraid of how the defendant might react. I felt as if I did not own my house any more. There was always loud music, banging, and shouting from the basement, especially from around midnight until two or three o'clock in the morning.

10.   I began keeping the kitchen door locked. I could not sleep and I lost my appetite. I suffered from headaches and anxiety attacks. If I went out, I dreaded going home. My physician prescribed diazepam and Prozac. True copies of the pharmacist's invoices for diazepam and Prozac are attached as Exhibits C and D.

11.   When the defendant did not pay the April rent, I called my daughter, Alice, in Penticton. Alice arrived late on April 5. On April 6, we got in touch with a paralegal firm specializing in residential tenancies law. The paralegal firm drafted and served a Form N4—Notice to End a Tenancy Early for Non-Payment of Rent on the defendant.

12.   On April 17, the defendant vacated the apartment, taking the keys to the side entrance and the basement apartment with her. She left the basement apartment in a filthy state. It cost me $1,059.00 to have a contractor come in to clean the apartment, replace the carpet, repair the damage, and repaint. I had to pay a locksmith $125.00 to rekey the locks. A true copy of the invoice for the contractor is attached as Exhibit E. A true copy of the locksmith's invoice is attached as Exhibit F.

13.   The paralegal's services cost me $300.00. A true copy of the invoice for paralegal services is attached as Exhibit G.

14.   My daughter stayed long enough to help me find me a reliable, quiet tenant for the basement apartment. The new tenant moved in on June 1. There have been no more problems.

APPENDIX 5.2   Form 15A Continued

15. I am sixty-two years old. I have lived on my own for fifteen years, since my husband died. I was in excellent health before the defendant moved into my house. I have always been very independent, which is why it took me so long to seek help from my family. I prefer to handle things myself; but I could not handle this situation.

16. Since the defendant moved out, I have stopped taking Prozac. I continue to have anxiety attacks and suffer from loss of appetite. I still need diazepam to get to sleep. Without diazepam, the anxiety attacks wake me up in the night, and I lie there sweating and shaking. My physician has advised me that diazepam is addictive over the long term, but there is no other way I can get to sleep.

17. As of the date this claim was issued, I was claiming special damages of $3,992.47, calculated as follows:

    Loss of income — unpaid rent

3 months × $775.00	$2,325.00
Medication	183.47
Cost of repairs	1,059.00
Rekey locks	125.00
Cost of drafting and serving N4	300.00
Total as of July 6, 20—	$3,992.47

18. Since the claim was issued, I have had to pay for another prescription for diazepam, costing $75.00. A true copy of the credit card invoice is attached as Exhibit H. This amount brings the total for special damages to $4,067.47.

19. The balance of the claim is for general damages for pain, suffering, and mental distress that I suffered as a direct result of the defendant's conduct. A true copy of my treating physician's report is attached as Exhibit I.

APPENDIX 5.2   Form 15A Concluded

Exhibits to the affidavit: [Note that a real affidavit would have copies of documents stamped

as exhibits (dated and signed by the commissioner of oaths) attached to it.]

Exhibit A   Tenancy agreement dated January 13, 20—

Exhibit B   Notice of NSF cheque dated February 15, 20—

Exhibit C   Pharmacist's invoice for diazepam

Exhibit D   Pharmacist's invoice for Prozac

Exhibit E   Invoice from contractor for repairs

Exhibit F   Invoice from locksmith

Exhibit G   Invoice from Prior Mustafa LLP

Exhibit H   Pharmacist's invoice for renewal of diazepam prescription

Exhibit I   Treating physician's report

Acting for the Defendant

LEARNING OBJECTIVES

After reading this chapter, you will understand:

- The time for filing a defence
- When to dispute the entire claim
- When to admit all or part of the claim and make a proposal of terms of payment
- Making a proposal of terms of payment
- The basic rules of pleading for a defence
- What a defendant's claim is used for
- The basic rules of pleading for a defendant's claim
- The consequences for the defendant of being noted in default

INTRODUCTION

A defendant who is served personally with the plaintiff's claim has 20 days from the date of service to file a defence with the court.

If the defendant is served by an alternative to personal service, the time for filing a defence will vary, depending on how the plaintiff's claim is served. See table 6.1 at page 201 for the time periods for delivering a defence to a plaintiff's or defendant's claim.

A defendant who wishes to make a claim against the plaintiff or any other person may issue a defendant's claim within 20 days after filing the defence, unless the court orders otherwise. Generally speaking, the defendant's claim will be issued on the same day that the defence is filed.

The court will serve the defence on all other parties. The defendant is responsible for serving the defendant's claim. The defendant's claim must be served personally or by an alternative to personal service.

A defendant who has been noted in default and/or had default judgment signed against him may make a motion for an order setting aside the noting in default and other relief. The motion should be made as soon as is reasonably possible in all of the circumstances. The supporting affidavit must provide a reasonable explanation for the default, and satisfy the court that the defendant has a meritorious defence.

DEFENDANT NOT IN DEFAULT

General

The defendant should bring the plaintiff's claim with her to the initial consultation. If she intends to dispute all or part of the claim, she should also bring originals of any documents she intends to rely on in her defence. The original documents should be placed in the documents subfile for the client matter. Copies of the documents will be attached to the defence.

As early as possible in the matter, you must find out when your client was served, because this tells you how much time you have left to file the defence. The general rule is that a defendant has 20 days from the date of being served to file a defence. This is not a big window, so you should draft and file the defence as soon as possible after being retained.

If the plaintiff is represented, you should contact the plaintiff's lawyer or paralegal and advise them that you are in the process of obtaining instructions. If the initial contact with the defendant does not take place until the time for filing a defence has almost expired, you should also request an extension of time. Professional courtesy requires that, if asked to do so, a party's legal representative should seek their client's instructions to consent to a brief extension of the deadline for delivering a defence, if they have been made aware that the defendant is taking reasonable steps to defend the action.

If the client declines to retain you, or you decline the retainer on grounds of a conflict of interest or for some other reason, you must advise the client in the non-engagement letter of the procedural consequences of failing to file a defence within the prescribed time, and also of any limitation periods.

Drafting the Defence

GENERAL

The defence must be filed with the clerk within 20 days of service of the plaintiff's claim. If there are multiple plaintiffs and co-defendants, enough copies should be provided to serve all parties to the proceeding (Rule 9.01(1) of the *Rules of the Small Claims Court*).

If the defence is based in whole or in part on a document, a copy of the document shall be attached to each copy of the defence. If the document is not available, the defence shall state the reason why the document is not attached (Rule 9.02(1)2). Note that the Rule 9.02 obligation to disclose is mandatory.

TABLE 6.1   Time for Delivering a Defence to a Plaintiff's Claim or Defendant's Claim

Type of service	Rule	Method of service	Time for delivering defence	Rule
Personal service	8.01(1)	Document is handed to person being served	20 days after date of service (including holidays and ending on a business day)	8.01(1)
Alternative to personal service: service on person's lawyer	8.03(5)	Leaving a copy with the lawyer or an employee in the lawyer's office (acceptance of service must be endorsed on a copy of the document)	20 days after date of service (including holidays and ending on a business day)	
Alternative to personal service: service at place of residence	8.03(2)	(a) Leaving a copy in a sealed envelope addressed to the individual with an apparently adult member of same household; and (b) On the same day or following day, serving the document by mail or by commercial courier	5 days after date of mailing or date that delivery by courier is verified (excluding holidays and ending on a business day) *plus* 20 days (including holidays and ending on a business day)	8.03(4)
Alternative to personal service: corporation	8.03(3)	Ontario corporation: (a) Service of copy by mail or courier to address of head office or principal place of business; and (b) Service of copy by mail or courier to each director at that director's address on record with the Ministry of Government Services Extra-provincial corporation: (a) Service by mail or courier to the attorney for service in Ontario; and (b) Service by mail or courier to each director at that director's address on record with the Ministry of Government Services	5 days after date of mailing or date that delivery by courier is verified (excluding holidays and ending on a business day) *plus* 20 days (including holidays and ending on a business day)	8.03(4)
Alternative to personal service: service on an individual by mail or courier to individual's place of residence	8.03(7)	Sending a copy by registered mail or by commercial courier to the individual's place of residence Note: this form of service is valid only if the individual's signature verifying receipt is obtained	20 days after the date on which the individual verifies receipt by signature on a delivery confirmation provided by Canada Post or the commercial courier	8.03(8)
Substituted service	8.04	Pursuant to a court order where it is shown that it is impractical to carry out service personally or by an alternative to personal service	By court order	

The current court fee for filing a defence is $40.00.

The clerk will serve all parties with the defence by mail or fax (Rules 9.01(2) and 8.01(3)).

During the initial consultation, you must go over the substance of the plaintiff's claim carefully with your client. The defence (Form 9A) gives the defendant a number of options (see figure 6.1). You have to determine which of these options is appropriate in your client's case:

1. dispute the entire claim;

FIGURE 6.1   Disputing the Plaintiff's Claim

FORM / FORMULE 9A   **PAGE 2**

Claim No. / N° de la demande

THIS DEFENCE IS BEING FILED ON BEHALF OF: (Name(s) of defendant(s))
LA PRÉSENTE DÉFENSE EST DÉPOSÉE AU NOM DE : (Nom du/de la ou des défendeur(s)/défenderesse(s))

and I/we: (Check as many as apply)
et je/nous : (Cochez la ou les cases qui s'appliquent)

☐   Dispute the claim made against me/us.
    conteste/contestons la demande présentée contre moi/nous.

☐   Admit the full claim and propose the following terms of payment:
    reconnais/reconnaissons être redevable(s) de la totalité de la demande et propose/proposons les
    modalités de paiement suivantes :

    $ _____ per _____ commencing _____ , 20 _____ .
       (Amount / Montant) $ par   (Week/month / semaine/mois)   à compter du

☐   Admit part of the claim in the amount of $ _____ and propose the following terms of payment:
    reconnais/reconnaissons être redevable(s)   (Amount / Montant) $ et propose/proposons les modalités de
    d'une partie de la demande, soit   paiement suivantes :

    $ _____ per _____ commencing _____ , 20 _____ .
       (Amount / Montant) $ par   (Week/month / semaine/mois)   à compter du

REASONS FOR DISPUTING THE CLAIM AND DETAILS:
MOTIFS DE CONTESTATION DE LA DEMANDE ET PRÉCISIONS :

Explain what happened, including where and when. Explain why you do not agree with the claim made against you.
Expliquez ce qui s'est passé, en précisant où et quand. Expliquez pourquoi vous contestez la demande
présentée contre vous.

If you are relying on any documents, you **MUST** attach copies to the Defence. If evidence is lost or unavailable,
you **MUST** explain why it is not attached.
Si vous vous appuyez sur des documents, vous **DEVEZ** en annexer des copies à la défense. Si une preuve est
perdue ou n'est pas disponible, vous **DEVEZ** expliquer pourquoi elle n'est pas annexée.

What happened?
Where?
When?
Que s'est-il
passé?

2. admit the claim and make a proposal of terms of payment of the amount claimed; or

3. admit part of the claim, make a proposal of terms of payment of that part of the claim, and defend the remainder of the claim.

If all or part of the plaintiff's claim is disputed, the defence should state the material facts the defendant is relying on in concise non-technical language with a reasonable amount of detail (Rule 9.02(1)1). Copies of any documents on which the defendant intends to rely shall be attached (Rule 9.02(1)2).

If the plaintiff is self-represented, the grounds for the claim are not likely to comply with formal rules for drafting pleadings. They may consist of nothing more than five or six handwritten sentences. This does not mean that the self-represented plaintiff does not have a good cause of action, and you should still go over the claim carefully with the defendant, with a view to drafting a persuasive defence.

DEFENDANT DISPUTES ALL OR PART OF THE CLAIM

For the overall structure of a disputed action, see figure 6.2.

Small Claims Court Rule 9 does not require the allegations in support of a full or partial defence to be typed and double-spaced, and set out in separate, numbered paragraphs in a schedule to the Form 9A. Rule 9 requires only that the defence contain contact information for the defendant or the defendant's agent or lawyer; the reasons why the defendant disputes all or part of the plaintiff's claim, stated in concise non-technical language with a reasonable amount of detail (Rule 9.02(1)1); and disclosure of any documents upon which the defence is based (Rule 9.02(1)2). This is appropriate for a court intended to be user-friendly for the self-represented.

Nevertheless, you, as a professional paralegal, should use professional standards when drafting pleadings. The grounds for the defence should be set out in a separate schedule. The schedule should begin with **admissions** and **denials** (if the claim is drafted in such a way as to permit this), and should then set out, in separate, numbered paragraphs, the allegations of material fact on which the defendant relies.

In a properly drafted defence, it is standard practice to begin by making admissions and denials. This gives the plaintiff a "snapshot" of what is and is not in dispute. See, for example, Rule 25.07 of the *Rules of Civil Procedure*, which applies to defences in Superior Court of Justice proceedings:

Rules of Pleading—Applicable to Defences

Admissions

25.07(1) In a defence, a party shall admit every allegation of fact in the opposite party's pleading that the party does not dispute.

Denials

(2) Subject to subrule (6), all allegations of fact that are not denied in a party's defence shall be deemed to be admitted unless the party pleads having no knowledge in respect of the fact.

Different Version of Facts

(3) Where a party intends to prove a version of the facts different from that pleaded by the opposite party, a denial of the version so pleaded is not sufficient, but the party shall plead the party's own version of the facts in the defence.

FIGURE 6.2   Small Claims Court Procedure: Defendant Disputes Claim

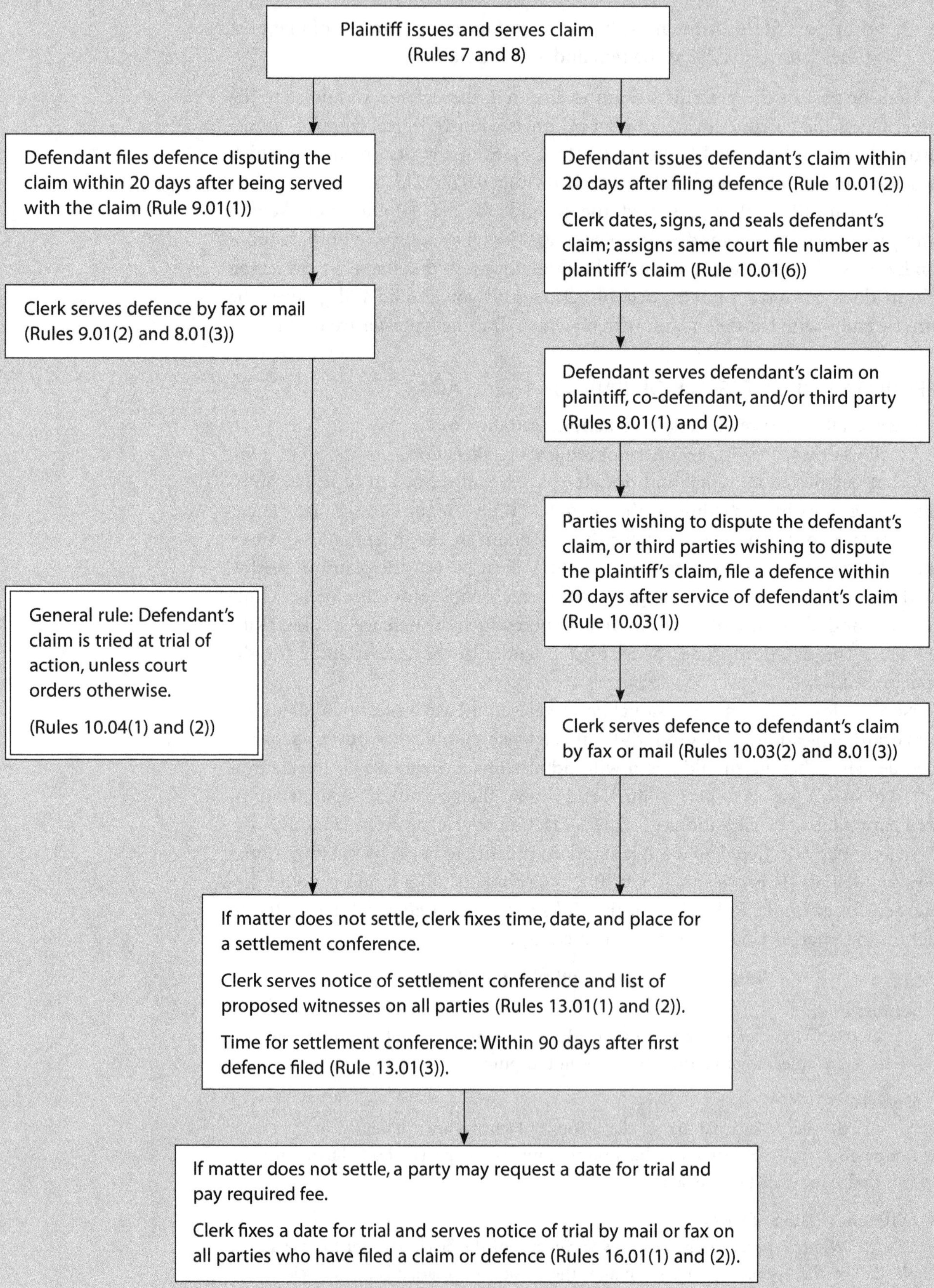

```
                    ┌─────────────────────────────────┐
                    │     Plaintiff issues and serves claim    │
                    │           (Rules 7 and 8)               │
                    └─────────────────────────────────┘
```

Plaintiff issues and serves claim (Rules 7 and 8)

Defendant files defence disputing the claim within 20 days after being served with the claim (Rule 9.01(1))

Defendant issues defendant's claim within 20 days after filing defence (Rule 10.01(2))

Clerk dates, signs, and seals defendant's claim; assigns same court file number as plaintiff's claim (Rule 10.01(6))

Clerk serves defence by fax or mail (Rules 9.01(2) and 8.01(3))

Defendant serves defendant's claim on plaintiff, co-defendant, and/or third party (Rules 8.01(1) and (2))

Parties wishing to dispute the defendant's claim, or third parties wishing to dispute the plaintiff's claim, file a defence within 20 days after service of defendant's claim (Rule 10.03(1))

General rule: Defendant's claim is tried at trial of action, unless court orders otherwise.

(Rules 10.04(1) and (2))

Clerk serves defence to defendant's claim by fax or mail (Rules 10.03(2) and 8.01(3))

If matter does not settle, clerk fixes time, date, and place for a settlement conference.

Clerk serves notice of settlement conference and list of proposed witnesses on all parties (Rules 13.01(1) and (2)).

Time for settlement conference: Within 90 days after first defence filed (Rule 13.01(3)).

If matter does not settle, a party may request a date for trial and pay required fee.

Clerk fixes a date for trial and serves notice of trial by mail or fax on all parties who have filed a claim or defence (Rules 16.01(1) and (2)).

Affirmative Defences

(4) In a defence, a party shall plead any matter on which the party intends to rely to defeat the claim of the opposite party and which, if not specifically pleaded, might take the opposite party by surprise or raise an issue that has not been raised in the opposite party's pleading.

Effect of Denial of Agreement

(5) Where an agreement is alleged in a pleading, a denial of the agreement by the opposite party shall be construed only as a denial of the making of the agreement or of the facts from which the agreement may be implied by law, and not as a denial of the legality or sufficiency in law of the agreement.

Damages

(6) In an action for damages, the amount of damages shall be deemed to be in issue unless specifically admitted.

If the plaintiff's claim has been drafted by a lawyer or paralegal, the substance of the claim should be set out in double-spaced, numbered paragraphs on the Form 7A or in a separate schedule to the form. It is good practice to make a separate copy of the substance of the claim, and go through it paragraph by paragraph with your client, marking the allegations he admits with an A and the allegations he denies with a D.

Stating the admissions and denials enables you and the other party or parties to assess the issues that are or are not in dispute, and to respond appropriately.

BOX 6.1

How Much Should the Defendant Admit?

The defendant should admit any allegations in the plaintiff's claim that are not in dispute. An admission is just an admission of one particular allegation of fact. It is not an admission of liability. The defendant is just letting the plaintiff and the court know that he acknowledges the truth of certain things the plaintiff has said, while reserving his right to defend against other allegations.

The defendant may admit some of the plaintiff's allegations, deny others, and still dispute the claim. Disputed allegations of fact must be supported by the plaintiff's evidence and accepted by the judge as true on a balance of probabilities if the plaintiff wishes to succeed at trial.

You need to take complete notes of the defendant's version of the facts. For one thing, sometimes a plaintiff's allegation, as stated, is true (and thus admitted by the defendant). However, it is incomplete. If all you do is admit the allegation, you may harm your client's defence. By interviewing your client carefully, you may discover additional information that either neutralizes the plaintiff's allegation or turns it to the defendant's advantage.

Even if a plaintiff's allegation is denied by the defendant, the defence should contain alternative allegations that provide the defendant's version of the facts. Denying everything is not, by itself, a defence. You must also put forward allegations of fact that support the **theory of the defence**—that is, the defendant's grounds for disputing the plaintiff's claim.

BOX 6.2

Drafting the Defence: What Is Relevant?

In the paragraphs below, the fact situation according to the defendant in *Greco v. Hardwick* is given with the relevant facts emphasized in bold type. A brief explanation of why the facts are relevant follows each paragraph.

> You work for Paxton Limones PC, 82 Main Street, Suite 11, Brampton, Ontario L1N 2P3 TEL: 905 888 9999 FAX: 905 888 0000.
>
> Your client is James Hardwick. **James lives at 128 George Court in Brampton. He was recently served with a claim for $5,000.00 plus interest by the plaintiff, Juliette Greco, who is his neighbour and who lives at 126 George Court.**

This information has procedural relevance, but it is not relevant for purposes of drafting the defence.

The information is relevant because it is an admission by the defendant that he received the claim. Your next question should be, when and how was he served? You need to know in order to decide whether the deadline for delivering a defence is approaching or has passed. If the deadline has passed, you should contact the court immediately to find out if he has been noted in default.

> **James tells you that he asked Juliette for the money last spring** because she had always been friendly with them, and seemed like a nice person. She had the Hardwick family over for supper a few times, and let their sons use her pool. He needed the money to pay off some old credit card debts.
>
> When **he borrowed the money**, he thought he would be getting a lot more back on his income tax refund than he ended up getting. That is why **he signed the promissory note agreeing to the August 2, 20— repayment date**. If he had known that he was going to be audited and end up paying tax, he would never have signed the note.

The action is a liquidated claim for collection of a debt. The bold pieces above are relevant to the defence, because they are admissions that James asked for, and accepted, the money, and signed the promissory note. None of those allegations are in dispute.

James's motives for asking for and accepting the money are irrelevant to any issue in this action. His family's relationship with the plaintiff, and his personal opinion as to Juliette's "niceness" or otherwise, are also irrelevant.

> As soon as he got the tax assessment from the CRA, **he spoke to Juliette about his situation, and offered to do chores around her house and yard instead of paying her cash. She seemed to be pleased with this arrangement. The agreement was that he would perform general yard maintenance (including some late-season snow removal and spring yard clean-up), take care of the pool, and take care of her pets (including walking the dog twice a day and cleaning up after him) for the rest of the summer, and that would take care of the loan. He insists that Juliette agreed to this, although he never got anything from her in writing. He thought a written agreement was unnecessary, because they were friends.**

This information is relevant because, if it can be proven, it establishes (1) that upon defaulting in payment of the note, James took prompt action to remedy the default; (2) that the remedy proposed by James was providing services in lieu of cash payment; and (3) the terms of the unwritten (oral) agreement between the parties. Unwritten contracts are enforceable, so long as there is persuasive evidence of offer, acceptance, and consideration.

Some of the information is personal opinion (for example, the last sentence), but it goes to establishing the "neighbourly" relationship and provides plausible grounds for the informal, unwritten contract for services between the plaintiff and the defendant.

More detail is required about the nature and extent of the services performed. Also, the defendant will have to provide estimates from contractors or some other form of evidence as to the monetary value of those services.

> **When Juliette went away on a couple of trips, she left him her house key and the code to the security system, so that he could get into the house while she was away. He completed all the work they had agreed upon. Then he got a letter from her by registered mail in August, demanding payment of the promissory note. He didn't know what was going on, and when he tried to speak to Juliette about it, she got very impatient and would not answer his questions.**

Giving her house key and security code to James supports his allegation that his services were accepted by Juliette and performed with her knowledge and consent.

The allegation that he completed all the work agreed on goes to proving that he complied with the terms of the unwritten contract, as does his request for an explanation when she sent him the first demand letter.

> James's wife, Pamela, was the one who opened the letter from Juliette demanding payment. She was furious. One evening when they were having a few drinks with friends in the backyard, they said some things they probably shouldn't have. Juliette must have overheard, because shortly after that she left a message on their answering machine telling the boys not to use her pool. **That was when James stopped doing any work for her. And shortly after that, he got another letter, demanding payment.**

This is relevant because it provides the approximate date at which he stopped providing services (mid-August).

The demand letters may also go to establishing the plaintiff's breach of the terms of the oral contract. This will have to be expressed in neutral terms in the defendant's claim.

> James thinks it's all a "woman problem." He thinks Pamela was jealous of Juliette, and Juliette was resentful of Pamela because Pamela has a husband and two children, and she doesn't. **He reckons he performed at least $6,000.00 worth of unpaid work for Juliette since he signed the promissory note.**

The value of the services performed is relevant if it is supported by the evidence. The defendant will have to obtain qualified contractors' estimates as to the value of the work done, or some equivalent.

If, as James alleges, the value of the services provided by James is greater than the amount he owes Juliette, he may have grounds for a defendant's claim against Juliette.

DRAFTING THE DEFENCE

Go back and read the fact situation and discussion in *Greco v. Hardwick* in chapter 4 at pages 118-119. Also read the plaintiff's claim in *Greco v. Hardwick* in appendix 4.3.

Now, assume that you have been retained to act for the defendant, James Hardwick (see box 6.2).

When going over the client notes in box 6.2 above, you must also decide which paragraphs in the plaintiff's claim are admitted by the defendant, and which are denied. Excerpts from Schedule A to Ms. Greco's claim are provided below. Each is followed by a discussion of how you should consider dealing with the plaintiff's allegations when drafting the defence.

Schedule A

1. The plaintiff claims:
   (a) Liquidated damages of $5,000.00;
   (b) Pre- and post-judgment interest at a rate of 10% per annum from the date of default until such time as any amounts owing are paid in full in accordance with the terms of the promissory note dated April 1, 20—;
   (c) In the alternative, pre- and post-judgment interest in accordance with the *Courts of Justice Act*;
   (d) Her costs of this action; and
   (e) Such further and other relief as this Honourable Court deems just.

The prayer for relief does not contain allegations of fact. It does not have to be admitted or denied.

2. The plaintiff is an individual residing in the City of Brampton in the Province of Ontario.

Admit. The plaintiff's address is not in dispute.

3. The defendant is an individual residing at 128 George Court in the City of Brampton in the Province of Ontario.

Admit. The defendant's address is not in dispute.

4. Pursuant to a promissory note dated April 1, 20—, the plaintiff loaned the defendant the sum of $5,000.00. According to the terms of the note, the entire sum was to be repaid in full by the defendant on or before August 2, 20—. In the event of default, interest became due and owing on the balance owing at a rate of 10% per annum from the date of default until such time as all amounts owing were paid in full.

Admit. James does not dispute that he signed the note, nor does he dispute its terms.

5. The defendant failed to pay the amount owing on or before August 2, 20—.

6. In spite of repeated demands for payment, both spoken and written, the defendant has failed to pay anything whatsoever on account of the amount owing to the plaintiff.

What about these two paragraphs? Why does James believe that, although he took the money, he should not have to pay it back? What is the substance of his defence to the plaintiff's claim for money? James should admit that he failed to pay the amount owing but allege that he provided unpaid services in lieu of payment, with the plaintiff's knowledge and consent.

James's defence is reproduced in appendix 6.1 to this chapter.

Are There Grounds for a Defendant's Claim?

GENERAL

A defendant's claim is governed by Rule 10 of the *Rules of the Small Claims Court*.
A defendant may make a claim:

1. against the plaintiff (Rule 10.01(1)(a)); or

2. against any other person, including a co-defendant or a third party who is not named in the plaintiff's claim, based on a transaction or occurrence relied on by the plaintiff, or related to the plaintiff's claim (Rule 10.01(1)(b)); or

3. against the plaintiff and any other person in accordance with Rule 10.01(1)(b).

A defendant making a defendant's claim may bring any person into the action commenced by the plaintiff, so long as the basis for the defendant's claim against that person arises out of a transaction or occurrence relied on by the plaintiff or is related to the plaintiff's claim (Rule 10.01(1)(b)).

The defendant's claim must be issued (that is, sealed, dated, and signed) by the clerk in the same way as a plaintiff's claim. This must take place within 20 days of the date on which the defence is filed, or after that time but before trial or default, with leave of the court (Rule 10.01(2)). Often a defence will be filed and a defendant's claim issued at the same time. Occasionally the grounds for a defendant's claim will not come to your attention until after the defence has been filed. If this occurs when you are outside the 20-day limit set by Rule 10.01(2), the court may order an extension of the time for making a defendant's claim, so long as the court is satisfied that you have good grounds for making a defendant's claim and a reasonable explanation for the delay.

The court file number assigned to a defendant's claim will be the same as that assigned to the plaintiff's claim. On the Form 10A, the defendant and plaintiff in the plaintiff's action switch roles. The defendant becomes the plaintiff by defendant's claim, and the plaintiff becomes the defendant by defendant's claim.

The defendant's claim will be tried with the plaintiff's claim unless to do so will complicate or delay the trial of the plaintiff's claim or cause undue prejudice to any party, in which case the court may order separate trials or direct that the defendant's claim proceed as a separate action (Rule 10.04).

The defendant's claim must be served personally or by an alternative to personal service on the other parties. A party who wishes to dispute the defendant's claim or a third party who wishes to dispute the plaintiff's claim may, within 20 days after service of the defendant's claim, file a defence with the clerk, together with copies for all parties or persons against whom the defendant's or plaintiff's claim is made (Rule 10.03(1)). If a defendant by defendant's claim fails to file a defence within the prescribed time, she may be noted in default. However, the clerk cannot sign default judgment against a defendant by defendant's claim who has been noted in default. Judgment against a defendant by defendant's claim who has been noted in default must be obtained at trial or on motion (Rules 10.05(2) and 11.04).

DRAFTING A DEFENDANT'S CLAIM: WHAT IS RELEVANT?

The principles for drafting a defendant's claim are the same as those for drafting a plaintiff's claim. You must review the plaintiff's claim and your notes of what the defendant said, and pick out the pieces that form a basis for the defendant's claim. You must also ensure that the defendant has provided documentary or other evidence to substantiate a claim for money.

See box 4.10 in chapter 4 at pages 118-119, and review the annotated client notes in *Greco v. Hardwick* in box 6.2 at pages 206-207 of this chapter. The defendant's claim of James Hardwick is reproduced in appendix 6.2 to this chapter.

DEFENCE TO DEFENDANT'S CLAIM

A party who wishes to dispute the defendant's claim or a third party who wishes to dispute the plaintiff's claim may, within 20 days after service of the defendant's claim, file a defence with the clerk (Rule 10.03(1)). The party filing the defence shall attach to the defence any documents upon which the defence is based. The party shall provide copies of the defence for all other parties or persons against whom the defendant's or plaintiff's claim is made. The clerk shall serve a copy of the defence on each party by mail or by fax (Rules 10.03(2) and 8.01(3)).

A **third party** is a person who is not a party to an agreement or transaction, but who may have rights or obligations with respect to the agreement or transaction, or whose presence is necessary to enable the court to adjudicate effectively on the issues in the proceeding.

See appendix 6.3 for Ms. Greco's defence to the defendant's claim.

When Should You Make a Proposal of Terms of Payment?

A good defence is a defence that has legal merit and that can be supported by the evidence.

Many Small Claims Court cases are for the collection of an unpaid debt of some kind. The range of defences to a claim for money are limited. For example, it is not a defence to say, "Yes, I owe the plaintiff the money, but I can't afford to pay her back right now." Inability to pay does not, by itself, absolve a debtor from liability for a debt.

As a paralegal, you have a professional duty to encourage compromise and settlement. If you are advising a defendant who does not have a good defence, you should encourage your client to make a proposal of terms of payment. Page 2 of Form 9A gives the defendant the option of making a proposal of terms of payment for all or part of the plaintiff's claim. If the defendant makes a proposal of terms of payment for part of the plaintiff's claim, the other part of the claim remains in dispute. The factual grounds for the partial dispute must be clearly stated in the schedule to the defence. Copies of any documentary evidence on which you intend to rely in support of the partial dispute should be attached to the defence.

Before advising a client to file a partial dispute, you must be satisfied that there are legal grounds for the partial dispute, and that there is evidence to support it.

See figure 6.3 for an overview of what happens when a defendant admits all or partial liability.

Proposal of Terms of Payment—No Dispute by Plaintiff (Rules 9.03(1) and (2))

LUMP SUM PAYMENT

A defendant who admits liability for all or part of the claim may choose to pay the entire amount admitted to be owing in one lump sum payment, instead of in installments. You should consider requesting that your client pay the settlement funds to you in trust by certified cheque. The funds may then be deposited to your mixed trust account, and paid by you to the plaintiff or the plaintiff's representative.

If the client pays the settlement funds to you in trust by regular cheque, you should make sure the cheque has cleared before paying the money out of trust to the other side.

When the amount agreed to be owing has been paid in full, both parties should sign full and final releases. You should also consider filing a Request for Clerk's Order on Consent (Form 11.2A) signed by the parties with the court indicating that payment has been made in full. See figure 6.4.

FIGURE 6.3 Small Claims Court Procedure: Defendant Admits All or Partial Liability

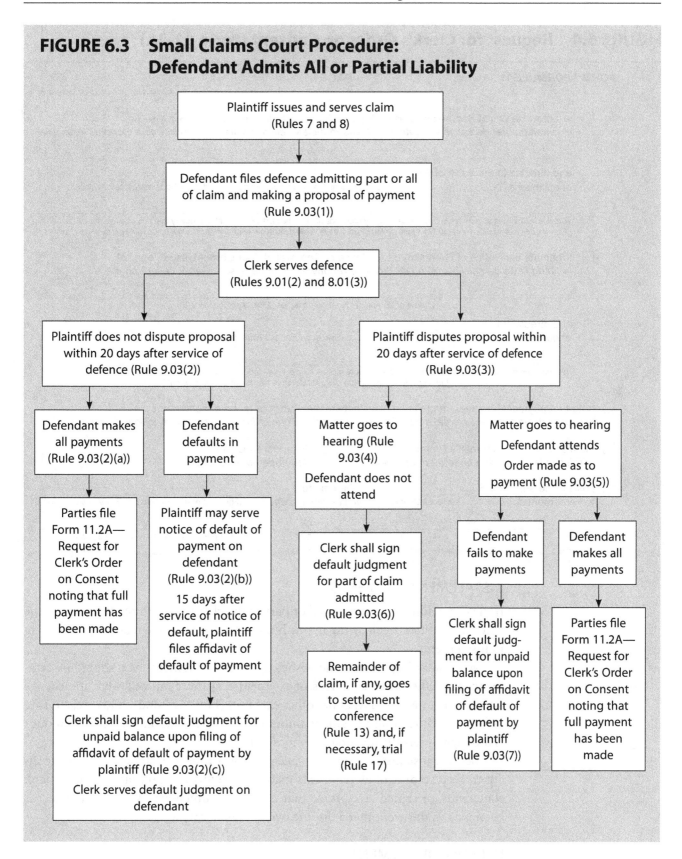

FIGURE 6.4   Request for Clerk's Order on Consent (Form 11.2A)

FORM / *FORMULE* 11.2A   PAGE 3

Claim No. / *N° de la demande*

☐ withdraw the Writ of Seizure and Sale of Personal Property issued against: (Name of debtor(s)
   le retrait du bref de saisie-exécution de biens meubles délivré contre :   (*Nom du/de la/des débiteur(s)/débitrice(s)*)

and directed to the bailiff of the   :
et adressé à l'huissier de   (Small Claims Court location / *Emplacement de la Cour des petites créances*)

(Provide instructions about what is to be done with any proceeds held by the clerk of the court or property that has been seized by the bailiff.
/ *Donnez des instructions sur ce qu'il faut faire de tout produit de la vente détenu par le greffier du tribunal ou de tout bien saisi par l'huissier.*)

☐ terminate the Notice of Garnishment or Notice of Renewal of Garnishment issued against:
   la fin de l'avis de saisie-arrêt ou de l'avis de renouvellement de la saisie-arrêt délivré contre :

(Name of debtor(s) / *Nom du/de la/des débiteur(s)/débitrice(s)*)

and directed to   :
et adressé à   (Name of garnishee / *Nom du tiers saisi*)

(Provide instructions about what is to be done with any money held by the clerk of the court. / *Donnez des instructions sur ce qu'il
faut faire de toute somme d'argent détenue par le greffier du tribunal.*)

☐ note that payment has been made in full satisfaction of an order or terms of settlement
   le constat qu'un paiement intégral a été effectué en exécution d'une ordonnance ou des conditions de la transaction

☐ dismiss the: ☐ Plaintiff's Claim   ☐ Defendant's Claim
   le rejet de la :   *demande du demandeur*   *demande du défendeur*

☐ costs in the amount of $ _____ , to be paid to _____
   le versement de   (Amount / *Montant*) $ *au titre des dépens à*   (Name of party(ies) / *Nom de la ou des parties*)

by _____
par   (Name of party(ies) / *Nom de la ou des parties*)

INSTALLMENT PAYMENTS

If the client admits liability for all or part of the claim but cannot afford to pay the amount admitted to be owing in one lump sum payment, she may propose paying in installments.

When advising a client who wishes to pay in installments, you should be careful to make the proposed terms of payment realistic. Find out what the client's after-tax income is and what her other expenses (housing, food, child care, etc.) are before recommending a payment amount. If the agreed-upon installment amount is too high, it sets the defendant up for failure.

Because installment payments take place over time, you should advise your client to keep records of all payments made, in the form of cancelled cheques, bank statements, or signed receipts, so that there is documentary evidence of what has been paid in the event that a dispute over payment arises.

DEFAULT OF PAYMENT

If the plaintiff does not dispute the defendant's proposal of terms of payment within 20 days after service of the defence, the proposal is deemed to be accepted and the defendant is required to make the payments as if the proposal were a court order (Rules 9.03(2)(a) and 9.03(3)).

BOX 6.3

Sample Proposal of Terms of Payment

France Nguyen advanced $3,000.00 to Mavis Mirren on January 1, 20—. The parties agreed that interest would be charged on the money at a rate of 7% per year, and that the entire amount plus interest would be paid in full on or before June 1, 20—. Ms. Mirren failed to pay the amount owing on or before June 1, 20—. After several demands for payment, Ms. Nguyen commenced an action in Newmarket Small Claims Court for the amount owing. Ms. Mirren was served with the plaintiff's claim on July 20, 20—.

On July 28, 20—, Ms. Mirren filed a defence with a proposal for payment of the entire amount owing in installments of $300.00 per month, payable on the first day of each month. See appendix 6.4 for the proposal of terms of payment in *Nguyen v. Mirren*.

If the defendant defaults on any payment, the plaintiff may serve the defendant with a notice of default of payment (Form 20L). If the defendant does not pay within 15 days of receiving the notice of default of payment, the plaintiff may file an affidavit of default of payment (Form 20M) with the court. The affidavit of default states the following:

1. that the defendant failed to make a payment in accordance with the proposal;

2. the amount paid by the defendant and the unpaid balance; and

3. that 15 days have passed since the defendant was served with a notice of default of payment.

The affidavit of service of the notice of default of payment should be filed along with the affidavit of default of payment.

On the filing of the affidavit of default and the affidavit of service of the notice of default, the clerk is required to sign judgment for the unpaid balance of the undisputed amount. The judgment may be enforced against the defendant under Rule 20.

BOX 6.4

Proposal for Payment: Default of Payment

See box 6.3 above, and appendix 6.4. The defence was served on the plaintiff by mail on August 1, 20—. As of August 27, the plaintiff had failed to file a dispute. The defendant made two payments, one on September 1 and one on October 1, each in the amount of $300.00. She defaulted on the November payment.

See appendix 6.5 for examples of a notice of default of payment (Form 20L), an affidavit of default of payment (Form 20M) with detailed calculation of the amount owing, and a default judgment (Form 11B).

Pre-judgment interest was discussed in chapter 5 at pages 162-165. For the affidavit of default of payment (Form 20M), note that when calculating interest owing, you are required to adjust the amount owing from time to time as payments are received. See figure 6.5 below, and the detailed calculation of the amount owing attached to the Form 20M at appendix 6.5.

FIGURE 6.5   Affidavit of Default of Payment (Form 20M)

4. The unpaid balance is calculated as follows:
Le solde impayé est calculé de la façon suivante :

(A) **DEBT** (amount of judgment) $ _____
   LA CRÉANCE (montant du jugement) $

(B) **PRE-JUDGMENT INTEREST** calculated
   LES INTÉRÊTS ANTÉRIEURS AU JUGEMENT calculés

   on the sum of $ _____   at the rate of _____ %
   sur la somme de $ *au taux de*   *pour cent*

   per annum from _____ , 20 ___ to _____ , 20 ___ ,
   par an du   *au*

   being _____ days. $ _____
   soit   *jours.* $

> **NOTE:**   Calculation of interest is always on the amount owing from time to time as
>   payments are received. This is true for both pre-judgment and post-judgment
>   interest. Attach a separate sheet setting out how you calculated the total amount
>   of any pre/post-judgment interest.
>
> **REMARQUE :**   *Les intérêts doivent toujours être calculés sur la somme due. Le calcul doit tenir*
>   *compte des paiements reçus de temps à autre. Ceci s'applique autant aux intérêts*
>   *antérieurs au jugement qu'aux intérêts postérieurs au jugement. Annexez une*
>   *feuille distincte indiquant comment vous avez calculé le montant total des intérêts*
>   *antérieurs et postérieurs au jugement.*

SCR 9.03-20M (June 1, 2009 / *1er juin 2009*) CSD   **Continued on next page / *Suite à la page suivante***

Proposal of Terms of Payment—Dispute by Plaintiff (Rules 9.03(3) to (7))

The plaintiff may refuse to accept the defendant's proposal of terms of payment by filing a request to the clerk for a terms of payment hearing (Form 9B) within 20 days after service of the defence (Rule 9.03(3)). See figure 6.6.

On receiving a request for a terms of payment hearing, the clerk shall fix a date and time for the hearing and serve a notice of hearing on the parties by mail or by fax. When fixing the date, the clerk must allow for a reasonable notice period from the date the request is received (Rule 9.03(4)).

If the defendant is an individual, the clerk is also required to serve a financial information form (Form 20I) on the defendant (Rule 9.03(5)). The defendant is required to complete the financial information form and serve it on the plaintiff/creditor before the terms of payment hearing (Rules 9.03(4.2) and (4.3)). The financial information form *shall not* be filed with the court.

A blank financial information form can be found in appendix 6.6 to this chapter. The form is intended to give the plaintiff/creditor information about the de-

FIGURE 6.6   Request to Clerk for Terms of Payment Hearing (Form 9B)

ONTARIO

Superior Court of Justice
Cour supérieure de justice

Request to Clerk
Demande au greffier

Form / *Formule* 9B Ont. Reg. No. / *Règl. de l'Ont.* : 258/98

Small Claims Court / *Cour des petites créances de*   Claim No. / *N° de la demande*

Address / *Adresse*

Phone number / *Numéro de téléphone*

BETWEEN / *ENTRE*

Plaintiff(s) / *Demandeur(s)/demanderesse(s)*

and / *et*

Defendant(s) / *Défendeur(s)/défenderesse(s)*

TO THE CLERK OF THE _____   **SMALL CLAIMS COURT:**
AU GREFFIER DE LA COUR   (Name of Small Claims Court location / *Emplacement de la*
DES PETITES CRÉANCES DE   *Cour des petites créances*) :

My name is _____   **and I request that the clerk of the court:**
Je m'appelle   (Name of party/representative / *Nom de la partie ou du/de la*   *et je demande au greffier du tribunal*
                              représentant(e))   *de faire ce qui suit :*

(Check appropriate box(es). / Cochez la ou les cases appropriées.*)*

☐   note defendant(s) _____
    constater le ou les défendeurs   (Name of defendant(s) / *Nom du/de la/des défendeur(s)/défenderesse(s)*)

    in default for failing to file a Defence (Form 9A) within the prescribed time period [R. 11.01(1)].
    en défaut pour n'avoir pas déposé de défense (formule 9A) dans le délai prescrit [par. 11.01 (1)].

☐   schedule an assessment hearing (all defendants have been noted in default) [R. 11.03(2)(b)].
    fixe▢ date d'une audience d'évaluation (tous les défendeurs ont été constatés en défaut) [alinéa
    1▢3 (2) b)].

☐   schedule a terms of payment hearing because I dispute the defendant's proposed terms of payment
    contained in the Defence (Form 9A) [R. 9.03(3)].

fendant's financial situation, her ability to pay the amount owing, whether she has any assets against which a judgment can be enforced, etc.

The terms of payment hearing is not a formal trial. It is more in the nature of a settlement conference—in other words, an informal meeting with the object of working out terms of payment that are acceptable to the plaintiff and payable by the defendant.

A terms of payment hearing may be heard by a referee or "other person" (someone other than a judge or deputy judge). A **referee** is a non-judge who is authorized by the Rules to hear terms of payment hearings.

If the defendant does not appear at the hearing, the clerk may sign a default judgment against the defendant for the part of the claim that has been admitted (Rule 9.03(6)). The default judgment for that part of the claim is served by the clerk on all parties named in the claim by mail or fax (Rule 8.01(4)).

If both parties appear, they may make submissions as to the defendant's ability to pay and in what amount, and an order may be made by the referee as to terms of payment by the defendant (Rule 9.03(5)).

If the defendant fails to make payments in accordance with the order, the plaintiff may file an affidavit of default stating the amount paid and the balance owing, and the clerk shall sign judgment for the amount owing, unless the referee or other person presiding at the terms of payment hearing specifies otherwise in the order as to terms of payment (Rule 9.03(7)).

Summary—Defendant Not in Default

A defendant who is not in default has the following options:

1. dispute the full claim;

2. dispute part of the claim and propose terms of payment for the part that is not disputed; or

3. admit the full claim and propose terms of payment.

A defendant who disputes the full claim must file a defence. If the defendant has a claim against the plaintiff or a claim against any other person (including a co-defendant or a third party not named in the plaintiff's claim), the defendant must also issue a defendant's claim within 20 days of filing the defence.

The clerk will serve the defence. The defendant is responsible for serving the defendant's claim on all parties named in the defendant's claim by personal service or by an alternative to personal service (Rule 8.01(1)).

A defendant who disputes part of the plaintiff's claim must file a defence for the disputed portion of the claim. The defendant must indicate on the Form 9A that she does not dispute the remainder of the claim, and make a proposal of terms of payment. The defendant may pay the undisputed part of the plaintiff's claim by a lump sum payment of the full amount that is not in dispute, or she may propose payment by installments. If the plaintiff does not dispute the defendant's proposal of terms of payment within 20 days after service of the defence, the plaintiff is deemed to accept the terms of the proposal and the defendant may make payment in accordance with the terms of the proposal as if it were a court order.

A defendant who admits the entire claim must file a defence indicating the non-dispute and proposing terms of payment. If the plaintiff does not dispute the defendant's proposal of terms of payment within 20 days after service of the defence, the plaintiff is deemed to accept the terms of the proposal and the defendant may make payment in accordance with the terms of the proposal as if it were a court order.

A plaintiff who receives a proposal of terms of payment may dispute the proposed terms and request a terms of payment hearing. This must be done within 20 days after service of the defence. The clerk will schedule a hearing and serve all parties by mail or fax. An individual defendant will be required to complete a financial information form and serve it on the creditor before the hearing. The defendant shall not file the financial information form with the court.

At the terms of payment hearing, the referee or another person may make an order as to terms of payment by the defendant.

DEFENDANT NOTED IN DEFAULT

A defendant who has been noted in default should bring the plaintiff's claim with him to the client interview, along with the default judgment if one has been entered, and any **enforcement documents** that he has been served with. Enforcement documents are notices of steps taken by the plaintiff/creditor or ordered by the court to enforce the judgment. For example, a debtor may receive notice of a garnishment of his employment income by service of a notice of garnishment. Other examples of enforcement documents are a notice of garnishment hearing, a notice of examination of debtor, and a notice of contempt hearing. Enforcement of orders will be discussed in chapter 11.

The procedural consequences of being noted in default are significant. A defendant who has been noted in default is not entitled to file a defence or take any other steps in the proceeding, except making a motion to set aside the noting in default and default judgment, if any, without leave (permission) of the court or the plaintiff's consent (Rule 11.05(1)).

Any step in the proceeding may be taken without the consent of a defendant who has been noted in default (Rule 11.05(2)).

A defendant who has been noted in default is not entitled to notice of any step in the proceeding taken by other parties, except the following (Rule 11.05(3)):

1. service of default judgment (Rule 11.02(3));

2. amendment of claim or defence (Rule 12.01);

3. motion after judgment (Rule 15.01(6)); and

4. post-judgment enforcement proceedings against a debtor (Rule 20).

As is the case whenever your client is a defendant, the first thing you have to do is go over the plaintiff's claim with him, and satisfy yourself that he has a good defence and a reasonable explanation for the default. You should then contact the other side to see if they will consent to a setting aside of the noting in default, the default judgment (if any), and any steps taken to enforce the judgment under Rule 20. If they are willing to consent, a consent for clerk's order (Form 11.2B) may be completed, signed by both parties or their paralegals or lawyers, and filed with the court. The defendant may then file a defence on whatever terms the parties agree to. These terms should be included in the clerk's order.

If the plaintiff does not consent to a clerk's order setting aside the noting in default, you must make a motion to the court for an order setting aside the noting in default and any other appropriate relief. Motions, including motions for set aside of a noting in default, will be discussed in more detail in chapter 7.

CHAPTER SUMMARY

A defendant who was served personally with the plaintiff's claim has 20 days from the date of service to file a defence with the court. If the defendant was served by an alternative to personal service, the time for filing a defence will vary, depending on the type of service.

A defendant may dispute the full claim, or admit all or part of the claim and make a proposal of terms of payment. Where only part of the claim is admitted, a defence must be filed with respect to the part in dispute. The defence or partial defence should state all the facts the defendant is relying on in brief sentences using non-technical language. Copies of any documents the defendant intends to rely on should be attached to the defence.

The defendant may make a claim against the plaintiff, or against any other person (including a co-defendant or a third party who is not named in the plaintiff's claim), or against the plaintiff and any other person, based on a transaction or occurrence relied on by the plaintiff or related to the plaintiff's claim. This is called a defendant's claim. On the defendant's claim, the defendant becomes the plaintiff by defendant's claim, and the plaintiff becomes the defendant by defendant's claim. The defendant's claim must be issued within 20 days of the date on which the defence is filed, unless the court extends the time. The court file number assigned to the defendant's claim will be the same as that assigned to the plaintiff's claim.

Defendants named in a defendant's claim must file defences within 20 days of service of the defendant's claim. If they fail to do so and are noted in default, judgment against them may only be obtained at trial or on a motion for judgment. The clerk may not sign judgment against a defendant who is in default in a defendant's claim.

If the defendant admits all or part of the claim and makes a proposal of terms of payment, the plaintiff has 20 days from service of the defence to dispute the proposal. If the plaintiff does not dispute the proposal during the 20-day period, the plaintiff is deemed to accept the proposal, and the defendant may begin making payments as if the proposal were a court order. If the defendant defaults in payment, the plaintiff may serve a notice of default of payment on the defendant. When 15 days have passed after service of the notice of default of payment, the plaintiff may file an affidavit of default of payment with the court, and the clerk is required to sign judgment against the defendant for the part of the claim that was admitted. Any part of the claim that was disputed will go to settlement conference and, if necessary, to trial.

The plaintiff may dispute the defendant's proposal of terms of payment within 20 days from service of the defence and request a terms of payment hearing. The clerk will serve a notice of hearing on all parties. The clerk will also serve individual defendants with a financial information form, which must be completed by the defendant and served on the plaintiff before the hearing. The financial information form shall not be filed with the court.

If the defendant does not attend at the terms of payment hearing, the clerk may sign judgment for the part of the claim that has been admitted.

If the defendant attends at the hearing, the court may hear submissions from both parties and make an order for terms of payment. If the defendant fails to make a payment, the plaintiff may file an affidavit of default of payment with the court, and the clerk is required to sign judgment against the defendant for the part of the claim that was admitted.

If the defendant fails to file a defence within the time prescribed by the Rules, the plaintiff may note the defendant in default. In a liquidated claim, the plaintiff may also request that default judgment be signed against the defendant. A defendant who has been noted in default shall not file a defence or take any other step in the proceeding, except for a motion to set aside the noting in default, without leave of the court or the plaintiff's consent.

KEY TERMS

admission

denial

enforcement documents

referee

theory of the defence

third party

REFERENCES

Courts of Justice Act, RSO 1990, c. C.43.

Rules of Civil Procedure, RRO 1990, Reg. 194.

Rules of the Small Claims Court, O. Reg. 258/98.

IN-CLASS EXERCISE

You work for Prior Mustafa LLP, 22 County Court Boulevard, Brampton, Ontario A1A 2B3 TEL: 905 111 2222 FAX: 905 111 2233.

Your client is Jeanne Renoir. Ms. Renoir lives at 78 Calculator Crescent, Milton, Ontario L2M 1S4 TEL: 905 880 9999.

One week ago, on January 9, 20—, Ms. Renoir was served with the attached plaintiff's claim. Please read the plaintiff's claim. Then review Ms. Renoir's comments, which follow the plaintiff's claim. Draft a defence and defendant's claim for Ms. Renoir. Date the defence and defendant's claim January 15, 20—. Make a list of the documents you would need to attach to the defendant's claim as part of your documentary disclosure pursuant to Rule 10.01(4)2.

IN-CLASS EXERCISE—Form 7A

ONTARIO

Superior Court of Justice
Cour supérieure de justice

Plaintiff's Claim
Demande du demandeur

Form / *Formule* 7A Ont. Reg. No. / *Règl. de l'Ont.* : 258/98

Seal / *Sceau*

Milton

Small Claims Court / *Cour des petites créances de*
491 Steeles Ave. E.
Milton, Ontario
L9T 1Y7

Address / *Adresse*

905 878 4165

Phone number / *Numéro de téléphone*

9876

Claim No. / *N° de la demande*

Plaintiff No. 1 / *Demandeur n° 1*

☐ Additional plaintiff(s) listed on attached Form 1A.
Le ou les demandeurs additionnels sont mentionnés sur la formule 1A ci-jointe.

☐ Under 18 years of age.
Moins de 18 ans.

Last name, or name of company / *Nom de famille ou nom de la compagnie*		
Excellent Fences Inc.		
First name / *Premier prénom*	Second name / *Deuxième prénom*	Also known as / *Également connu(e) sous le nom de*
Address (street number, apt., unit) / *Adresse (numéro et rue, app., unité)*		
c/o Franklin Kafka PC		
City/Town / *Cité/ville*	Province	Phone no. / *N° de téléphone*
Postal code / *Code postal*		Fax no. / *N° de télécopieur*
Representative / *Représentant(e)*		LSUC # / *N° du BHC*
Franklin Kafka PC Attention: Frank Kafka		**######**
Address (street number, apt., unit) / *Adresse (numéro et rue, app., unité)*		
1238 Hausmann Boulevard, Suite 2		
City/Town / *Cité/ville*	Province	Phone no. / *N° de téléphone*
Milton	**Ontario**	**905 663 4444**
Postal code / *Code postal*		Fax no. / *N° de télécopieur*
L6V 8Z9		**905 663 5555**

Defendant No. 1 / *Défendeur n° 1*

☐ Additional defendant(s) listed on attached Form 1A.
Le ou les défendeurs additionnels sont mentionnés sur la formule 1A ci-jointe.

☐ Under 18 years of age.
Moins de 18 ans.

Last name, or name of company / *Nom de famille ou nom de la compagnie*		
Renoir		
First name / *Premier prénom*	Second name / *Deuxième prénom*	Also known as / *Également connu(e) sous le nom de*
Jeanne	**Marie**	**Jean Renoir**
Address (street number, apt., unit) / *Adresse (numéro et rue, app., unité)*		
78 Calculator Crescent		
City/Town / *Cité/ville*	Province	Phone no. / *N° de téléphone*
Milton	**Ontario**	**905 880 9999**
Postal code / *Code postal*		Fax no. / *N° de télécopieur*
L2M 1S4		
Representative / *Représentant(e)*		LSUC # / *N° du BHC*
Address (street number, apt., unit) / *Adresse (numéro et rue, app., unité)*		
City/Town / *Cité/ville*	Province	Phone no. / *N° de téléphone*
Postal code / *Code postal*		Fax no. / *N° de télécopieur*

IN-CLASS EXERCISE—Form 7A   Continued

FORM / *FORMULE* 7A   **PAGE 2**   <u>9876</u>

Claim No. / *N° de la demande*

REASONS FOR CLAIM AND DETAILS / *MOTIFS DE LA DEMANDE ET PRÉCISIONS*

Explain what happened, including where and when. Then explain how much money you are claiming or what goods you want returned.

Expliquez ce qui s'est passé, en précisant où et quand. Ensuite indiquez la somme d'argent que vous demandez ou les biens dont vous demandez la restitution, explication à l'appui.

If you are relying on any documents, you **MUST** attach copies to the claim. If evidence is lost or unavailable, you **MUST** explain why it is not attached.

*Si vous vous appuyez sur des documents, vous **DEVEZ** en annexer des copies à la demande. Si une preuve est perdue ou n'est pas disponible, vous **DEVEZ** expliquer pourquoi elle n'est pas annexée.*

What happened?   **See Schedule A attached**
Where?
When?

Que s'est-il
passé?
Où?
Quand?

IN-CLASS EXERCISE—Form 7A   Continued

FORM / *FORMULE* 7A   PAGE 3   9876
Claim No. / *N° de la demande*

How much? $ 3523.00
Combien?   (Principal amount claimed / *Somme demandée*) $

☒   ADDITIONAL PAGES ARE ATTACHED BECAUSE MORE ROOM WAS NEEDED.
     DES FEUILLES SUPPLÉMENTAIRES SONT ANNEXÉES EN RAISON DU MANQUE D'ESPACE.

The plaintiff also claims pre-judgment interest from September 1, 20--   **under:**
Le demandeur demande aussi des intérêts   (Date)   *conformément à :*
antérieurs au jugement de

(Check only   ☐ the *Courts of Justice Act*
one box /   *la* **Loi sur les tribunaux judiciaires**
Cochez une
seule case)   ☒ **an agreement at the rate of** 10   **% per year**
                       un accord au taux de   **% par an**

and post-judgment interest, and court costs.
et des intérêts postérieurs au jugement, ainsi que les dépens.

Prepared on: **January 7**   , 20 --   _____
Fait le :   (Signature of plaintiff or representative / *Signature du*
                                                          demandeur/de la demanderesse ou du/de la représentant(e))

Issued on: _____ , 20 _____   _____
Délivré le :   (Signature of clerk / *Signature du greffier*)

┌───┐
| **CAUTION TO**   **IF YOU DO NOT FILE A DEFENCE** (Form 9A) with the court within twenty (20) calendar
| **DEFENDANT:**   days after you have been served with this Plaintiff's Claim, judgment may be obtained
| without notice and enforced against you. Forms and self-help materials are available at the
| Small Claims Court and on the following website: www.ontariocourtforms.on.ca.
|
| *AVERTISSEMENT*   *SI VOUS NE DÉPOSEZ PAS DE DÉFENSE* (formule 9A) *auprès du tribunal au plus tard*
| *AU DÉFENDEUR :*   *vingt (20) jours civils après avoir reçu signification de la présente demande du demandeur,*
| *un jugement peut être obtenu sans préavis et être exécuté contre vous. Vous pouvez*
| *obtenir les formules et la documentation à l'usage du client à la Cour des petites créances*
| *et sur le site Web suivant : www.ontariocourtforms.on.ca.*
└───┘

IN-CLASS EXERCISE—Form 7A   Continued

Schedule A

1. The plaintiff claims:

   (a)   The liquidated amount of $3,523.00;

   (b)   Pre- and post-judgment interest at a rate of 10% per year, in accordance with a contract dated April 30, 20— between the parties;

   (c)   In the alternative, pre- and post-judgment interest in accordance with the *Courts of Justice Act*;

   (d)   Its costs of this action; and

   (e)   Such further and other relief as this Honourable Court deems just.

2. The plaintiff is a corporation incorporated under the laws of Ontario carrying on business as a landscape designer.

3. The defendant resides at 78 Calculator Crescent, Milton, Ontario L2M 1S4.

4. By a contract dated April 30, 20—, the plaintiff and the defendant agreed that the plaintiff should provide the following services to the defendant:

   (1)   Build a privacy fence across the bottom of her lot (approximately 50 feet in length), no gate, pressure-treated wood, privacy lattice, 6'0" in height, all posts to be properly anchored and finished with finials;

   (2)   Build a gate on the east side of the house at the top of the garden between neighbour's fence and house, posts to be properly anchored and finished with finials;

   (3)   Build a privacy fence at the top of the lot with gate (approximately 15 feet in length), pressure-treated wood, privacy lattice, 6'0" in height, all posts to be properly anchored and finished with finials.

5. The total cost of the above services was $4,123.00 including applicable taxes.

IN-CLASS EXERCISE—Form 7A   Concluded

6. The defendant paid a deposit of $600.00 at the time of signing the contract on April 30, 20—. In spite of repeated demands, no further payment has been received from the defendant since the job was completed.

7. All services under the contract were completed in a good and workmanlike fashion by September 1, 20—.

8. The amount owing as of this date is $3,523.00 plus interest at a rate of 10% per year in accordance with the terms of the contract dated April 30, 20—.

9. The defendant uses both "Jeanne Renoir" and "Jean Renoir" as her name. The name on her personal cheque is Jeanne Renoir, and she signed the cheque using that name. The name she uses on her business cards is Jean Renoir.

Attached document:

Copy of contract dated April 30, 20— signed by Bill Withers for the plaintiff and Jeanne Renoir

IN-CLASS EXERCISE—Defendant's Comments

Ms. Renoir admits the contents of paragraphs 2 and 3 of the plaintiff's claim.

She admits that she signed a contract with the plaintiff dated April 30, 20— on the terms stated in paragraphs 4 and 5.

She denies the contents of paragraphs 7 and 8.

With respect to the contents of paragraph 6, she admits that she paid a deposit of $600.00 at the time of signing the contract. She denies that any further amount is owing.

The contract dated April 30, 20— stated that all work was to be completed by June 30, 20—. As of that date, the fences were only partly completed. Ms. Renoir adopts rescued greyhounds who have been retired from the track, and requires a large, secure, fenced running space for the dogs. As a direct result of the plaintiff's failure to complete the fence in accordance with the terms of the contract, Ms. Renoir had to board her dogs at a kennel from July 1 to September 17, 20—, at a cost of $2,100.00 including applicable taxes.

While boarding, one of her dogs contracted a skin infection. The cost of veterinary treatment was $517.00.

The work was not done in a good and workmanlike fashion. The contract provided that the supporting posts for the fence were to be properly anchored. Ms. Renoir discussed this with Bill Withers, owner of Excellent Fences Inc., in early June. They agreed that proper anchoring meant in-ground concrete or four-foot bolted metal anchors for the supporting posts. When the fence at the bottom of the property was partly completed, Ms. Renoir inspected it and asked the workers what was being used to anchor it, as she could see no sign of bolted metal anchors. She was assured that the posts were embedded in 12 inches of in-ground concrete.

During a high wind in early October, two of the posts at the top of the property became loose. The hinges on both gates were damaged because of the instability of the supporting posts and the fact that the bottom hinges were installed upside down. When the supporting posts began to shift in the high wind, the hinge pins fell out and the gates came loose and started banging back and forth, damaging the hardware. Ms. Renoir had to hire another contractor to correct the damage. Both gates had to be taken down, reassembled, rehinged, and rehung, at a cost of $976.00. Before this could be done, the supporting posts had to be restabilized with additional concrete, at a cost of $654.00. When the new contractor dug out the area around the supporting posts, he discovered that they were anchored in approximately six inches of concrete.

Please draft a defence and defendant's claim for Ms. Renoir. For the defendant's claim, you will ask for pre- and post-judgment interest at a rate of 10% per year in accordance with the contract dated April 30, 20—, and, in the alternative, pre- and post-judgment interest in accordance with the *Courts of Justice Act* in the prayer for relief.

APPENDIX 6.1   Greco v. Hardwick: Defence (Form 9A)

ONTARIO

Superior Court of Justice
Cour supérieure de justice

Defence / *Défense*
Form / *Formule* 9A Ont. Reg. No. / *Règl. de l'Ont.* : 258/98

Brampton
Small Claims Court / *Cour des petites créances de*
7755 Hurontario Street
Brampton, Ontario
L6W 4T6
Address / *Adresse*

905 456 4700
Phone number / *Numéro de téléphone*

7891
Claim No. / *N° de la demande*

Plaintiff No. 1 / *Demandeur n° 1*

☐ Additional plaintiff(s) listed on attached Form 1A.
Le ou les demandeurs additionnels sont mentionnés sur la formule 1A ci-jointe.

☐ Under 18 years of age.
Moins de 18 ans.

Last name, or name of company / *Nom de famille ou nom de la compagnie*		
Greco		
First name / *Premier prénom* **Juliette**	Second name / *Deuxième prénom*	Also known as / *Également connu(e) sous le nom de*
Address (street number, apt., unit) / *Adresse (numéro et rue, app., unité)* **c/o Prior Mustafa LLP**		
City/Town / *Cité/ville*	Province	Phone no. / *N° de téléphone*
Postal code / *Code postal*		Fax no. / *N° de télécopieur*
Representative / *Représentant(e)* **Prior Mustafa LLP Attention: Paralegal name**		LSUC # / *N° du BHC* **######**
Address (street number, apt., unit) / *Adresse (numéro et rue, app., unité)* **22 County Court Boulevard**		
City/Town / *Cité/ville* **Brampton**	Province **Ontario**	Phone no. / *N° de téléphone* **905 111 2222**
Postal code / *Code postal* **A1A 2B3**		Fax no. / *N° de télécopieur* **905 111 2233**

Defendant No. 1 / *Défendeur n° 1*

☐ Additional defendant(s) listed on attached Form 1A.
Le ou les défendeurs additionnels sont mentionnés sur la formule 1A ci-jointe.

☐ Under 18 years of age.
Moins de 18 ans.

Last name, or name of company / *Nom de famille ou nom de la compagnie*		
Hardwick		
First name / *Premier prénom* **James**	Second name / *Deuxième prénom*	Also known as / *Également connu(e) sous le nom de*
Address (street number, apt., unit) / *Adresse (numéro et rue, app., unité)* **c/o Paxton Limones PC**		
City/Town / *Cité/ville*	Province	Phone no. / *N° de téléphone*
Postal code / *Code postal*		Fax no. / *N° de télécopieur*
Representative / *Représentant(e)* **Paxton Limones PC Attention: Paralegal name**		LSUC # / *N° du BHC* **######**
Address (street number, apt., unit) / *Adresse (numéro et rue, app., unité)* **82 Main Street, Suite 11**		
City/Town / *Cité/ville* **Brampton**	Province **Ontario**	Phone no. / *N° de téléphone* **905 888 9999**
Postal code / *Code postal* **L1N 2P3**		Fax no. / *N° de télécopieur* **905 888 0000**

SCR 9.01-10.03-9A (June 1, 2009 / *1er juin 2009*) CSD

APPENDIX 6.1 Continued

FORM / *FORMULE* 9A **PAGE 2** 7891

Claim No. / *N° de la demande*

THIS DEFENCE IS BEING FILED ON BEHALF OF: (Name(s) of defendant(s))
LA PRÉSENTE DÉFENSE EST DÉPOSÉE AU NOM DE : (Nom du/de la ou des défendeur(s)/défenderesse(s))

James Hardwick

and I/we: (Check as many as apply)
et je/nous : (Cochez la ou les cases qui s'appliquent)

☒ Dispute the claim made against me/us.
  conteste/contestons la demande présentée contre moi/nous.

☐ Admit the full claim and propose the following terms of payment:
  *reconnais/reconnaissons être redevable(s) de la totalité de la demande et propose/proposons les
  modalités de paiement suivantes :*

  $ _____ per _____ commencing _____ , 20 ____ .
  (Amount / *Montant*) *$ par* (Week/month / *semaine/mois*) *à compter du*

☐ Admit part of the claim in the amount of $ _____ and propose the following terms of payment:
  reconnais/reconnaissons être redevable(s) (Amount / *Montant*) *$ et propose/proposons les modalités de
  d'une partie de la demande, soit* *paiement suivantes :*

  $ _____ per _____ commencing _____ , 20 ____ .
  (Amount / *Montant*) *$ par* (Week/month / *semaine/mois*) *à compter du*

REASONS FOR DISPUTING THE CLAIM AND DETAILS:
MOTIFS DE CONTESTATION DE LA DEMANDE ET PRÉCISIONS :

Explain what happened, including where and when. Explain why you do not agree with the claim made against you.
*Expliquez ce qui s'est passé, en précisant où et quand. Expliquez pourquoi vous contestez la demande
présentée contre vous.*

If you are relying on any documents, you **MUST** attach copies to the Defence. If evidence is lost or unavailable,
you **MUST** explain why it is not attached.
*Si vous vous appuyez sur des documents, vous **DEVEZ** en annexer des copies à la défense. Si une preuve est
perdue ou n'est pas disponible, vous **DEVEZ** expliquer pourquoi elle n'est pas annexée.*

What happened?   **See Schedule A attached**
Where?
When?

*Que s'est-il
passé?
Où?
Quand?*

    Continued on next page / *Suite à la page suivante*

APPENDIX 6.1   Continued

Why I/we disagree   See Schedule A attached
with all or part of
the claim: /

Je conteste/Nous
contestons la
totalité ou une
partie de la
demande pour les
motifs suivants :

⊠   ADDITIONAL PAGES ARE ATTACHED BECAUSE MORE ROOM WAS NEEDED.
     DES FEUILLES SUPPLÉMENTAIRES SONT ANNEXÉES EN RAISON DU MANQUE D'ESPACE.

Prepared on: **November 15**   , 20 --   _____
Fait le :   (Signature of defendant or representative /
                                                     Signature du défendeur/de la défenderesse ou du/de la représentant(e))

NOTE:	Within seven (7) calendar days of changing your address for service, notify the court and all other parties in writing.
REMARQUE :	*Dans les sept (7) jours civils qui suivent tout changement de votre adresse aux fins de signification, veuillez en aviser par écrit le tribunal et les autres parties.*

CAUTION TO PLAINTIFF(S):	If this Defence contains a proposal of terms of payment, you are deemed to have accepted the terms **unless** you file with the clerk and serve on the defendant(s) a Request to Clerk (Form 9B) for a terms of payment hearing **WITHIN TWENTY (20) CALENDAR DAYS** of service of this Defence [R. 9.03(3)].
AVERTISSEMENT AU(X) DEMANDEUR(S) :	*Si la présente défense comprend une proposition à l'égard des modalités de paiement, vous êtes réputé(e)(s) les avoir acceptées, **sauf** si vous déposez auprès du greffier et signifiez au(x) défendeur(s) une demande au greffier (formule 9B) pour la tenue d'une audience relative aux modalités de paiement **DANS LES VINGT (20) JOURS CIVILS** de la signification de la présente défense [par. 9.03 (3)].*

SCR 9.01-10.03-9A (June 1, 2009 / *1er juin 2009*) CSD

APPENDIX 6.1   Concluded

Schedule A

1. The defendant, James Hardwick, admits the allegations contained in paragraphs 2, 3, and 4 of the plaintiff's claim.

2. With respect to paragraphs 5 and 6, the defendant admits that he failed to pay the amount owing on the due date. However, the defendant states, and the fact is, that during the period from April 15, 20— to August 19, 20—, he provided unpaid services to the plaintiff in the amount of $5,700.00. By an informal oral agreement, the plaintiff agreed that the value of these services would be set off against any amounts owing pursuant to the promissory note dated April 1, 20—.

3. The services provided included the following: snow removal, general yard clean-up and maintenance, pool care and maintenance, general repairs, and pet care and clean-up. These services were provided with the plaintiff's knowledge and consent.

4. The defendant asks that the plaintiff's claim be dismissed with costs payable to the defendant.

APPENDIX 6.2   Greco v. Hardwick: Defendant's Claim (Form 10A)

ONTARIO
Su☐e☐i☐☐C☐u☐t of Justice
Cour supérieure de justice

Defendant's Claim
Demande du défendeur

Form / *Formule* 10A Ont. Reg. No. / *Règl. de l'Ont. :* 258/98

Seal / *Sceau*

Brampton

Small Claims Court / *Cour des petites créances de*
7755 Hurontario Street
Brampton, Ontario
L6W 4T6

Address / *Adresse*

905 456 4700

Phone number / *Numéro de téléphone*

7891

Claim No. / *N° de la demande*

Plaintiff by Defendant's Claim No. 1 /
Demandeur dans la demande du défendeur n° 1

☐ Additional plaintiff(s) listed on attached Form 1A. *Le ou les demandeurs additionnels sont mentionnés sur la formule 1A ci-jointe.*

☐ Under 18 years of age. *Moins de 18 ans.*

Last name, or name of company / *Nom de famille ou nom de la compagnie* **Hardwick**		
First name / *Premier prénom* **James**	Second name / *Deuxième prénom*	Also known as / *Également connu(e) sous le nom de*
Address (street number, apt., unit) / *Adresse (numéro et rue, app., unité)* **c/o Paxton Limones PC**		
City/Town / *Cité/ville*	Province	Phone no. / *N° de téléphone*
Postal code / *Code postal*		Fax no. / *N° de télécopieur*
Representative / *Représentant(e)* **Paxton Limones PC Attention: Paralegal name**		LSUC # / *N° du BHC* **######**
Address (street number, apt., unit) / *Adresse (numéro et rue, app., unité)* **82 Main Street, Suite 11**		
City/Town / *Cité/ville* **Brampton**	Province **Ontario**	Phone no. / *N° de téléphone* **905 888 9999**
Postal code / *Code postal* **L1N 2P3**		Fax no. / *N° de télécopieur* **905 888 0000**

Defendant by Defendant's Claim No. 1 /
Défendeur dans la demande du défendeur n° 1

☐ Additional defendant(s) listed on attached Form 1A. *Le ou les défendeurs additionnels sont mentionnés sur la formule 1A ci-jointe.*

☐ Under 18 years of age. *Moins de 18 ans.*

Last name, or name of company / *Nom de famille ou nom de la compagnie* **Greco**		
First name / *Premier prénom* **Juliette**	Second name / *Deuxième prénom*	Also known as / *Également connu(e) sous le nom de*
Address (street number, apt., unit) / *Adresse (numéro et rue, app., unité)* **c/o Prior Mustafa LLP**		
City/Town / *Cité/ville*	Province	Phone no. / *N° de téléphone*
Postal code / *Code postal*		Fax no. / *N° de télécopieur*
Representative / *Représentant(e)* **Prior Mustafa LLP Attention: Paralegal name**		LSUC # / *N° du BHC* **######**
Address (street number, apt., unit) / *Adresse (numéro et rue, app., unité)* **22 County Court Boulevard**		
City/Town / *Cité/ville* **Brampton**	Province **Ontairo**	Phone no. / *N° de téléphone* **905 111 2222**
Postal code / *Code postal* **A1A 2B3**		Fax no. / *N° de télécopieur* **905 111 2233**

SCR 10.01-10A (June 1, 2009 / *1er juin 2009*) CSD

APPENDIX 6.2 Continued

FORM / *FORMULE* **10A**	**PAGE 2**	7891

Claim No. / *N° de la demande*

REASONS FOR CLAIM AND DETAILS / *MOTIFS DE LA DEMANDE ET PRÉCISIONS*

Explain what happened, including where and when. Then explain how much money you are claiming or what goods you want returned.

Expliquez ce qui s'est passé, en précisant où et quand. Ensuite indiquez la somme d'argent que vous demandez ou les biens dont vous demandez la restitution, explication à l'appui.

If you are relying on any documents, you **MUST** attach copies to the claim. If evidence is lost or unavailable, you **MUST** explain why it is not attached.

*Si vous vous appuyez sur des documents, vous **DEVEZ** en annexer des copies à la demande. Si une preuve est perdue ou n'est pas disponible, vous **DEVEZ** expliquer pourquoi elle n'est pas annexée.*

What happened?　　　**See Schedule A attached**
Where?
When?

Que s'est-il passé?
Où?
Quand?

APPENDIX 6.2   Continued

FORM / *FORMULE* 10A   PAGE 3   7891
                                                                     Claim No. / *N° de la demande*

See Schedule A attached

How much? $ ....990.00 *$*
Combien?   (Principal amount claimed / *Somme demandée*)

⊠   **ADDITIONAL PAGES ARE ATTACHED BECAUSE MORE ROOM WAS NEEDED.**
     DES FEUILLES SUPPLÉMENTAIRES SONT ANNEXÉES EN RAISON DU MANQUE D'ESPACE.

**The plaintiff by defendant's claim also claims pre-judgment interest
from**   August 19, 20--   **under:**
Le demandeur dans la demande du défendeur demande aussi des   (Date)   *conformément à :*
intérêts antérieurs au jugement à compter du

(Check only   ⊠   the *Courts of Justice Act*
one box /   *la* **Loi sur les tribunaux judiciaires**
Cochez une
seule case)   ☐   an agreement at the rate of _____ **% per year**
                         un accord au taux de   **% par an**

and post-judgment interest, and court costs.
et des intérêts postérieurs au jugement, ainsi que les dépens.

Prepared on: **November 15**_____, 20 **--** _____
Fait le :   (Signature of plaintiff or representative / *Signature du*
                                                         demandeur/de la demanderesse ou du/de la représentant(e))

Issued on: _____, 20 _____   _____
Délivré le :   (Signature of clerk / *Signature du greffier*)

CAUTION TO DEFENDANT BY DEFENDANT'S CLAIM: *AVERTISSEMENT AU DÉFENDEUR DANS LA DEMANDE DU DÉFENDEUR :*	**IF YOU DO NOT FILE A DEFENCE** (Form 9A) with the court within twenty (20) calendar days after you have been served with this Defendant's Claim, judgment may be obtained by Defendant's Claim without notice and enforced against you. Forms and self-help materials are available at the Small Claims Court and on the following website: www.ontariocourtforms.on.ca. *SI VOUS NE DÉPOSEZ PAS DE DÉFENSE (formule 9A) auprès du tribunal au plus tard vingt (20) jours civils après avoir reçu signification de la présente demande du défendeur, un jugement peut être obtenu par suite de cette demande sans préavis et être exécuté contre vous. Vous pouvez obtenir les formules et la documentation à l'usage du client à la Cour des petites créances et sur le site Web suivant : www.ontariocourtforms.on.ca.*

SCR 10.01-10A (June 1, 2009 / *1er juin 2009*) CSD

APPENDIX 6.2 Continued

Schedule A

1. The plaintiff by defendant's claim claims:

    (a)   Damages of $990.00;

    (b)   Pre- and post-judgment interest in accordance with the *Courts of Justice Act*;

    (c)   His costs of this action; and

    (d)   Such further and other relief as this Honourable Court deems just.

2. After the promissory note dated April 1, 20— was signed, the plaintiff by defendant's claim ("Mr. Hardwick") approached the defendant by defendant's claim ("Ms. Greco") and offered to perform services in lieu of repayment in cash. Ms. Greco agreed to accept Mr. Hardwick's services.

3. Between April 15, 20— and August 19, 20—, when he received the first demand letter by registered mail from Ms. Greco, Mr. Hardwick performed the following services.

4. Mr. Hardwick cleared the lawns and garden beds of winter debris, and prepared them for spring planting where necessary.

5. Mr. Hardwick mowed Ms. Greco's grass on a weekly basis commencing the week of May 1 and ending the week of August 21. Mr. Hardwick maintained Ms. Greco's in-ground pool. Said services included general maintenance, bi-weekly cleaning, and some mechanical repairs.

6. Mr. Hardwick performed other maintenance on Ms. Greco's property, including hedge trimming, pruning, and disposal of yard waste. Mr. Hardwick scraped and painted Ms. Greco's garden shed. Mr. Hardwick also lifted the floor of the shed to remove and dispose of the remains of dead animals.

7. Mr. Hardwick cared for Ms. Greco's dog and two cats when Ms. Greco was out of town on business. Ms. Greco travels a good deal in the course of her employment. During the period in question, she was out of town from May 20 to May 31, and from June 10 to on

APPENDIX 6.2   Concluded

or about June 30. She provided Mr. Hardwick with a key to her house and the code to the security system for the times when she was away.

8. All services were performed with Ms. Greco's knowledge and consent.

9. Based on current prices charged by yard maintenance and pet care contractors, the unpaid services performed by Mr. Hardwick and accepted by Ms. Greco have a cash value of $5,990.00, calculated as follows:

    (a)   Sixteen weeks of yard maintenance at $155.00 per week for a total of $2,480.00;

    (b)   Five weeks of pet care at $250.00 per week for a total of $1,250.00;

    (c)   Eleven weeks of pool maintenance at $120.00 per week for a total of $1,320.00; and

    (d)   Miscellaneous services (mail, mending fence, attending to alarm system, painting garden shed, clearing out and disposing of dead animals, etc.) valued at $940.00.

Attached documents:

Quote of $1,850.00 for twelve weeks of general yard maintenance, including mowing, hedge trimming, pruning, etc. by Green Tree Yard and Garden Inc.

Quote of $350.00 per week for in-house pet care from Serene Beasts Pet Services.

Quote of $95.00 per week for general pool maintenance from Mermaids R Us.

APPENDIX 6.3 Greco v. Hardwick: Defence to Defendant's Claim (Form 9A)

ONTARIO

puperior Court of Justice
Cour supérieure de justice

Defence / *Défense*
Form / *Formule* 9A Ont. Reg. No. / *Règl. de l'Ont.* : 258/98

Brampton
Small Claims Court / *Cour des petites créances de*
7755 Hurontario Street
Brampton, Ontario
L6W 4T6
Address / *Adresse*

905 456 4700
Phone number / *Numéro de téléphone*

7891
Claim No. / *N° de la demande*

☐ Additional plaintiff(s) listed on attached Form 1A.
Le ou les demandeurs additionnels sont mentionnés sur la formule 1A ci-jointe.

☐ Under 18 years of age.
Moins de 18 ans.

Plaintiff No. 1 / *Demandeur n° 1*

Last name, or name of company / *Nom de famille ou nom de la compagnie*		
Hardwick **Plaintiff by defendant's claim**		
First name / *Premier prénom* **James**	Second name / *Deuxième prénom*	Also known as / *Également connu(e) sous le nom de*
Address (street number, apt., unit) / *Adresse (numéro et rue, app., unité)* **c/o Paxton Limones PC**		
City/Town / *Cité/ville*	Province	Phone no. / *N° de téléphone*
Postal code / *Code postal*		Fax no. / *N° de télécopieur*
Representative / *Représentant(e)* **Paxton Limones PC Attention: Paralegal name**		LSUC # / *N° du BHC* **######**
Address (street number, apt., unit) / *Adresse (numéro et rue, app., unité)* **82 Main Street, Suite 11**		
City/Town / *Cité/ville* **Brampton**	Province **Ontario**	Phone no. / *N° de téléphone* **905 888 9999**
Postal code / *Code postal* **L1N 2P3**		Fax no. / *N° de télécopieur* **905 888 0000**

☐ Additional defendant(s) listed on attached Form 1A.
Le ou les défendeurs additionnels sont mentionnés sur la formule 1A ci-jointe.

☐ Under 18 years of age.
Moins de 18 ans.

Defendant No. 1 / *Défendeur n° 1*

Last name, or name of company / *Nom de famille ou nom de la compagnie*		
Greco **Defendant by defendant's claim**		
First name / *Premier prénom* **Juliette**	Second name / *Deuxième prénom*	Also known as / *Également connu(e) sous le nom de*
Address (street number, apt., unit) / *Adresse (numéro et rue, app., unité)* **c/o Prior Mustafa LLP**		
City/Town / *Cité/ville*	Province	Phone no. / *N° de téléphone*
Postal code / *Code postal*		Fax no. / *N° de télécopieur*
Representative / *Représentant(e)* **Prior Mustafa LLP Attention: Paralegal name**		LSUC # / *N° du BHC* **######**
Address (street number, apt., unit) / *Adresse (numéro et rue, app., unité)* **22 County Court Boulevard**		
City/Town / *Cité/ville* **Brampton**	Province **Ontario**	Phone no. / *N° de téléphone* **905 111 2222**
Postal code / *Code postal* **A1A 2B3**		Fax no. / *N° de télécopieur* **905 111 2233**

SCR 9.01-10.03-9A (June 1, 2009 / *1er juin 2009*) CSD

APPENDIX 6.3   Continued

FORM / *FORMULE* 9A   PAGE 2   7891

Claim No. / *N° de la demande*

THIS DEFENCE IS BEING FILED ON BEHALF OF: (Name(s) of defendant(s))
LA PRÉSENTE DÉFENSE EST DÉPOSÉE AU NOM DE :   (Nom du/de la ou des défendeur(s)/défenderesse(s))

Juliette Greco (Defendant by defendant's claim)

and I/we: (Check as many as apply)
et je/nous :   (Cochez la ou les cases qui s'appliquent)

☒   Dispute the claim made against me/us.
      conteste/contestons la demande présentée contre moi/nous.

☐   Admit the full claim and propose the following terms of payment:
      reconnais/reconnaissons être redevable(s) de la totalité de la demande et propose/proposons les
      modalités de paiement suivantes :

      $ _____ per _____ commencing _____, 20 ____ .
      (Amount / *Montant*)   *$ par*   (Week/month / *semaine/mois*)   *à compter du*

☐   Admit part of the claim in the amount of $ _____ and propose the following terms of payment:
      reconnais/reconnaissons être redevable(s)   (Amount / *Montant*)   *$ et propose/proposons les modalités de*
      d'une partie de la demande, soit   *paiement suivantes :*

      $ _____ per _____ commencing _____, 20 ____ .
      (Amount / *Montant*)   *$ par*   (Week/month / *semaine/mois*)   *à compter du*

REASONS FOR DISPUTING THE CLAIM AND DETAILS:
MOTIFS DE CONTESTATION DE LA DEMANDE ET PRÉCISIONS :

Explain what happened, including where and when. Explain why you do not agree with the claim made against you.
Expliquez ce qui s'est passé, en précisant où et quand. Expliquez pourquoi vous contestez la demande
présentée contre vous.

If you are relying on any documents, you **MUST** attach copies to the Defence. If evidence is lost or unavailable,
you **MUST** explain why it is not attached.
*Si vous vous appuyez sur des documents, vous **DEVEZ** en annexer des copies à la défense. Si une preuve est*
*perdue ou n'est pas disponible, vous **DEVEZ** expliquer pourquoi elle n'est pas annexée.*

What happened?   See Schedule A attached
Where?
When?
Que s'est-il
passé?
Où?
Quand?

SCR 9.01-10.03-9A (June 1, 2009 / *1ᵉʳ juin 2009*) CSD   **Continued on next page / *Suite à la page suivante***

APPENDIX 6.3   Continued

FORM / *FORMULE* 9A   PAGE 3   7891
                                                          Claim No. / *N° de la demande*

Why I/we disagree   See Schedule A attached
with all or part of
the claim: /

Je conteste/Nous
contestons la
totalité ou une
partie de la
demande pour les
motifs suivants :

⊠   **ADDITIONAL PAGES ARE ATTACHED BECAUSE MORE ROOM WAS NEEDED.**
    DES FEUILLES SUPPLÉMENTAIRES SONT ANNEXÉES EN RAISON DU MANQUE D'ESPACE.

Prepared on: **November 28**   , 20 **--**   _____
Fait le :   (Signature of defendant or representative /
                                                            Signature du défendeur/de la défenderesse ou du/de la représentant(e))

| **NOTE:** | Within seven (7) calendar days of changing your address for service, notify the court and all other parties in writing. |
| **REMARQUE :** | *Dans les sept (7) jours civils qui suivent tout changement de votre adresse aux fins de signification, veuillez en aviser par écrit le tribunal et les autres parties.* |

| **CAUTION TO PLAINTIFF(S):** | If this Defence contains a proposal of terms of payment, you are deemed to have accepted the terms **unless** you file with the clerk and serve on the defendant(s) a Request to Clerk (Form 9B) for a terms of payment hearing **WITHIN TWENTY (20) CALENDAR DAYS** of service of this Defence [R. 9.03(3)]. |
| **AVERTISSEMENT AU(X) DEMANDEUR(S) :** | *Si la présente défense comprend une proposition à l'égard des modalités de paiement, vous êtes réputé(e)(s) les avoir acceptées, **sauf** si vous déposez auprès du greffier et signifiez au(x) défendeur(s) une demande au greffier (formule 9B) pour la tenue d'une audience relative aux modalités de paiement **DANS LES VINGT (20) JOURS CIVILS** de la signification de la présente défense [par. 9.03 (3)].* |

APPENDIX 6.3   Continued

Schedule A

1. With respect to paragraph 2 of the defendant's claim, the defendant by defendant's claim ("Ms. Greco") admits that shortly after signing the promissory note dated April 1, 20—, the plaintiff by defendant's claim ("Mr. Hardwick") advised her that he would not be able to pay the full amount owing on the due date of August 1, 20—. He proposed doing yard and pool maintenance in partial payment of the amount owing, and paying what he could in cash installments commencing on the due date. Ms. Greco agreed to this arrangement.

2. With respect to paragraphs 3, 4, 5, 6, and 8, Ms. Greco admits that Mr. Hardwick performed the services stated during the period from April 15 to August 19, 20—. In past years, she has always hired Glenn Woods Garden Services to maintain the yard and pool. The annual fee charged to her by Glenn Woods for lawn care, landscaping, and pool maintenance from April 15 to October 15 has always been in the range of $1,500.00. Before agreeing to accept his services, Ms. Greco obtained Mr. Hardwick's assurance that the charge for his services would be in that range. She also advised him that her acceptance of these services would constitute partial payment only of the amount due on the note. She accepted his services instead of those of Glenn Woods for one summer only on those terms.

3. The garden shed required a fresh coat of stain only. It did not have to be scraped and painted. Ms. Greco's nephew offered to do the work for free.

4. With respect to the contents of paragraph 7, Ms. Greco states and the fact is that Mr. Hardwick's children have often cared for her pets when she was away on business trips. She always leaves the key and security code with Mr. Hardwick or his wife so that the boys can get into her house to feed the cats and dog, clean the litter box, change the water, and let the dog out. The dog is elderly and arthritic, and does not need to be walked.

APPENDIX 6.3   Concluded

5. Ms. Greco has never been charged for this assistance in the past. Her nephew or nieces would have taken care of the animals for nothing while she was gone. They have done so in the past, when the Hardwick children were unable to help out.

6. On August 1, 20—, Ms. Greco approached Mr. Hardwick and asked when she could start expecting payments on the amount still owing on the note. Mr. Hardwick said he would pay $500.00 on or before August 10, 20—. When she received no payment, Ms. Greco sent the first demand letter, dated August 15, 20—.

7. With respect to paragraph 9, Ms. Greco states and the fact is that the values assigned by Mr. Hardwick to the services provided are grossly inflated. She asks that the defendant's claim be dismissed with costs to Ms. Greco.

Attached documents:

20— invoice from Glenn Woods Garden Services in the amount of $1,455.00, marked "Paid in full"

20— invoice from Glenn Woods Garden Services in the amount of $1,450.00, marked "Paid in full"

20— invoice from Glenn Woods Garden Services in the amount of $1,550.00, marked "Paid in full"

APPENDIX 6.4   Nguyen v. Mirren: Defence with Proposal of Terms of Payment (Form 9A)

ONTARIO

ouperior Court of Justice
Cour supérieure de justice

Defence / *Défense*
Form / *Formule* 9A Ont. Reg. No. / *Règl. de l'Ont.* : 258/98

Newmarket

Small Claims Court / *Cour des petites créances de*
50 Eagle Street West
Newmarket, Ontario
L3Y 6B1

Address / *Adresse*

905 853 4809

Phone number / *Numéro de téléphone*

8899

Claim No. / *N° de la demande*

Plaintiff No. 1 / *Demandeur n° 1*

☐ Additional plaintiff(s) listed on attached Form 1A.
Le ou les demandeurs additionnels sont mentionnés sur la formule 1A ci-jointe.

☐ Under 18 years of age.
Moins de 18 ans.

Last name, or name of company / *Nom de famille ou nom de la compagnie*		
Nguyen		
First name / *Premier prénom*	Second name / *Deuxième prénom*	Also known as / *Également connu(e) sous le nom de*
France		
Address (street number, apt., unit) / *Adresse (numéro et rue, app., unité)*		
c/o Prior Mustafa LLP		
City/Town / *Cité/ville*	Province	Phone no. / *N° de téléphone*
Postal code / *Code postal*		Fax no. / *N° de télécopieur*
Representative / *Représentant(e)*		LSUC # / *N° du BHC*
Prior Mustafa LLP Attention: Paralegal name		**######**
Address (street number, apt., unit) / *Adresse (numéro et rue, app., unité)*		
22 County Court Boulevard		
City/Town / *Cité/ville*	Province	Phone no. / *N° de téléphone*
Brampton	**Ontario**	**905 111 2222**
Postal code / *Code postal*		Fax no. / *N° de télécopieur*
A1A 2B3		**905 111 2233**

Defendant No. 1 / *Défendeur n° 1*

☐ Additional defendant(s) listed on attached Form 1A.
Le ou les défendeurs additionnels sont mentionnés sur la formule 1A ci-jointe.

☐ Under 18 years of age.
Moins de 18 ans.

Last name, or name of company / *Nom de famille ou nom de la compagnie*		
Mirren		
First name / *Premier prénom*	Second name / *Deuxième prénom*	Also known as / *Également connu(e) sous le nom de*
Mabel		
Address (street number, apt., unit) / *Adresse (numéro et rue, app., unité)*		
89 Oliver Crescent, Unit 442		
City/Town / *Cité/ville*	Province	Phone no. / *N° de téléphone*
Newmarket	**Ontario**	**905 222 3333**
Postal code / *Code postal*		Fax no. / *N° de télécopieur*
E1H 2F2		
Representative / *Représentant(e)*		LSUC # / *N° du BHC*
Address (street number, apt., unit) / *Adresse (numéro et rue, app., unité)*		
City/Town / *Cité/ville*	Province	Phone no. / *N° de téléphone*
Postal code / *Code postal*		Fax no. / *N° de télécopieur*

SCR 9.01-10.03-9A (June 1, 2009 / *1er juin 2009*) CSD

APPENDIX 6.4   Continued

FORM / *FORMULE* 9A	PAGE 2	8899

Claim No. / *N° de la demande*

THIS DEFENCE IS BEING FILED ON BEHALF OF: (Name(s) of defendant(s))
LA PRÉSENTE DÉFENSE EST DÉPOSÉE AU NOM DE :   (Nom du/de la ou des défendeur(s)/défenderesse(s))

Mabel Mirren

and I/we: (Check as many as apply)
et je/nous :   (Cochez la ou les cases qui s'appliquent)

☐ Dispute the claim made against me/us.
   conteste/contestons la demande présentée contre moi/nous.

☒ Admit the full claim and propose the following terms of payment:
   reconnais/reconnaissons être redevable(s) de la totalité de la demande et propose/proposons les modalités de paiement suivantes :

$ _____300.00_____ per __month__   commencing **September 1**_____ , 20 _--_ .
   (Amount / *Montant*)   *$ par*   (Week/month / *semaine/mois*)   *à compter du*

☐ Admit part of the claim in the amount of $ _____   and propose the following terms of payment:
   reconnais/reconnaissons être redevable(s)   (Amount / *Montant*)   *$ et propose/proposons les modalités de*
   d'une partie de la demande, soit   *paiement suivantes :*

$ _____ per _____   commencing _____ , 20 ____ .
   (Amount / *Montant*)   *$ par*   (Week/month / *semaine/mois*)   *à compter du*

REASONS FOR DISPUTING THE CLAIM AND DETAILS:
MOTIFS DE CONTESTATION DE LA DEMANDE ET PRÉCISIONS :

Explain what happened, including where and when. Explain why you do not agree with the claim made against you.
Expliquez ce qui s'est passé, en précisant où et quand. Expliquez pourquoi vous contestez la demande présentée contre vous.

If you are relying on any documents, you **MUST** attach copies to the Defence. If evidence is lost or unavailable, you **MUST** explain why it is not attached.
*Si vous vous appuyez sur des documents, vous **DEVEZ** en annexer des copies à la défense. Si une preuve est perdue ou n'est pas disponible, vous **DEVEZ** expliquer pourquoi elle n'est pas annexée.*

What happened?   n/a
Where?
When?
Que s'est-il
passé?
Où?
Quand?

APPENDIX 6.4   Concluded

FORM / *FORMULE* 9A	PAGE 3	<u>8899</u>
		Claim No. / *N° de la demande*

Why I/we disagree with all or part of the claim: /

Je conteste/Nous contestons la totalité ou une partie de la demande pour les motifs suivants :

☐   **ADDITIONAL PAGES ARE ATTACHED BECAUSE MORE ROOM WAS NEEDED.**
DES FEUILLES SUPPLÉMENTAIRES SONT ANNEXÉES EN RAISON DU MANQUE D'ESPACE.

Prepared on: <u>July 28</u>   , 20   --

Fait le :   <u>   </u>

(Signature of defendant or representative /
Signature du défendeur/de la défenderesse ou du/de la représentant(e))

NOTE:	Within seven (7) calendar days of changing your address for service, notify the court and all other parties in writing.
REMARQUE :	*Dans les sept (7) jours civils qui suivent tout changement de votre adresse aux fins de signification, veuillez en aviser par écrit le tribunal et les autres parties.*

CAUTION TO PLAINTIFF(S):	If this Defence contains a proposal of terms of payment, you are deemed to have accepted the terms **unless** you file with the clerk and serve on the defendant(s) a Request to Clerk (Form 9B) for a terms of payment hearing **WITHIN TWENTY (20) CALENDAR DAYS** of service of this Defence [R. 9.03(3)].
AVERTISSEMENT AU(X) DEMANDEUR(S) :	*Si la présente défense comprend une proposition à l'égard des modalités de paiement, vous êtes réputé(e)(s) les avoir acceptées, **sauf** si vous déposez auprès du greffier et signifiez au(x) défendeur(s) une demande au greffier (formule 9B) pour la tenue d'une audience relative aux modalités de paiement **DANS LES VINGT (20) JOURS CIVILS** de la signification de la présente défense [par. 9.03 (3)].*

SCR 9.01-10.03-9A (June 1, 2009 / *1er juin 2009*) CSD

APPENDIX 6.5   Nguyen v. Mirren: Procedures on Default of Payment by Defendant (Forms 20L, 20M, and 11B)—Form 20L

ONTARIO

Sup⬚ri⬚r Court of Justice
Cour supérieure de justice

Notice of Default of Payment
Avis de défaut de paiement

Form / *Formule* 20L Ont. Reg. No. / *Règl. de l'Ont.* : 258/98

Newmarket	**8899**
Small Claims Court / *Cour des petites créances de*	Claim No. / *N° de la demande*
50 Eagle Street West	
Newmarket, Ontario	
L3Y 6B1	

Address / *Adresse*

905 853 4809

Phone number / *Numéro de téléphone*

BETWEEN / *ENTRE*

France Nguyen

Plaintiff(s)/Creditor(s) / *Demandeur(s)/demanderesse(s)/Créancier(s)/créancière(s)*

and / *et*

Mabel Mirren

Defendant(s)/Debtor(s) / *Défendeur(s)/défenderesse(s)/Débiteur(s)/débitrice(s)*

TO: **Mabel Mirren**

DESTINATAIRE(S) :   (Name of defendant(s)/debtor(s) / *Nom du/de la/des défendeur(s)/défenderesse(s)/débiteur(s)/débitrice(s)*)

TAKE NOTICE that you defaulted in your payment(s) to
VEUILLEZ PRENDRE NOTE que vous n'avez pas effectué le ou les paiements que vous deviez verser à

France Nguyen

(Name of plaintiff(s)/creditor(s) / *Nom du/de la/des demandeur(s)/demanderesse(s)/créancier(s)/créancière(s)*)

(Check appropriate box. / Cochez la case appropriée.*)*

☐ under an order for periodic payment, dated _____ , 20 _____ .
en vertu d'une ordonnance prescrivant des versements périodiques datée du

According to Rule 20.02(4) of the *Rules of the Small Claims Court*, the order for periodic payment terminates on the day that is 15 days after the creditor serves the debtor with this notice, unless before that date, a Consent (Form 13B) is filed in which the creditor waives the default.
Conformément au paragraphe 20.02 (4) des Règles de la Cour des petites créances, l'ordonnance prescrivant des versements périodiques prend fin le 15ᵉ jour qui suit la signification par le créancier au débiteur du présent avis, sauf si, avant cette date, le créancier dépose le consentement (formule 13B) dans lequel il renonce à la constatation du défaut.

☒ under a proposal of terms of payment in the Defence (Form 9A) dated **July 28** _____ , 20 -- .
en vertu d'une proposition à l'égard des modalités de paiement dans la défense (formule 9A) datée du

According to Rule 9.03(2)(c) the clerk may sign judgment for the unpaid balance of the undisputed amount on the day that is 15 days after the plaintiff serves the defendant with this notice.
Conformément à l'alinéa 9.03 (2) c), le greffier peut consigner un jugement relativement au solde impayé de la somme non contestée le 15ᵉ jour qui suit la signification par le demandeur au défendeur du présent avis.

SCR 20.02-20L (June 1, 2009 / *1ᵉʳ juin 2009*) CSD

APPENDIX 6.5—Form 20L   Concluded

FORM / *FORMULE* **20L**   **PAGE 2**   **8899**

Claim No. / *N° de la demande*

You can get forms and self-help materials at the Small Claims Court or online at: www.ontariocourtforms.on.ca. *Vous pouvez obtenir les formules et la documentation à l'usage du client auprès de la Cour des petites créances ou en ligne à l'adresse :* www.ontariocourtforms.on.ca.

NOTE TO DEFENDANT/DEBTOR: / *REMARQUE AU DÉFENDEUR/DÉBITEUR :*

If you / *Si, selon le cas :*

- failed to make payments but intend to do so; or
  vous n'avez pas effectué de paiements mais vous avez l'intention de le faire;

- made payments but the payments were not received by the creditor;
  vous avez effectué des paiements mais le créancier ne les a pas reçus;

contact the plaintiff/creditor to make payment arrangements or correct the reason for non-receipt of payments. You may obtain the plaintiff/creditor's written consent (Form 13B may be used) to waive the default and file it with the court within 15 days of being served with this notice. Failure to do so may result in the following: *communiquez avec le demandeur/créancier pour prendre les dispositions de paiement ou pour régler le motif de la non-réception des paiements. Vous pouvez obtenir le consentement écrit du demandeur/créancier (vous pouvez utiliser la formule 13B) pour renoncer à la constatation du défaut et le déposer au tribunal dans les 15 jours de la signification du présent avis. Si vous ne le faites pas, vous pourriez subir l'une ou l'autre des conséquences suivantes :*

- in the case of default under a proposal of terms of payment in the Defence (Form 9A), the plaintiff may obtain default judgment for the unpaid balance of the undisputed amount; or
  si vous n'effectuez pas les paiements conformément aux modalités de paiement proposées dans la défense (formule 9A), le demandeur pourra obtenir un jugement par défaut relativement au solde impayé de la somme non contestée;

- in the case of default under an order for periodic payment, the order will terminate and the creditor may take other steps to enforce the order.
  si vous n'effectuez pas les paiements conformément à une ordonnance prescrivant des versements périodiques, l'ordonnance prendra fin et le créancier pourra prendre d'autres mesures en vue de l'exécution forcée de l'ordonnance.

November 5 _____ , 20 --

_____
(Signature of plaintiff/creditor or representative / *Signature du demandeur/de la demanderesse/du créancier/de la créancière ou du/de la représentant(e)*)
Prior Mustafa LLP
22 County Court Boulevard
Brampton, Ontario A1A 2B3
TEL: 905 111 2222
Attention: Paralegal name
(Name, address and phone number of plaintiff/creditor or representative / *Nom, adresse et numéro de téléphone du demandeur/de la demanderesse/du créancier/de la créancière ou du/de la représentant(e)*)

SCR 20.02-20L (June 1, 2009 / *1ᵉʳ juin 2009*) CSD

APPENDIX 6.5—Form 20M

ONTARIO
Superior Court of Justice
Cour supérieure de justice

Affidavit of Default of Payment
Affidavit de défaut de paiement
Form / *Formule* 20M Ont. Reg. No. / *Règl. de l'Ont.* : 258/98

Newmarket
Small Claims Court / *Cour des petites créances de*

8899
Claim No. / *N° de la demande*

50 Eagle Street West
Newmarket, Ontario
L3Y 6B1
Address / *Adresse*

905 853 4809
Phone number / *Numéro de téléphone*

BETWEEN / *ENTRE*

France Nguyen
Plaintiff(s)/Creditor(s) / *Demandeur(s)/demanderesse(s)/Créancier(s)/créancière(s)*

and / *et*

Mabel Mirren
Defendant(s)/Debtor(s) / *Défendeur(s)/défenderesse(s)/Débiteur(s)/débitrice(s)*

My name is France Nguyen
Je m'appelle   (Full name / *Nom et prénoms*)

I live in Newmarket, Ontario
J'habite à   (Municipality & province / *Municipalité et province*)

and I swear/affirm that the following is true:
et je déclare sous serment/j'affirme solennellement que les renseignements suivants sont véridiques :

1. In this action, I am the
Dans la présente action, je suis le/la

(Check one box only. / Cochez une seule case.)

☒ plaintiff/creditor.
demandeur/demanderesse/créancier/créancière.

☐ representative of the
plaintiff(s)/creditor(s)
représentant(e) du/de la/des demandeur(s)/demanderesse(s) ou du/de la/des créancier(s)/créancière(s)

(Name of plaintiff(s)/creditor(s) / *Nom du/de la/des demandeur(s)/demanderesse(s) ou du/de la/des créancier(s)/créancière(s)*)

2. To date, I have received from the defendant(s)/debtor(s) $ **600.00** , the last payment being made
À ce jour, j'ai reçu du ou des défendeurs/débiteurs   (Amount / *Montant*) *$, soit le dernier paiement ayant*

on or about **October 1**   , 20 **--** .
été effectué le ou vers le

3. I make this affidavit in support of a request that:
Je fais le présent affidavit à l'appui d'une demande visant à :

(Check appropriate box and complete paragraph. / Cochez la case appropriée et remplissez le point.)

☒ the clerk of the court issue a Default Judgment (Form 11B) [R. 9.03(2)(c)]. The defendant(s)
enjoindre au greffier du tribunal de rendre un jugement par défaut (formule 11B) [alinéa 9.03 (2) c)].
Le ou les défendeurs

Mabel Mirren
(Name(s) of defendant(s) / *Nom du/de la/des défendeur(s)/défenderesse(s)*)

failed to make payment in accordance with the proposed terms of payment in the Defence
n'ont pas effectué les paiements conformément aux modalités de paiement proposées dans la défense

(Form 9A) dated **July 28**   , 20 **--**   and fifteen (15) days have passed since the
(formule 9A) datée du   *et quinze (15) jours se sont écoulés depuis*

defendant was served with a Notice of Default of Payment (Form 20L).
la signification de l'avis de défaut de paiement au défendeur (formule 20L).

SCR 9.03-20M (June 1, 2009 / *1er juin 2009*) CSD

APPENDIX 6.5—Form 20M   Continued

FORM / *FORMULE* 20M	PAGE 2	8899
		Claim No. / *N° de la demande*

☐ the clerk of the court issue a Default Judgment (Form 11B) [R. 9.03(7)]. The defendant(s)
enjoindre au greffier du tribunal de rendre un jugement par défaut (formule 11B) [par. 9.03 (7)]. Le ou les défendeurs

(Name of defendant(s) / *Nom du/de la/des défendeur(s)/défenderesse(s)*)

failed to make payment in accordance with the terms of payment order
n'ont pas effectué les paiements conformément à l'ordonnance relative aux modalités de paiement

(Check appropriate box and complete paragraph. / Cochez la case appropriée et remplissez le point.)

dated _____, 20 _____ .
datée du

☐ I may enforce the judgment [R. 20.02(3)]. The debtor(s)
m'autoriser à exécuter le jugement [par. 20.02 (3)]. Le ou les débiteurs

(Name(s) of debtor(s) / *Nom du/de la/des débiteur(s)/débitrice(s)*)

failed to make payment in accordance with the order for periodic payment dated
n'ont pas effectué les paiements conformément à l'ordonnance prescrivant des versements périodiques datée du

_____, 20 _____, and fifteen (15) days have passed since the debtor(s) has/have
et quinze (15) jours se sont écoulés depuis la signification

been served with a Notice of Default of Payment (Form 20L). A Consent (Form 13B) in which the creditor waives the default has not been filed.
de l'avis de défaut de paiement (formule 20L) au ou aux débiteurs. Un consentement (formule 13B) dans lequel le créancier renonce à la constatation du défaut n'a pas été déposé.

4.   The unpaid balance is calculated as follows:
Le solde impayé est calculé de la façon suivante :

(A) **DEBT** (amount of judgment) $ _____ 2,400.00
     LA CRÉANCE (montant du jugement) $

(B) **PRE-JUDGMENT INTEREST** calculated
     LES INTÉRÊTS ANTÉRIEURS AU JUGEMENT calculés

on the sum of $ _____ 3,000.00   at the rate of 7 _____ %
sur la somme de $ *au taux de*   *pour cent*

per annum from **January 1** _____, 20 -- to **November 27** _____, 20 -- ,
par an du   *au*

being **330** _____ days. $ _____ 181.57
soit   *jours.* $

┌──┐
│ **NOTE:**   Calculation of interest is always on the amount owing from time to time as │
│   payments are received. This is true for both pre-judgment and post-judgment │
│   interest. Attach a separate sheet setting out how you calculated the total amount │
│   of any pre/post-judgment interest. │
│ **REMARQUE :** *Les intérêts doivent toujours être calculés sur la somme due. Le calcul doit tenir* │
│   *compte des paiements reçus de temps à autre. Ceci s'applique autant aux intérêts* │
│   *antérieurs au jugement qu'aux intérêts postérieurs au jugement. Annexez une* │
│   *feuille distincte indiquant comment vous avez calculé le montant total des intérêts* │
│   *antérieurs et postérieurs au jugement.* │
└──┘

APPENDIX 6.5—Form 20M   Concluded

FORM / *FORMULE* 20M	PAGE 3	8899

Claim No. / *N° de la demande*

(C) **COSTS** to date of judgment
LES DÉPENS à la date du jugement $ 105.00
                                                              $

                                       SUBTOTAL $ 2,686.57
                                       TOTAL PARTIEL $

(D) **TOTAL AMOUNT OF PAYMENTS RECEIVED FROM DEBTOR**
    after judgment (if any)   (minus) $ 0
    LE MONTANT TOTAL DES PAIEMENTS REÇUS DU DÉBITEUR *(moins)* $
    après le jugement (le cas échéant)

(E) **POST-JUDGMENT INTEREST** to date calculated
    LES INTÉRÊTS POSTÉRIEURS AU JUGEMENT à ce jour, calculés

    on the sum of $ _____   at the rate of _____ %
    sur la somme de $ *au taux de*   *pour cent*

    per annum from _____, 20 ___ to _____, 20 ___ ,
    par an du   *au*

    being _____ days. $
    soit   *jours.* $

(F) **SUBSEQUENT COSTS** incurred after judgment (including the cost of issuing
    the Notice of Default of Payment (Form 20L)) $
    LES DÉPENS SUBSÉQUENTS engagés après le jugement (y compris le coût de $
    délivrance de l'avis de défaut de paiement (formule 20L))

(This figure must match the total figure identified in the Default Judgment
(Form 11B) or Affidavit of Enforcement Request (Form 20P). / *Ce montant*
doit correspondre au montant total énoncé dans le jugement par défaut
(formule 11B) ou l'affidavit relatif à une demande d'exécution forcée (formule
20P).)

                                       TOTAL DUE $ 2,686.57
                                       SOLDE DÛ $

Sworn/Affirmed before me at   **Brampton**
Déclaré sous serment/Affirmé
solennellement devant moi à   (Municipality / *municipalité*)

in   **Ontario**
en/à/au   (Province, state, or county / *province, État ou pays*)

on   **November 27**   , 20 --
le   _____
                Commissioner for taking affidavits
                Commissaire aux affidavits
                (Type or print name below if signature is
                illegible.)
                (Dactylographiez le nom ou écrivez-le en
                caractères d'imprimerie ci-dessous si la
                signature est illisible.)

Signature
(This form is to be signed in front of a
lawyer, justice of the peace, notary public
or commissioner for taking affidavits.)
(La présente formule doit être signée en
présence d'un avocat, d'un juge de paix,
d'un notaire ou d'un commissaire aux
affidavits.)

WARNING:	IT IS AN OFFENCE UNDER THE *CRIMINAL CODE* TO KNOWINGLY SWEAR OR AFFIRM A FALSE AFFIDAVIT.
AVERTISSEMENT :	*FAIRE SCIEMMENT UN FAUX AFFIDAVIT CONSTITUE UNE INFRACTION AU CODE CRIMINEL.*

SCR 9.03-20M (June 1, 2009 / *1er juin 2009*) CSD

APPENDIX 6.5—Form 20M Adjusted Calculation of Interest

Principal $3,000.00

Interest   7.0% per year (simple interest)

Convert interest rate to a decimal = 7 ÷ 100 = 0.07

Calculate interest on $3,000.00 from January 1 to August 31:

Per diem (interest per day) = (3,000.00 × 0.07) ÷ 365 = 0.575

Number of days from Jan. 1 to Aug. 31 (using table of days at table 5.2, page 160) = 243

Interest from Jan. 1 to Aug. 31 = 0.575 × 243 = 139.80

Adjust for September 1 payment:

Principal =	3,000.00
minus September 1 payment	300.00
equals	2,700.00

Calculate interest on $2,700.00 from September 1 to October 1:

Per diem = (2,700.00 × 0.07) ÷ 365 = 0.518

Number of days from Sept. 1 to Oct. 1 = 30

Interest from Sept. 1 to Oct. 1 = 0.518 × 30 = 15.54

Adjust for October 1 payment:

Principal =	2,700.00
minus October 1 payment	300.00
equals	2,400.00

Calculate interest on $2,400.00 from October 1 to November 27:

Per diem = (2,400.00 × 0.07) ÷ 365 = 0.46

Number of days from Oct. 1 to Nov. 27 = 57

Interest from Oct. 1 to Nov. 27 = 0.46 × 57 = 26.23

As of Nov. 27 (the date of the affidavit of default), the debt owing is 3,000.00 – 600.00 = 2,400.00

The total interest owing, adjusted for payments received, is 139.80 + 15.54 + 26.23 = 181.57

Numbers for completing Form 20M and Form 11B:

Debt (minus payment):	$2,400.00
Interest rate:	7% per year (simple interest compounded annually)
From / to:	January 1 to November 27
Total days:	330
Total pre-judgment interest:	$181.57 (total of all interest charged according to detailed calculation above)
Total payments after judgment:	0
Costs:	Fee for filing claim (infrequent claimant) and default judgment

APPENDIX 6.5—Form 11B

<table>
<tr>
<td colspan="2">

ONTARIO

Superior Court of Justice
Cour supérieure de justice
</td>
<td>

Default Judgment
Jugement par défaut
Form / *Formule* 11B Ont. Reg. No. / *Règl. de l'Ont.* : 258/98
</td>
</tr>
<tr>
<td>

Seal / *Sceau*
</td>
<td>

Newmarket
Small Claims Court / *Cour des petites créances de*
50 Eagle Street West
Newmarket, Ontario
L3Y 6B1
Address / *Adresse*

905 853 4809
Phone number / *Numéro de téléphone*
</td>
<td>

8899
Claim No. / *N° de la demande*
</td>
</tr>
</table>

Plaintiff No. 1 / *Demandeur n° 1* ☐ Additional plaintiff(s) listed on attached Form 1A.
Le ou les demandeurs additionnels sont mentionnés sur la formule 1A ci-jointe.

Last name, or name of company / *Nom de famille ou nom de la compagnie*		
Nguyen		
First name / *Premier prénom*	Second name / *Deuxième prénom*	Also known as / *Également connu(e) sous le nom de*
France		
Address (street number, apt., unit) / *Adresse (numéro et rue, app., unité)*		
c/o Prior Mustafa LLP		
City/Town / *Cité/ville*	Province	Phone no. / *N° de téléphone*
Postal code / *Code postal*		Fax no. / *N° de télécopieur*
Representative / *Représentant(e)*		LSUC # / *N° du BHC*
Prior Mustafa LLP Attention: Paralegal name		**######**
Address (street number, apt., unit) / *Adresse (numéro et rue, app., unité)*		
22 County Court Boulevard		
City/Town / *Cité/ville*	Province	Phone no. / *N° de téléphone*
Brampton	**Ontario**	**905 111 2222**
Postal code / *Code postal*		Fax no. / *N° de télécopieur*
A1A 2B3		**905 111 2233**

Defendant No. 1 / *Défendeur n° 1* ☐ Additional defendant(s) listed on attached Form 1A.
Le ou les défendeurs additionnels sont mentionnés sur la formule 1A ci-jointe.

Last name, or name of company / *Nom de famille ou nom de la compagnie*		
Mirren		
First name / *Premier prénom*	Second name / *Deuxième prénom*	Also known as / *Également connu(e) sous le nom de*
Mabel		
Address (street number, apt., unit) / *Adresse (numéro et rue, app., unité)*		
89 Oliver Crescent, Unit 442		
City/Town / *Cité/ville*	Province	Phone no. / *N° de téléphone*
Newmarket	**Ontario**	**905 222 3333**
Postal code / *Code postal*		Fax no. / *N° de télécopieur*
E1H 2F2		
Representative / *Représentant(e)*		LSUC # / *N° du BHC*
Address (street number, apt., unit) / *Adresse (numéro et rue, app., unité)*		
City/Town / *Cité/ville*	Province	Phone no. / *N° de téléphone*
Postal code / *Code postal*		Fax no. / *N° de télécopieur*

SCR 11.02-11B (June 1, 2009 / *1er juin 2009*) CSD

APPENDIX 6.5—Form 11B   Continued

FORM / FORMULE 11B   PAGE 2   8899

<div align="right">Claim No. / N° de la demande</div>

NOTICE TO THE DEFENDANT(S):
AVIS AU(X) DÉFENDEUR(S) :

(*Check one box only. / Cochez une seule case.*)

☐ You have been noted in default according to Rule 11.01.
   vous avez été constaté(e) en défaut aux termes de la règle 11.01.

☒ You have defaulted in your payment according to Rule 9.03(2)(b), pursuant to
   vous n'avez pas effectué vos paiements aux termes de l'alinéa 9.03 (2) b), conformément à/au

   a defence _____   dated **July 28**_____ , 20 **--** ,
   <span>   (Name of document / *Titre du document*)</span>   *daté(e) du*

   and 15 days have passed since you were served with a Notice of Default of Payment (Form 20L).
   et 15 jours se sont écoulés depuis qu'un avis de défaut de paiement vous a été signifié (formule 20L).

DEFAULT JUDGMENT IS GIVEN against the following defendant(s):
UN JUGEMENT PAR DÉFAUT EST RENDU contre le ou les défendeurs suivants :

Last name, or name of company / *Nom de famille ou nom de la compagnie*		
Mirren		
First name / *Premier prénom*	Second name / *Deuxième prénom*	Also known as / *Également connu(e) sous le nom de*
Mabel		

Last name, or name of company / *Nom de famille ou nom de la compagnie*		
First name / *Premier prénom*	Second name / *Deuxième prénom*	Also known as / *Également connu(e) sous le nom de*

Last name, or name of company / *Nom de famille ou nom de la compagnie*		
First name / *Premier prénom*	Second name / *Deuxième prénom*	Also known as / *Également connu(e) sous le nom de*

☐ Additional defendant(s) listed on attached page (*list in same format*).
   Défendeur(s) additionnel(s) mentionné(s) sur une feuille annexée (énumérez-les en suivant le même format).

THE DEFENDANT(S) MUST PAY to the plaintiff(s) the following sums:
LE OU LES DÉFENDEURS DOIVENT VERSER au(x) demandeur(s) les sommes suivantes :

(A) **DEBT** (principal amount claimed minus any payments received since the plaintiff's
    claim was issued) $ **2,400.00**
    LA CRÉANCE (somme demandée moins tout paiement reçu depuis la délivrance $
    de la demande du demandeur)

(B) **PRE-JUDGMENT INTEREST** calculated
    LES INTÉRÊTS ANTÉRIEURS AU JUGEMENT calculés

    on the sum of $ **3,000.00** at the rate of **7**   %
    sur la somme de $ *au taux de*   *pour cent*

    per annum from **January 1**_____ , 20 **--** , to **November 27**_____ , 20 **--** ,
    par an du   *au*

    being **330**_____ days. $ **181.57**
    soit   *jours.* $

APPENDIX 6.5—Form 11B   Concluded

FORM / *FORMULE* 11B   PAGE 3   8899

                                                                          Claim No. / *N° de la demande*

(C) **COSTS** to date $ 105.00
    LES DÉPENS à ce jour $

                                                        TOTAL $ 2,686.57
                                                                                                 $

This judgment bears post-judgment interest at **7**   % per annum commencing this date.
Le présent jugement porte des intérêts postérieurs   *pour cent à partir de la date du présent jugement.*
au jugement calculés au taux annuel de

November 27   , 20 **--**   _____
                                                          (Signature of clerk / *Signature du greffier*)

CAUTION TO DEFENDANT:	**YOU MUST PAY THE AMOUNT OF THIS JUDGMENT DIRECTLY TO THE PLAINTIFF(S) IMMEDIATELY.** Failure to do so may result in additional post-judgment interest and enforcement costs.
AVERTISSEMENT AU DÉFENDEUR :	*VOUS DEVEZ VERSER DIRECTEMENT AU(X) DEMANDEUR(S) LE MONTANT DÛ AUX TERMES DU PRÉSENT JUGEMENT IMMÉDIATEMENT,* à défaut de quoi d'autres intérêts postérieurs au jugement et dépens de l'exécution forcée pourront vous être imputés.

SCR 11.02-11B (June 1, 2009 / *1er juin 2009*) CSD

APPENDIX 6.6   Financial Information Form (Form 20I)

FINANCIAL INFORMATION FORM
FORMULE DE RENSEIGNEMENTS FINANCIERS
Form / *Formule* 20I Ont. Reg. No. / *Règl. de l'Ont.* : 258/98

This form is to be completed by the debtor and served on the creditor.
La présente formule doit être remplie par le débiteur et signifiée au créancier.

This form is not to be filed in the court file.
Cette formule ne doit pas être déposée au dossier du greffe.

MONTHLY INCOME / *REVENU MENSUEL*		MONTHLY EXPENSES / *DÉPENSES MENSUELLES*	
Employer(s) / *Employeur(s)*		Rent/Mortgage / *Loyer/Hypothèque*	$
Employer(s) / *Employeur(s)*		Maintenance/Support Payments / *Versements d'aliments*	$
Net salary / *Salaire net*	$	Property taxes / *Impôts fonciers*	$
Commissions / *Commissions*	$	Utilities (heat, water & light) / *Services d'utilité publique (chauffage, eau et éclairage)*	$
Tips and gratuities / *Pourboires et gratifications*	$	Phone / *Téléphone*	$
Employment insurance / *Prestations d'assurance-emploi*	$	Cable / *Câblodistribution*	$
Pension income / *Revenu de pension*	$	House/Tenant insurance / *Assurance-habitation /assurance de responsabilité locative*	$
Investment income / *Revenu de placements*	$	Life insurance / *Assurance-vie*	$
Rental income / *Revenu de location*	$	Food / *Nourriture*	$
Business income / *Revenu tiré d'une entreprise*	$	Childcare/Babysitting / *Garderie/gardiennage d'enfants*	$
Child tax benefit / *Prestation fiscale pour enfants*	$	Motor vehicle (lease or loan) / *Véhicule automobile (location à bail ou prêt)*	$
Maintenance *(if any)* / *Aliments* (le cas échéant)	$	(licence, insurance, fuel & maintenance) / *(permis, assurance, essence et entretien)*	$
Monthly income of other adult household members / *Revenu mensuel des autres membres adultes du ménage*	$	Transportation (public) / *Transports (en commun)*	$
Other / *Autre*	$		
Income assistance / *Aide au revenu*	$		
INCOME TOTAL / ***REVENU TOTAL***	$	**EXPENSES TOTAL** / ***DÉPENSES TOTALES***	$

Continued on next page / *Suite à la page suivante*

APPENDIX 6.6—Form 20I   Concluded

FORM / *FORMULE* 20I   **PAGE 2**

MONTHLY DEBTS *DETTES MENSUELLES*	VALUE OF ASSETS *VALEUR DES AVOIRS*
Credit card(s) payments *(please specify):* *Paiements de carte(s) de crédit (Veuillez préciser.)*	Real estate equity $ *Valeur nette réelle des biens immobiliers* $

_____ $
                                              $
	Market value $
	   Valeur marchande $

_____ $
                                              $
	Mortgage balance $
	   Solde de l'hypothèque $

_____ $ $	Automobile equity $ *Valeur nette réelle des véhicules automobiles* $
Bank or finance company loan payments *(please specify):* *Remboursement de prêt(s) d'une banque ou d'une compagnie de financement (Veuillez préciser.)*	Make and year _____ *Marque et année*

_____ $
                                              $
	Loan balance $
	   Solde du/des prêts $

_____ $ $	Bank or other account balance(s) *(include RRSP's)* $ *Solde de compte(s) bancaire(s) ou autre(s) compte(s) (Incluez les REÉR.)* $
Department store(s) payments *(please specify):* *Versements à un ou des grands magasins (Veuillez préciser.)*	Stocks & bonds $ *Actions et obligations* $
_____ $ $	Life insurance (cash value) $ *Assurance-vie (valeur de rachat)* $
_____ $ $	Money owing to you $ *Sommes qui vous sont dues* $
	Name of debtor _____ *Nom du débiteur/de la débitrice*
DEBTS TOTAL $ ***DETTES TOTALES*** $	Personal property $ *Biens meubles* $
	Cash $ *Argent comptant* $
	Other $ *Autre* $
	TOTAL VALUE OF ASSETS $ ***VALEUR TOTALE DES AVOIRS*** $

Motions

LEARNING OBJECTIVES

After reading this chapter, you will understand:

- When to use a request for clerk's order on consent
- What a motion is
- What a supporting affidavit is used for
- What an exhibit is
- Time for service and filing of a motion
- *Ex parte* motions
- Contested motions
- Motions in writing for an assessment of damages

WHAT IS A MOTION?

General

A motion is a procedural step that is usually taken while the action is still going on. It is used to obtain a judge's order to resolve an issue in the action that cannot wait until trial. You may also use a motion to resolve an issue that arises after trial. For example, if the trial judge made a purely arithmetical error in calculating the amount of the judgment, a party may make a motion for an order amending the judgment (Rules 17.04(4)(a)(ii) and (5)1).

Motions are governed by Rule 15 of the *Rules of the Small Claims Court*. The form used on a motion is a notice of motion and supporting affidavit (Form 15A).

Any party to an action may make a motion. It does not matter whether you are a plaintiff or a defendant—you have the right to make a motion to the court if you require the court's assistance in resolving an issue. The party making the motion is called the **moving party**, regardless of whether that party is a plaintiff or a defendant. The other party is called the **responding party**, because that party answers, or responds to, the motion.

Judges may make a wide range of orders on a motion. These orders are intended to help the parties resolve issues and move the proceeding along.

For example, a plaintiff who has been unable to serve the plaintiff's claim personally or by an alternative to personal service on a defendant may make a motion to obtain directions from the judge as to an acceptable form of substituted service. If the plaintiff can demonstrate to the court that good faith efforts have been made to comply with Rule 8, and that it is impractical to effect prompt service of the claim personally or by an alternative to personal service, the court may allow substituted service (Rule 8.04).

No Further Motions Without Leave of the Court (Rule 15.04)

Generally, it is up to a party or the party's representative to determine whether it is necessary to bring a motion before the court. However, motions are intended to be used in good faith. That is, they are intended to expedite the action, not slow it down while adding to another party's legal expenses.

Motions that are brought for the sole purpose of harassing another party—that is, delaying the action while adding to another party's costs—are an abuse of court process. (This type of procedural abuse used to be called **motioning the other party to death**.) Rule 15.04 provides that if the court is satisfied that a party has tried to delay the action, add to its costs, or otherwise abuse the court's process by making numerous motions without merit, the court may, on a motion by the party being harassed, make an order prohibiting the other party from making any further motions in the action without leave of the court.

Request for Clerk's Order on Consent (Rule 11.2, Form 11.2A)

Some procedural issues may be resolved by a request for clerk's order on consent (Form 11.2A). The request for clerk's order on consent must be signed by all parties, including added, deleted, or substituted parties. It must state that each party has received a copy of the request, and that no party that would be affected by the order is under disability (Rule 11.2.01(1)2).

If the above conditions are met, the clerk shall, on the filing of a request for clerk's order on consent, make an order granting the relief sought, including costs, if the relief sought is (Rule 11.2.01(1)1):

  i. amending a claim or defence less than 30 days before the originally scheduled trial date,

  ii. adding, deleting or substituting a party less than 30 days before the originally scheduled trial date,

  iii. setting aside the noting in default or default judgment against a party and any specified step to enforce the judgment that has not yet been completed,

  iv. restoring a matter that was dismissed as abandoned under rule 11.1 to the list,

   v.   noting that payment has been made in full satisfaction of a judgment or terms of settlement, or

   vi. dismissing an action.

The clerk shall serve a copy of an order made under Rule 11.2.01(1) on any party who requests it and provides a stamped, self-addressed envelope (Rules 11.2.01(2) and 8(14)).

Where an order is made under Rule 11.2.01(1)1(iii) to set aside a specified step to enforce the judgment and the enforcement step has not been completed, a party shall file a copy of the order at each court location where the enforcement step has been requested (Rule 11.2.01(4)).

BOX 7.1

Reminder: Parties Under Disability

Rule 1.02(1) states that "disability," where used in respect of a person or party, means that the person or party is (a) a minor, (b) mentally incapable within the meaning of s. 6 or 45 of the *Substitute Decisions Act, 1992,* or (c) an absentee within the meaning of the *Absentees Act.* Special procedures for parties under disability are set out at Rule 4. Parties under disability are discussed in chapter 4.

The clerk may refuse to make an order on consent under Rule 11.2.01(1). If the clerk refuses to make the order requested, the clerk shall serve a copy of the request for clerk's order on consent, with reasons for the refusal, on all parties (Rule 11.2.01(3)).

You will find a sample request for clerk's order on consent at appendix 7.1 to this chapter.

Notice of Motion and Supporting Affidavit (Form 15A)

The form that is used on a motion is a notice of motion and supporting affidavit (Form 15A).

The notice of motion states

- the parties and their legal representatives, if any;

- the date, time, and location (including courtroom number) of the hearing of the motion; and

- the order sought by the moving party.

SUPPORTING AFFIDAVIT

Evidence in support of the motion is submitted in writing in the form of a supporting affidavit. Any documents that the moving party intends to rely upon at the hearing of the motion must be attached to the affidavit as **exhibits**.

An individual who makes an affidavit is called a **deponent**. The supporting affidavit on a motion tells the deponent's story about why an order is needed and why it should be granted by the court. Affidavits are written using the first person (I, me, my). The contents of the affidavit, including the exhibits, may be referred to in the moving party's **submissions** on the motion. Submissions are legal arguments put before the judge, for her consideration when deciding whether or not to grant the relief requested.

The allegations made in the supporting affidavit must be sworn or affirmed in the same manner as oral (spoken) evidence given on the witness stand—that is, the deponent (the person making the affidavit) must swear or affirm the truth of the contents of the affidavit in the presence of a commissioner of oaths.

Rule 15 of the *Small Claims Court Rules* does not specifically address formal requirements for affidavits. You may wish to consider using a separate Schedule A attached to and forming part of the Form 15A when drafting a supporting affidavit. With respect to formatting and other issues, you should also consider Rule 4.06 of the *Rules of Civil Procedure*.

AFFIDAVITS
Format

4.06(1) An affidavit used in a proceeding shall,

(a) [deleted];

(b) be expressed in the first person;

(c) state the full name of the deponent and, if the deponent is a party or a lawyer, officer, director, member or employee of a party, shall state that fact;

(d) be divided into paragraphs, numbered consecutively, with each paragraph being confined as far as possible to a particular statement of fact; and

(e) be signed by the deponent and sworn or affirmed before a person authorized to administer oaths or affirmations.

Contents

(2) An affidavit shall be confined to the statement of facts within the personal knowledge of the deponent or to other evidence that the deponent could give if testifying as a witness in court, except where these rules provide otherwise.

Exhibits

(3) An exhibit that is referred to in an affidavit shall be marked as such by the person taking the affidavit and where the exhibit,

(a) is referred to as being attached to the affidavit, it shall be attached to and filed with the affidavit;

(b) is referred to as being produced and shown to the deponent, it shall not be attached to the affidavit or filed with it, but shall be left with the registrar for the use of the court, and on the disposition of the matter in respect of which the affidavit was filed, the exhibit shall be returned to the lawyer or party who filed the affidavit, unless the court orders otherwise; and

(c) is a document, a copy shall be served with the affidavit, unless it is impractical to do so.

The statements made in the affidavit should, for the most part, be within the personal knowledge of the deponent. **Statements of information and belief** are acceptable, so long as the source of the information and the fact of the deponent's belief in its truth are specified in the affidavit. See Rule 39.01(4) of the *Rules of Civil Procedure*.

EXHIBITS

Copies of any documents relied on in support of the motion are attached to the supporting affidavit as exhibits.

The supporting affidavit should identify the document that is attached as an exhibit in sufficient detail. Documents should be identified by the type of document (contract, invoice, cancelled cheque, and so on), the date of the document, the name of the signatory or signatories if any, and any other relevant details. A **signatory** is someone who signs a document. Exhibits should be identified as they occur in the narrative, and copies should be stamped as exhibits and attached to the affidavit in the same order. The deponent must attest to the fact that the copy is a **true copy**—that is, an accurate copy of the original document.

BOX 7.2

What Is a Statement of Information and Belief?

The role of the deponent of an affidavit is the same as the role of a witness who takes the stand and gives evidence under oath at trial, except that the evidence in the affidavit is written, and the evidence at trial is usually spoken.

The general rule is that a witness can give evidence only about matters within her personal knowledge. That rule is relaxed for a deponent of a supporting affidavit on a motion. She is allowed to state, as a fact, information not within her personal knowledge that she has received from another individual or some other source—that is, make statements of information and belief.

A statement of information and belief must be identified as such, by naming the source of the information and the fact that the deponent believes the statement to be true.

When to use a statement of information and belief: The defendant is served with a plaintiff's claim on May 1, 20—. She has a good defence, but does not seek legal representation until May 23, 20—, when she is already out of time for filing a defence. Her paralegal contacts the plaintiff's paralegal by telephone and email on May 23 to advise the plaintiff's paralegal that he has been retained and will require a short extension of the deadline for filing a defence. The plaintiff's paralegal does not respond. When the defendant's paralegal attempts to file the defence on May 25, he is advised by the court clerk that the defendant was noted in default on May 24.

If the matter cannot be resolved on consent, a motion for an order setting aside the default must be brought by the defendant. The defendant will be the deponent in the supporting affidavit. The excerpt below from her supporting affidavit contains an example of a statement of information and belief:

3. I am advised by my paralegal, Joseph Mustafa, and believe that he contacted the plaintiff's paralegal, Frances Douglas, by telephone and email on May 23, 20— to advise Ms. Douglas that I had retained him and to request a short extension of the deadline for filing a defence. A true copy of the email dated May 23, 20— is attached as Exhibit 1.

4. Ms. Douglas did not respond to Mr. Mustafa's telephone call and email. When Mr. Mustafa tried to file my defence on May 25, 20—, he was informed that I had been noted in default on May 24, 20—.

The deponent has no personal knowledge of the events described in paragraphs 3 and 4 above— she was not present when her paralegal tried to contact the plaintiff's paralegal on May 23, 20—, she only knows about Ms. Douglas's failure to respond because Mr. Mustafa told her about it, and she was not present when Mr. Mustafa attempted to file her defence. Her affidavit indicates this by using the language of information and belief—"I am advised by [name of informant] and believe that ..."—specifying the source of the deponent's information, and that she believes the information to be true.

In the body of the affidavit, the document will be identified using language along the following lines:

4. Pursuant to a residential tenancy agreement dated January 13, 20—, I agreed to rent the basement apartment in my home at 67 Harmony Avenue, Toronto, Ontario to the defendant. The tenancy commenced February 1, 20— at a monthly rent of $775.00, including water, heat, and hydro. A true copy of the tenancy agreement dated January 13, 20— is attached as Exhibit 1.

Each exhibit to the original affidavit is stamped. The exhibits are dated and signed by the commissioner of oaths at the same time the affidavit is sworn or affirmed by the deponent. Once sworn or affirmed, exhibits form part of the affidavit, and may be referred to during argument on the motion.

Exhibit stamps may be purchased from a legal stationer such as Dye & Durham, or they may be computer-generated. The standard language of an exhibit stamp is as follows:

This is Exhibit 1
to the affidavit of Om Chandra Prakash
sworn before me at Brampton, Ontario
on November 14, 20—
Ruth Prawer
A commissioner etc.

PERJURY

The deponent of a supporting affidavit has the same moral duty to tell the truth as a witness who takes the stand at trial and swears or affirms that in his testimony to the court he will tell the truth, the whole truth, and nothing but the truth.

Any witness or deponent who knowingly swears or affirms a false affidavit commits **perjury**. Perjury is a criminal offence. Everyone who commits perjury is guilty of an indictable offence and liable to imprisonment for a term not exceeding 14 years.

See page 4 of the Form 15A, excerpted below. See also the *Criminal Code*, ss. 131 and 132.

FIGURE 7.1   Warning: Perjury (Form 15A)

Sworn/Affirmed before me at _____
Déclaré sous serment/Affirmé   (Municipality / *municipalité*)
solennellement devant moi à

in _____
en/à/au   (Province, state or country / *province, État ou pays*)   Signature

on _____ , 20 _____   (This form is to be signed in front of a
le   Commissioner for taking affidavits   lawyer, justice of the peace, notary public
                              Commissaire aux affidavits   or commissioner for taking affidavits.)
                      (Type or print name below if signature is illegible.) (*La présente formule doit être signée en*
                      (*Dactylographiez le nom ou écrivez-le en*   *présence d'un avocat, d'un juge de paix,*
                      caractères d'imprimerie ci-dessous si la   *d'un notaire ou d'un commissaire aux*
                              signature est illisible.)   *affidavits.*)

| WARNING: | IT IS AN OFFENCE UNDER THE *CRIMINAL CODE* TO KNOWINGLY SWEAR OR AFFIRM A FALSE AFFIDAVIT. |
| *AVERTISSEMENT :* | *FAIRE SCIEMMENT UN FAUX AFFIDAVIT CONSTITUE UNE INFRACTION AU* CODE CRIMINEL. |

Types of Motions

GENERAL

In Small Claims Court, there are three types of motions:

1. a motion without notice to other parties (also called an ***ex parte* motion**);

2. a motion on notice to other parties; and

3. a motion in writing for an assessment of damages in an unliquidated claim where all defendants have been noted in default.

MOTION WITHOUT NOTICE (RULE 15.03)

A motion without notice (also known as an *ex parte* motion) is a motion made without notifying the other parties to the action—that is, without serving the motion materials on other parties or giving them any other notice that the motion is being brought.

In Small Claims Court, motions without notice are permitted if the nature or circumstances of the motion make notice unnecessary or not reasonably possible (Rule 15.03(1)). If you appear before a judge on an *ex parte* motion, be prepared to make submissions to the judge as to why the motion should be allowed to proceed without notice to other parties. If the judge decides that notice to the other parties is required, you must follow the procedures for a motion on notice, discussed below.

If you are representing the moving party on an *ex parte* motion, you must ensure that the motion materials filed by the moving party with the court make full and fair disclosure of all material facts upon which the moving party is relying. A paralegal shall not knowingly attempt to deceive a tribunal or influence the course of justice by misstating facts or law, presenting or relying upon a deceptive affidavit, or suppressing what ought to be disclosed (Rule 4.01 of the *Paralegal Rules of Conduct*).

A party who obtains an order on a motion without notice must serve the order, along with a copy of the notice of motion and supporting affidavit, on all other parties within five days after the order is signed (Rule 15.03(2)). Service is by mail, by courier, by fax, by personal service, or by an alternative to personal service, unless the court orders otherwise (Rule 8.01(14)).

Any party affected by the *ex parte* order may make a motion to **set aside** (cancel or have declared null and void) or **vary** (change the terms of) the order, within 30 days after service (Rule 15.03(3)).

On a responding party's motion to set aside or vary an *ex parte* order, a failure by the moving party's representative to make full and fair disclosure of all material facts in the material filed in support of the motion without notice should be raised as a ground for setting aside the order. The *Rules of the Small Claims Court* are silent on this issue, but you may argue by analogy with reference to Rule 1.03(2) of the *Rules of the Small Claims Court* and Rule 39.01(6) of the *Rules of Civil Procedure*.

MOTION ON NOTICE

Before serving the notice of motion and supporting affidavit on other parties, the moving party must contact the court clerk or the court scheduling office to obtain a date and time for hearing the motion (Rule 15.01(2)). The date, time, and location (including the room number of the courtroom where the motion will be heard) must be stated on the notice of motion.

Before contacting the clerk to set a date, you should consider contacting all other parties, including self-represented parties, to obtain a range of dates when they will be available to attend on the motion. That way, a responding party has no excuse for requesting an **adjournment** of the motion—that is, putting it off to a later date—because he or his representative is unavailable on the hearing date.

The notice of motion and the supporting affidavit shall be served at least seven days before the hearing date on all parties who have filed a claim and any defendant who has not been noted in default (Rule 15.01(3)(a)). The notice of motion and supporting affidavit shall be filed with proof of service at least three days before the hearing of the motion (Rule 15.01(3)(b)).

BOX 7.3

Reminder: Counting Time

When counting time under the Rules, it is good practice to refer to Rule 3.01 of the *Rules of Civil Procedure*. Rule 3.01(b) states that, where a period of seven days or less is prescribed, holidays shall not be counted.

For the definition of "holidays," refer to Rule 1.02 of the *Small Claims Court Rules*.

Although the *Small Claims Court Rules* are silent about this, when counting the seven-day minimum period for serving other parties with the motion materials, you should consider excluding holidays. This gives other parties a reasonable amount of time to review the motion materials and prepare for the hearing.

When counting the three-day period for filing the notice of motion and supporting affidavit with proof of service with the court, it is prudent to exclude holidays, including statutory holidays and weekends, from the count. The same principle applies when counting the two-day period for filing a responding affidavit or supplementary affidavit.

The notice of motion and supporting affidavit may be served by personal service, an alternative to personal service, mail, courier, or fax, unless the court orders otherwise (Rule 8.01(14)). Keep in mind that you must count the seven-day minimum notice period from the date service becomes effective. This will vary depending on the type of service, so carefully review Rule 8 if you are unsure about how much time you have before the hearing date to get the motion served and filed.

A party who has been served with motion materials may respond to the moving party's motion by serving an affidavit in response (Form 15B) on every party who has filed a claim or defence. An affidavit in response contains the evidence (including documents) that the responding party intends to rely on when opposing the motion. The affidavit in response must be filed, with proof of service, at least two days before the hearing date (Rule 15.01(4)).

The moving party may serve a supplementary affidavit on every party who has filed a claim or defence and file it with proof of service at least two days before the hearing date (Rule 15.01(5)). A supplementary affidavit may be used to respond to an affidavit filed by a responding party, and/or to put additional evidence before the court for use on the motion.

MOTION AFTER JUDGMENT HAS BEEN SIGNED

If a motion is made after judgment has been signed (that is, after default judgment has been signed or the court has made a final order), the motion materials must be served on all parties, including parties who have been noted in default (Rule 15.01(6)). See also Rule 11.05(3)3.

SAMPLE MOTION FOR SET ASIDE (PARRISH V. THURSTON)

Background

The following is a summary of what has happened so far.

On March 1, 20—, the plaintiff, Maxwell Parrish, loaned Frank Thurston $27,000.00. Mr. Thurston signed a promissory note dated March 1, 20— acknowledging that he had received the money, and promising to pay it back in full on September 1, 20—. The note provided that, in the event of default, interest at a rate of 12% per annum would accrue on any outstanding balance commencing September 1, 20— and continuing until such time as all amounts owing were paid in full.

Mr. Thurston failed to pay the amount owing on September 1, 20—. A demand letter dated October 13, 20— was sent to Mr. Thurston by the plaintiff's paralegal. A plaintiff's claim was issued on November 1, 20— in Brampton Small Claims Court for $25,000.00 plus pre-judgment interest in accordance with the promissory note dated March 1, 20—. The plaintiff waived the amount owing over and above the Small Claims Court monetary jurisdiction.

New Developments

Service of the plaintiff's claim took place on November 3, 20—. The defendant failed to file a defence within the prescribed time. Default judgment was signed on December 1, 20—.

Mr. Thurston receives the default judgment in the mail on December 8, 20—. He immediately contacts Anna Limones at Paxton Limones PC, 82 Main Street, Suite 11, Brampton, Ontario L1N 2P3 TEL: 905 888 9999 FAX: 905 888 0000 for legal advice. Mr. Thurston tells Ms. Limones that he did not receive the plaintiff's claim.

Mr. Thurston's story is that he lost his job on June 15, 20—. To save on expenses, he moved in with some friends at the address on the plaintiff's claim in September, but it did not work out. He moved back home to Brampton in early October. He received the default judgment because it was forwarded to his Brampton address by Canada Post. He has no idea what happened to the plaintiff's claim. When he tried to get in touch with a former roommate at the Labrador Court address, the number was out of service.

By the time the amount owing under the note became due on September 1, Mr. Thurston had been looking for work for two months, with no luck. The market for his type of work is very competitive, and he decided that he should set aside the money he had saved from his employment earnings and freelance work to be used if he was still unemployed when his employment insurance benefits ran out.

Mr. Thurston says he phoned Mr. Parrish several times in July and August and left voicemails advising him that he had lost his job and would not be able to pay off the note until he found another one. Mr. Parrish did not return his calls.

On December 1, 20—, Mr. Thurston found another job, with an annual salary of $39,000.00. He wants to make a motion to set aside the noting in default and default judgment. If the motion is granted, he wants to file a defence making a proposal of terms of payment.

Mr. Thurston's notice of motion and supporting affidavit are at appendix 7.2 to this chapter.

HEARING OF THE MOTION

Method of Hearing (Rule 15.02(1))

A motion may be heard in a number of ways, depending on the relief being asked for and the technology available. Rule 15.02(1) states that a motion may be heard:

(a) In person. The parties or their representatives attend at court before a judge to argue the motion.

(b) By telephone or video conference if telephone or video conference facilities are available at the court. A party must file a request for telephone or video conference (Form 1B) giving reasons for the request. When deciding whether or not to grant the request, the judge shall consider the balance of convenience between the party requesting the telephone or video conference and any party who opposes it; plus any other relevant matter (Rule 1.07(3)).

   If the court makes an order directing a telephone or video conference, the court shall make the necessary arrangements and notify the parties (Rule 1.07(4)).

   A judge presiding at a proceeding or a step in a proceeding may set aside or vary an order directing a telephone or video conference (Rule 1.07(5)).

(c) By a motion in writing for an assessment of damages. In an action where all defendants have been noted in default, the plaintiff may obtain judgment for the unliquidated portion of a claim by filing a motion in writing for an assessment of damages (Rule 11.03(2)(a)). A date must be obtained from the court for the motion to be scheduled before a judge. The attendance of the parties is not required (Rule 15.02(2)). An **assessment order** shall be served by the clerk to the moving party if the moving party provides a stamped, self-addressed envelope with the notice of motion (Rule 8.01(5)). An assessment order is not required to be served on a defendant in default.

An assessment order is an order made by a judge on a motion in writing for an assessment of damages in an unliquidated claim where all defendants have been noted in default.

(d) By any other method that the judge determines is fair and reasonable. This is in keeping with the general principle stated in Rule 1.03(1) that the Rules shall be liberally construed to secure the just, most expeditious, and least expensive determination of every proceeding on its merits in accordance with s. 25 of the *Courts of Justice Act.*

Arguing a Motion in Person or by Telephone or Video Conference (Rules 15.02(1)(a) and (b))

The procedure on a motion is very different from the procedure at a trial.

At a trial, the witnesses for the plaintiff and the defendant take the stand, give sworn evidence in support of the claim or defence, and are cross-examined by the other side.

When all the evidence has been heard and tested by cross-examination, the plaintiff and defendant, or their legal representatives, make submissions as to the order the court should make, with reference to the evidence. The judge then summarizes the findings of fact (that is, the parts of the evidence that the judge accepts as true on a balance of probabilities), applies legal principles to those findings of fact, and makes an order.

When a motion is argued in person, the parties or their representatives are required to be present at the court at the time stated on the notice of motion, and to wait until their matter is called. When the matter is called, the parties or their representatives take their places at the counsel tables facing the judge's bench. The moving party or her representative speaks first. Usually the moving party's submissions to the judge will consist of a brief summary of what she is asking for, and arguments as to why the court should grant the order, with reference to the affidavit and exhibits filed, and any relevant law.

The other party or parties then present arguments as to why the order should not be granted, with reference to any materials they have filed.

The judge may interrupt submissions from time to time to ask questions of either side.

Having heard the parties' submissions, the judge makes an order. The judge may give brief reasons for the order.

Where the technology is available, the same procedure will be followed on a motion by telephone or video conference, except that the time for the telephone or video conference will be fixed, so that the parties and their representatives do not have to waste time sitting around in a courthouse waiting for their matter to be called on the list.

Motion in Writing for an Assessment of Damages (Rules 11.03(2)(a) and 15.02(1)(c))

A motion in writing for an assessment of damages may be made where (1) all or part of the claim is for an unliquidated amount; (2) all defendants have been served with the claim; (3) none of the defendants have filed a defence within the time required; and (4) all defendants have been noted in default. Keep in mind that, in many cases, there will be only one defendant in an unliquidated claim in Small Claims Court. If that defendant goes into default, the plaintiff may note the defendant in default and make a motion in writing for an assessment of damages.

A date must be obtained from the court for the motion to be scheduled before a judge. The attendance of the parties is not required (Rule 15.02(2)). An assessment order shall be served by the clerk to the moving party if the moving party provides a stamped, self-addressed envelope with the notice of motion (Rule 8.01(5)). An assessment order is not required to be served on a defendant in default.

In an unliquidated claim where one or more defendants have filed a defence, a plaintiff requiring an assessment of damages against a defendant noted in default shall proceed to a settlement conference under Rule 13 and, if necessary, to trial in accordance with Rule 17 (Rule 11.03(7)). In other words, the liability of the defendant in default is subject to review and approval by the judge at the settlement conference, or adjudication by the trial judge.

Motions in writing for an assessment of damages were discussed in detail in chapter 5 at pages 166-167. A sample motion for an assessment of damages can be found at appendix 5.2.

CHAPTER SUMMARY

A motion is used to obtain a judge's order or direction resolving an issue in the action that cannot wait until final resolution by trial or settlement.

A motion is not always necessary to determine an issue. Where all parties (including added, deleted, or substituted parties) consent, an issue may be resolved by a request for clerk's order on consent (Form 11.2A), so long as the relief sought falls within Rule 11.2.01(1)1. The request for clerk's order on consent must be signed by all parties (including added, deleted, or substituted parties). It must state that all parties have received a copy of the request, and that no party who would be affected by the order is under disability.

Motions are governed by Rule 15. The form filed on a motion is a notice of motion and supporting affidavit (Form 15A).

Any party to an action may make a motion. The party making the motion is called the moving party. The other party or parties are called responding parties.

The notice of motion sets out the time, date, and place where the motion will be heard, and the relief being asked for on the motion. The supporting affidavit contains the written evidence in support of the motion. Any documents used in support of the motion should be attached to the affidavit as exhibits.

A motion without notice is a motion made without notifying the other party or parties. A motion without notice (also known as an *ex parte* motion) may be made if the nature and circumstances of the motion make notice unnecessary or not reasonably possible. The party making the motion must serve a copy of the order and the motion materials on every party affected by the order within five days after the order is signed. A party affected by an order made on an *ex parte* motion may make a motion to set aside or vary the order within 30 days of being served with the order.

Where a motion is on notice to the other party or parties, the moving party must contact the clerk to obtain a date and time for hearing the motion before serving the motion materials. It is advisable to contact the other party or parties and agree on some mutually convenient dates before contacting the clerk.

The motion materials must be served on all parties, except a defendant who has been noted in default, at least seven days before the hearing date, and filed with proof of service at least three days before the hearing date.

A responding party may serve an affidavit in response and file it, with proof of service, at least two days before the hearing date.

The moving party may serve a supplementary affidavit and file it, with proof of service, at least two days before the hearing date.

A motion on notice may be heard in person, or by telephone or video conference where those facilities are available, or by any other method that a judge determines is fair and reasonable in the circumstances.

KEY TERMS

adjournment

assessment order

deponent

ex parte motion

exhibit

motioning the other party to death

moving party

perjury

responding party

set aside

signatory

statement of information and belief

submission

true copy

vary a court order

REFERENCES

Absentees Act, RSO 1990, c. A2.

Courts of Justice Act, RSO 1990, c. C.43.

Criminal Code, RSC 1985, c. C-46.

Law Society of Upper Canada (LSUC), *Paralegal Rules of Conduct* (Toronto: LSUC, 2007, as amended); available online at http://www.lsuc.on.ca.

Rules of Civil Procedure, RRO 1990, Reg. 194.

Rules of the Small Claims Court, O. Reg. 258/98.

Substitute Decisions Act, 1992, SO 1992, c. S22.

IN-CLASS EXERCISE: Dante v. Herrero—Motion to Set Aside Default Judgment

Background

Francesca Dante loaned $4,000.00 to her best friend, Suzanne Herrero, on December 1, 20—. The loan is secured by a promissory note dated December 1, 20— signed by Ms. Herrero. The terms of the note are as follows:

> By her signature hereto, the undersigned SUZANNE HERRERO acknowledges receipt of the sum of FOUR THOUSAND DOLLARS ($4,000.00), paid by Francesca Dante to Suzanne Herrero on today's date. Interest shall be payable on said sum at a rate of 12% per annum, commencing December 1, 20—. The entire principal amount plus interest thereon shall be due and payable in full on March 1, 20—. In the event of default by Suzanne Herrero, interest shall continue to accrue at a rate of 12% per annum until such time as all amounts owing are paid in full or judgment is obtained, and post-judgment interest shall accrue on the judgment amount, including costs, at a rate of 12% per annum until such time as the amount owing is paid in full.

On March 1, 20—, Ms. Herrero gave Ms. Dante a cheque in the amount of $4,120.00, on account of the principal and interest then owing. The cheque was returned due to insufficient funds.

Ms. Dante commenced a claim for $4,000.00 plus interest at a rate of 12% per year commencing December 1, 20— in claim number 6638 on April 3, 20—.

Ms. Herrero was personally served with the plaintiff's claim on April 5, 20—. She failed to file a defence within the prescribed time. On April 27, 20—, the plaintiff obtained default judgment.

See also chapter 4, box 4.1 at page 97, and the drafting exercises at chapter 4, page 134 and chapter 5, page 174.

New Developments

Ms. Herrero receives the default judgment in the mail on May 3, 20—.

She immediately contacts Paxton Limones PC, 82 Main Street, Suite 11, Brampton, Ontario L1N 2P3 TEL: 905 888 9999 FAX: 905 888 0000 for legal advice.

According to Ms. Herrero, shortly after signing the note dated December 1, 20—, she had some unexpected expenses, and realized that she would not be able to pay the whole amount back in full on the due date of March 1, 20—. She phoned and emailed Ms. Dante several times during January and February to discuss repaying the loan in installments. Ms. Dante insisted that the money be paid in full on March 1. "I need that money for other things!" she told Ms. Herrero during a telephone conversation in early February. She did not respond to Ms. Herrero's email messages.

Frustrated, Ms. Herrero mailed Ms. Dante the cheque dated March 1, 20— for $4,120.00, knowing that it would probably be returned for insufficient funds. She did not return Ms. Dante's phone calls and emails because she was tired of arguing with Ms. Dante about a situation she could not change.

When she was served with the plaintiff's claim, she was so angry she tossed it in a drawer and forgot about it. She realizes now that that was not a very sensible thing to do.

Her telephone number and email address have not changed. She cannot understand why Ms. Dante did not just get in touch with her to talk about payment terms. "We used to be friends, you know," she said. "I don't know what's up with Francesca all of a sudden."

Please draft a notice of motion and supporting affidavit for Ms. Herrero. You are seeking an order for set aside of the noting in default and other relief. Refer to the precedent motion and affidavit at appendix 7.2 for assistance in completing the documents. Keep in mind that the documents at appendix 7.2 are precedents only—they should be used as a guideline, not copied word for word.

The motion is scheduled for May 21, 20— at 9:30 a.m. at Courtroom 10B at Brampton Small Claims Court. The notice of motion and supporting affidavit are prepared on May 7, 20—. The affidavit will be sworn on the same date.

REVIEW QUESTIONS

1. What is a motion? What is it used for?

2. What is the party who makes a motion called? What is the other party called? Can a defendant make a motion?

3. What form is served and filed on a motion? Cite the applicable rule.

4. A plaintiff wishes to use a request for clerk's order on consent to obtain an order amending the claim and adding a party. The added party refuses to sign the request for clerk's order on consent. Can the plaintiff obtain her order using a request for clerk's order on consent? Cite the applicable rule.

5. A defendant wishes to use a request for clerk's order on consent to obtain an order amending the defence. The plaintiff is a party under disability. Can the defendant obtain the order using a request for clerk's order on consent? Cite the applicable rule.

6. What is an affidavit? What is the person who makes an affidavit called?

7. What is the supporting affidavit used for on a motion?

8. What are submissions?

9. What are exhibits? How is an exhibit identified in an affidavit?

10. What is a motion without notice? When may a motion without notice to other parties be made? Please refer to any relevant rule or rules.

11. Give a brief description of the procedure on a motion without notice. Must the moving party file proper motion materials? What are the obligations of a party who obtains an order on a motion without notice? Please refer to any relevant rule or rules.

12. Give a brief description of the procedure at the hearing of a motion on notice that is being heard in person.

APPENDIX 7.1   Chakravarty v. Complete Home Renovations: Request for Clerk's Order on Consent (Form 11.2A)

ONTARIO

Superior Court of Justice
Cour supérieure de justice

Request for Clerk's Order on Consent
Demande d'ordonnance du greffier sur consentement

Form / *Formule* 11.2A Ont. Reg. No. / *Règl. de l'Ont.* : 258/98

Brampton	**4586**
Small Claims Court / *Cour des petites créances de*	Claim No. / *N° de la demande*
7755 Hurontario Street	
Brampton, Ontario	
L6W 4T6	
Address / *Adresse*	
905 456 4700	
Phone number / *Numéro de téléphone*	

Plaintiff No. 1 / *Demandeur n° 1*

☐ Additional plaintiff(s) listed on attached Form 1A.
Le ou les demandeurs additionnels sont mentionnés sur la formule 1A ci-jointe.

Last name, or name of company / *Nom de famille ou nom de la compagnie*		
Chakravarty		

First name / *Premier prénom*	Second name / *Deuxième prénom*	Also known as / *Également connu(e) sous le nom de*
Amrita		

Address (street number, apt., unit) / *Adresse (numéro et rue, app., unité)*		
c/o Prior Mustafa LLP		

City/Town / *Cité/ville*	Province	Phone no. / *N° de téléphone*

Postal code / *Code postal*		Fax no. / *N° de télécopieur*

Representative / *Représentant(e)*	LSUC # / *N° du BHC*
Prior Mustafa LLP Attention: Paralegal name	**######**

Address (street number, apt., unit) / *Adresse (numéro et rue, app., unité)*		
22 County Court Boulevard		

City/Town / *Cité/ville*	Province	Phone no. / *N° de téléphone*
Brampton	**Ontario**	**905 111 2222**

Postal code / *Code postal*		Fax no. / *N° de télécopieur*
A1A 2B3		**905 111 2233**

Defendant No. 1 / *Défendeur n° 1*

☐ Additional defendant(s) listed on attached Form 1A.
Le ou les défendeurs additionnels sont mentionnés sur la formule 1A ci-jointe.

Last name, or name of company / *Nom de famille ou nom de la compagnie*		
Complete Home Renovations		

First name / *Premier prénom*	Second name / *Deuxième prénom*	Also known as / *Également connu(e) sous le nom de*

Address (street number, apt., unit) / *Adresse (numéro et rue, app., unité)*		
455 Lonsdale Court		

City/Town / *Cité/ville*	Province	Phone no. / *N° de téléphone*
Mississauga	**Ontario**	**905 123 4444**

Postal code / *Code postal*		Fax no. / *N° de télécopieur*
X2X 3Y4		**905 123 5555**

Representative / *Représentant(e)*	LSUC # / *N° du BHC*

Address (street number, apt., unit) / *Adresse (numéro et rue, app., unité)*		

City/Town / *Cité/ville*	Province	Phone no. / *N° de téléphone*

Postal code / *Code postal*		Fax no. / *N° de télécopieur*

NOTE: This request must be signed by all parties and anyone being added, deleted or substituted.
REMARQUE : *La présente demande doit être signée par toutes les parties et par toute personne qui est jointe, radiée ou substituée.*

APPENDIX 7.1   Continued

FORM / *FORMULE* 11.2A   **PAGE 2**   **4586**

Claim No. / *N° de la demande*

TO THE PARTIES:
AUX PARTIES :

THIS REQUEST IS FILED BY: Amrita Chakravarty

LA PRÉSENTE DEMANDE EST DÉPOSÉE PAR :   (Name of party / *Nom de la partie*)

I state that:
Je déclare que :

☒   Each party has received a copy of this form.
     Chaque partie a reçu une copie de la présente formule.

☒   No party that would be affected by the order is under disability.
     Aucune partie sur laquelle l'ordonnance aurait une incidence n'est incapable.

☒   This form has been signed and consented to by all parties, including any parties to be added, deleted or substituted.
     Toutes les parties, y compris celles qui doivent être jointes, radiées ou substituées, ont signé la présente formule et y ont consenti.

I request that the clerk make the following order(s) on the consent of all parties:
Je demande au greffier de rendre l'ordonnance ou les ordonnances suivantes sur consentement de toutes les parties :
(Check appropriate boxes. / Cochez les cases appropriées.)

☒   set aside the noting in default of   **Complete Home Renovations**
     l'annulation de la constatation du défaut de   (Name of defendant(s) / *Nom du/de la/des défendeur(s)/défenderesse(s)*)

☐   set aside Default Judgment against
     l'annulation du jugement par défaut prononcé contre   (Name of defendant(s) / *Nom du/de la/des défendeur(s)/défenderesse(s)*)

☐   restore to the list the following matter that was dismissed under Rule 11.1:   (Specify.)
     la réinscription au rôle de l'affaire suivante qui a été rejetée aux termes de la règle 11.1 :   *(Précisez.)*

☐   cancel the examination hearing regarding
     l'annulation de l'interrogatoire concernant   (Name of person to be examined / *Nom de la personne qui doit être interrogée*)

☐   with respect to the following step(s) taken to enforce the default judgment that are not yet completed:
     à l'égard de la ou des mesures suivantes qui ont été prises pour exécuter le jugement par défaut et qui ne sont pas encore menées à terme :

     ☐   withdraw the Writ of Seizure and Sale of Land issued against: (Name of debtor(s))
        le retrait du bref de saisie-exécution de biens-fonds délivré contre :   (*Nom du/de la/des débiteur(s)/débitrice(s)*)

     and directed to the sheriff of the   :
     et adressé au shérif de   (Name of county/region in which the sheriff(enforcement office) is located / *Nom du comté/de la région où se trouve le shérif (bureau de l'exécution)*)

     (Provide instructions about what is to be done with any proceeds held or property seized by the sheriff. / *Donnez des instructions sur ce qu'il faut faire de tout produit de la vente détenu ou bien saisi par le shérif.*)

APPENDIX 7.1   Continued

☐ withdraw the Writ of Seizure and Sale of Personal Property issued against: (Name of debtor(s)
le retrait du bref de saisie-exécution de biens meubles délivré contre :   *(Nom du/de la/des débiteur(s)/débitrice(s))*

and directed to the bailiff of the _____   :
et adressé à l'huissier de   (Small Claims Court location / *Emplacement de la Cour des petites créances*)

(Provide instructions about what is to be done with any proceeds held by the clerk of the court or property that has been seized by the bailiff.
/ Donnez des instructions sur ce qu'il faut faire de tout produit de la vente détenu par le greffier du tribunal ou de tout bien saisi par l'huissier.)

☐ terminate the Notice of Garnishment or Notice of Renewal of Garnishment issued against:
la fin de l'avis de saisie-arrêt ou de l'avis de renouvellement de la saisie-arrêt délivré contre :

_____
(Name of debtor(s) / *Nom du/de la/des débiteur(s)/débitrice(s))*

and directed to _____   :
et adressé à   (Name of garnishee / *Nom du tiers saisi)*

(Provide instructions about what is to be done with any money held by the clerk of the court. / *Donnez des instructions sur ce qu'il*
faut faire de toute somme d'argent détenue par le greffier du tribunal.)

☐ note that payment has been made in full satisfaction of an order or terms of settlement
le constat qu'un paiement intégral a été effectué en exécution d'une ordonnance ou des conditions de la transaction

☐ dismiss the: ☐ Plaintiff's Claim   ☐ Defendant's Claim
le rejet de la :   *demande du demandeur*   *demande du défendeur*

☒ costs in the amount of $ _____**200.00**_____ , to be paid to   **Amrita Chakravarty**
le versement de   (Amount / *Montant)* $ *au titre des dépens à*   (Name of party(ies) / *Nom de la ou des parties)*

_____ by   **Complete Home Renovations**
par   (Name of party(ies) / *Nom de la ou des parties)*

**The originally scheduled trial date is less than 30 days away and I request that the clerk make the
following order(s) on the consent of all parties and any person to be added or substituted :**
*La date du procès fixée à l'origine tombe dans moins de 30 jours et je demande au greffier de rendre
l'ordonnance ou les ordonnances suivantes sur consentement de toutes les parties et de toute personne
qui doit être jointe ou substituée :*
(Check appropriate boxes. / Cochez les cases appropriées.)

☐ amend a Plaintiff's Claim issued on _____ , 20 _____ .
la modification de la demande d'un demandeur délivrée le
(Attach two (2) copies of the amended Plaintiff's Claim. / Annexez deux (2) copies de la demande du demandeur modifiée.)

☐ amend a Defence filed on _____ , 20 _____ .
la modification d'une défense déposée le
(Attach two (2) copies of the amended Defence. / Annexez deux (2) copies de la défense modifiée.)

APPENDIX 7.1   Continued

FORM / *FORMULE* **11.2A**   **PAGE 4**   4586

Claim No. / *N° de la demande*

☐ amend a Defendant's Claim issued on _____ , 20 _____ .
la modification de la demande d'un défendeur délivrée le
(Attach two (2) copies of the amended Defendant's Claim. / Annexez deux (2) copies de la demande du défendeur modifiée.)

☐ add _____
la jonction de   (Name of party / *Nom de la partie*)

    to the   ☐ Plaintiff's Claim   ☐ Defendant's Claim
    à la   *demande du demandeur*   *demande du défendeur*

    as a   ☐ defendant   ☐ Plaintiff
    à titre de   *défendeur/défenderesse*   *demandeur/demanderesse*

☐ delete _____
la radiation de   (Name of party / *Nom de la partie*)

    from the   ☐ Plaintiff's Claim   ☐ Defendant's Claim
    de la   *demande du demandeur*   *demande du défendeur*

☐ substitute _____
la substitution à   (Name of party / *Nom de la partie*)

    with _____
    de   (Name of party / *Nom de la partie*)

    in the   ☐ Plaintiff's Claim   ☐ Defendant's Claim
    dans la   *demande du demandeur*   *demande du défendeur*

December 15 _____ , 20 --	_____ , 20 _____
(Signature of party consenting / *Signature de la partie qui consent*)	(Signature of party consenting / *Signature de la partie qui consent*)
Amrita Chakravarty	**Franklin Butler for Complete Home Renovations**
(Name of party consenting / *Nom de la partie qui consent*)	(Name of party consenting / *Nom de la partie qui consent*)
(Signature of witness / *Signature du témoin*)	(Signature of witness / *Signature du témoin*)
Paralegal name	**Witness name**
(Name of witness / *Nom du témoin*)	(Name of witness / *Nom du témoin*)
_____ , 20 _____	_____ , 20 _____
(Signature of party consenting / *Signature de la partie qui consent*)	(Signature of party consenting / *Signature de la partie qui consent*)
(Name of party consenting / *Nom de la partie qui consent*)	(Name of party consenting / *Nom de la partie qui consent*)
(Signature of witness / *Signature du témoin*)	(Signature of witness / *Signature du témoin*)
(Name of witness / *Nom du témoin*)	(Name of witness / *Nom du témoin*)

APPENDIX 7.1   Concluded

DISPOSITION: *The clerk of the court will complete this section.*
DÉCISION :   Le greffier du tribunal remplit cette partie.

☐ order to go as asked
ordonnance de procéder comme il a été demandé

☐ order refused because:
ordonnance refusée pour les motifs suivants :

_____, 20 _____   _____

(Signature of clerk / *Signature du greffier*)

APPENDIX 7.2   Parrish v. Thurston: Motion for Set Aside of Noting in Default and Default Judgment (Form 15A)

ONTARIO

Superior Court of Justice
Cour supérieure de justice

Notice of Motion and Supporting Affidavit
Avis de motion et affidavit à l'appui
Form / *Formule* 15A Ont. Reg. No. / *Règl. de l'Ont.* : 258/98

Brampton	**4567**
Small Claims Court / *Cour des petites créances de*	Claim No. / *N° de la demande*
7755 Hurontario Street	
Brampton, Ontario	
L6W 4T6	
Address / *Adresse*	
905 456 4700	
Phone number / *Numéro de téléphone*	

Plaintiff No. 1 / *Demandeur n° 1*   ☐ Additional plaintiff(s) listed on attached Form 1A.
Le ou les demandeurs additionnels sont mentionnés sur la formule 1A ci-jointe.

Last name, or name of company / *Nom de famille ou nom de la compagnie*		
Parrish		
First name / *Premier prénom*	Second name / *Deuxième prénom*	Also known as / *Également connu(e) sous le nom de*
Maxwell		
Address (street number, apt., unit) / *Adresse (numéro et rue, app., unité)*		
c/o Prior Mustafa LLP		
City/Town / *Cité/ville*	Province	Phone no. / *N° de téléphone*
Postal code / *Code postal*		Fax no. / *N° de télécopieur*
Representative / *Représentant(e)*		LSUC # / *N° du BHC*
Prior Mustafa LLP Attention: Marie Prior		**######**
Address (street number, apt., unit) / *Adresse (numéro et rue, app., unité)*		
22 County Court Boulevard		
City/Town / *Cité/ville*	Province	Phone no. / *N° de téléphone*
Brampton	**Ontario**	**905 111 2222**
Postal code / *Code postal*		Fax no. / *N° de télécopieur*
A1A 2B3		**905 111 2233**

Defendant No. 1 / *Défendeur n° 1*   ☐ Additional defendant(s) listed on attached Form 1A.
Le ou les défendeurs additionnels sont mentionnés sur la formule 1A ci-jointe.

Last name, or name of company / *Nom de famille ou nom de la compagnie*		
Thurston		
First name / *Premier prénom*	Second name / *Deuxième prénom*	Also known as / *Également connu(e) sous le nom de*
Frank		
Address (street number, apt., unit) / *Adresse (numéro et rue, app., unité)*		
c/o Paxton Limones PC		
City/Town / *Cité/ville*	Province	Phone no. / *N° de téléphone*
Postal code / *Code postal*		Fax no. / *N° de télécopieur*
Representative / *Représentant(e)*		LSUC # / *N° du BHC*
Paxton Limones PC Attention: Anna Limones		**######**
Address (street number, apt., unit) / *Adresse (numéro et rue, app., unité)*		
82 Main Street, Suite 11		
City/Town / *Cité/ville*	Province	Phone no. / *N° de téléphone*
Brampton	**Ontario**	**905 888 9999**
Postal code / *Code postal*		Fax no. / *N° de télécopieur*
L1N 2P3		**905 888 0000**

APPENDIX 7.2   Continued

FORM / *FORMULE* 15A   **PAGE 2**   **4567**

Claim No. / *N° de la demande*

THIS COURT WILL HEAR A MOTION on December 21 _____ , 20 -- , **at** 9:30 a.m. _____ ,
LE TRIBUNAL PRÉCITÉ ENTENDRA UNE MOTION le _____ , *à* _____ (Time / *heure*)

or as soon as possible after that time, at   **7755 Hurontario Street, Brampton, Ontario, Courtroom 7A**
ou dès que possible par la suite à/au   (Address of court location and courtroom number / *Adresse du tribunal et numéro de la salle d'audience*)

Complete Part A or Part B below, then complete the affidavit in support of motion on page 3. / *Remplissez la partie A ou la partie B ci-dessous. Remplissez ensuite l'affidavit à l'appui de la motion à la page 3.*

A.   This motion will be made in person
     by   Frank Thurston   ,
     La motion sera présentée en personne par :   (Name of party / *Nom de la partie*)

     for the following order : / *en vue d'obtenir l'ordonnance suivante :*

☒   the court's permission to extend time to   (Specify)
     l'autorisation du tribunal de proroger le délai pour   (Précisez)

     file a defence _____ .

☒   set aside default judgment and noting in default.
     l'annulation du jugement par défaut et la constatation du défaut.

☐   set aside noting in default.
     l'annulation de la constatation du défaut.

☒   permission to file a Defence.
     l'autorisation de déposer une défense.

☐   permission to file a Defendant's Claim.
     l'autorisation de déposer une demande du défendeur.

☐   terminate garnishment and/or withdraw writ(s).
     la mainlevée de la saisie-arrêt ou le retrait d'un ou de plusieurs brefs, ou les deux.

☒   Other:
     Autre :

     Costs of this motion to be paid by the plaintiff to the defendant.

☒   **ADDITIONAL PAGES ARE ATTACHED BECAUSE MORE ROOM WAS NEEDED.**
     DES FEUILLES SUPPLÉMENTAIRES SONT ANNEXÉES EN RAISON DU MANQUE D'ESPACE.

☐   **DOCUMENTS ARE ATTACHED.**
     PIÈCES JOINTES.

NOTE: **IF YOU FAIL TO ATTEND AN IN-PERSON MOTION,** an order may be made against you, with costs, in your absence. If you want to attend the motion by telephone or video conference, complete and file a Request for Telephone or Video Conference (Form 1B). If the court permits it, the clerk will make the necessary arrangements and notify the parties [R. 1.07(5)].

REMARQUE :   *SI VOUS NE VOUS PRÉSENTEZ PAS EN PERSONNE À L'AUDITION DE LA MOTION, une ordonnance peut être rendue contre vous en votre absence, avec dépens. Si vous voulez assister à l'audition de la motion par conférence téléphonique ou vidéoconférence, remplissez et déposez la Demande de conférence téléphonique ou vidéoconférence (formule 1B). Si le tribunal l'autorise, le greffier prendra les dispositions nécessaires et en avisera les parties [par. 1.07 (5)].*

SCR 15.01-15A (June 1, 2009 / *1er juin 2009*) CSD   **Continued on next page / *Suite à la page suivante***

APPENDIX 7.2　Continued

FORM / *FORMULE* 15A　　　　　　　PAGE 3　　　　　　　4567
Claim No. / *N° de la demande*

B.　This motion in writing for an assessment of damages is made by
La présente motion par écrit en vue d'une évaluation des dommages-intérêts est présentée par

_____ ,
(Name of plaintiff / *Nom du demandeur/de la demanderesse*)

who asks the court for an order assessing damages against
qui demande au tribunal de rendre une ordonnance d'évaluation des dommages-intérêts contre

_____
(Name of defendant(s) / *Nom du/de la/des défendeur(s)/défenderesse(s)*)

who have/has been noted in default.
qui a/ont été constaté(e)(s) en défaut.

AFFIDAVIT IN SUPPORT OF MOTION / *AFFIDAVIT À L'APPUI DE LA MOTION*

My name is Frank Thurston
Je m'appelle 　　　　　　　　　(Full name / *Nom et prénoms*)

I live in Brampton, Ontario
J'habite à 　　　　　　　　　(Municipality & province / *Municipalité et province*)

I swear/affirm that the following is true:
Je déclare sous serment/j'affirme solennellement que les renseignements suivants sont véridiques :

Set out the facts in numbered paragraphs. If you learned a fact from someone else, you must give that person's name and state that you believe that fact to be true.
Indiquez les faits sous forme de dispositions numérotées. Si vous avez pris connaissance d'un fait par l'entremise d'une autre personne, vous devez indiquer le nom de cette personne et déclarer que vous croyez que ce fait est véridique.

See Schedule A attached

APPENDIX 7.2   Continued

FORM / *FORMULE* 15A	PAGE 4	**4567**
		Claim No. / *N° de la demande*

AFFIDAVIT IN SUPPORT OF MOTION, continued / *AFFIDAVIT À L'APPUI DE LA MOTION, suite*

See Schedule A attached

If more space is required, attach and initial extra pages. / Si vous avez besoin de plus d'espace, annexez une ou des feuilles supplémentaires et paraphez-les.

Sworn/Affirmed before me at **Brampton**
Déclaré sous serment/Affirmé   (Municipality / municipalité)
solennellement devant moi à

in **Ontario**
en/à/au   (Province, state or country / province, État ou pays)

on **December 9**   , 20 **--**
le   Commissioner for taking affidavits
                                                    Commissaire aux affidavits
                                        (Type or print name below if signature is illegible.)
                                        (Dactylographiez le nom ou écrivez-le en caractères d'imprimerie ci-dessous si la signature est illisible.)

Signature
(This form is to be signed in front of a lawyer, justice of the peace, notary public or commissioner for taking affidavits.)
(La présente formule doit être signée en présence d'un avocat, d'un juge de paix, d'un notaire ou d'un commissaire aux affidavits.)

WARNING: IT IS AN OFFENCE UNDER THE *CRIMINAL CODE* **TO KNOWINGLY SWEAR OR AFFIRM A FALSE AFFIDAVIT.**
AVERTISSEMENT : FAIRE SCIEMMENT UN FAUX AFFIDAVIT CONSTITUE UNE INFRACTION AU CODE CRIMINEL.

SCR 15.01-15A (June 1, 2009 / *1er juin 2009*) CSD

APPENDIX 7.2   Continued

Schedule A

1.   I am the defendant in this action and have personal knowledge of the following.

2.   On March 1, 20—, the plaintiff loaned me $27,000.00 pursuant to a promissory note of the same date. Under the terms of the note, the entire amount was due in full on September 1, 20—. Interest at a rate of 12% per annum began to accrue in the event of default of payment on September 1, 20—. Interest continues to accrue until such time as any amounts owing pursuant to the note are paid in full. A true copy of the promissory note dated March 1, 20— is attached as Exhibit 1.

3.   When I borrowed the money, I was employed full-time by XRZ Networks Inc. at an annual salary of $40,000.00. I was also doing freelance work. I used the money to pay some business debts and purchase necessary equipment and supplies for my business. I anticipated that I would be able to pay the full amount back on the due date, with the proceeds from a couple of the freelance projects.

4.   My employment with XRZ Networks Inc. was terminated abruptly on June 15, 20—. I immediately began seeking other employment, but the market for my type of work is very competitive, and the results of my job search were disappointing. Because of the uncertainty about when I would find paid employment, I decided to use my employment insurance benefits for my living expenses, and set aside the money that I had saved from my employment earnings and freelance work to be used if I was still unemployed when my benefits ran out.

5.   I phoned Mr. Parrish several times in July and August and left voicemails advising him that I had lost my job and would not be able to pay the amount due on the note on September 1. He did not return my calls.

6.   I am advised by my paralegal, Anna Limones, and believe that according to the affidavit of service in the court file, the plaintiff's claim was served on November 3, 20— by

APPENDIX 7.2   Continued

leaving a copy with one of my former roommates at Unit 103, 45 Labrador Court and delivering another copy to that address by courier. I did not receive the plaintiff's claim. I lived at the Labrador Court address for a brief period in September, 20—. I moved back to Brampton in early October. I have been living at my parents' home in Brampton since then.

7. I received the default judgment dated December 1, 20— because it was forwarded to my Brampton address by Canada Post. When I received the default judgment, I promptly sought legal assistance. I have tried to contact a former roommate at the Labrador Court address to find out what happened with the plaintiff's claim, but the number is out of service.

8. On December 1, 20—, I found full-time employment, at an annual salary of $39,000.00. I am in a position to pay the amount claimed by the plaintiff in installments. I wish to file a defence with a proposal of terms of payment.

APPENDIX 7.2 Concluded

By his signature hereto, the undersigned FRANK THURSTON acknowledges receipt of the sum of TWENTY-SEVEN THOUSAND DOLLARS ($27,000.00), paid by Maxwell Parrish to Frank Thurston on today's date. The entire principal amount shall be due and payable in full on September 1, 20—. In the event of default by Frank Thurston, interest shall accrue at a rate of 12% per annum until such time as all amounts owing are paid in full or judgment is obtained, and post-judgment interest shall accrue on the judgment amount at a rate of 12% per annum until such time as the judgment is paid in full.

Date: *March 1, 20—*   Signed: *Frank Thurston*

                                              Frank Thurston

This is Exhibit 1
to the affidavit of Frank Thurston
sworn before me at Brampton, Ontario
on December 9, 20—
Anna Limones
A commissioner etc.

Offers to Settle and Settlement Conferences

LEARNING OBJECTIVES

After reading this chapter, you will understand:

- The duty to encourage compromise and settlement

- Restrictions on disclosure of settlement discussions

- When and how to make or accept an offer to settle

- How to finalize settlement

- The consequences of failing to comply with the terms of settlement

- The costs consequences of failing to accept an offer to settle

- The purpose of the settlement conference

- The role of the court at the settlement conference

INTRODUCTION

If a reasonable outcome for the client can be achieved by negotiation, paralegals have a duty to encourage clients to settle their differences.

The *Small Claims Court Rules* encourage compromise and settlement. Defendants are encouraged to settle by Rule 9.03, which states that a defendant may admit liability for all or part of the amount claimed and make a proposal of terms of payment in the defence. If the plaintiff does not dispute the defendant's proposal within 20 days of service of the defence, the proposal of terms of payment is deemed to be accepted and the defendant may begin paying money into court in accordance with its terms, as if it were a court order.

If the matter does not settle at the pleadings stage, the parties are given another opportunity at the settlement conference. The Small Claims Court settlement conference is intended, among other things, to narrow and resolve the issues and to facilitate settlement of the action (Rule 13.03(1)).

Rule 14—Offer to Settle sets up a detailed process for making and accepting offers to settle as the action goes forward. Rule 14.01.1 states that an offer, an acceptance, and a notice of withdrawal of offer shall be in writing. There are court forms that may be used for each of these steps (Forms 14A, 14B, and 14C). There is also a court form for recording the terms of a settlement in writing (Form 14D).

The parties may continue to negotiate settlement up until any time before a final disposition of the matter. Depending on the result obtained at trial, there may be adverse costs consequences for a party who does not accept an offer to settle that is made seven or more days before the trial and remains open until the trial. See Rule 14.07, discussed below.

THE PROFESSIONAL DUTY TO ENCOURAGE SETTLEMENT

The *Paralegal Rules of Conduct* (the "Paralegal Rules") and the *Paralegal Professional Conduct Guidelines* (the "Guidelines") impose a professional obligation on paralegals to encourage compromise and settlement. Paralegal Rule 3.02(5) states that a paralegal shall advise and encourage a client to compromise or settle a dispute whenever it is possible to do so on a reasonable basis, and shall discourage a client from commencing ill-advised legal proceedings.

Compromise and Settlement

The costs of legal proceedings are not just monetary. There is also a certain amount of wear and tear on the parties and on others associated with the matter. Litigation tends to keep alive grievances and ill-feeling that might otherwise dissipate over time. It can be very stressful, and it is often time-consuming. **Compromise and settlement** (also called "compromising your damages") means that a party to a dispute agrees to waive some part of what is owing or make other concessions in order to resolve a matter without the additional costs, delay, and uncertainty of continuing a legal proceeding.

You should encourage your client to make an offer to settle as early as possible in a proceeding (Paralegal Guideline 7 at paragraph 7). Before making an offer to settle, you should discuss possible terms with your client, and obtain his informed instructions as to what those terms should be. You should confirm those instructions in writing. You should allow the other party reasonable time for review and acceptance of the offer.

When you receive an offer to settle from another party, you should review the offer with your client. You should explain its terms, the implications of accepting the offer, and the possibility of making a counter-offer. If you think the offer is reasonable and the client should accept the offer, you should discuss your reasons with the client and ensure that he understands them. You must obtain his clear and informed instructions before accepting the offer, and you should confirm those instructions in writing.

If you receive an offer to settle from another party and you think your client should make a counter-offer, you should discuss your reasons with the client and ensure that he understands them. Before making the counter-offer, you must obtain the client's clear and informed instructions to do so. You should confirm those instructions in writing.

When making an offer to settle or a counter-offer, you should include a term stating a date and time when the offer or counter-offer expires.

NEGOTIATING SETTLEMENT (RULE 14)

General

A settlement agreement in a court action is a contract that is intended to bring the litigation to an end, so long as the parties perform its terms.

As with any contract, for a settlement agreement to be legally binding, there must be an offer, acceptance, and **consideration**. Consideration is something that causes a party to enter into a contract or agreement. It has been defined as "some right, interest, profit or benefit accruing to the one party, or some forbearance, detriment, loss or responsibility given, suffered or undertaken by the other" (see *Currie v. Misa*).

Consent by the parties to the terms of the settlement agreement must be *informed*—that is, the parties must have enough information about what they are signing and any risks or benefits to themselves to make an intelligent decision about whether or not to sign. There must be no **duress** or **misrepresentation**. Duress is threatening someone or otherwise forcing her to agree to something she would not have agreed to without the threat or use of force. Misrepresentation is giving an inaccurate, untrue, or incomplete version of the facts—in the case of a

---

BOX 8.1

What Exactly Is Consideration?

Consideration is a legal concept deriving from the 19th-century common law of contract. You will find a list of things that the courts have called consideration below. The list is not exhaustive.

Note: A **promisor** is a person who makes a promise. A **promisee** is a person who receives a promise.

Consideration may be:

- a right bargained for by the promisee;

- indirect benefits to the promisor;

- liability or risk assumed, right relinquished, disadvantage experienced, or change of legal status by promisee, so long as the detriment is at the promisor's request; or

- 10 peppercorns (Lord Denning).

settlement, an inaccurate or incomplete version of the terms of the agreement, with the result that one or more of the parties signing does not have a real understanding of the potential risks or disadvantages of what he is agreeing to do.

Contract law also applies to the negotiation itself. You must know the rules of offer and acceptance, and when they add up to an agreement.

To begin with, you need to know the difference between an **offer** and an **invitation to treat**. An offer contains all essential terms. If an offer is accepted, the result is a binding contract that can be performed. An invitation to treat, on the other hand, is intended to do nothing more than open up negotiations. An invitation to treat lacks at least some essential terms, such as a fixed amount of money to be paid, terms of payment, and so on.

BOX 8.2

Invitation to Treat

A common example of an invitation to treat is an advertisement of a house for resale in a newspaper or on the Internet. There are pictures of the house, along with a brief description of its best features, and, in some cases, a price. In most housing markets, it is understood that the description is intended to emphasize the house's best features (and may not be accurate), that the price (whether or not it is advertised) is negotiable, and that closing the deal will be subject to certain conditions, including clear title to the land and a satisfactory report by a building inspector. In other words, the advertisement is designed to invite negotiation with potential purchasers—it is not a firm offer.

Table 8.1 is a basic outline of the law of offer and acceptance. Keep in mind that contracts or settlement agreements are often the result of prolonged negotiation.

When negotiating a settlement with opposing parties, you must negotiate in good faith—that is, with a view to achieving a settlement that both parties can live with. Negotiation is about ascertaining the goals of the parties, and working towards an agreement that will achieve those goals. When negotiating, you should represent your client's interests resolutely and fearlessly, but that does not mean trying to hammer the other party into the ground. This is why a settlement negotiation is also called *compromise* and settlement—because a settlement cannot be achieved unless both parties compromise, or make trade-offs, in order to achieve their own goals and avoid the expense, stress, and uncertain outcomes of litigation.

Negotiating settlement with self-represented parties presents unique challenges. The self-represented party must understand that you are acting exclusively in the interests of your own client. Unsophisticated individuals will sometimes mistake politeness and professionalism for sympathy with their own case. You must be very careful not to encourage this misconception, and you must be very careful also not to say anything to a self-represented party that could be mistaken for legal advice.

TABLE 8.1 Negotiating an Agreement

Action	Response	Legal result
Party A makes an invitation to treat or negotiate	Party B responds	Negotiation begins; may or may not result in a binding contract
Party A makes an offer containing all the essential terms, including the offer's expiry date	Party B does not respond	Offer expires on the date stated in the offer*
Party A makes an offer containing all the essential terms No expiry date	Party B does not respond	Party A may withdraw the offer by serving notice of withdrawal of offer (Form 14C) on Party B*
Party A makes an offer containing all the essential terms	Party B rejects the offer	Party A's offer becomes void when it is rejected
Party A makes an offer containing all the essential terms	Party B accepts the offer	The parties have a binding agreement
Party A makes an offer containing all the essential terms	Party B makes a counter-offer containing all the essential items	If Party A accepts Party B's counter-offer, there is a binding agreement If Party A rejects Party B's counter-offer, there is no deal and negotiations end or start all over again with a new offer by one of the parties

* Exception: A defendant makes a proposal of terms of payment in the defence. If the plaintiff does not dispute the proposal within 20 days, the plaintiff is deemed to have accepted the proposal, and the defendant may commence making the payments as if the proposal were a court order.

Offer to Settle (Form 14A)

GENERAL

An offer to settle, an acceptance of an offer to settle, and a withdrawal of an offer to settle shall be made in writing (Rule 14.01.1(1)). An offer may be made using Form 14A. An acceptance of an offer to settle may be made using Form 14B. A withdrawal of an offer to settle may be made in Form 14C.

An offer to settle may be made at any time after the action is started (Rule 14.02(1)).

An offer to settle does not have to be made using Form 14A. However, it must be in writing, and it must be signed and dated by the party making the offer or her legal representative.

Never make an offer to settle on a client's behalf without first discussing the offer with your client and ensuring that the client understands the risks and benefits of the offer, and agrees to its terms. You should obtain the client's written instructions to make the offer.

BOX 8.3

Is a Proposal of Terms of Payment in a Defence the Same Thing as an Offer to Settle?

The answer is yes. The proposal of terms of payment in a defence is in writing, and it is signed and dated by the defendant or by the defendant's representative acting pursuant to the client's written instructions. If accepted by the plaintiff, or not disputed by the plaintiff within 20 days after service of the defence, the proposal of terms of payment is deemed to be binding upon the parties as if it were a court order (Rule 9.03(2)(a)). When advising a defendant about a proposal of terms of payment, you should ensure that its terms are reasonable and can be performed by the defendant.

TERMS OF AN OFFER TO SETTLE

When drafting an offer to settle for your client, you must remember that, if it is accepted, it becomes a binding agreement between the parties. You must take care to include all essential terms for performance of the agreement. At a minimum, the offer to settle should include the following:

1. The settlement amount, including interest and costs, if any.

2. How the settlement amount is to be paid.

   a. If the settlement amount is to be paid by lump sum (one payment), that should be stated in the offer, along with the manner of payment (money order or certified cheque), who the cheque or money order should be made out to, and the date by which the payment is to be paid. If the settlement funds are to be paid into your trust account, the offer should state that the money is to be paid to you in trust.

   b. If the settlement amount is to be paid in installments, the installments must be specified by amount, frequency, and payment date. If appropriate, there may also be a term as to payment by postdated cheques.

   c. If the settlement amount is to be paid into court, there should be a term to that effect. See Rules 14.05(2) and (3), and discussion below.

3. If interest is accruing on the settlement amount, the interest rate, the document authorizing the interest rate (loan agreement, promissory note, and so on), and how interest is calculated.

4. A date and time at which the offer expires if not accepted. If the date and time of expiry are not stated in the offer, you must serve a notice of withdrawal of offer on the other side if you wish to withdraw it. Where an offer contains an expiry date—that is, a date after which it can no longer be accepted—it expires on the day after that date (Rule 14.03(2)).

5. Where the settlement amount is being paid in installments, the consequences of default, including additional costs, if any.

BOX 8.4

When May You Pay Yourself Out of Settlement Funds Held in Your Trust Account?

You are permitted to pay outstanding legal fees and disbursements out of settlement funds held in your trust account to the credit of a client matter if:

- the settlement funds are payable to the client;

- you discussed the arrangement with the client at the initial consultation and confirmed it in writing in the retainer agreement or engagement letter;

- all parties have signed full and final releases; and

- you deliver a final invoice for fees and disbursements to the client before moving the money from your trust account to your general account.

The balance remaining should be paid to the client by trust cheque and delivered with the final reporting letter and invoice.

In no circumstances may you pay yourself from settlement funds held in your trust account to be paid by the client to another party.

TERMS SET OUT IN THE RULES

Many of the terms that should be contained in an offer to settle are stated in the Rules. This means that, if a party fails to include an important term in the offer (such as the deadline for accepting the offer), the Rules will fill in the gaps. This protects self-represented parties who are not accustomed to drafting offers to settle or settlement agreements.

Here are the terms set out in the Rules:

1. Withdrawal of offer (Rule 14.03(1)): If the offer does not state a date and time when the offer expires, the party making the offer may withdraw the offer at any time by serving a notice of withdrawal (Form 14C).

2. Deemed withdrawal (Rule 14.03(2)): If the offer contains a deadline for acceptance, and it is not accepted on or before that date, it is deemed to be withdrawn on the day after the stated deadline. Form 14A contains a term stating when the offer expires. All the party making the offer has to do is fill in the date.

3. No acceptance of offer after court has disposed of the claim (Rule 14.03(3)): Disposition of a claim happens when the court makes a final order in the matter. Offers to settle may remain open until the court makes a final order.

   Rule 14.05(1) complements Rules 14.03(1), (2), and (3). Rule 14.05(1) states that an offer to settle may be accepted by serving acceptance of the offer on the party who made it at any time before the offer is withdrawn or expires, or the court disposes of the action. An acceptance of offer must be in writing (Rule 14.01.1(1)), and may be made using Form 14B.

4. Payment into court (Rules 14.05(2) and (3)): A plaintiff's offer to settle may include a term that the money shall be paid into court. If the defendant pays the money into court and notifies the plaintiff, that is deemed to be acceptance of the plaintiff's offer (Rule 14.05(2)). The defendant's notification to the plaintiff of payment of money into court should be in writing.

   A request to clerk (Form 9B) must be completed when money is paid into court. A copy of the offer to settle should be attached when payment into court is made. See figure 8.1.

   If a defendant offers to pay money to a plaintiff to settle a claim, the plaintiff may make it a term of acceptance that the defendant pay the settlement amount into court. When paying the money into court, the defendant must complete and file a request to clerk (Form 9B), with a copy of the plaintiff's acceptance attached. If the defendant fails to pay the money into court, it is deemed to be a default, and the plaintiff may make a motion to the court for judgment in the terms of the accepted offer, or continue the proceeding as if there had been no offer to settle (Rules 14.05(3) and 14.06).

5. Costs (Rule 14.05(4)): A written offer to settle should always include a term as to costs. If the offer is silent as to costs, Rule 14.05(4) applies. Rule 14.05(4) restricts a costs award to disbursements—that is, the offering party's out-of-pocket expenses, such as court filing fees. Rule 14.05(4) does not address legal fees that must be paid by a party who is represented.

   If an accepted offer to settle does not deal with costs, a plaintiff who accepts a defendant's offer to settle is entitled to disbursements assessed to the date the plaintiff was served with the offer (Rule 14.05(4)(a)). If the accepted offer was made by the plaintiff, the plaintiff is entitled to disbursements assessed to the date that the notice of acceptance was served (Rule 14.05(4)(b)).

   Section 29 of the *Courts of Justice Act* states that a Small Claims Court award of costs, exclusive of disbursements, shall not exceed 15% of the amount claimed or the value of the property sought to be recovered. If s. 29 is applied to an offer to settle, then a party who is represented and who is claiming $25,000.00 may request costs, exclusive of disbursements, equal to 15% of the amount claimed—that is, $3,750.00.

   If you are using s. 29 to calculate the costs amount in an offer to settle, you should also consider Rule 19.04. Rule 19.04(2) states that if a successful party is represented by a paralegal at trial, the representation fee shall not exceed half of the maximum costs that may be awarded under s. 29 of the *Courts of Justice Act*. Applying Rule 19.04 to a term for costs in an offer to settle, the maximum amount a party who is

FIGURE 8.1   Request to Clerk: Payment of Money into Court Pursuant to a Written Offer to Settle (Form 9B)

FORM / *FORMULE* 9B   PAGE 2

Claim No. / *N° de la demande*

☐ accept payment in the amount of $ _____ into court
accepter que le paiement de   (Amount / *montant*)   *$ soit consigné au tribunal,*

☐ according to an order of the court, dated _____ , 20 ____ .
conformément à une ordonnance du tribunal datée du

☐ for a person under disability according to an order or settlement dated
au nom d'un incapable, conformément à une ordonnance ou à une transaction datée du

_____ , 20 ____ [R. 4.08(1)].
                              [par. 4.08 (1)].

☐ pursuant to the attached written offer to settle, dated _____ , 20 ____ [R. 14.05(2)].
aux termes de l'offre de transaction écrite ci-jointe datée du   *[par. 14.05 (2)].*

☐ according to the following legislation:
conformément à la disposition législative suivante :

_____ .

(Name of statute or regulation and section / *Titre de la loi ou du règlement et mention de l'article*)

☐ Other: (Specify.)
Autre :   (*Précisez.*)

_____ , 20 ____   _____

                                     (Signature of party or representative / *Signature de la partie ou du/de la représentant(e)*)

represented by a paralegal may ask for is $1,875.00 exclusive of disbursements.

A costs provision that complies with s. 29 and Rule 19.04(2) may not cover all of the successful party's costs, but it is better than being limited to recovery of disbursements only under Rule 14.05(4).

You will find a sample of an offer to settle in Form 14A in appendix 8.1 to this chapter.

BOX 8.5

Why Is a Term About Payment of Costs Important in an Offer to Settle?

Plaintiff commences a claim for $10,000.00 plus pre- and post-judgment interest of 12% on February 1, 20—. Plaintiff is an infrequent claimant, who has retained a paralegal as its representative. The court fee for issuing the claim is $75.00.

Defendant files a defence and serves a defendant's claim for $2,500.00. Plaintiff files a defence to defendant's claim. The court filing fee for the defence to defendant's claim is $40.00.

Plaintiff makes a written offer to settle for $9,000.00, which is served on Defendant on April 4, 20—. Defendant accepts the offer.

If there is no term as to costs in the plaintiff's offer to settle, what is the plaintiff entitled to under Rule 14.05(4)(b)?

Plaintiff is entitled to the total disbursements assessed to the date the offer was served—that is,

$75.00 for issuing the plaintiff's claim, and $40.00 for filing the defence to defendant's claim, for a total of $115.00.

If there is a term as to costs in the plaintiff's offer to settle, what is the plaintiff entitled to?

Applying s. 29 of the *Courts of Justice Act*, if Plaintiff is represented by a lawyer, Plaintiff may ask for costs in any amount up to 15% of the original amount claimed—that is, 15% of $10,000.00, or $1,500.00, exclusive of disbursements. Applying s. 29 and Rule 19.04(2), if Plaintiff is represented by a paralegal, then Plaintiff may ask for half that amount—that is, $750.00, exclusive of disbursements.

ACCEPTING AN OFFER

An offer may be accepted at any time before the deadline for acceptance stated in the offer. If there is no deadline for acceptance stated in the offer, it may be accepted at any time up until a written notice of withdrawal is served.

Regardless of whether informal, spoken negotiations have been going on, both offer and acceptance shall be in writing. If you are acting for the party making the offer, you must discuss the risks and advantages of making the offer with your client; obtain informed, written instructions from the client as to the terms of the offer; and if appropriate arrange for the client to review and approve the written offer before it is forwarded to the other side. If you are acting for the party accepting the offer, you must review the offer with your client; discuss the risks and advantages of accepting the offer; and obtain informed, written instructions to accept or reject the offer, or to make a counter-offer.

You will find a sample of an acceptance of offer to settle in Form 14B in appendix 8.2 to this chapter.

FAILURE TO COMPLY WITH ACCEPTED OFFER (RULE 14.06)

If a party to an accepted offer to settle fails to comply with the terms of the offer, the other party may

1. make a motion to the court for judgment according to the terms of the accepted offer (Rule 14.06(a)); or

2. continue with the proceeding as if there had been no offer to settle (Rule 14.06(b)).

BOX 8.6

Reminder: Defendant's Proposal of Terms of Payment

A defendant may admit liability for all or part of a plaintiff's claim and propose terms of payment in the defence. If the plaintiff does not dispute the proposal within 20 days after service of the defence, the plaintiff is deemed to accept the defendant's proposal. Once there is deemed acceptance, the defendant is obliged to make payments as if the proposal were a court order (Rule 9.03(2)(a)). If the defendant fails to make a payment, the plaintiff may serve a notice of default of payment (Form 20L) on the defendant, and file an affidavit of default of payment (Form 20M) with the court. The clerk shall sign judgment for the unpaid balance of the undisputed amount on the filing of the affidavit of default of payment. The judgment is enforceable under Rule 20.

The plaintiff may dispute the proposal of terms of payment within 20 days after service of the defence by filing a request to clerk for a terms of payment hearing and serving it on the defendant. At the hearing, the referee may make an order as to terms of payment by the defendant. Unless the referee specifies otherwise in the order, if the defendant fails to make payment in accordance with the order, the plaintiff may file an affidavit confirming the default and stating the amount paid and the unpaid balance, and the clerk shall sign judgment for the unpaid balance.

DEADLINE FOR ACCEPTANCE OF OFFER

When making an offer to settle, it is standard practice to include a term stating the deadline for acceptance of the offer. If it is not accepted, the offer is deemed to have been withdrawn on the day after that date. The Form 14A—Offer to Settle contains a term to this effect. See figure 8.2.

If an offer to settle does not state a date at which it expires, then the party making the offer may withdraw the offer at any time before it is accepted, by serving a notice of withdrawal of an offer to settle on the party to whom it was made. A withdrawal of an offer to settle must be in writing. A withdrawal of an offer to settle may be made in Form 14C.

WHEN MAY SETTLEMENT DISCUSSIONS BE DISCLOSED TO A JUDGE? (RULE 14.04)

The general rule is that settlement discussions, including offers to settle, should never be disclosed to a judge at any stage of the action, subject to the exceptions discussed below. The assumption is that a judge who is aware of settlement discussions may develop a bias against a party he perceives as being unreasonable, which will prevent him from being an impartial adjudicator.

There are two exceptions to the rule that settlement discussions shall not be disclosed to judges:

1. Settlement negotiations and offers to settle may be revealed to the judge who presides at a settlement conference. This encourages free and frank

FIGURE 8.2   Offer to Settle (Form 14A)

FORM / *FORMULE* 14A   PAGE 2

Claim No. / *N° de la demande*

3. This offer to settle is available for acceptance until _____ , 20 _____ .
    L'acceptation de la présente offre de transaction peut se faire jusqu'au

This offer to settle may be accepted by serving an acceptance of offer to settle (Form 14B may be used) on the party who made it, at any time before it is withdrawn or before the court disposes of the claim to which the offer applies [R. 14.05(1)]. You can get forms at court offices or online at www.ontariocourtforms.on.ca.
La présente offre de transaction peut être acceptée en signifiant une acceptation de l'offre de transaction (la formule 14B peut être utilisée) à la partie qui l'a faite, avant que l'offre ne soit retirée ou avant que le tribunal ne décide la demande qui en fait l'objet [par. 14.05 (1)]. Vous pouvez obtenir des formules aux greffes des tribunaux ou en ligne à l'adresse www.ontariocourtforms.on.ca.

_____ , 20 _____   _____
                                    (Signature of party or representative making offer / *Signature de la partie ou du/de la représentant(e)*)

                                    _____
                                    (Name, address and phone number of party or representative / *Nom, adresse et numéro de téléphone de la partie ou du/de la représentant(e)*)

NOTE:	**IF YOU ACCEPT AN OFFER TO SETTLE, THEN FAIL TO COMPLY WITH ITS TERMS,** judgment in the terms of the accepted offer may be obtained against you on motion to the court, or the action may continue as if there has been no offer to settle [R. 14.06].
REMARQUE :	*SI VOUS ACCEPTEZ UNE OFFRE DE TRANSACTION MAIS QU'ENSUITE VOUS N'EN*

discussion of the issues and promotes settlement of the matter, which is one of the objectives of a settlement conference. See the discussion of Rule 13.02 below.

2. Settlement negotiations and offers to settle may be raised after the trial judge has made a final decision at trial (Rule 14.04). At that point, the reasonableness of a party in making offers to settle may be considered by the judge when making a decision about the amount of costs to be awarded to the **successful party**. The successful party is the party who succeeds, or wins, at trial. It may be the plaintiff or the defendant.

The costs consequences to an unsuccessful party of failing to accept an offer to settle by the successful party are set out at Rule 14.07.

BOX 8.7

What if There Is No Deadline for Acceptance in an Offer to Settle?

If no deadline for acceptance is stated in an offer to settle, the Rules provide that the offer may be withdrawn at any time before it is accepted by serving a notice of withdrawal of offer to settle in writing. A withdrawal of an offer to settle may be made in Form 14C.

An offer to settle drafted by a licensee should always contain a deadline for acceptance.

COSTS CONSEQUENCES OF FAILURE TO ACCEPT AN OFFER TO SETTLE (RULE 14.07)

Before discussing Rule 14.07, it will be useful to review what legal costs mean, and the general rule with respect to awards of costs.

BOX 8.8

Review: What Are Costs?

Costs are money amounts that the court orders one party to pay to the other party, as reimbursement for legal expenses. Costs are awarded in addition to any other relief that may be ordered.

The general rule is that costs are awarded to the successful party, to reimburse the successful party for expenses incurred in the course of the proceeding. These expenses include the party's representation fees, plus disbursements for out-of-pocket expenses such as court fees.

Rule 14.07 sets out special rules for costs awards to parties who refuse to accept reasonable offers to settle made prior to the trial. These special rules are set out in table 8.2 below.

The costs awards set out in Rule 14.07 are discretionary—that is, the court may choose to follow Rule 14.07 or not, depending on the circumstances.

How does Rule 14.07 play out in terms of real money? The first thing to remember is that Rule 14.07 will apply only after there has been a trial. This means it must be read together with Rule 19.

Rule 19.01(1) states that a successful party is entitled to have his reasonable disbursements, including the cost of effecting service, paid by the unsuccessful party, unless the court orders otherwise. The cost of effecting service is limited to $20.00 by Rule 19.01(3), unless the court decides that there are special circumstances that justify a greater amount.

Rule 19.04 states that, if the amount claimed by the successful party exceeds $500.00 (excluding interest and costs), and the party is represented by a lawyer, student-at-law, or agent, the court may allow a reasonable representation fee at trial or at an assessment hearing (Rule 19.04(1)). In the case of a student-at-law or an agent, the representation fee shall not exceed half of the maximum costs that may be awarded under s. 29 of the *Courts of Justice Act* (Rule 19.04(2)).

TABLE 8.2   Rule 14.07—Costs Consequences of Failure to Accept Offer

Rule number	Party making offer	Conditions	Result at trial	Potential costs consequences
14.07(1)	Plaintiff makes offer to defendant	■ Offer made at least 7 days before the trial ■ Offer is not withdrawn before the trial ■ Offer does not expire before the trial ■ Defendant does not accept offer	■ Plaintiff wins ■ Plaintiff obtains a judgment that is as favourable as or more favourable than the terms of the offer	■ Costs awarded to *plaintiff* ■ Court *may* award costs to successful plaintiff equal to twice the costs of the action (including disbursements) ■ Rule 14.07(1) costs award is *discretionary*, not mandatory—the court does not have to comply with Rule 14.07(1), but may instead consider other circumstances when making an order for costs
14.07(2)	Defendant makes offer to plaintiff	■ Offer made at least 7 days before the trial ■ Offer is not withdrawn before the trial ■ Offer does not expire before the trial ■ Plaintiff does not accept offer	■ Plaintiff wins ■ Plaintiff obtains a judgment that is as favourable as or less favourable than the terms of the offer	■ Costs awarded to *defendant* ■ Court *may* award costs to defendant equal to twice the costs the plaintiff (as successful party) is entitled to from the date the offer was served ■ Rule 14.07(2) costs award is *discretionary*, not mandatory—the court does not have to comply with Rule 14.07(2), but may instead consider other circumstances when making an order for costs

THE SETTLEMENT CONFERENCE (RULE 13)

General

A settlement conference is an informal meeting before a judge, deputy judge, or referee. A referee is a non-judge who is authorized by Rule 21.01(1)(b) to conduct settlement conferences. A referee shall not make a final decision at a settlement conference, but shall report her findings and recommendations to the court (Rule 21.01(2)).

A settlement conference must be held in every defended action—that is, every action where at least one party disputes another party's claim (Rule 13.01(1)). The court clerk is responsible for setting the date for the settlement conference (Rule 13.01(2)). The settlement conference must be held within 90 days after the first defence is filed (Rule 13.01(3)). If there is only one defendant, the settlement conference must be held within 90 days after the sole defendant files her defence.

The clerk is required to send each party a blank list of proposed witnesses (Form 13A) along with the notice of settlement conference (Rule 13.01(2)).

BOX 8.9

How Does Rule 14.07 Work?

Plaintiff's offer to settle (Rule 14.07(1)): Plaintiff sues Defendant for $4,000.00. Plaintiff is represented by a paralegal. Defendant is self-represented. Plaintiff makes an offer to settle for $3,500.00 including costs. The offer is made 30 days before the trial date, and has not expired at the time the trial commences. Defendant, who is self-represented, does not accept the offer.

Having heard the evidence at trial, the court awards the plaintiff $3,800.00 and requests submissions as to costs.

All issues of liability and the relief to be granted have now been determined, with the exception of costs. The parties may now disclose any offers to settle or related negotiations to the trial judge (Rule 14.04). Plaintiff is the successful party and is entitled to his costs, including a reasonable representation fee. Applying s. 29 of the *Courts of Justice Act* and Rule 19.04(2), Plaintiff is entitled to a maximum representation fee of one half of 15% of the amount claimed ($4,000.00), or $300.00. Plaintiff is also entitled to recover disbursements, including the following:

Filing the claim:	$75.00
Service of the claim (Rule 19.01(3)):	$20.00
Fixing a date for trial:	$100.00
Total	$195.00

Assuming that these are all of Plaintiff's disbursements, the maximum costs award that Plaintiff would ordinarily be entitled to is $495.00.

However, there was a plaintiff's offer to settle that was not accepted. When making submissions as to an appropriate award of costs, Plaintiff's paralegal may refer to Rule 14.07(1). The Rule 14.07(1) criteria are met—that is, Plaintiff obtained a judgment that is more favourable than the terms of the offer; the offer was made at least seven days before the trial, and the offer was not withdrawn and did not expire before the trial. Therefore, the court may award Plaintiff an amount not exceeding twice his costs of the action—that is, anything up to $990.00.

Defendant's offer to settle (Rule 14.07(2)): Plaintiff sues Defendant for $3,300.00. Defendant makes an offer to settle for $2,500.00, including costs. The offer is made 21 days before the trial date, and has not expired at the time the trial commences.

At trial, both Plaintiff and Defendant are represented by paralegals. After hearing the evidence, the court awards Plaintiff $2,200.00 and requests submissions as to costs.

All issues of liability and the relief to be granted have now been determined, with the exception of costs. The parties may now disclose any offers to settle or related negotiations to the trial judge (Rule 14.04). Plaintiff is the successful party, and is entitled to her costs, including a reasonable representation fee. Applying s. 29 of the *Courts of Justice Act* and Rule 19.04(2), Plaintiff is entitled to a maximum representation fee of one half of 15% of the amount claimed ($3,300.00), or $247.50. Plaintiff is also entitled to recover disbursements, including the following:

Filing the claim:	$75.00
Service of the claim (Rule 19.01(3)):	$20.00
Fixing a date for trial:	$100.00
Total	$195.00

Assuming that these are all of Plaintiff's disbursements, the maximum costs award that Plaintiff would ordinarily be entitled to is $442.50.

However, there was a defendant's offer to settle that was not accepted. When making submissions as to an appropriate award of costs, Defendant's paralegal may refer to Rule 14.07(2). The Rule 14.07(2) criteria are met—that is, Plaintiff obtained a judgment that is less favourable than the terms of Defendant's offer; the offer was made at least seven days before the trial, and the offer was not withdrawn and did not expire before the trial.

Therefore, the court may award Defendant an amount not exceeding twice the costs awardable to Plaintiff from the date the offer to settle was served.

In Conclusion: Where settlement discussions continue right up to trial, your client should be advised about Rule 14.07. And keep Rule 14.07 in mind when you are making submissions as to costs.

The parties and, if they are represented, their representatives shall participate in the settlement conference, unless the court orders otherwise (Rule 13.02(1)). A party who attends must have authority to settle the matter. If a party requires another person's approval before agreeing to settlement, that party shall arrange to have telephone access to the other person throughout the conference, whether the conference takes place during or after regular business hours (Rule 13.02(2)).

As its name indicates, the primary purpose of a settlement conference is to promote settlement of the action, where appropriate. The 90-day rule is intended to promote early settlement in matters where that is possible. Where settlement is not possible, or is not possible at the time when the settlement conference is held, the settlement conference may be used to decide

- which issues in the action are in dispute;

- whether there has been full disclosure of the relevant facts and evidence between the parties; and

- whether anything else is needed to help the parties prepare for a trial.

Because the settlement conference is intended to promote settlement, the parties and their legal representatives must be able to discuss all issues freely and frankly (Rule 13.03(3)), including any settlement discussions that have taken place to that point. Thereafter, except as otherwise provided or with the consent of the parties, the matters discussed at the settlement conference shall not be disclosed to others until after the action has been disposed of (Rule 13.03(4)).

The Purposes of a Settlement Conference

A settlement conference is an informal meeting for the purpose of discussing the action and talking about settlement. The settlement conference may take place in a court office or meeting room. Regardless of where the settlement conference takes place, it is a private meeting. No members of the public are allowed to attend. During the conference, the parties and their representatives sit at a table with the judge or referee.

Rule 13.03(1) sets out the purposes of the settlement conference:

(a) to resolve and narrow issues in the action;

(b) to bring about a speedy resolution of the action;

(c) to encourage settlement of the action;

(d) to help the parties prepare effectively for trial; and

(e) to provide full disclosure between the parties of relevant facts and evidence.

Preparing for a Settlement Conference

DISCLOSURE

The general rule in Small Claims Court actions is that full and fair disclosure should take place as early as possible in the proceeding. See Rules 7.01(2), 9.02(1), and 10.01(4), which require that copies of all documents on which a party intends to rely be attached to the claim or defence. Early, full disclosure lets the parties know the case they have to meet, and promotes early settlement because it helps them to assess the strengths and weaknesses of their own case and that of their opponent.

Rule 13.03(2) sets out an additional disclosure requirement. At least 14 days before the date of the settlement conference, each party or his legal representative shall serve the other parties with copies of any documents (including an expert report) that were not attached to the claim or defence, and file them with the court (Rule 13.03(2)(a)). Each party must also serve and file a list of proposed witnesses and any other persons with knowledge of the matters in dispute in the action (Rule 13.03(2)(b)).

The court may award costs against a person who attends a settlement conference without having filed the material required by Rule 13.03(2) (Rule 13.02(7)).

DISCUSSION WITH YOUR CLIENT

When you receive the notice of settlement conference, you should contact your client immediately with the date, time, and venue of the conference, and advise her that it is mandatory to attend the settlement conference. If you are unable to attend on the date set for the settlement conference, you should contact the court office and request an adjournment to another date. You should consider contacting the other side to advise them that you are asking for an adjournment and request some mutually convenient dates.

Before the scheduled date for the settlement conference, you should meet with or phone your client to discuss the purpose of the settlement conference, go over the facts and issues in the client matter, and explore the possibility of settlement. You should also remind her that her attendance is mandatory.

The Role of the Parties at a Settlement Conference

ATTENDANCE

It is mandatory for the parties and their legal representatives to attend the settlement conference (Rule 13.02(1)). Participation may be by personal attendance, or by telephone or video conference if those facilities are available at the court (Rules 13.02(1)(b) and 1.07). A party who wishes to conduct the settlement conference by telephone or video conference must file a request for telephone or video conference (Form 1B), stating the reasons for the request. If a judge grants the request, the court will make the necessary arrangements and notify the parties.

If a party who has received a notice of settlement conference fails to attend the settlement conference, the court may impose appropriate sanctions, including an order requiring her to pay the other party's costs (Rule 13.02(5)(a)). The costs of a settlement conference shall not exceed $100.00 unless the court orders otherwise because there are special circumstances (Rule 13.10). The court may also order that an additional settlement conference be held (Rules 13.02(3) and (5)(b)).

Rule 13.02(6) sets out special sanctions for a non-attending defendant in the following circumstances. If a defendant (1) fails to attend a first settlement conference, (2) receives notice of an additional settlement conference, and (3) fails to attend the additional settlement conference, the court may strike out the defence and dismiss the defendant's claim, if any, and allow the plaintiff to prove the plaintiff's claim without a trial, or make such other order as is just.

BE PREPARED

When you are getting ready for a settlement conference, you should do a thorough review of the contents of the client file, including the pleadings, disclosure, motions if any, offers to settle, counter-offers, and so on. This will help you to get a good result at the settlement conference. Even if no settlement is achieved, thorough preparation for the settlement conference gives you a head start on getting ready for trial.

When reviewing the client file, consider the following (the list is not exhaustive):

- What issues are in dispute? What issues are not in dispute?

- What are the strengths of the client's case? Are there any weaknesses?

- Are there any documents, written statements, or audio or visual records that you require from other parties?

- Are there any documents, written statements, or audio or visual records that you have not yet provided to other parties? If yes, you should ensure that you serve them on all other parties at least 14 days before the date of the settlement conference. If that is not possible, then at the settlement conference you should advise other parties that there will be additional disclosure. The additional disclosure shall be served at least 30 days before the trial date on all parties who were served with a notice of trial.

- Who are your witnesses? You must complete and serve the list of proposed witnesses on all other parties at least 14 days before the date of the settlement conference. If the matter goes to trial, you should contact your witnesses to review their evidence. Witnesses other than your client must be served with a summons to witness. A summons to witness must be served personally.

- Have you received a list of proposed witnesses from other parties? If not, why not? Follow up with other parties or their representatives, and, if necessary, with the judge at the settlement conference.

- Do you require an expert report? If you have not already obtained and disclosed an expert report, you shall serve it at least 30 days before the trial date on all parties who were served with a notice of trial.

- Have you received a list of proposed witnesses from other parties? If not, why not? Follow up with other parties or their representatives, and, if necessary, with the judge at the settlement conference.

If a person who attends a settlement conference is so ill-prepared that it frustrates the purposes of the conference set out in Rule 13.03(1) from being carried out, the court may order costs against that person (Rule 13.02(7)(a)).

The Role of the Court at a Settlement Conference

A judge, deputy judge, or referee may conduct a settlement conference. The judge or deputy judge who conducts the settlement conference is prohibited from presiding at the trial, if any (Rule 13.08). Referees cannot make court orders or preside at trials. A referee who presides at a settlement conference shall report his findings and recommendations to the court (Rule 21.01(2)). Based on those recommendations, a judge may make any order that may be made under Rule 13.05(1) or (2).

A settlement conference judge may make recommendations to the parties on any matter relating to the conduct of the action, in order to fulfill the purposes of the settlement conference as set out in Rule 13.03(1). Among other things, the judge may make recommendations with respect to (Rule 13.04):

(a) clarification and simplification of issues in the action;

(b) getting rid of claims or defences that appear to be unsupported by the evidence and/or the law; and

(c) admission of certain facts or documents without further proof at trial.

A settlement conference judge may make any order relating to the conduct of the action that the court could make, including but not limited to the following (Rules 13.05(1) and (2)):

1. adding or deleting parties;

2. consolidating actions (that is, taking two separate actions with the same parties and similar issues, and combining them into one action);

3. staying (or stopping) the action;

4. amending or striking out a claim or defence on grounds that it discloses no reasonable cause of action or defence, may delay or prejudice a fair trial, or has no legal merit (Rule 12.02(1));

5. staying or dismissing a claim;

6. directing production of documents;

7. changing the place of trial under Rule 6.01;

8. directing an additional settlement conference under Rule 13.02(3);

9. ordering costs; and

10. at an additional settlement conference, ordering judgment under Rule 13.02(6) against a defendant who fails to attend a first settlement conference, receives notice of an additional settlement conference, and fails to attend the additional settlement conference.

If you are acting for a defendant at a settlement conference, and you have concerns that the court where the action was commenced is not the proper place of trial, you should raise this issue at the settlement conference. That way, the settlement conference judge may, if appropriate, make an order that the action be tried at another venue. See Rules 6.01(2) and (3).

If the settlement conference is conducted by a referee, a judge may make any of the above orders on the referee's recommendation.

A judge may order final judgment at a settlement conference where the matter in dispute is for an amount under the appealable limit (currently $500.00 exclusive of interest and costs (*Courts of Justice Act*, s. 31)). A party must file a consent in Form 13B signed by all parties before the settlement conference stating that they wish to obtain a final determination of the matter at the settlement conference even if a mediated settlement is not reached (Rule 13.05(4)).

Within 10 days after the judge signs an order at a settlement conference, the order shall be served on any parties who were not present at the settlement conference by the clerk, by mail or fax in accordance with Rule 8.01(6).

At the end of the settlement conference, the court shall prepare a memorandum on the file (Rule 13.06(1)). The memorandum summarizes the following:

1. any recommendations made under Rule 13.04;

2. the issues remaining in dispute;

3. the matters agreed on by the parties;

4. any relevant evidentiary issues; and

5. information relating to scheduling of the remaining steps in the proceeding.

The memorandum shall be filed with the clerk, who is required to give a copy to the trial judge (Rule 13.06(2)).

A judge who conducts a settlement conference in an action shall not preside at the trial of the action (Rule 13.08).

Additional Matters

At or after the settlement conference, the clerk shall provide the parties with a notice stating that one of the parties must request a trial date if the action is not disposed of within 30 days after the settlement conference, and pay the fee required for setting the action down for trial (Rule 13.07). A request to clerk (Form 9B) is used to request a trial date. As of this writing, the fee for an infrequent claimant to fix a date for a trial is $100.00. The fee for a frequent claimant to do so is $130.00.

After a settlement conference has been held, a claim against a party who is not in default shall not be withdrawn or discontinued by the party making the claim without the written consent of the party against whom the claim is made, or leave of the court (Rule 13.09).

CHAPTER SUMMARY

Paralegals have a duty to encourage their clients to settle their differences, if a reasonable outcome for the client can be achieved by negotiation.

A settlement agreement in a court action is a contract. As with any contract, there must be an offer, acceptance, and consideration. The offer and acceptance must take place without duress or misrepresentation. The *Small Claims Court Rules* state that an offer to settle, an acceptance of an offer to settle, and a notice of withdrawal of an offer to settle shall be made in writing (Rule 14.01.1(1)). The parties may use Forms 14A, 14B, and 14C for these purposes.

A proposal of terms of payment in a defence is the same thing as an offer to settle. If accepted by the plaintiff, or not disputed by the plaintiff within 20 days after service of the defence, it becomes a binding agreement, which has the same effect as a court order.

When drafting an offer to settle, you must take care to include all essential terms for performance of the agreement, including but not limited to the settlement amount, including interest and costs, if any; the terms of payment; the interest rate, if interest is being paid on the outstanding balance; the date and time at which the offer expires; and the consequences of default in payment, including additional costs, if any.

A settlement conference must be held in every defended action. The purposes of a settlement conference are to resolve or narrow issues in the action, to expedite disposition of the action, to encourage settlement, to assist the parties in effective preparation for trial, and to ensure full disclosure between the parties of the relevant facts and evidence.

A judge who attends at a settlement conference shall not preside at trial.

Settlement negotiations may be revealed to and discussed with the judge at a settlement conference. Where the action is not settled at the settlement conference, settlement discussions may not be disclosed again until after a final order has been made at trial. At that time they may be raised as going to the issue of costs to be paid by one party to another.

KEY TERMS

compromise and settlement	invitation to treat	promisee
consideration	misrepresentation	promisor
duress	offer	successful party

REFERENCES

Courts of Justice Act, RSO 1990, c. C.43.

Currie v. Misa (1875), LR 10 Ex. 153; aff'd. 1 App. Cas. 554 (HL).

Law Society of Upper Canada (LSUC), *Paralegal Professional Conduct Guidelines* (Toronto: LSUC, 2008, as amended) ("the Guidelines"); available online at http://www.lsuc.on.ca.

Law Society of Upper Canada (LSUC), *Paralegal Rules of Conduct* (Toronto: LSUC, 2007, as amended); available online at http://www.lsuc.on.ca.

Rules of the Small Claims Court, O. Reg. 258/98.

REVIEW QUESTIONS

1. What is a settlement agreement in a court action?

2. What three things are needed for a settlement contract to be legally binding?

3. What is the difference between an offer and an invitation to treat?

4. Is a proposal of terms of payment in a defence the same thing as an offer to settle? If yes, why? If no, why not?

5. Name five terms that an offer to settle should include. Give brief details where necessary.

6. Name five terms that should be contained in an offer to settle, which are implied by the Rules, if they are not included in the offer to settle. Please provide the rule numbers.

7. What happens if a party to an accepted offer fails to comply with the terms of the offer (in other words, fails to perform the terms of the settlement agreement)?

8. What is the general rule with respect to revealing settlement discussions to a judge? What are two exceptions to the general rule?

9. What are the costs consequences to a plaintiff to whom Rule 14.07(1) applies?

10. What are the costs consequences to a plaintiff to whom Rule 14.07(2) applies?

11. What is a settlement conference, and when must it be held?

12. What are the purposes of a settlement conference? Name five, and cite the authority for your answer.

13. What must a party disclose prior to a settlement conference? Please state the authority for your answer.

14. What are the consequences for a party of failing to attend at a settlement conference?

15. What is the role of the court at a pretrial conference?

APPENDIX 8.1   Chakravarty v. Complete Home Renovations: Plaintiff's Offer to Settle (Form 14A)

ONTARIO

Superior Court of Justice
Cour supérieure de justice

Offer to Settle
Offre de transaction

Form / *Formule* 14A Ont. Reg. No. / *Règl. de l'Ont.* : 258/98

Brampton

Small Claims Court / *Cour des petites créances de*
7755 Hurontario Street
Brampton, Ontario
L6W 4T6

Address / *Adresse*

905 456 4700

Phone number / *Numéro de téléphone*

4586

Claim No. / *N° de la demande*

BETWEEN / *ENTRE*

Amrita Chakravarty

Plaintiff(s) / *Demandeur(s)/demanderesse(s)*

and / *et*

Complete Home Renovations

Defendant(s) / *Défendeur(s)/défenderesse(s)*

My name is   Amrita Chakravarty
Je m'appelle

(Full name / *Nom et prénoms*)

1. In this action, I am the
    Dans la présente action, je suis le/la

    ☒ Plaintiff
       demandeur/demanderesse

    ☐ Defendant
       défendeur/défenderesse

    ☐ representative of
       représentant(e) de _____
                            (Name of party(ies) / *Nom de la ou des parties*)

2. I offer to settle this action against   **Complete Home Renovations**
    Je présente une offre de transaction dans cette action contre   (Name of party(ies) / *Nom de la ou des parties*)

    on the following terms: *(Set out terms in numbered paragraphs, or on an attached sheet.)*
    selon les conditions suivantes : (Indiquez les conditions sous forme de paragraphes numérotés ou sur une feuille annexée.)

    a. The defendant, Complete Home Renovations, shall pay $2,500.00 plus $400.00 in costs for a total amount payable of $2,900.00, by certified cheque payable to Prior Mustafa LLP in trust in full and final settlement of this claim.

    b. Upon payment of this sum in accordance with paragraph (a) above on or before February 1, 20--, the plaintiff and defendant shall sign full and final waivers releasing each other from any further liability with respect to this matter.

    c. The parties shall sign terms of settlement which shall be entered as an order of this court. If the defendant accepts this offer but fails to pay the above amount in accordance with the above, the terms of settlement shall be enforceable as an order of this court.

APPENDIX 8.1—Form 14A   Concluded

FORM / *FORMULE* 14A   PAGE 2   4586

Claim No. / *N° de la demande*

3.   This offer to settle is available for acceptance until **February 1**   , 20 -- .
      L'acceptation de la présente offre de transaction peut se faire jusqu'au

This offer to settle may be accepted by serving an acceptance of offer to settle (Form 14B may be used) on the party who made it, at any time before it is withdrawn or before the court disposes of the claim to which the offer applies [R. 14.05(1)]. You can get forms at court offices or online at www.ontariocourtforms.on.ca.
La présente offre de transaction peut être acceptée en signifiant une acceptation de l'offre de transaction (la formule 14B peut être utilisée) à la partie qui l'a faite, avant que l'offre ne soit retirée ou avant que le tribunal ne décide la demande qui en fait l'objet [par. 14.05 (1)]. Vous pouvez obtenir des formules aux greffes des tribunaux ou en ligne à l'adresse www.ontariocourtforms.on.ca.

January 3   , 20 --

(Signature of party or representative making offer / *Signature de la partie ou du/de la représentant(e)*)

Prior Mustafa LLP
22 County Court Boulevard
Brampton, Ontario A1A 2B3
TEL: 905 111 2222
Attention: Paralegal name

(Name, address and phone number of party or representative / *Nom, adresse et numéro de téléphone de la partie ou du/de la représentant(e)*)

NOTE: **IF YOU ACCEPT AN OFFER TO SETTLE, THEN FAIL TO COMPLY WITH ITS TERMS,** judgment in the terms of the accepted offer may be obtained against you on motion to the court, or the action may continue as if there has been no offer to settle [R. 14.06].

REMARQUE : *SI VOUS ACCEPTEZ UNE OFFRE DE TRANSACTION MAIS QU'ENSUITE VOUS N'EN OBSERVEZ PAS LES CONDITIONS, un jugement suivant les conditions de l'offre acceptée peut être obtenu contre vous sur présentation d'une motion au tribunal ou l'action peut continuer comme s'il n'y avait jamais eu d'offre de transaction [règle 14.06].*

NOTE: **IF THIS OFFER TO SETTLE IS NOT ACCEPTED, IT SHALL NOT BE FILED WITH THE COURT OR DISCLOSED** to the trial judge until all questions of liability and relief (other than costs) have been determined [R. 14.04].

REMARQUE : *SI LA PRÉSENTE OFFRE DE TRANSACTION N'EST PAS ACCEPTÉE, ELLE NE DOIT PAS ÊTRE DÉPOSÉE AUPRÈS DU TRIBUNAL NI DIVULGUÉE au juge du procès tant que toutes les questions relatives à la responsabilité et aux mesures de redressement (à l'exclusion des dépens) n'ont pas été décidées [règle 14.04].*

APPENDIX 8.2   Chakravarty v. Complete Home Renovations: Defendant's Acceptance of Offer to Settle (Form 14B)

ONTARIO
Superior Court of Justice
Cour supérieure de justice

Acceptance of Offer to Settle
Acceptation de l'offre de transaction
Form / *Formule* 14B Ont. Reg. No. / *Régl. de l'Ont.* : 258/98

Brampton
Small Claims Court / *Cour des petites créances de*

4586
Claim No. / *N° de la demande*

7755 Hurontario Street
Brampton, Ontario
L6W 4T6
Address / *Adresse*

905 456 4700
Phone number / *Numéro de téléphone*

BETWEEN / *ENTRE*

Amrita Chakravarty

Plaintiff(s) / *Demandeur(s)/demanderesse(s)*

and / *et*

Complete Home Renovations

Defendant(s) / *Défendeur(s)/défenderesse(s)*

My name is Anna Limones
Je m'appelle   (Full name / *Nom et prénoms*)

1. In this action, I am the
   Dans la présente action, je suis le/la

   ☐ plaintiff
      demandeur/demanderesse

   ☐ defendant
      défendeur/défenderesse

   ☒ representative of **Complete Home Renovations**
      représentant(e) de   (Name of party(ies) / *Nom de la ou des parties*)

2. I accept the offer to settle from **Amrita Chakravarty**
   J'accepte l'offre de transaction faite par   (Name of party(ies) / *Nom de la ou des parties*)

   dated **January 3**   , 20 **--** .
   et datée du

3. This offer to settle has not expired and has not been withdrawn.
   Cette offre de transaction n'est pas expirée et n'a pas été retirée.

January 15   , 20 **--**
                                         (Signature of party or representative accepting offer / *Signature de la partie
                                          ou du/de la représentant(e) qui accepte l'offre*)
                                         Paxton Limones PC
                                         82 Main Street, Suite 11
                                         Brampton, Ontario L1N 2P3
                                         TEL: 905 888 9999
                                         Attention: Anna Limones
                                         (Name, address and phone number of party or representative / *Nom, adresse
                                          et numéro de téléphone de la partie ou du/de la représentant(e)*)

CAUTION:	**IF YOU ACCEPT AN OFFER TO SETTLE, THEN FAIL TO COMPLY WITH ITS TERMS,** judgment in the terms of the accepted offer may be obtained against you on motion to the Court, or this action may continue as if there has been no offer to settle [R. 14.06].
AVERTISSEMENT :	*SI VOUS ACCEPTEZ UNE OFFRE DE TRANSACTION MAIS QU'ENSUITE VOUS N'EN OBSERVEZ PAS LES CONDITIONS, un jugement suivant les conditions de l'offre acceptée peut être obtenu contre vous sur présentation d'une motion au tribunal ou la présente action peut continuer comme s'il n'y avait jamais eu d'offre de transaction [règle 14.06].*

SCR 14.01.1-14B (June 1, 2009 / *1er juin 2009*) CSD

Trials and Assessment Hearings

LEARNING OBJECTIVES

After reading this chapter, you will understand:

- Requesting and conducting an assessment hearing
- Requesting a date for trial
- Requesting adjournment of a trial date
- Preparing for trial
- The consequences of a party's failure to attend
- The consequences of a witness's failure to attend
- Courtroom etiquette
- Evidence at a Small Claims Court trial
- Direct examination, cross-examination, and re-examination
- Putting in exhibits
- Objections
- Costs

INTRODUCTION

If the action is not resolved at the settlement conference, the clerk shall provide the parties with a notice stating that one of the parties must request a trial date if the action is not disposed of within 30 days after the settlement conference, and pay the fee required for setting the action down for trial (Rule 13.07).

Any party may request that the clerk fix a date for trial. However, it is the plaintiff's action, and the plaintiff is responsible for moving it forward. The plaintiff or the plaintiff's representative may request a date for trial by attending at the court office, filing a request to clerk (Form 9B), and paying the fee. The clerk then fixes a date for trial and serves a notice of trial on each party who has filed a claim or defence.

Before requesting a date for trial, you should consider getting a list of available dates from the court clerk, and then contacting the other parties or their representatives, if they are represented, and obtaining some mutually agreeable dates for the trial. That way, adjournments and the resulting delay and expense can be avoided.

Full and fair disclosure of the parties' evidence should have taken place at or before the settlement conference. However, if a party intends to submit as evidence at trial a document, written statement, or audio or visual record that has not already been disclosed to all parties entitled to disclosure, the party wishing to introduce the evidence must serve it on all other parties served with the notice of trial at least 30 days before the trial date. The document or record shall then be received in evidence unless the trial judge orders otherwise (Rule 18.02(1)).

If you require an adjournment of the trial date because a witness is unavailable, or you have a scheduling conflict, or for some other good reason, you should contact the court as soon as possible and request that the court adjourn the trial to a later date. Before contacting the court to request an adjournment, you should consider contacting the other parties or their representatives, if they are represented, to advise them that you are asking for an adjournment and to obtain some mutually convenient dates for rescheduling the trial.

If another party advises you that they require an adjournment, you should seek instructions from your client to consent, if the request is reasonable, sufficient notice has been given, and no prejudice to the rights of your client would result. This is in keeping with your professional duty of courtesy and good faith to licensees and others (Paralegal Rule 7.01(2)).

If you require witnesses other than your client to be present at trial, you must serve them personally with a summons to witness and with attendance money at least 10 days before the trial date (Rule 8.01(7)).

The structure of a Small Claims Court trial is the same as that of other civil trials, except that the rules of evidence are relaxed in Small Claims Court. The plaintiff takes the stand and gives his evidence in support of the claim. He is then cross-examined by the defendant or the defendant's representative. At the end of cross-examination, he may give reply evidence to any new issue raised in cross-examination.

Any other witnesses for the plaintiff also take the stand, give evidence, are cross-examined, and give reply evidence if appropriate.

When the plaintiff's evidence is concluded, the defendant takes the stand, gives evidence under oath, is cross-examined, and gives reply evidence if appropriate.

If the parties are represented, their representatives may be asked to make opening or closing submissions.

Having heard the evidence and submissions, the court may take a brief recess before giving its reasons and making an order. When making its order, the court may also order that costs be awarded in accordance with s. 29 of the *Courts of Justice Act* and any applicable rules.

In a Small Claims Court action, an award of costs, not including disbursements, cannot exceed 15% of the amount claimed (*Courts of Justice Act*, s. 29; Rule 19.02).

A successful party who is self-represented may be awarded an amount not exceeding $500.00 as compensation for inconvenience and expense caused by another party, if the amount claimed in the action exceeds $500.00 excluding interest and costs (Rule 19.05).

If the court is satisfied that a party has unduly complicated or prolonged an action or has been unreasonable in some other way, the court may order that party to pay an amount as compensation to another party as a penalty (Rule 19.06).

GENERAL

Assessment Hearings

In a plaintiff's claim for unliquidated damages where all defendants have been noted in default, a plaintiff may

(a) file with the court a motion in writing for an assessment of damages and supporting affidavit, setting out the reasons why the motion should be granted and attaching any relevant documents (Rule 11.03(2)(a), Form 15A); or

(b) file a request to clerk requesting that an assessment hearing be arranged (Rule 11.03(2)(a), Form 9B).

The plaintiff may prefer to resolve the matter by way of a motion in writing, because it does not require a court attendance. On a motion in writing for an assessment of damages, the plaintiff is not required to prove liability against the defendant noted in default, but the affidavit evidence must be sufficiently detailed to

BOX 9.1

Application of Rule 11.03

Remember that an unliquidated amount is an amount that is not fixed and specified by a document or other evidence. It must be determined by the court based on all of the evidence.

Rule 11.03 does not apply unless all the defendants in a plaintiff's claim for an unliquidated amount have been noted in default. If there are multiple defendants, and one of them has delivered a defence, the plaintiff must proceed to a settlement conference under Rule 13 and if necessary to trial under Rule 17 in order to obtain a final disposition of the matter (Rule 11.03(7)). However, any defendant who has been noted in default is subject to the consequences set out in Rule 11.05.

Where part of a plaintiff's claim is for a debt or liquidated amount and part is for an unliquidated amount, and a defendant fails to file a defence within the prescribed time, the plaintiff may file proof of service and a request to clerk with the court. The clerk may note the defendant in default and sign judgment against the defendant for the part of the claim that is for a debt or liquidated amount. If all defendants have been noted in default, Rule 11.03 applies to the part of the claim that is for an unliquidated amount.

prove the amount of the claim (Rule 11.03(5)). For a discussion of the affidavit evidence to be filed in support of a Rule 11.03(2)(a) motion, see chapter 5, page 167. See also appendix 5.2 at pages 193-198. If a judge finds that a plaintiff's affidavit is inadequate or unsatisfactory, the judge may order that a further affidavit be provided, or an assessment hearing be held (Rule 11.03(3)).

An assessment hearing may be held:

1. where the plaintiff requests an assessment hearing (Rule 11.03(2)(b)); or

2. where a judge orders an assessment hearing. A judge will order an assessment hearing where the affidavit evidence filed in support of a Rule 11.03(2)(a) motion in writing is so inadequate or unsatisfactory that the judge requires oral evidence from the plaintiff in order to make a decision (Rule 11.03(3)(b)).

Where an assessment hearing is requested by the plaintiff or ordered by a judge, the plaintiff will be required to fix a date for the hearing. The plaintiff must complete a request to clerk (Form 9B) for an assessment hearing to be scheduled. See figure 9.1 below. The plaintiff or his paralegal then attends at the court office to file the Form 9B and pay the fee. As of this writing, the fee for fixing a date for an infrequent claimant is $100.00. A frequent claimant must pay $130.00.

An assessment hearing is like a trial (Rule 11.03(4)), except that the defendant is not present, and, as with a motion in writing, the plaintiff is not required to prove liability against a defendant noted in default, because the defendant by her default is deemed to admit liability (Rule 11.03(5)). The only issue before the court is how much money the defendant owes the plaintiff.

You should prepare for an assessment hearing as you would for a trial. You should contact your witnesses before the hearing to go over their evidence with them. Any witnesses other than the plaintiff must be properly summoned and provided with witness money.

At the hearing, the plaintiff, and the plaintiff's witnesses if any, will take the stand and give evidence under oath or affirmation. You must put all relevant evidence with respect to the damage suffered before the court, so that the money equivalent of the damage can be determined. Relevant evidence may include expert reports and other documentary evidence, if appropriate. The evidence should be presented in an organized and coherent fashion. Your closing remarks should summarize the evidence in support of the amount claimed. You should have the numbers, calculations, and legal principles at your fingertips, so that you can refer to them in your submissions.

Fixing a Date for Trial (Rule 16)

GENERAL

If the action is not resolved at the settlement conference, it should be set down for trial as soon as possible after that. The judge conducting the settlement conference may include instructions or a deadline for setting the action down for trial in her order (Rule 13.05(1)).

Any party may request that the clerk fix a date for trial (Rule 16.01(1)(b)). However, it is the plaintiff's action, so generally speaking the plaintiff is responsible for moving the matter forward, including fixing a date for trial, unless the court

FIGURE 9.1 Request to Clerk (Form 9B)

BETWEEN / ENTRE

....

Plaintiff(s) / *Demandeur(s)/demanderesse(s)*

and / et

....

Defendant(s) / *Défendeur(s)/défenderesse(s)*

TO THE CLERK OF THE _____ **SMALL CLAIMS COURT:**
AU GREFFIER DE LA COUR (Name of Small Claims Court location / *Emplacement de la*
DES PETITES CRÉANCES DE *Cour des petites créances*) :

My name is _____ **and I request that the clerk of the court:**
Je m'appelle (Name of party/representative / *Nom de la partie ou du/de la* *et je demande au greffier du tribunal*
représentant(e)) *de faire ce qui suit :*

(Check appropriate box(es). / Cochez la ou les cases appropriées.)

☐ note defendant(s) ....
constater le ou les défendeurs (Name of defendant(s) / *Nom du/de la/des défendeur(s)/défenderesse(s)*)

> Tick this box to request a date
> for an assessment hearing.

(Form 9A) within the prescribed time period [R. 11.01(1)].
défense (formule 9A) dans le délai prescrit [par. 11.01 (1)].

☐ schedule an assessment hearing (all defendants have been noted in default) [R. 11.03(2)(b)].
fixer la date d'une audience d'évaluation (tous les défendeurs ont été constatés en défaut) [alinéa 11.03 (2) b)].

☐ schedule a terms of payment hearing because I dispute the defendant's proposed terms of payment
contained in the Defence (Form 9A) [R. 9.03(3)].
fixer la date d'une audience relative aux modalités de paiement parce que je conteste les modalités de

> Tick this box to request a date for a trial.

éfense (formule 9A) [par. 9.03 (3)].

☐ schedule a trial [R. 16.01(1)(b)].
fixer une date de procès [alinéa 16.01 (1) b)].

orders otherwise or another party (for example, a defendant making a defendant's claim against the plaintiff) chooses to take this step.

When fixing a date for trial, the party or the party's legal representative must complete a request to clerk (Form 9B) for a trial date to be scheduled, and attend at the court office to file the Form 9B and pay the fee. As of this writing, the fee for fixing a trial date for an infrequent claimant is $100.00. A frequent claimant must pay $130.00.

The clerk then serves a notice of trial on each party who has filed a claim or defence.

WHAT TO DO WHEN YOU RECEIVE A NOTICE OF TRIAL

When you receive a notice of trial, you should contact your client and advise him of the date. Tell him that his attendance is mandatory, and advise him to note the date and time in his calendar.

The notice of trial should be filed in your pleadings subfile. The trial date should be noted in your calendar, along with suitable tickler periods. It should also be noted in the central tickler, if you maintain one, and on the checklist/tickler in the client file. You should review the settlement conference endorsement record to find out whether there are any directions, recommendations, or court orders by the settlement conference judge that require further action. You should diarize for and ensure that any further action is completed by the deadlines stated in the Rules or in the order.

If you intend to put in as evidence at trial a document, written statement, or audio or visual record that has not already been disclosed to all parties entitled to disclosure, you should consider whether you already have the document in your possession, or need to obtain it from a witness or other person, and diarize appropriately for follow-up. Your tickler period should give you time to obtain the document if you do not already have it, and serve it upon all other parties served with the notice of trial at least 30 days before the trial date, in accordance with Rule 18.02(1).

If you will require the presence of witnesses other than your client at the trial, you shall serve them personally at least 10 days before the trial date, along with attendance money (Rule 8.01(7)). You should consider serving them well before the deadline set by the Rules, to give them time to advise their employers and make any other arrangements necessary for attendance in court on that date.

Some of the above can be done by your personal assistant, if you have one and if he is experienced and reliable. When delegating, keep in mind that you are responsible for all business entrusted to you. You must directly supervise any work delegated to non-licensees (Paralegal Rule 8.01, Guideline 18).

ADJOURNMENT OF THE TRIAL DATE (RULE 17.02)

The court may postpone or adjourn a trial on such terms as are just, including the payment by one party to another of an amount as compensation for inconvenience and expense (Rule 17.02(1)). If the trial of an action has been adjourned two or more times, any further adjournment may be made only on motion with notice to all the parties who were served with the notice of trial, unless the court orders otherwise (Rule 17.02(2)).

Before requesting a date for trial, you should contact the other parties or their representatives, if they are represented, and obtain some mutually convenient dates for the trial before filing the request to clerk. You can then provide the clerk with a number of dates when both parties can attend. That way, you may avoid the delay and inconvenience of a request for an adjournment by a party who is not available on the trial date.

On receiving a request for an adjournment from another party or their representative, you should consider your duty to agree to reasonable requests concerning trial dates, adjournments, and waiver of procedural formalities and similar matters that do not prejudice the rights of your client (Paralegal Rule 7.01(2), Guideline 17). When deciding whether a request for an adjournment is reasonable, you should consider whether

1. the party requesting the adjournment has given you reasonable notice;

2. it is the first such request;

3. you are satisfied that they have a good reason for asking; and

4. there are any other relevant circumstances.

If you yourself require an adjournment of a trial date for a very good reason, you should advise all other parties well in advance of the trial date that you are requesting an adjournment, and obtain some mutually convenient dates for the adjournment, if possible. You should contact the court office with your request. If a judge grants your request and orders an adjournment, the clerk will notify all parties of the new date.

BOX 9.2

Adjournments

Remember, a judge is not bound to order an adjournment just because the parties have consented to one. The consent of the parties is just one factor that a judge will consider when deciding whether to allow an adjournment. The judge will also look at whether there is a good reason for the adjournment, and whether there have been previous adjournments. See the discussion of Rule 17.02(2) above.

If the judge does not grant the request for an adjournment, the trial will go ahead on the original date. All parties should be present and ready to go on that date. A paralegal who has a scheduling conflict must make any necessary arrangements to avoid prejudicing the client.

Where an adjournment has been agreed to by the parties before the scheduled trial date, the court office should be informed so that the matter can be referred to a judge. If the judge allows the adjournment, the clerk will notify the parties of the new trial date.

Sometimes a party will, without prior notice to other parties, turn up on the trial date to request an adjournment, or send a friend to do so. If the court exercises its discretion to grant the adjournment on such terms as are just under Rule 17.02(1), the other parties should, at a minimum, receive compensation for inconvenience and expense. The other parties should consider requesting that additional terms be imposed, if appropriate.

Failure to Attend at Trial (Rule 17.01)

The consequences of failure to attend at trial, and the remedial action that may be taken by the party who failed to attend, are set out in Rule 17.01 and table 9.1.

TABLE 9.1   Failure to Attend at Trial (Rule 17.01)

Who fails to attend?	What may the judge do?	Other issues	What may the absent party do?
All parties (Rule 17.01(1))	▪ Strike the action off the trial list ▪ Make such other order as is just		▪ Make a motion on notice to all other parties who were served with a notice of trial to have the matter restored to the trial list (Rules 1.03, 2.01, and 15)
A party (Rule 17.01(2)(a))	▪ Proceed with trial in party's absence ▪ Make such other order as is just		▪ Make a motion for an order setting aside or varying the judgment, on such terms as are just, where (1) a judgment is obtained against the absent party, and (2) the motion is made within 30 days after the absent party becomes aware of the judgment (Rules 17.01(4) and (5)(a)); or ▪ Make a motion for an order extending the 30-day period if there are special circumstances justifying the extension (Rules 17.01(4) and (5)(b))
Defendant (Rule 17.01(2)(b))	▪ Strike out defence and dismiss defendant's claim, if any ▪ Allow plaintiff to prove the plaintiff's claim ▪ Plaintiff is not required to prove liability against absent party but is required to prove the amount of the claim (Rule 17.01(2.1)) ▪ Make such other order as is just	▪ The judge must consider any issue as to proper place of trial raised under Rule 6.01(1) in the defence, and make a ruling	▪ Make a motion for an order setting aside or varying the judgment, on such terms as are just, where (1) a judgment is obtained against the absent party, and (2) the motion is made within 30 days after the absent party becomes aware of the judgment (Rules 17.01(4) and (5)(a)); or ▪ Make a motion for an order extending the 30-day period if there are special circumstances justifying the extension (Rules 17.01(4) and (5)(b))
Plaintiff (Rule 17.01(2)(c))	▪ Dismiss the plaintiff's action ▪ If there is a defendant's claim, allow the defendant to prove the claim ▪ Make such other order as is just	▪ The judge must consider any issue as to proper place of trial raised under Rule 6.01(1) in the defence, and make a ruling	▪ Make a motion for an order setting aside or varying the judgment, on such terms as are just, where (1) a judgment is obtained against the absent party, and (2) the motion is made within 30 days after the absent party becomes aware of the judgment (Rules 17.01(4) and (5)(a)); or ▪ Make a motion for an order extending the 30-day period if there are special circumstances justifying the extension (Rules 17.01(4) and (5)(b))

EVIDENCE AT TRIAL (RULE 18)

Application of Rule 18.01

At the trial of an undefended action, the plaintiff's case may be proved by affidavit, unless the trial judge orders otherwise (Rule 18.01).

Rule 18.01 has been carried over from the old *Rules of the Small Claims Court*, before the changes that came into effect on July 1, 2006. Before July 1, 2006, an unliquidated claim that was undefended went to trial. In those circumstances, Rule 18.01 allowed the plaintiff to prove her case by affidavit evidence, unless the trial judge ordered otherwise. Rule 11.03 of the current Rules permits a plaintiff in a claim for an unliquidated amount where all defendants have been noted in default to obtain judgment by filing a motion in writing for an assessment of damages or by requesting an assessment hearing.

Inspection of Property (Rule 17.03)

The trial judge may inspect any real or personal property concerning which a question arises in the action. Real property is land or buildings. Personal property is property that is movable—for example, vehicles, stocks, jewellery, furniture, etc. The inspection must take place in the presence of the parties or their representatives.

Written Statements, Documents, and Records (Rule 18.02)

DISCLOSURE—GENERAL

At every stage of a Small Claims Court action, full and fair disclosure of documents is required. The Rule 1.02 definition of "document" includes data and information in electronic form. If a plaintiff's claim is based in whole or in part on a document, the document is required to be attached to each copy of the claim. If the document is unavailable, the claim must state the reason why the document is not attached (Rule 7.01(2)2).

Similar disclosure obligations apply where a defence or defendant's claim is based in whole or in part on a document (Rules 9.02(1)2 and 10.01(4)2).

In a defended action, further disclosure is required at the settlement conference stage. At least 14 days before the date of the settlement conference, each party must serve on all other parties and file with the court (1) a copy of any document to be relied on at the trial, including an expert report, not attached to the party's claim or defence, and (2) a list of proposed witnesses and of other persons who know about the matters in dispute in the action (Rule 13.03(2)).

If the settlement conference judge is not satisfied with a party's disclosure, she may make an order directing further production of documents (Rule 13.05(2)(vi)). The order should state a deadline for completion of further disclosure and penalties for failure to comply. These conditions fall within a settlement conference judge's discretion to make any order relating to the conduct of the action that the court could make, as set out in Rule 13.05(1).

PRETRIAL DISCLOSURE—DOCUMENTS AND WRITTEN STATEMENTS (RULE 18.02)

A document or written statement or an audio or visual record that has been served, at least 30 days before the trial date, on all parties served with a trial notice, shall be received in evidence, unless the trial judge orders otherwise (Rule 18.02(1)).

Rule 18.02(1) applies to the following written statements and documents (Rule 18.02(2)):

1. The signed written statement of any witness, including the written report of an expert, to the extent that the written statement relates to facts and opinions that the witness would be permitted to testify about in person.

2. Any other document, including but not limited to

   - a hospital record or medical report made in the course of care and treatment,

   - a financial record,

   - a receipt,

   - a bill,

   - documentary evidence of loss of income or property damage, and

   - a repair estimate.

A party who serves a written statement or document described in Rule 18.02(2) on another party shall also provide the name, telephone number, and address for service of the witness or author (Rule 18.02(3)(a)). If the witness or author is giving expert evidence, a summary of his or her qualifications must also be provided (Rule 18.02(3)(b)).

The Ontario *Evidence Act* permits the following documents to be received in evidence as authentic, absent proof to the contrary (the list is not inclusive):

- consolidated statutes printed by the Queen's Printer for Ontario (s. 24.1(1)) or electronically published by the Queen's Printer for Ontario (s. 24.1(2));

- books and records of banks (s. 33);

- photographic prints of a promissory note, cheque, receipt, instrument, agreement, document, plan, or other record or book of entry kept by a person (s. 34);

- electronic records (including printouts) (s. 34.1);

- business records made in the usual and ordinary course of business (s. 35); and

- medical records, including a report signed by a practitioner that is obtained by or prepared for a party to an action, or any other report of a practitioner that relates to an action (s. 52).

What Is an Expert Witness?

An expert witness is not the same thing as an ordinary witness. Ordinarily, a witness is a person who has personal knowledge of a fact or event that is relevant to the issues in the action, and who gives testimony about that personal knowledge under oath or affirmation at trial. Their evidence is restricted to what they observed.

An **expert witness** is a witness who may not have personal knowledge of the facts themselves, but because of education, experience, specialization, and so on, has knowledge about an issue or issues in the action that the **trier of fact** does not have, because the matters in issue go beyond the range of ordinary knowledge. The expert witness gives **opinion evidence** about these issues to the trier of fact. Opinion evidence is evidence of what the expert witness thinks, believes, or infers with regard to facts in dispute.

The expert witness's opinion evidence must be relevant to issues in the action, and it must help the trier of fact to understand those issues.

BOX 9.3

What Is a Trier of Fact?

In a jury trial, the jury is the trier of fact, and the judge is the arbiter of law. The jury listens to the evidence and the trial judge's explanation of the relevant law. The jury then decides which evidence to believe and which evidence not to believe, makes **findings of fact** based on the evidence it believes to be true, and decides what the outcome of the proceeding should be.

A finding of fact is a determination that an allegation made by one party is supported by the evidence and is, therefore, true, even though that allegation is denied by another party. The finding must be based on a reasonable assessment of the evidence in the action.

Jury trials are expensive and time-consuming. There are no jury trials in Small Claims Court (*Courts of Justice Act*, s. 108(1)). At trials where no jury is permitted by the *Courts of Justice Act*, the judge is the trier of fact and law— that is, the judge listens to the evidence and decides what she does and does not believe. She then applies the relevant law to her findings of fact, and makes a decision based on her findings of fact and law.

The qualifications required to make a witness an expert will vary, depending on the nature of the expert evidence being given. An expert witness who is giving opinion evidence about a medical issue may provide educational qualifications, experience as a practitioner, areas of specialization, details of research, a list of publications, etc. An expert witness who is giving opinion evidence about how properly to construct a retaining wall or a concrete foundation may choose to emphasize her years of experience in building such structures, as opposed to, say, her educational qualifications.

An expert witness's qualifications may be proven by statements in the written report or an appendix to the report (Rule 18.02(3)(b)).

A party who has been served with a written statement or document described in Rule 18.02(2) and wishes to cross-examine the witness or author may summon the witness or author as set out in Rule 18.03.

> ## BOX 9.4
>
> ### What Is an Expert Witness?
>
> **Background:** Plaintiff is a homeowner who hires Careless Contractor Inc. to renovate Plaintiff's basement. The contract provides that all work is to be completed in a good and workmanlike fashion, in compliance with applicable codes and by-laws. The renovation is incomplete and shoddy. When Careless Contractor does not correct Plaintiff's list of deficiencies, Plaintiff hires We Care About You Ltd. to repair the work done by Careless.
>
> We Care has been doing home renovations for 15 years. We Care is insured, and has never had a complaint by a dissatisfied customer.
>
> Plaintiff sues Careless Contractor for damages for breach of contract and the cost of reasonable repairs.
>
> Thirty-five days before the trial date, Plaintiff serves a written statement by We Care describing the deficiencies in Careless Contractor's work, what had to be done to correct those deficiencies, and the cost of the corrections. The statement includes We Care's name, telephone number and address for service, and a summary of We Care's qualifications.
>
> **Discussion:** We Care is not an ordinary witness—that is, We Care has no personal knowledge of the shoddy work done by Careless Contractor. We Care was not standing by watching while Careless Contractor performed the deficient work. We Care came in after the fact, to assess what had been done wrong and perform necessary repairs.
>
> However, We Care has special knowledge about home renovations, based on 15 years of experience in home renovations. The trial judge, who is the trier of fact and law in a Small Claims Court trial, does not have this knowledge. We Care's opinion about what was wrong with the work done by Careless Contractor is relevant to the main issue in the case (failure to perform work contracted for in a good and workmanlike manner in accordance with applicable codes and by-laws). We Care's evidence will be helpful to the judge in making an informed decision about that issue, and any consequent damages. Therefore, We Care is an expert witness.
>
> If Careless Contractor wishes to cross-examine We Care, Careless may serve a summons to witness on the We Care representative who made the written report, along with attendance money, at least 10 days before the trial date (Rules 18.02(4) and 8.01(7)). A copy of the summons to witness shall be served on Plaintiff (Rule 18.02(5)). Service may be proven by filing an affidavit of service with the court (Rule 18.03(4)).

A party who serves a summons to witness on a witness or author referred to in Rule 18.02(3) shall, at the time the summons is served, also serve a copy of the summons on every other party. A party who is not served with a copy of the summons may request an adjournment of the trial, with costs (Rule 18.02(7)).

The summons to witness may also require the witness to produce at the trial the documents and other things in his or her possession, control, or power relating to the matters in question in the action that are specified in the summons (Rule 18.03(2)).

A summons to witness shall be served personally at least 10 days before the trial date, and it must be accompanied by attendance money (Rule 8.01(7)). As of this writing, attendance money (also called "witness money") for ordinary witnesses in Small Claims Court is $6.00 per day. Attendance money for a barrister, solicitor, physician, surgeon, engineer, or veterinary surgeon who is not a party to the action, for the purpose of giving evidence of a professional service rendered to give a professional opinion, is $15.00 per day.

Service of a summons to witness and payment of attendance money may be proven by an affidavit of service (Form 8A, Rule 18.03(4)). The summons to witness remains in effect until the attendance of the witness is no longer required (Rule 18.03(5)).

If an expert witness is summoned by a party to give evidence at trial under Rule 18.02, the expert witness will give evidence of her qualifications under oath on the stand. The expert witness may be cross-examined on her qualifications. The court will then make a determination about whether she has the necessary qualifications to give expert evidence on the issue in question. If she is qualified as an expert witness, she may give expert evidence and be cross-examined on that evidence.

Summons to Witness (Rule 18.03, Form 18A)

GENERAL

The general rule with respect to evidence at trial is that a person whose evidence is material to the conduct of an action should be present at the trial to give his evidence under oath or affirmation and be cross-examined on that evidence.

The parties to the action are required to attend at trial. Other witnesses must be served with a **summons to witness** (Form 18A), which compels their attendance. The summons to witness must be accompanied by attendance money. It must be personally served on the witness at least 10 days before the trial date. Service is proven by filing an affidavit of service with the court.

BOX 9.5

When Should You Serve a Summons to Witness?

You should always serve a summons to witness on any person whose evidence is material to the conduct of an action, regardless of whether the person is a relative, a personal friend, or a total stranger. A person who has not been served with a summons to witness is under no legal obligation to appear in court. If that person fails to show up on the trial date, the judge may order the trial to go ahead in her absence, and your client may be prejudiced as a result.

If a person who has been served with a summons to witness fails to show up on the trial date or remain until her attendance is no longer required, the trial judge may issue a warrant for arrest of defaulting witness (Form 18B) directed to all police officers in Ontario, requiring them to apprehend the witness anywhere within Ontario and promptly bring the witness before the court (Rule 18.03(6)).

Copies of a summons to witness served on a witness or author of a written statement or document referred to in Rule 18.02(3) shall be served on every other party (Rule 18.02(5)). A party who is not served with a copy of the summons in accordance with Rule 18.02(5) may request an adjournment of the trial, with costs.

The deadline for service of a summons should be noted on your file checklist/tickler when you receive the notice of trial, along with a bring-forward date. Noting a tickler period of at least three weeks before the trial date is good practice. This will give you ample time to arrange for service of summonses on all witnesses well before the 10-day deadline stated in Rule 8.01(7) expires.

Another good reason to serve the summons at least three weeks in advance of the trial date is that this gives the witness time to make whatever arrangements are necessary to allow her to be at court. As well, it gives you more time to get in touch with the witness, discuss her evidence with her, and properly prepare her for the approaching trial.

The summons to witness remains in effect until the attendance of the witness is no longer required (Rule 18.03(5)).

ATTENDANCE MONEY

Attendance money must be served with the summons to witness. Attendance money should be in the form of a firm cheque on the general account, payable to the witness being summoned. It is a disbursement that can be charged back to your client.

The amount of attendance money required to be paid in a Small Claims Court action is very modest. Attendance money for an ordinary witness is $6.00 per day plus mileage. If the witness is a barrister, solicitor, physician, surgeon, engineer, or veterinary surgeon who is not a party to the action and has been summoned to give evidence of a professional service rendered or to give a professional opinion, the

---

BOX 9.6

What Is Personal Service?

Your process server goes to serve Mr. Bill Witness with a summons to witness and witness money at his place of business at 10:30 a.m. The process server enters the place of business, approaches Bill Witness, and asks, "Are you Bill Witness?" Mr. Witness says, "Yes I am." The process server hands the summons to witness and the cheque for attendance money to Mr. Witness, and says, "I am serving you with a summons to witness and attendance money."

Bill Witness glances at the summons, and says, "I'm a busy man! I don't have time for this!" He tries to hand the summons and cheque back to the process server. When she refuses to accept them, he throws them on the floor. The process server leaves.

Has personal service taken place?

Yes. The process server obtained personal identification from the person to be served, described the documents being served, and handed them to the witness. What the witness does with the documents after service is irrelevant. Any person who has been served with a summons to witness should comply with the summons. A judge may issue a warrant for the arrest of a witness who fails to comply with a summons (Rule 18.03(6)).

BOX 9.7

Greco v. Hardwick: Summons to Witness (Form 18A)

The factual background to *Greco v. Hardwick* is in chapter 4 at box 4.10 and appendix 4.5, and in chapter 6 at box 6.2 and appendixes 6.1, 6.2, and 6.3.

The matter went to settlement conference, but the parties failed to come to an agreement. The trial is scheduled for April 18, 20—. There has been full documentary disclosure by both parties, including witness lists. The name and contact information for Glenn Woods was on the list of proposed witnesses served on the defendant and filed with the court by Ms. Greco's paralegal prior to the settlement conference, in accordance with Rule 13.03(2).

At appendix 9.1, you will find the summons to witness that is served on Glenn Woods along with the affidavit of service of Neela Subramaniam proving personal service on Mr. Woods of the summons to witness and attendance money. The affidavit of service is filed with the court to prove that Mr. Woods was served with a summons to witness and attendance money in accordance with Rule 8.01(7).

witness money payable is $15.00 per day plus kilometres travelled per day. Mileage is 30 cents per kilometre in southern Ontario, and 30.5 cents per kilometre in northern Ontario (*Kilometre Allowances* regulation to the *Administration of Justice Act*).

FAILURE TO ATTEND

A witness who has been properly summoned must attend at court on the specified date and remain in attendance in accordance with the requirements of the summons to witness. If a witness who has been served with a summons to witness fails to attend or does not remain in attendance, the trial judge may issue a warrant (Form 18B) directing all police officers in Ontario to apprehend the witness anywhere in Ontario and bring him or her promptly before the court (Rule 18.03(6)).

The party who summoned the witness may assist the police in apprehending the witness by filing an identification form with the clerk (Form 20K, Rule 18.03(6.1)).

When apprehended, the witness may be detained in custody (that is, put in jail) until her or his presence is no longer required; or the judge may release the witness on such terms as are just. In either case, the witness may be ordered to pay any costs arising out of the failure to attend or to remain in attendance (Rule 18.03(7)).

You will find a sample warrant for arrest of defaulting witness and identification form at appendix 9.2.

ABUSE OF POWER TO SUMMON A WITNESS (RULE 18.03(8))

Only persons whose evidence is material to the conduct of an action should be summoned to attend at trial. **Material evidence** is evidence that has a logical connection to an issue or issues in dispute in the action. It is evidence that, on its own or combined with other evidence, helps the trial judge to decide which party's allegations to accept as being true.

If a party summons a witness who has no material evidence to give with respect to the issues in dispute in the action, she wastes the time of the court, the other parties, and the witness. In such cases, the court may order that the party pay compensation for inconvenience and expense directly to the witness.

INTERPRETERS

The Ministry of the Attorney General is required to provide interpreters from English to French or French to English. Interpreters in other languages must be provided by the party requiring their presence.

If a party serves a summons to witness on a witness who requires an interpreter for a language other than English or French, the party must arrange for a qualified interpreter to attend at the trial (Rule 18.03(5.1)).

A **qualified interpreter** is someone who is trained to interpret in a courtroom environment. Interpreters are not under oath when they interpret. They must provide an unbiased and accurate version of what the witness under oath is saying on the stand.

Your client must understand that a qualified interpreter is required by the *Small Claims Court Rules*. If a party does not comply with Rule 18.03(5.1), every other party is entitled to request an adjournment of the trial, with costs (Rule 18.03(5.2)).

Preparing for Trial

PRETRIAL TASKS: REVIEW

Table 9.2 reviews the pretrial tasks in a defended action.

REVIEWING THE CLIENT MATTER

When preparing a file for a trial in a defended action, you should first ensure that all deadlines for disclosure, summoning witnesses, making offers to settle, and so on, have been complied with. All of these deadlines, along with bring-forward dates, should be recorded in your tickler system. As tasks are completed, they should be initialed by the person who completes the task and the date of completion noted. Supporting documents (such as proof of service) should be placed in the appropriate subfile of the client file.

You should review the pleadings, along with any witness notes and documents, and directions or comments by the settlement conference judge, to determine what evidence you need to put in. Keep in mind that an allegation in a pleading is just that—an unproven statement—unless it is supported under oath by spoken evidence or documentary evidence that is accepted by the Small Claims Court trial judge as true.

You should discuss with your client the issues raised in her claim or defence, with reference to the allegations the other party is making. Depending on the complexity of the matter, this may be done in person or over the phone. In either case, it should be done at least a week before the trial date, if time permits, and you should be careful to make notes of everything that is said. You should review those notes with your client before ending the interview.

TABLE 9.2   Pretrial Tasks in a Defended Action: Review

Task	Who?	When?	How?
Compliance with order for further disclosure made by the settlement conference judge (Rule 13.05(1)(vi))	▪ A party named in the order	▪ As soon as possible after the settlement conference, and before any deadline stated in the order	▪ Provide disclosure of documents, witnesses, etc., to other parties as set out in the order ▪ File proof of disclosure in client file and, if required, in court file
Obtain any documents, written statements, or audio or visual records that have not already been disclosed to other parties and that a party intends to rely on at trial	▪ Plaintiff or defendant	▪ As soon as possible after the settlement conference, and before the Rule 18.02(1) 30-day deadline for service expires	▪ Contact the witness or author ▪ If a fee will be charged for the document or written statement, discuss with the client how the fee is to be paid—any arrangement should be confirmed in writing
Disclosure of a document or written statement or audio or visual record that a party intends to rely on at trial (Rule 18.02)	▪ Plaintiff or defendant	▪ At least 30 days before the trial date (Rule 18.02(1))	▪ Service on all parties who were served with a notice of trial (Rule 18.02(1)) ▪ May be served by mail, by courier, personally, or by an alternative to personal service ▪ Written statement or document must include name, telephone number, and address for service of the witness/author (Rule 18.02(3)(a)) ▪ If witness or author is giving expert evidence, the written statement or document should also include a summary of his or her qualifications (Rule 18.02(3)(b))
Summon witness or author of a written document or statement served under Rules 18.02(1) and (2)	▪ Any party served with a written document or statement under Rules 18.02(1) and (2)	▪ At least 10 days before the trial date (Rule 8.01(7))	▪ Personal service of summons to witness plus attendance money on witness or author (Rule 8.01(7)) ▪ Service may be proven by affidavit (Form 8A) ▪ Service of a copy of the summons on every other party
Summon a witness (Rule 18.03)	▪ A party who requires the attendance of a person in Ontario to give evidence at the trial	▪ At least 10 days before the trial date (Rule 8.01(7)) ▪ Note: It is good practice to serve the summons to witness well in advance of the 10-day deadline	▪ Personal service of summons to witness plus attendance money on witness (Rule 8.01(7)) ▪ Service may be proven by affidavit (Form 8A)

(Table 9.2 is concluded on the next page.)

TABLE 9.2   Concluded

Task	Who?	When?	How?
Offer to settle (Rule 14.01)	■ Plaintiff or defendant	■ At any time up until after the court disposes of the action (Rule 14.03(3)) ■ At least seven days before the trial commences, if you want the Rule 14.07 costs consequences to apply	■ Serve a written offer to settle (Form 14A) on the other party ■ File proof of service in client file

With any non-party witness, ordinary or expert, keep in mind that there is no way that attendance money compensates a witness for a court attendance. Witnesses who are losing employment or business income to attend at court tend to be unhappy. You can manage some of that unhappiness by serving the summons to witness and attendance money well in advance of the trial date. This gives them a reasonable amount of time to get used to the idea of a court attendance, to arrange for missing a day's work, and to deal with any other inconveniences connected with the court appearance.

Interviewing Witnesses (Paralegal Rule 4.02)

GENERAL (PARALEGAL RULES 4.02(1) AND 4.01(5)(I), (J), (K), (M))

Subject to Paralegal Rules 4.02(2) and (3), a paralegal may seek information from any potential witness in a proceeding, including witnesses appearing for opposing parties. The witness need not be summoned.

You may not contact a witness who is represented, except as provided in Paralegal Rules 4.02(2) and (3).

When contacting witnesses, you should identify yourself to the witness, and explain that you are a paralegal. You must give the witness your client's name and status in the proceeding, and ensure that the witness understands that you are acting exclusively in your client's interest. You should make a special effort to be clear on these points when speaking to a person who is self-represented (Guideline 12).

A witness has no obligation to speak to you. If a witness tells you they do not want to talk to you, you should leave the witness alone. You are not permitted to **harass a witness** (Paralegal Rule 4.01(5)(j)).

When interviewing witnesses, you shall take care not to subvert or suppress any evidence. You must not coach a witness to leave out evidence or to say things that are not completely true, because it will benefit your client.

When interviewing witnesses, you shall take care not to procure the witness to stay out of the way—in other words, you shall not cause or persuade a witness not to give evidence at trial.

Additional restrictions on a paralegal advocate's conduct when dealing with witnesses are set out at Paralegal Rule 4.01(5), which requires that, when acting as an advocate, a paralegal shall not

- knowingly permit a witness or party to be presented in a false or misleading way, or to impersonate another;

- needlessly abuse, hector, harass, or inconvenience a witness; or

- persuade a witness not to give evidence, or encourage a witness not to attend a hearing.

Interviewing Represented Persons (Paralegal Rules 4.02(2), (3), and (6))

You shall not approach or deal with a person who is represented by another licensee, except through or with the consent of the licensee (Paralegal Rule 4.02(2)).

If you are acting for a party in a matter involving a corporation or organization represented by another licensee, you shall not, without the licensee's consent or unless otherwise authorized or required by law (Paralegal Rule 4.02(3)),

- approach directors, officers, or persons likely to be involved in the decision-making process for the corporation or organization; or

- approach employees and agents of the corporation or organization whose acts or omissions in connection with the matter may expose the corporation or organization to quasi-criminal, criminal, or civil liability.

For purposes of Paralegal Rule 4.02(3), "organization" includes a partnership, limited partnership, sole proprietorship, association, union, unincorporated group, government department, government agency, tribunal, and regulatory body (Paralegal Rule 4.02(6)).

Paralegal Rule 4.02 applies to communications with a party to a formal adjudicative proceeding, contract, or negotiation who is represented by a licensee in the matter to which the communication relates. Paralegal Rule 4.02 also applies to communications with any person who is represented by a licensee in the matter to which the communication relates (Paralegal Rule 4.02(4)).

A paralegal is prohibited from communicating with a represented person if the paralegal has direct knowledge that the person is represented, or where the circumstances are such that the paralegal should be able to determine that the person is represented (Paralegal Rule 4.02(5)).

DIRECT EXAMINATION— PREPARING YOUR QUESTIONS

The *Small Claims Court Rules* provide for disclosure at every stage of the action. This means that, by the time the matter gets to trial, you should have a good sense of the strengths and weaknesses of your client's case and that of the opposing party.

The best way to make a good case for your client at trial is by preparing your witnesses thoroughly and by putting complete, detailed evidence on every material issue before the court. If you prepare carefully, and use direct examination to present the evidence to the court as a concise, organized narrative, it is unlikely that cross-examination will do much to undermine your client's case.

BOX 9.8

Greco v. Hardwick: Preparing for Trial

The background and pleadings in this action can be found in chapter 4, at box 4.10 and appendix 4.3, and in chapter 6, at box 6.2 and appendixes 6.1, 6.2, and 6.3.

Assume that you are the paralegal for Juliette Greco, the plaintiff (defendant in defendant's claim). The date for trial is April 18, 20—.

You are reviewing the client file to determine what evidence is required at trial to tell the judge Ms. Greco's story and convince the judge that she should get what she is asking for.

When reviewing the factual background and the pleadings, ask yourself the following questions.

1. What is the basis for the plaintiff's action, as stated in the plaintiff's claim?

2. What evidence is needed to support the plaintiff's claim?

3. What evidence do we have in the present case to support the plaintiff's claim?

4. Is that evidence sufficient?

5. What is the basis for the defendant's dispute, as stated in the defence and defendant's claim?

6. What evidence is needed to support the defendant's dispute?

7. Is that evidence sufficient?

8. What is the basis for the defence to defendant's claim?

9. What evidence is needed to support Ms. Greco's defence to Mr. Hardwick's defendant's claim?

10. Is that evidence sufficient?

Question (1):	What is the basis for the plaintiff's action, as stated in the plaintiff's claim?
Answer:	▶ An unpaid debt.
Question (2):	What evidence is needed to support the plaintiff's claim?
Answer:	▶ Evidence that money was paid to the defendant. ▶ Evidence that the money was not paid back to the plaintiff.
Question (3):	What evidence do we have in the present case to support the plaintiff's claim?
Answer:	▶ A promissory note dated April 1, 20—. ▶ The defendant's admission that he took the money (see Schedule A to defence). ▶ The defendant's admission that he did not pay the money back.
Question (4):	Is that evidence sufficient?
Answer:	▶ No. See discussion of the defendant's dispute, below.
Question (5):	What is the basis for the defendant's dispute, as stated in the defence and defendant's claim?
Answer:	▶ That he performed services in lieu of payment, with the plaintiff's knowledge and consent. ▶ That these services had a value of $5,990.00, as calculated at paragraph 9 of the defendant's claim.
Question (6):	What evidence is needed to support the defendant's dispute?
Answer:	▶ The defendant's evidence that he performed the services with the plaintiff's knowledge and consent (particulars in defendant's claim). ▶ The estimates attached to the defendant's claim.

Question (7):	Is that evidence sufficient?
Answer:	▶ No.
Question (8):	What is the basis for the defence to defendant's claim?
Answer:	▶ There was no written contract with respect to the services to be provided or their value. ▶ The plaintiff disputes the terms of the spoken contract. ▶ The plaintiff disputes the value assigned to the services rendered.
Question (9):	What evidence is needed to support Ms. Greco's defence to Mr. Hardwick's defendant's claim?
Answer:	▶ There was a spoken agreement that the defendant/plaintiff by defendant's claim ("Mr. Hardwick") would perform the services for a fee in the range of the fee charged by Glenn Woods Garden Services for the same services. ▶ The plaintiff/defendant by defendant's claim ("Ms. Greco") accepted the services offered by Mr. Hardwick in partial payment only of the amount due on the note. ▶ Many of the services Mr. Hardwick or his children performed had been performed in the past for no charge. ▶ Many of the services Mr. Hardwick or his children performed could have been completed by others for no charge. ▶ When the note became due, Ms. Greco approached Mr. Hardwick regarding payment of the balance due on the note. ▶ She then began sending demands for payment (see documents attached to the plaintiff's claim). ▶ The values assigned by Mr. Hardwick to the services performed are grossly inflated. ▶ Glenn Woods performed identical services in the past for a fee ranging from $1,400.00 to $1,550.00.
Question (10):	Is that evidence sufficient?
Answer:	▶ See discussion below.
Evidentiary issue	The defendant intends to rely on the estimates attached to the defendant's claim as evidence at the trial.
Discussion	▶ We have summoned our own witness, Glenn Woods, to give evidence as to the value of services equivalent to those provided to the plaintiff by the defendant. ▶ If the defendant summons some or all of the authors of the estimates, the plaintiff's paralegal can cross-examine them on their quotes. Cross-examination may not achieve much, in the circumstances. The plaintiff should rely on the direct evidence of Glenn Woods contradicting the defendant's quotes. ▶ If the defendant relies on the written quotes only, that will go to the weight to be assigned to the quotes, as opposed to the weight to be given to Glenn Woods's spoken evidence under oath.
Evidentiary issue	What is a weakness in both parties' cases?
Answer:	▶ The absence of a written contract with respect to the services to be provided by the defendant in lieu of payment of the debt owing to the plaintiff. When a spoken agreement is at issue in the action, the judge as trier of fact must make **findings as to credibility**—that is, the judge must decide whose evidence to believe on a balance of probabilities. This makes for unpredictable outcomes.

Some of the issues can be dealt with by evidence led in direct examination of the plaintiff or her witnesses. Others will be dealt with by evidence led in direct examination, and then revisited in cross-examination of the defendant.

Direct examination and cross-examination are dealt with in more detail below.

Direct examination is the series of questions that you ask your own witnesses when they take the stand, to help them tell their story clearly and concisely, so that it can be easily understood by the court. When you have reviewed the file and decided what evidence you need to put before the court to tell your client's story, you should prepare a detailed list of the questions you need to ask in direct examination. When drafting your questions, it is a good rule to begin at the beginning and go through a witness's story step-by-step with her to the end, using your questions as prompts to elicit all evidence that is material in the process.

The questions you ask in direct examination provide the pieces of the story. If you miss one of the pieces, or get the pieces in the wrong order, the story becomes confusing. Breaking the narrative down into an orderly procession of facts is part of the difficult art of direct examination. You need to prepare your questions carefully, with this in mind.

At trial, as you go through your list of questions in direct examination, listen carefully to the witness's answers, and be prepared to depart from the script. If an answer is incomplete, ask the witness questions to clarify what he said. If a witness's answer to one question answers several other questions, cross those questions off the list.

Because the purpose of direct examination is to let the witness tell her story, you should draft your questions using open-ended questions only. With a few exceptions, those are the only questions you will be allowed to ask your witnesses in direct examination.

Open-ended, or direct, questions are questions that do not "lead" the witness—that is, they do not contain any language that implies certain facts or suggests a "correct" answer to the witness. Open-ended questions use "who," "what," "when," "where," and "how."

Questions that imply the existence of certain facts or suggest a correct answer to a witness (or to the trier of fact) are called **leading questions**. Leading questions are perfectly acceptable in cross-examination, but they are only permitted in direct examination when the question concerns information that is not in dispute.

Tables 9.3 and 9.4 contain some examples of the same question, phrased as an open-ended question and as a leading question. Assume that the witness in the stand is the plaintiff, Juliette Greco.

TABLE 9.3   Greco v. Hardwick: Asking Open-Ended Questions and Leading Questions

Open-ended question	Leading question
What is your name?	Your name is Juliette Greco?
Where do you live?	You live at 126 George Court in Brampton?
Who are your neighbours?	James and Pamela Hardwick are your neighbours?
What is their address?	They live at 128 George Court?

The leading questions in table 9.3 *are* permissible for use in direct examination, because they are about issues that are not in dispute (in the *Greco v. Hardwick* case, the parties' names and addresses). However, keep in mind that it is good practice to use open-ended questions in direct examination whenever possible. If your witness has been prepared properly, she should have no problem telling her story without being led.

TABLE 9.4   Greco v. Hardwick: Asking Open-Ended Questions and Leading Questions

Open-ended question	Leading question
Was the money due under the promissory note paid?	James Hardwick told you he could not pay the money?
Did he discuss this with you?	James Hardwick offered to perform services in lieu of payment?
When did the discussion take place?	He made the offer shortly after signing the promissory note?
What did he say?	He offered to do yard and pool maintenance instead of paying?
Did you accept his offer?	Before accepting his offer, you obtained Mr. Hardwick's assurance that the charge for his services would be in the range of what you had been charged in past years by Glenn Woods Garden Services?
Did you discuss a price?	(See above.)

The leading questions in table 9.4 *are not* permissible in direct examination, because they are about issues that are disputed in the action—that is, the terms of the spoken agreement between Juliette Greco and James Hardwick for performance of services instead of payment of money.

The open-ended questions in table 9.4 let the witness tell the court her story about the issues in dispute (the terms of her unwritten agreement with James Hardwick to accept services instead of payment, including the value to be assigned to those services). With the leading questions, all the witness gets to say is "yes" or "no." In other words, the paralegal asking the questions, who is not under oath and cannot be cross-examined, is putting in all the evidence.

When preparing your questions, you should note the places in the evidence where you intend to submit a document as an **exhibit**.

An exhibit is an original document that is material to an issue in the action. It must be identified by a witness with personal knowledge of its contents. The contents of the document may be referred to in the witness's spoken evidence. It is then marked as an exhibit by the court clerk and placed in the court file as part of the evidence.

Exhibits should be entered at the point in the witness's evidence where they support and confirm that evidence. That is why it is important to note their place in the evidentiary narrative when you are drafting your questions.

The procedure for entering documents as exhibits at trial is discussed in more detail in the section on introducing exhibits at trial below.

CROSS-EXAMINATION— PREPARING YOUR QUESTIONS

General

In direct examination, the relationship between the paralegal and the witness is usually friendly. When a paralegal puts a properly prepared witness on the stand, the paralegal should already know what the witness will say. The paralegal's questions are designed to help the witness tell the story.

Cross-examination is used to pinpoint weaknesses or inconsistencies in the testimony of another party or another party's witness. You should avoid using open-ended questions in cross-examination, because they leave the narrative in the witness's control. You should use leading questions exclusively, or as often as possible.

A successful Small Claims Court cross-examination may be very brief, because quite often there is not that much evidence that is susceptible to testing by cross-examination. The trick to successful cross-examination is to select the weaknesses in a witness's evidence that go to issues in dispute, and plan your questions carefully to explore and emphasize those weaknesses.

As with direct examination, you should prepare your questions for cross-examination ahead of time. You should listen carefully to the witness's testimony in direct examination, and take notes. Be prepared to revise and adapt your questions in response to what the witness says in direct examination and the answers the witness gives you in cross-examination.

Preparation

When you are preparing for cross-examination of the witnesses for the other party, the first question you should always ask yourself is: Will cross-examining this witness accomplish anything for my client's case? In a civil case, there is no absolute obligation to cross-examine. If cross-examination is unlikely to accomplish anything that assists your client's case, you should not cross-examine.

If you decide to cross-examine a witness, you should prepare carefully. You must focus on the issues where the opposing party's case is vulnerable and where cross-examination is likely to bring out evidence that is useful to your client's case or impugn evidence that is harmful to your client's case. Unless you are an experienced advocate, you should make a list of the questions you intend to ask ahead of time. Whether you ask all of these questions in cross-examination will depend largely upon what the witness says during direct examination and the witness's responses during cross-examination.

If the other party is represented by an experienced advocate, the other party's advocate will have advised his client ahead of time about what to expect in cross-examination, and will do his best to cover off those issues in direct examination. This means that you must listen carefully to the evidence of an opposing party or an opposing party's witness in direct examination, and edit and adapt your cross-examination accordingly.

If the witness gives evidence that is incomplete or ambiguous with respect to material issues in direct examination, you will want to question him on that evidence. If the witness gives evidence that is consistent and credible, you may decide not to question the witness on certain issues, or not to question the witness at all.

Courtesy

Paralegal Rule 4.01(5)(j) states that, when acting as an advocate, a paralegal shall not needlessly abuse, hector, harass, or inconvenience a witness. A well-prepared cross-examination is far more effective if conducted in a courteous manner. An ill-prepared cross-examination will not be saved by rude or abusive conduct toward the witness.

Conclusion

When preparing your cross-examination, analyze the issues and evidence carefully. You want to target weaknesses in the other party's evidence, with a view to emphasizing the strengths of your own party's case.

When cross-examining a witness, if you do not get the answer you want to a particular question, do not get into a debate with the witness about it or engage in any other form of bullying or harassment. Use your questions to probe the issue, and then move on to your next point. Stay calm, be polite, and be thorough.

Listen carefully to the other party's evidence during direct examination. If the witness gives evidence that is consistent and credible, you may decide to change your questions, not to question the witness on certain issues, or not to question the witness at all.

EXHIBITS

If you intend to rely on a document at trial, you should ensure that the document has been disclosed to all other parties. If you are aware of the document when you draft your claim or defence, a copy should be attached to the pleading. If you become aware of the document later in the action, you should disclose it along with any other additional disclosure at least 14 days before the settlement conference (Rule 13.03(2)) or, if that is impossible, in accordance with an order or direction from the settlement conference judge or at least 30 days before the trial date.

If you are putting an original document in as evidence at trial, it must be introduced as an exhibit. First, you show the original document to opposing parties or their representatives. You should distribute photocopies of the document to the judge and the opposing party or parties.

If the witness has personal knowledge of the document, you will show the original document to the witness, and ask him to identify it. You then question the witness with respect to those parts of the document's contents that are material to the action. When you have finished questioning him, you hand the original to the clerk, and request that the document be admitted into evidence. The clerk will mark the original as an exhibit and place it in the court file as part of the evidence.

An exhibit that has been identified by a sworn witness is marked by a number. If you plan to refer to an exhibit that will be identified by a later witness, you will ask that it be marked for identification. Exhibits for identification are marked with letters. You may request that an exhibit marked for identification be admitted into evidence when a witness who has personal knowledge of its contents takes the stand.

BOX 9.9

Greco v. Hardwick: Submitting a Document as an Exhibit

The following dialogue demonstrates how the promissory note in *Greco v. Hardwick* would be submitted as an exhibit at trial.

Plaintiff's paralegal:	What was the amount of the loan to Mr. Hardwick?
Ms. Greco:	$5,000.00.
Plaintiff's paralegal:	When was the money paid to Mr. Hardwick?
Ms. Greco:	April 1, 20—.
Plaintiff's paralegal:	Was there anything in writing with respect to the loan?
Ms. Greco:	Yes. The defendant signed a promissory note dated April 1, 20—.
Plaintiff's paralegal (to the judge):	Your Honour, I am showing the defendant's paralegal an original of a promissory note dated April 1, 20—. A photocopy of the note has already been disclosed to him.
The judge (to the defendant's paralegal):	You've received a copy of this document?
Defendant's paralegal (to the judge):	Yes, Your Honour. A photocopy of this document was attached to the plaintiff's claim. And my client has a duplicate original.
The judge (to the plaintiff's paralegal):	Proceed.
Plaintiff's paralegal (to Ms. Greco):	Can you identify this document for the court?
Ms. Greco:	Yes. It is a duplicate original of a promissory note signed by James Hardwick on April 1, 20—.
Plaintiff's paralegal:	Please tell the court about the terms of the note.
Ms. Greco:	The amount of the loan was $5,000.00. The due date was August 2, 20—. In the event of default, interest became payable at a rate of 10% per year until any balance owing was paid in full.
Plaintiff's paralegal:	When did Mr. Hardwick sign the note?
Ms. Greco:	He signed both copies of the note in my presence when I gave him the cheque for $5,000.00 on April 1, 20—. I gave him the original, and I kept the duplicate original.
Plaintiff's paralegal:	Your Honour, I would ask that the promissory note dated April 1, 20— signed by James Hardwick be marked as Exhibit 1.

The judge may then examine the document, or simply order the clerk to mark it as an exhibit.

When preparing for trial, you should put originals of all documents you intend to enter as exhibits in a subfile, clipped together in the order in which you intend to introduce them. You should have copies of the documents clipped together in the subfile in the same order as the originals. At trial, as you hand out copies to the other party and the judge, and enter the originals, you should mark your own copies with the exhibit numbers as they are assigned by the court, by hand or electronically.

TRIAL PROCEDURE

General

When you arrive at the courthouse, you should go to the courtroom where your trial is scheduled to be heard. A **docket** will be posted outside the courtroom listing the matters to be heard that day. You should note where your matter is on the list. You should then go into the courtroom, fill out a **counsel slip**, and give it to the clerk. A counsel slip is a piece of paper that tells the court what your name is, the matter you are there on, and who you are representing. It gives the court notice that there is someone appearing on the matter. If you have settled the matter, or if you are requesting an adjournment of the matter to a future date, you should advise the clerk of this as well.

If your client and/or any other witnesses are there, you should speak to them outside the courtroom. If the opposing party and her legal representative are there, you should greet them so that they know you are present.

When court starts, all parties will be called into the courtroom. The judge and clerk will then **purge the list**. Matters that have settled and adjournments will be dealt with first. Undisputed matters (that is, matters where one party does not appear) will be dealt with next.

Disputed matters will be held down until all of the above matters have been dealt with.

If you are still actively negotiating settlement with the other side, the negotiations should take place outside the courtroom. You may wish to inform the court clerk that you are outside talking, so that he can page you if your matter is called.

If there are no matters to discuss outside the courtroom, the parties, their legal representatives, and any additional witnesses should take seats in the public gallery until their matter is called.

What this means for you is that, if the other side shows up and wants a trial, it does not matter what number you are on the court docket. You must wait until the list has been purged before your trial will be heard by the judge.

Courtroom Etiquette

PROPER DRESS

Licensees should wear business attire on Small Claims Court appearances. Men should wear a suit and tie. Women should wear a suit or dress slacks with a suit jacket. Dark colours are preferable. Jewellery should be kept to a minimum.

CONDUCT IN THE COURTROOM

In the courtroom, you should behave with the utmost decorum and professionalism. You should not read newspapers, chew gum, or talk to others (except very briefly in an undertone) in a courtroom where a judge is sitting. Cellphones should be turned off.

If you need to talk to your client, a witness, another party, or another party's legal representative, you should do so outside the courtroom.

THE JUDGE

General

When acting as an advocate, you shall treat the judge with candour, fairness, courtesy, and respect (Paralegal Rule 4.01(1)).

You should rise when a judge enters or leaves the courtroom. You should rise whenever you address the bench or the bench addresses you. When entering or leaving a courtroom in which a judge is sitting, you should pause at the door and bow to the bench.

Experienced judges will be aware of the applicable law in most of the cases that come before them. However, occasionally a judge will ask you to explain a particular legal principle. If asked, you must inform her honestly and candidly about the law in question, to the best of your knowledge and ability.

The Role of the Judge at Trial

Small Claims Court judges tend to play an activist role in the courtroom. At a Small Claims Court trial, the judge will often intervene in the proceeding, questioning witnesses, clarifying issues, and taking any necessary steps to ensure that a self-represented party is not denied a fair trial because of lack of familiarity with court procedure. This is an appropriate role for a trial judge to play in a court where quite often one or both parties are self-represented and unsophisticated. It is in keeping with the general mandate of the court to hear and determine in a summary way all questions of law and fact in order to secure a just, speedy, and inexpensive determination of the matter before it (*Courts of Justice Act*, s. 25; Rule 1.03(1)).

Where one party is self-represented and the other has legal representation, the trial judge's role is to ensure procedural fairness for the self-represented party, and to discourage bullying or intimidation of the self-represented party by the other party's legal representative. The judge should never give legal advice to a litigant.

SELF-REPRESENTED PARTIES

You should treat self-represented parties with courtesy and respect.

You are not required to educate an unsophisticated, self-represented adversary as to the law. However, you do have a duty to be truthful, honest, and thorough in presenting your client's case and the law as it applies to your client's case, in order to ensure that the court is not misled.

As in other civil actions, settlement negotiations in Small Claims Court may continue right up until there is a final disposition of the matter. Negotiating settlement with self-represented parties presents unique challenges. The self-represented

FIGURE 9.2   What Does the Courtroom Look Like?

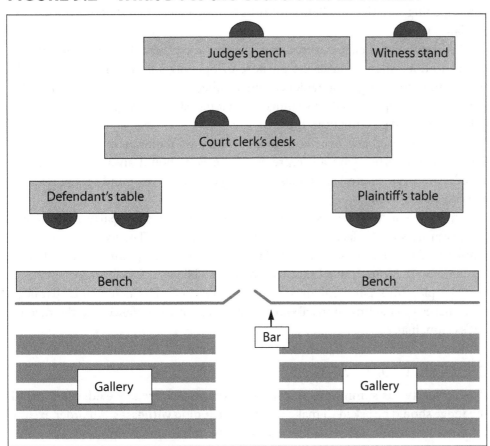

party must be advised and must understand that you are acting exclusively in the best interests of your client.

If a matter involving a self-represented party settles at trial, the trial judge must review the terms of settlement. The trial judge cannot give legal advice to the self-represented party with respect to the terms of the agreement. For example, she cannot comment on whether she thinks some of the terms are unclear or unduly harsh—that amounts to giving a legal opinion. She is restricted to ensuring that the self-represented party understands the terms of settlement, and satisfying herself that the court has legal jurisdiction to make an order in accordance with the terms of settlement.

Trial Procedure

INTRODUCTIONS AND OPENING SUBMISSIONS

When the matter is called, the parties take their places at the counsel tables facing the judge's bench. The plaintiff and her representative sit at the counsel table on the right facing the judge's bench. The defendant and his representative sit at the counsel table on the left facing the judge's bench.

The plaintiff's paralegal rises and introduces herself by last name and initial. The defendant's paralegal rises and introduces himself by last name and initial.

If requested to do so by the judge, the parties' representatives may then make brief opening submissions. The plaintiff's paralegal goes first, followed by the defendant's paralegal.

Self-represented parties, through no fault of their own other than lack of legal sophistication, often mistake the purpose of opening submissions. They use the opportunity to start giving evidence and arguing their case. In matters where the parties are self-represented, busy judges with long lists often dispense with opening submissions and go straight to the evidence.

An experienced and courteous judge will always request a brief opening submission from parties who are represented. So you should always have one prepared, because, if requested, it assists the judge to focus his mind on the issues in the case before him.

In this context, a submission is an explanation of what a party wants, and a brief summary of the facts that entitle the party to get it. The word "brief" needs emphasis. The judge does not wish to listen to details at this point—that is what the evidence is for. More detailed submissions should be saved for closing argument.

The plaintiff's paralegal makes submissions first. The defendant's paralegal then makes brief submissions about the grounds for the defence and the defendant's claim, if any.

ORDER EXCLUDING WITNESSES

If either party has summoned non-party witnesses, before any evidence is heard, the judge should be asked to make an **order excluding witnesses**. An order excluding witnesses requires all witnesses except the parties themselves to leave the courtroom and wait outside the courtroom until they are called to give evidence themselves. The purpose of an order excluding witnesses is to prevent witnesses who have not yet taken the stand from hearing, and being influenced by, the evidence of the witnesses who take the stand ahead of them. When a witness has given his evidence and has been cross-examined, he may remain in the courtroom and hear the remainder of the case if he wishes.

An order excluding witnesses is required only when there are witnesses other than the parties giving evidence. If the plaintiff and the defendant are the only witnesses, an order excluding witnesses is not required.

EVIDENCE

After introductions and opening submissions are finished, and, if required, an order excluding witnesses has been made, the plaintiff is invited to call her first witness. Usually, this will be the plaintiff herself. The plaintiff takes the stand, is sworn or affirmed, and gives her evidence in support of her claim during direct examination. If there is a defendant's claim, the plaintiff may give evidence in support of her defence to the defendant's claim at the same time as her evidence in support of the plaintiff's claim, if appropriate. The plaintiff's representative should consider requesting a direction from the judge regarding this before proceeding.

When direct examination is completed, the plaintiff may be cross-examined by the defendant's paralegal. If any new issues are raised in cross-examination, the plaintiff will be re-examined by her legal representative on those issues at the completion of cross-examination. The purpose of **re-examination** (also called reply or rebuttal evidence) is to clarify and, if necessary, neutralize or rebut any potentially damaging evidence brought out during cross-examination. Re-examination should be brief, and may deal only with issues that were raised in previous evidence. It may not be used to introduce new evidence; and if either party tries to use re-examination for this purpose, the other party should object.

The same procedure applies to any other witnesses the plaintiff calls.

When the plaintiff and any other witnesses for the plaintiff have given their evidence, the plaintiff's case is closed. The defendant and any other witnesses for the defendant then take the stand, are sworn or affirmed, give evidence for the defence and defendant's claim (if there is one), and are cross-examined.

When all of the defendant's evidence has been heard, the defendant's case is closed. The judge will then ask whether there is any reply. The plaintiff or a plain-

BOX 9.10

Objections

Objections are used to draw the court's attention to improper evidence or procedure. They should be made promptly. A paralegal who objects to a particular question or line of questioning by another licensee should raise the objection as soon as the other licensee has finished speaking, and before the witness has had a chance to answer.

Do not raise an objection unless you have reasonable grounds for doing so. Know what those grounds are, and state them when raising the objection. If you are objecting to the improper use of leading questions in direct examination by the opposing paralegal, rise and say: "Objection. My colleague is leading the witness." If you are objecting to improper use of re-examination by the opposing paralegal, rise and say: "Objection. My colleague cannot try to introduce new evidence during reply. He must restrict his questioning to evidence that is already before the court."

When you have raised an objection, the opposing party may be invited to make submissions. The judge will then make a ruling, sustaining the objection or dismissing the objection. When the judge has made that ruling, whether you agree with it or not, do not get into a debate with the judge about it. Thank the judge, and sit down.

When raising objections in Small Claims Court, keep s. 27 of the *Courts of Justice Act* in mind. Section 27 states that at a hearing, a Small Claims Court judge may admit and act on any oral testimony, document, or other thing so long as it is relevant and not unduly repetitious, regardless of whether that evidence would be admissible in any other court. In other words, in Small Claims Court, cases may be decided entirely or in part based on hearsay evidence, so long as any statutory rules with respect to evidence (as set out in the Ontario *Evidence Act*, for example) are complied with.

It is very important to keep this relaxed approach toward admissible evidence in mind when your opponent is self-represented. You have a duty to protect your client and promote your client's interests; but, if you use this duty as an excuse for objecting to every mistake a self-represented party makes, it will look like harassment. Restrict your objections to the most serious errors, and be polite and respectful when making them.

tiff's witness may take the stand and give reply evidence intended to rebut evidence by the defendant or a defendant's witness. The defendant has the right to respond to the rebuttal.

When all the evidence has been heard, the judge should request closing submissions from the parties' representatives.

COMMUNICATION WITH WITNESSES GIVING EVIDENCE (PARALEGAL RULE 4.03)

When preparing for a hearing, you may contact any witness, whether the witness is sympathetic to your client's cause or not. Different rules apply during a hearing. Your ability to speak to a witness who is giving testimony is restricted, to ensure that you do not influence what the witness says in the stand.

During a proceeding, whether you may speak to a witness depends upon

- whether the witness gives evidence that supports your (and your client's) cause, or the cause of an opposing party, and

- what stage the witness is at in giving evidence.

A witness who gives evidence that supports your cause is called a **sympathetic witness**. A witness who gives evidence that supports an opposing party's cause is called an **unsympathetic witness**.

Whether a paralegal is representing a plaintiff, a defendant, a third party, or an accused, there are certain key stages in the process which govern what the paralegal may discuss with the witness:

- During examination-in-chief (also known as direct examination), when a paralegal examines her own witness in support of her client's case.

- Any interval between commencement of examination-in-chief and completion of examination-in-chief—if, for example, the court takes a recess before examination-in-chief of the witness has been completed.

- After the paralegal has finished examination-in-chief of the witness but before cross-examination of the witness by another licensee.

- During cross-examination of a witness by an opposing licensee.

- After an opposing licensee has finished cross-examination of the witness, but before the paralegal begins any re-examination of the witness.

- During re-examination, when the paralegal re-examines her own witness on matters arising out of the cross-examination.

Subject to the direction of the tribunal, you shall observe the rules respecting communication with witnesses giving evidence set out in Paralegal Rule 4.03(1). For a summary of these rules, see table 9.5.

If you are uncertain whether you may speak to a witness under Paralegal Rule 4.03(1), you should obtain the consent of the opposing licensee or leave of the tribunal before entering into discussions with a witness that might otherwise be inappropriate under the rule (Paralegal Rule 4.03(2)).

Paralegal Rule 4.03(1) applies, with necessary modifications, to examinations out of court (Paralegal Rule 4.03(3)).

TABLE 9.5 Communication with Witnesses (Paralegal Rule 4.03(1))

Rule 4.03(1)	Stage of proceeding?	Who is in the witness stand?	Called by whom?	Communication?
1.	Examination-in-chief conducted by you	Your witness	You	During an interval, you may only discuss with the witness any matter not covered in the examination to that point.
3.	Interval between completion of examination-in-chief and commencement of cross-examination	Your witness	You	You shall not discuss with the witness the evidence given in chief or relating to any matter touched on during examination-in-chief.
4.	Cross-examination by opposing licensee	Your witness	You	You shall have no conversation with the witness about the witness's evidence or any issue in the proceeding.
5.	Interval between completion of cross-examination and commencement of re-examination	Your witness	You	You shall have no conversation with the witness about evidence to be dealt with on re-examination.
2.	Examination-in-chief conducted by another licensee	Witness unsympathetic to your cause	Another licensee	You may discuss the witness's evidence with the witness.*
6.	Cross-examination conducted by you	Witness unsympathetic to your cause	Another licensee	You may discuss the witness's evidence with the witness.*
8.	Re-examination by opposing licensee	Witness unsympathetic to your cause	Opposing licensee	You may discuss the witness's evidence with the witness.*
7.	Cross-examination conducted by you	Witness sympathetic to your cause	Another licensee	You may only discuss with the witness any matter not covered in the cross-examination to that point.*
8.	Re-examination by opposing licensee	Witness sympathetic to your cause	Opposing licensee	You shall not discuss with the witness the evidence to be given during re-examination.

* Reminder: A witness has no obligation to speak to you. If a witness tells you they do not want to talk to you, you should leave the witness alone. You are not permitted to harass a witness (Paralegal Rule 4.01(5)).

CLOSING SUBMISSIONS

When the parties' witnesses have been called, have given evidence, and have been cross-examined and re-examined, and both parties' cases are closed, the judge may ask for closing submissions from each party. The plaintiff makes closing submissions first.

In order to be persuasive, a party's closing submission should review the issues in dispute, summarize the evidence that supports the party's claim or defence, and present arguments as to why the relief the party is seeking should be granted by the court based on that evidence.

You should prepare a draft closing submission in advance. Depending on the evidence at trial, you may have to alter your draft submission, but it will still provide a useful framework for your closing arguments.

If you intend to refer to case law in your closing submission, you should disclose the cases to which you will be referring to other parties or their representatives before the trial date. At trial, you should have enough copies in your file for the judge, for other parties, and for yourself. Any passages you intend to refer to during legal argument should be highlighted on all copies, and you should have page number references at your fingertips.

COSTS

General

Costs are money amounts that the court orders one party to pay to the other party. Costs are awarded in addition to any other relief, monetary or otherwise, that may be ordered. The general rule is that costs are awarded to the successful party, to reimburse the successful party for representation fees, if any, and disbursements incurred by that party to conduct the action.

Costs were discussed in chapter 8 at pages 290-292, in the context of offers to settle. This discussion deals with costs awards at trial.

Disbursements

A successful party is entitled to recover all reasonable disbursements, including costs of effecting service, travel expenses, accommodation, photocopying, and experts' reports, from the unsuccessful party, unless the court orders otherwise (Rule 19.01(1)).

The clerk shall assess disbursements in accordance with the regulations to the *Administration of Justice Act* and Rule 19.01(3). The relevant regulations are *Kilometre Allowances* and *Small Claims Court—Fees and Allowances*. Rule 19.01(3) states that the amount of disbursements assessed for effecting service shall not exceed $20.00 for each person served unless it is the court's opinion that there are special circumstances that justify assessing a greater amount. The clerk's assessment is subject to review by the court.

In addition to disbursements assessed by the clerk, the court may award a successful party an amount not exceeding $50.00 for preparation and filing of pleadings (Rule 19.03).

Limit on Award of Costs Exclusive of Disbursements

Any authority to award costs under Rule 19 is subject to s. 29 of the *Courts of Justice Act* (Rule 19.02). Section 29 of the *Courts of Justice Act* states that, in Small Claims Court, an award of costs, other than disbursements, shall not exceed 15% of the amount claimed or the value of the property sought to be recovered, unless the court considers it necessary in the interests of justice to penalize a party or a party's representative for unreasonable behaviour in the proceeding.

Section 29 limits an award of costs, other than disbursements, to 15% of the amount claimed, not 15% of the amount the court actually awards. Fifteen percent of the current Small Claims Court maximum monetary jurisdiction of $25,000.00 is $3,750.00. $3,750.00 is the maximum award of costs, other than disbursements, that the court may order to be paid to a successful party by an unsuccessful party in a Small Claims Court action, unless the exception for unreasonable behaviour by a party or a party's representative applies, in which case the court may make a higher costs award.

Representation Fee (Rule 19.04)

If the amount claimed in an action exceeds $500, excluding interest and costs, and the successful party is represented by a lawyer, student-at-law, or agent, the court may award the party a reasonable representation fee at trial or at an assessment hearing (Rule 19.04(1)).

In the case of an agent (including a paralegal) or a student-at-law, the representation fee shall not exceed half of the maximum costs that may be awarded under s. 29 of the *Courts of Justice Act* (Rule 19.04(2)). In a claim for $25,000.00 where the successful party is represented by a paralegal, an award of costs other than disbursements—that is, a representation fee—may not exceed $1,875.00, unless the "unreasonable behaviour" exception in s. 29 of the *Courts of Justice Act* applies, in which case the court has discretion to increase the amount of the representation fee.

Compensation for Inconvenience and Expense (Rule 19.05)

If the amount claimed exceeds $500.00 and the successful party is self-represented, the court may order an unsuccessful party to pay an amount not exceeding $500.00 to the successful party as compensation for inconvenience and expense.

Penalty (Rule 19.06)

If the court is satisfied that any party (self-represented or represented, successful or unsuccessful) has unduly complicated or prolonged an action or has otherwise acted unreasonably, the court may order the party to pay an amount as compensation to another party.

Submission as to Costs at Trial

When both parties have made their closing submissions, the judge will give his decision. He will then ask the successful party for a submission as to costs, unless Rule 14.07 applies, in which case the party who raises Rule 14.07 may be asked for a submission.

If Rule 19.06 applies, any party (self-represented or represented, successful or unsuccessful) who has unduly complicated or prolonged the action or has otherwise acted unreasonably may be ordered by the court to pay compensation to another party (whether that party is self-represented or represented, successful or unsuccessful). When preparing your submission on costs, you should review Rule 19.06 if you think it may be applicable, and include details of the party's unreasonable behaviour in your submission.

You should prepare your submission as to costs ahead of time. Your submission should refer to any rules of the *Small Claims Court Rules* or sections of the *Courts of Justice Act* you are relying on, so that you are prepared for any questions the judge may ask. A successful client may not recover all of her representation fees, but she is entitled to recover 7.5% of the amount claimed exclusive of disbursements under s. 29 of the *Courts of Justice Act*, and you should draft your submission on costs with that in mind. The clerk will assess proper disbursements.

CHAPTER SUMMARY

In an action for unliquidated damages where all defendants in the proceeding have been noted in default, a plaintiff may (1) file a motion in writing for an assessment of damages, with an affidavit in support setting out reasons why the motion should be granted, including details as to the amount of damages owed; or (2) request an assessment hearing.

An assessment hearing may be held:

1. where the plaintiff requests an assessment hearing (Rule 11.03(2)(b)); or

2. where a judge orders an assessment hearing. A judge will order an assessment hearing where the affidavit evidence filed in support of a Rule 11.03(2)(a) motion in writing is so inadequate or unsatisfactory that the judge requires oral evidence from the plaintiff in order to make a decision (Rule 11.03(3)(b)).

Where an assessment hearing is requested by the plaintiff or ordered by a judge, the plaintiff will be required to fix a date for the hearing. An assessment hearing is like a trial (Rule 11.03(4)), except that the defendant is not present, and, as with a motion in writing, the plaintiff is not required to prove liability against a defendant noted in default, because the defendant by her default is deemed to admit liability (Rule 11.03(5)). The only issue before the court is how much money the defendant owes the plaintiff.

If a disputed action is not resolved at the settlement conference, the general rule is that it should be set down for trial as soon as possible after that. The settlement conference judge may include instructions or a deadline for setting the action down for trial in her order.

When you receive a notice of trial in a defended action, you should contact your client immediately and advise him of the date. The notice of trial should be filed in your pleadings subfile. The trial date should be noted in your calendar and on the file information sheet in the client file. You should do a quick review of the settlement conference endorsement record, to find out if there are any directions, recommendations, or court orders by the settlement conference judge that require further action. You should ensure that any further action required is taken.

At every stage of a Small Claims Court action, full and fair disclosure is encouraged. If a plaintiff's claim is based in whole or in part on a document, the document is required to be attached to each copy of the claim. If the document is unavailable, the claim must state the reason why the document is not attached (Rule 7.01(2)2). Similar disclosure obligations apply where a defence or defendant's claim is based in whole or in part on a document (Rules 9.02(1)2 and 10.01(4)2).

In a defended action, further disclosure is required at the settlement conference stage. At least 14 days before the date of the settlement conference, each party must serve on all other parties and file with the court (1) a copy of any document to be relied on at the trial, including an expert report, if these were not attached to the party's claim or defence, and (2) a list of proposed witnesses and of other persons who know about the matters in dispute in the action (Rule 13.03(2)).

Rule 18.02(1) continues the obligation to disclose. Rule 18.02(1) states that any document or written statement that has been served at least 30 days before the trial date on all parties served with a trial notice shall be received in evidence, unless the trial judge orders otherwise on evidentiary grounds.

The general rule with respect to evidence at trial is that a witness should be present at the trial to give his evidence and be cross-examined on that evidence. Rule 13.03(2) requires each party to serve on every other party and file with the court a list of proposed witnesses (Form 13A) and of other persons with knowledge of the matters in dispute at least 14 days before the date of the settlement conference.

Any witness who is required to attend in person to give spoken evidence at trial and/or to produce documents relating to the matters in question should be served with a summons to witness and attendance money.

At the courthouse on the trial date, the parties take their places at the counsel tables facing the judge's bench when the matter is called. The paralegals for the plaintiff and defendant introduce themselves, and give brief opening submissions if invited by the trial judge to do so.

If either party has summoned additional witnesses, before any evidence is heard, the judge should be asked to make an order excluding those witnesses from hearing evidence. An order excluding witnesses is required only when there are witnesses other than the parties giving evidence.

The plaintiff is then invited to call her first witness. Usually, this will be the plaintiff herself. The plaintiff takes the stand, is sworn or affirmed, and gives her evidence in support of her claim in direct examination. If there is a defendant's claim, the plaintiff should give evidence in support of her defence to the defendant's claim at the same time as her evidence in support of the plaintiff's claim, if it is appropriate to do so.

When direct examination is completed, the plaintiff may be cross-examined by the defendant or the defendant's representative. If any new issues are raised in cross-examination, the plaintiff will be re-examined by her legal representative on those issues at the completion of cross-examination. The same procedure applies to any other witnesses the plaintiff calls.

When the plaintiff and her witnesses, if any, have given their evidence, the plaintiff's case is closed. The defendant and the defendant's witnesses, if any, then take the stand, are sworn or affirmed, give evidence in support of the defence and the defendant's claim, if any, and are cross-examined and, where appropriate, re-examined.

When all of the defendant's evidence has been heard, the defendant's case is closed. If the parties are represented, the judge should then request closing submissions from the parties' legal representatives.

A party's closing submission should review the issues in dispute, summarize the evidence that supports the party's claim or defence, and present arguments as to why the relief the party is seeking should be granted by the court based on that evidence. The successful party should be prepared to make submissions as to costs.

KEY TERMS

counsel slip

direct examination

docket

exhibit

expert witness

findings as to credibility

findings of fact

harass a witness

leading questions

material evidence

open-ended, or direct, questions

opinion evidence

order excluding witnesses

purge the list

qualified interpreter

re-examination

summons to witness

sympathetic witness

trier of fact

unsympathetic witness

REFERENCES

Administration of Justice Act, RSO 1990, c. A.6.

Courts of Justice Act, RSO 1990, c. C.43.

Evidence Act, RSO 1990, c. E.23.

Kenkel, Joseph F., and William S. Chalmers, *Small Claims and Simplified Procedure Litigation*, 4th ed. (Markham, ON: Butterworths, 2002), at 72.

Kilometre Allowances, RRO 1990, Reg. 11.

Law Society of Upper Canada (LSUC), *Paralegal Professional Conduct Guidelines* (Toronto: LSUC, 2008, as amended); available online at http://www.lsuc.on.ca.

Law Society of Upper Canada (LSUC), *Paralegal Rules of Conduct* (Toronto: LSUC, 2007, as amended); available online at http://www.lsuc.on.ca.

Rules of the Small Claims Court, O. Reg. 258/98.

Small Claims Court—Fees and Allowances, O. Reg. 432/93.

REVIEW QUESTIONS

When answering the following questions, you should note the numbers of any rules you are relying on.

1. a. What is an assessment hearing?

    b. When will an assessment hearing be held?

    c. What must the plaintiff prove at an assessment hearing?

2. In a defended action, who may set a date for trial? What form must be filed?

3. You have just received a notice of trial in Small Claims Court. You are already booked to appear on several matters in Provincial Offences Court on that date. What should you do?

4. You are acting for the defendant in a Small Claims Court matter. The plaintiff is self-represented. You receive a notice of trial. You and your client, along with two witnesses, show up on the trial date. You are ready to go. When the matter is called, the plaintiff's son appears in the courtroom, and requests an adjournment. The son says that his father had to leave the province suddenly, to attend the funeral of a close relative. If the judge decides to grant the adjournment, what should you ask for?

5. You are acting for the plaintiff in a Small Claims Court action in Thunder Bay. After the settlement conference, and 45 days before the trial date, your client produces documents that you have never seen before. One of them is a written statement by a witness who lives in Toronto. You intend to rely on these documents at trial. What should you do?

6. What is an expert witness?

7. If a party requires a witness to attend at trial in person to give evidence, what should that party do? What is the deadline for doing so?

8. What happens if a witness who has been properly summoned fails to attend?

9. Name six things that you should do when preparing for trial.

10. Summarize the rules for communication with witnesses, including self-represented parties.

11. What is direct examination? What sort of questions do you use in direct examination?

12. What are leading questions? When may they be used in direct examination?

13. In a Small Claims Court trial, what should you focus on in cross-examination? How should you prepare your cross-examination?

14. What is an order excluding witnesses? When is it required? Why is it required?

15. What is an objection? When should you use an objection?

16. a. When are closing submissions made?

    b. What are some guidelines for making closing submissions persuasive?

    c. If you intend to refer to case law in your closing submission, what procedures should you follow?

APPENDIX 9.1   Greco v. Hardwick: Summons to Witness (Form 18A) and Affidavit of Service (Form 8A)

ONTARIO

Superior Court of Justice
Cour supérieure de justice

Seal / *Sceau*

Summons to Witness
Assignation de témoin
Form / *Formule* 18A Ont. Reg. No. / *Règl. de l'Ont.* : 258/98

Brampton
Small Claims Court / *Cour des petites créances de*
7755 Hurontario Street
Brampton, Ontario
L6W 4T6
Address / *Adresse*

905 456 4700
Phone number / *Numéro de téléphone*

7891
Claim No. / *N° de la demande*

BETWEEN / *ENTRE*

Juliette Greco

Plaintiff(s) / *Demandeur(s)/demanderesse(s)*

and / *et*

James Hardwick

Defendant(s) / *Défendeur(s)/défenderesse(s)*

TO: Glenn Woods
DESTINATAIRE :
(Name of witness / *Nom du témoin*)

YOU ARE REQUIRED TO ATTEND AND TO GIVE EVIDENCE IN COURT at the trial of this action on
*VOUS ÊTES REQUIS(E) DE VOUS PRÉSENTER DEVANT LE TRIBUNAL POUR TÉMOIGNER à l'instruction
de cette action le*

April 18   , 20 --   **at** 9:30 a.m.   , at
                                      à   (Time / *heure*)   **à/au**

7765 Hurontario Street, Brampton, Ontario L6W 4T1
(Address of court location / *Adresse du tribunal*)

and to remain until your attendance is no longer required. You may be required to return to court from time to time.
*et d'y demeurer jusqu'à ce que votre présence ne soit plus requise. Vous pourriez être requis(e) de vous
présenter à nouveau devant le tribunal à l'occasion.*

YOU ARE ALSO REQUIRED TO BRING WITH YOU AND PRODUCE AT THE TRIAL the following documents
or other things in your possession, control or power: (Identify and describe particular documents and other things required)
*VOUS ÊTES EN OUTRE REQUIS(E) D'APPORTER AVEC VOUS ET DE PRODUIRE LORS DE
L'INSTRUCTION les documents ou autres objets suivants dont vous avez la garde, la possession ou le contrôle :*
(Indiquez et décrivez les documents et autres objets particuliers qui sont requis)

Fee schedules for lawn care, landscaping and pool maintenance services

SCR 18.03-18A (June 1, 2009 / *1er juin 2009*) CSD

APPENDIX 9.1—Form 18A   Concluded

FORM / *FORMULE* 18A	PAGE 2	7891
		Claim No. / *N° de la demande*

and all other documents or other things in your possession, control or power relating to the action.
ainsi que tous les autres documents ou autres objets dont vous avez la garde, la possession ou le contrôle et qui se rapportent à l'action.

Juliette Greco
_____
(Name of party / *Nom de la partie*)

has requested the clerk to issue this summons.
a demandé au greffier de délivrer la présente assignation.

_____ , 20 _____   _____
                                 (Signature of clerk / *Signature du greffier*)

NOTE: **THIS SUMMONS MUST BE SERVED** personally, at least 10 days before the trial date, on the person to be summoned together with attendance money calculated in accordance with the Small Claims Court Schedule of Fees, which is a regulation under the *Administration of Justice Act*. To obtain a copy of the regulation, attend the nearest Small Claims Court or access the following website: www.e-laws.gov.on.ca.

REMARQUE :   *LA PRÉSENTE ASSIGNATION DOIT ÊTRE SIGNIFIÉE à personne, au moins 10 jours avant la date du procès, à la personne devant être assignée, avec l'indemnité de présence calculée conformément au barème des honoraires et frais de la Cour des petites créances qui constitue un règlement pris en application de la Loi sur l'administration de la justice. Vous pouvez obtenir un exemplaire du règlement auprès de la Cour des petites créances de votre localité ou en consultant le site Web suivant : www.lois-en-ligne.gouv.on.ca.*

CAUTION: **IF YOU FAIL TO ATTEND OR REMAIN IN ATTENDANCE AS REQUIRED BY THIS SUMMONS, A WARRANT MAY BE ISSUED FOR YOUR ARREST.**

AVERTISSEMENT :   *SI VOUS NE VOUS PRÉSENTEZ PAS OU SI VOUS NE DEMEUREZ PAS PRÉSENT(E) COMME L'EXIGE LA PRÉSENTE ASSIGNATION, UN MANDAT D'ARRÊT PEUT ÊTRE DÉLIVRÉ CONTRE VOUS.*

SCR 18.03-18A (June 1, 2009 / *1er juin 2009*) CSD

APPENDIX 9.1—Form 8A

ONTARIO

Superior Court of Justice
Cour supérieure de justice

Affidavit of Service
Affidavit de signification

Form / *Formule* 8A Ont. Reg. No. / *Règl. de l'Ont.* : 258/98

Brampton

Small Claims Court / *Cour des petites créances de*

7755 Hurontario Street
Brampton, Ontario
L6W 4T6

Address / *Adresse*

905 456 4700

Phone number / *Numéro de téléphone*

7891

Claim No. / *N° de la demande*

BETWEEN / *ENTRE*

Juliette Greco

Plaintiff(s) / *Demandeur(s)/demanderesse(s)*

and / *et*

James Hardwick

Defendant(s) / *Défendeur(s)/défenderesse(s)*

My name is Neela Subramaniam
Je m'appelle
(Full name / *Nom et prénoms*)

I live in Toronto, Ontario
J'habite à
(Municipality & province / *Municipalité et province*)

and I swear/affirm that the following is true:
et je déclare sous serment/j'affirme solennellement que les renseignements suivants sont véridiques :

1. **I served** Glenn Woods   , on **March 15**   , 20 -- ,
   J'ai signifié à (Full name of person/corporation served / *Nom et prénoms*   , *le*   (Date)
   de la personne/nom au complet de la personne morale
   qui a reçu la signification)

   at **78 Bosky Dell Crescent, Mississauga, Ontario**
   au   (Address (street and number, unit, municipality, province) / *Adresse (numéro et rue, unité, municipalité, province)*)

   which is ☒ the address of the person's home
   soit   *l'adresse du domicile de la personne*

   ☐ the address of the corporation's place of business
   l'adresse du lieu de travail de l'établissement de la personne morale

   ☐ the address of the person's or corporation's representative on record with the court
   l'adresse du/de la représentant(e) de la personne ou de la personne morale figurant au
   dossier du tribunal

   ☐ the address on the document most recently filed in court by the party
   l'adresse figurant sur le document déposé le plus récemment au tribunal par la partie

   ☐ the address of the corporation's attorney for service in Ontario
   l'adresse du fondé de pouvoir de la personne morale aux fins de signification en Ontario

   ☐ other address:
   autre adresse :   (Specify. / *Précisez.*)

   with **Summons to witness and attendance money**
   ce qui suit :   (Name(s) of document(s) served / *Titre(s) du ou des documents signifiés*)

SCR 8.06-8A (November 1, 2009 / *1er novembre 2009*) CSD

APPENDIX 9.1—Form 8A   Continued

FORM / *FORMULE* 8A   **PAGE 2**   7891

Claim No. / *N° de la demande*

2. I served the document(s) referred to in paragraph one by the following method:
J'ai signifié le ou les documents mentionnés au numéro un de la façon suivante :
(Tell how service took place by checking appropriate box(es).)
(Indiquez la façon dont la signification a été effectuée en cochant la ou les cases appropriées.)

Personal service / *Significa-tion à personne*

☒ leaving a copy with the person.
   en laissant une copie à la personne.

☐ leaving a copy with the _____ of the corporation.
   en laissant une copie au/à la   (Office or position / *Charge ou poste*)   *de la personne morale.*

☐ leaving a copy with: _____
   en laissant une copie à :   (Specify person's name and office or position. / *Indiquez le nom de la personne ainsi que sa charge ou son poste.*)

Service at place of residence / *Significa-tion au domicile*

☐ leaving a copy in a sealed envelope addressed to the person at the person's place of residence with a person who appeared to be an adult member of the same household, and sending another copy of the same document(s) to the person's place of residence on the same day or the following day by:
   en laissant une copie au domicile de la personne, dans une enveloppe scellée adressée à celle-ci, auprès d'une personne habitant sous le même toit qui semblait majeure et en envoyant une autre copie du ou des mêmes documents au domicile de la personne le même jour ou le jour suivant :

   ☐ regular lettermail.
      par courrier ordinaire.

   ☐ registered mail.
      par courrier recommandé.

   ☐ courier.
      par messagerie.

Service by registered mail / *Significa-tion par courrier recom-mandé*

☐ registered mail.
   par courrier recommandé.
   (If a copy of a plaintiff's claim or defendant's claim was served by registered mail, attach a copy of the Canada Post delivery confirmation showing the signature of the person being served to this affidavit.)
   (Si une copie de la demande du demandeur ou de la demande du défendeur a été signifiée par courrier recommandé, annexez au présent affidavit une copie de la confirmation de livraison remise par Postes Canada sur laquelle figure la signature du destinataire de la signification.)

Service by courier / *Significa-tion par messa-gerie*

☐ courier.
   par messagerie.
   (If a copy of a plaintiff's claim or defendant's claim was served by courier, attach a copy of the courier's delivery confirmation showing the signature of the person being served to this affidavit.)
   (Si une copie de la demande du demandeur ou de la demande du défendeur a été signifiée par messagerie, annexez au présent affidavit une copie de la confirmation de livraison remise par le service de messagerie sur laquelle figure la signature du destinataire de la signification.)

Service on lawyer / *Significa-tion à l'avocat*

☐ leaving a copy with a lawyer who accepted service on the person's behalf.
   en laissant une copie avec l'avocat qui a accepté la signification au nom de la personne.
   (Attach a copy of the document endorsed with the lawyer's acceptance of service.)
   (Annexez une copie du document, sur lequel l'avocat a inscrit qu'il a accepté la signification.)

Service by regular lettermail / *Significa-tion par courrier ordinaire*

☐ regular lettermail.
   par courrier ordinaire.

SCR 8.06-8A (November 1, 2009 / *1er novembre 2009*) CSD   **Continued on next page /** *Suite à la page suivante*

APPENDIX 9.1—Form 8A   Concluded

FORM / *FORMULE* 8A	PAGE 3	7891
		Claim No. / *N° de la demande*

Service by fax / *Signification par télécopie* ☐ fax sent at _____   *par télécopie envoyée à*   (Time / *heure*)   at the following fax number: _____   *au numéro de télécopieur suivant :*   (Fax number / *numéro de télécopieur*)

Service to last known address of corporation or attorney for service, and to the directors / *Signification à la dernière adresse connue de la personne morale ou de son fondé de pouvoir aux fins de signification et aux administrateurs*

☐ mail/courier to corporation or attorney for service at last known address recorded with the Ministry of Government Services, and
d'une part, par la poste/par messagerie à la personne morale ou à son fondé de pouvoir aux fins de signification, à la dernière adresse connue figurant dans les dossiers du ministère des Services gouvernementaux;

mail/courier to each director, as recorded with the Ministry of Government Services, as set out below:
d'autre part, par la poste/par messagerie à chaque administrateur mentionné dans les dossiers du ministère des Services gouvernementaux et dont le nom et l'adresse sont indiqués ci-dessous :

Name of director / *Nom de l'administrateur*	Director's address as recorded with the Ministry of Government Services (street & number, unit, municipality, province) / *Adresse de l'administrateur figurant dans les dossiers du ministère des Services gouvernementaux (numéro et rue, unité, municipalité, province)*
....	....
....	....
....	....
....	....

(Attach separate sheet for additional names if necessary. / *Joignez au besoin une feuille séparée s'il y a d'autres noms à ajouter.*)

Substituted service / *Signification indirecte* ☐ substituted service as ordered by the court on _____ , 20 ____ ,
par signification indirecte ordonnée par le tribunal le   (Date)

as follows: (Give details.)
comme suit :   (*Précisez.*)

Sworn/Affirmed before me at **Brampton**
Déclaré sous serment/Affirmé solennellement devant moi à   (Municipality / *municipalité*)

in **Ontario**
en/à/au   (Province, state, or country / *province, État ou pays*)

on **March 20** , 20 -- _____
le   Commissioner for taking affidavits
Commissaire aux affidavits
(Type or print name below if signature is illegible.)
(*Dactylographiez le nom ou écrivez-le en caractères d'imprimerie ci-dessous si la signature est illisible.*)

_____
Signature
(This form is to be signed in front of a lawyer, justice of the peace, notary public or commissioner for taking affidavits.)
(*La présente formule doit être signée en présence d'un avocat, d'un juge de paix, d'un notaire ou d'un commissaire aux affidavits.*)

SCR 8.06-8A (November 1, 2009 / *1er novembre 2009*) CSD

APPENDIX 9.2   Warrant (Form 18B) and Identification Form (Form 20K)

ONTARIO

Superior Court of Justice
Cour supérieure de justice

Warrant for Arrest of Defaulting Witness
Mandat d'arrêt d'un témoin défaillant
Form / *Formule* 18B Ont. Reg. No. / *Règl. de l'Ont.* : 258/98

Seal / *Sceau*

Thunder Bay
Small Claims Court / *Cour des petites créances de*
277 Camelot Street
Thunder Bay, Ontario
P7A 4B3
Address / *Adresse*

807 343 2710
Phone number / *Numéro de téléphone*

5432
Claim No. / *N° de la demande*

BETWEEN / ENTRE

Emma Flood

Plaintiff(s) / *Demandeur(s)/demanderesse(s)*

and / et

Christine Michaeli

Defendant(s) / *Défendeur(s)/défenderesse(s)*

TO ALL POLICE OFFICERS IN ONTARIO AND TO THE OFFICERS OF ALL CORRECTIONAL INSTITUTIONS IN ONTARIO:
À TOUS LES AGENTS DE POLICE DE L'ONTARIO ET AUX AGENTS DE TOUS LES ÉTABLISSEMENTS CORRECTIONNELS DE L'ONTARIO :

The witness   **Anton Zupetti, also known as Andy Zupetti**
Le témoin   (Name / *Nom*)

of   **343 King's Cross Road, Thunder Bay, Ontario A2B 3C4**
de   (Address / *Adresse*)

was served with a Summons to Witness (Form 18A) to give evidence at the trial of this action, and the prescribed attendance money was paid or tendered.
a reçu signification d'une assignation de témoin (formule 18A) pour témoigner à l'instruction de la présente action, et l'indemnité de présence prescrite lui a été versée ou offerte.

The witness failed to attend or to remain in attendance at the trial, and I am satisfied that the evidence of this witness is material to this proceeding.
Le témoin ne s'est pas présenté ou n'est pas demeuré présent au procès, et je suis convaincu(e) que son témoignage est essentiel à l'instance.

YOU ARE ORDERED TO ARREST AND BRING this person before the court to give evidence in this action, and if the court is not then sitting or if the person cannot be brought before the court immediately, to deliver the person to a provincial correctional institution or other secure facility, to be admitted and detained there until the person can be brought before the court.
JE VOUS ORDONNE D'ARRÊTER CETTE PERSONNE ET DE L'AMENER devant le tribunal afin qu'elle témoigne dans l'action et, si le tribunal ne siège pas ou si la personne ne peut être amenée devant le tribunal immédiatement, de la livrer à un établissement correctionnel provincial ou à un autre établissement de garde en milieu fermé, afin qu'elle y soit admise et détenue jusqu'à ce qu'elle puisse être amenée devant le tribunal.

I FURTHER ORDER YOU TO HOLD this person in custody and to detain him/her only so long as necessary to bring this person before a court as ordered above.
JE VOUS ORDONNE EN OUTRE DE MAINTENIR cette personne sous garde et de la détenir tant et aussi longtemps qu'il sera nécessaire pour l'amener devant un tribunal, comme il est ordonné ci-dessus.

_____ , 20 _____   _____

(Signature of judge / *Signature du juge*)

APPENDIX 9.2—Form 20K

ONTARIO

Superior Court of Justice
Cour supérieure de justice

Identification Form
Formule de renseignements signalétiques

Form / *Formule* 20K Ont. Reg. No. / *Règl. de l'Ont.* : 258/98

Thunder Bay
Small Claims Court / *Cour des petites créances de*
277 Camelot Street
Thunder Bay, Ontario
P7A 4B3
Address / *Adresse*

5432
Claim No. / *N° de la demande*

807 343 2710
Phone number / *Numéro de téléphone*

BETWEEN / *ENTRE*

Emma Flood
Plaintiff(s)/Creditor(s) / *Demandeur(s)/demanderesse(s)/Créancier(s)/créancière(s)*

and / *et*

Christine Michaeli
Defendant(s)/Debtor(s) / *Défendeur(s)/défenderesse(s)/Débiteur(s)/débitrice(s)*

TO HELP PROCESS A CIVIL WARRANT FOR COMMITTAL, the following information, or **as much information as is reasonably available should be provided**. This is necessary for the police to identify the person to be arrested. Without this information it will be difficult to enforce the warrant.
POUR FACILITER LA DÉLIVRANCE D'UN MANDAT DE DÉPÔT AU CIVIL, les renseignements suivants ou autant de renseignements qui sont raisonnablement disponibles devraient être fournis. Ces renseignements sont nécessaires pour que la police puisse identifier la personne à arrêter. Sans ces renseignements, il sera difficile d'exécuter le mandat.

1. Name   **Zupetti**   **Anton**   **Leopold**
   Nom   (Last name of individual / *Nom de famille du particulier*)   (First name / *Premier prénom*)   (Second name / *Deuxième prénom*)

2. Also known as names (if any)   **Andy Zupetti**
   Nom(s) sous lequel/lesquels la personne est également connue (le cas échéant)

3. Last known address and telephone number
   Dernière adresse connue et dernier numéro de téléphone connu
   343 King's Cross Road, Thunder Bay, Ontario A2B 3C4

4. (a) Date of birth *(d, m, y)*   **22/04/1980**
        Date de naissance (j, m, a)

5. Physical description
   Description physique

   (a) Gender **M**   (b) Height **5' 8"**   (c) Weight **195**   (d) Build **stocky**
        Sexe   *Taille*   *Poids*   *Corpulence*

   (e) Colour of eyes **green**   (f) Hair colour **brown**   (g) Complexion **fair**
        Couleur des yeux   *Couleur des cheveux*   *Teint*

   (h) Clean-shaven **yes**   (i) Wears glasses **no**
        Rasé de près   *Porte des lunettes*

   (j) Clothing habits and tastes **casual (blue jeans)**
        Habitudes et goûts vestimentaires

APPENDIX 9.2—Form 20K   Concluded

FORM / *FORMULE* 20K   PAGE 2   **5432**

Claim No. / *N° de la demande*

(k) Distinguishing marks, scars, tattoos, etc.   **head shaved, goatee, facial piercings, tattoos on neck, arms and upper torso**
Marques distinctives, cicatrices, tatouages, etc.

(l) Other **Slight limp (right leg)**
Autre   (Specify / *Précisez.*)

6. Usual occupation **unemployed**
Profession habituelle

7. Last known place of employment **unemployed**
Dernier lieu de travail connu

8. Vehicle description
Description du véhicule

(a) Make, model and year **Honda Civic 2003**   (b) Colour **Black**
Marque, modèle et année   *Couleur*

(c) Licence plate number **BFAD 439**   Province or state **Ontario**
Numéro de la plaque d'immatriculation   *Province ou État*

(d) Driver's licence number   Province or state
Numéro du permis de conduire   *Province ou État*

(e) Distinguishing features on the vehicle (dents, car stereo, etc.)
Caractéristiques distinctives du véhicule (bosses, autoradio, etc.)

Customized, tinted glass, some rust

9. Other information
Autres renseignements

10. Photograph of the person provided in the box below, if available.
Une photographie de la personne figure dans la case ci-dessous, si elle est disponible.

The information supplied above is true to the best of my knowledge and belief.
Au mieux de ma connaissance et de ce que je tiens pour véridique, les renseignements ci-dessus sont exacts.

_____
(Signature of party / *Signature de la partie*)

Emma Flood
(Name of party / *Nom de la partie*)

February 10   , 20 **--**

SCR 20.11-20K (June 1. 2009 / *1ᵉʳ juin 2009*) CSD

Motions for New Trial and Appeals

LEARNING OBJECTIVES

After reading this chapter, you will understand:

- Grounds for a Rule 17.04 motion for a new trial or amendment of judgment

- Procedure on a Rule 17.04 motion

- Drafting documents on a Rule 17.04 motion

- Appeal to the Divisional Court

INTRODUCTION

A motion for a new trial or for an amendment of the judgment pursuant to Rule 17.04 of the *Rules of the Small Claims Court* may be made in the following circumstances. If the trial judge made a purely arithmetical error in calculating the amount of damages awarded, you may make a motion for an amendment of the judgment. If you discover relevant evidence that was not available at the time of the original trial and could not reasonably have been expected to be available at that time, you may make a motion for a new trial.

If a party believes that the trial judge's decision was incorrect or faulty for reasons other than those set out in Rule 17.04, the judgment must be appealed. Appeals of Small Claims Court trial decisions are governed by s. 31 of the *Courts of Justice Act*, and by Rule 61 of the *Rules of Civil Procedure*.

An appeal of a final order in a Small Claims Court action lies to the Divisional Court. The Divisional Court is the appellate branch of the Superior Court of Justice. It hears appeals in matters that involve amounts of not more than $50,000.00, exclusive of costs.

An appeal to the Divisional Court shall be heard in the region where the hearing of the action that led to the decision appealed from took place, unless the parties agree otherwise or the Chief Justice of the Superior Court of Justice orders otherwise because it is necessary to do so in the interests of justice.

An appeal of a Small Claims Court decision may be heard by one judge of the Superior Court of Justice.

At present, paralegals are not allowed to appear on appeals in Divisional Court. Parties who choose to appeal a Small Claims Court decision must represent themselves or hire a lawyer.

MOTION FOR A NEW TRIAL OR AMENDMENT OF THE JUDGMENT (RULE 17.04)

Where there was a purely arithmetical error in the determination by the court of the amount of damages awarded, a party may make a motion for an amendment of the judgment (Rule 17.04(5)1). Where there is relevant evidence that was not available to the party at the time of the original trial and could not reasonably have been expected to be available at that time, a party may make a motion for a new trial (Rule 17.04(5)2).

A motion for a new trial or an order amending the judgment must be made within 30 days after the date the final order is made (Rule 17.04(1)). The motion is made to a Small Claims Court judge or deputy judge.

The moving party shall make a request to a court reporter to make a transcript of the reasons for judgment and any other portion of the proceeding that is relevant. The transcript can be ordered by contacting the court office. The current charge for a transcript is $3.20 per page for the first copy, and $0.55 per page for each additional copy. For a schedule of fees, see *Court Reporters and Court Monitors*, O. Reg. 587/91 to the *Administration of Justice Act*. The court reporter will notify you when the transcript is ready. The transcript will not be released to you until you have paid the court reporter's fee for the transcription.

The moving party shall serve the notice of motion and supporting affidavit, along with proof that a request has been made for a transcript of the reasons for judgment and any other portion of the proceeding that is relevant, on all parties at least seven days before the hearing date, and file it with the court at least three days before the hearing date (Rules 15.01(3), 15.01(6), and 17.04(2)).

If available, a copy of the transcript or partial transcript shall be served on all parties who were served with the original notice of trial and filed, with proof of service, at least three days before the hearing date of the motion (Rule 17.04(3)).

If the motion is for an order amending the judgment based on an arithmetical error, the supporting affidavit must show the error in calculating the judgment, as well as the correct calculation of the judgment.

If the motion is for an order for a new trial on grounds of new evidence, the supporting affidavit should address all of the elements of the test for admitting new evidence (see Rule 17.04(5)2).

On the hearing of the motion, if the moving party demonstrates that

1. there was a purely arithmetical error in the determination of the amount of damages awarded, or

2. there is relevant evidence that was not available to the party at the time of the original trial and could not reasonably have been expected to be available at that time,

the court may

(i) grant a new trial, or

(ii) pronounce the judgment that ought to have been given at trial and order judgment accordingly.

Otherwise, the court shall dismiss the motion (Rule 17.04(4)).

Arithmetical Error (Rule 17.04(5)1)

A purely arithmetical error is a miscalculation of the amount owing to a successful party by the judge or the party—for example, a mistake in addition or subtraction. Any party may make a Rule 17.04 motion to have the error corrected.

Rule 17.04(5)1 should be used only where there is an arithmetical error in calculating the amount of the award. It should not be used to request that the judge on the motion reconsider the trial judge's decision as to the amount owing because the moving party thinks that amount is wrong for some other reason.

BOX 10.1

Greco v. Hardwick: What Is a Purely Arithmetical Error?

Background: Juliette Greco sues her neighbour, James Hardwick, for $5,000.00 when he defaults in payment of a promissory note for a loan in that amount. The note provided for pre-judgment interest of 10% per year on the amount owing in the event of default. The due date stated in the note is August 2, 20—.

In his defence and counterclaim, James Hardwick admits that he signed the note and received the money. He states that he realized shortly after taking the money that he would not be able to pay it back on the due date. He then entered into a spoken agreement with Ms. Greco that he would perform services instead of making money payments. He performed those services, and their fair market value exceeds the amount owing under the promissory note. He has produced written quotations that the fair market value of the services provided totals $5,990.00.

In her defence to the defendant's claim, Ms. Greco disputes the value of Mr. Hardwick's services. She alleges that she could have obtained similar services for $1,500.00 from Glenn Woods of Glenn Woods Garden Services, the person who usually provides those services to her. She could have obtained other services allegedly provided by Mr. Hardwick for free.

The matter goes to trial on April 18, 20—. In his reasons for judgment, the trial judge states that he accepts Ms. Greco's evidence with respect to the value of Mr. Hardwick's services, and orders that Mr. Hardwick shall pay Ms. Greco $5,000.00 minus $1,500.00, for a total owing of $2,500.00, plus pre- and post-judgment interest at a rate of 10% per year in accordance with the promissory note, and costs fixed at $660.00.

The mistake is discovered by Ms. Greco's paralegal when he requests a copy of the judge's endorsement from the clerk.

Discussion: This is a purely arithmetical error. The judge clearly intended to award Ms. Greco $3,500.00, but made a mistake in his subtraction. To correct the error, a motion must be brought under Rule 17.04(1), requesting that the court amend the final order to correct the amount owing to $3,500.00, pursuant to Rules 17.04(4)(a)(ii) and 17.04(5). The motion must be made within 30 days after April 18, 20—.

You will find the notice of motion and supporting affidavit at appendix 10.1 to this chapter.

Additional issue: The defendant, Mr. Hardwick, thinks the judge's decision is completely wrong, because he believes that the judge should have accepted his evidence that the services he performed were worth more than the amount owing under the note. May he make a Rule 17.04 motion to have the trial judge's error corrected?

Discussion: No. Mr. Hardwick's objections are legal and/or factual—they are not based on a simple arithmetical error. If he wishes to challenge the trial judge's order, he must do so by way of an appeal.

New Evidence (Rule 17.04(5)2)

For a Rule 17.04 motion to succeed on this ground, the court must be satisfied that the evidence (1) is new—that is, it is evidence that the moving party did not know about at the time of the trial; (2) is relevant to the issues in the action; (3) is credible; (4) was not available to the party at the time of the original trial; and (5) could not reasonably have been expected to be available at that time.

Some examples of new evidence are:

1. a witness whose evidence is material to issues in the case, but who was not discovered until after the trial (*Applecrest Investments Ltd. v. Guardian Insurance Co.*);

2. a document that is material to issues in the action, but that is not discovered until after the trial, in spite of the moving party's diligent efforts to discover all relevant documents (*R. Clancy Heavy Equipment Sales Ltd. v. Joe Gourley Construction Ltd.*).

APPEAL OF A SMALL CLAIMS COURT JUDGMENT

The appeal of a final order in a Small Claims Court action to the Divisional Court is governed by s. 31 of the *Courts of Justice Act* and by Rule 61 of the *Rules of Civil Procedure*. The Divisional Court is the appellate branch of the Superior Court of Justice. It hears appeals in matters that involve amounts of not more than $50,000.00, exclusive of costs.

Section 31 applies to a final order in an action

1. for the payment of money in excess of $500.00, excluding costs; or

2. for the recovery of possession of personal property exceeding $500.00 in value.

In actions to which s. 31 applies, an appeal to the Divisional Court is as of right. An **appeal as of right** is an automatic right to appeal. In other words, the party making the appeal (the appellant) can do so without first seeking permission (leave) to do so from the appeal court.

At present, paralegals are not allowed to provide any form of legal services to clients with respect to Divisional Court appeals. Providing legal services includes giving legal advice on the merits of an appeal and drafting documents on the appeal. Parties who wish to appeal a Small Claims Court order must represent themselves or hire a lawyer.

If you are a paralegal whose client wishes to appeal a final order in a Small Claims Court action, or if you are contacted by a person seeking legal advice about whether to appeal a final order in a Small Claims Court action, you should advise him to seek the services of a lawyer. You may wish to direct him to the Lawyer Referral Service (1-800-268-8326) or to the Lawyer and Paralegal Directory at the Law Society website. There is no charge for the Lawyer Referral Service. You should consider sending the person a non-engagement letter confirming that you have declined the retainer on grounds of unauthorized practice. The non-engagement letter should advise him of any limitation periods, and suggest that he seek the services of a lawyer. You will find a sample non-engagement letter at appendix 10.2.

CHAPTER SUMMARY

A motion for a new trial or for an amendment of the judgment (Rule 17.04 of the *Rules of the Small Claims Court*) may be made in the following circumstances. If the trial judge made a purely arithmetical error in calculating the amount of damages awarded, you may make a motion for an amendment of the judgment. If you discover relevant evidence that was not available at the time of the original trial and could not reasonably have been expected to be available at that time, you may make a motion for an amendment of the judgment or for a new trial.

The motion must be made within 30 days after the final order is made. The moving party shall serve the notice of motion and supporting affidavit, along with proof that a request has been made for a transcript of the reasons for judgment and any other portion of the proceeding that is relevant, on all parties at least seven days before the hearing date, and file it with the court at least three days before the hearing date (Rules 15.01(3), 15.01(6), and 17.04(2)). If available, copies of the transcript or partial transcript shall be served on all the parties who were served with the original notice of motion and filed, with proof of service, at least three business days before the hearing date for the motion (Rule 17.04(3)).

If the motion is for an order amending the judgment based on an arithmetical error, the supporting affidavit must show the error in calculating the judgment, as well as the correct calculation of the judgment.

If the motion is for an order for a new trial on grounds of new evidence, the evidence in the supporting affidavit should demonstrate that there is relevant evidence that was not available to the party at the time of the original trial and could not reasonably have been expected to be available at that time.

A final order in a Small Claims Court action for the payment of money in excess of $500.00, excluding costs, or for recovery of possession of personal property exceeding $500.00 in value may be appealed to the Divisional Court. The Divisional Court is the appellate branch of the Superior Court of Justice. It hears appeals in matters that involve amounts of not more than $50,000.00, exclusive of costs. The appeal is as of right—that is, the party making the appeal has an automatic right to do so, without seeking leave from the appeal court.

At present, paralegals are not allowed to provide any form of legal services to clients with respect to Divisional Court appeals. Providing legal services includes giving legal advice on the merits of an appeal and drafting documents on the appeal. Persons who wish to appeal a Small Claims Court order must represent themselves or hire a lawyer.

KEY TERMS

appeal as of right

REFERENCES

Administration of Justice Act, RSO 1990, c. A.6.

Applecrest Investments Ltd. v. Guardian Insurance Co., [1992] OJ no. 1060 (Gen. Div.).

Court Reporters and Court Monitors, O. Reg. 587/91.

Courts of Justice Act, RSO 1990, c. C.43.

R. Clancy Heavy Equipment Sales Ltd. v. Joe Gourley Construction Ltd., [2001] AJ no. 638 (Alta. CA).

Rules of Civil Procedure, RRO 1990, Reg. 194.

Rules of the Small Claims Court, O. Reg. 258/98.

REVIEW QUESTIONS

1. What are the grounds for making a motion under Rule 17.04?

2. What is the deadline for making a Rule 17.04 motion?

3. What documents must be served and filed in support of a Rule 17.04 motion?

4. You are a licensed paralegal. What should you do if a client or other person approaches you for advice about appealing a final order in a Small Claims Court action?

APPENDIX 10.1   Greco v. Hardwick—Notice of Motion and Supporting Affidavit (Form 15A)

ONTARIO

Superior Court of Justice
Cour supérieure de justice

Notice of Motion and Supporting Affidavit
Avis de motion et affidavit à l'appui
Form / *Formule* 15A Ont. Reg. No. / *Règl. de l'Ont.* : 258/98

Brampton

Small Claims Court / *Cour des petites créances de*

7755 Hurontario Street
Brampton, Ontario
L6W 4T6

Address / *Adresse*

905 456 4700

Phone number / *Numéro de téléphone*

7891

Claim No. / *N° de la demande*

Plaintiff No. 1 / *Demandeur n° 1*   ☐ Additional plaintiff(s) listed on attached Form 1A.
Le ou les demandeurs additionnels sont mentionnés sur la formule 1A ci-jointe.

Last name, or name of company / *Nom de famille ou nom de la compagnie*		
Greco		

First name / *Premier prénom*	Second name / *Deuxième prénom*	Also known as / *Également connu(e) sous le nom de*
Juliette		

Address (street number, apt., unit) / *Adresse (numéro et rue, app., unité)*		
c/o Prior Mustafa LLP		

City/Town / *Cité/ville*	Province	Phone no. / *N° de téléphone*

Postal code / *Code postal*		Fax no. / *N° de télécopieur*

Representative / *Représentant(e)*	LSUC # / *N° du BHC*
Prior Mustafa LLP Attention: Paralegal name	**######**

Address (street number, apt., unit) / *Adresse (numéro et rue, app., unité)*		
22 County Court Boulevard		

City/Town / *Cité/ville*	Province	Phone no. / *N° de téléphone*
Brampton	**Ontario**	**905 111 2222**

Postal code / *Code postal*	Fax no. / *N° de télécopieur*
A1A 2B3	**905 111 2233**

Defendant No. 1 / *Défendeur n° 1*   ☐ Additional defendant(s) listed on attached Form 1A.
Le ou les défendeurs additionnels sont mentionnés sur la formule 1A ci-jointe.

Last name, or name of company / *Nom de famille ou nom de la compagnie*		
Hardwick		

First name / *Premier prénom*	Second name / *Deuxième prénom*	Also known as / *Également connu(e) sous le nom de*
James		

Address (street number, apt., unit) / *Adresse (numéro et rue, app., unité)*		
c/o Paxton Limones PC		

City/Town / *Cité/ville*	Province	Phone no. / *N° de téléphone*

Postal code / *Code postal*		Fax no. / *N° de télécopieur*

Representative / *Représentant(e)*	LSUC # / *N° du BHC*
Paxton Limones PC Attention: Paralegal name	**######**

Address (street number, apt., unit) / *Adresse (numéro et rue, app., unité)*		
82 Main Street, Suite 11		

City/Town / *Cité/ville*	Province	Phone no. / *N° de téléphone*
Brampton	**Ontario**	**905 888 9999**

Postal code / *Code postal*	Fax no. / *N° de télécopieur*
L1N 2P3	**905 888 0000**

SCR 15.01-15A (June 1, 2009 / *1er juin 2009*) CSD

APPENDIX 10.1   Continued

FORM / *FORMULE* 15A   PAGE 2   7891
_____
                                                                    Claim No. / *N° de la demande*

THIS COURT WILL HEAR A MOTION on May 10   , 20 --   , **at** 9:30 a.m.   ,
LE TRIBUNAL PRÉCITÉ ENTENDRA UNE MOTION le   , *à*   (Time / *heure*)

or as soon as possible after that time, at   Courtroom 5, 7765 Hurontario Street, Brampton, Ontario
ou dès que possible par la suite à/au   (Address of court location and courtroom number / *Adresse du tribunal et numéro de la*
                                                                salle d'audience)

Complete Part A or Part B below, then complete the affidavit in support of motion on page 3. / *Remplissez la partie A ou la partie B ci-dessous. Remplissez ensuite l'affidavit à l'appui de la motion à la page 3.*

This motion will be made in person
A.   by   Juliette Greco   ,
*   La motion sera présentée en personne par :*   (Name of party / *Nom de la partie*)

for the following order : / *en vue d'obtenir l'ordonnance suivante :*

☐   the court's permission to extend time to (Specify)
    l'autorisation du tribunal de proroger le délai pour (*Précisez*)
    _____.

☐   set aside default judgment and noting in default.
    l'annulation du jugement par défaut et la constatation du défaut.

☐   set aside noting in default.
    l'annulation de la constatation du défaut.

☐   permission to file a Defence.
    l'autorisation de déposer une défense.

☐   permission to file a Defendant's Claim.
    l'autorisation de déposer une demande du défendeur.

☐   terminate garnishment and/or withdraw writ(s).
    la mainlevée de la saisie-arrêt ou le retrait d'un ou de plusieurs brefs, ou les deux.

☒   Other:
    Autre :
    Order amending judgment dated April 18, 20-- due to arithmetical error (Rule 17.04).

☒   **ADDITIONAL PAGES ARE ATTACHED BECAUSE MORE ROOM WAS NEEDED.**
    DES FEUILLES SUPPLÉMENTAIRES SONT ANNEXÉES EN RAISON DU MANQUE D'ESPACE.

☐   **DOCUMENTS ARE ATTACHED.**
    PIÈCES JOINTES.

| NOTE: | **IF YOU FAIL TO ATTEND AN IN-PERSON MOTION,** an order may be made against you, with costs, in your absence. If you want to attend the motion by telephone or video conference, complete and file a Request for Telephone or Video Conference (Form 1B). If the court permits it, the clerk will make the necessary arrangements and notify the parties [R. 1.07(5)]. |
| *REMARQUE :* | *SI VOUS NE VOUS PRÉSENTEZ PAS EN PERSONNE À L'AUDITION DE LA MOTION,* une ordonnance peut être rendue contre vous en votre absence, avec dépens. Si vous voulez assister à l'audition de la motion par conférence téléphonique ou vidéoconférence, remplissez et déposez la Demande de conférence téléphonique ou vidéoconférence (formule 1B). Si le tribunal l'autorise, le greffier prendra les dispositions nécessaires et en avisera les parties [par. 1.07 (5)]. |

APPENDIX 10.1   Continued

FORM / *FORMULE* 15A   PAGE 3   7891

Claim No. / *N° de la demande*

B.   This motion in writing for an assessment of damages is made by
La présente motion par écrit en vue d'une évaluation des dommages-intérêts est présentée par

_____ ,

(Name of plaintiff / *Nom du demandeur/de la demanderesse*)

who asks the court for an order assessing damages against
qui demande au tribunal de rendre une ordonnance d'évaluation des dommages-intérêts contre

_____

(Name of defendant(s) / *Nom du/de la/des défendeur(s)/défenderesse(s)*)

who have/has been noted in default.
qui a/ont été constaté(e)(s) en défaut.

AFFIDAVIT IN SUPPORT OF MOTION / *AFFIDAVIT À L'APPUI DE LA MOTION*

My name is   Juliette Greco
Je m'appelle   (Full name / *Nom et prénoms*)

I live in   Brampton, Ontario
J'habite à   (Municipality & province / *Municipalité et province*)

I swear/affirm that the following is true:
Je déclare sous serment/j'affirme solennellement que les renseignements suivants sont véridiques :

Set out the facts in numbered paragraphs. If you learned a fact from someone else, you must give that person's name and state that you believe that fact to be true.
Indiquez les faits sous forme de dispositions numérotées. Si vous avez pris connaissance d'un fait par l'entremise d'une autre personne, vous devez indiquer le nom de cette personne et déclarer que vous croyez que ce fait est véridique.

See Schedule A attached

SCR 15.01-15A (June 1, 2009 / *1er juin 2009*) CSD   **Continued on next page /** *Suite à la page suivante*

APPENDIX 10.1   Continued

FORM / *FORMULE* **15A**   **PAGE 4**   <u>7891</u>
                                                                            Claim No. / *N° de la demande*

AFFIDAVIT IN SUPPORT OF MOTION, continued / *AFFIDAVIT À L'APPUI DE LA MOTION, suite*

See Schedule A attached

If more space is required, attach and initial extra pages. / Si vous avez besoin de plus d'espace, annexez une ou des feuilles supplémentaires et paraphez-les.

Sworn/Affirmed before me at **Brampton**
Déclaré sous serment/Affirmé   (Municipality / *municipalité*)
solennellement devant moi à

in **Ontario**
en/à/au   (Province, state or country / *province, État ou pays*)

on **April 28**   , 20 **--**   _____
le   Commissioner for taking affidavits
                                        Commissaire aux affidavits
                                        (Type or print name below if signature is illegible.)
                                        (Dactylographiez le nom ou écrivez-le en caractères d'imprimerie ci-dessous si la signature est illisible.)

_____
Signature
(This form is to be signed in front of a lawyer, justice of the peace, notary public or commissioner for taking affidavits.)
(La présente formule doit être signée en présence d'un avocat, d'un juge de paix, d'un notaire ou d'un commissaire aux affidavits.)

WARNING: **IT IS AN OFFENCE UNDER THE** *CRIMINAL CODE* **TO KNOWINGLY SWEAR OR AFFIRM A FALSE AFFIDAVIT.**
AVERTISSEMENT :   *FAIRE SCIEMMENT UN FAUX AFFIDAVIT CONSTITUE UNE INFRACTION AU CODE CRIMINEL.*

SCR 15.01-15A (June 1, 2009 / *1er juin 2009*) CSD

APPENDIX 10.1   Concluded

Schedule A

1. I am the plaintiff in this proceeding, and as such have personal knowledge of the following.

2. At the trial of this matter on April 18, 20—, it was not disputed that I loaned $5,000.00 to the defendant pursuant to a promissory note dated April 1, 20—. The due date for the loan was August 2, 20—. In the event of any default, interest at a rate of 10% per year became due and payable on any balance outstanding. The issues before the court were:

    (a)   the terms of an alleged spoken agreement between the defendant and me that the defendant should provide services in lieu of payment of the note;

    (b)   the services that were provided pursuant to that alleged agreement; and

    (c)   the value, if any, to be assigned to those services.

3. The defendant was present at trial, and gave evidence in support of his defence and defendant's claim.

4. Having heard all of the evidence at trial and closing submissions for both parties, Smith J. made the following order (at page 3, lines 5 to 14 of the transcript of the reasons for judgment):

    "I accept the plaintiff's evidence with respect to the value of Mr. Hardwick's services. Both Ms. Greco and Mr. Woods were credible witnesses. I do not find Mr. Hardwick's evidence with respect to the terms of the alleged agreement wholly credible; nor do I find the written estimates of the value of the services he provided credible. I value those services at $1,500.00. Order to go that the defendant, James Hardwick, shall pay to the plaintiff, Juliette Greco, $5,000.00 minus $1,500.00, for a total owing of $2,500.00, plus pre- and post-judgment interest at a rate of 10% per year in accordance with the promissory note dated April 1, 20—, and costs fixed at $660.00."

5. Upon reviewing his notes, my paralegal, Joseph Mustafa, discovered the trial judge's error in calculating the damages owing.

6. Under the terms of the court order dated April 18, 20—, the amount of damages owing to me is $5,000.00 − $1,500.00 = $3,500.00.

7. I make this affidavit in support of a motion for an order amending the April 18, 20— judgment to state that the defendant, James Hardwick, shall pay me the amount of $3,500.00 plus pre- and post-judgment interest at a rate of 10% per year in accordance with the promissory note dated April 1, 20—, and costs fixed at $660.00, and for no other or improper purpose.

APPENDIX 10.2 Non-Engagement Letter (Unauthorized Practice—Paralegal Firm Declines Retainer)

[Date]

[File number]

[Client name and address]

Dear **[Client name]**:

Re: [Matter name]

You are the defendant in Claim No. 9086 in London Small Claims Court. You contacted us on **[date]** to discuss appealing the final order dated June 3, 20—. As we discussed during our **[telephone conversation/meeting/initial consultation]**, an appeal of a final order in a Small Claims Court action lies to the Divisional Court. We are a paralegal firm. At present, paralegals are not permitted to appear before the Divisional Court.

We therefore cannot represent you and we must decline to do so in this matter.

The time for appealing a Small Claims Court decision is 30 days after a final order is made. Since time limitations may be critical to your case, we recommend that you immediately contact a lawyer for assistance regarding your matter. If you do not have a lawyer in mind to represent you, the Law Society maintains a directory of lawyers who may be available to assist you at its website (http://www.lsuc.on.ca), or you may wish to call the Lawyer Referral Service at 1-800-268-8326. There is no charge for the Lawyer Referral Service.

We confirm that we do not have any documents belonging to you.

Although we were not able to assist you in this matter, we hope that you will consider **[paralegal firm name]** in the event that you require legal services in the future.

Thank you again for your interest in this firm.

Yours truly,

[PARALEGAL FIRM NAME]

[Signature]

[Signatory name]
Paralegal

[Adapted from the Law Society of British Columbia website (http://www.lawsociety.bc.ca) and the Law Society of Upper Canada website (http://www.lsuc.on.ca).]

Enforcing Small Claims Court Judgments

LEARNING OBJECTIVES

After reading this chapter, you will understand:

- What enforcement of a judgment is, and what it is for
- Conducting searches
- General powers of the court in an enforcement
- Periodic payments
- Enforcement of orders made outside of Ontario
- Certificate of judgment
- Consolidation orders
- Post-judgment interest
- Examination of the debtor or other person
- Contempt hearings
- Delivery of personal property
- Seizure and sale of personal property
- Seizure and sale of land
- Garnishment

INTRODUCTION

A Small Claims Court order for payment of money to an unsecured creditor is just a piece of paper unless the person who is ordered to pay the money is willing to pay, or has income or assets against which the order can be enforced.

In Small Claims Court, enforcement of orders is governed by Rule 20 of the *Rules of the Small Claims Court.*

A party who is entitled to enforce a Small Claims Court order for the payment or recovery of money against another person is called a **creditor**. A party against whom a Small Claims Court order for the payment or recovery of money may be enforced is called a **debtor** (Rule 20.01).

Enforcement of a court order by seizing a debtor's income, by seizing and selling her assets, or by any other lawful method, is also called **execution of an order**.

A creditor who does not have current information about the income and assets of a debtor may schedule an examination of the debtor or any other person with knowledge of the financial circumstances of the debtor (Rule 20.10). The debtor and/or other persons with knowledge of the debtor's circumstances may be examined with respect to the reason for non-payment; the debtor's income and property; the debts owed to and by the debtor; any transfers of property the debtor has made before or after a court order; the debtor's present, past, and future means to satisfy the order; whether the debtor intends to obey the order or has any reason for not doing so; and any other matter pertinent to the enforcement of the order.

A person who is served with a notice of examination shall (1) inform themselves about the matters set out in Rule 20.10(4) and be prepared to answer questions; and (2) where the debtor is an individual, complete a financial information form and serve it on the creditor requesting the examination. The financial information form shall not be filed with the court.

The examination takes place in the presence of the court. It is conducted under oath, and is recorded. When the examination is concluded, the court may make an order as to payment. While the order is in force, no step to execute the judgment may be taken, other than issuing and filing a writ of seizure and sale of land with the sheriff.

A person who has been properly summoned to a notice of examination but (1) fails to attend or (2) fails to answer questions or produce documents may be ordered to attend at a contempt hearing (Rule 20.11). Possible penalties include (1) a finding that the person is in contempt of court; (2) an order requiring the person to attend at an examination under Rule 20.10; (3) incarceration for a period not exceeding 40 days; (4) attending an additional contempt hearing; or (5) complying with any other order that the judge considers just or necessary.

A creditor who intends to enforce a judgment in another jurisdiction may do so by filing a certificate of judgment in that jurisdiction (Rule 20.04).

An order for the delivery of personal property may be enforced by a writ of delivery of personal property issued by the clerk to a bailiff on the request of the person in whose favour the order was made, supported by an affidavit for enforcement request of the person or the person's representative stating that the property has not been delivered (Rule 20.05).

If there is a default under an order for the payment or recovery of money, the creditor may request that the clerk issue a writ of seizure and sale of personal property, supported by an affidavit for enforcement request stating the amount still owing. The clerk shall issue to a bailiff a writ of seizure and sale of personal property and the bailiff shall enforce the writ for the amount owing, post-judgment interest, and the bailiff's fees and expenses (Rule 20.06(1)).

A writ of seizure and sale of personal property remains in force for six years after the date of its issue and for a further six years after each renewal (Rule 20.06(2)). It may be renewed before it expires by filing a request to renew a writ of seizure and sale with the bailiff. The creditor may request enforcement by filing a direction to enforce with the bailiff.

If an order for the payment or recovery of money is unsatisfied, the creditor may request that the clerk issue a writ of seizure and sale of land, supported by an affidavit for enforcement request stating the amount still owing. The clerk shall issue a writ of seizure and sale of land directed to the sheriff specified by the creditor (Rule 20.07(1)).

A writ of seizure and sale of land remains in force for six years from the date of its issue and for a further six years after each renewal. It may be renewed before it expires by filing a request to renew a writ of seizure and sale with the sheriff.

A creditor may enforce an order for the payment or recovery of money by garnishment of debts, including employment income, payable to the debtor by other persons. If a debt is payable to the debtor and to one or more co-owners (for example, if the debtor has a bank account held jointly with a spouse or partner), one half of the indebtedness, or a greater or lesser amount specified in a court order, may be garnished (Rule 20.08).

A creditor who wishes to enforce an order by garnishment shall file with the clerk of a court in the territorial division in which the debtor resides or carries on business an affidavit for enforcement request and, if the order was made in another territorial division, a certificate of judgment, and the clerk shall issue a notice of garnishment directed to the garnishee named in the affidavit.

The garnishee is liable to pay to the clerk any debt of the garnishee to the debtor, within 10 days after service of the notice on the garnishee or 10 days after the debt becomes payable, whichever is later.

A debtor against whom there are two or more unsatisfied orders for the payment of money may make a motion to the court for a consolidation order (Rule 20.09). At the hearing of the motion, the court may make a consolidation order setting out a list of all unpaid orders; the amounts to be paid into court by the debtor under the consolidation order; and the times of payment. All payments made by the debtor are shared equally among creditors named in the consolidation order.

While the consolidation order is in force, no step to enforce the judgment may be taken or continued against the debtor by a creditor named in the order, except issuing a writ of seizure and sale of land and filing it with the sheriff.

A consolidation order terminates immediately if (1) an order for payment of money is obtained against the debtor after the date of the consolidation order for a debt incurred after the consolidation order; or (2) the debtor is in default for 21 days.

GENERAL

In Small Claims Court, enforcement of orders is governed by Rule 20. Orders by some other courts, tribunals, and boards for payment of $25,000.00 or less may also be enforced under Rule 20. Section 68 of the *Provincial Offences Act* states that unpaid fines levied in provincial offences proceedings may be collected by civil enforcement in Small Claims Court. Section 19 of the *Statutory Powers Procedure Act* states that a certified copy of a tribunal's decision or order in a proceeding may be filed in the Superior Court of Justice (of which Small Claims Court is a branch) by the tribunal or by a party and on filing shall be deemed to be an order of that court and is enforceable as such.

As of this writing, the fee for receiving a process from the Ontario Court of Justice or an order or judgment as provided by statute is $25.00. Refer to the Small Claims Court fee schedule published as a regulation to the *Administration of Justice Act*. The fee schedule is also published at the website of the Ministry of the Attorney General.

Types of Creditors

There are three main types of creditors:

1. secured creditors;
2. preferred creditors; and
3. ordinary creditors (also known as judgment or execution creditors).

SECURED CREDITORS

Secured creditors are creditors whose loans are secured against real or personal property. If the debtor defaults in payment, the secured creditor may **realize on her security** under the terms of the security agreement.

The real or personal property against which the loan is pledged is known as **collateral**.

Security against land may take the form of a mortgage, a lien, a construction lien, and so on. The secured creditor's interest in the land is registered against title to the land, and shows up on a standard title search.

If the form of security is a mortgage, the person who holds the security is called the **mortgagee**. The person who receives the loan or other benefit and pledges the security is called the **mortgagor**.

Security for a loan against personal property (also known as a **chattel mortgage**) is registered under the *Personal Property Security Act* (PPSA). The holder of a security interest registered under the PPSA takes priority over other creditors with respect to the personal property that is the security.

Priority of Secured Interests

The general rule with respect to security registered against land or personal property is that priority is ranked by order of the time of registration of the security, unless there is an agreement stating otherwise. For example, a mortgagee whose interest is registered chronologically first against the title to land is called a first mortgagee. The security interest of a first mortgagee will rank ahead of the interest of any second, third, or subsequent mortgagees whose mortgages are registered later.

PREFERRED CREDITORS

Preferred creditors are unsecured creditors who rank ahead of ordinary unsecured creditors in a debt collection or a bankruptcy because of priority and special rights conferred by a statute. For example, special rules apply to support creditors in a debt collection. A **support creditor** is a person to whom child or spousal support is owed by the debtor.

ORDINARY CREDITORS

Ordinary creditors are unsecured creditors with no preferred status. This is the type of creditor who is most likely to be encountered in a Small Claims Court collection. How much an ordinary creditor can collect on a judgment debt will depend on what assets or income, if any, the debtor possesses against which the judgment may be enforced.

A debtor who has no income or assets against which a judgment may be enforced is said to be **judgment-proof**.

Sometimes a debtor is judgment-proof simply because he has no money or other assets. In other words, he is poor.

In other cases, a debtor may deliberately arrange her affairs so that creditors cannot get at her assets. She may transfer her title in any real property she owns to a spouse, or to a trust set up for her children. She may lease her car in the name of her business. She may pay herself income through a management company. For many business people, these types of arrangements are just good planning—for tax purposes, or as a way of protecting yourself and your assets from the ordinary risks of business.

This type of debtor is not poor, but she too may be judgment-proof, because she has arranged her affairs with a view to managing business risk by limiting her personal and business liability to creditors.

Finding Out About the Debtor: Searches

Some creditors collect essential information about the debtor before they advance money, approve a residential tenancy agreement, or sell a computer to the debtor. They already have the correct name, address, birth date, social insurance number, driver's licence number, and so on, verified by documentation, when they send the file to you for collection. If they have obtained the debtor's informed consent or if they are permitted to do so by legislation, they may also have a credit bureau check, showing what other debts the debtor owes, and the debtor's credit ranking.

If the creditor did not collect this information before loaning money or providing services, or if it is the kind of claim where that information would not necessarily have been obtained ahead of time (for example, damage to property or personal injury), you should confirm, at a minimum, the debtor's correct name and address before commencing the action.

Having obtained judgment against the debtor in this scenario of scarce information, you should consider conducting additional searches to find out whether it is cost-effective for your client to enforce judgment against the debtor, and by what means.

CREDIT BUREAU SEARCH

If you are a member of a credit bureau such as Equifax, you may search the defendant's credit status online, subject to compliance with the *Personal Information Protection and Electronic Documents Act*, discussed in chapter 3 at pages 71-72. A standard credit bureau report will give you a record of the defendant's credit history, including loans, defaults, etc., and will rank the defendant with respect to her creditworthiness. A poor credit rating is a reliable indicator that it may be difficult to enforce a judgment against the defendant.

EXECUTION SEARCH

Outstanding judgments from other proceedings against the defendant may be registered as writs of seizure and sale with the Sheriff's Office in the district or county where the defendant lives or carries on business. An execution search will provide information about outstanding writs and the creditors who filed them. Execution searches can be conducted online through websites such as ServiceOntario and Cyberbahn. They may be conducted on a county-specific basis, or province-wide.

Execution searches are done by name. An execution search on a debtor with a common name, such as Ahmed, Brown, Singh, or Wong, may turn up a plethora of executions that were filed against judgment debtors with the same name as your debtor. Before relying on an execution search, you must be careful to determine which executions were filed against your particular debtor.

If your execution search turns up outstanding executions against a person who you are satisfied is your debtor, this will tell you that there are other creditors out there. The proceeds of an enforcement against the defendant's income or assets, if any, may have to be shared with these creditors. Your client should be advised of this.

PERSONAL PROPERTY SECURITY ACT SEARCH

Property may be **real property**—that is, immovable (land, houses, etc.)—or **personal property**—that is, movable (vehicles, home entertainment centres, computers, books, stocks and bonds, business inventory, etc.). (A third category, intellectual property, is a person's intangible right of ownership in the products of her own creativity. Intellectual property is not addressed in this chapter.) An outstanding loan against personal property such as a motor vehicle is called a **chattel mortgage.** The **chattel mortgagee** (the holder of the loan) may secure its interest by registering the chattel mortgage under the *Personal Property Security Act* (PPSA). Registration of the chattel mortgagee's interest under the PPSA means that, if the debtor defaults on the loan, the chattel mortgagee has the right to seize and sell the property to satisfy the balance owing. The chattel mortgagee's secured interest ranks ahead of that of other creditors.

If you are aware that the defendant owns personal property, such as a motor vehicle, a PPSA search will tell you if there are any **encumbrances** (that is, outstanding loans) secured against that vehicle. If there is a secured creditor with a registered interest in the vehicle, your client's chances of recovering some part or all of his judgment by seizing and selling the vehicle are slim to nil.

BOX 11.1

Online Searches

All of the searches discussed below are available online, through websites such as ServiceOntario and Cyberbahn.

BANKRUPTCY SEARCH

A person who has assigned or been petitioned into bankruptcy turns over all her rights to deal with her property to the trustee in bankruptcy, who deals with the bankrupt's estate. Secured creditors may realize their interest in the property against which their interest has been secured (by way of a mortgage against land or a PPSA registration, for example) outside of the bankruptcy. If there is money left after they have realized on their security, they must turn the surplus over to the trustee. If there is a deficiency—that is, there is still money owing after they have seized and sold the secured property—they may file a claim as ordinary creditors in the bankruptcy.

A bankruptcy search may be done by mail, by telephone, or online using websites such as Cyberbahn. If the search reveals that your defendant has assigned or been petitioned by other creditors into bankruptcy, you should consider advising your client not to proceed with litigation. Even if the litigation is permitted to go forward, judgment creditors rank with ordinary creditors in a bankruptcy.

BANK ACT SEARCH

This search will be used only if the debtor is a large business that has borrowed large sums over a long period. It will not be used for consumer debtors or small businesses.

Section 427 of the federal *Bank Act* provides that a business that borrows money from a chartered bank may pledge its assets to the bank as a s. 427 security. The debtor business remains in possession of the collateral and uses it to run the business; however, title to the collateral is transferred to the chartered bank until the loan is repaid.

OTHER CONSIDERATIONS: SHELL CORPORATIONS

Often, small-business owners will incorporate their businesses to protect their personal assets from seizure in the event of a business failure. The corporation is a separate legal person who may enter into contracts, be named as a party in a court action, and so on. It is called a shell corporation because it has no or negligible assets.

Any client who is doing business with a small, incorporated business should be advised to obtain personal guarantees of the business's contractual obligations from its principal or principals and/or their spouses, children, or any other person to whom they may have transferred their assets. A client without guarantees should be advised that a judgment against a shell corporation may be unenforceable.

General Power of the Court

The Small Claims Court may order the times and the proportions in which money payable under an order of the court shall be paid (*Courts of Justice Act*, s. 28). In an enforcement, the court may (Rule 20.02(1)):

(a) stay the enforcement of an order of the court, for such time and on such terms as are just; and

(b) vary the times and proportions in which money payable under an order of the court shall be paid, if the court is satisfied that the debtor's circumstances have changed.

A **stay of enforcement** stops a creditor or creditors from enforcing their judgments against the debtor, for so long as the debtor complies with the terms of the court order.

If the court makes an order for **periodic payment** of money, no step to enforce the judgment may be taken or continued against the debtor by a creditor named in the order, except issuing a writ of seizure and sale of land and filing it with the sheriff (Rule 20.02(2)). An order for periodic payment is an order that the money shall be paid in fixed amounts at regular intervals until such time as all amounts owing are paid in full.

The court may vary, or change, the times of payment and the amounts to be paid, if the court is satisfied that the debtor's circumstances have changed. If the debtor's financial circumstances have deteriorated since the order for periodic payment was made, the amount of a periodic payment may be reduced. If the debtor's financial circumstances have improved since the order for periodic payment was made, the amount of the periodic payment may be increased.

If the debtor fails to make a payment under an order for periodic payment, the creditor may serve the debtor with a notice of default of payment (Form 20L). A notice of default of payment may be served by mail, by courier, by fax, personally (Rule 8.02), or by an alternative to personal service (Rule 8.03), unless the court orders some other type of service (Rule 8.01(14)).

An order for periodic payment terminates on the day that is 15 days after the creditor serves the debtor with the notice of default of payment, unless a consent (Form 13B) in which the creditor waives the default is filed within the 15-day period (Rule 20.02(4)). If no consent is filed within the 15-day period, the creditor may then file with the court an affidavit of default of payment (Form 20M), together with a copy of the notice of default of payment and proof of service (Rule 20.02(3)).

To **waive the default** means to give up the right to terminate the order for periodic payment based on the debtor's failure to pay. A creditor should consider waiving the default if the creditor is satisfied that the debtor's failure to pay was inadvertent and will continue making payments if the order for periodic payment is left in place.

You will find examples of a notice of default of payment and affidavit of default of payment, along with an adjusted calculation of interest, at appendix 6.5 in chapter 6.

Consolidation Order (Rule 20.09)

A debtor against whom there are two or more unsatisfied orders for payment of money may make a motion to the court for a consolidation order (Rule 20.09(1)).

A debtor who wishes to make a motion for a consolidation order shall contact the court clerk in the territorial division where the debtor lives to schedule a hearing date for the motion. The debtor must complete and file a notice of motion and supporting affidavit (Form 15A) with the court, and serve copies of the motion and supporting affidavit on all creditors named in the supporting affidavit at least seven days before the hearing date (Rule 20.09(3)).

The supporting affidavit must include the following information (Rule 20.09(2)):

(a) the names and addresses of the creditors who have obtained an order for payment of money against the debtor;

(b) the amount owed to each creditor;

(c) the amount of the debtor's income from all sources, identifying the sources; and

(d) the debtor's current financial obligations and any other relevant facts.

You will find an example of a notice of motion and supporting affidavit (Form 15A) for a consolidation order at appendix 11.1 to this chapter.

All creditors named in the supporting affidavit must be served with the notice of motion and affidavit at least seven days before the date the motion is scheduled to be argued (Rule 20.09(3)).

At the hearing of the motion, the court may make a consolidation order setting out (Rule 20.09(4)):

1. a list of all unsatisfied judgments, including the date, court, and amount, and the amount unpaid;

2. the amounts to be paid into court by the debtor under the consolidation order; and

3. the times of the payments.

The total of the amounts to be paid into court by the debtor on account of the consolidation order may not exceed 20% of the debtor's wages as set out in s. 7 of the *Wages Act* (discussed below at table 11.1, pages 384-385). The *Wages Act* defines "wages" as the debtor's wages after all lawful deductions—that is, the debtor's **net wages** after income tax, employment insurance premiums, Canada Pension Plan contributions, pension adjustments, and so on, have been deducted.

At the hearing of the motion, a creditor may make submissions as to the amount and times of payment (Rule 20.09(6)). All payments into a consolidation account belong to the creditors named in the consolidation order. The creditors share equally in the distribution of the money (Rule 20.09(12)). The clerk shall distribute the money paid into the consolidation account at least once every six months (Rule 20.09(13)).

While the consolidation order is in force, no step to enforce the judgment may be taken by a creditor named in the order, except issuing a writ of seizure and sale of land and filing it with the sheriff (Rule 20.09(9)).

If an order for payment of money is made against the debtor after the date of the consolidation order, for a debt incurred before the date of the consolidation order, the creditor may file a certified copy of the new order with the clerk. The creditor shall be added to the list of creditors in the consolidation order, and the creditor is entitled to share in distribution under the order from the time his name is added (Rule 20.09(7)).

A consolidation order terminates immediately if

- an order for payment of money is obtained against the debtor for a debt incurred after the date of the consolidation order (Rule 20.09(8)), or

- the debtor is in default under it for 21 days (Rule 20.09(10)).

If a consolidation order terminates, the clerk shall notify the creditors named in the order, and no further consolidation order shall be made in respect of the debtor for one year after the date of the termination (Rule 20.09(11)). The notice that the consolidation order is terminated shall be served by mail or fax (Rule 20.09(11.2)).

BOX 11.2

Consolidation Order: Events of Termination

SCENARIO ONE

Debtor obtains a consolidation order for payments of money to Creditors One, Two, and Three on December 3, 20—. On December 20, 20—, Creditor Four obtains an order for payment of money against Debtor, for a debt incurred on August 1, 20—.

Question: Does the consolidation order dated December 3, 20— terminate because of the December 20, 20— order for payment of money in favour of Creditor Four?

Answer: No, because the debt to Creditor Four was incurred by Debtor before the date of the consolidation order (Rule 20.09(7)).

Question: Is Creditor Four entitled to share in the proceeds of the December 3 consolidation order?

Answer: Yes. Creditor Four may file a certified copy of the new order with the clerk, and the clerk will add Creditor Four to the consolidation order, entitling Creditor Four to share equally in any distributions from that time forward (Rule 20.09(7)).

SCENARIO TWO

Debtor obtains a consolidation order for payments of money to Creditors One, Two, and Three on February 5, 20—. On September 13, 20—, Creditor Four obtains an order for payment of money against Debtor, for a debt incurred on May 13, 20—.

Question: Does the consolidation order dated February 5, 20— terminate because of the September 13, 20— order for payment of money in favour of Creditor Four?

Answer: Yes, because the debt to Creditor Four was incurred by Debtor after the date of the consolidation order (Rule 20.09(8)).

Question: What are the consequences of termination of the order?

Answer: The clerk shall serve a notice of termination of the consolidation order on all creditors named in the order by mail or fax. No further consolidation order may be made in respect of the debtor for one year after the date of termination (Rule 20.09(11)). On termination of the order, all creditors may enforce their orders in any way they see fit.

When a consolidation order with respect to a debtor terminates, a creditor may enforce the debt in any way she sees fit.

If payment is made in full satisfaction of the consolidation order, the debtor may, with the consent of all parties, file a request for clerk's order on consent (Form 11.2A) indicating that payment has been made in full satisfaction of the order. If the debtor cannot obtain the consent of all parties, she may make a motion for an order confirming that payment has been made in full satisfaction of the order (Rule 20.12).

Reasonable Force

Some types of enforcement require enforcement staff to enter a private dwelling to seize personal property for delivery or sale pursuant to a writ. Section 20(2) of the *Execution Act* states that a sheriff acting under a writ of seizure and sale or a writ of delivery in respect of property on premises that is used as a dwelling shall not use force to enter the dwelling or execute the writ except under the authority of an order of the court by which the writ was issued. The court may make the order where in the opinion of the court there are reasonable and probable grounds to believe that there is property on the premises that is liable to be taken in execution under the writ.

Enforcement of Orders Made in Another Canadian Province or Territory

An order for payment of $25,000.00 or less or return of property with a value of $25,000.00 or less made by a court in another Canadian province or territory (except Quebec) may be filed in the Ontario Small Claims Court under the *Reciprocal Enforcement of Judgments Act* and enforced in Ontario as if it were an order of the Small Claims Court. The application to register the judgment may be made at any time within six years after the date of the judgment.

If the judgment debtor was not personally served with the originating process in the original action and did not appear or defend the action, reasonable notice of the application shall be given to the judgment debtor. An **originating process** is the document that commences the action. An **originating court**, or **original court**, is the court where the judgment is made. For purposes of an application under the *Reciprocal Enforcement of Judgments Act*, a **registering court** is the court in which the judgment is registered.

You must obtain permission to file the order from a judge of the Small Claims Court where you wish to file the order. You may request permission by filing a notice of motion and supporting affidavit, along with a certified copy of the order, at the Small Claims Court office where the order is to be filed.

No judgment shall be registered if the registering court is satisfied that any of the following apply:

(a) the court where the order originated acted without jurisdiction;

(b) the judgment debtor was a person who was neither carrying on business nor ordinarily resident within the jurisdiction of the original court, and did not voluntarily appear or otherwise submit to the jurisdiction of the court;

(c) the judgment debtor, being the defendant in the proceeding, was not duly served with the originating process and did not appear, despite the fact that the judgment debtor was ordinarily resident or was carrying on business within the jurisdiction of the court or agreed to submit to the jurisdiction of the court;

(d) the judgment was obtained by fraud;

(e) an appeal is pending, or the judgment debtor is entitled to appeal and intends to appeal against the judgment;

(f) the judgment was in respect of a cause of action which for reasons of public policy or for some other similar reason would not have been entertained by the registering court; or

(g) the judgment debtor would have a good defence if an action were brought on the original judgment.

Your supporting affidavit should contain evidence that is sufficient to satisfy the registering court that none of the above conditions apply.

You do not have to attend at the motion, but you may attend if you wish. The court will notify you by mail if permission has been granted to file the order in Ontario for enforcement. There is a fee for the motion and for receiving the judgment for enforcement.

A judgment registered under the Act is of the same force and effect as if it had been made by the registering court.

Enforcement of a Small Claims Court Judgment in Another Territorial Division

A creditor who has obtained an order for payment of money in one territorial division, and who wishes to enforce it in another territorial division, may do so by issuing a certificate of judgment (Form 20A) in the originating court, directed to the clerk at the court location specified by the creditor. As of this writing, the fee for issuing a certificate of judgment is $19.00.

The certificate of judgment must be supported by an affidavit for enforcement request stating the amount still owing pursuant to the order.

When you file your certificate of judgment with the court in another territorial division, your order becomes enforceable as if it were an order of the court in that territorial division.

You will find examples of a certificate of judgment and affidavit for enforcement request at appendix 11.2 to this chapter.

METHODS OF ENFORCING AN ORDER

General (Rule 20.03)

In addition to any other lawful method of enforcing an order for payment of money, a creditor may enforce the order by:

1. a writ of seizure and sale of personal property (Rule 20.06);

2. a writ of seizure and sale of land (Rule 20.07); and

3. a garnishment (Rule 20.08).

Assets Exempt from Seizure

Certain assets of a debtor cannot be seized by the sheriff or bailiff under a writ, nor may they be garnished. Assets that can be seized or garnished are called **exigible assets**. Assets that cannot be seized or garnished are called **non-exigible assets**. See table 11.1 on the following pages for an overview of assets that are exempt from seizure.

Calculating Post-judgment Interest

Post-judgment interest starts to run on the total judgment amount from the date of judgment. The *total judgment amount* is the money award plus pre-judgment interest plus costs (*Courts of Justice Act*, s. 129(1)).

If there is a contractual interest rate, you will calculate post-judgment interest using that rate.

If there is no agreement setting out the rate of interest that applies in the event of a default, then pre- and post-judgment interest rates must be determined in accordance with ss. 127 to 130 of the *Courts of Justice Act*, using the rates published pursuant to O. Reg. 339/07. Current tables of post-judgment and pre-judgment interest rates can be found at the Ministry of the Attorney General's website.

Calculating Post-judgment Interest Under the Courts of Justice Act

When calculating interest under the *Courts of Justice Act*, you must read the applicable sections carefully. Section 129(1) states that money owing under an order, including costs to be assessed or costs fixed by the court, bears interest at the post-judgment interest rate, calculated from the date of the order. In other words, s. 129(1) gives you the *time period* for calculating post-judgment interest.

However, if you want to know the *rate of interest*, you must go to the definition of post-judgment interest in s. 127(1). The s. 127(1) definition states that the interest rate for post-judgment interest under the *Courts of Justice Act* is the bank rate at the end of the first day of the last month of the quarter preceding the quarter in which the date of the order falls.

TABLE 11.1 Assets Exempt from Seizure

Authority	Exempt from Seizure
Federal—Pensions, Benefits	
Canada Pension Plan, RSC 1985, c. C-8	Pension benefits
Canadian Forces Superannuation Act, RSC 1985, c. C-17	Pensions
Old Age Security Act, RSC 1985, c. O-9	Benefits
Pension Fund Societies Act, RSC 1985, c. P-8	Interest of a member in the fund of a society is exempt and cannot be assigned to a creditor or others
RCMP Superannuation Act, RSC 1985, c. R-11	Benefits
Employment Insurance Act, SC 1996, c. 23	Benefits
War Veterans Allowances Act, RSC 1985, c. W-3	Allowances
Federal—Other Assets	
Indian Act, RSC 1985, c. I-5	Real and personal property of status natives cannot be seized by a non-native creditor

Exceptions: Most federal pensions may be garnished in an enforcement of a family support order (*Garnishment, Attachment and Pension Diversion Act*, RSC 1995, c. G-2). Employment insurance benefits are considered income under the *Family Responsibility and Support Arrears Enforcement Act, 1996* (SO 1996, c. 31) and are also subject to garnishment by support creditors.

Authority	Exempt from Seizure
Provincial—Wages	
Wages Act, RSO 1990, c. W-1	80% of a person's wages. "Wages" does not include an amount that an employer is required by law to deduct from wages. The exemption amount may be increased or decreased on motion by a debtor or a creditor. **Exception:** Support creditors may garnish up to 50% of a person's wages.
Provincial—Insurance Benefits	
Workplace Safety and Insurance Act, 1997, SO 1997, c. 16	Benefits are not assignable. **Exception:** Support creditors may garnish up to 50% of a person's benefits.
Insurance Act, RSO 1990, c. I-8	Where a beneficiary is designated, insurance money does not form part of insured's estate and is not subject to claims of creditors of the insured. If beneficiary is a family member of the insured, the rights and interests of the insured in the insurance money and in the contract are exempt from execution or seizure.

TABLE 11.1 Concluded

Authority	Exempt from Seizure
Provincial—Pensions, Benefits	
Compensation for Victims of Crime Act, RSO 1990, c. C-24	Victim's compensation
Courts of Justice Act, RSO 1990, c. C-43, s. 143.1	Welfare benefits under *Family Benefits Act* or *Ontario Works Act, 1997*
Pension Benefits Act, RSO 1990, c. P-8	Pension benefits **Exception:** A party to a domestic contract or subject to a court order may claim up to 50% of a former spouse's benefits accumulated during the spousal relationship.
Provincial—Other Assets	
Execution Act, RSO 1990, c. E-24	Clothing up to a certain amount ($5,650.00); Household furniture, utensils, equipment, food, and fuel up to a certain amount ($11,300.00); Tools and instruments ordinarily used by the debtor in the debtor's business, profession, or calling up to a certain amount ($11,300.00); If a person earns a living through farming or agriculture, the livestock, fowl, bees, books, tools, implements, and seed ordinarily used by the debtor in the debtor's business, up to a certain amount ($28,300.00); and One motor vehicle worth less than the prescribed amount ($5,650.00). **Note:** Amounts prescribed by regulation as of the date of this writing.

A quarter is a three-month period. There are four quarters in any year:

- First quarter: January, February, March

- Second quarter: April, May, June

- Third quarter: July, August, September

- Fourth quarter: October, November, December.

If the order for payment of money is made in September, during the third quarter of the year, then the applicable post-judgment interest rate under the *Courts of Justice Act* is the interest rate for the preceding quarter—that is, the second quarter of that year. If the order for payment of money is made in February, during the first quarter of the year, then the applicable post-judgment interest rate under the *Courts of Justice Act* is the interest rate for the fourth, or last, quarter of the preceding year.

If you have difficulty keeping all these dates and formulas in mind when calculating post-judgment interest, read the relevant sections of the *Courts of Justice Act*. Statutes are there to tell you what to do.

BOX 11.3

Calculating Post-judgment Interest Using the Courts of Justice Act

At trial on September 8, 2010 the plaintiff is awarded $7,000.00 plus pre-judgment interest of $28.86 and costs fixed at $283.00, for a total judgment amount of $7,311.86.

CALCULATING POST-JUDGMENT INTEREST

Because there is no written loan agreement, the plaintiff must use the pre- and post-judgment interest rates set out in the *Courts of Justice Act*.

Pursuant to s. 127(1) of the *Courts of Justice Act*, the post-judgment interest rate is the adjusted bank rate at the end of the first day of the last month of the quarter preceding the quarter in which the date of the order falls. In this case, the order falls in September—that is, the third quarter of 2010. So the post-judgment interest rate will be the published rate for the second quarter of 2010—that is, 2.0%.

Pursuant to s. 129(1), post-judgment interest is calculated from the date of the order—that is, September 8, 2010. Post-judgment interest continues to be calculated so long as there is any balance owing on the judgment amount.

Calculation of simple interest on both pre- and post-judgment interest is on the amount owing from time to time as payments are received. After every payment, you should recalculate the per diem interest, to determine whether the per diem is being reduced as payments are applied to reduce the balance owed. See the detailed calculations of interest in appendix 6.5 at page 248 and appendix 11.8 at pages 449-450.

Step One: Calculate the per diem interest.

Per diem means per day. **Per diem interest** is the amount of interest that accrues on a daily basis. To calculate per diem interest, you must first convert the interest rate from a percentage out of 100 to a decimal.

You calculate per diem interest using the following steps.

▶ Convert the interest rate to a decimal. To do this, you divide the interest rate by 100.

▶ Multiply the amount owing by the interest rate expressed as a decimal.

▶ Divide the result by the number of days in a year—that is, 365.

In this case, the post-judgment interest rate under the *Courts of Justice Act* is 2.0%. Following the above steps:

▶ Convert 2.0% to a decimal: 2.0 ÷ 100 = 0.02

▶ Multiply the total judgment amount by the interest rate expressed as a decimal: 0.02 × ($7,000 + $28.86 + $283.00 = $7,311.86) = $146.24

▶ Divide the result by the number of days in a year: $146.24 ÷ 365 = $0.40 per day in interest.

Step Two: Calculate the number of days that have elapsed since post-judgment interest began to run.

You issue a notice of garnishment on September 15. You must calculate post-judgment interest to the date of the enforcement for the affidavit for enforcement request. The start date for post-judgment interest is the date the order was made—that is, September 8. The end date for purposes of this particular calculation is September 15 (although post-judgment interest will continue to accrue until all amounts owing are paid in full). Use the table of days at page 160 to calculate the number of days that elapsed between the start date and the end date for purposes of filling out the forms for this particular enforcement.

Find the number (from 1 to 365) for the start date (that is, the date the order was made—in this case, September 8), and subtract that number from the number for the date of the notice of garnishment (in this case, September 15).

September 15 is the 258th day of the year. September 8 is the 251st day of the year.

▶ 258 − 251 = 7 days

Step Three: Calculate the amount of post-judgment interest that has accrued from September 8, 2010 to September 15, 2010.

The post-judgment interest that accrues from the date the order was made to the date the garnishment forms were prepared = 7 days × $0.40 per day = $2.80.

Finding Out About the Debtor: Examination of Debtor or Other Person (Rule 20.10)

ARRANGING AN EXAMINATION OF DEBTOR

An examination of the debtor is not really an enforcement. Rather, it is an investigative tool to help the creditor find out about the debtor's financial circumstances for purposes of enforcement.

Where there is an order for payment or recovery of money and the debtor has (1) failed to pay anything, or (2) made some payments and then stopped paying, leaving a balance owing, the creditor may request an examination of the debtor or other person with relevant information about the debtor's financial circumstances.

In addition to individual debtors, the following persons may be examined (Rule 20.10(5)):

1. an officer or director of a corporate debtor;

2. any partner of a debtor that is a partnership; or

3. the sole proprietor of a debtor that is a sole proprietorship.

The creditor arranges an examination by requesting that the clerk of the court where the debtor resides or carries on business issue a notice of examination (Form 20H) directed to the debtor or another person.

The notice of examination must be accompanied by an affidavit for enforcement request (Form 20P) setting out (Rule 20.10(2)):

1. the date of the order and the amount awarded;

2. the territorial division where the order was made;

3. the rate of post-judgment interest payable;

4. the total amount of any payments received since the order was made; and

5. the amount owing, including post-judgment interest.

If the order was made in another territorial jurisdiction, the creditor seeking the examination shall file a certificate of judgment (Form 20A) at the court location where the examination is scheduled to be held. Certificates of judgment were discussed above.

The notice of examination shall be served on the debtor or person to be examined by mail, by courier, personally as provided in Rule 8.02, or by an alternative to personal service as provided in Rule 8.03 (Rule 20.10(10)).

If the person to be examined is the debtor and the debtor is an individual, the creditor will serve a blank financial information form (Form 20I) on the debtor along with the notice of examination (Rule 20.10(11)). The financial information form is for the information of the creditor only. It shall not be filed with the court.

The notice of examination and the financial information form, if applicable, shall be served at least 30 days before the date fixed for the examination. The notice of examination shall be filed, with proof of service, at least three days before the date fixed for the examination (Rule 20.10(12)).

You will find examples of a notice of examination, blank financial information form, and affidavit for enforcement request at appendix 11.3 to this chapter.

PROCEDURE AT THE EXAMINATION OF DEBTOR

The examination may be conducted in person by the creditor and the debtor, or by video conference if facilities for video conferencing are available at the court (Rules 1.07(1.1) and 20.10(5.1)). The examination shall be (Rule 20.10(6)):

(a) held in the absence of the public, unless the court orders otherwise;

(b) conducted under oath; and

(c) recorded.

The debtor, any other persons to be examined, and any witnesses whose evidence the court considers necessary may be examined in relation to (Rule 20.10(4)):

1. the reason for non-payment;

2. the debtor's income and property;

3. the debts owed to and by the debtor;

4. the sale or transfer of any property by the debtor before or after the order was made;

5. the debtor's present, past, and future resources available to satisfy the order;

6. whether the debtor intends to pay the order or has any reason for not doing so; and

7. any other matter pertinent to enforcing the order.

A person who is served with a notice of examination shall inform himself about the matters set out above and be prepared to answer questions about them. In the case of a debtor who is an individual, the debtor shall complete the financial information form and serve it on the creditor requesting the examination, but shall not file it with the court (Rule 20.10(4.1)). The debtor should be prepared to produce any documents or records, such as pay stubs, bank statements or passbooks, credit card statements, and so on, that are relevant to her financial circumstances.

For standard scripts of the questions that should be asked on an examination of a debtor, see appendixes 11.4 (individual debtor) and 11.5 (corporate debtor). When examining an individual debtor, go over the information on the financial information form in detail. Obtain documents such as pay stubs, income tax returns, deeds, mortgages, residential and commercial leases, and so on, to confirm the numbers on the form.

The creditor or the creditor's representative should take detailed notes of what is said at the examination. A debtor should also consider taking notes of the examination.

The examination will be conducted in the presence of a judge. After the examination or if the debtor's consent is filed, the court may make an order as to payment (Rule 20.10(7)). While the court order as to payment is in force, the only enforcement step a creditor named in the order may take is to issue a writ of seizure and sale of land and file it with the sheriff (Rule 20.10(8)).

If the debtor fails to make a payment under an order for periodic payment, the creditor may serve the debtor with a notice of default of payment (Form 20L). A notice of default of payment may be served by mail, by courier, by fax, personally (Rule 8.02), or by an alternative to personal service (Rule 8.03), unless the court orders some other type of service (Rule 8.01(14)).

An order for periodic payment terminates on the day that is 15 days after the creditor serves the debtor with the notice of default of payment, unless a consent (Form 13B) in which the creditor waives the default is filed within the 15-day period (Rule 20.02(4)). If no consent is filed within the 15-day period, the creditor may file with the court an affidavit of default of payment (Form 20M), together with a copy of the notice of default of payment and proof of service (Rule 20.02(3)).

CONTEMPT HEARING (RULE 20.11)

If a person who has been served with a notice of examination attends at the examination but refuses to answer questions or produce documents or records, the court may order that person to attend before the court for a contempt hearing (Rule 20.11(1)).

If a person who has been served with a notice of examination fails to show up for the examination, the court may order that person to attend before a judge of the Superior Court of Justice for a contempt hearing (Rule 20.11(2)).

In the context of a court proceeding, a **contempt** is any act that obstructs or hinders the court in the administration of justice, or that shows disrespect for the court. There must be an element of deliberation for an act to amount to a contempt.

If the court makes an order for a contempt hearing, the clerk shall provide the creditor with a notice of contempt hearing setting out the time, date, and place of the hearing. The creditor shall serve the debtor or other person personally with the notice of contempt hearing and file the affidavit of service at least seven days before the hearing (Rules 20.11(3)(b) and 8.01(13)).

A person who has been ordered to attend a contempt hearing may make a motion to set aside the order. The motion may be made before or after receiving the notice of contempt hearing; but it must be made before the date of the hearing. On the motion, the court may set aside the order to attend at a contempt hearing, and order that the person attend instead at another examination under Rule 20.10 (Rule 20.11(4)).

At a contempt hearing of a debtor or other person for refusing to answer questions or produce documents and records under Rule 20.11(1), the court may find the person to be in contempt of court if the person fails to show cause why he should not be held in contempt for refusing to answer questions or produce documents and records (Rule 20.11(5)).

At a contempt hearing of a debtor or other person for failure to attend on an examination, a judge of the Superior Court of Justice may find the person to be in contempt of court if the judge is satisfied (1) that the person failed to attend as required by the notice of examination, and (2) that the failure to attend was wilful (Rule 20.11(6)). If the court is satisfied that the person failed to attend because of an honest mistake or due to inadvertence, the court will not make a finding of contempt.

At a contempt hearing, the court may order that the person (Rule 20.11(7))

(a) attend an examination under Rule 20.10;

(b) be jailed for a period not exceeding 40 days;

(c) attend at an additional contempt hearing; or

(d) comply with any other order that the judge considers necessary or just.

If a warrant of committal is ordered under Rule 20.11(7)(b), the creditor may complete and file with the clerk an identification form (Form 20K) to assist the police in apprehending the person named in the warrant of committal. The clerk shall issue the warrant of committal (Form 20J), accompanied by the identification form if one is filed. The warrant of committal directs all police officers in Ontario to apprehend the person named in the warrant anywhere in Ontario and promptly bring the person to the nearest correctional institution.

A person who is apprehended under a warrant of committal shall be discharged from custody on order of the court or when the time set out in the warrant expires, whichever is earlier. In either case, the period of incarceration cannot exceed 40 days (Rules 20.11(9) and 20.11(7)(b)).

The warrant of committal remains in force for 12 months after the date of its issue and may be renewed by the court on a motion by the creditor for further 12-month periods thereafter, unless the court orders otherwise (Rule 20.11(10)). A warrant issued pursuant to an order of a judge of the Superior Court of Justice may be discharged or renewed only by a judge of that court (Rule 20.11(11)).

You will find examples of a warrant of committal and identification form at appendix 11.6 to this chapter.

A debtor who has been served with a notice of contempt hearing should consider seeking legal representation.

Delivery of Personal Property (Rule 20.05)

The Small Claims Court has jurisdiction in any action for the recovery of possession of personal property where the value of the property is $25,000.00 or less (*Courts of Justice Act*, s. 23). Where a person wrongfully retains possession of personal property with a value of $25,000.00 or less belonging to another person, the owner may commence an action for an order for delivery of the personal property. In the claim, the plaintiff must provide the court with a full description of the personal property to be seized, including its exact location; proof of ownership; make, model, and serial number; and photographs, if available.

When the court order for delivery of the property has been granted, it may be enforced by a writ of delivery (Form 20B) issued by the clerk to the bailiff. The writ of delivery must be supported by an affidavit for enforcement request (Form 20P) by the owner or the owner's paralegal

- stating that the property has not been delivered (Rule 20.05(1));

- providing a full description of the personal property to be seized and where it can be located; and

- stating whether the order being enforced is an interim order or a final judgment.

The clerk will sign the writ of delivery and return it to the owner or the owner's representative. The original writ and copies of the affidavit for enforcement request and the court order granting the writ are filed with the enforcement office.

There is a fee for issuing the writ of delivery. As of this writing, the bailiff charges $36.00 plus mileage for each attempt, whether successful or not, to enforce a writ of delivery.

When a date is set for execution of the writ, the bailiff will contact the owner. The owner is responsible for attending at the premises with the bailiff at the date and time specified. The owner is also responsible for making arrangements for removal of the items to be seized quickly and efficiently, and for paying for those arrangements, which may include:

- hiring a locksmith to gain access to the property;

- hiring a moving company or rental vehicle to remove large pieces such as furniture; and/or

- if the property must be dismantled before being removed, arranging to have people present to dismantle it quickly.

If the property referred to in a writ of delivery cannot be found or taken by the bailiff, the creditor may make a motion to the court for an order directing the bailiff to seize any other personal property of the person against whom the order was made (Rule 20.05(2)). The bailiff will require a deposit in advance for storage costs. The bailiff will hold the property seized in storage until the court makes a further order for its disposition (Rule 20.05(3)). While the property is being held by the bailiff pending a further court order, the owner must continue to pay storage costs from time to time. If he fails to do so, the seizure will be deemed to be abandoned (Rule 20.05(4)).

Section 20(2) of the *Execution Act* states that a sheriff acting under a writ of seizure and sale or a writ of delivery in respect of property on premises that is used as a dwelling shall not use force to enter the dwelling or execute the writ except under the authority of an order of the court by which the writ was issued. The court may make the order where in the opinion of the court there are reasonable and probable grounds to believe that there is property on the premises that is liable to be taken in execution under the writ.

You will find examples of a writ of delivery and affidavit for enforcement request at appendix 11.7 to this chapter.

A person who has been served with a writ of delivery and who disagrees with the order may make a motion to the court for an order rescinding the writ of delivery.

Writ of Seizure and Sale of Personal Property (Rule 20.06)

A writ of seizure and sale of personal property (Form 20C) is used to seize personal property of the debtor and sell it at public auction to satisfy all or part of an order for payment of money in favour of the creditor.

If there is a default under an order for payment or recovery of money, the creditor may make a request, supported by an affidavit for enforcement request

(Form 20P), for the clerk to issue to a bailiff a writ of seizure and sale of personal property (Form 20C). The bailiff shall enforce the writ for the amount owing, post-judgment interest, and the bailiff's fees and expenses (Rule 20.06(1)).

A writ of seizure and sale of personal property remains in force for six years after the date of its issue, and is renewable at six-year intervals thereafter (Rule 20.06(2)). It may be renewed before its expiration by filing a request to renew writ of seizure and sale (Form 20N) with the bailiff (Rule 20.06(3)). You should diarize for the renewal date and seek instructions from the client in advance of the deadline.

If more than six years have passed since the order for payment or recovery of money was made, a writ of seizure and sale of personal property may be issued only with leave of the court on motion by the creditor (Rule 20.06(1.1)). If the writ of seizure and sale of personal property is not issued within one year after the date on which an order granting leave to issue it was made, the order ceases to have effect and a writ of seizure and sale of personal property may be issued only with leave of the court on a subsequent motion (Rule 20.06(1.2)).

When the clerk has issued the writ of seizure and sale of personal property, you must file it with the enforcement office. You must inform the bailiff in writing of the property of the debtor that you wish to seize, and provide detailed information to assist enforcement staff in locating and seizing the property. This information is set out in the direction to enforce writ of seizure and sale of personal property (Form 20O), which is filed with the enforcement office.

The bailiff will require an enforcement fee and a deposit to cover anticipated expenses of enforcing the writ. These expenses will include insurance, locksmith, freight, storage, and advertising the sale of the property seized. The creditor will also be charged for every attempt, successful or not, to enforce the writ, plus mileage. If the initial deposit is not sufficient to cover the expenses incurred in enforcing the writ, the creditor will be required to make an additional deposit.

If the creditor is trying to seize a motor vehicle, snowmobile, or boat, she must provide the court with the following:

- A current PPSA search and a *Repair and Storage Liens Act* search, indicating whether there are liens or security interests registered against the vehicle, and the amount of the lien or security. These searches can be carried out online at the ServiceOntario website.

- A vehicle abstract search to prove that the vehicle is owned by the debtor.

- In the case of a motor vehicle, an up-to-date copy of a used-vehicle information package that is not more than one week old (available from the Ministry of Transportation).

If there are any liens or security interests registered against the vehicle, an ordinary creditor who is considering seizing the vehicle should think carefully about whether it will be worthwhile to do so. The secured creditor or lien claimant is entitled to have any balance due on their security paid out of the proceeds of the sale before ordinary execution creditors take their share. There may be little or nothing left for an ordinary execution creditor after the secured creditor and the bailiff's fees and charges have been paid.

Certain assets are exempt from seizure under s. 2 of the *Execution Act*:

1. clothing up to a certain amount ($5,650.00);

2. household furniture, utensils, equipment, food, and fuel up to a certain amount ($11,300.00);

3. tools and instruments ordinarily used by the debtor in the debtor's business, profession, or calling up to a certain amount ($11,300.00);

4. if a person earns a living through farming or agriculture, the livestock, fowl, bees, books, tools, implements, and seed ordinarily used by the debtor in the debtor's business, up to a certain amount ($28,300.00); and

5. one motor vehicle worth less than the prescribed amount ($5,650.00).

The values in parentheses are prescribed from time to time by regulation.

The bailiff must be satisfied that the personal property being seized is owned by the debtor, and is free and clear of any claims by co-owners. If the debtor disputes the seizure on grounds that an asset is jointly owned by a spouse, other family member, or the debtor's business, the bailiff will refuse to seize the asset, and return the writ to you with a brief report to that effect. Where there is a title dispute, you must apply to the court for an order authorizing you to seize the asset in question. All of this takes time and money, and may prove not to be cost-effective in the context of a Small Claims Court collection.

The bailiff may refuse to seize the debtor's personal property if the bailiff is not satisfied that the value of the property when sold will exceed the costs of executing the writ of seizure and sale.

Where a debtor's personal property has been seized pursuant to a writ of seizure and sale of personal property, the bailiff must deliver an inventory of the property seized within a reasonable time after a request is made by the debtor or the debtor's agent (Rule 20.06(5)).

Personal property seized under a writ of seizure and sale shall not be sold by the bailiff unless notice of the time and place of sale has been (Rule 20.06(6)):

(a) mailed at least 10 days before the sale

  (i) to the creditor at the address shown on the writ, or to the creditor's lawyer or paralegal, and

  (ii) to the debtor at the debtor's last known address; and

(b) advertised in a manner that is likely to bring it to the attention of the public.

The costs of advertising are paid for by the creditor.

You will find examples of a writ of seizure and sale of personal property, affidavit for enforcement request, and detailed calculation of interest at appendix 11.8.

Writ of Seizure and Sale of Land (Rule 20.07)

A writ of seizure and sale can be used to encumber any real property (land or buildings) already owned by a debtor in the county or district where the writ is registered, or which may be purchased by the debtor in the future in that county or district. A writ of seizure and sale of land can be a very effective way of enforcing a judgment. If the debtor tries to sell or mortgage the land, the writ will show up on a routine execution search against the debtor's name. The debtor will be required to pay off the amount owing on the execution before the sale can be completed or the mortgage registered.

A creditor may request that the clerk issue a writ of seizure and sale of land (Form 20D) directed to the sheriff in any region where the debtor may own land. The creditor's request must be supported by an affidavit for enforcement request. If you are filing a writ of seizure and sale of land in more than one county or district, you will need to complete an affidavit and writ for each location where the debtor may own land. There is a fee for issuing the writ (currently $35.00) and a fee for filing it with the sheriff (currently $100.00). Sheriff's fees are published as a regulation to the *Administration of Justice Act*.

You do not require a certificate of judgment in order to register your writ of seizure and sale of land in a territorial division other than the division where the order for payment or recovery of money was made.

A writ of seizure and sale of land remains in force for six years from the date of issue, and is renewable indefinitely for further terms of six years (Rule 20.07(3)). It may be renewed before it expires by filing a request to renew a writ of seizure and sale (Form 20N) with the sheriff. You should diarize for the renewal date and seek instructions from the client in advance of the deadline.

If more than six years have passed since the order for payment or recovery of money was made, a writ of seizure and sale of land may be issued only with leave of the court on motion by the creditor (Rule 20.07(1.1)). If the writ of seizure and sale of land is not issued within one year after the date on which an order granting leave to issue it was made, the order ceases to have effect and a writ of seizure and sale of land may be issued only with leave of the court on a subsequent motion (Rule 20.07(1.2)).

A creditor who has filed a writ of seizure and sale against land has a right to direct the sheriff to seize and sell the land. The procedure for sale of land is set out at Rule 60.07(17) of the *Rules of Civil Procedure*. Seizing and selling land is a costly and complicated process. Other encumbrances against the land, including mortgages and liens, must be satisfied before an execution creditor gets to collect anything from the sale proceeds. A Small Claims Court creditor who is considering this method of enforcement should be referred to a real estate lawyer or to the Lawyer Referral Service at 1-800-268-8326 or 416-947-3330 (within the GTA). There is no charge for the Lawyer Referral Service.

Rule 60.07(17) is excerpted at appendix 11.9. You will find a writ of seizure and sale of land and an affidavit for enforcement request at appendix 11.10 to this chapter.

Garnishment (Rule 20.08)

A creditor may enforce an order for payment or recovery of money by garnishment of debts payable to the debtor by other persons. If a debt is payable to the debtor and to one or more co-owners, one half of the indebtedness or a greater or lesser amount specified in a court order may be garnished.

KEY TERMS

In order to understand how a garnishment works, you must understand certain key terms and concepts.

First of all, in a garnishment, the **garnishee** is any person who owes money to the debtor. If the debtor is employed, then the employer is the garnishee, because the employer owes employment income to the debtor from time to time. If the debtor has a bank account, the bank is the garnishee, because the bank owes the debtor the money held in the bank account.

The **garnishor** is any creditor who is trying to enforce an order for payment of money by way of a garnishment.

Garnishee is a noun. Garnish is a verb (action word). A garnishor (creditor) garnishes money owed to the debtor when the garnishor seizes that money in a garnishment.

WHAT CAN BE GARNISHED?

The following sources of money may be attached in a garnishment:

1. wages paid by an employer to an employee;

2. commissions and tips;

3. bank accounts, whether solely owned by the debtor, or owned jointly with other persons;

4. money paid out of an RRSP;

5. money paid from a mutual fund;

6. accounts receivable of the debtor;

7. cash value of a life insurance policy owned by the debtor; and

8. payments to the debtor from an estate.

Employment income and bank accounts are frequently garnished by creditors. To garnish employment income, the creditor must have the correct legal name and address of the debtor's current employer. Garnishment against a debtor's bank account must be made at the branch where the account is held. It is essential that the creditor have current information about the debtor's bank accounts.

Joint debts may be garnished (Rule 20.08(2)). An example of a joint debt owed to a debtor is a joint bank account. Bank accounts may be garnished if the creditor has current, accurate information about where the debtor's bank accounts are located. A bank account owned solely by the debtor is garnishable for its entire contents. If a bank account or any other debt is payable to the debtor and to one or more co-owners, one half of the indebtedness or a greater or lesser amount specified in an order made by the court at a garnishment hearing may be garnished (Rule 20.08(2)). A **co-owner of debt** is a person who is entitled to part of a debt also payable to the debtor.

If more than six years have passed since the order for payment or recovery of money was made, a notice of garnishment may be issued only with leave of the court on motion by the creditor (Rule 20.08(2.1)). If a notice of garnishment is not issued within one year after the date on which an order granting leave to issue it was made, the order ceases to have effect and a notice of garnishment may be issued only with leave of the court on a subsequent motion (Rule 20.08(2.2)).

A notice of garnishment may be renewed before its expiration by filing with the clerk of the court in which the notice was issued a notice of renewal of garnishment (Form 20E.1) together with an affidavit for enforcement request (Rule 20.08(5.2)). When the notice of renewal of garnishment and affidavit for enforcement request are filed, the clerk shall issue the notice of renewal of garnishment, naming as garnishee the person named in the affidavit (Rule 20.08(5.3)). The rules that apply to notices of garnishment also apply to notices of renewal of garnishment (Rule 20.08(5.4)).

PROCEDURE ON A GARNISHMENT

A creditor who wishes to enforce an order by garnishment shall file with the clerk of a court in the territorial division in which the debtor resides or carries on business an affidavit for enforcement request (Form 20P) naming one debtor and one garnishee, and a certificate of judgment (Form 20A) if the order was made in another territorial division (Rule 20.08(3)). The clerk shall issue a notice of garnishment (Form 20E) naming as garnishee the person named in the affidavit for enforcement request (Rule 20.08(4)). The notice of garnishment shall name only one debtor and one garnishee (Rule 20.08(5)).

If there is more than one garnishee, you must fill out an affidavit for enforcement request and a notice of garnishment for each garnishee.

The court clerk issues the notice of garnishment by signing and dating it. There is a fee for issuing each separate notice of garnishment, which is recoverable in the garnishment. The fee per notice is currently $100.00. This is quite expensive for Small Claims Court, so you should carefully consider whether there is a good chance that you will recover something before recommending a garnishment to a client.

The clerk will return your copies of the issued notice of garnishment to you. You will then serve the garnishee (that is, the person who owes the debtor money) with the notice of garnishment and a blank garnishee's statement (Form 20F). Service is by mail, by courier, personally as provided in Rule 8.02, or by an alternative to personal service as provided in Rule 8.03 (Rule 8.01(8)(b)). If the garnishee is a financial institution, the address for service of the notice of garnishment and all further notices required to be served shall be served at the branch at which the debt is payable (for example, where the bank account is) (Rule 20.08(6.2)).

You shall serve the notice of garnishment and affidavit for enforcement request on the debtor within five days of serving the notice of garnishment on the garnishee (Rule 20.08(6.1)). Service is by mail, by courier, personally as provided in

Rule 8.02, or by an alternative to personal service as provided in Rule 8.03 (Rule 8.01(8)(a)).

Proof of service of the notice of garnishment in the form of affidavits of service on the garnishee and the debtor should be filed promptly with the court. The clerk must be satisfied that proper service of the notice of garnishment has taken place before she will start making payments out of court.

The garnishment attaches a debt payable by the garnishee to the debtor at the time the notice of garnishment is served, and any debts payable within six years after the notice is served (Rule 20.08(8)). The garnishee is liable to pay to the clerk any debt of the garnishee to the debtor, up to the total amount shown in the notice of garnishment, within 10 days after service of the notice, or 10 days after the debt becomes payable, whichever is later (Rule 20.08(7)).

The garnishee is personally liable to the creditor for any missed payments. If the garnishee does not make payments to the clerk and does not send a garnishee's statement, the creditor is entitled to an order against the garnishee for payment of the entire amount set out in the notice of garnishment, unless a court orders otherwise (Rule 20.08(17)). If a garnishee who has been served with a notice of garnishment pays a debt attached by the notice to a person other than the clerk, the garnishee remains liable to pay the debt in accordance with the notice (Rule 20.08(18)).

If the garnishee is the debtor's employer, the amount being paid into court shall not exceed 20% of the debtor's wages, as set out in the *Wages Act* (see table 11.1 at pages 384-385 above) (Rule 20.08(9)). The other 80% of the debtor's wages are exempt from garnishment, except by support creditors, who may garnish up to 50% of a debtor's wages. For purposes of the *Wages Act*, "wages" does not include an amount that an employer is required by law to deduct from wages. In other words, the exemption applies to net wages—that is, whatever is left after lawful deductions. Payments from an insurance or indemnity scheme that are intended to replace income lost because of disability are deemed to be wages, whether the scheme is administered by the employer or another person (*Wages Act*, s. 7(1.1)).

A judge may decrease the exemption on motion by the creditor, if the judge is satisfied that it is just to do so, having regard to the nature of the debt owed to the creditor, the person's financial circumstances, and any other matter the judge considers relevant.

A judge may increase the exemption on motion by the debtor on notice to the creditor, if the judge is satisfied that it is just to do so, having regard to the debtor's financial circumstances and any other matter the judge considers relevant.

When a garnishee starts paying money into court, the money is paid into the court's account in trust for the creditor. If proof of service has been filed, after an initial 30-day holding period for the first payment received, the clerk will begin making payments out of court to the creditor or creditors (Rule 20.08(20.1)). Subsequent payments will be made as the money is received. Payment is by cheque.

If two or more creditors have filed requests for garnishment at the same court location against the same debtor, any amount paid into court under any of the notices of garnishment issued to those creditors will be divided equally among all creditors who have not been paid in full.

Payment of creditors will be delayed if (Rule 20.08(20))

(a) a creditor, debtor, garnishee, co-owner of a debt, or any other interested person has requested a garnishment hearing under Rule 20.08(15);

(b) a notice of motion and supporting affidavit has been filed under

- Rule 8.10 (failure to receive document),
- Rule 11.06 or 11.2.01(1)1(iii) (setting aside of noting in default and default judgment, if any), or
- Rule 17.04 (motion for new trial or amendment of judgment); or

(c) a request for clerk's order on consent (Form 11.2A) has been filed setting aside the noting in default or default judgment against a party or any specified step to enforce a judgment that has not yet been completed.

You will find examples of a notice of garnishment, affidavit for enforcement request, and blank garnishee's statement at appendix 11.11.

GARNISHMENT HEARING

A creditor, debtor, garnishee, co-owner of the debt, or any other interested party may request a garnishment hearing. For example, a co-owner of a debt may request a garnishment hearing to obtain a determination of her rights with respect to the debt.

To set up a garnishment hearing, the person requesting the hearing shall call the court office and obtain a hearing date from the clerk. The person shall then complete the notice of garnishment hearing (Form 20Q) and serve it on the creditor, debtor, garnishee and co-owner of the debt, if any, and any other interested persons. Service is by mail, by courier, personally as provided in Rule 8.02, or by an alternative to personal service as provided in Rule 8.03 (Rules 8.01(9), 20.08(15), and 20.08(15.1)).

The notice of garnishment hearing shall be filed at the court office before the hearing date.

At a garnishment hearing, the court may (Rule 20.08(15.2))

(a) if it is alleged that the garnishee's debt to the debtor has been **assigned** or **encumbered**, order the **assignee** or **encumbrancer** to appear and state the nature and particulars of the claim;

(b) determine the rights and liabilities of the garnishee, any co-owner of the debt, the debtor, and any assignee or encumbrancer;

(c) vary or suspend periodic payments under a notice of garnishment; or

(d) determine any other matter in relation to a notice of garnishment.

To assign a legal right or entitlement (including wages owed or the money in a bank account) is to transfer it to another person. The person to whom the right or entitlement is assigned is called the assignee. To encumber is to mortgage or place a lien or other security interest against property. The person holding the lien or security interest is called the encumbrancer.

An assignment by a person when insolvent or unable to pay the person's debts in full or when the person knows that he, she, or it is on the eve of insolvency, with intent to defeat, hinder, delay, or prejudice creditors, or any one or more of them, is void as against the creditor or creditors injured, delayed, or prejudiced under the *Assignments and Preferences Act*. Every transfer of real property or personal property made with intent to defeat, hinder, delay, or defraud creditors or others is void as against such persons and their assigns under the *Fraudulent Conveyances Act*. If satisfied that the assignment or transfer was made with intent to defraud creditors, a court may set aside the transaction.

PAYMENT WHERE A DEBT IS JOINTLY OWNED

A co-owner of a debt is a person to whom a debt is jointly owed along with the debtor—for example, a person who holds a bank account jointly with the debtor.

A garnishee (that is, the person who owes money to the debtor) is required to identify any co-owners of a debt to the creditor in the garnishee's statement. The creditor must serve a co-owner of debt with a notice to co-owner of debt (Form 20G) and a copy of the garnishee's statement.

A person who has been served with a notice to co-owner of debt must request a garnishment hearing within 30 days after the notice is sent. If she fails to do so, she loses her right to dispute the enforcement of the creditor's order for the payment of money or a payment made by the clerk (Rule 20.08(16)).

If a debt is owed to the debtor and one or more co-owners, and (Rule 20.08(21))

- a payment of the jointly owned debt has been made to the clerk,

- no request for a garnishment hearing is made, and

- the 30-day period from service of the notice to co-owner of debt required by Rule 20.08(16) has expired,

then the creditor may file with the clerk, within 30 days after expiry of the Rule 20.08(16) notice period,

(a) proof of service of the notice to co-owner; and

(b) an affidavit stating that the creditor believes that no co-owner of the debt is a person under disability, and the grounds for the belief.

The affidavit required by Rule 20.08(21) may contain statements of the deponent's information and belief, specifying the source of the information and the fact of the belief (Rule 20.08(22)).

If the creditor does not file the material referred to above, the clerk shall return the money to the garnishee.

When dealing with a co-owner or co-owners of a debt in a garnishment, you should diarize for the above deadlines with appropriate tickler periods for follow-up.

SATISFACTION OF A DEBT BY GARNISHMENT (RULE 20.08(20.2))

When the amount owing under an order that is enforced by garnishment is paid, the creditor shall immediately serve a notice of termination of garnishment (Form 20R) on the garnishee and on the clerk.

Satisfaction of Order (Rule 20.12)

If you are a creditor enforcing an order or terms of settlement under Rule 20, it is your responsibility to notify the court and the enforcement office to advise that payment has been made in full, and to stop or withdraw any further enforcement steps. If the debtor requests your consent to a request for clerk's order on consent indicating that full payment has been made, you should cooperate.

If you have been enforcing the order or terms of settlement by way of a garnishment, you shall comply with Rule 20.08(20.2), discussed above.

If you are a debtor and payment has been made in full satisfaction of an order or terms of settlement,

(a) where all parties consent, you may file a request for clerk's order on consent (Form 11.2A) indicating that payment has been made in full satisfaction of the order or terms of settlement; or

(b) you may make a motion for an order confirming that payment has been made in full satisfaction of the order or terms of settlement.

CHAPTER SUMMARY

Rule 20 of the *Rules of the Small Claims Court* sets out the procedures for ordinary creditors to follow when enforcing orders for payment of money or other relief.

There are three main types of creditors: secured, preferred, and ordinary. Secured creditors are creditors whose loans are secured against real or personal property. Preferred creditors are unsecured creditors who rank ahead of ordinary unsecured creditors because of a priority conferred by a statute. Ordinary creditors are unsecured creditors without preferred status. This is the type of creditor most likely to be encountered in a Small Claims Court proceeding.

A creditor who does not have current information about the income and assets of a debtor may request an examination of debtor or other person (Rule 20.10). The examination may be conducted in person or by video conference where facilities for a video conference are available. The examination shall be held in the absence of the public unless the court orders otherwise, conducted under oath, and recorded. The debtor or any other person may be examined in relation to the reason for non-payment of the debt; the debtor's income and property; other debts owed to and by the debtor; the debtor's past, present, and future means to satisfy the order, and any other matter pertinent to the enforcement of the order.

A creditor who intends to enforce a judgment in another territorial division may do so by issuing a certificate of judgment in the court location where the order originated and filing it in the court location where the order is to be enforced (Rule

20.04). A certificate of judgment is not required to register a writ of seizure and sale of land at another court location.

An order for delivery of personal property may be enforced by a writ of delivery of personal property (Rule 20.05).

A writ of seizure and sale of personal property authorizes the bailiff to seize any personal property of the debtor, sell it by public auction, and apply the proceeds to the cost of enforcement and satisfaction of the order (Rule 20.06).

A writ of seizure and sale of personal property remains in force for six years after the date of its issue, and for a further six years after each renewal (Rule 20.06(2)).

A writ of seizure and sale of land may be filed with the sheriff in any county or region where the debtor may own land (Rule 20.07(1)). A writ of seizure and sale of land remains in force for six years after the date of its issue and for a further six years after each renewal (Rule 20.07(3)). The writ will show up on a standard execution search against the property. Before the property can be transferred, refinanced, or dealt with in any other way, the amount owing must be paid by the debtor.

A creditor may enforce an order for payment or recovery of money by garnishment of debts payable to the debtor by other persons (Rule 20.08). If a debt is payable to the debtor and to one or more co-owners, one half of the indebtedness or a greater or lesser amount specified in a court order may be garnished.

Where more than one creditor has filed a notice of garnishment against the same debtor, all creditors share equally in any proceeds of the garnishment, regardless of how much they are actually owed.

When the amount owing under an order that is enforced by a garnishment is paid, the creditor shall immediately serve a notice of termination of garnishment on the garnishee and the clerk.

A debtor against whom there are two or more unsatisfied orders for the payment of money may make a motion to the court for a consolidation order (Rule 20.09). The motion shall be served on all creditors named in the supporting affidavit at least seven days before the hearing date. At the hearing of the motion, the court may make a consolidation order setting out a list of all unsatisfied orders; the amount to be paid into court by the debtor under the consolidation order; and the times of payment. All payments into a consolidation account are shared equally among the creditors named in the consolidation order.

Payments made under a consolidation order are periodic payments. While an order for periodic payment is in effect, the only enforcement step available to creditors named in the order is to issue and file a writ of seizure and sale of land.

If payment is made in full satisfaction of an order, including a consolidation order, and where all parties consent, a party may file a request for clerk's order on consent indicating that payment has been made in full satisfaction of the order or terms of settlement; or the debtor may make a motion for an order confirming that payment has been made in full.

KEY TERMS

assign

assignee

chattel mortgage

chattel mortgagee

collateral

contempt

co-owner of debt

creditor

debtor

encumber

encumbrancer

encumbrances

execution of an order

exigible assets

garnishee

garnishor

judgment-proof

mortgagee

mortgagor

net wages

non-exigible assets

original court

originating court

originating process

per diem

per diem interest

periodic payments

personal property

preferred creditor

real property

registering court

realize on the security

secured creditor

stay of enforcement

support creditor

waive the default

REFERENCES

Administration of Justice Act, RSO 1990, c. A.6.

Administration of Justice Act, Small Claims Court—Fees and Allowances, O. Reg. 432/93.

Assignments and Preferences Act, RSO 1990, c. A.33.

Bank Act, SC 1991, c. 46.

Canada Pension Plan, RSC 1985, c. C-8.

Canadian Forces Superannuation Act, RSC 1985, c. C-17.

Compensation for Victims of Crime Act, RSO 1990, c. C-24.

Courts of Justice Act, RSO 1990, c. C.43.

Employment Insurance Act, SC 1996, c. 23.

Execution Act, RSO 1990, c. E.24.

Execution Act—Exemptions, O. Reg. 657/05.

Family Benefits Act, RSO 1990, c. F.2.

Family Responsibility and Support Arrears Enforcement Act, 1996, SO 1996, c. 31.

Fraudulent Conveyances Act, RSO 1990, c. F.29.

Garnishment, Attachment and Pension Diversion Act, RSC 1995, c. G-2.

Indian Act, RSC 1985, c. I-5.

Insurance Act, RSO 1990, c. I-8.

Old Age Security Act, RSC 1985, c. O-9.

Ontario Works Act, 1997, SO 1997, c. 25.

Pension Benefits Act, RSO 1990, c. P-8.

Pension Fund Societies Act, RSC 1985, c. P-8.

Personal Property Security Act, RSO 1990, c. P.10.

Provincial Offences Act, RSO 1990, c. P.33.

RCMP Superannuation Act, RSC 1985, c. R-11.

Reciprocal Enforcement of Judgments Act, RSO 1990, c. R.5.

Reciprocal Enforcement of Judgments Act—Application, O. Reg. 322/92.

Repair and Storage Liens Act, RSO 1990, c. R.23.

Rules of Civil Procedure, RRO 1990, Reg. 194.

Rules of the Small Claims Court, O. Reg. 258/98.

Small Claims Court Guide to Procedures: After Judgment—Guide to Getting Results
    (Queen's Printer for Ontario, 2009); available online at
    http://www.attorneygeneral.jus.gov.on.ca.

Statutory Powers Procedure Act, RSO 1990, c. S.22.

Wages Act, RSO 1990, c. W.1.

War Veterans Allowances Act, RSC 1985, c. W-3.

Workplace Safety and Insurance Act, 1997, SO 1997, c. 16.

DRAFTING EXERCISE

On November 15, 20— in Brampton Small Claims Court claim number 6638, the plaintiff, Francesca Dante, is awarded judgment against the defendant, Suzanne Herrero, for $4,000.00 plus pre-judgment interest in the amount of $458.96 and costs fixed at $630.00.

Use the table of days at page 160 to calculate post-judgment interest.

Claim number:	6638
Court:	Brampton
Address:	7755 Hurontario Street Brampton, Ontario L6W 4T6
Telephone:	905 456 4700
Plaintiff:	Francesca Dante
Address:	c/o Prior Mustafa LLP
Representative:	Prior Mustafa LLP Attention: Paralegal name
LSUC #:	######
Address:	22 County Court Boulevard Brampton, Ontario A1A 2B3
Telephone:	905 111 2222
Fax:	905 111 2233
Defendant:	Suzanne Herrero
Address:	105 Morton Avenue Mississauga, Ontario L2X 4Y5

The debtor, Suzanne Herrero, works for XYZ Staffing Enterprises, 42 Adelaide Street West, Suite 345, Toronto, Ontario M5X 8Z9 TEL: 416 777 8888 FAX: 416 777 8899.

Draft an affidavit for enforcement request and a certificate of judgment dated November 24, 20—, directed to the clerk of the Brampton Small Claims Court.

Your additional costs on the affidavit for enforcement request will be the cost of issuing the certificate of judgment.

Also draft an affidavit for enforcement request and notice of garnishment for enforcement in the territorial division of Toronto. These documents should be dated December 12, 20—. Note: You would also serve a blank garnishee's statement on the garnishee.

Your additional costs on the affidavit for enforcement request in the garnishment will be the fees for the certificate of judgment and the notice of garnishment.

You will find Small Claims Court addresses, forms, and fees at the Attorney General's website (http://www.attorneygeneral.jus.gov.on.ca).

REVIEW QUESTIONS

When answering the following questions, make a note of the numbers of any rules or other authorities in support of your answers.

1. What is enforcement of a judgment? Why is enforcement necessary?

2. If a Small Claims Court creditor needs to obtain a wide range of current information about a debtor's financial circumstances and ability to pay a judgment, what is the most efficient way of doing so?

3. Debtor has four orders for payment of money outstanding against her. Debtor is employed, but is struggling to make payments to all four creditors and pay for living expenses. What should Debtor do? Please provide details of the appropriate procedure.

4. When is a certificate of judgment used in an enforcement?

5. When should you use a writ of delivery? What is the difference between a writ of delivery and a writ of seizure and sale of personal property?

6. a. Creditor obtains a judgment in Newmarket Small Claims Court. Creditor wishes to file a writ of seizure and sale of land in Toronto. What is the procedure?

   b. How does a writ of seizure and sale of land assist Creditor in enforcing her judgment?

7. a. When is a garnishment used to enforce a judgment?

   b. What are five sources of money that can be garnished?

   c. What are five sources of money that cannot be garnished by an ordinary creditor?

8. a. Creditor serves a notice of garnishment on the branch of the bank at which Debtor has an account. The bank account is jointly owned. How does Creditor find out that there is a co-owner of the debt?

   b. What must Creditor do upon receiving notice from the branch?

   c. What must the co-owner of the debt do if he wishes to protect his interest in the debt?

APPENDIX 11.1   Notice of Motion and Supporting Affidavit (Form 15A) with Additional Parties (Form 1A)

ONTARIO

Superior Court of Justice
Cour supérieure de justice

Notice of Motion and Supporting Affidavit
Avis de motion et affidavit à l'appui
Form / *Formule* 15A Ont. Reg. No. / *Règl. de l'Ont.* : 258/98

Newmarket
Small Claims Court / *Cour des petites créances de*

50 Eagle Street West
Newmarket, Ontario
L3Y 6B1
Address / *Adresse*

905 853 4809
Phone number / *Numéro de téléphone*

8899
Claim No. / *N° de la demande*

Plaintiff No. 1 / *Demandeur n° 1*   ☒ Additional plaintiff(s) listed on attached Form 1A.
Le ou les demandeurs additionnels sont mentionnés sur la formule 1A ci-jointe.

Last name, or name of company / *Nom de famille ou nom de la compagnie* **Nguyen**		
First name / *Premier prénom* **France**	Second name / *Deuxième prénom*	Also known as / *Également connu(e) sous le nom de*
Address (street number, apt., unit) / *Adresse (numéro et rue, app., unité)* **c/o Prior Mustafa LLP**		
City/Town / *Cité/ville*	Province	Phone no. / *N° de téléphone*
Postal code / *Code postal*		Fax no. / *N° de télécopieur*
Representative / *Représentant(e)* **Prior Mustafa LLP Attention: Paralegal name**		LSUC # / *N° du BHC* **######**
Address (street number, apt., unit) / *Adresse (numéro et rue, app., unité)* **22 County Court Boulevard**		
City/Town / *Cité/ville* **Brampton**	Province **Ontario**	Phone no. / *N° de téléphone* **905 111 2222**
Postal code / *Code postal* **A1A 2B3**		Fax no. / *N° de télécopieur* **905 111 2233**

Defendant No. 1 / *Défendeur n° 1*   ☐ Additional defendant(s) listed on attached Form 1A.
Le ou les défendeurs additionnels sont mentionnés sur la formule 1A ci-jointe.

Last name, or name of company / *Nom de famille ou nom de la compagnie* **Mirren**		
First name / *Premier prénom* **Mabel**	Second name / *Deuxième prénom*	Also known as / *Également connu(e) sous le nom de*
Address (street number, apt., unit) / *Adresse (numéro et rue, app., unité)* **89 Oliver Crescent, Unit 442**		
City/Town / *Cité/ville* **Newmarket**	Province **Ontario**	Phone no. / *N° de téléphone* **905 222 3333**
Postal code / *Code postal* **E1H 2F2**		Fax no. / *N° de télécopieur*
Representative / *Représentant(e)*		LSUC # / *N° du BHC*
Address (street number, apt., unit) / *Adresse (numéro et rue, app., unité)*		
City/Town / *Cité/ville*	Province	Phone no. / *N° de téléphone*
Postal code / *Code postal*		Fax no. / *N° de télécopieur*

APPENDIX 11.1 Continued

ONTARIO **Superior Court of Justice** *Cour supérieure de justice*	**PAGE 1A**	**Additional Parties** ***Parties additionnelles*** Form / *Formule* 1A Ont. Reg. No. / *Règl. de l'Ont.* : 258/98

<u>8899</u>
Claim No. / *N° de la demande*

☒ **Plaintiff No. /** *Demandeur n°* 2 Claim No. 9001 ☐ **Defendant No. /** *Décendeur n°*

Last name, or name of company / *Nom de famille ou nom de la compagnie* **National Bank of Canada MasterCard**		
First name / *Premier prénom*	Second name / *Deuxième prénom*	Also known as / *Également connu(e) sous le nom de*
Address (street number, apt., unit) / *Adresse (numéro et rue, app., unité)* **P.O. Box 4700**		
City/Town / *Cité/ville* **Rexdale**	Province **Ontario**	Phone no. / *N° de téléphone* **416 453 6666**
Postal code / *Code postal* **X1X 2Y3**		Fax no. / *N° de télécopieur*
Representative / *Représentant(e)*		LSUC # / *N° du BHC*
Address (street number, apt., unit) / *Adresse (numéro et rue, app., unité)*		
City/Town / *Cité/ville*	Province	Phone no. / *N° de téléphone*
Postal code / *Code postal*		Fax no. / *N° de télécopieur*

☒ **Plaintiff No. /** *Demandeur n°* 3 Claim No. 9089 ☐ **Defendant No. /** *Décendeur n°*

Last name, or name of company / *Nom de famille ou nom de la compagnie* **Ferndale Property Management**		
First name / *Premier prénom*	Second name / *Deuxième prénom*	Also known as / *Également connu(e) sous le nom de*
Address (street number, apt., unit) / *Adresse (numéro et rue, app., unité)* **47 Mary Street**		
City/Town / *Cité/ville* **Newmarket**	Province **Ontario**	Phone no. / *N° de téléphone* **905 855 2361**
Postal code / *Code postal* **L3Y 3Y4**		Fax no. / *N° de télécopieur*
Representative / *Représentant(e)*		LSUC # / *N° du BHC*
Address (street number, apt., unit) / *Adresse (numéro et rue, app., unité)*		
City/Town / *Cité/ville*	Province	Phone no. / *N° de téléphone*
Postal code / *Code postal*		Fax no. / *N° de télécopieur*

☐ **Plaintiff No. /** *Demandeur n°* ☐ **Defendant No. /** *Décendeur n°*

Last name, or name of company / *Nom de famille ou nom de la compagnie*		
First name / *Premier prénom*	Second name / *Deuxième prénom*	Also known as / *Également connu(e) sous le nom de*
Address (street number, apt., unit) / *Adresse (numéro et rue, app., unité)*		
City/Town / *Cité/ville*	Province	Phone no. / *N° de téléphone*
Postal code / *Code postal*		Fax no. / *N° de télécopieur*
Representative / *Représentant(e)*		LSUC # / *N° du BHC*
Address (street number, apt., unit) / *Adresse (numéro et rue, app., unité)*		
City/Town / *Cité/ville*	Province	Phone no. / *N° de téléphone*
Postal code / *Code postal*		Fax no. / *N° de télécopieur*

SCR 1.05-1A (June 1, 2009 / *1er juin 2009*) CSD

APPENDIX 11.1   Continued

FORM / *FORMULE* 15A   PAGE 2   <u>8899</u>
Claim No. / *N° de la demande*

THIS COURT WILL HEAR A MOTION on <u>January 11</u>   , 20 <u>--</u> , **at** <u>9:30 a.m.</u>   ,
LE TRIBUNAL PRÉCITÉ ENTENDRA UNE MOTION le   **, à**   (Time / *heure*)

or as soon as possible after that time, at   <u>50 Eagle Street West, Newmarket, Ontario, Courtroom 5A</u>
ou dès que possible par la suite à/au   (Address of court location and courtroom number / *Adresse du tribunal et numéro de la salle d'audience*)

Complete Part A <u>or</u> Part B below, then complete the affidavit in support of motion on page 3. / *Remplissez la partie A <u>ou</u> la partie B ci-dessous. Remplissez ensuite l'affidavit à l'appui de la motion à la page 3.*

A.   **This motion will be made in person**
        by   <u>Mabel Mirren</u>   ,
        La motion sera présentée en personne par :   (Name of party / *Nom de la partie*)
        for the following order : / *en vue d'obtenir l'ordonnance suivante :*

☐   the court's permission to extend time to   (Specify)
        l'autorisation du tribunal de proroger le délai pour   (Précisez)
        _____   .

☐   set aside default judgment and noting in default.
        l'annulation du jugement par défaut et la constatation du défaut.

☐   set aside noting in default.
        l'annulation de la constatation du défaut.

☐   permission to file a Defence.
        l'autorisation de déposer une défense.

☐   permission to file a Defendant's Claim.
        l'autorisation de déposer une demande du défendeur.

☐   terminate garnishment and/or withdraw writ(s).
        la mainlevée de la saisie-arrêt ou le retrait d'un ou de plusieurs brefs, ou les deux.

☒   Other:
        Autre :
        Consolidation order (Rule 20.09)

☐   **ADDITIONAL PAGES ARE ATTACHED BECAUSE MORE ROOM WAS NEEDED.**
    DES FEUILLES SUPPLÉMENTAIRES SONT ANNEXÉES EN RAISON DU MANQUE D'ESPACE.

☐   **DOCUMENTS ARE ATTACHED.**
    PIÈCES JOINTES.

NOTE:	**IF YOU FAIL TO ATTEND AN IN-PERSON MOTION,** an order may be made against you, with costs, in your absence. If you want to attend the motion by telephone or video conference, complete and file a Request for Telephone or Video Conference (Form 1B). If the court permits it, the clerk will make the necessary arrangements and notify the parties [R. 1.07(5)].
REMARQUE :	*SI VOUS NE VOUS PRÉSENTEZ PAS EN PERSONNE À L'AUDITION DE LA MOTION, une ordonnance peut être rendue contre vous en votre absence, avec dépens. Si vous voulez assister à l'audition de la motion par conférence téléphonique ou vidéoconférence, remplissez et déposez la Demande de conférence téléphonique ou vidéoconférence (formule 1B). Si le tribunal l'autorise, le greffier prendra les dispositions nécessaires et en avisera les parties [par. 1.07 (5)].*

APPENDIX 11.1   Continued

FORM / *FORMULE* 15A   **PAGE 3**   8899

                                                                                        Claim No. / *N° de la demande*

B.   This motion in writing for an assessment of damages is made by
     La présente motion par écrit en vue d'une évaluation des dommages-intérêts est présentée par

                                                                                                                    ,

                          (Name of plaintiff / *Nom du demandeur/de la demanderesse*)

who asks the court for an order assessing damages against
qui demande au tribunal de rendre une ordonnance d'évaluation des dommages-intérêts contre

                          (Name of defendant(s) / *Nom du/de la/des défendeur(s)/défenderesse(s)*)

who have/has been noted in default.
qui a/ont été constaté(e)(s) en défaut.

AFFIDAVIT IN SUPPORT OF MOTION / *AFFIDAVIT À L'APPUI DE LA MOTION*

My name is Mabel Mirren
Je m'appelle   (Full name / *Nom et prénoms*)

I live in Newmarket, Ontario
J'habite à   (Municipality & province / *Municipalité et province*)

I swear/affirm that the following is true:
Je déclare sous serment/j'affirme solennellement que les renseignements suivants sont véridiques :

Set out the facts in numbered paragraphs. If you learned a fact from someone else, you must give that person's name and state that you believe that fact to be true.
Indiquez les faits sous forme de dispositions numérotées. Si vous avez pris connaissance d'un fait par l'entremise d'une autre personne, vous devez indiquer le nom de cette personne et déclarer que vous croyez que ce fait est véridique.

 See Schedule A attached

APPENDIX 11.1   Continued

FORM / *FORMULE* 15A   PAGE 4   8899
_____
                                                    Claim No. / *N° de la demande*

AFFIDAVIT IN SUPPORT OF MOTION, continued / *AFFIDAVIT À L'APPUI DE LA MOTION, suite*
See Schedule A attached

If more space is required, attach and initial extra pages. / Si vous avez besoin de plus d'espace, annexez une ou des feuilles supplémentaires et paraphez-les.

Sworn/Affirmed before me at **Newmarket**
Déclaré sous serment/Affirmé   (Municipality / *municipalité*)
solennellement devant moi à

in **Ontario**
en/à/au   (Province, state or country / *province, État ou pays*)

on **December 11**   , 20 **--**   _____
le   Commissioner for taking affidavits
                                          Commissaire aux affidavits
                                          (Type or print name below if signature is illegible.)
                                          (Dactylographiez le nom ou écrivez-le en
                                          caractères d'imprimerie ci-dessous si la
                                          signature est illisible.)

_____
Signature
(This form is to be signed in front of a
lawyer, justice of the peace, notary public
or commissioner for taking affidavits.)
(La présente formule doit être signée en
présence d'un avocat, d'un juge de paix,
d'un notaire ou d'un commissaire aux
affidavits.)

WARNING: **IT IS AN OFFENCE UNDER THE** *CRIMINAL CODE* **TO KNOWINGLY SWEAR OR**
                      AFFIRM A FALSE AFFIDAVIT.
AVERTISSEMENT :   *FAIRE SCIEMMENT UN FAUX AFFIDAVIT CONSTITUE UNE INFRACTION AU CODE*
                      CRIMINEL.

SCR 15.01-15A (June 1, 2009 / *1ᵉʳ juin 2009*) CSD

APPENDIX 11.1 Concluded

Schedule A

1. I am the debtor in the following actions and as such have personal knowledge of the following.

2.

Creditor	Claim No.	Judgment Amount	Date
France Nguyen 92 Friendship Court Newmarket, Ontario L3Z 3X5	Newmarket 8899	$ 2,744.08	Nov. 27, 20—
National Bank of Canada MasterCard P.O. Box 4700 Rexdale, Ontario X1X 2Y3	Newmarket 9001	$ 5,378.48	Dec. 2, 20—
Ferndale Property Management 47 Mary Street Newmarket, Ontario L3Y 3Y4	Newmarket 9089	$ 2,500.00	Dec. 5, 20—
TOTAL OWING		$10,622.56	

3. My net monthly employment income is $2,478.00. I have no other sources of income.

4. My current monthly expenses are as follows:

Rent	$ 975.00
Food	500.00
Vehicle lease	250.00
Car insurance, fuel	250.00
Clothing	100.00
TOTAL	$2,075.00

5. When I have paid my living expenses in every month, I have $403.00 left with which to pay any additional expenses.

APPENDIX 11.2   Certificate of Judgment (Form 20A) and Affidavit for Enforcement Request (Form 20P)

ONTARIO

Superior Court of Justice
Cour supérieure de justice

Certificate of Judgment
Certificat de jugement

Form / *Formule* 20A Ont. Reg. No. / *Règl. de l'Ont.* : 258/98

Seal / *Sceau*

Thunder Bay

Small Claims Court / *Cour des petites créances de*

277 Camelot Street
Thunder Bay, Ontario
P7A 4B3

Address / *Adresse*

807 343 2710

Phone number / *Numéro de téléphone*

5432

Claim No. / *N° de la demande*

BETWEEN / *ENTRE*

Emma Flood

Creditor(s) / *Créancier(s)/créancière(s)*

and / *et*

Christine Michaeli

Debtor(s) / *Débiteur(s)/débitrice(s)*

A judgment was made in this action on March 20 **, 20** -- **, in the**
Un jugement a été rendu dans la présente action le   *, à la*

Thunder Bay

(Name of court where judgment was made / *Nom de la cour où le jugement a été rendu*)

against / *contre*

Last name of debtor, or name of company / *Nom de famille du débiteur/de la débitrice ou nom de la compagnie*		
Michaeli		
First name / *Premier prénom*	Second name / *Deuxième prénom*	Third name / *Troisième prénom*
Christine		

Last name of debtor, or name of company / *Nom de famille du débiteur/de la débitrice ou nom de la compagnie*		
First name / *Premier prénom*	Second name / *Deuxième prénom*	Third name / *Troisième prénom*

Last name of debtor, or name of company / *Nom de famille du débiteur/de la débitrice ou nom de la compagnie*		
First name / *Premier prénom*	Second name / *Deuxième prénom*	Third name / *Troisième prénom*

☐   Additional debtor(s) and also known as names are listed on attached Form 1A.1.
Le ou les débiteur(s) additionnel(s) et le ou les noms sous lesquels les débiteurs sont également connus sont mentionnés sur la formule 1A.1 ci-jointe.

APPENDIX 11.2—Form 20A

FORM / *FORMULE* 20A   PAGE 2   5432

Claim No. / *N° de la demande*

Judgment was made for the following sums:
Un jugement a été rendu à l'égard des sommes suivantes :

(A) **AMOUNT OF JUDGMENT** (debt and pre-judgment interest) $ 8,210.96
     LE MONTANT DU JUGEMENT (créance et intérêts antérieurs au jugement) $

(B) **COSTS** to date of judgment $ 359.00
     LES DÉPENS à la date du jugement $

                                                    SUBTOTAL $ 8,569.96
                                                    TOTAL PARTIEL $

Post-judgment interest continues to accrue at **2.0**   % per annum.
Les intérêts postérieurs au jugement continuent   (Interest rate /   % *par an.*
à courir au taux de   *Taux d'intérêt*)

May 5   , 20 **--**   _____
                                                   (Signature of clerk / *Signature du greffier*)

TO THE CLERK OF THE Sault Ste. Marie   **SMALL CLAIMS COURT:**
AU GREFFIER DE LA COUR DES PETITES   (Name of court to where the judgment is to be filed
CRÉANCES DE   / *Nom du tribunal où le jugement doit être déposé*)

The person requesting this certificate is **Emma Flood**
La personne qui demande le présent certificat est   (Name of party requesting certificate / *Nom de la partie qui demande le certificat*)

53 Edward Street, Thunder Bay, Ontario P2B 1J3
                (Address of party requesting certificate / *Adresse de la partie qui demande le certificat*)

SCR 20.04-20A (June 1, 2009 / *1ᵉʳ juin 2009*) CSD

APPENDIX 11.2—Form 20P

ONTARIO

Superior Court of Justice
Cour supérieure de justice

Affidavit for Enforcement Request
Affidavit relatif à une demande d'exécution forcée
Form / *Formule* 20P Ont. Reg. No. / *Règl. de l'Ont.* : 258/98

Thunder Bay
Small Claims Court / *Cour des petites créances de*
277 Camelot Street
Thunder Bay, Ontario
P7A 4B3
Address / *Adresse*

807 343 2710
Phone number / *Numéro de téléphone*

5432
Claim No. / *N° de la demande*

BETWEEN / *ENTRE*

Emma Flood
Plaintiff(s)/Creditor(s) / *Demandeur(s)/demanderesse(s)/Créancier(s)/créancière(s)*

and / *et*

Christine Michaeli
Defendant(s)/Debtor(s) / *Défendeur(s)/défenderesse(s)/Débiteur(s)/débitrice(s)*

My name is Emma Flood
Je m'appelle
(Full name / *Nom et prénoms*)

I live in Thunder Bay, Ontario
J'habite à
(Municipality & province / *Municipalité et province*)

and I swear/affirm that the following is true:
et je déclare sous serment/j'affirme solennellement que les renseignements suivants sont véridiques :

1. **In this action, I am the**
   Dans la présente action, je suis le/la

   (Check one
   box only. /
   *Cochez une
   seule case.*)

   ☒ plaintiff/creditor.
   demandeur/demanderesse/créancier/créancière.

   ☐ representative of the plaintiff(s)/creditor(s).
   représentant(e) du/de la/des demandeur(s)/demanderesse(s)/créancier(s)/créancière(s).

   I make this affidavit in support of a request that the clerk of the court issue the following enforcement process(es):
   Je fais le présent affidavit à l'appui d'une demande visant à enjoindre au greffier du tribunal de délivrer l'acte ou les actes de procédure portant exécution forcée suivants :

   ☒ Certificate of Judgment (Form 20A) to the clerk of the   **Sault Ste. Marie**
   Certificat de jugement (formule 20A), au greffier   (Name of court where the judgment is to be filed / *Nom du tribunal*
   de la Cour des petites créances de   *où le jugement doit être déposé*)

   Small Claims Court.

   ☐ Writ of Seizure and Sale of Personal Property (Form 20C) directed to the bailiff of
   Bref de saisie-exécution de biens meubles (formule 20C) adressé à l'huissier de la Cour des petites créances de

   Small Claims Court.

   (Name of court location / *Emplacement du tribunal*)

   ☐ Writ of Seizure and Sale of Land (Form 20D) directed to the sheriff of
   Bref de saisie-exécution de biens-fonds (formule 20D) adressé   (Name of county/region in which the
   au shérif du/de la   enforcement office is located / *Comté/région où*
   est situé le bureau de l'exécution)

APPENDIX 11.2—Form 20P   Continued

FORM / *FORMULE* **20P**   **PAGE 2**   **5432**

Claim No. / N° de la demande

☐ Notice of Garnishment (Form 20E)/Notice of Renewal of Garnishment (Form 20E.1).
Avis de saisie-arrêt (formule 20E)/Avis de renouvellement de la saisie-arrêt (formule 20E.1).

I believe that the garnishee
Je crois que le tiers saisi _____

(Name of garnishee / Nom du tiers saisi)

at _____
à/au

(Address of garnishee / Adresse du tiers saisi)

is indebted to the debtor or will become indebted to the debtor for the following reasons:
est ou sera redevable d'une dette au débiteur pour les motifs suivants :

The Notice will be served on the debtor _____
L'avis sera signifié au débiteur,

(Name of debtor / Nom du débiteur/de la débitrice)

at _____
à/au

(Address of debtor for service / Adresse du débiteur/de la débitrice aux fins de signification)

within five days of serving it on the garnishee.
dans les cinq jours qui suivent sa signification au tiers saisi.

☐ Notice of Examination (Form 20H).
Avis d'interrogatoire (formule 20H).

☐ Writ of Delivery (Form 20B).
Bref de délaissement (formule 20B).

☐ Other *(Set out the nature of your request):*
Autre (Indiquez la nature de votre demande) *:*

Complete this section if you are requesting a Writ of Delivery.
Remplissez la présente section si vous demandez un bref de délaissement.

2. An order for the delivery of the following personal property:
   Une ordonnance de délaissement des biens meubles suivants :
   (According to the court order, set out a description of the property to be delivered. Identify any marks or serial numbers. / Selon l'ordonnance du tribunal, donnez la description des biens qui doivent être restitués. Indiquez toute marque d'identification ou tout numéro de série y figurant.*)*

SCR 20.04-10-20P (June 1, 2009 / *1er juin 2009*) CSD   **Continued on next page /** *Suite à la page suivante*

APPENDIX 11.2—Form 20P   Continued

FORM / *FORMULE* 20P   PAGE 3   5432

Claim No. / *N° de la demande*

was made in this action against: _____
a été rendue dans l'action contre :   (Name of person against whom the order was made / *Nom de la personne contre qui l'ordonnance a été rendue*)

on _____ , 20 ____ , in the _____
le   *à la Cour des petites*   (Name of court location where order was made / *Emplacement*
créances de   *du tribunal où l'ordonnance a été rendue*)

Small Claims Court. Since the above listed personal property has not been delivered, I make this affidavit in support of a request that the clerk of the court issue a Writ of Delivery (Form 20B) to the bailiff of the
Étant donné que les biens meubles susmentionnés n'ont pas été restitués, je fais le présent affidavit à l'appui d'une demande visant à enjoindre au greffier du tribunal de délivrer un bref de délaissement (formule 20B) à l'huissier de la Cour des petites créances de

_____ Small Claims Court.
(Name of court location / *Emplacement du tribunal*)

Complete this section if you are requesting a Certificate of Judgment, Writ of Seizure and Sale of Personal Property, Writ of Seizure and Sale of Land, Notice of Garnishment, Notice of Renewal of Garnishment or Notice of Examination.
Remplissez la présente section si vous demandez un certificat de jugement, un bref de saisie-exécution de biens meubles, un bref de saisie-exécution de biens-fonds, un avis de saisie-arrêt, un avis de renouvellement de la saisie-arrêt ou un avis d'interrogatoire.

3.   A judgment was made in this action against **Christine Michaeli**
Un jugement a été rendu dans l'action contre   (Name of debtor(s) / *Nom du/de la/des débiteur(s)/débitrice(s)*)

on **March 20**   , 20 **--** in the
le   *à la Cour des petites créances de*

Thunder Bay _____ Small Claims Court
(Name of court where judgment was made / *Nom du tribunal où le jugement a été rendu*)

for the following sums:
à l'égard des sommes suivantes :

(A) **DEBT** $ 8,000.00
     LA CRÉANCE $

(B) **PRE-JUDGMENT INTEREST** calculated
     LES INTÉRÊTS ANTÉRIEURS AU JUGEMENT calculés

     on the sum of $ **8,000.00**   at the rate of **2.5**   %
     sur la somme de $ *au taux de*   *pour cent*

     per annum from **February 28** , 20 **--** to **March 20**   , 20 **--** ,
     par an du   *au*

     being **385**   days. $ 210.96
     soit   *jours.* $

                    SUBTOTAL (Amount of Judgment) $ 8,210.96
                    TOTAL PARTIEL (montant du jugement) $

(C) **COSTS** to date of judgment $ 359.00
     LES DÉPENS à la date du jugement $

SCR 20.04-10-20P (June 1, 2009 / *1ᵉʳ juin 2009*) CSD   **Continued on next page /** *Suite à la page suivante*

APPENDIX 11.2—Form 20P Concluded

FORM / *FORMULE* 20P   PAGE 4   5432

(D) **TOTAL AMOUNT OF PAYMENTS RECEIVED FROM DEBTOR**
after judgment (if any)   (minus) $ 8,569.96
LE MONTANT TOTAL DES PAIEMENTS REÇUS DU   *(moins)* $
DÉBITEUR après le jugement (le cas échéant)

(E) **POST-JUDGMENT INTEREST** to date calculated
LES INTÉRÊTS POSTÉRIEURS AU JUGEMENT à ce jour, calculés

on the sum of $ 8,569.96   at the rate of **2.0**   %
sur la somme de $ *au taux de*   *pour cent*

per annum from **March 20**   , 20 -- to **May 5**   , 20 -- ,
par an du   *au*

being **46**   days. $ 21.60
soit   *jours.* $

> **NOTE:** Calculation of interest is always on the amount owing from time to time as payments are received. This is true for both pre-judgment and post-judgment interest. Attach a separate sheet setting out how you calculated the total amount of any pre/post-judgment interest.
> *REMARQUE : Les intérêts doivent toujours être calculés sur la somme due. Le calcul doit tenir compte des paiements reçus de temps à autre. Ceci s'applique autant aux intérêts antérieurs au jugement qu'aux intérêts postérieurs au jugement. Annexez une feuille distincte indiquant comment vous avez calculé le montant total des intérêts antérieurs et postérieurs au jugement.*

(F) **SUBSEQUENT COSTS** incurred after judgment (including the cost of issuing
the requested enforcement(s)) $ 19.00
LES DÉPENS SUBSÉQUENTS engagés après le jugement (y compris le $
coût de la délivrance de la ou des mesures d'exécution forcée demandées)

                                        TOTAL DUE $ 8,610.56
                                        SOLDE DÛ $

Sworn/Affirmed before me at **Thunder Bay**
Déclaré sous serment/Affirmé   (Municipality / *municipalité*)
solennellement devant moi à

in **Ontario**   _____
en/à/au   (Province, state or country / *province, État ou pays*)   Signature
                                                            (This form is to be signed in front of a
on **May 5**   , 20 --   _____   lawyer, justice of the peace, notary public
le   Commissioner for taking affidavits   or commissioner for taking affidavits.)
                                Commissaire aux affidavits   *(La présente formule doit être signée en*
                            (Type or print name below if signature is illegible.)   *présence d'un avocat, d'un juge de paix, d'un*
                            (Dactylographiez le nom ou écrivez-le en caractères   *notaire ou d'un commissaire aux affidavits.)*
                            d'imprimerie ci-dessous si la signature est illisible.)

> **WARNING:**   **IT IS AN OFFENCE UNDER THE *CRIMINAL CODE* TO KNOWINGLY SWEAR OR AFFIRM A FALSE AFFIDAVIT.**
> *AVERTISSEMENT : FAIRE SCIEMMENT UN FAUX AFFIDAVIT CONSTITUE UNE INFRACTION AU CODE CRIMINEL.*

APPENDIX 11.3   Notice of Examination (Form 20H), Financial Information Form (Form 20I), and Affidavit for Enforcement Request (Form 20P)

ONTARIO

Superior Court of Justice
Cour supérieure de justice

Notice of Examination
Avis d'interrogatoire
Form / *Formule* 20H Ont. Reg. No. / *Règl. de l'Ont.* : 258/98

(Seal / *Sceau*)

Sault Ste. Marie
Small Claims Court / *Cour des petites créances de*
426 Queen Street East
Sault Ste. Marie, Ontario
P6A 6W2
Address / *Adresse*

705 945 8000
Phone number / *Numéro de téléphone*

2000
Claim No. / *N° de la demande*

BETWEEN / *ENTRE*

Emma Flood

Creditor(s) / *Créancier(s)/créancière(s)*

and / *et*

Christine Michaeli

Debtor(s) / *Débiteur(s)/débitrice(s)*

TO: Christine Michaeli
DESTINATAIRE :   (Name of person to be examined / *Nom de la personne qui doit être interrogée*)

of **55A Tranquillity Boulevard, Sault Ste. Marie, Ontario P6S 1C5**
de/du   (Address of person to be examined / *Adresse de la personne qui doit être interrogée*)

The creditor has obtained a judgment against **Christine Michaeli**
Le créancier a obtenu un jugement contre   (Name of debtor / *Nom du débiteur/de la débitrice*)

on **March 20**   , 20 **--**   in the
le   *à la Cour des petites créances de*

Thunder Bay   Small Claims Court.
                   (Name of court where judgment was made / *Nom du tribunal où le jugement a été rendu*)

According to the supporting affidavit filed by the creditor, the total unpaid balance on the judgment is
Selon l'affidavit à l'appui déposé par le créancier, le solde total impayé aux termes du jugement s'élève à

$ **8,645.56** .   *(This amount must match the total amount identified in the supporting affidavit.)*
    (Total)   **$.**   *(Ce montant doit correspondre au montant total énoncé dans l'affidavit à l'appui.)*

This total unpaid balance takes into account all money received, accrued post-judgment interest and costs to
Ce solde total impayé tient compte de toutes les sommes reçues, des intérêts postérieurs au jugement courus et des dépens

this date: **May 5**   , 20 **--**   .   *(This date must match the date of the supporting affidavit.)*
à cette date :   *(Cette date doit correspondre à celle de l'affidavit à l'appui.)*

YOU ARE REQUIRED TO ATTEND AN EXAMINATION HEARING to explain how the debtor will pay this judgment and if there are any reasons for not doing so.
VOUS ÊTES REQUIS(E) DE VOUS PRÉSENTER À UN INTERROGATOIRE *pour expliquer de quelle façon le débiteur acquittera la somme due aux termes de ce jugement et s'il existe quelque motif que ce soit de ne pas le faire.*

APPENDIX 11.3—Form 20H   Concluded

FORM / *FORMULE* 20H   PAGE 2   **2000**

Claim No. / *N° de la demande*

THIS COURT WILL HOLD AN EXAMINATION HEARING
LE TRIBUNAL PRÉCITÉ TIENDRA UN INTERROGATOIRE

or as soon as possible after that time,

on   June 19   , 20 --   , at 9:30 a.m.   **at**

le   , à   (Time / *heure*)   *ou dès que possible par la suite à/au*

426 Queen Street East, Sault Ste. Marie, Ontario P6A 6W2

(Address of court location / *Adresse du tribunal*)

1A

(Courtroom number / *Numéro de la salle d'audience*)

                                , 20

(Signature of clerk / *Signature du greffier*)

CAUTION TO PERSON BEING EXAMINED:	If you fail to attend the examination hearing or attend and refuse to answer questions or produce documents, you may be ordered to attend a contempt hearing. At the contempt hearing, you may be found in contempt of court and the court may order you to be jailed for up to 40 days.
AVERTISSEMENT À LA PERSONNE QUI EST INTERROGÉE :	*Si vous ne vous présentez pas à l'interrogatoire ou si vous vous présentez mais que vous refusez de répondre aux questions ou de produire des documents, le tribunal peut ordonner que vous vous présentiez à une audience pour outrage. Lors de l'audience pour outrage, vous pouvez être reconnu(e) coupable d'outrage au tribunal et le tribunal peut ordonner que vous soyez incarcéré(e) pour une période maximale de 40 jours.*

NOTE TO DEBTOR:	A debtor who is an individual must serve on the creditor a completed Financial Information Form (Form 20I) prior to the hearing. This form must **not** be filed with the court.
REMARQUE AU DÉBITEUR :	*Le débiteur qui est un particulier doit signifier au créancier une formule de renseignements financiers remplie (formule 20I) avant l'interrogatoire. Cette formule ne doit **pas** être déposée auprès du tribunal.*

SCR 20.10-20H (June 1, 2009 / *1er juin 2009*) CSD

APPENDIX 11.3—Form 20I

FINANCIAL INFORMATION FORM
FORMULE DE RENSEIGNEMENTS FINANCIERS
Form / *Formule* 20I Ont. Reg. No. / *Règl. de l'Ont.* : 258/98

This form is to be completed by the debtor and served on the creditor.
La présente formule doit être remplie par le débiteur et signifiée au créancier.

This form is not to be filed in the court file.
Cette formule ne doit pas être déposée au dossier du greffe.

MONTHLY INCOME *REVENU MENSUEL*		MONTHLY EXPENSES *DÉPENSES MENSUELLES*	
Employer(s) *Employeur(s)*		Rent/Mortgage *Loyer/Hypothèque*	$ ____ $
Employer(s) *Employeur(s)*		Maintenance/Support Payments *Versements d'aliments*	$ ____ $
Net salary *Salaire net*	$ ____ $	Property taxes *Impôts fonciers*	$ ____ $
Commissions *Commissions*	$ ____ $	Utilities (heat, water & light) *Services d'utilité publique (chauffage, eau et éclairage)*	$ ____ $
Tips and gratuities *Pourboires et gratifications*	$ ____ $	Phone *Téléphone*	$ ____ $
Employment insurance *Prestations d'assurance-emploi*	$ ____ $	Cable *Câblodistribution*	$ ____ $
Pension income *Revenu de pension*	$ ____ $	House/Tenant insurance *Assurance-habitation /assurance de responsabilité locative*	$ ____ $
Investment income *Revenu de placements*	$ ____ $	Life insurance *Assurance-vie*	$ ____ $
Rental income *Revenu de location*	$ ____ $	Food *Nourriture*	$ ____ $
Business income *Revenu tiré d'une entreprise*	$ ____ $	Childcare/Babysitting *Garderie/gardiennage d'enfants*	$ ____ $
Child tax benefit *Prestation fiscale pour enfants*	$ ____ $	Motor vehicle (lease or loan) *Véhicule automobile (location à bail ou prêt)*	$ ____ $
Maintenance *(if any)* *Aliments* (le cas échéant)	$ ____ $	(licence, insurance, fuel & maintenance) *(permis, assurance, essence et entretien)*	$ ____ $
Monthly income of other adult household members *Revenu mensuel des autres membres adultes du ménage*	$ ____ $	Transportation (public) *Transports (en commun)*	$ ____ $
Other *Autre*	$ ____ $		
Income assistance *Aide au revenu*	$ ____ $		
INCOME TOTAL *REVENU TOTAL*	$ ____ $	**EXPENSES TOTAL** *DÉPENSES TOTALES*	$ ____ $

Continued on next page / *Suite à la page suivante*

APPENDIX 11.3—Form 20I   Concluded

FORM / *FORMULE* **20I**   **PAGE 2**

MONTHLY DEBTS *DETTES MENSUELLES*	VALUE OF ASSETS *VALEUR DES AVOIRS*
Credit card(s) payments *(please specify):* *Paiements de carte(s) de crédit (Veuillez préciser.)*	Real estate equity $ _____ $ *Valeur nette réelle des biens immobiliers*
_____ $ _____ $	Market value $ _____ $ *Valeur marchande*
_____ $ _____ $	Mortgage balance $ _____ $ *Solde de l'hypothèque*
_____ $ _____ $	Automobile equity $ _____ $ *Valeur nette réelle des véhicules automobiles*
Bank or finance company loan payments *(please specify):* *Remboursement de prêt(s) d'une banque ou d'une compagnie de financement (Veuillez préciser.)*	Make and year _____ *Marque et année*
	Loan balance $ _____ $ *Solde du/des prêts*
_____ $ _____ $	Bank or other account balance(s) *(include RRSP's)* $ _____ $ *Solde de compte(s) bancaire(s) ou autre(s) compte(s) (Incluez les REÉR.)*
_____ $ _____ $	
Department store(s) payments *(please specify):* *Versements à un ou des grands magasins (Veuillez préciser.)*	Stocks & bonds $ _____ $ *Actions et obligations*
_____ $ _____ $	Life insurance (cash value) $ _____ $ *Assurance-vie (valeur de rachat)*
_____ $ _____ $	Money owing to you $ _____ $ *Sommes qui vous sont dues*
	Name of debtor _____ *Nom du débiteur/de la débitrice*
DEBTS TOTAL $ _____ *DETTES TOTALES* $	Personal property $ _____ $ *Biens meubles*
	Cash $ _____ $ *Argent comptant*
	Other $ _____ $ *Autre*
	TOTAL VALUE OF ASSETS $ _____ *VALEUR TOTALE DES AVOIRS* $

APPENDIX 11.3—Form 20P

ONTARIO

Superior Court of Justice
Cour supérieure de justice

Affidavit for Enforcement Request
Affidavit relatif à une demande d'exécution forcée
Form / *Formule* 20P Ont. Reg. No. / *Règl. de l'Ont.* : 258/98

Sault Ste. Marie
Small Claims Court / *Cour des petites créances de*
426 Queen Street East
Sault Ste. Marie, Ontario
P6A 6W2
Address / *Adresse*

705 945 8000
Phone number / *Numéro de téléphone*

2000
Claim No. / *N° de la demande*

BETWEEN / *ENTRE*

Emma Flood
Plaintiff(s)/Creditor(s) / *Demandeur(s)/demanderesse(s)/Créancier(s)/créancière(s)*

and / *et*

Christine Michaeli
Defendant(s)/Debtor(s) / *Défendeur(s)/défenderesse(s)/Débiteur(s)/débitrice(s)*

My name is Emma Flood
Je m'appelle   (Full name / *Nom et prénoms*)

I live in Thunder Bay, Ontario
J'habite à   (Municipality & province / *Municipalité et province*)

and I swear/affirm that the following is true:
et je déclare sous serment/j'affirme solennellement que les renseignements suivants sont véridiques :

1. **In this action, I am the**
   Dans la présente action, je suis le/la

   (Check one box only. / *Cochez une seule case.*)

   ☒ plaintiff/creditor.
   demandeur/demanderesse/créancier/créancière.

   ☐ representative of the plaintiff(s)/creditor(s).
   représentant(e) du/de la/des demandeur(s)/demanderesse(s)/créancier(s)/créancière(s).

   I make this affidavit in support of a request that the clerk of the court issue the following enforcement process(es):
   Je fais le présent affidavit à l'appui d'une demande visant à enjoindre au greffier du tribunal de délivrer l'acte ou les actes de procédure portant exécution forcée suivants :

   ☐ Certificate of Judgment (Form 20A) to the clerk of the
   Certificat de jugement (formule 20A), au greffier
   de la Cour des petites créances de

   Small Claims Court.

   (Name of court where the judgment is to be filed / *Nom du tribunal où le jugement doit être déposé*)

   ☐ Writ of Seizure and Sale of Personal Property (Form 20C) directed to the bailiff of
   Bref de saisie-exécution de biens meubles (formule 20C) adressé à l'huissier de la Cour des petites créances de

   Small Claims Court.

   (Name of court location / *Emplacement du tribunal*)

   ☐ Writ of Seizure and Sale of Land (Form 20D) directed to the sheriff of
   Bref de saisie-exécution de biens-fonds (formule 20D) adressé
   au shérif du/de la

   (Name of county/region in which the enforcement office is located / *Comté/région où est situé le bureau de l'exécution*)

SCR 20.04-10-20P (June 1, 2009 / *1er juin 2009*) CSD

APPENDIX 11.3—Form 20P   Continued

FORM / *FORMULE* **20P**   **PAGE 2**   __2000__
Claim No. / *N° de la demande*

☐ Notice of Garnishment (Form 20E)/Notice of Renewal of Garnishment (Form 20E.1).
Avis de saisie-arrêt (formule 20E)/Avis de renouvellement de la saisie-arrêt (formule 20E.1).

I believe that the garnishee _____
Je crois que le tiers saisi   (Name of garnishee / *Nom du tiers saisi*)

at _____
à/au   (Address of garnishee / *Adresse du tiers saisi*)

is indebted to the debtor or will become indebted to the debtor for the following reasons:
est ou sera redevable d'une dette au débiteur pour les motifs suivants :

The Notice will be served on the debtor _____
L'avis sera signifié au débiteur,   (Name of debtor / *Nom du débiteur/de la débitrice*)

at _____
à/au   (Address of debtor for service / *Adresse du débiteur/de la débitrice aux fins de signification*)

within five days of serving it on the garnishee.
dans les cinq jours qui suivent sa signification au tiers saisi.

☒ Notice of Examination (Form 20H).
Avis d'interrogatoire (formule 20H).

☐ Writ of Delivery (Form 20B).
Bref de délaissement (formule 20B).

☐ Other *(Set out the nature of your request)*:
Autre (Indiquez la nature de votre demande) :

Complete this section if you are requesting a Writ of Delivery.
Remplissez la présente section si vous demandez un bref de délaissement.

2. An order for the delivery of the following personal property:
Une ordonnance de délaissement des biens meubles suivants :
(According to the court order, set out a description of the property to be delivered. Identify any marks or serial numbers. / Selon l'ordonnance du tribunal, donnez la description des biens qui doivent être restitués. Indiquez toute marque d'identification ou tout numéro de série y figurant.*)*

APPENDIX 11.3—Form 20P   Continued

FORM / *FORMULE* 20P   PAGE 3   **2000**

Claim No. / *N° de la demande*

was made in this action against:
a été rendue dans l'action contre :   (Name of person against whom the order was made / *Nom de la personne contre qui l'ordonnance a été rendue*)

on _____, 20 ____, in the _____
le   *à la Cour des petites*   (Name of court location where order was made / *Emplacement du tribunal où l'ordonnance a été rendue*)
                        créances de

Small Claims Court. Since the above listed personal property has not been delivered, I make this affidavit in support of a request that the clerk of the court issue a Writ of Delivery (Form 20B) to the bailiff of the
Étant donné que les biens meubles susmentionnés n'ont pas été restitués, je fais le présent affidavit à l'appui d'une demande visant à enjoindre au greffier du tribunal de délivrer un bref de délaissement (formule 20B) à l'huissier de la Cour des petites créances de

_____ Small Claims Court.
                (Name of court location / *Emplacement du tribunal*)

Complete this section if you are requesting a Certificate of Judgment, Writ of Seizure and Sale of Personal Property, Writ of Seizure and Sale of Land, Notice of Garnishment, Notice of Renewal of Garnishment or Notice of Examination.
Remplissez la présente section si vous demandez un certificat de jugement, un bref de saisie-exécution de biens meubles, un bref de saisie-exécution de biens-fonds, un avis de saisie-arrêt, un avis de renouvellement de la saisie-arrêt ou un avis d'interrogatoire.

3. A judgment was made in this action against **Christine Michaeli**
   Un jugement a été rendu dans l'action contre   (Name of debtor(s) / *Nom du/de la/des débiteur(s)/débitrice(s)*)

   on **March 20**_____, 20 **--** in the _____
   le   *à la Cour des petites créances de*

   Thunder Bay_____ Small Claims Court
            (Name of court where judgment was made / *Nom du tribunal où le jugement a été rendu*)

   for the following sums:
   à l'égard des sommes suivantes :

   (A) **DEBT** $ _____ 8,000.00
       LA CRÉANCE $

   (B) **PRE-JUDGMENT INTEREST** calculated
       LES INTÉRÊTS ANTÉRIEURS AU JUGEMENT *calculés*

       on the sum of $ _____ **8,000.00**   at the rate of **2.5**   %
       sur la somme de $ *au taux de*   *pour cent*

       per annum from **February 28**, 20 **--** to **March 20**, 20 **--** ,
       par an du   *au*

       being **385**_____ days. $ _____ 210.96
       soit   *jours.* $

                    SUBTOTAL (Amount of Judgment) $ 8,210.96
                    TOTAL PARTIEL (montant du jugement) $

   (C) **COSTS** to date of judgment $ _____ 359.00
       LES DÉPENS *à la date du jugement* $

APPENDIX 11.3—Form 20P   Concluded

FORM / *FORMULE* 20P   PAGE 4   2000

                                                                        Claim No. / *N° de la demande*

(D) **TOTAL AMOUNT OF PAYMENTS RECEIVED FROM DEBTOR**
     after judgment (if any)   (minus) $ _____ 0
     LE MONTANT TOTAL DES PAIEMENTS REÇUS DU   *(moins)* $
     DÉBITEUR après le jugement (le cas échéant)

(E) **POST-JUDGMENT INTEREST** to date calculated
     LES INTÉRÊTS POSTÉRIEURS AU JUGEMENT à ce jour, calculés

     on the sum of $ _____ 8,569.96   at the rate of **2.0**   %
     sur la somme de $ *au taux de*   *pour cent*

     per annum from **March 20** , 20 **--** to **May 5** , 20 **--** ,
     par an du   *au*

     being **46**   days. $ _____ 21.60
     soit   *jours.* $

     > **NOTE:** Calculation of interest is always on the amount owing from time to time as payments are
     > received. This is true for both pre-judgment and post-judgment interest. Attach a separate sheet
     > setting out how you calculated the total amount of any pre/post-judgment interest.
     > *REMARQUE : Les intérêts doivent toujours être calculés sur la somme due. Le calcul doit tenir*
     > *compte des paiements reçus de temps à autre. Ceci s'applique autant aux intérêts antérieurs au*
     > *jugement qu'aux intérêts postérieurs au jugement. Annexez une feuille distincte indiquant comment*
     > *vous avez calculé le montant total des intérêts antérieurs et postérieurs au jugement.*

(F) **SUBSEQUENT COSTS** incurred after judgment (including the cost of issuing
     the requested enforcement(s)) $ _____ 54.00
     LES DÉPENS SUBSÉQUENTS engagés après le jugement (y compris le $
     coût de la délivrance de la ou des mesures d'exécution forcée demandées)

                                              TOTAL DUE $ 8,645.56
                                              SOLDE DÛ $

Sworn/Affirmed before me at **Thunder Bay**
Déclaré sous serment/Affirmé   (Municipality / *municipalité*)
solennellement devant moi à

in **Ontario**   _____
en/à/au   (Province, state or country / *province, État ou pays*)   Signature
                                                                       (This form is to be signed in front of a
on **May 5** , 20 **--**   lawyer, justice of the peace, notary public
le   _____   or commissioner for taking affidavits.)
                                               Commissioner for taking affidavits   *(La présente formule doit être signée en*
                                               Commissaire aux affidavits   *présence d'un avocat, d'un juge de paix, d'un*
                                               (Type or print name below if signature is illegible.)   *notaire ou d'un commissaire aux affidavits.)*
                                               (Dactylographiez le nom ou écrivez-le en caractères
                                               d'imprimerie ci-dessous si la signature est illisible.)

> **WARNING:**   IT IS AN OFFENCE UNDER THE *CRIMINAL CODE* TO KNOWINGLY SWEAR OR
>   AFFIRM A FALSE AFFIDAVIT.
> *AVERTISSEMENT :*   *FAIRE SCIEMMENT UN FAUX AFFIDAVIT CONSTITUE UNE INFRACTION AU CODE*
>   *CRIMINEL.*

APPENDIX 11.4   Examination of Individual Debtor

The following script is a list of standard questions to be used on a judgment debtor examination of an individual debtor. You will need to adapt it to the information provided by the debtor in the financial information form. When examining the debtor, remember to obtain documentary backup for as much information as possible. Any amount stated on the financial information form should be supported by documentation. Any statement made under oath during the examination should be supported by documentation, to the best of the debtor's ability to produce such documentation.

If the debtor fails to provide photocopies of documents such as a deed, mortgage/charge, apartment lease agreement, vehicle lease agreement, bank loans, or lines of credit, etc., request the judge's permission to keep and photocopy the originals, on your undertaking to return them in good order and within a reasonable time to the debtor.

PERSONAL INFORMATION   **[Comments]**

Full name:

Are you the same person as _____ ,

who owes money to _____

according to this judgment in court file number _____

dated _____?

Are the details contained in the financial information form you have provided true and complete?

Do you ever use any other name(s)? If yes, what are they?

Birth date: [birth certificate]

S.I.N.:   [social insurance card]

Home telephone:

Work telephone:

Home address:

Spousal status (unmarried, cohabiting, married, divorced, separated):

Name of spouse or partner (if any):

Dependants (names, ages, nature of relationship):

EMPLOYMENT STATUS AND INCOME

– employed, unemployed, self-employed

– full-time or part-time

If employed, name and address of employer:

Name of person you report to:

Your position:

Salary: [If the debtor is employed, you should ask for three current pay stubs and tax returns for the past three years]

What is the pay period?

Any commissions, bonuses, etc.?

How long with this employer?

How long in this position?

Previous positions with this employer and their duration?

Are you related in any way to your employer?

APPENDIX 11.4 Continued

Do you have any sources of income other than employment income?

[If yes, obtain details and documentation]

[If the debtor has disclosed any other forms of income in the Monthly Income column on the file information form, confirm the amount for the record and obtain documentation or the debtor's undertaking to disclose documentation for each type of income]

DEBTOR'S SPOUSE OR PARTNER

Full name:

Address:

Telephone:

– employed, unemployed, self-employed

– full-time or part-time

If employed, name and address of employer:

Name of person they report to:

Their position:

Salary:

What is the pay period? [three recent pay stubs]

Any commissions, bonuses, etc.?

How long with this employer?

How long in this position?

MONTHLY EXPENSES

Rent/Mortgage

Municipal address:

Own or lease?

Details of ownership: [copy of deed, mortgage/charge, recent mortgage statements]

– type of ownership (joint tenancy, tenant in common, etc.)

– date of purchase

– particulars of purchase [closing letter]

Current value? [market value of similar properties, recent notice of property tax assessment]

Mortgage payments?

– amount

– when due

– current mortgage balance due

Do you own any other real estate? [If yes, go through the above questions and documentary disclosure again]

Details of leased residence: [copy of tenancy agreement, plus notices of any legal rent increases]

Name of landlord/owner:

Address:

Rent and due date: [If there is no tenancy agreement, copies of cancelled rent cheques, money orders, receipts for cash]

Is the landlord related to you?

Who pays the rent?

APPENDIX 11.4   Continued

How is it paid?

Any rent arrears?

If yes, how much?

Is there an application to the
Landlord and Tenant Board
pending?   [notice of early termination, landlord application, etc.]

Other Monthly Expenses

For each of the following

– confirm the monthly amount due

– are there any arrears?   [must be supported by documentation]

Support payments: [copy of order plus three current pay stubs showing
                                            deduction]

Property taxes: [copy of recent tax bills]

Utilities, phone, cable, property
insurance, etc.:   [at least three recent invoices]

Motor vehicle (lease or loan):

Year, make, and model:

Own or lease?   [purchase and loan documents]

Details of ownership:

– purchase price

– balance owing on loan

Details of lease: [vehicle lease agreement]

– monthly payments

– balance owing

Routine costs:

– insurance

– plates

– licence

– maintenance

– fuel

– monthly payments   [see below]

– insurance, licence, etc.   [copy of most recent policy, etc.]

MONTHLY DEBTS

Credit card debts: [at least three months of statements]

– name of card

– account number

– how much owing

– how much paid each month

Bank or finance company loans: [at least three months of statements]

– particulars of debt

– how much owing

– how much paid each month

VALUE OF ASSETS

Real estate equity (see above):

Automobile equity (see above):

APPENDIX 11.4   Concluded

Bank accounts: [statements and passbooks]

– sole owner or joint owner

– particulars of accounts

Accounts receivable: [unpaid invoices or other proof of money owing]

– names and addresses of debtor
  and amounts owing

Life insurance (cash value):   [copy of policy]

Personal property:

– particulars of ownership (chattel mortgage, free and clear)

– value

– location

– sole owner or co-owner?

LIST OF OTHER CREDITORS

For each creditor not mentioned above, obtain the following information:

– name and address of creditor

– amount owed

– security held (if any)

– judgment (if any), including amount and court file number

TRANSFER OF ASSETS

Have you sold any assets within the past two years?

– provide particulars of the sale,
  including purchaser, purchase
  price, date, etc.   [copy of contract or any other documents confirming the
                                 sale or transfer]

Have you transferred any assets within the past two years?

– provide terms of transfer, including transferee,
  date, terms of transfer, etc.

APPENDIX 11.5   Examination of Corporate Debtor

An officer or director of a corporate debtor will be examined on behalf of the corporation.

PRELIMINARY

Name of officer?

Address and telephone number?

Position with the company?

How long have you been in that position?

You are an officer of _____ [name of corporation]?

You are aware of the amount owing to _____

[name of creditor] pursuant to a judgment dated _____

in court file number _____ in

_____ [name of court]?

MINUTE BOOK

Location of minute book?

Will you make the minute books of the corporation available to me if I wish to examine them?

FINANCIAL STATEMENTS

Required for the present period: the books of accounting, general ledger, etc.

Required for the past five years:

(a) Particulars of revenues.

(b) Particulars of expenses.

(c) Salaries paid to officers and directors.

(d) Loans, advances, or dividends to shareholders.

(e) Any extraordinary expenses or revenues during the five-year period.

(f) Whether company has returned any goods to creditors or paid creditors out of the normal course of business.

(g) Bank statements.

Who are the company's current auditors/accountants/solicitors?

Have there been any changes over the past five years?

PARTICULARS OF CORPORATION

Date of incorporation?

Original share issue (including kinds, numbers, and values of original shares)?

Original and past shareholders?

Present shareholders?

Was there ever a time when there was only one shareholder?

Is there a shareholders' agreement? If yes, can you please disclose a copy?

Details regarding share transfers?

Where the transferred shares were paid for in full?

Directors, officers, and employees:

(a) Original and past directors.

(b) Present directors.

(c) Original and past officers.

(d) Present officers.

APPENDIX 11.5 Concluded

Office and premises:

(a) Where is the head office?

(b) Are the premises owned or leased? Please provide details plus documentation.

(c) Did the company ever own the premises?

Business:

(a) Type of business?

(b) What was the nature of the financial difficulties which caused the company to default on the debt?

(c) Has the company ceased to carry on business, and, if yes, on what date did that occur?

Other creditors:

(a) Names and addresses of all secured creditors of the company, and the nature of their security.

(b) Names and addresses of all ordinary creditors of the company, including other execution creditors.

(c) Details of any money owed to a bank, in the form of an overdraft or a bank loan, and, if yes, what form of security does the bank hold?

(d) Any mortgages or liens against assets, including vehicles, equipment, trade fixtures, inventory?

Corporate assets:

Does the company own any of the following:

(a) Real property?

(b) Motor vehicles?

(c) Machinery, equipment, tools, etc.?

(d) Inventory?

(e) Accounts receivable or other debts or obligations owing to the company?

APPENDIX 11.6   Warrant of Committal (Form 20J) and Identification Form (Form 20K)

ONTARIO

Superior Court of Ju☐tice
C☐ur supérieure de justice

Warrant of Committal
Mandat de dépôt

Form / *Formule* 20J Ont. Reg. No. / *Règl. de l'Ont.* : 258/98

Seal / *Sceau*

Toronto

Small Claims Court / *Cour des petites créances de*

47 Sheppard Avenue East
Toronto, Ontario
M2N 5X5

Address / *Adresse*

416 326 3554

Phone number / *Numéro de téléphone*

5678

Claim No. / *N° de la demande*

BETWEEN / *ENTRE*

Maxine Chong

Plaintiff(s) / *Demandeur(s)/demanderesse(s)*

and / *et*

LeeAnn Kingman

Defendant(s) / *Défendeur(s)/défenderesse(s)*

TO ALL POLICE OFFICERS IN ONTARIO AND TO THE OFFICERS OF ALL CORRECTIONAL INSTITUTIONS IN ONTARIO:
À TOUS LES AGENTS DE POLICE DE L'ONTARIO ET AUX AGENTS DE TOUS LES ÉTABLISSEMENTS CORRECTIONNELS DE L'ONTARIO :

THIS WARRANT IS FOR THE COMMITTAL OF / *LE PRÉSENT MANDAT EST DÉCERNÉ POUR L'INCARCÉRATION DE*

Last name / *Nom de famille*			
Kingman			
First name / *Premier prénom*	Second name / *Deuxième prénom*		Also known as / *Également connu(e) sous le nom de*
LeeAnn			
Address (street number, apt., unit) / *Adresse (numéro et rue, app., unité)*			
48 Brimley Road, Apt. 1306			
City/Town / *Cité/ville*	Province		Phone no. / *N° de téléphone*
Toronto	**Ontario**		**416 444 5555**
Postal code / *Code postal*			Fax no. / *N° de télécopieur*
L2L 3T6			

A Notice of Contempt Hearing was issued from this court which required
Un avis d'audience pour outrage a été délivré par le tribunal précité ordonnant à

LeeAnn Kingman

(Name of person required to attend contempt hearing / *Nom de la personne tenue de se présenter à l'audience pour outrage*)

to attend the sittings of this court at   **9:30 a.m.**   on   **October 15**   , 20 **--**   .
de se présenter aux séances du   (Time / *Heure*)   *le*   (Date)
tribunal à

At a contempt hearing *(Check appropriate box.)*
Lors d'une audience pour outrage (Cochez
la case appropriée.)

☒ before a judge of the Superior Court of Justice,
devant un juge de la Cour supérieure de justice

☐ before a provincial judge or deputy judge of the
Small Claims Court,
*devant un juge provincial ou un juge suppléant de la Cour des
petites créances,*

(a)   it was duly proven that the Notice of Contempt Hearing was properly served, and
d'une part, il a été dûment prouvé que l'avis d'audience pour outrage a été signifié en bonne et due forme,

SCR 20.11-20J (June 1, 2009 / *1er juin 2009*) CSD

APPENDIX 11.6—Form 20J   Concluded

FORM / *FORMULE* **20J**   **PAGE 2**   5678

(b)   this court found this person to be in contempt of court because he/she:
d'autre part, le tribunal a reconnu la personne susmentionnée coupable d'outrage au tribunal pour l'un des motifs suivants :

☒ wilfully failed to attend an examination hearing as required by a Notice of Examination (Form 20H), although properly served.
elle a délibérément omis de se présenter à un interrogatoire comme l'exigeait un avis d'interrogatoire (formule 20H), bien que l'avis lui ait été signifié en bonne et due forme.

(Check appropriate box. / Cochez la case appropriée.)

☐ attended an examination hearing and refused to answer questions or produce documents or records.
elle s'est présentée à un interrogatoire mais a refusé de répondre aux questions ou de produire des documents ou des dossiers.

At the contempt hearing, a judge of this court ordered this person to be committed.
Lors de l'audience pour outrage, un juge du tribunal a ordonné l'incarcération de la personne susmentionnée.

YOU ARE ORDERED to take the person named above to the nearest correctional institution and admit and
IL VOUS EST ORDONNÉ d'amener la personne susmentionnée à l'établissement correctionnel le plus proche

detain him or her there for **7**   days.
et de l'y admettre et l'y détenir pendant   jours.

This warrant expires twelve (12) months from the date of issue, unless renewed by court order. If renewed, the warrant expires twelve (12) months from the date of the renewal.
Le présent mandat expire douze (12) mois à compter de la date de sa délivrance, sauf si le tribunal le renouvelle par ordonnance. S'il est renouvelé, le mandat expire douze (12) mois à compter de la date du renouvellement.

_____ , 20 _____   _____

(Signature of clerk / *Signature du greffier*)

APPENDIX 11.6—Form 20K

ONTARIO

Superior Court of Justice
Cour supérieure de justice

Identification Form
Formule de renseignements signalétiques
Form / *Formule* 20K Ont. Reg. No. / *Règl. de l'Ont.* : 258/98

Toronto
Small Claims Court / *Cour des petites créances de*

5678
Claim No. / *N° de la demande*

47 Sheppard Avenue East
Toronto, Ontario
M2N 5X5
Address / *Adresse*

416 326 3554
Phone number / *Numéro de téléphone*

BETWEEN / *ENTRE*

Maxine Chong
Plaintiff(s)/Creditor(s) / *Demandeur(s)/demanderesse(s)/Créancier(s)/créancière(s)*

and / *et*

LeeAnn Kingman
Defendant(s)/Debtor(s) / *Défendeur(s)/défenderesse(s)/Débiteur(s)/débitrice(s)*

TO HELP PROCESS A CIVIL WARRANT FOR COMMITTAL, the following information, or **as much information as is reasonably available should be provided**. This is necessary for the police to identify the person to be arrested. Without this information it will be difficult to enforce the warrant.
POUR FACILITER LA DÉLIVRANCE D'UN MANDAT DE DÉPÔT AU CIVIL, les renseignements suivants ou autant de renseignements qui sont raisonnablement disponibles devraient être fournis. Ces renseignements sont nécessaires pour que la police puisse identifier la personne à arrêter. Sans ces renseignements, il sera difficile d'exécuter le mandat.

1. Name **Kingman**   **LeeAnn**
   Nom   (Last name of individual / *Nom de famille*   (First name / *Premier prénom*)   (Second name / *Deuxième prénom*)
             du particulier)

2. Also known as names (if any) **n/a**
   Nom(s) sous lequel/lesquels la personne est également connue (le cas échéant)

3. Last known address and telephone number
   Dernière adresse connue et dernier numéro de téléphone connu
   48 Brimley Road, Apt. 1306, Toronto, Ontario L2L 3T6 TEL: 416 444 5555

4. (a) Date of birth *(d, m, y)* **24 April 1978**
   Date de naissance (j, m, a)

5. Physical description
   Description physique

   (a) Gender **female**   (b) Height **5' 7"**   (c) Weight **170 lbs**   (d) Build **heavy set**
       Sexe   *Taille*   *Poids*   *Corpulence*

   (e) Colour of eyes **blue**   (f) Hair colour **light brown**   (g) Complexion **fair**
       Couleur des yeux   *Couleur des cheveux*   *Teint*

   (h) Clean-shaven   (i) Wears glasses **no**
       Rasé de près   *Porte des lunettes*

   (j) Clothing habits and tastes **business casual**
       Habitudes et goûts vestimentaires

APPENDIX 11.6—Form 20K   Concluded

FORM / *FORMULE* 20K   PAGE 2   5678

Claim No. / *N° de la demande*

(k) Distinguishing marks, scars, tattoos, etc. **scorpion tattoo on upper right arm**
Marques distinctives, cicatrices, tatouages, etc.

(l) Other **loud, distinctive laugh**
Autre   (Specify / *Précisez.*)

6. Usual occupation **office assistant**
Profession habituelle

7. Last known place of employment **Tenants R Us Legal Services**
Dernier lieu de travail connu

8. Vehicle description
Description du véhicule

(a) Make, model and year _____ (b) Colour _____
Marque, modèle et année   *Couleur*

(c) Licence plate number _____ Province or state _____
Numéro de la plaque d'immatriculation   *Province ou État*

(d) Driver's licence number _____ Province or state _____
Numéro du permis de conduire   *Province ou État*

(e) Distinguishing features on the vehicle (dents, car stereo, etc.)
Caractéristiques distinctives du véhicule (bosses, autoradio, etc.)

_____

9. Other information _____
Autres renseignements

10. Photograph of the person provided in the box below, if available.
Une photographie de la personne figure dans la case ci-dessous, si elle est disponible.

The information supplied above is true to the best of my knowledge and belief.
Au mieux de ma connaissance et de ce que je tiens pour véridique, les renseignements ci-dessus sont exacts.

_____
(Signature of party / *Signature de la partie*)

Maxine Chong
_____
(Name of party / *Nom de la partie*)

_____ , 20 ____

APPENDIX 11.7   Writ of Delivery (Form 20B) and Affidavit for Enforcement Request (Form 20P)

ONTARIO

Superior Court of Justice
Cour supérieure de justice

Writ of Delivery
Bref de délaissement
Form / *Formule* 20B Ont. Reg. No. / *Règl. de l'Ont.* : 258/98

Seal / *Sceau*

Newmarket
Small Claims Court / *Cour des petites créances de*
50 Eagle Street West
Newmarket, Ontario
L3Y 6B1
Address / *Adresse*

7777
Claim No. / *N° de la demande*

905 853 4809
Phone number / *Numéro de téléphone*

BETWEEN / *ENTRE*

Merry Clayton

Plaintiff(s) / *Demandeur(s)/demanderesse(s)*

and / *et*

Richard Parker

Defendant(s) / *Défendeur(s)/défenderesse(s)*

TO THE BAILIFF OF **Newmarket**
À L'HUISSIER DE LA COUR
DES PETITES CRÉANCES DE
(Name of Small Claims Court location / *Emplacement de la Cour des petites créances*)

SMALL CLAIMS COURT:

Under an order of this court made on **May 16** , 20 **--**
En vertu d'une ordonnance rendue par le tribunal précité le

YOU ARE DIRECTED to seize from **Richard Parker**
NOUS VOUS ENJOIGNONS de saisir auprès de   (Name of person against whom the order was made / *Nom de la personne contre qui l'ordonnance a été rendue*)

and to deliver without delay to
et de remettre sans retard à

Name of person in whose favour the order was made / *Nom de la personne en faveur de qui l'ordonnance a été rendue*   **Merry Clayton**
Street and number / *Numéro et rue*   **255 Pelican Court**
City, province, postal code / *Ville, province, code postal*   **Newmarket, Ontario L2M 3N4**
Phone number and fax number, if any / *Numéro de téléphone et numéro de télécopieur, le cas échéant*   **905 853 4455**

possession of the following personal property:
la possession des biens meubles suivants :

(According to the court order, set out a description of the property to be delivered. Identify any marks or serial numbers. If the order refers to items set out in the issued claim, attach a copy of the issued claim.)
(Conformément à l'ordonnance du tribunal, donnez la description des biens qui doivent être remis. Indiquez toute marque d'identification ou tout numéro de série y figurant. Si l'ordonnance vise des articles énoncés dans la demande délivrée, annexez une copie de la demande délivrée.)

Model: Doinel LN52B750 LCD TV
Description: 1920 X 1080 52" LCD Television
Value: $1,699.89
Serial number: 123458XYZ

APPENDIX 11.7—Form 20B   Concluded

FORM / *FORMULE* 20B   PAGE 2   7777
                                                         Claim No. / *N° de la demande*

45 Longtree Street, Basement apartment
The above personal property is located at: **Newmarket, Ontario B2B 3C4**
Les biens meubles susmentionnés se trouvent à/au :   (Address / *Adresse*)

If the address provided does not clearly identify where the items are located, please attach a detailed map that shows the nearest intersection.
Si l'adresse fournie n'indique pas clairement l'emplacement des articles, veuillez annexer un plan détaillé qui montre l'intersection la plus rapprochée.

(To be completed by the clerk of the court. / Section à remplir par le greffier du tribunal.)	☒ **THE COURT HAS EXPRESSLY ORDERED** that you are authorized to use reasonable force to enter a private dwelling to execute this writ of delivery, if necessary [*Execution Act*, s. 20(2)]. A copy of the court's order on the endorsement record is attached. ***EN VERTU D'UNE ORDONNANCE EXPRESSE DU TRIBUNAL,*** *vous êtes autorisé(e) à avoir recours à la force raisonnable pour pénétrer dans un logement privé pour exécuter le présent bref de délaissement, si cela est nécessaire [Loi sur l'exécution forcée, par. 20 (2)]. Une copie de l'ordonnance du tribunal qui figure au dossier des inscriptions est annexée.*

_____ , 20 _____   _____
                                                     (Signature of clerk / *Signature du greffier*)

SCR 20.05-20B (June 1, 2009 / *1ᵉʳ juin 2009*) CSD

APPENDIX 11.7—Form 20P

ONTARIO

Superior Court of Justice
Cour supérieure de justice

Affidavit for Enforcement Request
Affidavit relatif à une demande d'exécution forcée

Form / *Formule* 20P Ont. Reg. No. / *Règl. de l'Ont. :* 258/98

Newmarket
....
Small Claims Court / *Cour des petites créances de*
50 Eagle Street
Newmarket, Ontario
L3Y 6B1
....
Address / *Adresse*

905 853 4809
....
Phone number / *Numéro de téléphone*

7777
....
Claim No. / *N° de la demande*

BETWEEN / *ENTRE*

Merry Clayton
....
Plaintiff(s)/Creditor(s) / *Demandeur(s)/demanderesse(s)/Créancier(s)/créancière(s)*

and / *et*

Richard Parker
....
Defendant(s)/Debtor(s) / *Défendeur(s)/défenderesse(s)/Débiteur(s)/débitrice(s)*

My name is Merry Clayton
Je m'appelle
....
(Full name / *Nom et prénoms*)

I live in Newmarket, Ontario
J'habite à
....
(Municipality & province / *Municipalité et province*)

and I swear/affirm that the following is true:
et je déclare sous serment/j'affirme solennellement que les renseignements suivants sont véridiques :

1. **In this action, I am the**
    Dans la présente action, je suis le/la

    (Check one box only. / *Cochez une seule case.*)

    ☒ plaintiff/creditor.
    demandeur/demanderesse/créancier/créancière.

    ☐ representative of the plaintiff(s)/creditor(s).
    représentant(e) du/de la/des demandeur(s)/demanderesse(s)/créancier(s)/créancière(s).

    I make this affidavit in support of a request that the clerk of the court issue the following enforcement process(es):
    Je fais le présent affidavit à l'appui d'une demande visant à enjoindre au greffier du tribunal de délivrer l'acte ou les actes de procédure portant exécution forcée suivants :

    ☐ Certificate of Judgment (Form 20A) to the clerk of the
    Certificat de jugement (formule 20A), au greffier
    de la Cour des petites créances de
    Small Claims Court.

    (Name of court where the judgment is to be filed / *Nom du tribunal où le jugement doit être déposé*)

    ☐ Writ of Seizure and Sale of Personal Property (Form 20C) directed to the bailiff of
    Bref de saisie-exécution de biens meubles (formule 20C) adressé à l'huissier de la Cour des petites créances de
    Small Claims Court.

    (Name of court location / *Emplacement du tribunal*)

    ☐ Writ of Seizure and Sale of Land (Form 20D) directed to the sheriff of
    Bref de saisie-exécution de biens-fonds (formule 20D) adressé
    au shérif du/de la

    (Name of county/region in which the enforcement office is located / *Comté/région où est situé le bureau de l'exécution*)

SCR 20.04-10-20P (June 1, 2009 / *1ᵉʳ juin 2009*) CSD

APPENDIX 11.7—Form 20P Continued

FORM / *FORMULE* 20P   **PAGE 2**   **7777**
Claim No. / *N° de la demande*

☐ Notice of Garnishment (Form 20E)/Notice of Renewal of Garnishment (Form 20E.1).
Avis de saisie-arrêt (formule 20E)/Avis de renouvellement de la saisie-arrêt (formule 20E.1).

I believe that the garnishee
Je crois que le tiers saisi   (Name of garnishee / *Nom du tiers saisi*)

at
à/au   (Address of garnishee / *Adresse du tiers saisi*)

is indebted to the debtor or will become indebted to the debtor for the following reasons:
est ou sera redevable d'une dette au débiteur pour les motifs suivants :

The Notice will be served on the debtor
L'avis sera signifié au débiteur,   (Name of debtor / *Nom du débiteur/de la débitrice*)

at
à/au   (Address of debtor for service / *Adresse du débiteur/de la débitrice aux fins de signification*)

within five days of serving it on the garnishee.
dans les cinq jours qui suivent sa signification au tiers saisi.

☐ Notice of Examination (Form 20H).
Avis d'interrogatoire (formule 20H).

☒ Writ of Delivery (Form 20B).
Bref de délaissement (formule 20B).

☐ Other *(Set out the nature of your request):*
Autre (Indiquez la nature de votre demande) *:*

Complete this section if you are requesting a Writ of Delivery.
Remplissez la présente section si vous demandez un bref de délaissement.

2. An order for the delivery of the following personal property:
Une ordonnance de délaissement des biens meubles suivants :
(According to the court order, set out a description of the property to be delivered. Identify any marks or serial numbers. / Selon l'ordonnance du tribunal, donnez la description des biens qui doivent être restitués. Indiquez toute marque d'identification ou tout numéro de série y figurant.)

Model: Doinel LN52B750 LCD TV

Description: 1920 X 1080 52" LCD Television
Value: $1,699.89
Serial number: 123458XYZ

APPENDIX 11.7—Form 20P   Continued

FORM / *FORMULE* 20P   PAGE 3   <u>7777</u>

Claim No. / *N° de la demande*

was made in this action against: **Richard Parker**
a été rendue dans l'action contre :   (Name of person against whom the order was made / *Nom de la personne contre qui*
l'ordonnance a été rendue)

on <u>May 16</u>   , 20 **--** , in the <u>Newmarket</u>
le   *à la Cour des petites*   (Name of court location where order was made / *Emplacement*
créances de   *du tribunal où l'ordonnance a été rendue*)

Small Claims Court. Since the above listed personal property has not been delivered, I make this affidavit in
support of a request that the clerk of the court issue a Writ of Delivery (Form 20B) to the bailiff of the
Étant donné que les biens meubles susmentionnés n'ont pas été restitués, je fais le présent affidavit à l'appui
d'une demande visant à enjoindre au greffier du tribunal de délivrer un bref de délaissement (formule 20B) à
l'huissier de la Cour des petites créances de

<u>Newmarket</u>   Small Claims Court.
          (Name of court location / *Emplacement du tribunal*)

Complete this section if you are requesting a Certificate of Judgment, Writ of Seizure and Sale of Personal Property, Writ of Seizure and Sale of Land, Notice of Garnishment, Notice of Renewal of Garnishment or Notice of Examination.
Remplissez la présente section si vous demandez un certificat de jugement, un bref de saisie-exécution de biens meubles, un bref de saisie-exécution de biens-fonds, un avis de saisie-arrêt, un avis de renouvellement de la saisie-arrêt ou un avis d'interrogatoire.

3. A judgment was made in this action against
   Un jugement a été rendu dans l'action contre   (Name of debtor(s) / *Nom du/de la/des débiteur(s)/débitrice(s)*)

on _____ , 20 ____ in the
le   *à la Cour des petites créances de*

                                                                      Small Claims Court
          (Name of court where judgment was made / *Nom du tribunal où le jugement a été rendu*)

for the following sums:
à l'égard des sommes suivantes :

(A) **DEBT** $ _____
     LA CRÉANCE $

(B) **PRE-JUDGMENT INTEREST** calculated
     LES INTÉRÊTS ANTÉRIEURS AU JUGEMENT calculés

     on the sum of $ _____ at the rate of _____ %
     sur la somme de $ *au taux de*   *pour cent*

     per annum from _____ , 20 ____ to _____ , 20 ____ ,
     par an du   *au*

     being _____ days. $ _____
     soit   *jours.* $

                              SUBTOTAL (Amount of Judgment) $ ⋯⋯⋯⋯⋯⋯⋯
                              TOTAL PARTIEL (montant du jugement) $

(C) **COSTS** to date of judgment $ _____
     LES DÉPENS à la date du jugement $

SCR 20.04-10-20P (June 1, 2009 / *1er juin 2009*) CSD   **Continued on next page /** *Suite à la page suivante*

APPENDIX 11.7—Form 20P   Concluded

FORM / *FORMULE* 20P	PAGE 4	7777
		Claim No. / *N° de la demande*

(D) **TOTAL AMOUNT OF PAYMENTS RECEIVED FROM DEBTOR**
after judgment (if any)   (minus) $ _____
LE MONTANT TOTAL DES PAIEMENTS REÇUS DU   *(moins)* $
DÉBITEUR après le jugement (le cas échéant)

(E) **POST-JUDGMENT INTEREST** to date calculated
LES INTÉRÊTS POSTÉRIEURS AU JUGEMENT à ce jour, calculés

on the sum of $ _____   at the rate of _____ %
sur la somme de $ *au taux de*   *pour cent*

per annum from _____ , 20 ___ to _____ , 20 ___ ,
par an du   *au*

being _____ days. $ _____
soit   *jours.* $

> **NOTE:** Calculation of interest is always on the amount owing from time to time as payments are received. This is true for both pre-judgment and post-judgment interest. Attach a separate sheet setting out how you calculated the total amount of any pre/post-judgment interest.
> **REMARQUE :** *Les intérêts doivent toujours être calculés sur la somme due. Le calcul doit tenir compte des paiements reçus de temps à autre. Ceci s'applique autant aux intérêts antérieurs au jugement qu'aux intérêts postérieurs au jugement. Annexez une feuille distincte indiquant comment vous avez calculé le montant total des intérêts antérieurs et postérieurs au jugement.*

(F) **SUBSEQUENT COSTS** incurred after judgment (including the cost of issuing
the requested enforcement(s)) $ _____
LES DÉPENS SUBSÉQUENTS engagés après le jugement (y compris le $
coût de la délivrance de la ou des mesures d'exécution forcée demandées)

                                                        TOTAL DUE $ _____
                                                        SOLDE DÛ $

Sworn/Affirmed before me at **Newmarket**
Déclaré sous serment/Affirmé   (Municipality / *municipalité*)
solennellement devant moi à

in **Ontario**
en/à/au   (Province, state or country / *province, État ou pays*)

on **May 22** , 20 -- _____

                    Commissioner for taking affidavits
                    Commissaire aux affidavits
                    (Type or print name below if signature is illegible.)
                    (Dactylographiez le nom ou écrivez-le en caractères
                    d'imprimerie ci-dessous si la signature est illisible.)

Signature
(This form is to be signed in front of a lawyer, justice of the peace, notary public or commissioner for taking affidavits.)
(La présente formule doit être signée en présence d'un avocat, d'un juge de paix, d'un notaire ou d'un commissaire aux affidavits.)

> **WARNING:**   **IT IS AN OFFENCE UNDER THE *CRIMINAL CODE* TO KNOWINGLY SWEAR OR AFFIRM A FALSE AFFIDAVIT.**
> *AVERTISSEMENT : FAIRE SCIEMMENT UN FAUX AFFIDAVIT CONSTITUE UNE INFRACTION AU CODE CRIMINEL.*

APPENDIX 11.8 Writ of Seizure and Sale of Personal Property (Form 20C) and Affidavit for Enforcement Request (Form 20P)

ONTARIO

Superior Court of Justice
Cour supérieure de justice

Writ of Seizure and Sale of Personal Property
Bref de saisie-exécution de biens meubles
Form / *Formule* 20C Ont. Reg. No. / *Règl. de l'Ont.* : 258/98

Seal / *Sceau*

Brampton
Small Claims Court / *Cour des petites créances de*
7755 Hurontario Street
Brampton, Ontario
L6W 4T6
Address / *Adresse*

905 456 4700
Phone number / *Numéro de téléphone*

4567
Claim No. / *N° de la demande*

Creditor No. 1 / *Créancier n° 1*

☐ Additional party(ies) listed on attached Form 1A.
La ou les parties additionnelles sont mentionnées sur la formule 1A ci-jointe.

Last name, or name of company / *Nom de famille ou nom de la compagnie* **Parrish**		
First name / *Premier prénom* **Maxwell**	Second name / *Deuxième prénom*	Also known as / *Également connu(e) sous le nom de*
Address (street number, apt., unit) / *Adresse (numéro et rue, app., unité)* **c/o Prior Mustafa LLP**		
City/Town / *Cité/ville*	Province	Phone no. / *N° de téléphone*
Postal code / *Code postal*		Fax no. / *N° de télécopieur*
Representative / *Représentant(e)* **Prior Mustafa LLP Attention: Marie Prior**		LSUC # / *N° du BHC* **######**
Address (street number, apt., unit) / *Adresse (numéro et rue, app., unité)* **22 County Court Boulevard**		
City/Town / *Cité/ville* **Brampton**	Province **Ontario**	Phone no. / *N° de téléphone* **905 111 2222**
Postal code / *Code postal* **A1A 2B3**		Fax no. / *N° de télécopieur* **905 111 2233**

Debtor No. 1 / *Débiteur n° 1*

☐ Additional party(ies) listed on attached Form 1A.
La ou les parties additionnelles sont mentionnées sur la formule 1A ci-jointe.

Last name, or name of company / *Nom de famille ou nom de la compagnie* **Thurston**		
First name / *Premier prénom* **Frank**	Second name / *Deuxième prénom*	Also known as / *Également connu(e) sous le nom de*
Address (street number, apt., unit) / *Adresse (numéro et rue, app., unité)* **66 Clay Brick Crescent, basement apartment**		
City/Town / *Cité/ville* **Brampton**	Province **Ontario**	Phone no. / *N° de téléphone* **905 123 7654**
Postal code / *Code postal* **R2D 3P0**		Fax no. / *N° de télécopieur*
Representative / *Représentant(e)*		LSUC # / *N° du BHC*
Address (street number, apt., unit) / *Adresse (numéro et rue, app., unité)*		
City/Town / *Cité/ville*	Province	Phone no. / *N° de téléphone*
Postal code / *Code postal*		Fax no. / *N° de télécopieur*

SCR 20.06-20C (June 1, 2009 / *1er juin 2009*) CSD

APPENDIX 11.8—Form 20C   Continued

FORM / *FORMULE* **20C**   PAGE 2   4567
Claim No. / N° de la demande

TO THE BAILIFF OF THE Brampton   **SMALL CLAIMS COURT:**
À L'HUISSIER DE LA COUR   (Small Claims Court location / *Emplacement de la Cour des*
DES PETITES CRÉANCES DE   *petites créances*)

Under an order of this court made on **May 23**   , 20 **--** , in favour of
En vertu d'une ordonnance rendue par ce tribunal le   *, en faveur de*

Maxwell Parrish
(Name of creditor(s) / *Nom du/de la/des créancier(s)/créancière(s)*)

YOU ARE DIRECTED to seize and sell the personal property of
NOUS VOUS ENJOIGNONS de saisir les biens meubles de

Last name, or name of company / *Nom de famille ou nom de la compagnie*		
Thurston		
First name / *Premier prénom*	Second name / *Deuxième prénom*	Third name / *Troisième prénom*
Frank		

☐   Additional debtor(s) and also known as names listed on attached Form 1A.1.
Le ou les débiteurs additionnels et le ou les noms sous lesquels ils sont également connus sont mentionnés sur la formule 1A.1 ci-jointe.

situated within your jurisdiction and to realize from the seizure and sale the following sums:
qui se trouvent dans votre ressort et de procéder à leur vente pour réaliser les sommes suivantes :

(A) **AMOUNT OF JUDGMENT** (debt and pre-judgment interest) $ 25,629.39
   LE MONTANT DU JUGEMENT (créance et intérêts antérieurs au jugement) $

(B) **COSTS** to date of judgment $ 145.00
   LES DÉPENS à la date du jugement $

(C) **TOTAL AMOUNT OF PAYMENTS RECEIVED FROM DEBTOR** after
   judgment (if any) $ 0
   LE MONTANT TOTAL DES PAIEMENTS REÇUS DU DÉBITEUR après le $
   jugement (le cas échéant)

   Post-judgment interest continues to accrue
   Les intérêts postérieurs au jugement continuent à courir

   at the rate of **12**   % per annum from **May 23**   , 20 **--** .
   au taux de   *% par an à compter du*

(D) **SUBSEQUENT COSTS** incurred after judgment (including the cost of issuing this writ) $ 35.00
   LES DÉPENS SUBSÉQUENTS engagés après le jugement (y compris le coût $
   de délivrance du présent bref)

(E) Your fees and expenses in enforcing this writ.
   Les honoraires et frais qui vous sont dus pour l'exécution forcée du présent bref.

APPENDIX 11.8—Form 20C   Concluded

FORM / *FORMULE* 20C   PAGE 3   4567
                                                                          Claim No. / *N° de la demande*

YOU ARE DIRECTED to calculate the amount owing at the time of enforcement and to pay the proceeds over to the clerk of this court for the creditor.
ET NOUS VOUS ENJOIGNONS de calculer la somme due au moment de l'exécution forcée et de verser le produit de la vente au greffier du tribunal précité pour le compte du créancier.

May 29 _____ , 20 **--**   _____
                                              (Signature of clerk / *Signature du greffier*)

Reasonable disbursements necessarily incurred to enforce this writ $ .... $
Débours raisonnables qui ont dû être engagés pour exécuter le présent bref   (filled in and initialled by
(Bailiff (enforcement office) fees and expenses / *Honoraires et frais de l'huissier (bureau de l'exécution)*)   the enforcement office /
                                                                                              à remplir et à parapher
                                                                                              par le bureau de
                                                                                              l'exécution)

NOTE:	**THIS WRIT REMAINS IN FORCE FOR SIX YEARS** after the date of its issue and for a further six years after each renewal. The writ may be renewed before it expires by filing a Request to Renew a Writ of Seizure and Sale (Form 20N) with the bailiff (enforcement office).
REMARQUE :	*LE PRÉSENT BREF RESTE EN VIGUEUR PENDANT SIX ANS après la date de sa délivrance ou après chaque renouvellement. Le bref peut être renouvelé avant qu'il n'expire en déposant une demande de renouvellement du bref de saisie-exécution (formule 20N) auprès de l'huissier (bureau de l'exécution).*

APPENDIX 11.8—Form 20P

ONTARIO

Superior Court of Justice
Cour supérieure de justice

Affidavit for Enforcement Request
Affidavit relatif à une demande d'exécution forcée
Form / *Formule* 20P Ont. Reg. No. / *Règl. de l'Ont.* : 258/98

Brampton
Small Claims Court / *Cour des petites créances de*
7755 Hurontario Street
Brampton, Ontario
L6W 4T6
Address / *Adresse*

905 456 4700
Phone number / *Numéro de téléphone*

4567
Claim No. / *N° de la demande*

BETWEEN / *ENTRE*

Maxwell Parrish
Plaintiff(s)/Creditor(s) / *Demandeur(s)/demanderesse(s)/Créancier(s)/créancière(s)*

and / *et*

Frank Thurston
Defendant(s)/Debtor(s) / *Défendeur(s)/défenderesse(s)/Débiteur(s)/débitrice(s)*

My name is Marie Prior
Je m'appelle   (Full name / *Nom et prénoms*)

I live in Brampton, Ontario
J'habite à   (Municipality & province / *Municipalité et province*)

and I swear/affirm that the following is true:
et je déclare sous serment/j'affirme solennellement que les renseignements suivants sont véridiques :

1. **In this action, I am the**
   Dans la présente action, je suis le/la

   (Check one box only. / *Cochez une seule case.*)

   ☐ plaintiff/creditor.
   demandeur/demanderesse/créancier/créancière.

   ☒ representative of the plaintiff(s)/creditor(s).
   représentant(e) du/de la/des demandeur(s)/demanderesse(s)/créancier(s)/créancière(s).

   I make this affidavit in support of a request that the clerk of the court issue the following enforcement process(es):
   Je fais le présent affidavit à l'appui d'une demande visant à enjoindre au greffier du tribunal de délivrer l'acte ou les actes de procédure portant exécution forcée suivants :

   ☐ Certificate of Judgment (Form 20A) to the clerk of the
   Certificat de jugement (formule 20A), au greffier
   de la Cour des petites créances de   (Name of court where the judgment is to be filed / *Nom du tribunal où le jugement doit être déposé*)

   Small Claims Court.

   ☒ Writ of Seizure and Sale of Personal Property (Form 20C) directed to the bailiff of
   Bref de saisie-exécution de biens meubles (formule 20C) adressé à l'huissier de la Cour des petites créances de

   Brampton   Small Claims Court.
   (Name of court location / *Emplacement du tribunal*)

   ☐ Writ of Seizure and Sale of Land (Form 20D) directed to the sheriff of
   Bref de saisie-exécution de biens-fonds (formule 20D) adressé   (Name of county/region in which the
   au shérif du/de la   enforcement office is located / *Comté/région où est situé le bureau de l'exécution*)

APPENDIX 11.8—Form 20P   Continued

FORM / *FORMULE* **20P**   **PAGE 2**   <u>4567</u>

Claim No. / N° de la demande

☐ Notice of Garnishment (Form 20E)/Notice of Renewal of Garnishment (Form 20E.1).
   Avis de saisie-arrêt (formule 20E)/Avis de renouvellement de la saisie-arrêt (formule 20E.1).

   I believe that the garnishee
   Je crois que le tiers saisi ....
   (Name of garnishee / Nom du tiers saisi)

   at ....
   à/au ....
   (Address of garnishee / Adresse du tiers saisi)

   is indebted to the debtor or will become indebted to the debtor for the following reasons:
   est ou sera redevable d'une dette au débiteur pour les motifs suivants :

   The Notice will be served on the debtor
   L'avis sera signifié au débiteur, ...
   (Name of debtor / Nom du débiteur/de la débitrice)

   at ....
   à/au ....
   (Address of debtor for service / Adresse du débiteur/de la débitrice aux fins de signification)

   within five days of serving it on the garnishee.
   dans les cinq jours qui suivent sa signification au tiers saisi.

☐ Notice of Examination (Form 20H).
   Avis d'interrogatoire (formule 20H).

☐ Writ of Delivery (Form 20B).
   Bref de délaissement (formule 20B).

☐ Other *(Set out the nature of your request):*
   Autre (Indiquez la nature de votre demande) *:*

Complete this section if you are requesting a Writ of Delivery.
Remplissez la présente section si vous demandez un bref de délaissement.

2. An order for the delivery of the following personal property:
   Une ordonnance de délaissement des biens meubles suivants :
   (According to the court order, set out a description of the property to be delivered. Identify any marks or serial numbers. / Selon l'ordonnance du tribunal, donnez la description des biens qui doivent être restitués. Indiquez toute marque d'identification ou tout numéro de série y figurant.)

APPENDIX 11.8—Form 20P   Continued

FORM / *FORMULE* **20P**   **PAGE 3**   <u>4567</u>
                                                                        Claim No. / *N° de la demande*

was made in this action against: _____
a été rendue dans l'action contre :   (Name of person against whom the order was made / *Nom de la personne contre qui*
                                              l'ordonnance a été rendue)

on _____, 20 ____ , in the _____
le   *à la Cour des petites*   (Name of court location where order was made / *Emplacement*
                                        créances de   *du tribunal où l'ordonnance a été rendue*)

Small Claims Court. Since the above listed personal property has not been delivered, I make this affidavit in
support of a request that the clerk of the court issue a Writ of Delivery (Form 20B) to the bailiff of the
Étant donné que les biens meubles susmentionnés n'ont pas été restitués, je fais le présent affidavit à l'appui
d'une demande visant à enjoindre au greffier du tribunal de délivrer un bref de délaissement (formule 20B) à
l'huissier de la Cour des petites créances de

_____ Small Claims Court.
            (Name of court location / *Emplacement du tribunal*)

**Complete this section if you are requesting a Certificate of Judgment, Writ of Seizure
and Sale of Personal Property, Writ of Seizure and Sale of Land, Notice of
Garnishment, Notice of Renewal of Garnishment or Notice of Examination.**
*Remplissez la présente section si vous demandez un certificat de jugement, un bref de
saisie-exécution de biens meubles, un bref de saisie-exécution de biens-fonds, un avis
de saisie-arrêt, un avis de renouvellement de la saisie-arrêt ou un avis d'interrogatoire.*

3. A judgment was made in this action against **Frank Thurston** _____
Un jugement a été rendu dans l'action contre   (Name of debtor(s) / *Nom du/de la/des débiteur(s)/débitrice(s)*)

on **May 23** _____ , 20 **--** in the _____
le   *à la Cour des petites créances de*

Brampton _____ Small Claims Court
        (Name of court where judgment was made / *Nom du tribunal où le jugement a été rendu*)

for the following sums:
à l'égard des sommes suivantes :

(A) **DEBT** $ _____ 23,500.00
    LA CRÉANCE $

(B) **PRE-JUDGMENT INTEREST** calculated
    LES INTÉRÊTS ANTÉRIEURS AU JUGEMENT calculés

    on the sum of $ _____ 25,000.00 at the rate of **12** %
    sur la somme de $ *au taux de*   *pour cent*

    per annum from **September 1** , 20 **--** to **May 23** , 20 **--** ,
    par an du   *au*

    being **264** _____ days. $ _____ 2,129.39
    soit   *jours.* $

                        SUBTOTAL (Amount of Judgment) $ ········ 25,629.39
                        TOTAL PARTIEL *(montant du jugement)* $

(C) **COSTS** to date of judgment $ _____ 145.00
    LES DÉPENS à la date du jugement $

APPENDIX 11.8—Form 20P   Concluded

FORM / *FORMULE* **20P**   PAGE 4   **4567**

Claim No. / *N° de la demande*

(D) **TOTAL AMOUNT OF PAYMENTS RECEIVED FROM DEBTOR**
after judgment (if any)   (minus) $ **0**
LE MONTANT TOTAL DES PAIEMENTS REÇUS DU   *(moins)* $
DÉBITEUR après le jugement (le cas échéant)

(E) **POST-JUDGMENT INTEREST** to date calculated
LES INTÉRÊTS POSTÉRIEURS AU JUGEMENT à ce jour, calculés

on the sum of $ **25,774.39**   at the rate of **12**   %
sur la somme de $ *au taux de*   *pour cent*

per annum from **May 23**   , 20 **--**   to **May 29**   , 20 **--** ,
par an du   *au*

being **6**   days. $ **50.84**
soit   *jours.* $

> **NOTE:** Calculation of interest is always on the amount owing from time to time as payments are
> received. This is true for both pre-judgment and post-judgment interest. Attach a separate sheet
> setting out how you calculated the total amount of any pre/post-judgment interest.
> *REMARQUE : Les intérêts doivent toujours être calculés sur la somme due. Le calcul doit tenir
> compte des paiements reçus de temps à autre. Ceci s'applique autant aux intérêts antérieurs au
> jugement qu'aux intérêts postérieurs au jugement. Annexez une feuille distincte indiquant comment
> vous avez calculé le montant total des intérêts antérieurs et postérieurs au jugement.*

(F) **SUBSEQUENT COSTS** incurred after judgment (including the cost of issuing
the requested enforcement(s)) $ **35.00**
LES DÉPENS SUBSÉQUENTS engagés après le jugement (y compris le $
coût de la délivrance de la ou des mesures d'exécution forcée demandées)

TOTAL DUE $ **25,860.23**
SOLDE DÛ $

Sworn/Affirmed before me at **Brampton**
Déclaré sous serment/Affirmé   (Municipality / *municipalité*)
solennellement devant moi à

in **Ontario**
en/à/au   (Province, state or country / *province, État ou pays*)

on **May 29**   , 20 **--**   _____
le   Commissioner for taking affidavits
Commissaire aux affidavits
(Type or print name below if signature is illegible.)
*(Dactylographiez le nom ou écrivez-le en caractères
d'imprimerie ci-dessous si la signature est illisible.)*

_____
Signature
(This form is to be signed in front of a
lawyer, justice of the peace, notary public
or commissioner for taking affidavits.)
*(La présente formule doit être signée en
présence d'un avocat, d'un juge de paix, d'un
notaire ou d'un commissaire aux affidavits.)*

> **WARNING:**   **IT IS AN OFFENCE UNDER THE** *CRIMINAL CODE* **TO KNOWINGLY SWEAR OR
> AFFIRM A FALSE AFFIDAVIT.**
> *AVERTISSEMENT :*   *FAIRE SCIEMMENT UN FAUX AFFIDAVIT CONSTITUE UNE INFRACTION AU* CODE
> CRIMINEL.

SCR 20.04-10-20P (June 1, 2009 / *1er juin 2009*) CSD

APPENDIX 11.8—Form 20P Adjusted Calculation of Interest

Debt $25,000.00

Interest 12.0% per year (simple interest)

Order for set aside of default judgment dated December 1, 20—granted on December 21, 20—.

Payments made in accordance with proposal for terms of payment in defence dated Jan. 2, 20—:

February 1	$500.00
March 1	500.00
April 1	500.00
May 1	default

Convert interest rate to a decimal = 12 ÷ 100 = 0.12

This is a simple interest calculation. The principal amount upon which interest is calculated will be adjusted as payments are made.

Calculate interest on $25,000.00 from September 1 to January 31:

Per diem (interest per day) = (25,000 × 0.12) ÷ 365 = 8.219

Number of days from Sept. 1 to Feb. 1 (using table of days at table 5.2, page 160) = 121 + 32 = 153

Interest from Sept. 1 to Feb. 1 = 8.219 × 153 = 1,257.51

Adjust for February 1 payment:

Principal	25,000.00
minus February 1 payment	500.00
equals	24,500.00

Calculate interest on $24,500.00 from February 1 to March 1:

Per diem = (24,500 × 0.12) ÷ 365 = 8.055

Number of days from Feb. 1 to Mar. 1 = 28

Interest from Feb. 1 to Mar. 1 = 8.055 × 28 = 225.53

Adjust for March 1 payment:

Principal	24,500.00
minus March 1 payment	500.00
equals	24,000.00

Calculate interest on $24,000.00 from March 1 to April 1:

Number of days from Mar. 1 to April 1 = 31

Per diem = (24,000 × 0.12) ÷ 365 = 7.89

Interest from Mar. 1 to April 1 = 7.89 × 31 = 244.60

Adjust for April 1 payment:

Principal	24,000.00
minus April 1 payment	500.00
equals	23,500.00

APPENDIX 11.8—Form 20P Adjusted Calculation of Interest   Concluded

Background: The debtor defaults on the May 1 payment. The creditor serves a notice of default of payment. After the 15-day period has elapsed, the creditor files an affidavit of default of payment with the clerk. The clerk signs judgment on May 23. On May 29, the creditor issues the writ of seizure and sale of personal property.

Calculate interest on $23,500.00 from April 1 to May 23 (date of default judgment):

Number of days from April 1 to May 23 = 52

Per diem = (23,500 × 0.12) ÷ 365 = 7.726

Interest from April 1 to May 23 = 7.726 × 52 = 401.75

Total pre-judgment interest as of date of default judgment = 1,257.51 + 225.53 + 244.60 + 401.75 = $2,129.39

Numbers for completing the Form 20C:

Debt including pre-judgment interest to May 23 ($23,500 + 2,129.39): $25,629.39

Total payments after judgment: 0

Costs to date of judgment: $145.00

Subsequent costs: Fee for issuing writ of seizure and sale of personal property

Numbers for completing the Form 20P:

Pre-judgment interest:

Debt:	$23,500.00
Pre-judgment interest rate:	12% per year
From/to:	September 1 to May 23 of the following year
Total days:	264
Pre-judgment interest to May 23, 20—:	$2,129.39 (adjusted for pre-judgment payments)
Costs to date of judgment:	$145.00
Total payments received after judgment:	0

Post-judgment interest:

Calculated on the sum of:	23,500.00 + 2,129.39 + 145.00 = 25,774.39
Post-judgment interest rate:	12% per year (simple interest compounded annually)
From/to:	May 23 to May 29, 20—
Total days:	6
Per diem:	(25,774.39 × 0.12) ÷ 365 = 8.474
Post-judgment interest to May 29:	8.474 × 6 = 50.84
Subsequent costs:	Fee for issuing writ of seizure and sale of personal property

APPENDIX 11.9 Rule 60.07 Sale of Land

Courts of Justice Act
RRO 1990, Reg. 194

RULES OF CIVIL PROCEDURE

Sale of Land

60.07(17) A creditor may not take any step to sell land under a writ of seizure and sale until four months after the writ was filed with the sheriff or, where the writ has been withdrawn, four months after the writ was re-filed.

(18) No sale of land under a writ of seizure and sale may be held until six months after the writ was filed with the sheriff or, where the writ has been withdrawn, six months after the writ was re-filed.

(19) A sale of land shall not be held under a writ of seizure and sale unless notice of the time and place of sale has been,

(a) mailed to the creditor at the address shown on the writ or to the creditor's lawyer and to the debtor at the debtor's last known address, at least thirty days before the sale;

(b) published in *The Ontario Gazette* once at least thirty days before the sale and in a newspaper of general circulation in the place where the land is situate, once each week for two successive weeks, the last notice to be published not less than one week nor more than three weeks before the date of sale; and

(c) posted in a conspicuous place in the sheriff's office for at least thirty days before the sale.

(20) The notice shall set out,

(a) a short description of the property to be sold;

(b) the short title of the proceeding;

(c) the time and place of the intended sale; and

(d) the name of the debtor whose interest is to be sold.

(21) The sheriff may adjourn a sale to a later date where the sheriff considers it necessary in order to realize the best price that can be obtained in all the circumstances, and where the sale is adjourned, it may be conducted on the later date with such further notice, if any, as the sheriff considers advisable.

(22) Where notice of a sale of land under a writ of seizure and sale is published in *The Ontario Gazette* before the writ expires, the sale may be completed by a sale and transfer of the land after the writ expires.

APPENDIX 11.10   Writ of Seizure and Sale of Land (Form 20D) and Affidavit for Enforcement Request (Form 20P)

ONTARIO
Superior Court of Justice
C☐ur supérieure de justice

Writ of Seizure and Sale of Land
Bref de saisie-exécution de biens-fonds
Form / *Formule* 20D Ont. Reg. No. / *Règl. de l'Ont.* : 258/98

Seal / *Sceau*

Sault Ste. Marie
Small Claims Court / *Cour des petites créances de*
426 Queen Street East
Sault Ste. Marie, Ontario
P6A 6W2
Address / *Adresse*
705 945 8000
Phone number / *Numéro de téléphone*

2000
Claim No. / *N° de la demande*

☐ Additional party(ies) listed on attached Form 1A.
La ou les parties additionnelles sont mentionnées sur la formule 1A ci-jointe.

Creditor No. 1 / *Créancier n° 1*

Last name, or name of company / *Nom de famille ou nom de la compagnie* **Flood**		
First name / *Premier prénom* **Emma**	Second name / *Deuxième prénom*	Also known as / *Également connu(e) sous le nom de*
Address (street number, apt., unit) / *Adresse (numéro et rue, app., unité)* **53 Edward Street**		
City/Town / *Cité/ville* **Thunder Bay**	Province **Ontario**	Phone no. / *N° de téléphone* **807 555 3333**
Postal code / *Code postal* **P2B 1J3**		Fax no. / *N° de télécopieur*
Representative / *Représentant(e)*		LSUC # / *N° du BHC*
Address (street number, apt., unit) / *Adresse (numéro et rue, app., unité)*		
City/Town / *Cité/ville*	Province	Phone no. / *N° de téléphone*
Postal code / *Code postal*		Fax no. / *N° de télécopieur*

☐ Additional party(ies) listed on attached Form 1A.
La ou les parties additionnelles sont mentionnées sur la formule 1A ci-jointe.

Debtor No. 1 / *Débiteur n° 1*

Last name, or name of company / *Nom de famille ou nom de la compagnie* **Michaeli**		
First name / *Premier prénom* **Christine**	Second name / *Deuxième prénom*	Also known as / *Également connu(e) sous le nom de*
Address (street number, apt., unit) / *Adresse (numéro et rue, app., unité)* **55A Tranquillity Boulevard**		
City/Town / *Cité/ville* **Sault Ste. Marie**	Province **Ontario**	Phone no. / *N° de téléphone* **705 333 5555**
Postal code / *Code postal* **P6S 1C5**		Fax no. / *N° de télécopieur*
Representative / *Représentant(e)*		LSUC # / *N° du BHC*
Address (street number, apt., unit) / *Adresse (numéro et rue, app., unité)*		
City/Town / *Cité/ville*	Province	Phone no. / *N° de téléphone*
Postal code / *Code postal*		Fax no. / *N° de télécopieur*

NOTE: **THIS WRIT REMAINS IN FORCE FOR SIX YEARS** after the date of its issue and for a further six years after each renewal. The writ may be renewed before it expires by filing a Request to Renew a Writ of Seizure and Sale (Form 20N) with the sheriff (enforcement office.)

REMARQUE :   *LE PRÉSENT BREF RESTE EN VIGUEUR PENDANT SIX ANS après la date de sa délivrance ou après chaque renouvellement. Le bref peut être renouvelé avant qu'il n'expire en déposant une demande de renouvellement du bref de saisie-exécution (formule 20N) auprès du shérif (bureau de l'exécution).*

SCR 20.07-20D (June 1, 2009 / *1er juin 2009*) CSD

APPENDIX 11.10—Form 20D   Concluded

FORM / *FORMULE* **20D**   PAGE 2   **2000**

Claim No. / *N° de la demande*

TO THE SHERIFF OF Algoma   :
AU SHÉRIF DE   (Name of county/region in which the enforcement office is located / *Nom du comté/de la région où est situé*
                         le bureau de l'exécution)

Under an order of this court made on **March 20**   , 20 -- , in favour of
En vertu d'une ordonnance rendue par ce tribunal le   , *en faveur de*

Emma Flood
                              (Name of creditor(s) / *Nom du/de la/des créancier(s)/créancière(s)*)

YOU ARE DIRECTED to seize and sell the real property of
NOUS VOUS ENJOIGNONS de saisir les biens immeubles de

Last name, or name of company / *Nom de famille ou nom de la compagnie*		
Michaeli		
First name / *Premier prénom*	Second name / *Deuxième prénom*	Third name / *Troisième prénom*
Christine		

☐ Additional debtor(s) and also known as names listed on attached Form 1A.1.
Le ou les débiteurs additionnels et le ou les noms sous lesquels ils sont également connus sont mentionnés sur la formule 1A.1 ci-jointe.

situated within your jurisdiction and to realize from the seizure and sale the following sums:
qui se trouvent dans votre ressort et de procéder à leur vente pour réaliser les sommes suivantes :

(A) **AMOUNT OF JUDGMENT** (debt and pre-judgment interest) $ 8,210.96
    MONTANT DU JUGEMENT (créance et intérêts antérieurs au jugement) $

(B) **COSTS** to date of judgment $ 359.00
    LES DÉPENS à la date du jugement $

(C) **TOTAL AMOUNT OF PAYMENTS RECEIVED FROM DEBTOR** after
    judgment (if any) $ 0
    LE MONTANT TOTAL DES PAIEMENTS REÇUS DU DÉBITEUR après le $
    jugement (le cas échéant)

    Post-judgment interest continues to accrue
    Les intérêts postérieurs au jugement continuent à courir

    at the rate of **2.0**   % per annum from **March 20**   , 20 -- .
    au taux de   % *par an à compter du*

(D) **SUBSEQUENT COSTS** incurred after judgment (including the cost of issuing this writ) $ 89.00
    LES DÉPENS SUBSÉQUENTS engagés après le jugement (y compris le coût $
    de délivrance du présent bref)

(E) Your fees and expenses in enforcing this writ.
    Les honoraires et frais qui vous sont dus pour l'exécution forcée du présent bref.

YOU ARE DIRECTED to calculate the amount owing at the time of enforcement and pay out the proceeds according to law and to report on the execution of this writ if required by a party who filed this writ.
ET NOUS VOUS ENJOIGNONS de calculer la somme due au moment de l'exécution forcée et de verser le produit de la vente conformément à la loi et de faire un rapport sur l'exécution forcée du présent bref si la partie qui l'a déposé l'exige.

_____ , 20 _____   _____
                                           (Signature of clerk / *Signature du greffier*)

SCR 20.07-20D (June 1, 2009 / *1er juin 2009*) CSD

APPENDIX 11.10—Form 20P

ONTARIO

Superior Court of Justice
Cour supérieure de justice

Affidavit for Enforcement Request
Affidavit relatif à une demande d'exécution forcée
Form / *Formule* 20P Ont. Reg. No. / *Règl. de l'Ont.* : 258/98

Sault Ste. Marie
Small Claims Court / *Cour des petites créances de*
426 Queen Street East
Sault Ste. Marie, Ontario
P6A 6W2
Address / *Adresse*

705 945 8000
Phone number / *Numéro de téléphone*

2000
Claim No. / *N° de la demande*

BETWEEN / *ENTRE*

Emma Flood
Plaintiff(s)/Creditor(s) / *Demandeur(s)/demanderesse(s)/Créancier(s)/créancière(s)*

and / *et*

Christine Michaeli
Defendant(s)/Debtor(s) / *Défendeur(s)/défenderesse(s)/Débiteur(s)/débitrice(s)*

My name is Emma Flood
Je m'appelle
(Full name / *Nom et prénoms*)

I live in Thunder Bay, Ontario
J'habite à
(Municipality & province / *Municipalité et province*)

and I swear/affirm that the following is true:
et je déclare sous serment/j'affirme solennellement que les renseignements suivants sont véridiques :

1. **In this action, I am the**
   Dans la présente action, je suis le/la

   (Check one box only. / *Cochez une seule case.*)

   ☒ plaintiff/creditor.
   demandeur/demanderesse/créancier/créancière.

   ☐ representative of the plaintiff(s)/creditor(s).
   représentant(e) du/de la/des demandeur(s)/demanderesse(s)/créancier(s)/créancière(s).

   I make this affidavit in support of a request that the clerk of the court issue the following enforcement process(es):
   Je fais le présent affidavit à l'appui d'une demande visant à enjoindre au greffier du tribunal de délivrer l'acte ou les actes de procédure portant exécution forcée suivants :

   ☐ Certificate of Judgment (Form 20A) to the clerk of the
   Certificat de jugement (formule 20A), au greffier
   de la Cour des petites créances de
   (Name of court where the judgment is to be filed / *Nom du tribunal où le jugement doit être déposé*)

   Small Claims Court.

   ☐ Writ of Seizure and Sale of Personal Property (Form 20C) directed to the bailiff of
   Bref de saisie-exécution de biens meubles (formule 20C) adressé à l'huissier de la Cour des petites créances de

   Small Claims Court.
   (Name of court location / *Emplacement du tribunal*)

   ☒ Writ of Seizure and Sale of Land (Form 20D) directed to the sheriff of **Algoma**
   Bref de saisie-exécution de biens-fonds (formule 20D) adressé
   au shérif du/de la
   (Name of county/region in which the enforcement office is located / *Comté/région où est situé le bureau de l'exécution*)

APPENDIX 11.10—Form 20P   Continued

FORM / *FORMULE* **20P**   **PAGE 2**   **2000**

Claim No. / *N° de la demande*

☐ Notice of Garnishment (Form 20E)/Notice of Renewal of Garnishment (Form 20E.1).
Avis de saisie-arrêt (formule 20E)/Avis de renouvellement de la saisie-arrêt (formule 20E.1).

I believe that the garnishee
Je crois que le tiers saisi

(Name of garnishee / *Nom du tiers saisi*)

at
à/au

(Address of garnishee / *Adresse du tiers saisi*)

is indebted to the debtor or will become indebted to the debtor for the following reasons:
est ou sera redevable d'une dette au débiteur pour les motifs suivants :

The Notice will be served on the debtor
L'avis sera signifié au débiteur,

(Name of debtor / *Nom du débiteur/de la débitrice*)

at
à/au

(Address of debtor for service / *Adresse du débiteur/de la débitrice aux fins de signification*)

within five days of serving it on the garnishee.
dans les cinq jours qui suivent sa signification au tiers saisi.

☐ Notice of Examination (Form 20H).
Avis d'interrogatoire (formule 20H).

☐ Writ of Delivery (Form 20B).
Bref de délaissement (formule 20B).

☐ Other *(Set out the nature of your request)*:
Autre (Indiquez la nature de votre demande) :

Complete this section if you are requesting a Writ of Delivery.
Remplissez la présente section si vous demandez un bref de délaissement.

2. An order for the delivery of the following personal property:
Une ordonnance de délaissement des biens meubles suivants :
(According to the court order, set out a description of the property to be delivered. Identify any marks or serial numbers. / Selon l'ordonnance du
tribunal, donnez la description des biens qui doivent être restitués. Indiquez toute marque d'identification ou tout numéro de série y figurant.)

APPENDIX 11.10—Form 20P   Continued

FORM / *FORMULE* 20P   PAGE 3   <u>2000</u>

Claim No. / *N° de la demande*

was made in this action against:
a été rendue dans l'action contre :   (Name of person against whom the order was made / *Nom de la personne contre qui l'ordonnance a été rendue*)

on _____ , 20 ____ , in the _____
le   *à la Cour des petites*   (Name of court location where order was made / *Emplacement*
                                  créances de   *du tribunal où l'ordonnance a été rendue*)

Small Claims Court. Since the above listed personal property has not been delivered, I make this affidavit in support of a request that the clerk of the court issue a Writ of Delivery (Form 20B) to the bailiff of the
Étant donné que les biens meubles susmentionnés n'ont pas été restitués, je fais le présent affidavit à l'appui d'une demande visant à enjoindre au greffier du tribunal de délivrer un bref de délaissement (formule 20B) à l'huissier de la Cour des petites créances de

_____   Small Claims Court.
(Name of court location / *Emplacement du tribunal*)

Complete this section if you are requesting a Certificate of Judgment, Writ of Seizure and Sale of Personal Property, Writ of Seizure and Sale of Land, Notice of Garnishment, Notice of Renewal of Garnishment or Notice of Examination.
Remplissez la présente section si vous demandez un certificat de jugement, un bref de saisie-exécution de biens meubles, un bref de saisie-exécution de biens-fonds, un avis de saisie-arrêt, un avis de renouvellement de la saisie-arrêt ou un avis d'interrogatoire.

3. A judgment was made in this action against <u>Christine Michaeli</u>
    Un jugement a été rendu dans l'action contre   (Name of debtor(s) / *Nom du/de la/des débiteur(s)/débitrice(s)*)

    on <u>March 20</u>_____ , 20 <u>--</u> in the
    le   *à la Cour des petites créances de*

    <u>Thunder Bay</u>_____   Small Claims Court
    (Name of court where judgment was made / *Nom du tribunal où le jugement a été rendu*)

    for the following sums:
    à l'égard des sommes suivantes :

    (A) **DEBT** $ _____ 8,000.00
         LA CRÉANCE $

    (B) **PRE-JUDGMENT INTEREST** calculated
         LES INTÉRÊTS ANTÉRIEURS AU JUGEMENT *calculés*

         on the sum of $ _____ 8,000.00   at the rate of <u>2.5</u>   %
         sur la somme de $ *au taux de*   *pour cent*

         per annum from <u>February 28</u> , 20 <u>--</u> to <u>March 20</u>_____ , 20 <u>--</u> ,
         par an du   *au*

         being <u>385</u>_____ days. $ _____ 210.96
         soit   *jours.* $

                              SUBTOTAL (Amount of Judgment) $ 8,210.96
                              TOTAL PARTIEL *(montant du jugement)* $

    (C) **COSTS** to date of judgment $ _____ 359.00
         LES DÉPENS *à la date du jugement* $

APPENDIX 11.10—Form 20P   Concluded

FORM / *FORMULE* 20P   PAGE 4   **2000**
Claim No. / *N° de la demande*

(D) **TOTAL AMOUNT OF PAYMENTS RECEIVED FROM DEBTOR**
after judgment (if any)   (minus) $ _____ 0
LE MONTANT TOTAL DES PAIEMENTS REÇUS DU   *(moins)* $
DÉBITEUR après le jugement (le cas échéant)

(E) **POST-JUDGMENT INTEREST** to date calculated
LES INTÉRÊTS POSTÉRIEURS AU JUGEMENT à ce jour, calculés

on the sum of $ _____8,569.96_____ at the rate of _2.0____ %
sur la somme de $ *au taux de*   *pour cent*

per annum from **March 20** ___, 20 -- to **July 15** _____, 20 -- ,
par an du   *au*

being **117** _____ days. $ _____54.94
soit   *jours.* $

> **NOTE:** Calculation of interest is always on the amount owing from time to time as payments are received. This is true for both pre-judgment and post-judgment interest. Attach a separate sheet setting out how you calculated the total amount of any pre/post-judgment interest.
> *REMARQUE : Les intérêts doivent toujours être calculés sur la somme due. Le calcul doit tenir compte des paiements reçus de temps à autre. Ceci s'applique autant aux intérêts antérieurs au jugement qu'aux intérêts postérieurs au jugement. Annexez une feuille distincte indiquant comment vous avez calculé le montant total des intérêts antérieurs et postérieurs au jugement.*

(F) **SUBSEQUENT COSTS** incurred after judgment (including the cost of issuing
the requested enforcement(s)) $ _____89.00
LES DÉPENS SUBSÉQUENTS engagés après le jugement (y compris le $
coût de la délivrance de la ou des mesures d'exécution forcée demandées)

TOTAL DUE $ 8,713.90
SOLDE DÛ $

Sworn/Affirmed before me at **Thunder Bay**
Déclaré sous serment/Affirmé   (Municipality / *municipalité*)
solennellement devant moi à

in **Ontario**
en/à/au   (Province, state or country / *province, État ou pays*)

on **July 15** _____ , 20 -- _____
le   Commissioner for taking affidavits
                                                       Commissaire aux affidavits
                                         (Type or print name below if signature is illegible.)
                                         (Dactylographiez le nom ou écrivez-le en caractères
                                         d'imprimerie ci-dessous si la signature est illisible.)

Signature
(This form is to be signed in front of a lawyer, justice of the peace, notary public or commissioner for taking affidavits.)
(La présente formule doit être signée en présence d'un avocat, d'un juge de paix, d'un notaire ou d'un commissaire aux affidavits.)

WARNING:	**IT IS AN OFFENCE UNDER THE *CRIMINAL CODE* TO KNOWINGLY SWEAR OR AFFIRM A FALSE AFFIDAVIT.**
AVERTISSEMENT :	*FAIRE SCIEMMENT UN FAUX AFFIDAVIT CONSTITUE UNE INFRACTION AU CODE CRIMINEL.*

SCR 20.04-10-20P (June 1, 2009 / *1er juin 2009*) CSD

APPENDIX 11.11   Notice of Garnishment (Form 20E), Affidavit for Enforcement Request (Form 20P), and Garnishee's Statement (Form 20F)

ONTARIO

Superior Court of Justice
Cour supérieure de justice

Notice of Garnishment
Avis de saisie-arrêt

Form / *Formule* 20E Ont. Reg. No. / *Règl. de l'Ont.* : 258/98

(Seal / *Sceau*)

Sault Ste. Marie
Small Claims Court / *Cour des petites créances de*
426 Queen Street East
Sault Ste. Marie, Ontario
P6A 6W2
Address / *Adresse*

705 945 8000
Phone number / *Numéro de téléphone*

2000
Claim No. / *N° de la demande*

Creditor / *Créancier*

Last name, or name of company / *Nom de famille ou nom de la compagnie* **Flood**		
First name / *Premier prénom* **Emma**	Second name / *Deuxième prénom*	Also known as / *Également connu(e) sous le nom de*
Address (street number, apt., unit) / *Adresse (numéro et rue, app., unité)* **53 Edward Street**		
City/Town / *Cité/ville* **Thunder Bay**	Province **Ontario**	Phone no. / *N° de téléphone* **807 555 3333**
Postal code / *Code postal* **P2B 1J3**		Fax no. / *N° de télécopieur*
Representative / *Représentant(e)*		LSUC # / *N° du BHC*
Address (street number, apt., unit) / *Adresse (numéro et rue, app., unité)*		
City/Town / *Cité/ville*	Province	Phone no. / *N° de téléphone*
Postal code / *Code postal*		Fax no. / *N° de télécopieur*

Debtor / *Débiteur*

Last name, or name of company / *Nom de famille ou nom de la compagnie* **Michaeli**		
First name / *Premier prénom* **Christine**	Second name / *Deuxième prénom*	Also known as / *Également connu(e) sous le nom de*
Address (street number, apt., unit) / *Adresse (numéro et rue, app., unité)* **55A Tranquillity Boulevard**		
City/Town / *Cité/ville* **Sault Ste. Marie**	Province **Ontario**	Phone no. / *N° de téléphone* **705 333 5555**
Postal code / *Code postal* **P6S 1C5**		Fax no. / *N° de télécopieur*

Garnishee / *Tiers saisi*

Last name, or name of company / *Nom de famille ou nom de la compagnie* **Anton's Hot Yoga and Meditation Centre**		
First name / *Premier prénom*	Second name / *Deuxième prénom*	Also known as / *Également connu(e) sous le nom de*
Address (street number, apt., unit) / *Adresse (numéro et rue, app., unité)* **77 Spirit Road North**		
City/Town / *Cité/ville* **Sault Ste. Marie**	Province **Ontario**	Phone no. / *N° de téléphone* **705 333 5544**
Postal code / *Code postal* **P0S 1Z2**		Fax no. / *N° de télécopieur*

NOTE: **THE CREDITOR SHALL SERVE THIS NOTICE** on the debtor with an Affidavit for Enforcement Request (Form 20P) and serve on the garnishee this notice with a blank Garnishee's Statement (Form 20F).

REMARQUE : *LE CRÉANCIER SIGNIFIE LE PRÉSENT AVIS au débiteur conjointement avec un affidavit en vue d'une demande d'exécution (formule 20P) et signifie au tiers saisi le présent avis avec une déclaration du tiers saisi (formule 20F) en blanc.*

SCR 20.08-20E (June 1, 2009 / *1er juin 2009*) CSD

APPENDIX 11.11—Form 20E   Continued

FORM / *FORMULE* 20E   PAGE 2   **2000**
....
.... Claim No. / *N° de la demande*

TO THE GARNISHEE:
AU TIERS SAISI :

The creditor has obtained a court order against the debtor. The creditor claims that you owe or will owe the debtor a debt in the form of wages, salary, pension payments, rent, annuity or other debt that you pay out in a lump-sum, periodically or by instalments. (A debt to the debtor includes both a debt payable to the debtor alone and a joint debt payable to the debtor and one or more co-owners.)
Le créancier a obtenu une ordonnance du tribunal contre le débiteur. Le créancier prétend que vous êtes ou serez redevable au débiteur d'une dette sous forme de salaire, de prestations de retraite, de loyer, de rente ou autre que vous payez par somme forfaitaire, périodiquement ou par versements échelonnés. (Une dette envers le débiteur comprend à la fois une dette payable au débiteur seul et une dette payable conjointement au débiteur et à un ou plusieurs autres cotitulaires de la créance.)

YOU ARE REQUIRED TO PAY to the clerk of the _____ Small Claims Court
VOUS ÊTES REQUIS(E) DE PAYER au greffier   (Garnishment issuing court / *Tribunal qui prononce la*
de la Cour des petites créances de   *saisie-arrêt*)

(a)   all debts now payable by you to the debtor, **within 10 days** after this notice is served on you; **and**
       *d'une part, toutes les dettes dont vous êtes maintenant redevable au débiteur, **dans les 10 jours** qui suivent la signification du présent avis;*

(b)   all debts that become payable by you to the debtor after this notice is served on you and **within 6 years** after this notice is issued, **within 10 days** after they become payable.
       *d'autre part, toutes les dettes dont vous deviendrez redevable au débiteur après la signification du présent avis et **dans les 6 années** qui suivent sa délivrance, **dans les 10 jours** qui suivent la date à laquelle elles deviennent exigibles.*

The total amount of all your payments to the clerk is not to exceed $ ....
La totalité des paiements que vous ferez au greffier ne doit pas dépasser   (Amount unsatisfied /   **$.**
                                                                              Montant impayé)

THIS NOTICE IS LEGALLY BINDING ON YOU until it expires or is changed, renewed, terminated or satisfied. If you do not pay the total amount or such lesser amount as you are liable to pay, you must serve a Garnishee's Statement (Form 20F) on the creditor and debtor, and file it with the clerk within 10 days after this notice is served on you.
LE PRÉSENT AVIS VOUS LIE LÉGALEMENT jusqu'à ce qu'il expire ou qu'il soit modifié, renouvelé ou résilié, ou qu'il y soit satisfait. Si vous ne payez pas le montant total ou le montant moindre dont vous êtes redevable, vous devez signifier une déclaration du tiers saisi (formule 20F) au créancier et au débiteur et la déposer auprès du greffier dans les 10 jours qui suivent la signification du présent avis.

EACH PAYMENT, payable to the Minister of Finance, MUST BE SENT with a copy of the attached garnishee's payment notice to the clerk at the above court address.
CHAQUE PAIEMENT, libellé à l'ordre du ministre des Finances, DOIT ÊTRE ENVOYÉ au greffier, à l'adresse du tribunal indiquée ci-dessus, avec une copie de l'avis de paiement du tiers saisi ci-joint.

If your debt is jointly owed to the debtor and to one or more co-owners, you must pay the debtor's appropriate share of the amount now payable, or which becomes payable, or such a percentage as the court may order.
Si votre dette est payable conjointement au débiteur et à un ou plusieurs autres cotitulaires de la créance, vous devez payer la quote-part appropriée du débiteur du montant dont vous êtes maintenant redevable, ou qui devient redevable, ou le pourcentage que le tribunal ordonne.

SCR 20.08-20E (June 1, 2009 / *1er juin 2009*) CSD   **Continued on next page /** *Suite à la page suivante*

APPENDIX 11.11—Form 20E   Continued

The amounts paid into court shall not exceed the portion of the debtor's wages that are subject to seizure or garnishment under Section 7 of the *Wages Act* (information available at: www.attorneygeneral.jus.gov.on.ca and www.e-laws.gov.on.ca). The portion of wages that can be garnished may be increased or decreased only by order of the court. If such a court order is attached to this notice or is served on you, you must follow the direction in that court order.

Les montants consignés au tribunal ne doivent pas dépasser la partie du salaire du débiteur qui peut faire l'objet d'une saisie ou d'une saisie-arrêt aux termes de l'article 7 de la Loi sur les salaires *(pour de plus amples renseignements, reportez-vous aux adresses : www.attorneygeneral.jus.gov.on.ca et www.lois-en-ligne.gouv.on.ca). La partie saisissable du salaire ne peut être augmentée ou réduite que sur ordonnance du tribunal. Si une telle ordonnance du tribunal est annexée au présent avis ou vous est signifiée, vous devez vous conformer à la directive qui y est énoncée.*

_____, 20 _____   _____
                                            (Signature of clerk / *Signature du greffier*)

CAUTION TO GARNISHEE:	**IF YOU FAIL TO PAY** to the clerk the amount set out in this notice and do not file a Garnishee's Statement (Form 20F) disputing garnishment, **JUDGMENT MAY BE OBTAINED AGAINST YOU BY THE CREDITOR** for payment of the amount set out above, plus costs. If you make a payment to anyone other than the clerk of the court, you may be liable to pay again [R. 20.08(17) and (18)].
AVERTISSEMENT AU TIERS SAISI :	*SI VOUS NE VERSEZ PAS au greffier le montant précisé dans le présent avis et ne déposez pas la déclaration du tiers saisi (formule 20F) contestant la saisie-arrêt, LE CRÉANCIER PEUT OBTENIR CONTRE VOUS UN JUGEMENT ordonnant le paiement du montant précisé ci-dessus et des dépens. Si vous effectuez un paiement à une personne qui n'est pas le greffier du tribunal, vous pouvez être tenu(e) de payer de nouveau [par. 20.08 (17) et (18)].*

NOTE:	Any party or interested person may complete and serve a Notice of Garnishment Hearing (Form 20Q) to determine any matter related to this notice. To obtain forms and self-help materials, attend the nearest Small Claims Court or access the following website: www.ontariocourtforms.on.ca.
REMARQUE :	*Toute partie ou personne intéressée peut remplir et signifier un avis d'audience sur la saisie-arrêt (formule 20Q) en vue de décider une question relative au présent avis. Vous pouvez obtenir les formules et la documentation à l'usage du client auprès de la Cour des petites créances de votre localité ou en consultant le site Web suivant : www.ontariocourtforms.on.ca.*

APPENDIX 11.11—Form 20E   Concluded

FORM / *FORMULE* **20E**   **PAGE 4**   **2000**

Claim No. / *N° de la demande*

The top portion of the garnishee's payment notice, below, is to be completed by the creditor before the Notice of Garnishment is issued. Where it is anticipated that more than one payment will be made by the garnishee, the creditor should supply extra copies of the garnishee's payment notice. Additional copies of the garnishee's payment notice are available at court offices or online at www.ontariocourtforms.on.ca (see Form 20E or 20E.1). *Le créancier doit remplir la partie supérieure de l'avis de paiement du tiers saisi figurant ci-dessous avant la délivrance de l'avis de saisie-arrêt. S'il est prévu que le tiers saisi fera plus d'un paiement, le créancier doit fournir des exemplaires supplémentaires de l'avis de paiement du tiers saisi. Vous pouvez obtenir des exemplaires supplémentaires de l'avis de paiement du tiers saisi aux greffes des tribunaux ou en ligne à l'adresse www.ontariocourtforms.on.ca (consultez la formule 20E ou 20E.1).*

GARNISHEE'S PAYMENT NOTICE / *AVIS DE PAIEMENT DU TIERS SAISI*

Make payment by cheque or money order payable to the Minister of Finance and send it, along with this payment notice to the clerk of the court at the following address:
Effectuez le paiement par chèque ou mandat-poste à l'ordre du ministre des Finances et envoyez-le, avec une copie du présent avis de paiement, au greffier du tribunal à l'adresse suivante :

Court address: ....
Adresse du tribunal :

Claim No.: ....
N° de la demande :

Creditor: ....
Créancier/créancière :

Debtor: ....
Débiteur/débitrice :

Garnishee: ....
Tiers saisi :

TO BE COMPLETED BY GARNISHEE FOR EACH PAYMENT
À REMPLIR PAR LE TIERS SAISI LORS DE CHAQUE PAIEMENT

Date of payment: .... , 20 ....
Date du paiement :

Amount enclosed: $ ....
Montant inclus : $

APPENDIX 11.11—Form 20P

ONTARIO

Superior Court of Justice
Cour supérieure de justice

Affidavit for Enforcement Request
Affidavit relatif à une demande d'exécution forcée
Form / *Formule* 20P Ont. Reg. No. / *Règl. de l'Ont.* : 258/98

Sault Ste. Marie
Small Claims Court / *Cour des petites créances de*
426 Queen Street East
Sault Ste. Marie, Ontario
P6A 6W2
Address / *Adresse*

705 945 8000
Phone number / *Numéro de téléphone*

2000
Claim No. / *N° de la demande*

BETWEEN / *ENTRE*

Emma Flood
Plaintiff(s)/Creditor(s) / *Demandeur(s)/demanderesse(s)/Créancier(s)/créancière(s)*

and / *et*

Christine Michaeli
Defendant(s)/Debtor(s) / *Défendeur(s)/défenderesse(s)/Débiteur(s)/débitrice(s)*

My name is Emma Flood
Je m'appelle
                                            (Full name / *Nom et prénoms*)

I live in Thunder Bay, Ontario
J'habite à
                                            (Municipality & province / *Municipalité et province*)

and I swear/affirm that the following is true:
et je déclare sous serment/j'affirme solennellement que les renseignements suivants sont véridiques :

1. **In this action, I am the**
   Dans la présente action, je suis le/la

   (Check one box only. / *Cochez une seule case.*)

   ☒ plaintiff/creditor.
   demandeur/demanderesse/créancier/créancière.

   ☐ representative of the plaintiff(s)/creditor(s).
   représentant(e) du/de la/des demandeur(s)/demanderesse(s)/créancier(s)/créancière(s).

   I make this affidavit in support of a request that the clerk of the court issue the following enforcement process(es):
   Je fais le présent affidavit à l'appui d'une demande visant à enjoindre au greffier du tribunal de délivrer l'acte ou les actes de procédure portant exécution forcée suivants :

   ☐ Certificate of Judgment (Form 20A) to the clerk of the
   *Certificat de jugement (formule 20A), au greffier
   de la Cour des petites créances de*

   (Name of court where the judgment is to be filed / *Nom du tribunal où le jugement doit être déposé*)

   Small Claims Court.

   ☐ Writ of Seizure and Sale of Personal Property (Form 20C) directed to the bailiff of
   Bref de saisie-exécution de biens meubles (formule 20C) adressé à l'huissier de la Cour des petites créances de

   Small Claims Court.

   (Name of court location / *Emplacement du tribunal*)

   ☐ Writ of Seizure and Sale of Land (Form 20D) directed to the sheriff of
   *Bref de saisie-exécution de biens-fonds (formule 20D) adressé
   au shérif du/de la*

   (Name of county/region in which the enforcement office is located / *Comté/région où est situé le bureau de l'exécution*)

APPENDIX 11.11—Form 20P   Continued

FORM / *FORMULE* **20P**   **PAGE 2**   **2000**

Claim No. / *N° de la demande*

☒ Notice of Garnishment (Form 20E)/Notice of Renewal of Garnishment (Form 20E.1).

Avis de saisie-arrêt (formule 20E)/Avis de renouvellement de la saisie-arrêt (formule 20E.1).

I believe that the garnishee   **Anton's Hot Yoga and Meditation Centre**

Je crois que le tiers saisi   (Name of garnishee / *Nom du tiers saisi*)

at   **77 Spirit Road North, Sault Ste. Marie, Ontario P0S 1Z2**

à/au   (Address of garnishee / *Adresse du tiers saisi*)

is indebted to the debtor or will become indebted to the debtor for the following reasons:

est ou sera redevable d'une dette au débiteur pour les motifs suivants :

Wages

The Notice will be served on the debtor   **Christine Michaeli**

L'avis sera signifié au débiteur,   (Name of debtor / *Nom du débiteur/de la débitrice*)

at   **55A Tranquillity Boulevard, Sault Ste. Marie, Ontario P6S 1C5**

à/au   (Address of debtor for service / *Adresse du débiteur/de la débitrice aux fins de signification*)

within five days of serving it on the garnishee.

dans les cinq jours qui suivent sa signification au tiers saisi.

☐ Notice of Examination (Form 20H).

Avis d'interrogatoire (formule 20H).

☐ Writ of Delivery (Form 20B).

Bref de délaissement (formule 20B).

☐ Other *(Set out the nature of your request):*

Autre (Indiquez la nature de votre demande) :

Complete this section if you are requesting a Writ of Delivery.
Remplissez la présente section si vous demandez un bref de délaissement.

2. An order for the delivery of the following personal property:

Une ordonnance de délaissement des biens meubles suivants :

(According to the court order, set out a description of the property to be delivered. Identify any marks or serial numbers. / Selon l'ordonnance du tribunal, donnez la description des biens qui doivent être restitués. Indiquez toute marque d'identification ou tout numéro de série y figurant.*)*

SCR 20.04-10-20P (June 1, 2009 / *1er juin 2009*) CSD   **Continued on next page /** *Suite à la page suivante*

APPENDIX 11.11—Form 20P   Continued

FORM / *FORMULE* 20P	PAGE 3	**2000**
		Claim No. / *N° de la demande*

was made in this action against:
a été rendue dans l'action contre :   (Name of person against whom the order was made / *Nom de la personne contre qui l'ordonnance a été rendue*)

on _____, 20 _____, in the _____
le   à *la Cour des petites*   (Name of court location where order was made / *Emplacement créances de*   *du tribunal où l'ordonnance a été rendue*)

Small Claims Court. Since the above listed personal property has not been delivered, I make this affidavit in support of a request that the clerk of the court issue a Writ of Delivery (Form 20B) to the bailiff of the
Étant donné que les biens meubles susmentionnés n'ont pas été restitués, je fais le présent affidavit à l'appui d'une demande visant à enjoindre au greffier du tribunal de délivrer un bref de délaissement (formule 20B) à l'huissier de la Cour des petites créances de

_____ Small Claims Court.

(Name of court location / *Emplacement du tribunal*)

Complete this section if you are requesting a Certificate of Judgment, Writ of Seizure and Sale of Personal Property, Writ of Seizure and Sale of Land, Notice of Garnishment, Notice of Renewal of Garnishment or Notice of Examination.
Remplissez la présente section si vous demandez un certificat de jugement, un bref de saisie-exécution de biens meubles, un bref de saisie-exécution de biens-fonds, un avis de saisie-arrêt, un avis de renouvellement de la saisie-arrêt ou un avis d'interrogatoire.

3. A judgment was made in this action against **Christine Michaeli**
Un jugement a été rendu dans l'action contre   (Name of debtor(s) / *Nom du/de la/des débiteur(s)/débitrice(s)*)

on **March 20** _____, 20 **--** in the
le   à *la Cour des petites créances de*

Thunder Bay _____ Small Claims Court

(Name of court where judgment was made / *Nom du tribunal où le jugement a été rendu*)

for the following sums:
à l'égard des sommes suivantes :

(A) **DEBT** $ _____ 8,000.00
LA CRÉANCE $

(B) **PRE-JUDGMENT INTEREST** calculated
LES INTÉRÊTS ANTÉRIEURS AU JUGEMENT *calculés*

on the sum of $ _____ 8,000.00   at the rate of **2.5**   %
sur la somme de $ *au taux de*   *pour cent*

per annum from **February 28** , 20 **--** to **March 20** , 20 **--** ,
par an du   *au*

being **385** _____ days. $ _____ 210.96
soit   *jours.* $

SUBTOTAL (Amount of Judgment) $ _____ 8,210.96
TOTAL PARTIEL (montant du jugement) $

(C) **COSTS** to date of judgment $ _____ 359.00
LES DÉPENS *à la date du jugement* $

APPENDIX 11.11—Form 20P   Concluded

FORM / *FORMULE* **20P**   **PAGE 4**   **2000**

Claim No. / *N° de la demande*

(D) **TOTAL AMOUNT OF PAYMENTS RECEIVED FROM DEBTOR**
after judgment (if any)   (minus) $ 0
LE MONTANT TOTAL DES PAIEMENTS REÇUS DU   *(moins)* $
DÉBITEUR après le jugement (le cas échéant)

(E) **POST-JUDGMENT INTEREST** to date calculated
LES INTÉRÊTS POSTÉRIEURS AU JUGEMENT à ce jour, calculés

on the sum of $ 8,569.96   at the rate of **2.0**   %
sur la somme de $ *au taux de*   *pour cent*

per annum from **March 20**   , 20 **--** to **August 5**   , 20 **--** ,
par an du   *au*

being **138**   days. $ 64.80
soit   *jours.* $

> **NOTE:** Calculation of interest is always on the amount owing from time to time as payments are received. This is true for both pre-judgment and post-judgment interest. Attach a separate sheet setting out how you calculated the total amount of any pre/post-judgment interest.
> **REMARQUE :** *Les intérêts doivent toujours être calculés sur la somme due. Le calcul doit tenir compte des paiements reçus de temps à autre. Ceci s'applique autant aux intérêts antérieurs au jugement qu'aux intérêts postérieurs au jugement. Annexez une feuille distincte indiquant comment vous avez calculé le montant total des intérêts antérieurs et postérieurs au jugement.*

(F) **SUBSEQUENT COSTS** incurred after judgment (including the cost of issuing
the requested enforcement(s)) $ 189.00
LES DÉPENS SUBSÉQUENTS engagés après le jugement (y compris le $
coût de la délivrance de la ou des mesures d'exécution forcée demandées)

TOTAL DUE $ 8,823.76
SOLDE DÛ $

Sworn/Affirmed before me at **Thunder Bay**
Déclaré sous serment/Affirmé   (Municipality / *municipalité*)
solennellement devant moi à

in **Ontario**
en/à/au   (Province, state or country / *province, État ou pays*)

on **August 5**   , 20 **--**
le
                                        Commissioner for taking affidavits
                                        Commissaire aux affidavits
                                        (Type or print name below if signature is illegible.)
                                        (Dactylographiez le nom ou écrivez-le en caractères
                                        d'imprimerie ci-dessous si la signature est illisible.)

Signature
(This form is to be signed in front of a
lawyer, justice of the peace, notary public
or commissioner for taking affidavits.)
(La présente formule doit être signée en
présence d'un avocat, d'un juge de paix, d'un
notaire ou d'un commissaire aux affidavits.)

> **WARNING:**   **IT IS AN OFFENCE UNDER THE** *CRIMINAL CODE* **TO KNOWINGLY SWEAR OR AFFIRM A FALSE AFFIDAVIT.**
> *AVERTISSEMENT :* *FAIRE SCIEMMENT UN FAUX AFFIDAVIT CONSTITUE UNE INFRACTION AU* CODE *CRIMINEL.*

APPENDIX 11.11—Form 20F

ONTARIO
Superior Court of Justice
Cour supérieure de justice

Garnishee's Statement
Déclaration du tiers saisi
Form / *Formule* 20F Ont. Reg. No. / *Règl. de l'Ont.* : 258/98

Sault Ste. Marie
Small Claims Court / *Cour des petites créances de*
426 Queen Street East
Sault Ste. Marie, Ontario
P6A 6W2
Address / *Adresse*

705 945 8000
Phone number / *Numéro de téléphone*

2000
Claim No. / *N° de la demande*

BETWEEN / *ENTRE*

Emma Flood

Creditor(s) / *Créancier(s)/créancière(s)*

and / *et*

Christine Michaeli

Debtor(s) / *Débiteur(s)/débitrice(s)*

A Notice of Garnishment was issued on _____ , 20 _____ , naming me/us as garnishee.
Un avis de saisie-arrêt a été délivré le , *me/nous désignant comme tiers saisi(s).*

☐ **I/WE DO NOT OWE** and do not expect to owe to the debtor the amount set out in the Notice of Garnishment
for the following reason(s):
JE NE SUIS/NOUS NE SOMMES PAS REDEVABLE(S) et je ne m'attends/nous ne nous attendons pas à être redevable(s) au débiteur du montant énoncé dans l'avis de saisie-arrêt pour le ou les motifs suivants :

☐ **I/WE OWE OR WILL OWE** the debtor (or the debtor and one or more co-owners), wages or periodic
payments based on the terms explained below:
JE SUIS OU SERAI/NOUS SOMMES OU SERONS REDEVABLE(S) au débiteur (ou au débiteur et à un ou plusieurs autres cotitulaires de la créance) des montants suivants exigibles à titre de salaire ou de versements périodiques et selon les modalités suivantes :
(State the amount(s) and how often the debtor is paid. If the debtor is paid wages, state the gross amount of the debtor's wages before any deductions required by law and the net amount after those deductions, and attach a copy of a pay slip. If you owe or will owe the debtor a lump sum, state when and how much will be paid.)
(Indiquez le ou les montants et la fréquence des paiements faits au débiteur. Si le débiteur touche un salaire, indiquez son salaire brut avant les retenues que vous êtes tenu(e)(s) de déduire, selon la loi, ainsi que le montant net après les retenues, et annexez une copie d'un bordereau de paie. Si vous êtes ou serez redevable(s) d'une somme forfaitaire au débiteur, indiquez-en le montant et à quel moment le paiement sera effectué.)

☐ **I/We are making payment of less than** the amount stated because the debt is owed to the debtor and to
one or more co-owners, or for another reason explained below:
J'effectue/Nous effectuons un paiement inférieur au montant indiqué parce qu'il s'agit d'une dette envers le débiteur et envers un ou plusieurs autres cotitulaires de la créance, ou pour un autre motif indiqué ci-dessous :

(Identify the amount(s) and percentage owed to the debtor and each co-owner / *Précisez le ou les montants et le pourcentage redevable au débiteur et à chaque autre cotitulaire de la créance*)

APPENDIX 11.11—Form 20F Concluded

FORM / *FORMULE* **20F**   PAGE 2   _____ 2000

Claim No. / *N° de la demande*

Co-owner(s) of the debt: _____
Cotitulaire(s) de la créance :   (Full legal name(s) / *Nom et prénoms officiels*)

_____
(Address (street & number, unit, municipality, province) / *Adresse (numéro et rue, unité, municipalité, province))*

☐ **I/We are not making a payment at this time or are making a payment of less than the amount stated** because I/we have been served with other notice(s) of garnishment against the debtor. (Provide details below.)
Je n'effectue/Nous n'effectuons aucun paiement présentement ou j'effectue/nous effectuons un paiement inférieur au montant indiqué parce que j'ai/nous avons reçu signification d'un ou de plusieurs autres avis de saisie-arrêt contre le débiteur. (Donnez-en les détails ci-dessous.)

Name of creditor *Nom du créancier*	Name of issuing court *Nom du tribunal délivreur*	Location of court or Sheriff's Office where payment is currently being made *Emplacement du tribunal ou bureau du shérif où le paiement est actuellement effectué*	Date Notice of Garnishment received *Date de réception de l'avis de saisie-arrêt*

☐ **I/We will dispute the garnishment** by completing and serving a Notice of Garnishment Hearing (Form 20Q) on the creditor, debtor and co-owner(s) of the debt (if any) and any other interested person, and filing it with the clerk of the court.
Je contesterai/Nous contesterons la saisie-arrêt en remplissant et en signifiant un avis d'audience sur la saisie-arrêt (formule 20Q) au créancier, au débiteur et au(x) cotitulaire(s) de la créance (le cas échéant) et à tout autre intéressé et en le déposant auprès du greffier du tribunal.

_____, 20 _____   _____

(Signature of garnishee or representative / *Signature du tiers saisi ou du/de la représentant(e))*

_____

(Full legal name of garnishee / *Nom et prénoms officiels du tiers saisi)*

_____

(Address, phone and fax number of garnishee or representative / *Adresse, numéro de téléphone et de télécopieur du tiers saisi ou du/de la représentant(e))*

NOTE TO GARNISHEE: ***REMARQUE AU TIERS SAISI :***	The garnishee must serve a copy of the Garnishee's Statement on the creditor and the debtor and file it with the court. You can get an electronic version of this form online at <u>www.ontariocourtforms.on.ca</u>. *Le tiers saisi doit signifier une copie de la déclaration du tiers saisi au créancier et au débiteur et la déposer auprès du tribunal. Vous pouvez obtenir une version électronique de la présente formule en ligne à l'adresse <u>www.ontariocourtforms.on.ca</u>.*

NOTE TO CREDITOR: ***REMARQUE AU CRÉANCIER :***	A creditor who is served with a Garnishee's Statement must send it to the co-owners of the debt, if any, together with a Notice to Co-owner of Debt (Form 20G). You can get forms at court offices or online at <u>www.ontariocourtforms.on.ca</u>. *Le créancier qui reçoit signification de la déclaration du tiers saisi doit la faire parvenir aux cotitulaires de la créance, le cas échéant, avec l'avis au cotitulaire d'une créance (formule 20G). Vous pouvez obtenir des formules aux greffes des tribunaux ou en ligne à l'adresse <u>www.ontariocourtforms.on.ca</u>.*

APPENDIX

Small Claims Court Timelines

Procedural Step	Time Period	Start Date	Authority
Issue plaintiff's claim	2 years	The day the claim is discovered	*Limitations Act, 2002*, SO 2002, c. 24, sched. B, as amended, s. 4
		"Claim" is defined as "a claim to remedy an injury, loss or damage that occurred as a result of an act or omission."	*Limitations Act, 2002*, s. 1
Serve plaintiff's claim	6 months	The day the claim is issued	*Rules of the Small Claims Court* (RSCC), O. Reg. 258/98, Rule 8.01(2)
	Court may extend time for service before or after 6-month period ends		
File defence to plaintiff's claim or defendant's claim	Personal service: 20 days	The day personal service takes place	RSCC, Rule 9.01(1)
	Alternative to personal service: Depends on method of service	The day service is effective	
	Substituted service: By court order	By court order	RSCC, Rule 8.04
Issue defendant's claim	20 days	The day the defence is filed	RSCC, Rule 10.01(2)(a)
	After the 20-day period has expired but before trial or default judgment, with leave of the court	By court order	RSCC, Rule 10.01(2)(b)
File defence to defendant's claim	20 days	The day service of defendant's claim becomes effective	RSCC, Rule 10.03

Small Claims Court Timelines (concluded)

Procedural Step	Time Period	Start Date	Authority
File defence to plaintiff's claim—third party added by defendant's claim	20 days	The day service of defendant's claim becomes effective	RSCC, Rule 10.03
Default proceedings	Noting in default: Immediately after the time for filing a defence has expired, if no defence to a plaintiff's claim or a defendant's claim has been filed.		RSCC, Rule 11.01(1)
	Default judgment: In a plaintiff's claim for a debt or liquidated amount, if a defendant has been noted in default, the clerk may sign default judgment for all or part of the amount claimed, plus interest if claimed.		RSCC, Rule 11.02(1)
Settlement conference **Note:** This date is set by the clerk	90 days	The day the first defence is filed	RSCC, Rule 13.01(3)
Offer to settle	May be made any time up until the court makes a final disposition of the matter. May be accepted any time up until the offer is withdrawn or expires, or the court makes a final disposition of the matter.		RSCC, Rule 14.03
Request a trial date	ASAP by plaintiff upon receipt of notice from the clerk stating that a party must request a trial date if the matter does not settle within 30 days after the settlement conference.		RSCC, Rule 13.07
Motion for new trial	30 days	The day the final order is made	RSCC, Rule 17.04
Appeal to Divisional Court **Note:** The Divisional Court is the appeals branch of the Superior Court of Justice	30 days	The day the order appealed from is made, unless a statute or the *Rules of Civil Procedure* provide otherwise	*Courts of Justice Act,* RSO 1990, c. C.43, s. 31 *Rules of Civil Procedure,* RRO 1990, Reg. 194, Rule 61.04(1)
	At present, paralegals are not allowed to appear on appeals to the Divisional Court. However, if your client indicates that she wishes to appeal an order, you should advise her of the 30-day window and tell her to seek the services of a lawyer. You may wish to direct her to the Lawyer Referral Service (1-800-268-8326 or 416-947-3330 (within the GTA)).		

Glossary

action
a proceeding brought in a court

action splitting
dividing an action into two or more actions in order to bring it within the Small Claims Court monetary jurisdiction

adjournment
putting a court procedure, such as a motion, settlement conference, or trial, off to a later date

admission
a voluntary acknowledgement by a party that an allegation of fact made by another party is true—in other words, that the allegation is not in dispute

affidavit
a written statement of facts that is confirmed under oath or by affirmation by the person making the affidavit

allegation
an assertion made in a pleading by a party to an action, setting out what she hopes to prove

alternative to personal service
alternative method of delivery of a legal document to another party in a proceeding; may be used when the party being served has a lawyer with instructions to accept service of documents or when personal service has been attempted and has failed

amend
to change or correct a pleading, with the object of improving it or making it more complete

appeal as of right
an automatic right to appeal, without first seeking permission to do so from the appeal court

assessment of damages
a determination of the money damages owed to the plaintiff by the defaulting defendant(s); may be done by a motion in writing or by an assessment hearing

assessment order
an assessment order is an order made by a judge on a motion in writing for an assessment of damages in an unliquidated claim where all defendants have been noted in default

assign
to transfer a legal right or entitlement (including wages owed or the money in a bank account) to another person

assignee
a person to whom something is transferred

attorney
person authorized to act pursuant to a power of attorney

balance of convenience
a common law test; a court applying this test will balance the prejudice to one party of denying the relief asked for, against the prejudice to the opposing party if the relief is granted

binding authority
a judicial decision by a higher court that must be followed by lower courts (also known as binding precedent)

candid
forthright and sincere, able to look at both sides of an issue without bias

casual client
a client who consults you regarding a legal issue, but then decides not to proceed, or not to hire you to act as his legal representative

cause of action

the factual and legal grounds for seeking a remedy from a court

chattel mortgage

a loan that is secured against personal property; in Ontario, such security interests are registered under the *Personal Property Security Act*

chattel mortgagee

one who holds a loan secured against personal property or chattels

claimant

another word for plaintiff; a claimant is anyone who commences a claim

client

a person who consults with you and hires you to represent her in a matter or a number of matters

client identification

information obtained from the client regarding who the client is and what the client does

client matter number

a unique number assigned by the paralegal firm (or the file management software) to a particular client matter in order to identify that matter for filing, docketing, and billing purposes

client verification

obtaining documentary or other confirmation that the client is who he says he is

collateral

real or personal property against which a loan is pledged

competent paralegal

a paralegal who has and applies the relevant skills, attributes, and values appropriate to each matter undertaken on behalf of a client

compromise and settlement

when a party agrees to waive some part of what is owing or make other concessions in order to resolve a matter without the additional costs, delay, and uncertainty of a court proceeding

conflict of interest

any circumstance that may negatively affect a paralegal's ability to adequately represent the client's best interests

consideration

something that causes a party to enter into a contract; sometimes, but not always, a party's expectation of profiting from or receiving a benefit from the contract

construe

to interpret

contempt

any act that obstructs or hinders the court in the administration of justice, or that shows disrespect for the court; there must be an element of deliberation for an act to amount to contempt

co-owner of debt

a person who is entitled to part of the debt payable to the debtor

costs

the expenses connected with a legal proceeding; costs include a party's legal fees, plus disbursements, or out-of-pocket expenses, including court filing fees

counsel slip

a form that must be filled out on a court appearance and given to the court clerk; it gives the court notice that there is someone appearing on the matter, and tells the court what your name is, the matter you are there on, and who your client is

creditor

a person to whom money is owed; also, a person who is entitled to enforce an order for the payment or recovery of money

date of default

the date the cause of action arose

debtor

a person who owes money to another person; also, a person against whom an order for the payment of money may be enforced

defendant

the party who defends a civil action

defendant's claim

a claim by a defendant against any party named in the plaintiff's claim, including the plaintiff or a co-defendant, or against a third party not named in the plaintiff's claim

denial

an assertion by a party that an allegation of fact made by another party is not true—in other words, that the allegation is disputed

deponent

the person who makes an affidavit

direct examination

the questions that you ask your own witnesses when they take the stand to shape the evidence into a clear, concise narrative that can be easily understood by the court

disbursements

the out-of-pocket expenses of a legal proceeding; these include court filing fees, charges for service of documents, photocopying charges, postage, etc.

discretionary

where an action is discretionary, the court may make up its own mind about a particular matter, giving due regard to all relevant factors

dispute

an argument or disagreement between two or more sides in which the interest of one side is in direct opposition to the interest of another side

docket

a list of matters to be heard on a particular day in a particular courtroom; it will be posted outside the courtroom for the date those matters are scheduled to be heard

due diligence

exercising the prudence and vigilance that a reasonable and prudent paralegal would exercise in similar circumstances

duress

threatening someone or otherwise forcing her to agree to something she would not have agreed to without the threat or use of force

effect service

carry out or perform valid service of a document

encumber

to mortgage or place a lien or other security interest against property

encumbrances

outstanding loans or mortgages against property

encumbrancer

the person holding the lien or security interest

enforcement document

a notice to a judgment debtor of any steps taken by a judgment creditor or ordered by a court to enforce a judgment; for example, a notice of garnishment of employment income

engagement letter

confirms the terms of the paralegal–client retainer, but is not signed back by the client

equitable relief

remedies other than money damages; for example, an order compelling a person to do something (specific performance) or to stop doing something (injunction)

ex parte **motion**

a motion made without notice to other parties

execution of an order

enforcement of a court order by seizing a debtor's income, or by seizing and selling her assets

exhibit

an original document that is material to an issue in the action; it must be identified by a witness with personal knowledge of its contents, which may be referred to in her spoken evidence; it is then marked as an exhibit by the court clerk and placed in the court file as part of the evidence

exigible assets

assets that can be seized or garnished

expert witness

a witness who, because of education and/or specialization, has knowledge about an issue or issues in the action that the trial judge or other trier of fact does not have; the expert witness's evidence must be helpful to the court and necessary to a proper determination of the issue(s) about which the expert witness gives an opinion

express consent

also known as explicit consent, written authorization from your client to disclose particular information to specified third parties

fiduciary

a person who is required to act with scrupulous good faith, honesty, and integrity for the benefit of another person

fiduciary relationship

a relationship of absolute trust and confidence between two persons, in which one person (the fiduciary) is required to act with scrupulous good faith, honesty and integrity for the benefit of another person (the beneficiary)—in the paralegal–client relationship, the paralegal is the fiduciary and the client is the beneficiary

final reporting letter

sent to the client at the conclusion of the client matter, along with the final invoice for fees and disbursements incurred since the last interim invoice—provides a summary of the client matter, steps taken, and results achieved

finding as to credibility

where there is conflicting evidence from witnesses, a decision by the trier of fact (the judge in a non-jury trial) about whose evidence to believe, in all of the circumstances; factors to be considered are the witness's demeanour on the witness stand, knowledge of the circumstances, and relationship to the matters in question, including any issues of bias

finding of fact
a determination that an allegation made by one party to an action is true, even though that allegation is denied by another party; the finding must be based on a reasonable assessment of the evidence in the action

frequent claimant
anyone who files 10 or more claims in a Small Claims Court office on or after January 1 in any calendar year

frivolous and vexatious objection
an objection that has no legal merit and is made to annoy, harass, or embarrass the other side

funds
cash, currency, securities, negotiable instruments, or other financial instruments

garnishee
any person who owes money to the debtor; if the debtor is employed, then the employer is the garnishee, because the employer owes the debtor employment income; if the debtor has a bank account, then the bank is the garnishee, because the bank owes the debtor the money held in the bank account

garnishor
any creditor who is trying to enforce an order for payment of money by way of a garnishment

general account
a bank account used to pay for ongoing business expenses, such as salaries, rent, client disbursements that have not been billed, etc.

general damages
damages for pain and suffering caused by the injury or harm, and for future losses and expenses, such as future care costs and loss of future income; general damages cannot be quantified precisely, but they must be itemized and explained to the extent that it is possible to do so

harass a witness
engage in conduct that is coercive or threatening toward a witness at any stage of a proceeding

hearsay rule
a witness is not allowed to repeat in court what they were told by a third party, if the reason for putting the evidence in is to prove the truth of the contents of the third-party statement

implied consent
unwritten consent to disclose confidential information because it is required by the professional relationship (e.g., disclosure to employees) or because the matter requires it

(e.g., disclosure in pleadings and other documents filed with the court)

informed consent
consent based on information that is sufficient to allow the client to assess the situation and make an informed decision

infrequent claimant
anyone who files fewer than 10 Small Claims Court claims in a Small Claims Court office on or after January 1 in any calendar year

inherent jurisdiction
judicial powers that are essential for the administration of justice

installment (or partial) payments
a partial payment of a sum of money owing at regular intervals over a period of time until the amount owing is paid in full

interim invoice
a bill delivered to the client before the client matter is concluded—usually sent with with an interim reporting letter

interim reporting letter
a letter sent to the client before the client matter is concluded, usually with an interim invoice—reports the steps taken in the client matter to that point, the results obtained, and the likely next steps

invitation to treat
an invitation intended to do nothing more than open up negotiations; usually does not contain essential terms, such as a fixed amount of money to be paid, terms of payment, etc.

joint and several liability
form of liability where each partner is liable for any amount up to the full amount of any judgment obtained against the partnership

judgment debtor
any person who owes money to another pursuant to a court order

judgment-proof
having no income or assets against which a judgment may be enforced

judicial notice
matters of common knowledge (also referred to as "notorious facts") that a judge may accept as true without hearing

evidence and without inquiry—lesser known facts (for example, matters that can be checked in a standard reference work and are not easily disputed) may be judicially noticed after inquiry

jurisdiction
a court's area of legal authority; in Ontario, jurisdiction is established by the *Courts of Justice Act* and by the common law

justice
a justice is the same thing as a judge; "justice," "judge," and "court" are often used interchangeably in reported decisions

lawyer
a person who has been called to the Bar of Ontario and who is licensed to practise law in Ontario

leading question
a question that implies the existence of certain facts or suggests a correct answer to a witness (or to the trier of fact); the general rule is that leading questions may be used only in cross-examination of a witness

leave of the court
permission from the court, by way of a court order, to do something; usually obtained on motion by a party

legal fees
fees charged by a lawyer or paralegal for legal representation and advice

liberal construction
means that, when applying the Rules, the court goes beyond the exact meaning of the language in order to implement the principles behind the Rules

liberally construed
interpreting the Rules without undue emphasis on strict compliance with all procedural requirements and technicalities, with a view to bringing about a resolution that is just and fair to all parties within a reasonable time

liquidated claim
claim for a debt or fixed amount of money that does not require valuation by a court

liquidated damages
a specific amount of money that may be established by unpaid invoices, NSF cheques, or other documentation proving a debt or fixed amount

litigant
a party to a civil action; someone engaged in civil litigation

litigation guardian
a competent person who undertakes to direct a legal proceeding on behalf of a person under disability

lump sum payment
payment of the entire amount owing in a single payment, as opposed to payment in installments

mandatory
where an action is mandatory, the court must do something if certain preconditions exist; the court has no choice

material evidence
evidence that has a logical connection to an issue or issues in dispute in the action; evidence that will assist the trier of fact to make a determination about whose allegations to believe

merits of the case
the legal principles upon which a party's assertion of rights is based

misrepresentation
an inaccurate, untrue, or incomplete version of the facts; in contract law, an inaccurate or incomplete description of the terms of the agreement, with the result that the person signing does not have a real understanding of what he is signing

mixed trust account
a trust bank account into which money from many different clients will be deposited and held in trust, until such time as invoices are rendered on their files or you are directed to pay out the money by the client to whom the money belongs

monetary jurisdiction
the amount of money that the court may order one party to pay another, not including interest and costs

money retainer
money paid to you by the client on account of future legal services and/or disbursements to be incurred; it is a deposit to secure your legal services

mortgagee
the person who holds a mortgage

mortgagor
the person who receives a mortgage

motion
an application to a court or a judge for the purpose of obtaining an order directing that some kind of relief be granted to the party making the motion

motioning the other party to death
using motions to delay the action, add to the costs of other parties, or otherwise abuse the process of the court

moving party
the party in a proceeding who makes a motion

negotiable instrument
an unconditional order or promise to pay an amount of money, which can be transferred—for example, cheques or banknotes (paper money)

net wages
wages subject to garnishment under the *Wages Act*; the amount of a person's wages left after all lawful deductions (*Wages Act*, s. 7(1))

non-engagement letter
a letter confirming that the paralegal has declined to accept the retainer, or that the client has declined to retain the paralegal

non-exigible assets
assets that cannot be seized or garnished

notice
service of documents on other parties to make them aware of an intended procedural step or other matter

notice period
the minimum period of time for serving documents on other parties before a procedural step takes place

numbered company
a corporation that uses its registration number as its corporate name—for example, 123456 Ontario Limited

objection
an argument by a party that a particular piece of evidence, line of questioning, or other matter is improper or illegal and should not be allowed by the court

offer
in the context of contracts, an offer containing all essential terms; if accepted, a binding contract is the result

open-ended, or direct, question
a question that lets the witness give his own answer without prompting; a question that does not contain any language suggesting a "correct" answer to the witness

opinion evidence
in the case of an expert witness, testimony of what the expert witness thinks, believes, or infers with regard to facts in dispute

order excluding witnesses
an order that all witnesses except the parties themselves shall leave the courtroom and wait outside the courtroom until they are called to give evidence; the purpose of an order excluding witnesses is to prevent witnesses who have not yet taken the stand from hearing, and being influenced by, the evidence of the witnesses who take the stand ahead of them; required only when there are witnesses other than the parties giving evidence; if the plaintiff and the defendant are the only witnesses, an order excluding witnesses is not required

order for substituted service
a court order permitting the plaintiff to serve the claim in a manner that is not set out in the Rules

original court
the court where the judgment is made

originating court
the court where the judgment is made

originating process
the document that commences an action

paralegal
a non-lawyer who is not an articling student and who is licensed to provide legal services in permitted areas of practice to clients for a fee in the province of Ontario

paralegal–client retainer
the terms of the contractual arrangement between the paralegal and the client, including but not limited to the scope of the legal services to be provided, fees, billing practices, and the amount of the money retainer

partnership
a business that is owned by two or more persons; in most partnerships, the partners are jointly and severally liable for its debts and liabilities

partnership agreement
a contract that allocates liability among the partners, and specifies other terms and conditions of the partnership; binding only on the parties to the agreement

party
a person who commences or defends an action or proceeding

party under disability
in Small Claims Court, a person or party who is (a) a minor, (b) mentally incapable within the meaning s. 6 or 45 of the *Substitute Decisions Act, 1992*, or (c) an absentee within the meaning of the *Absentees Act*

payment into court
money paid to the accountant of the Superior Court of Justice pursuant to a court order, to be paid out to creditors or other parties in accordance with a court order

payment out of court
when money paid into court is paid out by the accountant of the Superior Court of Justice, in accordance with a court order

per diem
per day [Latin]

per diem interest
the amount of interest that accrues on a daily basis

periodic payments
fixed amounts of money that must be paid at regular intervals, usually on a stated date such as the first day of each and every month

perjury
swearing or affirming a statement (including a document) that you know is not true; perjury is a criminal offence

person under disability *see* **party under disability**

personal property
property that is movable—vehicles, stocks, jewellery, furniture, etc.; also called "chattels"

personal service
personal delivery of a copy of a document (e.g., an issued plaintiff's claim) to another party in accordance with the procedures set out in Rule 8.02; the requirements for personal service vary, depending upon who the other party is (e.g., an individual, a corporation, a municipality, etc.)

plaintiff
the party who commences a civil action

plaintiff's claim
the document that sets out the names of the parties and their addresses for service, the amount of the claim, any other relief being sought, and the allegations of fact in support of the claim

pleadings
the documents filed at the commencement of a proceeding, in which the parties plead, or state, the allegations of fact on which they rely in support of their case; in a Small Claims Court proceeding, the pleadings are the plaintiff's claim, the defence, the defendant's claim, and the defence to the defendant's claim, if any

post-judgment interest
interest that accrues on the judgment amount, including costs, or on any outstanding balances, until such time as any balance owing has been paid in full

power of attorney
a document authorizing an individual to act on another person's behalf in a legal or business matter

prayer or request for relief
the first paragraph in a claim, setting out in separate subparagraphs particulars of the damages, interest, and other relief that the plaintiff thinks she is entitled to

precedent document
a legal document that is used as a template or guide for drafting subsequent documents with a similar purpose

preferred creditor
an unsecured creditor who ranks ahead of ordinary unsecured creditors in a debt collection or a bankruptcy because of priority and special rights conferred by a statute

pre-judgment interest
interest that accrues on the amount determined to be owing commencing with the date of default and ending with the date of judgment

private corporation
a corporation whose shares are not publicly traded—its incorporating documents (1) restrict the right to sell shares, (2) limit the number of its shareholders (excluding employees) to 50, and (3) prohibit public trading of its shares or securities; also called a closely held corporation

promisee
a person who receives a promise

promisor
a person who makes a promise

promissory note
a promise to pay that is signed and dated by the debtor; it should contain the following terms: the names of the payor and the debtor, the amount advanced to the debtor, and the date on which it was advanced, and the terms of the loan, including payment terms, interest rates, penalties on default, if any, etc.

prospective client
a person who consults you about a legal issue but has not yet retained you

public company

a corporation whose shares are for sale to the general public—public companies are subject to rigorous disclosure requirements under securities legislation

purging the list

the judge and the clerk go through the matters listed on the court docket, and reorder them according to whether the matter has settled, will be adjourned on consent, will be adjourned subject to argument by the parties, or is undisputed (i.e., one of the parties has not appeared); undisputed matters will be dealt with by means of a brief trial at which the party who is present may give evidence; disputed matters at which all parties have shown up will be held down until all of the above have been dealt with

qualified interpreter

a person who is trained to interpret in a courtroom environment; interpreters are not under oath when they interpret; they must provide an unbiased and accurate version of what the witness under oath is saying on the stand

quantifying damages

calculating damages—that is, determining all of the different kinds of damage or injury that a party has suffered because of another's wrongdoing, and assigning money values to the different kinds of damage, based on the evidence

quash

to declare something null and void, and of no legal force and effect

question of fact

a factual dispute; in jury trials, questions of fact are determined by the jury; in non-jury trials, questions of fact are determined by the trial judge

question of law

an issue that requires the application or interpretation of a law or legal principle; in both jury and non-jury trials, questions of law are determined by judges

real property

property that is immovable—land, houses, etc.

realize on the security

when a secured creditor seizes and sells the property pledged as security for a debt, and applies the proceeds of the sale to the balance owing on the debt

re-examination

evidence intended to clarify and, if necessary, neutralize or rebut any potentially damaging evidence brought out in cross-examination; also called "reply evidence" or "rebuttal evidence"

referee

a non-judge who is authorized by the Rules to preside at terms of payment hearings

registering court

the court in which a judgment is registered

remedy

a method of enforcing a right, or preventing or compensating for a wrong

responding party

a party who answers or responds to a motion made by another party

retainer agreement

a letter confirming services to be rendered, your fee or hourly rate, any additional charges (disbursements, etc.), and any other terms of the paralegal–client relationship; more detailed than a retainer letter, and it must be signed back to you by the client

running account

an account where a regular customer charges purchases against a standard account number on an ongoing basis; the defendant makes payments against the account from time to time (usually on a monthly basis)

secured creditor

a creditor whose loans are secured against real or personal property; if the debtor defaults in payment, the secured creditor may seize and sell the property, and pay the balance owing on the loan out of the proceeds of the sale, in accordance with the terms of the security agreement

service

delivery of a legal document to another party in a proceeding

set aside

to declare a court order or procedural step of no force and effect

signatory

someone who signs a document

sole proprietorship

a business owned and run by one person

special damages
damages that compensate the plaintiff for all losses, including out-of-pocket expenses connected with the injury or harm, up to the date of the trial; can usually be calculated fairly precisely

statement of information and belief
in a supporting affidavit on a motion, information that the deponent was told by another person or has read in a document that she did not write

statute-barred
to be prevented by the terms of a statute from commencing an action to assert your legal rights

stay of enforcement
stopping enforcement by creditors against a debtor for so long as the debtor complies with the terms of a court order

strict construction
means that the language of a rule is read and applied using its exact, technical meaning; also known as "narrow construction"

submissions
an explanation of the facts and law, designed to persuade the judge to grant the order asked for by a party

successful party
the party who succeeds, or wins, at trial; it may be the plaintiff or the defendant

such terms as are just
the court looks at the conduct of the parties, the legal issues, and the potential prejudice to the parties as a result of a particular court order, and imposes conditions and/or awards costs accordingly

summons to witness
a document compelling the attendance at trial of a person whose evidence is material to the conduct of an action

support creditor
a person to whom child or spousal support is owed by a debtor

sympathetic witness
a witness who gives evidence that supports your cause

theory of the defence
the defendant's grounds for disputing the plaintiff's claim

third party
person who is not a party to an agreement or transaction, but who may have rights or obligations with respect to the agreement or transaction, or whose presence is necessary to enable the court to adjudicate effectively on the issues in the proceeding

trier of fact
at trial, the trier of fact listens to the evidence, decides which evidence to believe and which evidence not to believe, and makes findings of fact based on those decisions; at a jury trial, the trier of fact is the jury, but there are no jury trials in Small Claims Court; at a Small Claims Court trial, the trier of fact is the trial judge

true copy
an accurate copy of an original document

unliquidated claim
claim for an indefinite amount that must be valued by the court based on the evidence

unliquidated damages
an amount that is not fixed and specified, which must be determined by the court based on the evidence

unsympathetic witness
a witness who gives evidence that supports an opposing party's cause

vary a court order
to change the terms of a court order

venue
the place where a trial is held

waive
to give up a certain legal or other right, usually in the expectation of some benefit

waive the default
a decision by a lender or creditor not to insist upon strict compliance by a debtor with the terms for payment of a debt or other obligation

waiving the excess
in a plaintiff's claim or defendant's claim, giving up the right to claim any money owing above $10,000.00 (exclusive of interest and costs), in order to bring the matter within Small Claims Court monetary jurisdiction

Index

THE USBORNE
INTERNET-LINKED
COMPLETE BOOK OF
CHESS

THE USBORNE
INTERNET-LINKED
COMPLETE BOOK OF
CHESS

Elizabeth Dalby

Designed by Adam Constantine and Ruth Russell

Consultant: Jonathan Rowson

Chess board illustrations by Verinder Bhachu
and Adam Constantine
Illustrations by Leonard Le Rolland
Digital imagery by Keith Furnival

Cover designer: Neil Francis
Managing designer: Ruth Russell
Managing editor: Judy Tatchell

Contents

Internet links

Throughout this book, we have suggested interesting Web sites where you can find out more about chess.

Web site links

To visit the sites, go to the Usborne Quicklinks Web site at **www.usborne-quicklinks.com** and type the keywords "complete chess". There you will find links to click on to take you to all the recommended sites. Here are some of the things you can do on the Web sites:

- Discover new chess tactics and tricks
- Read the latest chess news
- Find out all about the history of chess.

Chess puzzles

In Usborne Quicklinks there are also chess puzzles that you can print out to test the skills that you have learned from this book. Just go to **www.usborne-quicklinks.com** and follow the instructions there.

Online chess games

Lots of chess Web sites feature the chance to play chess online against opponents of all abilities. If you want to play chess online, you should ask permission of an adult before you do, and make sure you follow the safety guidelines given at the top of the next column.

Computer not essential

If you don't have access to the Internet, don't worry. This book is a complete, self-contained reference book on its own.

Internet safety

When using the Internet, please make sure you follow these guidelines:

- Ask your parent's or guardian's permission before you connect to the Internet.
- If you write a message in a Web site guest book or on a Web site message board, or take part in an online chess game, do not give out any personal information such as your full name, address or telephone number, and ask an adult before you give your e-mail address.
- If a Web site asks you to log in or register by typing your name or e-mail address, ask permission of an adult first.
- If you do receive an e-mail from someone you don't know, tell an adult and do not reply to the e-mail.
- Never arrange to meet anyone you talk to or play against on the Internet.

Note for parents and guardians

The Web sites described in this book are regularly reviewed and the links in Usborne Quicklinks are updated. However, the content of a Web site may change at any time and Usborne Publishing is not responsible for the content on any Web site other than its own.

We recommend that children are supervised while on the Internet, that they do not use Internet Chat Rooms, and that you use Internet filtering software to block unsuitable material.

Please ensure that your children read and follow the safety guidelines printed above. For more information, see the "Net Help" area on the Usborne Quicklinks Web site.

Using the Internet

Most of the Web sites listed in this book can be accessed with a standard home computer and a Web browser (the software that enables you to display information from the Internet). We recommend:

- A PC with Microsoft® Windows® 98 or later version, or a Macintosh computer with System 9.0 or later, and 64Mb RAM
- A browser such as Microsoft® Internet Explorer 5, or Netscape® 6, or later versions
- Connection to the Internet via a modem (preferably 56Kbps) or a faster digital or cable line
- An account with an Internet Service Provider (ISP)
- A sound card to hear sound files.

Extras

Some Web sites need additional free programs, called plug-ins, to play sounds, or to show videos, animations or 3-D images. If you visit a site and do not have a necessary plug-in, a message will come up on the screen. There is usually a button that you can click on to download the plug-in. Or, go to **www.usborne-quicklinks.com** and click on "Net Help". There you can find links to download plug-ins. Here is a list of plug-ins that you might need:

- RealPlayer® – lets you play video and hear sound files
- QuickTime – enables you to view video clips
- Flash™ – lets you play animations
- Shockwave® – lets you play animations and interactive programs.

Macintosh and QuickTime are trademarks of Apple Computer, Inc., registered in the US and other countries.
RealPlayer is a trademark of RealNetworks, Inc., registered in the US and other countries.
Flash and Shockwave are trademarks of Macromedia, Inc., registered in the US and other countries.

Site availability

The links in Usborne Quicklinks are regularly reviewed and updated, but occasionally you may get a message that a site is unavailable. This might be temporary, so try again later, or even the next day. If any of the sites close down, we will, if possible, replace them with suitable alternatives, so you will always find an up-to-date list of sites in Usborne Quicklinks.

Help

For general help and advice on using the Internet, go to Usborne Quicklinks at **www.usborne-quicklinks.com** and click on "Net Help". To find out more about how to use your Web browser, click on "Help" at the top of the browser, and then choose "Contents and Index". You'll find a searchable dictionary containing tips on how to find your way around the Internet easily.

Computer viruses

A computer virus is a program that can seriously damage your computer. A virus can get into your computer when you download programs from the Internet, or in an attachment (an extra file) that arrives with an e-mail. We strongly recommend that you buy anti-virus software to protect your computer and that you update the software regularly. For more information about viruses, go to Usborne Quicklinks and click on "Net Help".

Playing chess

The game of chess has been described as an art, a science and a sport. Almost anyone can learn how to play. Some top chess champions can earn millions – so it could be worth spending time on improving your game.

The mission

The main objective in chess is to trap your opponent's King. Don't forget – all the other moves that you make in the game should build toward this.

Stages of the game

The game has three stages:

The opening
When you try to bring all your pieces into play and develop your plan of attack. (See pages 32–43.)

Forward march!

The middlegame
When you and your opponent battle for control of the board by taking each other's pieces. (See pages 44–49.)

Out of my way!

The endgame
When there are very few pieces left. Your King may become a more active attacking piece as it is in less danger of being attacked. (See pages 62–69.)

Gotcha!

A way of thinking

Wherever you are in a game, you should have a plan that governs how you move your pieces. Stay flexible, though, and change your plan if your opponent does something unexpected.

Don't try to plan too many moves in advance. Even champions don't tend to think ahead very far during a game of chess. There are just too many possibilities.

You can use various tactics, tricks and traps to outwit your opponent.

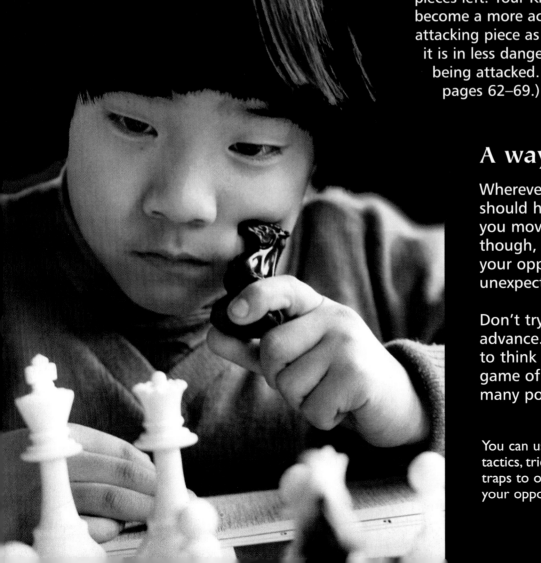

Setting up the board

The chess board has 64 squares of alternating colors. A "white", or lighter-colored, square is always positioned at the player's right. The pieces are placed as shown below.

Internet link
For a link to an excellent general chess Web site intended for new chess players go to **www.usborne-quicklinks.com**

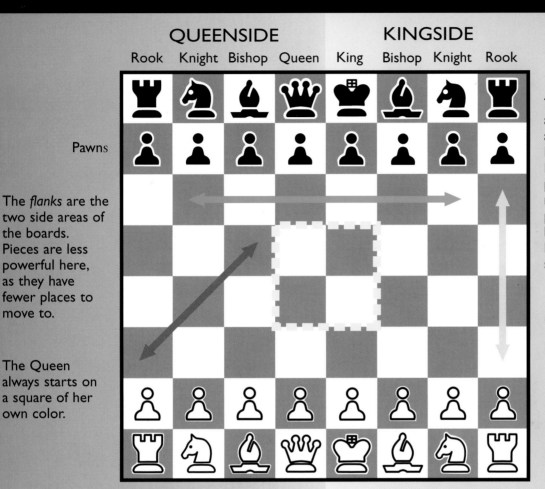

QUEENSIDE | **KINGSIDE**

Rook Knight Bishop Queen | King Bishop Knight Rook

Pawns

The *flanks* are the two side areas of the boards. Pieces are less powerful here, as they have fewer places to move to.

The Queen always starts on a square of her own color.

The "major pieces" are the Queens and the Rooks. Bishops and Knights are "minor pieces". All the major and minor pieces start on the back rank. The Pawns start on the second rank.

An *open file* is one that is not blocked by Pawns.

You will be at an advantage if you control the four central squares early in the game.

Key

A *rank* is a line of squares that runs across the board.

A *file* is a line of squares that runs from top to bottom of the board.

A line of squares that runs diagonally is called a *diagonal*.

The central part of the board.

Key words

diagonal A line of diagonal squares.

file A line of squares from top to bottom.

flank One of the side areas of the board.

Kingside The four files on the King's side.

open file A file that is not blocked by Pawns.

Queenside The four files on the Queen's side.

rank A line of squares from left to right.

Did you know?

Some chess sets are fabulously expensive, made of silver, gold, carved stone or jade. The pieces shown here are from a set made entirely of glass. The "white" pieces are clear and the "black" pieces are frosted.

9

Writing chess down

The standard way to record chess moves and games of chess is called *algebraic notation*. You will see this kind of notation in chess books, newsletters or on Web sites. Each square on the board has a different code, and so does each chess piece.

How the squares are coded

Each file is given a letter and each rank has a number. This means that each square has its own code. The letter comes first when you write down the code of a square. For example, the white King is on square **e1**.

In diagrams, White always starts on the first two ranks, at the bottom of the board. Black always starts on ranks seven and eight, at the top of the board.

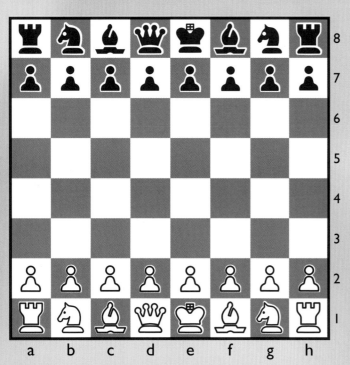

The board diagrams in this book are numbered and lettered to help you work out the code for each square.

How the pieces are coded

All the pieces except the Pawns have codes:

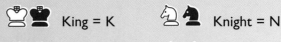

King = K	Knight = N
Queen = Q	Bishop = B
Rook = R	Pawn = no code

Other letters can be added after the move code to describe the move further:

+	Check	(Q)	Pawn promotes to Queen
++	Checkmate	(N)	Pawn promotes to Knight
0-0	Kingside castle		
0-0-0	Queenside castle	x	A capture (this is written immediately after the piece code)
!	Good move		
=	Neither side has the advantage		

All these terms are explained later on.

Writing moves down

Number each pair of moves – write White's move first. Write the code letter of the piece, then the letter and number of the square it is moving to. (For a Pawn, just write down the square it is moving to.) For example:

1. d4   d5   **2. e4   c6**   **3. e5   Bf5**

(Black's moves are written as **1... d5**. The dots after the number show that White's move is missing.)

Did you know?

The number of possible different games of chess is greater than the number of atoms in the known universe.

How the diagrams work

The games and puzzles in this book are described using diagrams as well as algebraic notation. Here is what the different symbols on the diagrams mean:

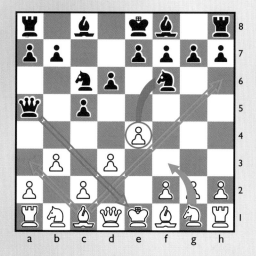

 A move The new position of a piece after one turn.

A capture A piece taken when an enemy lands on its square.

An attack A possible move that would result in capture.

A possible move A square that a piece could be moved to.

Key words

algebraic notation The standard method of writing down chess games, using letters and numbers to identify squares on the board, and letter codes for the pieces.

Internet link
For a link to a Web site where you can browse a selection of beginners' chess games, illustrated with diagrams and algebraic notation, go to **www.usborne-quicklinks.com**

How chess pieces move

The six types of chess piece have different moves:

 **King**

Can move one square in any direction. Cannot move to a square that is under attack from an opposing piece or jump over pieces.

 **Queen**

Can move any number of squares in a straight line along any open rank, file or diagonal. Cannot jump over pieces.

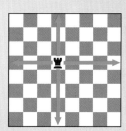 **Rook**

Can move any number of squares in a straight line along any open rank or file. Cannot jump over pieces.

 **Bishop**

Can move any number of squares in a straight line along open diagonals. Always stays on squares of the same color. Cannot jump over pieces.

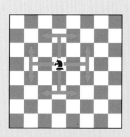 **Knight**

Can move in an "L" shape in any direction – two squares forward and one square to the left or right. Can jump over other pieces.

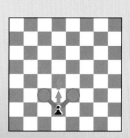 **Pawn**

Can move one square forward, except first move, when it may move forward two squares. Can capture on either of two squares diagonally ahead.

The King

The two Kings are the most important pieces on the board. If either is captured, the game is over. However, they are not the most powerful pieces. You should use your other pieces to protect the King from attack.

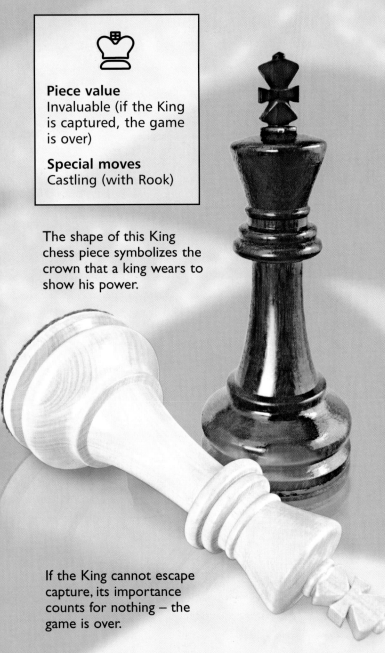

Piece value
Invaluable (if the King is captured, the game is over)

Special moves
Castling (with Rook)

The shape of this King chess piece symbolizes the crown that a king wears to show his power.

If the King cannot escape capture, its importance counts for nothing – the game is over.

The King's move in detail

The King can go in any direction, one square at a time. It therefore cannot move fast enough to be an attacking piece in the early stages of the game. In the endgame, when there are fewer pieces left on the board, you can use the King as part of your attack.

The King has more possible moves when it is near the middle of the board. However, it is also exposed to attack from all sides.

Be careful when your King is trapped near the edges or corners of the board. If it can't escape from attack you will lose the game.

King attack!

A King that could be taken by an enemy piece's next move is said to be in *check*.

Check!

If your King is in check, you must do one of the following to stop the check:

● Capture the *checking piece*.
● Move your King out of check.
● Position another piece between the attacking piece and your King.

You may never move the King into check.

If it is impossible for the King to escape check, then the game is over. This is called *checkmate*.

The King's role

A King has been part of the game of chess since it began in Asia. The piece was first called the *Rajah*, and later became the *Shah*.

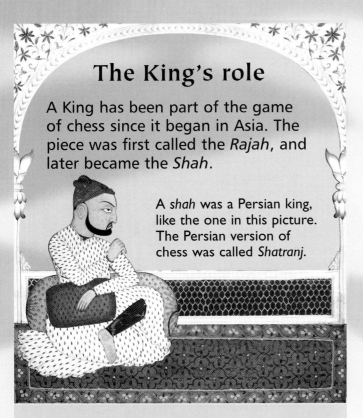

A *shah* was a Persian king, like the one in this picture. The Persian version of chess was called *Shatranj*.

When the modern game of chess evolved in Europe around the fifteenth century, this piece became known as the King. At the same time, it gained an extra move – castling (see right).

This picture of a medieval king shares some of the characteristics of the King in chess. His crown shows his importance. But he is still vulnerable and needs his people to protect him.

Key words

castling A special move for a King and Rook. They change places to protect the King and to bring the Rook into the middle to attack.

check An attack on the King.

checkmate When the King cannot escape from the attack (the game ends).

checking piece A piece that attacks the King.

Defending the King

Castling is a double move for the King and a Rook. It has several advantages. The King moves away from the exposed central files, to a square behind a wall of Pawns that can defend it. This move also brings the Rook to the middle, where it is most effective.

Stick with us.

Each player may only castle once, and only before the King and the Rook have been moved. You may not castle if your King is in check, or if any of the spaces between the King and the Rook are under attack.

Castling Kingside

When the two spaces between the King and the Kingside Rook are clear, the King moves two spaces toward the Rook. The Rook jumps to the space on the other side of the King.

Castling Queenside

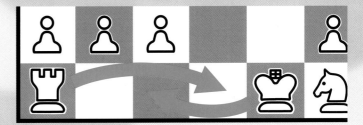

When the three spaces between the King and the Queenside Rook are clear, the King moves two spaces toward the Rook. The Rook jumps to the space on the other side of the King.

Internet link
For a link to a Web site with information and detailed diagrams explaining more about using the castling move, go to **www.usborne-quicklinks.com**

Kings on the attack

During the endgame, when most pieces have been taken, the two Kings take on a more attacking role. They may advance toward each other but can never occupy next-door squares. (This is because the two Kings would place each other in check.)

Grrr...

When there is only one square left between two advancing Kings, the player that moved last is said to have the *opposition*. This is an advantage – the other King cannot come any closer and must move in a different direction. It is possible to gain the opposition by *losing a tempo* (making an extra move to lose time), and this might happen in the following way:

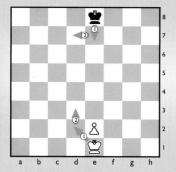

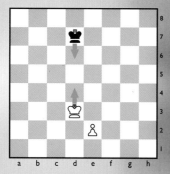

1. Kd2 Ke7
2. Kd3 Kd7
The two Kings advance. White's King has to go around the Pawn.

3. Kd4 Kd6
There is one square left between the Kings. Black has the opposition – White can advance no farther.

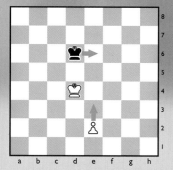

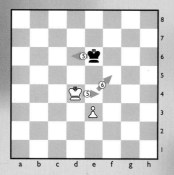

4. e3! Ke6
White moves a Pawn, loses a tempo and regains the opposition. It can now control Black's play.

5. Ke4! Kd6
6. Kf5
White forces Black's King to give way, and should now try to promote its Pawn.

Trapped King

If you have castled your King, it may seem safe behind a wall of Pawns. However, the Pawns that defend it can also trap it, resulting in *back rank mate* (see below).

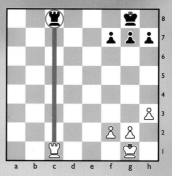

1. Rxc8++
White's Rook takes the black Rook, and checkmates Black at the same time. The black King is trapped on the back rank behind its own Pawns.

A good way to guard against this is to provide an escape route by moving the h-Pawn one square forward (or the b-Pawn if you have castled Queenside), as shown above by the white pieces.

No escape!

Although you should try to protect your King on all sides, remember that your own pieces could block your King's escape if you are not careful. If this happens it is known as *smothered mate*.

1. Nh6+ Kh8
Black has no choice but to move the King out of check.

2. Qg8+ Rxg8
3. Nf7++
The King is surrounded and can't escape mate.

Did you know?

The word "checkmate" comes from the Persian expression *shah mat* which means, literally, "the King is dead".

King puzzles

Can you solve these brainteasing puzzles involving the King?

1. How can White win a piece here?

2. How can White checkmate in one?

3. Can you spot Black's brilliant move to give checkmate?

4. Can you find a two-move checkmating sequence for White?

For puzzle solutions, see page 90.

 Do

● Castle early to protect your King.

● Use your army of pieces to help defend your King.

● Use your King as an attacking piece in the endgame.

 Don't

● Block your King's escape routes with your own pieces.

● Leave your King exposed or undefended.

● Try to use your King as an attacking piece too early in the game.

King defense tips

♕ Try to defend open files or diagonals that lead to the King, or it may be vulnerable to attack.

♕ Try not to let your opponent place pieces close to your King.

♕ You may be able to divert an attack on your King by attacking your opponent's King or other important pieces such as the Queen.

♕ Give your King an escape route to avoid either back rank mate or smothered mate.

♕ Try to see your King through the eyes of your opponent – as a moving target.

I'm coming to get you...

Key words

back rank mate The King is trapped on the back rank by other pieces, resulting in checkmate.

losing a tempo In the example shown on the opposite page, White loses a tempo by moving a Pawn instead of the King in order to gain the opposition. It actually means losing time – usually a bad thing, especially in the opening stage of the game, when the race is on to develop your pieces.

opposition When a square separates two advancing Kings, the player that moved last has the opposition.

smothered mate The King is completely surrounded by its own pieces and cannot move out of checkmate.

Internet link
For a link to a Web site that contains an exellent (but advanced) chess tactics glossary, including "gaining the opposition", go to **www.usborne-quicklinks.com**

The Queen

The Queen is the most powerful piece in your army. It is a devastatingly effective attacking piece, sometimes even able to threaten several pieces at once as it can move any distance in any direction. You should therefore use it wisely and avoid losing it at all costs.

Piece value
Nine (the most valuable piece on the board)

Special moves
None

The lady is a Queen

The English name for the most powerful chess piece is the Queen, because it stands beside the King. However, in French it is simply called *la dame* (lady), as it is in German (*die Dame*) and Italian (*la donna*).

When the Queen piece was first introduced in 1475, the new version of chess was called the "mad Queen game", as many chess players didn't like the new Queen piece.

The Queen's move in detail

The Queen can move in any direction, along ranks, files and diagonals. It is extremely powerful because it can move any number of squares, as long as its path is not blocked by another piece – its own pieces or the enemy's.

Sorry ma'am you can't pass!

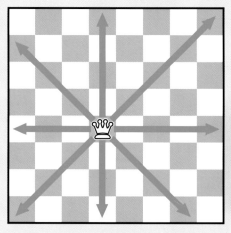

The powerful Queen can move in all directions, for any distance, but it cannot jump over pieces.

It is best not to bring the Queen into play too early, when the board is crowded with pieces and it may be forced to retreat. This would waste time that could be spent using other pieces to mount attacks, such as the Knights or the Bishops.

The Queen usually wears a coronet, and is the second-tallest piece on the board, after the King.

Certain capture

The Queen is a good piece with which to *fork* (threaten two or more pieces belonging to your opponent). Your opponent can only defend one piece at a time, so you will be able to capture the other with your next move. (For more about forks, see page 50.)

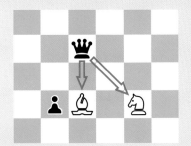

The black Queen forks the white Knight and Bishop. Whatever White does next, it will lose a piece.

 ## Do

● Use your Queen's attacking power during the middlegame.

● Consider forcing an *exchange* of Queens if you urgently need to take pressure off your King.

 ## Don't

● Bring your Queen into play too early. If you have to retreat, you may waste valuable time that could be spent developing other pieces.

● Let your Queen be taken without a very good reason, for example to divert attention away from your King if it is under attack.

Key words

fork A sneaky move – a piece moves to a square from where it can threaten two or more opposing pieces at once.

exchange Initiating the loss of one piece to enable you to capture a piece of the same type or value.

A Queen for a Queen

You should try not to allow your Queen to be taken – as far into the game as possible. However, you may decide to force the loss of both Queens (called an *exchange*). For example, if your King is under attack, a Queen exchange may divert your opponent's attention.

Once both Queens are out of the way, the King is safer and can move around the board more. The exchange itself may also divert your opponent from the course of the attack. Below is an example:

1... Qe5+
The black King may be attacked by White's Rook. Black creates a diversion and puts White in check.

2. Qxe5
The white Queen defends the white King by taking Black's threatening Queen...

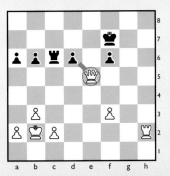

2... dxe5
...but is immediately taken by a black Pawn. Black has effectively forced a Queen exchange.

3. Rh7+ Kg6
White now attacks Black's King with its Rook, but Black can simply move away unscathed.

Internet link
For a link to an interactive Web site where you can try to place eight Queens on a chess board in such a way that none of them threaten each other, go to
www.usborne-quicklinks.com

The Rooks

Each player has two Rooks. They are extremely powerful – the only piece more powerful is the Queen. Rooks are especially deadly when they work as a team, and they can devastate your opponent's defense to bring checkmate if you use them well.

Piece value
Five

Special moves
Castling*
(with the King)

The name "Rook" came from the Persian word *ruhk*, meaning "chariot". The modern piece may be intended to resemble an ancient battering ram or moveable tower.

The Rook's move in detail

Rooks can move back and forth any number of squares, along ranks and files.

They are very powerful when placed on open files (those that are clear of Pawns and other pieces). Here, a Rook can threaten its opponent from a position deep within its own territory.

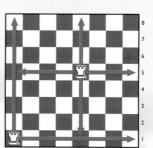

Rooks are powerful anywhere on the board, as long as they have open ranks or files to move along.

Pawn protectors

Rooks make good escorts for Pawns that are heading for promotion in the endgame (see page 25). They can give support from behind without blocking the Pawns' progress across the board.

A Rook on the same file as a Pawn protects it from behind.

*For more about castling, see page 13.

Doubly effective

Place your Rooks next to each other on ranks or files, where they can work as a pair to mow down your opponent's pieces. Rooks positioned in this way are called *doubled Rooks*.

I'm right behind you...

1. Rc8+ Rxc8
The first of White's doubled Rooks tears into enemy lines, giving check to the black King. Black is forced to retaliate by taking the Rook.

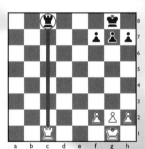

2. Rxc8++
White fires a follow-up shot with the second Rook, taking the black Rook. Black's King has no escape now – it is checkmated.

A well-positioned Rook

The Rooks' effectiveness depends on their position in relation to other pieces. Try to move Rooks to positions where they dominate open files, to control as many squares as possible.

I'm coming through...

1. Re1
The two sides have similar positions, but White moves first – its Rook to an open file. Black cannot now move its own Rook to that file without being taken by White.

Do

- Move Rooks to open files when you can.

- Use Rooks to give support to your Pawns from behind.

- Try to let your Rooks work together. Doubled Rooks are lethal weapons.

- Remember that your Rooks are the most powerful of your pieces after the Queen. Try to keep them until the endgame, when they will prove useful.

Don't

- Let your Rooks become trapped on blocked ranks or files.

- Hamper a Pawn's chances of promotion* by positioning your Rook in front of a Pawn that is trying to reach the other end of the board.

- Sacrifice Rooks carelessly – they are valuable.

Internet link
For a link to a Web site where you can find out the names of the chess pieces in over fifty different languages, go to **www.usborne-quicklinks.com**

Key words

doubled Rooks Two Rooks of the same color on the same rank or file (usually file). Together, they form an extremely powerful attacking force. If one of the Rooks launches an attack, but is taken, the other can immediately attack again from the same place.

*For more about Pawn promotion, see page 25.

The Bishops

The two Bishops are a powerful attacking force, especially when they work together to dominate the board. You should develop your Bishops quickly, but also try to keep both of them as long as you can.

These Bishops are from a chess set of the style, known as Staunton, that is used in tournaments.

Piece value Three

Special moves None

The top of the Bishop chess piece resembles the hat that a real bishop wears, called a *miter*.

The Bishop's move in detail

A Bishop can move any number of squares, along diagonals only. It cannot jump over other pieces.

Each player has two Bishops; one starts on a black square and one starts on a white square. As they only move diagonally, each Bishop always stays on squares the same color as it started on.

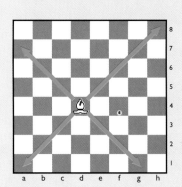

The Bishop can move as far as it likes along the diagonals but it cannot jump over pieces.

Working together

The Bishops can be powerfu because they have a long range. A pair of Bishops nea the center of the board can control many squares.

Mm... excellent plan!

When Bishops work togethe , they can control both the white and the black diagonals so there is no place for your opponent to hide! Remember that if your opponent only has one Bishop (for example, the black-squared Bishop), your pieces will be safer on squares of the other color (in this case, the white squares).

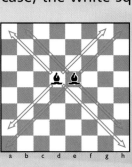

The two Bishops should work together to dominate the board. The diagram shows how many squares they can threaten.

Ready for attack

A sequence of two moves allows the Bishop to control the longest diagonal on the board. This is called *fianchetto*, and leaves the Bishop ready to attack while being protected on three sides by Pawns.

I'm in control here...

1. g3 e5
2. Bg2
The Bishop moves to the Pawn's starting square – *fianchetto*.

The word *fianchetto* comes from an Italian word meaning "side" or "flank" (because the Bishop moves to the side of the board).

> **Internet link**
> For a link to a Web site with a "user's guide to the *fianchetto*", that covers many different aspects of this type of opening move, go to
> **www.usborne-quicklinks.com**

Good Bishop, bad Bishop

A Bishop that is free to move is called a *good Bishop*. But the Bishop's diagonal move means there is a danger it may tangle with its own Pawns. If it becomes trapped behind them on *closed diagonals*, it is called a *bad Bishop*.

The black Pawns are not obstructing the movement of the black Bishop on this board. This is a good Bishop.

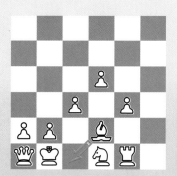

The white Bishop is trapped by its own Pawns. It cannot move freely or very far, so it is called a bad Bishop.

Do

● Develop your Bishops early in the game – possibly using an opening that involves them, like the King's Indian Defense (see page 43).

● Use your Bishops together – they are much more effective when attacking as a pair.

● Try to have good Bishops – don't block their progress with your own pieces.

● Try not to give up a Bishop unless you exchange it for the opposing Bishop on the same color squares, or you will be more vulnerable to attack.

Don't

● Sacrifice your Bishops if you can avoid it. They are a useful checkmating force in the endgame (for more on the endgame, see pages 62–69).

● Allow bad Bishops (Bishops blocked in by your own Pawns).

● Let your opponent take advantage of undefended diagonals if you only have one Bishop.

Key words

bad Bishop A Bishop that is trapped behind its own Pawns and cannot take part in attacks effectively.

closed diagonal A diagonal blocked by pieces.

fianchetto An opening move that places a Bishop on the longest diagonal.

good Bishop A Bishop that is not trapped by its own pieces and can move freely.

The Knights

The Knight's move in detail

Each player has two Knights. The Knights are good at squeezing into tight spaces on the board, where you can use their jumping power to launch surprise ambushes.

The Knights move in an "L" shape – two squares in any direction followed by one square to either right or left.

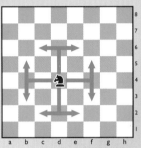

Knights can move in any direction, and may jump over other pieces.

Knights can move before any Pawns do, which can be a useful move during the opening.

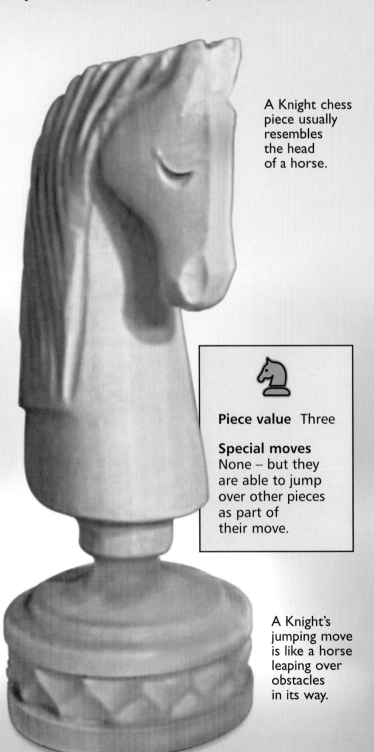

A Knight chess piece usually resembles the head of a horse.

Central role

Knights are less powerful near the edges of the board than in the middle. As you can see, the Knight in the middle can move to eight squares, while the one at the edge can move to only four.

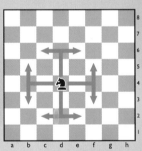

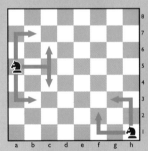

A Knight near the middle of the board can move in any direction.

A Knight's movement is limited when it is at the edge of the board.

Piece value Three

Special moves
None – but they are able to jump over other pieces as part of their move.

Strengths and weaknesses

A Knight's move makes it useful when the board is crowded with pieces. The agile Knights can hop between empty squares and weaken the enemy defense or force a smothered mate*.

When there are few pieces left, the Knights may move too slowly to make effective attacks, compared to Rooks or Bishops.

A Knight's jumping move is like a horse leaping over obstacles in its way.

*For more about smothered mate, see page 14.

Do

● Use your Knights to mount surprise attacks on your opponent – they are good at squeezing into gaps between pieces, especially in situations where the board is very crowded with both players' pieces.

● Support your Knights with Pawns. Otherwise, they can be vulnerable to attacks from longer-range pieces. This kind of Pawn support for more valuable pieces is called *anchorage*.

● Place your Knights in *outposts* – these are squares where they can't be attacked by opposing Pawns.

 ## Don't

● Confine your Knights to the edges of the board. The number of squares they can move to is limited. They are even more restricted in the corners where they only have two possible squares that they can move to.

? Knight puzzle

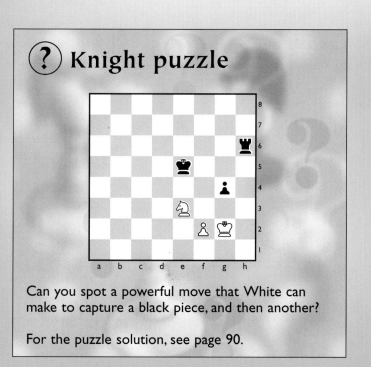

Can you spot a powerful move that White can make to capture a black piece, and then another?

For the puzzle solution, see page 90.

Key words

anchorage Support provided by Pawns for pieces that may be unable to escape from attack quickly, like Knights.

Cover me!

outpost A square that cannot be attacked by opposing Pawns.

Internet link
For a link to a Web site about the Knight's Tour – a famous mathematical problem based on the Knight's move in chess – with information and solutions, go to **www.usborne-quicklinks.com**

Knight wear

In some chess sets, the Knight piece is designed to look like a soldier on horseback. In medieval times, a knight was a mounted soldier who served and protected the King.

This ivory Knight piece is from a 12th-century set. It was found on the Isle of Lewis, in Scotland, and shows a knight on horseback.

The Pawns

ach player has eight Pawns. On their own, they are not very valuable but they can work as a team to attack and defend. If one of your Pawns reaches your opponent's end of the board it can be replaced by a more valuable piece, usually a Queen.

Piece value One

Special moves
- May move one or two squares on first move.
- Diagonal capture.
- The *en passant* rule.

Eight red Pawns line up at the start of a game. Red pieces are often used instead of black in chess sets.

The Pawn's move in detail

A Pawn can only ever move forward. Usually you can move it only one square; but on its first move you can move it two squares if you prefer.

This slow movement, in one direction only, restricts Pawns. However, if you use them carefully they can work together and support each other as well as providing cover for your other pieces.

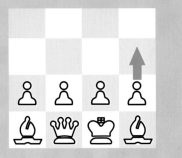

The basic Pawn move – one square forward along its file.

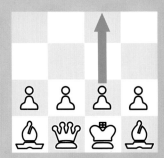

On its first move, a Pawn can move either one or two squares forward.

Devious capturing

The Pawns only deviate from their steady forward march to capture enemy pieces. They make captures by darting diagonally forward to either left or right.

The white Pawn moves one square diagonally forward to capture an enemy piece, in this case, a black Pawn.

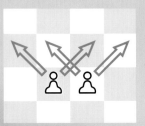

This diagram shows how two Pawns can dominate the important central part of the board by threatening four spaces.

No sneaking past!

There is one rule that allows a Pawn to make a special move, called *en passant*. On its first turn, a Pawn may move two squares forward. In doing this, it may be possible for the Pawn to sneak past an opposing Pawn. The *en passant* rule allows the Pawn that has been outsmarted to take the sneaky Pawn anyway.

Hey, you – come back here!

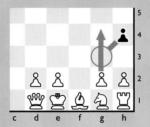

1. g4 xg3
White moves a Pawn forward two spaces, next to Black's Pawn. If White had moved the Pawn only one square, Black would have been able to capture it.

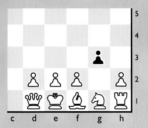

Using the *en passant* rule, Black has taken the white Pawn anyway. It ends up on the square where it would have landed if White had moved only one square ahead.

Pawn promotion

If one of your Pawns manages to reach the other end of the board (its *queening square*), it is *promoted*. This means that you may replace it with a more powerful piece, usually a Queen (because a Queen is the most powerful piece and therefore the most useful).

If your Queen has already been taken, you can have it back to replace the promoted Pawn. If you still have your Queen, you need to make the promoted Pawn look different. You could balance it on top of a Rook that has already been taken, put a ring over it, or even replace it with another small object.

Would you like a lift, your majesty?

Internet link
For a link to a Web site that contains frequently asked questions about the Pawn's moves in chess, go to
www.usborne-quicklinks.com

Key words

en passant The rule that allows a Pawn to capture another that has tried to evade capture by moving forward two squares.

promotion When a Pawn reaches the other end of the board and can be swapped for a more powerful piece, usually a Queen.

queening square The square that a Pawn must reach to gain promotion.

Do

● Use your Pawns to dominate the middle of the board during the opening stage of the game if you can.

● Activate your Pawns in the middlegame – use them to attack enemy pieces and defend your own.

● Give up your Pawns if necessary, to help your other pieces advance.

● Conserve some of your Pawns until the endgame, when they will become powerful if they can promote.

Don't

● Give up your Pawns unneccessarily. They may be worth more than you think – if not now, then later!

● Move the Pawns on the flanks during the opening if you can avoid it – concentrate on the central Pawns.

Strong Pawn positions

Each Pawn marches forward relentlessly throughout the game. As they cannot go backward, you need to think very carefully before you move any of your Pawns.

A strong *Pawn structure* can affect your entire strategy, allowing your pieces to work well together in the middlegame. It also means that you will find promoting Pawns easier in the endgame.

Everybody with me? Good.

 Do

- Use your Pawns to support each other. The white Pawns on a2, b3 and c4 form a *Pawn chain*. Black can only safely attack the base of the chain on a2 without risking capture.

- Try to have *passed Pawns* like the white Pawn on e5. This Pawn has no more enemy Pawns to pass on its own or next-door files. It is therefore more likely to reach the other end of the board and gain promotion.

- Use a Pawn on the seventh rank, like the one on g7, to threaten your opponent. This Pawn can safely promote with its next move – Black will be unable to take it immediately.

White's Pawns support each other, form a strong defense, and don't prevent the other pieces from launching attacks.

- Use Pawns to support more valuable pieces like Knights. The Pawn on h4 is supporting the Knight on g5. This method of support is called anchorage*.

- Dominate the middle of the board with Pawns during the opening, use them to attack and defend in the middlegame, and promote them in the endgame.

Did you know?

An unflattering word for an opponent who is a weaker chess player than yourself is a *patzer*. It comes from the German verb *patzen*, which means "to mess up".

Internet links
Go to **www.usborne-quicklinks.com** for links to the following Web sites:

Web site 1 A selection of fascinating chess records, including the most Pawn promotions in a game.

Web site 2 A biography page about Akiba Rubinstein, a chess player famous for his mastery of Pawn structures.

* For more about anchorage, see page 23.

Weak Pawn positions

Problems tend to arise when your Pawn structure gets broken up, or when a tightly-knit Pawn structure gets in the way of your other attacking pieces.

The placing of your Pawns directly affects your ability to attack or defend effectively. On the board below are some examples of Pawn structures to try to avoid.

We're losing it, men.

Don't

● Have *isolated Pawns*, like the one on h6, if you can help it. They make easy pickings for your opponent, especially if not supported by pieces.

● Scatter Pawns in small groups across the board in *Pawn islands*, as both players have done here. Your enemy will have little trouble capturing them. Black's Pawns especially are broken up and not supporting each other.

● Let your Pawns get left behind by the others, like the *backward Pawn* on a2. This Pawn cannot rely on the support of other Pawns in case of attack.

Both players have badly-placed Pawns on this board – they either block each other and other pieces or are separated from the others and so undefended.

● Structure your Pawns in such a way that they impede the movements of your other pieces, like the black-squared Bishop on f8, which can only move to the g7 square. A restricted Bishop is a bad Bishop*.

● Have *double* or *triple Pawns*, like White's double Pawns on the b-file. They cannot support each other.

Key words

backward Pawn A Pawn that has been left behind by the Pawns next to it, and so is undefended.

double Pawns Two Pawns of the same color on the same file.

isolated Pawn A lone Pawn that is undefended.

passed Pawn A Pawn that has left the opposing Pawns on next-door files behind.

Pawn chain Pawns arranged on next-door squares along a diagonal.

Pawn island A group of Pawns cut off from the others that are therefore vulnerable to attack.

Pawn structure Pawn arrangements on the board.

triple Pawns Three Pawns on the same file.

* For more about bad Bishops, see page 21.

Values, sacrifices and exchanges

Each chess piece has a value. For example, the Queen is given a value of nine, while each Pawn is given a value of one. These values are not used for anything in the game, but they help you to remember how important a piece is.

Piece values at a glance

 King Invaluable. When it is captured, the game is over.

 Queen Nine. The most valuable piece because it is also the most powerful.

 Rook Five. This piece is also very valuable because of its attacking power.

 Bishop Three. Similar in value to the Knights.

 Knight Three. Similar in value to the Bishops.

 Pawn One. Much more valuable if it can be promoted.

Internet link
For a link to a Web site that explains a chess variant for four people that reuses pieces that have been taken, go to **www.usborne-quicklinks.com**

A fair exchange?

The piece values help you to work out whether an *exchange* of pieces with your opponent is fair. (An exchange is a series of moves in which each of you loses a piece.) For example:

Bishop = three   **Knight** = three

Black exchanges a Bishop for a Knight. Pieces of equal value give a *fair exchange*.

Bishop = three   **Rook** = five

Black exchanges a Bishop for a more valuable Rook. Black has made an *advantageous exchange*.

Rook = five   **Knight** = three

Black exchanges a Rook for a Knight. The Rook is more valuable, so Black has made a *sacrifice*.

Key words

advantageous exchange Exchanging a low-value piece for one of higher value.

fair exchange Exchanging similar value pieces.

sacrifice Loss of a piece as part of a strategy.

material gain Having pieces of a higher total value than your opponent after a move or a series of moves.

Exceptions to the value rules

Although the piece values remain fixed, the real importance of a particular piece depends on the stage of the game and also where the piece is on the board at the time.

For example, a Pawn that is on the seventh rank can be promoted with its next move. This means that the Pawn is far more valuable than it would be if it were near the middle of the board.

Also, although a Bishop and a Knight both have a value of three, they may be more or less valuable to you. A Bishop is useful on a board with lots of open diagonals. A Knight is more useful on a board that is cluttered with pieces.

Do

● Use exchanges and sacrifices as part of your game plan.

● Try to outwit your opponent by making advantageous exchanges.

Don't

● Rely too much on the values of the pieces when you are trying to work out whether a sacrifice is a good idea – they are only intended as a guide.

● Forget that some pieces become more valuable later in the game – such as Pawns.

The decision to sacrifice

You may make a sacrifice for immediate *material gain* (to have more valuable pieces than your opponent), or to improve the position of your pieces on the board or to weaken your enemy's defense.

In this sequence, by sacrificing a Rook, White takes the pressure off its King and forces checkmate:

1. Rh8+! Kxh8
The white Rook places the black King in check. Black is forced to take the Rook.

2. Qh5+ Kg8
The white Queen now checks the King, forcing it to retreat.

3. Qh7++
One more advance from the Queen and Black is checkmated.

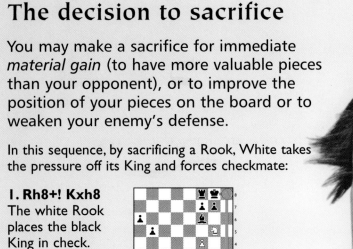

An eight year old girl studies the chess board in a tournament game. Many world champions take up chess at a young age.

Piece puzzles

On these two pages are some puzzles designed to test your knowledge of how the different chess pieces work best in game situations. When you are trying to solve the puzzles, consider the characteristics of each piece, and the way they move.

Knight puzzle

White can make an advantageous exchange by moving its Knight – how?

CLUE:
Look at the squares that the other white pieces are guarding.

Pawn puzzles

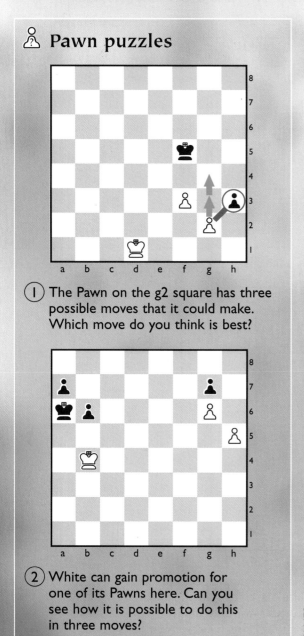

① The Pawn on the g2 square has three possible moves that it could make. Which move do you think is best?

② White can gain promotion for one of its Pawns here. Can you see how it is possible to do this in three moves?

CLUES:
1. Which black piece looks threatening?
2. You should consider sacrificing one Pawn in order to promote another.

Bishop puzzles

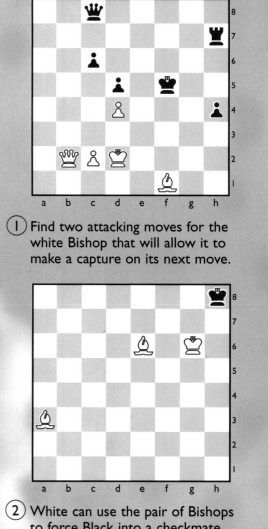

① Find two attacking moves for the white Bishop that will allow it to make a capture on its next move.

② White can use the pair of Bishops to force Black into a checkmate position. Can you see how to do this with one move?

CLUES:
1. A King cannot stay in check.
2. Remember that a King is an attacking piece too.

For puzzle solutions see page 90.

♖ Rook puzzle

What move can a black Rook make that will allow it to capture next turn?

CLUE: Seek the protection of a Pawn.

Did you know?

The first published chess puzzle was the "Indian Problem" (right). It was printed in *The Chess Player's Chronicle*, in 1845. Can you solve it?

White to move; mate in four.

Internet link

For a link to a Web site where you can find a browseable index of chess puzzles, go to **www.usborne-quicklinks.com**

♕ Queen puzzles

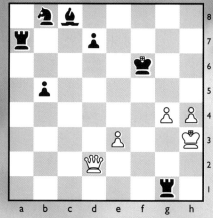

① How many ways can the white Queen check the black King, and take a piece with every subsequent move?

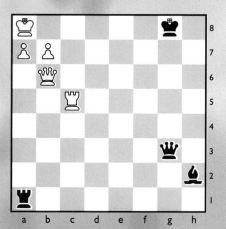

② How is it possible for the black Queen to force White into checkmate with only one move on this board?

CLUES:
1. Consider the flexibility of the Queen's move.
2. A Bishop acts as a bodyguard.

♔ King puzzles

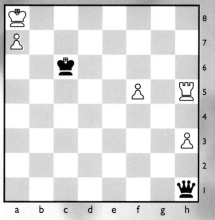

① What should the black player do here, if the goal is to reach checkmate in one?

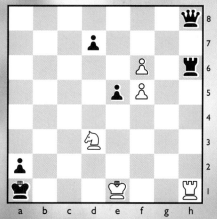

② This time it is possible for the white player to give checkmate to Black with only one move – but how? (This one is tricky.)

CLUES:
1. Think laterally to discover a solution.
2. This problem has an unusual solution involving a special move.

For puzzle solutions see page 90.

31

The opening

Every chess game has an *opening* stage. Both players should have clear plans from the start. In the opening stage, you will have different goals depending on whether you are playing as Black or White.

Opening goals

White plays first and so has a slight advantage in the game. White should try to hold this advantage in the opening stage of the game. Black, coming from behind, should try to end the opening stage at least on an equal footing with white.

All is quiet in the ranks, before battle commences.

Ready to go

Both players should use the opening stage to get into good positions. At the end of this stage, the King should be protected. Pieces should be *developed* (moved into positions to prepare for attack). Take control of the center by moving your pieces to places where they will dominate as many squares as possible.

Opening blunder

It is perfectly possible for a game to be won or lost in the opening stage. In 1997, IBM's "supercomputer", *Deep Blue*, beat the reigning World Champion, Garry Kasparov, because of a mistake that he made during the opening. He had never been beaten in a match before by a computer.

Television monitors display Kasparov as he takes on his computer opponent, *Deep Blue*.

Do

- Try to control the center of the board.

- Develop the minor pieces (Knights and Bishops) early on and prepare to use them to attack.

- Move Pawns carefully.*

- Castle as quickly as you safely can.

- Develop your pieces with a plan in mind.

 ## Don't

- Move pieces more than once at this stage, unless it is part of a plan. Otherwise you will waste time and fall behind in development.

- Sacrifice pieces for no reason at this stage.

- Start attacking too early.

- Expose the Queen to attack.

- Move without thinking – every move counts.

The end of the opening

This board shows how the pieces might be arranged at the end of the opening stage of the game.

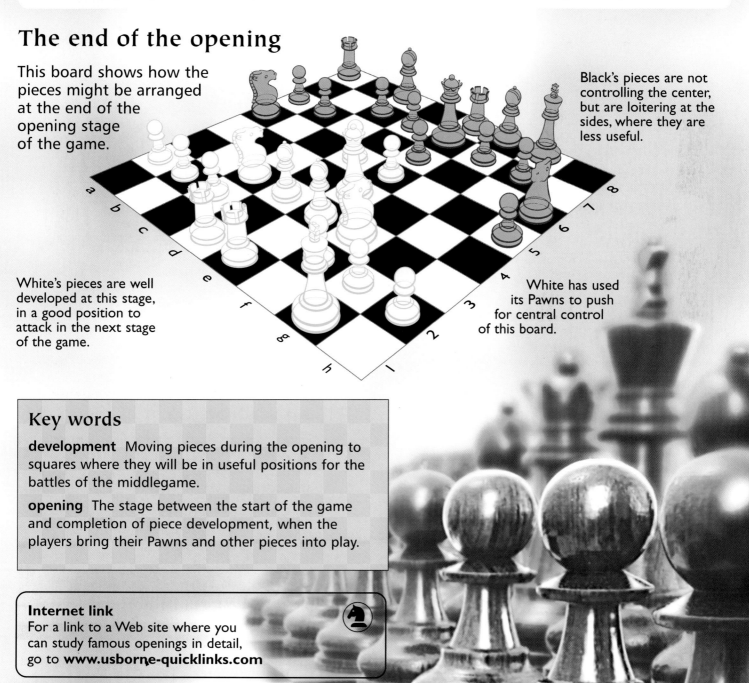

Black's pieces are not controlling the center, but are loitering at the sides, where they are less useful.

White's pieces are well developed at this stage, in a good position to attack in the next stage of the game.

White has used its Pawns to push for central control of this board.

Key words

development Moving pieces during the opening to squares where they will be in useful positions for the battles of the middlegame.

opening The stage between the start of the game and completion of piece development, when the players bring their Pawns and other pieces into play.

Internet link
For a link to a Web site where you can study famous openings in detail, go to **www.usborne-quicklinks.com**

*For more about Pawn structures, see pages 26–27.

Opening sequences

S ome distinctive combinations of moves played in the opening stages of chess games are famous and have been given names. Different openings influence what happens later in the game.

Naming openings

Opening sequences get their names in different ways:

● Some, like the *Giuoco Piano* (Italian for "quiet game"), get their name from the style of the game that follows the opening.
● Some are named after players, like the Caro-Kann (named after two nineteenth-century German players), or the Ruy Lopez (named after a Spanish priest).
● Others, like the King's Gambit, are named after the move that typifies them.

Each opening sequence tends to have a move that defines it. For example, the Ruy Lopez is defined by White's third move (3. Bb5). After this move, there can be different variations.

The Ruy Lopez opening allows White to carry on with piece development quickly, and then to castle on the Kingside.

Learn from openings

At first it is best to grasp the ideas behind an opening, rather than memorizing a series of moves. When you are playing, your opponent may not always make the moves you expect.

In the opening sequences on the next few pages, try to understand why the players make each move, to improve your own play.

Opening analysis

The only conclusion that experts have so far drawn from analysis of opening sequences seems to be that there is no such thing as the perfect opening!

There have been movements in chess theory in the same way that there have been in music or in art. The *hypermodern** approach, first written about by Aron Nimzowitsch in the 1920s, went against the traditional fight for occupation of the center of the board. Instead, hypermodernists aimed to control the center using pieces placed at a distance.

Hypermodernists Richard Réti and Aron Nimzowitsch face each other in the Marienbad Tournament in 1925.

Key words

closed game In the opening, a strategy that keeps the attacking pieces behind a strong Pawn structure until the game is in progress.

hypermodernism A movement in chess that started in the 1920s, where a player ignores the usual method of developing pieces to the middle squares, in order to control these squares from a distance.

open game In the opening, a strategy that develops the attacking pieces quickly, positioning them in front of the Pawns.

*For more about the hypermodern approach, see page 58.

Early decisions

Your opening moves affect the style of game that follows. If you keep most of your Pawns back and develop other pieces quickly so that they are in front, this is an *open game*. Open games tend to be quite fast and furious, with swift piece exchanges and fighting in the middle of the board.

Internet link
For a link to a Web site that lists many well-known openings and their defining moves, with a short description of each, go to
www.usborne-quicklinks.com

White and Black have both developed Knights and Bishops to positions in front of their Pawns, opening up lines of attack.

Black has started to build a strong Pawn defense, before advancing any other pieces. This should lead to a *closed game*.

The opposite of this is a *closed game*, where you develop a strong Pawn structure in front and keep the other pieces back until later on.

You can also choose either to push to occupy the middle part of the board or to hang back and wait for your opponent to charge in and – you hope – make mistakes.

Did you know?

The game of chess has made regular guest appearances in movies and novels over the years. Sometimes the game of chess itself is the star, and sometimes it features as just part of the story.

● *Through the Looking Glass* by Lewis Carroll. Alice steps through the looking glass into a world peopled by strange characters, including giant chess pieces. As she ventures further, she realizes that she is taking part in a giant game of chess.

● *Harry Potter and the Sorcerer's Stone* by J.K. Rowling – In their quest to protect the Philosopher's Stone, Harry and his friends Ron and Hermione risk their lives by taking part in a nightmarish game of Wizard Chess.

A still from the movie *Harry Potter and the Sorcerer's Stone*, showing Harry and his friends preparing to take part in a giant chess game.

The Italian – *Giuoco Piano*

The Italian opening is also called the *Giuoco Piano*, which means "quiet game" in Italian. However, this is misleading, as it is an opening that can lead to a game full of brutal attacks from both sides and plenty of excitement.

Basic opening strategy

In the Italian opening, White's e-Pawn moves to the center, and the minor pieces on the Kingside (the Kingside Knights and Bishops) develop quickly, allowing the King to castle. These early moves all fit in with the basic opening techniques that you learn when you start playing chess.

The first move of the Italian opening, (1. e4), is the most common opening move for White, for both new and experienced chess players.

I. e4 e5
These first Pawn moves prepare the way for both sides to get their pieces into play quickly.

2. Nf3 Nc6
The white Knight threatens Black's Pawn. Black defends the Pawn with a Knight of its own.

> **Internet link**
> For a link to a Web site where you can find an illustrated variation of the *Giuoco Piano*, go to **www.usborne-quicklinks.com**

How the board looks

With the third move, White launches its Kingside Bishop into the attack, aiming at the f7 Pawn that is defended only by the King. Black mirrors this move with its own Kingside Bishop, and the scene is set for battle to commence!

3. Bc4 Bc5
Let the battle begin!

The pieces are developing symmetrically. Both players have started attacking.

The Pawn on f7 is only protected by the King – this is a defensive weakness.

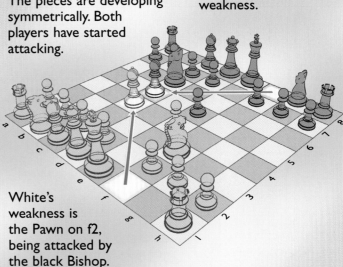

White's weakness is the Pawn on f2, being attacked by the black Bishop.

What's the idea?

This is an example of an open game. Both White and Black bring their pieces out quickly to seize attacking opportunities – at the same time exposing themselves to the enemy. This means there are likely to be plenty of exciting attacks and exchanges early on in the game. (So much for a "quiet game"!)

The Bishops that enter the battle on each player's third move attack crucial defensive squares, f7 and f2. These squares are weak points in each side's defense, guarded only by the King. Both players need to ensure that the enemy Bishop threat does not lure their King into a deadly trap later on.

The Spanish – Ruy Lopez

The Spanish opening was named after a sixteenth-century Spanish priest named Ruy Lopez. He wrote about his opening strategy in the first known book about chess.

Chess in print

The Spanish priest, Ruy Lopez, published this book about his opening theory in 1561. Since then, thousands of books have been published on all aspects of the game of chess, for players of all abilities.

Answering back

The Spanish opening is also a drive for control of the central squares by White.

1. e4 e5
2. Nf3 Nc6
The first two moves of the Spanish opening are the same as the first two moves of the Italian opening.

White leaps straight into the attack with the third move. Black has to decide how to respond to this attack before it can begin a retaliation. It has a choice of either defense or counter-attack...

Key words

pinned piece A piece that is forced to stay where it is in order to protect another piece.

Bishop on the attack!

3. Bb5
The white Bishop attacks the black Knight.

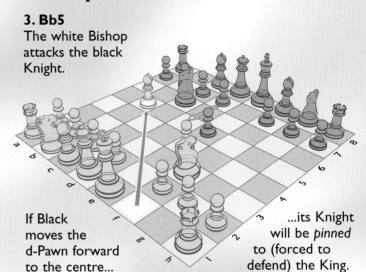

If Black moves the d-Pawn forward to the centre...

...its Knight will be *pinned* to (forced to defend) the King.

The white Bishop on b5 is a threat to Black's defense. This Bishop puts pressure on Black's Knight. If Black moves the d-Pawn (a crucial central Pawn), the Knight will be *pinned*. To move it would leave the Black King in check. (For more about pinned pieces see page 50.)

What happens next?

A common Black counter-attacking response to 3. Bb5 is the following:

3... a6
Black attacks the white Bishop with a Pawn.
4. Bxc6 dxc6
White takes Black's c-file Knight and Black retaliates by taking the white Bishop with its d-Pawn.

A fair exchange?

Here, White loses a Bishop and Black loses a Knight. This is a fair exchange – both pieces are worth three points. Black still has two Bishops, which may be useful to force checkmate later on in the game (see pages 68–69), but also now has doubled Pawns* on the c-file, to White's advantage.

*For more on doubled Pawns, see pages 26–27.

The Queen's Gambit

This opening sequence is characterized by White's second move, which involves a *gambit* – the offer of a Pawn to the opponent, in return for some kind of strategic advantage.

Queenside attack

This opening starts with a White bid for the central squares. Black responds solidly, but White's second move really begins to stir up trouble, in the form of tough decisions to be made early on, for Black.

1. d4 d5
The White and the Black Queenside Pawns advance to meet, head-on, in the middle of the board.

2. c4
This is the crucial move – the gambit. Black now has to decide whether or not to take the white c-Pawn.

Gambits – what's the point?

Playing a gambit in the opening can be positive for two main reasons:

♟ By losing a Pawn, you may open up the board and be able to develop your pieces more quickly than your opponent.

♟ Your opponent, enticed into taking one of your Pawns, may make a change of plan that upsets their strategy.

Offer accepted!

If Black takes the offered white c-Pawn, it will no longer have Pawns on both of the important two central files. This will give White an advantage in the battle for control of the center.

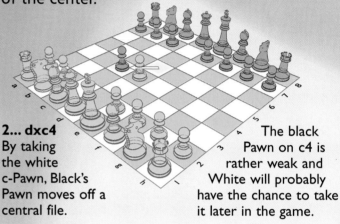

2... dxc4
By taking the white c-Pawn, Black's Pawn moves off a central file.

The black Pawn on c4 is rather weak and White will probably have the chance to take it later in the game.

Offer declined...

If Black does not take the white c-Pawn, that Pawn will continue to threaten the center. If White takes the black Pawn on d5, it will have a Pawn advantage in the center and may be able to use this later to undermine Black's Queenside defense.

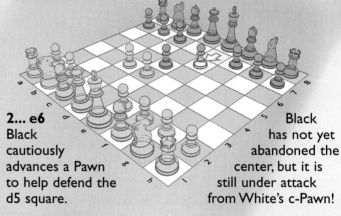

2... e6
Black cautiously advances a Pawn to help defend the d5 square.

Black has not yet abandoned the center, but it is still under attack from White's c-Pawn!

Key word

gambit A move made during the opening stage of the game, that offers a Pawn or a minor piece to the opponent, in return for better positions for the remaining pieces.

More White openings...

Once you understand the principles behind the basic opening strategies for White, you can begin to bend the rules to suit how you like to play. The following examples of opening sequences show some different approaches...

The Scandinavian opening

Black responds to White's 1. e4 opening with an immediate Pawn threat.

1. e4 d5
Black makes an aggressive reply to White's opening. But if the white player keeps a cool head, there may not be a problem...

2. exd5 Qxd5
White's Pawn takes the black d-Pawn, only to be taken by the black Queen. But Black's Queen is now developed rather early, and so may be vulnerable to a White attack.

The Four Knights game

Both sides move their pieces symmetrically, to logical positions. Black mirrors White's moves, and the game becomes gradually more tense as each side waits to see who will attack first.

1. e4 e5
2. Nf3 Nc6
3. Nc3 Nf6
After a push for central control, both players develop their Knights to positions where they can defend the Pawns.

Off-the-wall openings

As more and more opening sequences are described, so the need for different names grows. Here are some particularly wacky ones:

Elephant Gambit
Accelerated Dragon
Baby Orangutan
Bird's Invitation
Drunken Knight opening
Chameleon Sicilian
Latvian Corkscrew Counter-Gambit
English Double-Whammy
Grunfeld Spike
Hedgehog defense
Hippopotamus
Mad Dog Attack
Woodchuck

Ah... the Elephant Gambit.

The Reti opening

White's first move is a tricky one for Black to respond to. By not rushing into the center, the white player does not give away any plans. So, Black moves a Pawn into the center without delay. White hopes to control the center from a distance, with pieces rather than Pawns.

1. Nf3 d5
2. c4
White's second move provides a dilemma for Black's d-Pawn. It can either veer off-course to take the white c-Pawn, allow the challenge to stand or push on to d4.

Internet link
For a link to a Web site where you can browse a menu of chess openings for White and Black, go to **www.usborne-quicklinks.com**

The Caro-Kann defense

The Caro-Kann is a defensive opening for Black, which responds to White's opening 1. e4. It builds a solid Pawn structure, while allowing Black's major pieces to escape from the back rank to join the attack.

Let's see White try to get past us...

Rushing for power

Black's objective at the start of the game is to take things at its own pace and build a strong defense, before starting to attack the white Pawns that have rushed into the central part of the board.

1. e4 c6
Black responds to White's move in a laid-back way, choosing not to defend the center immediately with its d- or e-Pawn, but instead starting to build its own defense.

2. d4 d5
White charges in with its d-Pawn. Black pushes forward to attack the white Pawn on e4, its d-Pawn protected by the Pawn behind it.

3. e5
White advances the e-Pawn. (White could also have advanced a Knight to defend the attacked e-Pawn, or chosen to take the black Pawn on d5.)

Internet link
For a link to a Web site with illustrated variations on the Caro-Kann opening, go to
www.usborne-quicklinks.com

How it looks for Black

Black has already developed a strong Pawn structure, leading up to the center of the board. White would have to attack the base of this chain (b7) in order to upset these pieces without sacrificing material.

The way Black's Pawns are arranged also allows the Bishop on c8 to escape. However, the b8 Knight is deprived of the square that it would naturally develop to, by the Pawn on c6.

3... Bf5
Black's Queenside Bishop joins the attack...

...and threatens White's c-Pawn.

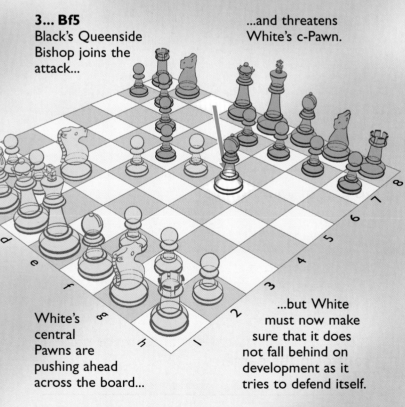

White's central Pawns are pushing ahead across the board...

...but White must now make sure that it does not fall behind on development as it tries to defend itself.

The fight for control of the center is raging – but not yet decided one way or the other. The kind of game that follows very much depends on White's next move at this point.

The Sicilian defense

The Sicilian defense has many *variations* (different combinations of moves), leading to games that are open or closed, depending on how White deals with Black's strategies. Some say it is the best opening defense against 1. e4.

A young Bobby Fischer* ponders the best move to make.

Defining moves

The Sicilian defense begins with a distinctive reply by Black to White's first move. This is shown below:

1. e4 c5
Black's first move doesn't threaten the white Pawn on e4. Instead, it looks ahead to White trying to push the other central Pawn to d4. White cannot now do this unchallenged.

Outwit your opponent

A large part of the game of chess involves trying to look ahead and think about what your opponent might do, as well as thinking about the moves that you are going to make as part of your own plan.

As Black, you start off by having to respond to your opponent's opening moves. Black should therefore try to win back the *initiative* in the opening stages of the game. By making a move that dictates what White should or should not do, such as 1... c5, Black can begin to take back some of the control in the game.

Internet link
For a link to a Web site that intoduces some variations on the Sicilian opening at an advanced level, go to **www.usborne-quicklinks.com**

A possible progression...

2. Nf3
White defends a potential white Pawn move to d4.

2... Nc6
Black moves a Knight to attack the same square.

Another possible route...

2. Nf3
White's Knight moves to attack the d4 square.

2... d6
Black builds a defensive Pawn structure.

Key words

initiative Control of the game. The player that is attacking has the initiative.

variation In opening strategy, a variation is a unique combination of moves that belong to a particular type of opening.

*For more about Bobby Fischer, see page 82.

41

The French defense

Black's pieces emerge slowly in this opening strategy, leaving White free to occupy the center of the board. Black begins a campaign to undermine this central dominance, by moving either Pawns or Knights to threaten the white Pawns.

Slow and steady

The French defense is a Black response to White's first move, 1. e4. Black builds a solid defense strategy before rushing into the center.

1. e4 e6
Black responds cautiously to White's central Pawn thrust, choosing to issue no immediate challenge with its own Pawns.

2. d4 d5
Now, with a Pawn on the e-file to provide support from behind, Black can respond with a head-on challenge to White's central Pawns.

The consequences:

♟ Remember – Black's Queenside Bishop will be blocked in during the early stages.

♟ There is likely to be Pawn gridlock in the center of the board at first.

♟ White will have more space initially; Black should plot to undermine this later.

♟ Usually one player will castle Kingside and the other Queenside in this opening.

What happens next?

In what is called the classic variation, both sides bring in their cavalry (the Knights) to support their clashing Pawns, setting the scene for a fight in the central battleground.

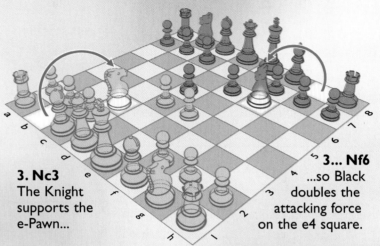

3. Nc3
The Knight supports the e-Pawn...

3... Nf6
...so Black doubles the attacking force on the e4 square.

In the advance variation, White pushes into black territory and locks the central Pawns. To break the deadlock, Black puts pressure on White's d-Pawn with a c-Pawn advance.

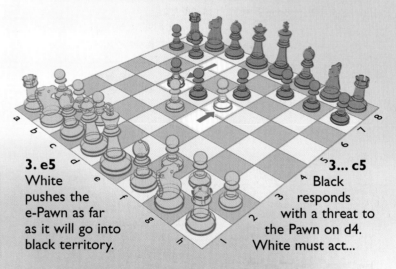

3. e5
White pushes the e-Pawn as far as it will go into black territory.

3... c5
Black responds with a threat to the Pawn on d4. White must act...

Internet link
For a link to a Web site where you can read about the French defense, including an analysis of the Pawn structures that arise, go to **www.usborne-quicklinks.com**

The King's Indian defense

O n this page is another opening idea for Black, in response to 1. d4. From a stealthy beginning it can quickly develop into a fierce *counter-attacking* strategy.

Slow and deadly

This opening sequence features what appears to be a fairly restrained series of moves from Black, which conceals the deadly weapon of a *fianchettoed** Bishop, ready to be unleashed on White's unsuspecting central Pawns.

1. d4 Nf6
Black does not rush headlong into the center with a Pawn, but instead threatens from a distance, using a Knight to prevent White occupying e4.

2. c4 g6
White continues to drive toward the center; Black quietly moves the g-Pawn forward one square, in preparation for *fianchetto*.

3. Nc3 Bg7
White's Knight moves to defend an anticipated Pawn move to e4. Black completes Kingside *fianchetto*.

Key words

counter-attack A response to an attack that poses a new attack.

What happens next?

White advances the e-Pawn to the center, to form a wall of Pawns. Black's d-Pawn moves forward one square, so the Queenside Bishop can get out, preparing for a central challenge.

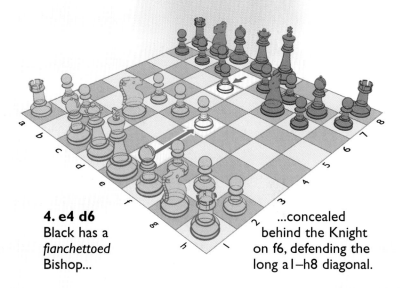

4. e4 d6
Black has a *fianchettoed* Bishop...

...concealed behind the Knight on f6, defending the long a1–h8 diagonal.

One to avoid!

One type of opening to avoid when you are playing as Black is the Scholar's Mate. This sequence of moves could end your chess game embarrassingly quickly if you don't spot it coming!

1. e4 e5
2. Bc4 Bc5
A calm, symmetrical opening, with no apparent threat on either side... but notice that Black's f7 Pawn is only protected by the King.

3. Qh5 Nf6
4. Qf7++ (or Bf7++)
White pounces on Black's weak Pawn, launching a vicious double attack on f7. Black cannot escape — the result is checkmate in only four moves!

*See pages 20–21 for more on the *fianchetto* move.

Thinking in the middlegame

The middlegame begins when both players have brought their pieces into play. Most attacks and exchanges take place during this phase of the game, so try to make sure that you have the upper hand in any ambushes that take place.

Taking charge

The player who is more in control of the game tends to have the *initiative*. The other player has to respond defensively to the attacker's plans instead of getting on with their own plans.

White has the initiative here because he has lots of resources to attack the black King, and Black will have to defend for a number of moves before getting around to his own plans.

Thinking for two

At this stage of the game you should work out what your opponent might do, so that you are less likely to be surprised by an attack.

BOO!

Internet link
For a link to a Web site with some chess rules and guidelines on etiquette for tournament players, go to **www.usborne-quicklinks.com**

Nerves of steel

During the fierce battles of the middlegame, try to remain calm. If you feel that you are doing badly, or even losing the game, you should try not to let your opponent see this.

If you appear to be confident, your opponent might be tricked into believing that you have an amazing plan up your sleeve. If your opponent then makes moves that are more cautious than necessary, you may be able to regain the advantage.

Intimidating opponents

In chess, a lot depends on staying focused and keeping cool. Just imagine trying to do that while playing against either of these:

Aron Nimzowitsch (1886–1935) could be an off-putting adversary. Upon entering a chess tournament room, he would stand on his head until it was time to start the game. Once he broke his leg during a match by getting it tangled with the leg of his chair.

Nimzowitsch thought of himself as a formidable opponent. His business card described him as "Crown Prince of the Chess World".

Vladimir Kramnik (1975–) has earned the nickname "Iceberg" for his ability to remain cool under great pressure. He claims that part of his success in beating former world champion Garry Kasparov lies in his ability not to be intimidated by him.

Chess etiquette

In chess tournaments, rules govern the way the players behave toward each other. Here are some examples:

● **The "touch-move" rule** If you touch a piece, you must move it. When you have taken your hand away after your move, you must leave the piece where it is.

● **Not saying "check"** It is polite to rely on your opponent noticing.

● **Saying "I adjust"** Say this first if you slightly adjust a piece on its square.

Time factors

If you are playing a friendly game of chess, you will have plenty of time to think about your moves – until your opponent gets bored and decides to do something else, that is!

In a chess competition, time is limited. It is measured using a *chess clock*. The game is lost if a player runs out of time.

Remember that once you touch a piece you are committed to moving it.

Key words

chess clock A special clock with two faces that records the time each player spends on moves in a chess game.

initiative Had by the player who is directing the course of the game by making moves that force certain responses.

Did you know?

After each player has moved four times, there are over 288 billion different possible positions for the pieces on a chess board. So don't feel too frustrated if you can't decide on the right move! Try to narrow down your choices quickly so you only seriously consider two or three.

 ## Do

● Try to reassess the situation on the board after every move – the balance of power may shift in a short space of time.

● Consider what your opponent is planning as well as thinking of your own strategy.

 ## Don't

● Allow yourself to get caught by surprise attacks – keep your eyes peeled for ambushes and traps from every direction.

● Relax – even though things may be going to plan, this can change very quickly!

The board in the middlegame

When you go into the middlegame, your pieces should be well placed if you are to stand a chance in the battle that follows. On these two pages are some examples of good positions and ones to avoid.

Closed or open?

The middlegame (like the opening) can be described as either "open" or "closed".* A closed game has Pawns that are locked together in the middle of the board. An open game has fewer Pawns and so the other pieces are freer to attack each other.

A strong position

This board illustrates a strong position for White in the middlegame.

White's pieces are mobile – they have space and are not blocking each other.

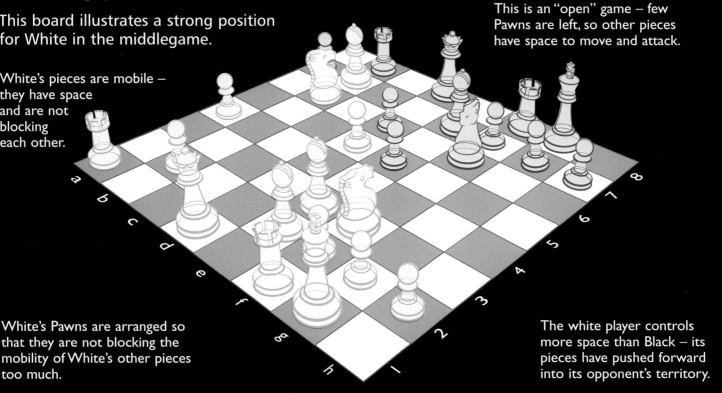

This is an "open" game – few Pawns are left, so other pieces have space to move and attack.

White's Pawns are arranged so that they are not blocking the mobility of White's other pieces too much.

The white player controls more space than Black – its pieces have pushed forward into its opponent's territory.

Points mean power

The pieces that a player has left on the board are called *material*. The player with the higher total piece value has the *material advantage* – and should have a more powerful army. (How powerful your pieces are also depends on how they are placed on the board.)

Advantage - us!

Mobilizing the troops

In the middlegame you should try for good piece *mobility* – pieces that are free to move and attack. One way to ensure this is to control as much space as possible, so that the pieces have room to move. Remember though, that you will have to work to defend the space you control.

*For more about closed and open games, see page 35.

Too much responsibility

In your drive to obliterate your opponent's defense, it helps if you can exploit any weaknesses that you spot. For example, your opponent may have a piece that is working to defend more than one other piece. This is an *overloaded piece*, and it is a weakness. If it moves to defend a piece, it will leave another undefended.

I don't know what to do!

Internet link
For a link to a Web site providing general advice on the middlegame, go to **www.usborne-quicklinks.com**

Did you know?

Some chess games are over well before the middlegame... the quickest checkmate of all only takes two moves!

A weak position

This board illustrates a weak position for Black in the middlegame.

Black has a bad Pawn structure. There are two pairs of doubled Pawns on the c- and f-files.

Black's pieces have poor mobility, so Black is less able to launch an effective attack.

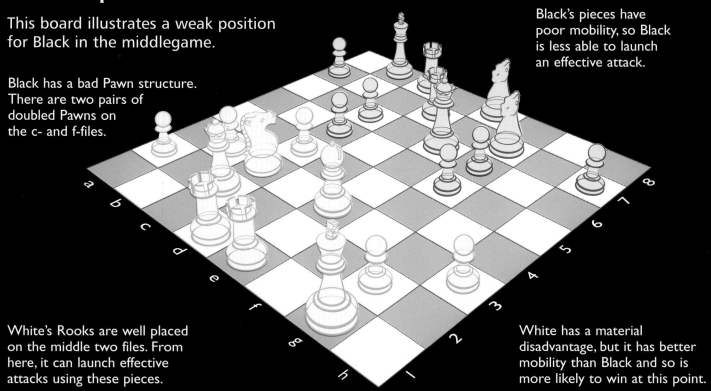

White's Rooks are well placed on the middle two files. From here, it can launch effective attacks using these pieces.

White has a material disadvantage, but it has better mobility than Black and so is more likely to win at this point.

Vulnerable King

Your King may look well defended, if you castled* during the opening and it is tucked behind a wall of Pawns. But during the middlegame there are still many powerful, dangerous pieces on the board. Be vigilant and defend your King at all times.

Can I stay here?

Key words

material The pieces that are left on the board.

material advantage/disadvantage Having pieces of a greater/lesser value than the enemy's.

mobility The ability of pieces to move freely.

overloaded piece A piece that has more than one defensive job to do, leaving it (or the pieces it is defending) open to attack.

*For more about castling, see page 13.

Middlegame puzzles

The middlegame is a battlefield, where you need to keep one eye on your attacking chances and the other firmly fixed on your own King's defenses. Watch out for sneaky ways to deliver an early checkmate to your opponent.

Did you know?

Some people study "fairy chess" problems, using board positions that could not arise in a normal game. They may also feature extra, made-up pieces, with special moves.

Internet link
For a link to a Web site with more chess puzzles, go to **www.usborne-quicklinks.com**

The right move

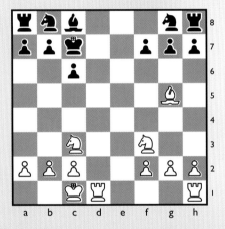

Can you spot the most devastating move for White to make here?

CLUE: The black King should watch his back!

Well-placed piece

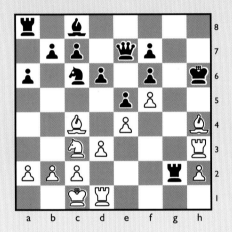

How can White use two pieces at once to annihilate the black King?

CLUE: Find a mobile attacking piece and use it.

Nowhere to run

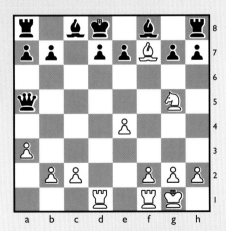

All looks calm here, but can you see how White can finish off the black King?

CLUE: How can you block the black King's escape?

Two-move mate

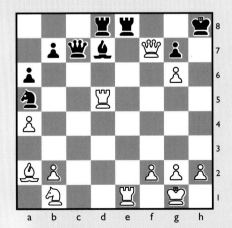

Can you find a way for White to give checkmate in two moves?

CLUE: Consider making a sacrifice.

For puzzle solutions see page 90.

♚? Defending the King

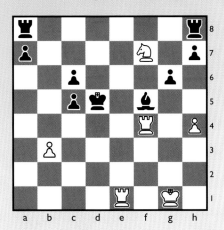

1 It might seem as if the black King has plenty of escape options, but can you see how White can use its pieces to trap it in checkmate?

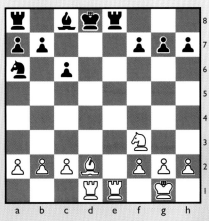

2 How can the white player here make the most of Black's vulnerable uncastled King, and force checkmate with only one move?

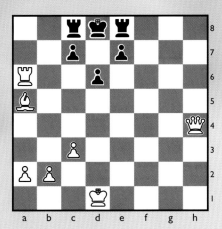

3 Which of White's pieces ends it all for Black here?

For puzzle solutions see pages 90–91.

CLUES:
1. Your Rooks need to support each other.

2. Use a double check to give mate.

3. Which of White's three pieces can attack at close range without risk?

♟ Square overload

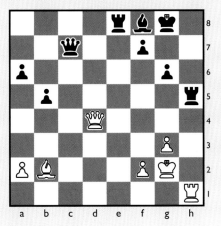

Can White checkmate in two moves?

CLUE:
Exploit the overloaded square, h8.

♟ Noble sacrifice

How can a White sacrifice be used to give mate in two moves?

CLUE:
Lose the Queen!

♟ Deadly initiative

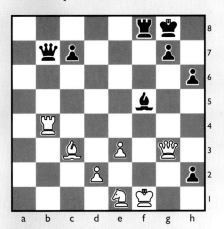

White is powerless to escape mate. Can you see Black's move?

CLUE:
Go for a double check.

Tactical tricks

Try using these tactical tricks to outwit your enemy. The objective of each is to unleash an attack so cunning and deadly that there is no way your opponent can escape without losing pieces.

Pinned down

An attack on a piece that is shielding a piece of greater value is called a *pin*. The *pinned piece* must stay where it is until the piece that is attacking it moves or is captured. If the pinned piece moves, it will leave the more valuable piece behind open to capture.

Black's Knight is an example of a pinned piece in this illustration.

The white Bishop is attacking the Black Knight. If the Knight moves, it will expose the black Queen.

Skewered!

A *skewer* is a kind of reverse pin. It is an attack on a valuable piece, that forces that piece to move. When this valuable piece moves, it exposes another, less valuable piece behind, to be attacked and captured.

As with the pin, the defending player is bound to lose a piece one way or the other, and can only act to limit the damage. (For information on defending against pins and skewers, see page 58.)

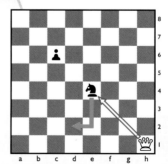

1 ... Nd2
Black's Knight moves swiftly away from an attack by the white Queen, leaving a black Pawn vulnerable.

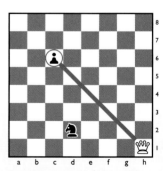

2. Qxc6
With no other pieces left defending it, the isolated black Pawn makes easy pickings for the white Queen.

Two-pronged attack

A *fork* is an attack on two or more pieces at the same time by a single enemy piece. The player that is under this double attack usually has no way of avoiding a capture. Its irregular move makes the Knight a good forking piece.

White's pieces both fall victim to Black's Knight fork, though they are not on the same rank, file or diagonal.

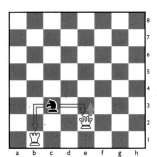

1. Qe3
Black's Knight forks White's Rook and Queen. The Queen escapes and attacks the Knight...

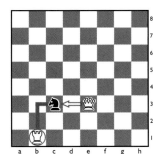

1... NxRb1
...but Black can now take White's Rook with its Knight and evade the Queen's attack.

Tactic tip

Look for ways to use your Knights to fork your opponents, who will be powerless to stop the attack by blocking a Knight's way with pieces. The Knight can simply leap over them! Its irregular jumping move also makes it hard for your opponent to see it coming in for such an attack.

Internet link
For a link to a Web site with more illustrated examples of pins, skewers and forks, go to **www.usborne-quicklinks.com**

Concealed threat

When one piece is moved to reveal an attack by another piece lurking behind, this is called a *discovered attack*. A discovered attack might take your opponent by surprise so that they do not see the threat until it is too late.

If the black Bishop moves, it will reveal a discovered attack on the white Queen from the black Rook.

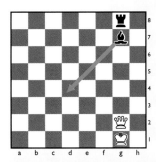

1... Bd4+
Black's Bishop moves to reveal a discovered attack on the white Queen by the Rook.

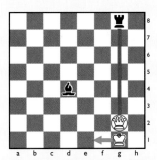

2. Kf1 Rxg2
The white King must move out of check, so Black's Rook is free to take the white Queen.

Key words

discovered attack A piece moves to reveal another attack from a different piece.
fork A simultaneous attack on two or more pieces by one enemy piece. Only one piece can escape the attack – the other will be captured.
pin An attack on a piece that is shielding one of greater value.
pinned piece A piece that must stay still to protect another piece of greater value.
skewer An attack that forces a valuable piece to move, exposing one of less value to attack.

Tactical trick puzzles

To solve the puzzles on these two pages you will need to use tactical moves like forks, pins and skewers to win important pieces from your opponent and even give checkmate. Watch out – some of the puzzles are quite tricky!

Did you know?

Until the beginning of last century, it was a rule that you had to announce a check. The rule was that if you didn't announce a check, it didn't count.

Internet link
For a link to a Web site with more chess puzzles, go to **www.usborne-quicklinks.com**

♟ Slice the defense

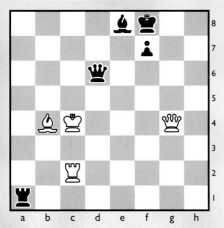

Can you find two moves for White that end in the capture of a black Rook?

CLUE: Fork the King, then skewer it!

♟ Lethal weapon

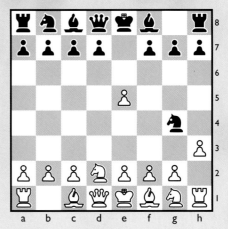

The black Knight must move – how can Black turn this into a three-move mate?

CLUE: A Queen fork disguises a more deadly trap.

♟ Don't get pinned down

Black's Queen is pinned – but which moves mean Black wins White's Queen?

CLUE: Escape a pin to set up a skewer.

♟ Cutlery crusade

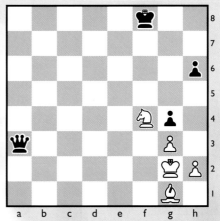

How can White fork twice to win Black's Queen?

CLUE: The black King and Queen share a diagonal.

For puzzle solutions see page 90.

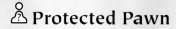 ## Protected Pawn

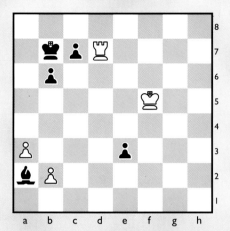

Black's Pawn hopes to promote. How can Black ensure the Pawn's safety?

CLUE: Sacrifice a piece to disable White's Rook.

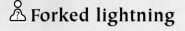 ## Forked lightning

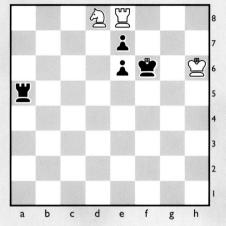

Can you find a two-move combination for White to take the black Rook?

CLUE: Plan to fork Black's Rook and King.

Rook revenge

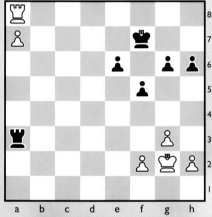

Can you see two moves for White that win a Rook?

CLUE: Ditch the passed Pawn and skewer the King.

Widen the gap

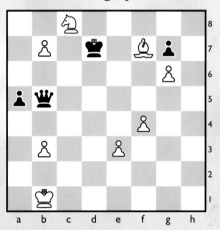

White can win the Queen (and ultimately the game) here – how?

CLUE: Try to set up a Knight fork.

Battle of the Bishops

How can White checkmate Black in two moves here?

CLUE: Two words – "Queen" and "sacrifice".

Inevitable capture

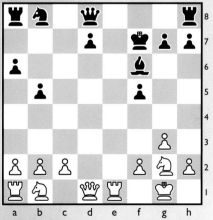

How can White guarantee winning a major piece with its next move?

CLUE: Get the King on one prong of your fork!

For puzzle solutions see page 90.

Making plans

If you want to get the edge on your opponent in a game of chess, you need to make every single move count. To ensure this, the moves that you make during a game should all be part of a *plan*.

Goals and objectives

To make a plan, you need to decide on what you want to achieve. Your plan will probably depend on what stage of the game you are at. Examples of plans include exchanging pieces, promoting a Pawn or checkmating your opponent.

1. b7 Qd8
2. b8(Q)
White's plan here was simple – to promote a Pawn. Black moved the Queen to attack the queening square, but White had planned for this and had back-up in the form of a Rook on b1.

Using tempo

The number of moves it takes you to achieve a particular aim is important in chess. You should try to be ahead in piece development and the race for occupation of territory on the board.

A *tempo* is a chess unit equal to a single move. A player loses a tempo by wasting a move – for example by using two moves to get a piece to a position that it could have reached in one move. If several moves are wasted, the player loses *tempi*. (The other player gains tempi.)

You may choose to lose a tempo*, to stall for time or to wrongfoot your opponent.

*For more about losing a tempo, see page 14.

Pole position

Your plan might be to improve your general *position*. A simple way to assess your position is to count the number of squares that your pieces could safely attack. If your pieces have more attacking scope than your opponent's, then you probably have a positional advantage.

The Black player has a positional advantage here. The blue shaded areas show all the squares that it could safely attack. The red shaded areas show all the squares White can safely attack.

Target weaknesses

One way to decide on a plan is to look for weaknesses in your enemy's army. Some examples of weaknesses that you could choose to exploit include a weak Pawn structure (where Pawns are undefended or blocking the movement of other pieces) or an exposed King.

Here, Black has an isolated Pawn on the d-file. White can make a plan to take this Pawn, leaving the way clear for its own d-Pawn to advance.

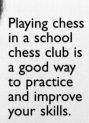

Playing chess in a school chess club is a good way to practice and improve your skills.

An attacking plan for White

On this board, White has the positional advantage and should plan attacks on Black. (Black should plan to weaken this advantage.)

 Dominant central Pawns that can be used to hold off Black attacks on the center.

 A Queenside Pawn majority that can advance and attack, while the Kingside Pawns defend.

 A passed Pawn on the a-file, approaching its queening square. White should try to protect and ultimately promote this Pawn.

 A well-protected King. White has guarded against the King being trapped on the back rank by moving the h-Pawn forward one square.

A defensive plan for Black

On this board, Black is at a disadvantage and should plan to improve on the situation. (White's plan should exploit these weaknesses.)

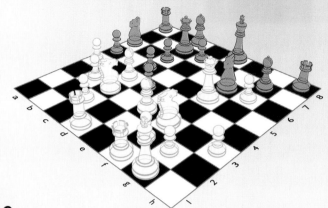

 Captured Pawns on the Kingside. Black should bolster its defense on this side with other pieces to keep White from promoting Pawns.

 Doubled Pawns on the c-file, that either need defending by other pieces, or may be sacrificed to open up better positions for Black.

 An isolated Pawn on the a-file. Black will need to defend this Pawn using other pieces.

 A King that has not yet castled to safety. Black should plan to castle Queenside soon.

Do

- Look for easy targets to exploit.

- Rectify weaknesses in your own position as quickly as you can.

- If you can't see anything more obvious to aim for, you could try to control more space, or create passed Pawns.

Don't

- Continue to pursue a plan if it doesn't work. Be flexible.

- Forget to foil your opponent's plans!

Key words

plan A series of moves designed to achieve a particular goal, for example to promote a Pawn.

position A measure of the amount of attacking control that you have over the squares on the board.

tempo (plural tempi) A unit of time in chess – equivalent to a single move.

Internet link
For a link to a Web site where you can find out more about the idea of tempo as it is used to measure time in chess games, with illustrated examples, go to
www.usborne-quicklinks.com

Combination puzzles

During the game, you should be on the lookout for clever combinations of moves that will deliver checkmate. Use tactical tricks and force checks to trap a vulnerable King, maybe even forcing it into a checkmate position.

Did you know?

Castling was originally two moves (first the King, then the Rook). It became one single move in 1561. You can still castle in two moves – called "castling by hand".

Internet link
For a link to a Web site with more chess puzzles, go to **www.usborne-quicklinks.com**

♟ Checkmate surprise

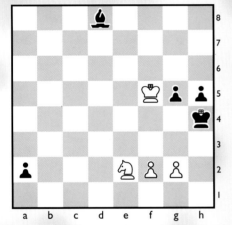

Black has a material advantage but can be checkmated in two moves – how?

CLUE: Make a cunning Knight move.

♟ Weak spot

How can White focus on Black's weaknesses to force mate in two?

CLUE: Make a major sacrifice.

♟ Push for victory

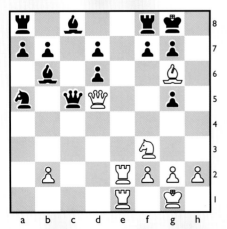

White is thrusting forward into Black territory – how does it mate in two?

CLUE: Build a back rank trap.

♟ Wrongfooted Rooks

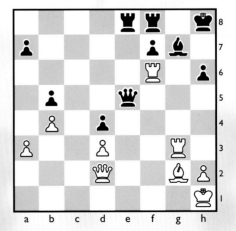

What scorching combination can White deliver to win from here?

CLUE: How can you keep the King trapped where it is?

For puzzle solutions see pages 90–91.

♟ Tragedy for the King

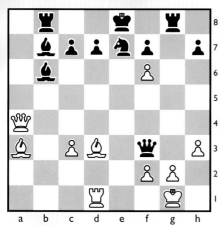

Find a winning combination for White featuring a sacrifice and a double check.

CLUE: Use a sacrifice to draw the King out to a vulnerable square.

♟ Inevitable defeat

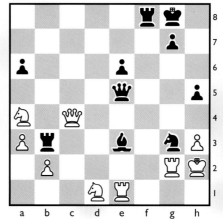

Black can sacrifice here to mate in four moves – what are they?

CLUE: In all three solutions, a Bishop makes the first move.

♟ Spoiled for choice

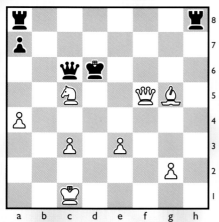

White has two two-move mate options here – can you find them?

CLUE: In both cases, White's Queen is all-important.

♟ Humble mate

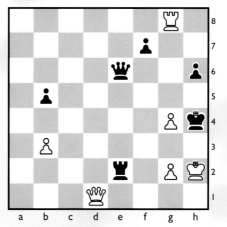

Can you see a two-move combination for White to give checkmate here?

CLUE: Release the white Pawns from the pin first.

♟ Early mate

Many pieces left, but White can mate in two, three or four – how?

CLUE: The first move is crucial to all three solutions.

♟ Long-term goal

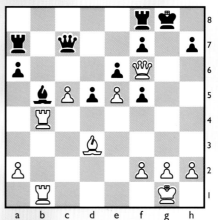

There are two ways to checkmate in four here – can you find them?

CLUE: Both solutions require a Rook sacrifice.

For puzzle solutions see pages 90–91.

Defense techniques

The best way to win a chess game is to seize the initiative and be the attacker. But there will be times when you need to play defensively, in response to an attack from your opponent.

Don't get pinned down

To avoid any of your valuable pieces being pinned* or skewered* by your opponent, be careful if two undefended pieces occupy the same rank, file or diagonal. In this kind of position they are most vulnerable to one of these types of attack.

1. Nd2
Here, White can pin the black Knight to the Queen on the next move by moving the Knight on f3. The Knight will not be able to move, until the Queen has moved away.

Watch out for forks

Forks* are quite tricky to guard against. The only way is to keep a very close eye on your opponent's attacking pieces, especially the Knights. The Knight's unusual move makes it difficult to see when it comes in for a fork attack. Because it can jump, it is also hard to defend against, as you cannot deter it by placing pieces to block its way.

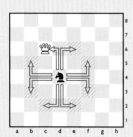

The Knight attacking the Queen could also attack another piece on any of the shaded squares.

Caught in a trap

If you find that you are the victim of a pin, fork or skewer, all is not lost. There are two things you can do to limit the damage:

● You could try to distract your opponent by launching an attack of your own on a different part of the board. While your opponent responds to this, you may have time to bring in reinforcements to defend the pieces that are under fire.

● Whatever kind of trap you are caught in, you will probably have to move a piece away from an immediate threat. By doing so, you will leave another piece exposed to attack. To limit the damage as much as possible, try to move the first piece to a place where it can defend the second piece, as in the examples below:

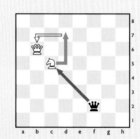

1. Nd7
The pinned white Knight moves, exposing the white Queen, but defending it at the same time. Black cannot capture the white Queen without losing its own.

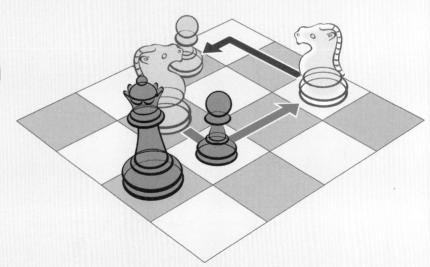

If you are caught in a skewer, try to move one of the attacked pieces away to a square from where it can defend the other attacked piece.

*For more about forks, pins and skewers, see pages 50–51.

Evade the Scholar's Mate

Checkmate in four moves, (Scholar's Mate*), spells doom for the unwary. Your opponent may disguise this deadly move sequence by adding extra moves, but if you know the danger signs you will be able to take evasive action before it is too late.

Help!

Scholar's Mate uses a double attack on the white f2 Pawn or the black f7 Pawn, by the Kingside Bishop and the Queen. If your opponent mobilizes both this Bishop and the Queen during the opening, you should be suspicious.

To defend against checkmate in this situation, you can do either of the following:

● Move your Knight to f6 (or f3) – this is a strong position for your Knight in the next stage of the game.

● Protect the f7 square at all costs – for example by moving your Queen to e7. Or block the White Queen's attack with a Pawn move to g6.

Danger for Black! White mounts a combined Bishop and Queen attack on the f7 square.

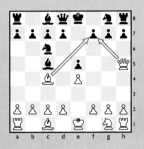

Internet link
For a link to a Web site where you can find a chess glossary that describes the idea of overprotection simply and effectively, go to **www.usborne-quicklinks.com**

*For more about Scholar's Mate, see page 43.

Defensive approach

Aron Nimzowitsch liked to play strategically in chess games. He used a technique called *overprotection*, which means that certain squares (for example the crucial central square e5) are heavily defended by several pieces.

This meant that any attack his opponent dared to launch on the e5 square would be quickly annihilated. Any of the defending pieces would also be able to carry out other duties elsewhere on the board at any time without leaving the square undefended.

This board illustrates one of Nimzowitsch's (playing White) favorite concepts – overprotection of the e5 square by a Bishop, a Knight and the Queen.

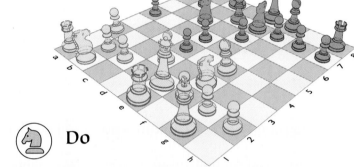

Do

● Be on the lookout for tactical traps like pins, forks and skewers.

● Defend aggressively – if your opponent attacks, do what they least expect and attack back.

Don't

● Panic... If you are caught in a trap, it may be possible to limit the damage or even turn the situation to your own advantage.

Key words
overprotection Defense of a square by more than one piece, making an attack on that square difficult for the opponent.

Sacrifice puzzles

Sometimes you will find you have to lose material to get ahead in a game of chess. Can you see how, in the puzzles on these two pages, you can force checkmate in either two or three moves by making a well-timed sacrifice?

Did you know?

The World Chess Federation estimates that there are at least 550 million people worldwide who play chess.

Internet link

For a link to a Web site with more chess puzzles, go to **www.usborne-quicklinks.com**

Seal Black's fate

Sacrifice a piece to give mate on White's second move.

CLUE: How can you bury the King?

Building a wall

How can White sacrifice a piece to allow the Queen to deliver checkmate?

CLUE: Make sure you move the right piece or all is lost!

Sacrificial barrage

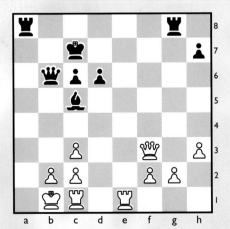

How can Black make a sacrifice here and mate on the second move?

CLUE: Make White's piled up Pawns work against the King.

King-baiting

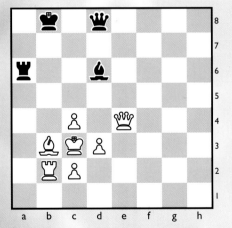

How can Black make a sacrifice here and mate in two?

CLUE: Try to draw the King toward a line of attack.

For puzzle solutions see page 91.

♙ Coming from behind

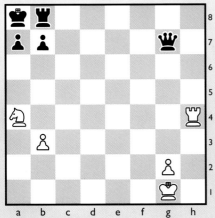

White is behind on material but can still checkmate Black in two – how?

CLUE: Sacrifice a piece to build a trap for Black.

♙ Brave monarch

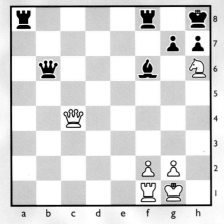

How can White make the highest sacrifice to win in two here?

CLUE: Send the Queen in.

♙ Danger all around

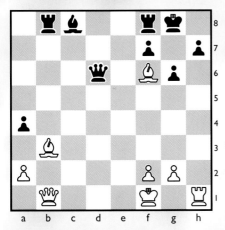

White can sacrifice and checkmate in two here – how?

CLUE: Remember your diagonal backup forces.

For puzzle solutions see page 91.

♙ Piledriver

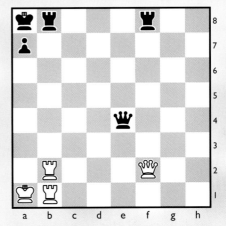

How can White sacrifice to force the loss of Black's Queen and checkmate?

CLUE: Dive straight to the heart of the black defense.

♙ Wriggling free

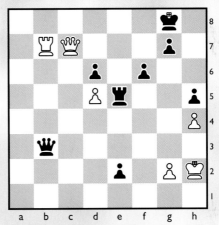

How can Black promote a Pawn and checkmate from this position?

CLUE: Make a sacrifice count by delivering check.

♙ Closing in

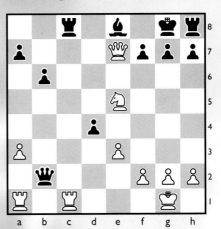

How can White use a sacrifice to mate in three here?

CLUE: Consider how Black must respond to what you do.

The endgame

The endgame is the stage when both players have lost most of their pieces, leaving the board fairly empty. Not all chess games reach this stage; sometimes the game ends in checkmate during the middlegame or even the opening.

More responsibility

In the endgame, you should use your King as an attacking piece. Your opponent now has fewer pieces left with which to threaten your King, so it can move around more. You also have fewer pieces left to attack your enemy, so you need to make full use of them all.

The King may not be able to move far, but it can attack eight squares at once.

Ambitious Pawns

Pawns become more valuable later in the game. This is because at this stage, the race for Pawn promotion* is really on. Promoting just one Pawn to a Queen is usually enough to tip the balance in your favor and enable you to win the game.

Ha ha! Power at last...

Keeping the pieces

During the endgame, it becomes vitally important that the few pieces that you do have left work together, providing support for each other without getting in each other's way.

For example, if you have a white-squared Bishop and a smattering of Pawns, try to keep the Pawns on black squares, to give the Bishop maximum freedom of movement (making it a good Bishop**).

As a general rule, try to keep your pieces near the center of the board, on *open lines*, where they can function at full power.

White is in a good position in this endgame, with a good Bishop, passed Pawns under the watchful eye of the King, and a mobile Rook.

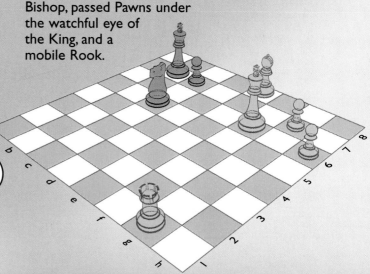

*For more about Pawn promotion, see page 25.

**For more about good and bad Bishops, see page 21.

A square fit for a Queen

A square a Pawn needs to reach to gain promotion is called a *queening square*. You should use your pieces to help your own Pawns to reach their queening squares safely.

Don't forget, though, to try to stop your opponent from promoting Pawns at the same time.

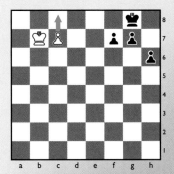

1. c8(Q)+

The white Pawn reaches its queening square. Black's King was too far away to have prevented this and cannot capture this dangerous new Queen.

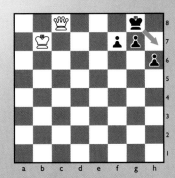

1... Kh7

The position of White's newly promoted Queen means that Black has to move the King. (If Black hadn't left the h7 square clear, this would have been back-rank mate.)

Key words

queening square The square on the far side of the board that a Pawn needs to reach to gain promotion (usually to a Queen).

open lines Ranks, files or diagonals that are clear of pieces.

Typical endgame

In the most common type of endgame each player has a King, a Rook and a few Pawns left. Make sure that your Rook is on an open file where it has as much influence as possible, or on a file behind a passed Pawn, to act as a bodyguard until the Pawn can promote.

In the example below. Black and White have almost identical positions, apart from the two Rooks.

White's Rook ties Black's to the defence of the f7 Pawn and also keeps the black King cut off on the back rank. Black's Rook, by contrast, has no mobility. It is behind a locked Pawn and blocked by a Pawn on the same rank.

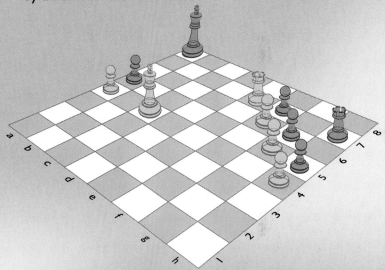

Internet link
For a link to a Web site where you can find out more about useful strategies to use in the endgame, go to **www.usborne-quicklinks.com**

 Do

● Use the King. In the endgame it can be a vital attacking piece.

● Guard your passed Pawns carefully. They are valuable and you should do everything you can to try to promote them.

 Don't

● Allow your opponent to promote Pawns or you will be at a disadvantage.

● Let your pieces get blocked in so you can't use them to their full attacking potential.

Endgame puzzles

When the game enters its final stage, you need to make all your remaining pieces work hard together to deliver checkmate. These endgame puzzles will test your ability to construct a trap, or mating net, using the material you have left.

Did you know?

The first chess game between Earth and Space (spaceship Soyuz 9) was on June 9th, 1970. Neither side won.

Internet link
For a link to a Web site where you can find more chess puzzles, go to
www.usborne-quicklinks.com

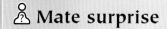 Mate surprise

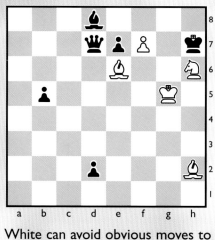

White can avoid obvious moves to give checkmate in two – how?

CLUE: The solution is not a Queen capture or Pawn promotion.

Cavalry charge

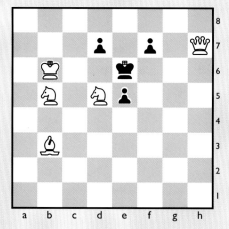

What move should White make here to force mate in two?

CLUE: The best move is not a direct attack.

Sticky end

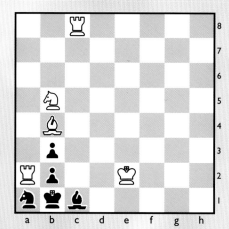

The Rook is threatened but White can still give checkmate in two – how?

CLUE: Remember – Black is moving down the board.

King pressure

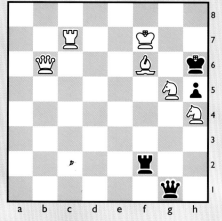

Again, White can mate in two if it chooses the right move – which?

CLUE: Move a piece into position to close the mating net.

For puzzle solutions see page 91.

♙ Forced to move

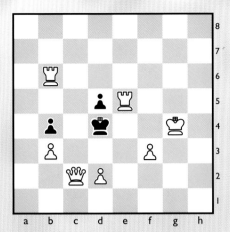

There are three possible two-move mates – can you find one for White?

CLUE: The right move for White makes the end inevitable for Black.

♙ Best move

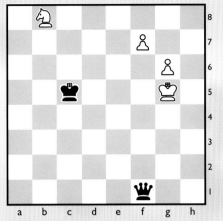

What is the best move for White in this endgame situation?

CLUE: Don't give Black a chance to move its Queen.

♙ Defensive collapse

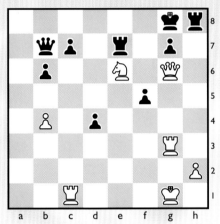

Can you see how White can give checkmate in two moves?

CLUE: Make a Queen sacrifice.

♖ Good clean fun

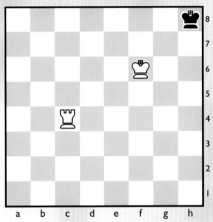

Can you find a two-move mating sequence for White in this endgame?

CLUE: Don't let the King wriggle free.

♙ Impending doom

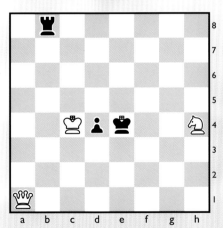

Pieces are scarce but White is one move away from a win – what is it?

CLUE: Make a King sandwich!

♔ Cornered King

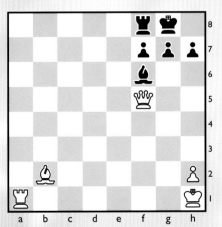

Can you find a three-move mate for White on the board shown here?

CLUE: Make a sacrifice to clear lines of attack for your pieces.

For puzzle solutions see page 91.

Attacking the King

An attack on the King is called *check*. Putting the enemy King in check does not mean you will definitely win the game, but it does mean that your opponent is forced to get out of check before making any other moves.

Take action

You must take evasive action if your King is in check. There are three ways to get out of check:

- Capture the checking piece.
- Place one of your own pieces between the checking piece and your King. (This will not work if the checking piece is a Knight.)
- Move your King away from the attack.

If you can't do any of these, it is checkmate.

Here, the white King is in check, but White has four options available – so all is not lost yet! Can you see what they are*?

Internet link
For a link to a Web site where you can see an animation that illustrates perpetual check, go to **www.usborne-quicklinks.com**

*Bxe3, Ne2, Kd1 or Kf1.

Sneaky checking

Your opponent might not see check coming if it is in the form of *discovered check* – when you move one of your pieces to reveal a piece behind that is giving check.

1. Bc7+
The white Bishop's move reveals a discovered check from the Rook. The black King will have to move out of check...

1... Kh8
2. Bxa5
The King moves, disastrously leaving the white Queen exposed to capture by the white Bishop.

Sneakier checking

An even more devastating surprise for your opponent is *double check* – when you move one piece into position to give check, revealing another checking piece behind.

If your King is double checked, you will have to move it. Taking one of the checking pieces with another of your pieces will not be enough. If you cannot move your King, you will be checkmated.

1. Ng6++
At first glance, Black seems to have a huge advantage. But one move from White gives double check from which there is no escape – so it is checkmate.

Forced moves

When you have to make a move, even though that move will put you in a worse position, this is known as *zugzwang* (German for "forced to move"). In this example, Black is in a *zugzwang* position that leads directly to checkmate by White.

Please don't make me do that...

1... h2
2. Nf2++
Black has no choice but to advance the h-Pawn. (The King cannot move to a safe square.) When the white Knight moves, Black's King is checkmated.

Slippery customer

When a player is put in check repeatedly, but cannot be checkmated, this is called *perpetual check*. This is a draw* – both sides can move but there is no way of resolving the situation.

1. Nf7+ Kg8
White was just about to be checkmated here (1... Qa3), but moves to put the black King in check.

2. Nh6+ Kh8
Black is in perpetual check. The Knight and the King could move back and forth forever – this is draw.

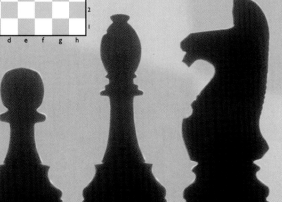

Did you know?

In a chess match between Crouch and Britton in the UK in 1984, Black gave check 43 times on consecutive turns!

The most checks recorded in a single match was 141, in a match between Johnsen and Gausdal in 1991. White gave check 100 times; Black 41 times. After all that, the game ended in draw.

Do

● Give check as a means of forcing your opponent to move. By moving, your opponent may lose time or neglect other pieces – and you can exploit this as part of a plan.

Don't

● Give check unnecessarily. It may make you feel powerful, but should only be done as part of a plan.

● Say "check" if you are playing in a chess competition. It is good manners to let your opponent notice this.

● Accidentally put your opponent in a perpetual check if you want to win the game – but it's fine if you want to draw.

Key words

check An attack on the King.

discovered check When a piece moves to reveal a piece behind that is giving check.

double check When a piece moves to give check, revealing a checking piece behind.

perpetual check When a player is checked repeatedly but cannot be checkmated – a draw.

zugzwang A situation where you are forced to move, even if there is no good move to make.

*For more about drawn games, see pages 72–73.

The King is dead – checkmate

Checkmating your opponent is the ultimate goal at the start of any game of chess. You may be able to force checkmate at any stage of the game. The examples on these two pages deal with checkmate in the endgame.

Playing to win

The endgame examples on these two pages show combinations of pieces with enough power to win. If your pieces don't have enough power the result will be a draw. (For more about drawn games see pages 72–73.)

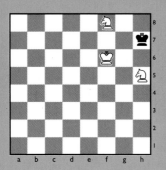

Two Knights and a King do not have enough combined force to give checkmate.

Using the opposition

If there is one square between your King and your opponent's after your move, you have the opposition* – the opposing King cannot move closer. Use the opposition to keep the King at the edge while your other pieces trap it.

Stay out of my way!

Internet link
For a link to a Web site where you can find out more about checkmating patterns, go to **www.usborne-quicklinks.com**

*For more about the opposition, see page 14.

Royal couple

It is fairly straightforward to checkmate a lone King with a King and a Queen. You will need to use them as a team, though. Try to drive the enemy King to a rank or file at the edge of the board. Use your own King to hold it there while you go in for the kill with the Queen. The Queen can sweep in to checkmate the King along a rank, file or diagonal.

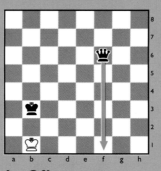

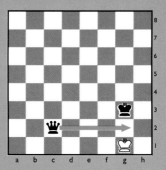

1... Qf1++
The black King holds the white King on the back rank, while the black Queen swoops in to give checkmate.

1... Qg2++
This time the black King keeps the white King still for the Queen to slide in from the side to give checkmate.

Rook and King v. King

It is also possible to checkmate your opponent using only one Rook and your King. The principle is similar to using your Queen – the only difference is that of course the Rook cannot sweep in for the kill along a diagonal in the same way that your Queen can. Again, you will need to use your King as part of your trap or *mating net*, as this example shows.

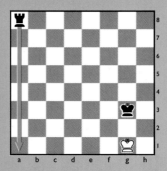

1... Ra1++
The black King holds the white King on the back rank, using the power of the opposition, while the black Rook glides in to seal the white King's fate.

Powerful pair

Two Rooks are powerful enough to force checkmate. Use them together to inch the enemy King to an edge rank or file, where it will be completely blockaded by the two Rooks.

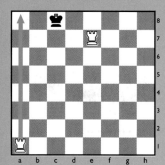

I. Ra8++
The black King is held on the back rank by the white Rook on the seventh rank, making it easy pickings for the other white Rook.

King and two Bishops v. King

Checkmate is more difficult with two Bishops and a King. You need to force the enemy King into a corner, and limit its movement using your King. The two Bishops together form a line of fire that it can't cross.

I. Bd5++
White's King is cornered by the glowering black King and the twin searchlights of the Bishop pair.

Mixed army

Push your opponent's King into a *dangerous corner* (the same color as your remaining Bishop) if all you have is a King, a Knight and a Bishop against a lone King. It might prove quite difficult to get your pieces arranged to produce checkmate – but it is possible!

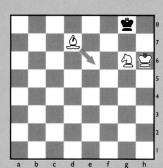

I. Be6++
The white King traps Black's King on the back rank. A Knight stops its sideways movement. When the white Bishop attacks, the black King has nowhere left to run – checkmate.

 Do

- Keep your King and minor pieces together for safety if they are all you have left.

- Use Bishops or Rooks together if you have both, to form a barrier that a King cannot cross.

 Don't

- Leave your King to cope on its own – if it becomes isolated it will be more vulnerable.

- Allow your opponent to get his King to a square where it will be safe from attack, or you will be unable to checkmate and will have to settle for a draw.

If you only have your King left, you will not be able to win but you may still be able to escape being checkmated.

Key words

dangerous/non-dangerous corner The corner square on which a King is exposed to/safe from the opposing Bishop.

mating net Pieces placed in such a way that wherever the enemy King moves, it will be trapped.

Checkmate puzzles

Most chess puzzles involve trying to give checkmate in a certain number of moves. By practicing these kinds of puzzles, you should improve your ability to spot checkmate opportunities that occur in your own games.

Did you know?

A poem published in 1763 told of how the Roman god Mars created chess and named it after a dryad called Caissa. She became known as the patron goddess of chess.

Internet link

For a link to a Web site with more chess puzzles, go to **www.usborne-quicklinks.com**

Walled-in King

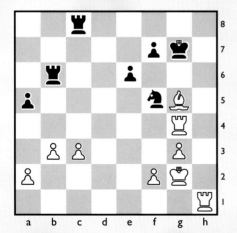

Can you spot a move for White that means checkmate for Black?

CLUE: Attack the King's exposed side – it can't run away.

Surrounded

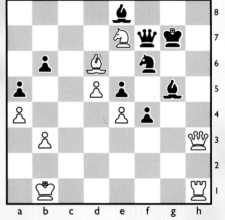

How can White infiltrate the King's defenses here to give mate in one?

CLUE: Surround the black King with attacking pieces.

Discovered doom

White can give checkmate in one on this board. What is the best move?

CLUE: Reveal a Rook.

Humble attacker

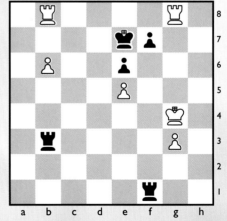

One little move for White here defeats Black. What is it?

CLUE: Use a Pawn as part of your mating net.

For puzzle solutions see page 91.

♟ Repeated blows

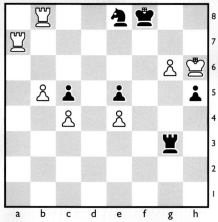

Which two punishing moves will checkmate Black here?

CLUE: Give your most powerful pieces a bit of Pawn support.

♔ King in the bag

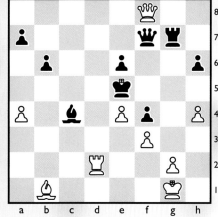

Can you find two moves for White that ensnare the black King?

CLUE: The final blow comes from a Pawn.

♟ Buried alive

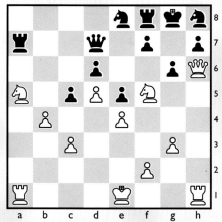

Can you find a two-move checkmate for White here?

CLUE: Make the ultimate sacrifice to win.

♟ Against the wall

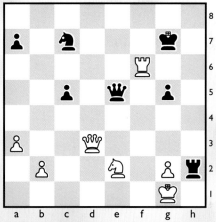

Can you find a two move sequence for White to checkmate Black?

CLUE: Corner the King.

♟ Sealed fate

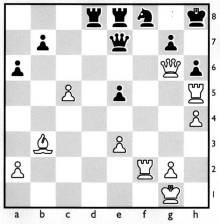

Which White move leaves Black unable to prevent checkmate?

CLUE: Use the distant protection of a Bishop.

♟ Death threat

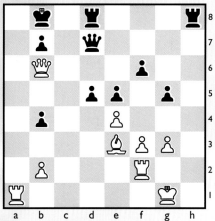

Can you see the two-move mate for White?

CLUE: Mate the black King in the corner.

For puzzle solutions see page 91.

71

Drawn games

The only way for a game of chess to be won or lost is if it ends in checkmate. A game that does not end in this way is called a *draw* – when neither player wins or loses. There are six different ways to draw in a game of chess:

No win situation

A game ends in *stalemate* if it is your turn to move, but there is no move that you can legally make. (You cannot move your King without placing it in check, and if you also have Pawns they are locked and unable to move at all.)

White to move – but neither the King nor the Pawn can move. This is stalemate.

Perpetual check

Perpetual check happens when one player continually puts the other in check. It is often used by the losing player to escape checkmate and force a draw.

1. **Kh1 Qf1+**
2. **Kh2 Qf2+**
3. **Kh1 Qf1+**
4. **Kh2 Qf2+**
Wherever the white King goes, the black Queen follows – perpetual check.

Repetition of moves

If the same position occurs three times in one game, a player can claim a draw. This is similar to perpetual check – the game has reached a situation that is impossible to resolve.

Draw by agreement

If both players agree that they are equally matched in terms of material and position, and unlikely to reach a checkmate situation, they may agree to a draw.

Grandmaster Viswanathan Anand claims a victory – however, more than half of all the chess games that are played at top levels end in a draw.

Nothing happening

When both players have made fifty moves without making a capture or a Pawn move, they may claim a draw. If they are still awake, that is. This is called the *fifty-move rule*.

Not enough firepower

Certain combinations of pieces in the endgame do not have the power to give checkmate. This is called having *insufficient mating material*. If players realize this, they can agree to a draw without having to chase each other around the board to find out that neither can win! The following piece combinations are not enough to give checkmate:

You'll never take me...

- King and Bishop v. King
- King and Knight v. King
- King and two Knights v. King
- King v. King

Internet link
For a link to a Web site where you can find details and illustrated examples of each of the six different types of draws, go to **www.usborne-quicklinks.com**

Chess tournaments

A chess competition is called a tournament. There are different types of tournaments, but they all follow similar basic rules that are set out by official chess organizations.

Swiss system As players win games, they play against progressively better players. (If they lose, they play against weaker players.) No one is knocked out of this type of tournament.

Quads Players are sorted into groups of similar ability. Each plays everyone else in the group to find a group winner. Gradually players are eliminated to leave one winner.

Correspondence Players send their moves to each other written on a postcard. Games can last for years!

Internet The Internet is a popular place to play chess for players of all levels, from beginners to Grandmasters.

Key words

draw A game that ends with no winner.

fifty-move rule If each player has made fifty consecutive moves without making a capture or a Pawn move, they may claim a draw.

insufficient mating material Too few pieces on the board for checkmate to be possible.

stalemate Happens when the player whose turn it is cannot move legally.

Internet link
For a link to a Web site where you can read about the 1993 Championship matches between Kasparov and Short, go to **www.usborne-quicklinks.com**

Garry Kasparov and Nigel Short took part in a fight for the title of World Champion in 1993. Chess at this level is exciting to watch and is often photographed or filmed for television.

KASPAROV   SHORT

THE TIMES WORLD CHESS CHAMPIONSHIP

Drawn game puzzles

Sometimes you will see that it is impossible for you to win a game of chess. In this kind of situation, the best thing to do is to force a draw. On these two pages are some puzzles that will help you spot the way to do this in different situations.

Did you know?

The shortest stalemate in theory in a game of chess would take only 12 moves – and no pieces would be exchanged.

Internet link

For a link to a Web site with more chess puzzles, go to **www.usborne-quicklinks.com**

♟ Playing to draw

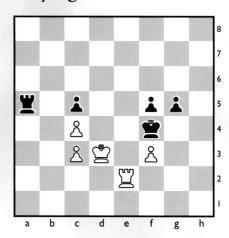

How can White force a stalemate to avoid eventual checkmate here?

CLUE: Sacrifice the Rook.

♟ Treacherous mate

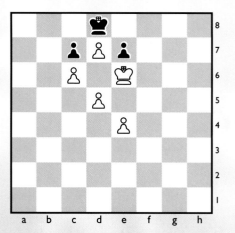

How can White checkmate in four – but avoid putting Black in stalemate?

CLUE: Move carefully to force responses from Black.

♟ Material loss

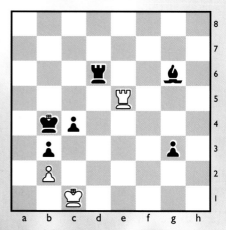

How can White turn its material disadvantage into a draw here?

CLUE: Use a check to force Black's move.

♔ Hidden King

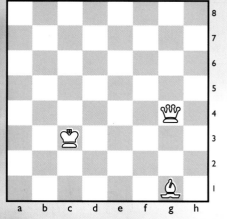

Where would you place the black King so it is in stalemate?

CLUE: In which corner does White control the most squares?

For puzzle solutions see page 91.

♙ Bouncing King

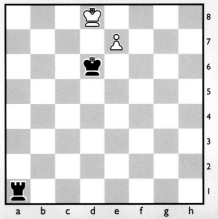

How can White use a sacrifice to good effect in forcing a draw here?

CLUE:
Go for perpetual check.

♙ Last-ditch attempt

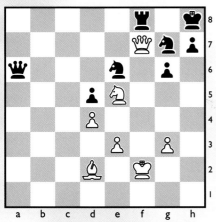

How should White move to prevent checkmate (and play for a draw)?

CLUE:
Underpromote the Pawn.

♙ Give it up

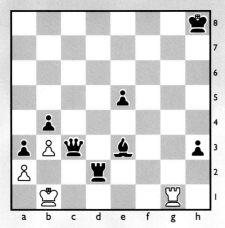

What can White do to force a stalemate position on this board?

CLUE:
A swift sacrifice is the key.

♙ Missing royal

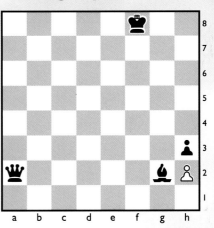

Where would a stalemated white King be found on this board?

CLUE:
It is in a place where its own Pawn restricts its movement.

♙ Futile promotion

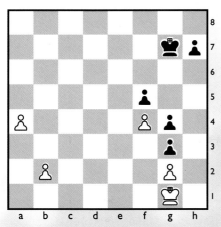

How can Black force a draw in four to escape death by promoted Pawn?

CLUE:
Black should use a Pawn to trap its own King.

♙ Fighting chance

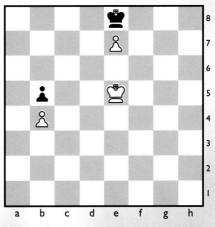

What do you think White's two best moves are here?

CLUE:
There is no need to play for stalemate – so don't!

For puzzle solutions see page 91.

The story of chess

The game of chess evolved from similar games over hundreds of years. People play different versions of chess all over the world. *Xiang Qi* (pronounced *shyang chi*), the Chinese version, is probably played by more people than any other game in the world.

Early games

Simple board games have been played for thousands of years, since the earliest civilizations. The game of chess appeared much later.

A fragment of a board game found at the site of Mohenjo-daro, an ancient city in Asia.

Shaturanga, the first truly chess-like game, is thought to have been invented in India, in the sixth century AD. It was a game for four players, designed to be played with a die on a checkered board with 64 squares, like a modern chess board.

In *Xiang Qi* (Chinese chess), the pieces are placed on points where lines cross, not on squares.

From Shaturanga to Shatranj

During the sixth century, changes were made to the rules of *Shaturanga* to accommodate Hindu law. Gambling was forbidden and so the use of dice was no longer allowed. The four armies merged to form two larger, opposing armies, in a game for two players. This new game was called *Shatranj*.

The birth of chess

There are different theories about how *Shatranj* evolved into the game of chess.

● Saracens (the Medieval name for Muslim Arabs) may have brought the game with them to Europe when they invaded Spain from North Africa.

● Charlemagne (King of the Holy Roman Empire in the ninth century, in what is now western and northern Europe) may have received a *Shatranj* set as a gift from a Byzantine empress. (The Byzantine Empire was in southern Europe, western Asia and northern Africa.)

● Knights may have brought the game back when they returned from the Crusades in the twelfth century.

This Isle of Lewis chess set was carved from walrus ivory. It dates from around the twelfth century and is one of the oldest-known chess set designs.

Key words

chess variant A game based on standard chess that has vital differences, for example different rules or a different board.

Internet link
For a link to a Web site where you can browse examples of the different chess variants from around the world, go to **www.usborne-quicklinks.com**

Setting the standard

The pieces that are used in international chess competitions are known as "Staunton" pieces. They were named after Howard Staunton, a famous chess player who approved their design in the 19th century. Staunton-type chess sets can be produced in almost any material but are usually wooden or plastic.

Staunton chess pieces have simple, stylized shapes.

A game for the world

From the Indian game of *Shatranj*, several distinct new games emerged all over the world, aside from chess:

● *Xiang Qi* (**Chinese chess**) This game uses points on its board instead of squares, and the opposing sides are separated by a central "river".

● *Shogi* (**Japanese chess**) A game in which pieces that have already been taken are allowed back onto the board.

● *Sittuyin* (**Burmese chess**) This version still makes use of the original horse and elephant pieces from *Shatranj*. In this game the players themselves decide how to arrange their pieces on the board at the start.

Variations on a theme

There are also many different games that are based on chess – these are collectively called *chess variants*:

● **Scotch game** The first player makes one move. The second player makes two moves. The first player goes again, with three moves, and so on. If either player gives check during their series of moves, their "turn" ends.

● **Fischerandom chess** In this variant, invented by Bobby Fischer, the back rank pieces are shuffled in random order, so that players cannot rely only on knowledge of opening lines to win a game.

● **Suicide chess** The objective in this variant is to be the first player to lose all your pieces!

● **Glinski's hexagonal chess** Invented in Poland, this is played mostly in eastern Europe, on a board made up of 91 hexagonal "cells".

● **Three-dimensional chess** *Raumschach* is the classic form of 3-D chess. It has also made appearances on *Star Trek*.

Mr. Spock thinks about his next move in a game of 3-D chess – he was beaten every time he played Captain Kirk on *Star Trek*.

The politics of chess

Chess might be "only a game", but some people take it very seriously indeed. It has been caught up in politics and riddled with cases of professional and personal rivalries and even long-standing feuds.

Governing chess

The *Fédération International des Echecs* (International Chess Federation), or FIDE* for short (pronounced *fee-day*) was set up in 1924 in Paris, to oversee chess playing internationally.

FIDE's motto is "we are one family". Its goal is to unite chess players worldwide.

Today, FIDE is still the main chess governing body, with 156 member federations from different countries, and over five million individual members worldwide. The president of FIDE is elected by its members. FIDE issues rules to tournaments and competitions, including the FIDE World Championship. It also awards titles like Grandmaster, International Master, Woman Grandmaster and others.

Chess rebels

● FIDE champion Bobby Fischer refused to play Anatoly Karpov, in 1975. FIDE made Karpov the new champion. However, Fischer and the US government claimed that the FIDE title was rightfully his.

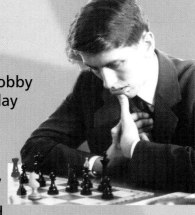

Bobby Fischer lost the title of World Chess Champion by refusing to defend it.

● Garry Kasparov broke away from FIDE to set up the Professional Chess Association in 1993. His first challenger was Nigel Short of the UK, but Kasparov held onto his title. He was beaten by Vladimir Kramnik in 2000. Kramnik now considers himself Champion.

Two champions

But who is the real World Champion? Since Kasparov left FIDE, there have been four FIDE World Champions:

1993–1999 Anatoly Karpov (Russia)
1999–2000 Alexander Khalifman (Russia)
2000–2001 Viswanathan Anand (India)
2001–   Ruslan Pomomariov (Ukraine) – at the age of only 18.

Moves are now being made to unify the World Championship title once more.

So what's the score?

Chess players are awarded an ELO rating according to their performance in tournament matches. Players with an ELO rating of 2,000 or above may be awarded a FIDE rating. The ELO rating system is named after the Hungarian chess player Arpad Elo, who devised it as a way of accurately comparing the skills of players. FIDE adopted his system in 1970. Titles like Grandmaster and International Master are awarded by FIDE. To become a Grandmaster you need to earn three Grandmaster "norms" – performances rated above 2,600 in a tournamnet where you play against three Grandmasters. You also need a FIDE rating of 2,500 or above.

*For the address of FIDE, see page 96.

A game for the masses

Chess became popular in the USSR (Soviet Union) after the Bolsheviks (communist workers) took power in the Russian Revolution in 1917. Lenin, the first Communist Party leader, was an avid chess player, describing the game as "the gymnasium of the mind". He was known for being gracious even in defeat.

Lenin supported the Bolsheviks' plan to encourage chess playing among the people of the USSR. Previously it had been a game played only by the rich and privileged members of society.

The Bolsheviks hoped that playing chess would encourage rational, logical thoughts among the Soviet people that would help them to follow the ideals of communism.

Legacy of champions

The USSR joined FIDE for the first time in 1946. Soon after, Mikhail Botvinnik became the first in a long line of Soviet champions. He went on to found a chess school that would later be attended by Karpov, Kasparov and Kramnik.

Since 1948, chess players from Russia and other former Soviet republic states have completely dominated the World Championships. (Between 1948 and 1972 no non-Soviet player claimed the title.)

Since the break up of the Soviet Union in 1991, less money has been spent on chess training for young players by Russia and the former Soviet republics. However, the legacy of generations of great chess players remains, and players from this region continue to dominate the chess world even today.

Illegal yogurt

In a tense match between fellow Russians Viktor Korchnoi and Anatoly Karpov in 1978, Korchnoi's team accused Karpov's team of cheating. How? By allegedly supplying Karpov with coded messages in the form of yogurt.

The chess authorities took quick action, and Karpov was, from that point in the tournament on, allowed only one particular variety of yogurt, served at a specified time by a waiter. He went on to win the match anyway.

Listen very carefully...

Internet link
For a link to a Web site where you can read all the latest FIDE news and information, go to
www.usborne-quicklinks.com

This is a swimming pool in Hungary, where a group of men are playing chess. Chess is popular in many eastern European countries.

Chess celebrities

The players on the next four pages have all been World Champion. The dates in brackets show when they held their titles.

Internet link
For a link to a Web site with links to biographical information about Chess Champions from Steinitz to Kasparov, go to **www.usborne-quicklinks.com**

Wilhelm Steinitz (1886–1894)

Wilhelm Steinitz of Bohemia (now the Czech Republic) was the first professional chess player, playing chess to earn money while he was a student in Vienna, in Austria. However, he never made enough to retire, and played chess until he had a mental breakdown. He developed the idea that a series of small advantages eventually add up to a large positional advantage in a game situation. This revolutionized the way people thought about chess at the time.

Emanuel Lasker (1894–1921)

The German Emanuel Lasker became World Champion at the age of 25. At first, people doubted his victory over the much older defending champion, Steinitz. He silenced his critics by beating Steinitz when they next played.

Lasker demanded large fees for appearances. After retiring from chess, he played bridge professionally. At the age of 65, he was forced to leave Nazi Germany for America, and had to return to playing chess for money.

José Raúl Capablanca (1921–1927)

José Raúl Capablanca was born in Cuba and learned chess at the age of four. At twelve years old, he beat the Cuban chess champion. He went to a university in America and beat the US champion at the age of 20.

In 1921, Lasker resigned his title to Capablanca, who became known for his apparently effortless style of play. After Capablanca's death, Alekhine, his great rival, conceded that the world had lost "a very great chess genius".

Alexander Alekhine (1927–1935, 1937–1946)

At the time when Alexander Alekhine (born in the Soviet Union) challenged Capablanca for the title of World Champion, there were more world-class chess players around than ever before.

He took the title from Capablanca, but later lost it to Max Euwe, possibly as a result of poor preparation or alcoholism. In a rematch, he managed to beat Euwe, regaining his title.

Max Euwe (1935–1937)

Max Euwe, from the Netherlands, was an amateur chess player. In his day job, he was a professor of mathematics and mechanics. He succeeded in beating Alekhine to win the champion's title (which Alekhine later won back from him).

When he retired from his academic profession, he became the president of FIDE* (*Fédération Internationale des Echecs*), between 1970 and 1978.

Mikhail Botvinnik (1948–1957, 1958–1960, 1961–1963)

Following the death of Alekhine, a tournament was organized to find the new World Champion, which Mikhail Botvinnik won – the first Russian to hold the title. Botvinnik set up a training program for Russian chess players**. Training included physical exercise, playing against strong players, studying analyses of games and playing under difficult conditions.

Vasily Smyslov (1957–1958)

The Russian Vasily Smyslov held the title of World Champion for only a year. As well as chess, he loved music, and during the break in his match against Botvinnik for the champion's title, he sang opera to the audience. He had almost become an opera singer with the Bolshoi, but had decided to take up chess as his career after narrowly failing the audition. He continued to play chess competitively until an old age – he was still playing in his seventies.

Mikhail Tal (1960–1961)

Latvian Mikhail Tal didn't play chess seriously until he was a teenager, but once he did take it up he found it hard to stop. Even when he was in the hospital after an operation, he managed to slip out to a nearby chess club.

When he became World Champion he was only 24, making him the youngest champion up until then. He was famous for the complicated combinations he used to obliterate the opposition.

Tigran Petrosian (1963–1969)

Tigran Petrosian was born in Georgia, to Armenian parents. His style of chess was influenced by the hypermodern*** theories of Aron Nimzowitsch, and he liked to play closed games that challenged other Grandmasters very effectively but were difficult for non-masters to understand. For this reason, he was not a particularly popular World Champion, although he held the title for six years.

*For more about FIDE, see page 78.
**For more about the Russians and chess, see page 79.
***For more about hypermodernism, see page 34.

Boris Spassky (1969–1972)

The Russian Boris Spassky was admired as a World Champion not only for his chess playing abilities, but also for being polite and friendly!

The American Bobby Fischer challenged him for the title in 1972. This was during the Cold War between East and West, so both players were under pressure from their countries to win. The Russians suspected that Fischer's chair had been tampered with to make it affect Spassky's play – but never proved anything.

Robert Fischer (1972–1975)

American Bobby Fischer started playing chess when he was six, and at fifteen became the youngest ever Grandmaster up until then. He was Champion for three years, but lost the title when he refused to play the challenger, Anatoly Karpov, in 1975. Since then, Bobby Fischer has not played in public. People sometimes report playing him on the Internet but it is difficult to prove this. He is still highly-rated and some people consider him to be the best chess player of all time. It is said that he can remember every detail and move of every game he has ever played.

Anatoly Karpov (1975–1985, FIDE 1993–1999)

Although the Russian Anatoly Karpov gained the title of World Champion by default, after Bobby Fischer refused to play for it, he quickly proved that he deserved the title by winning many subsequent chess tournaments.

He was beaten in 1985 by Garry Kasparov, after the longest tournament match in chess history (six months). However, he later regained the FIDE* title of World Champion when Kasparov split with FIDE to form his own Professional Chess Association in 1993.

Garry Kasparov (FIDE 1985–1993, PCA 1993–1998, unofficial 1998–2000)

Russian Garry Kasparov attended the Botvinnik Chess School, and became a Grandmaster on his seventeenth birthday. He was FIDE Champion for eight years, after beating Anatoly Karpov, at the age of 22.

In 1993, Kasparov set up the PCA*. He was PCA World Champion until it disbanded in 1998, and then continued to call himself World Champion until Vladimir Kramnik beat him in 2000.

*For more about FIDE and the PCA, see page 78.

Alexander Khalifman (FIDE 1999–2000)

Alexander Khalifman was born in 1966 in Leningrad (now called St. Petersburg) in Russia, and started playing chess at the age of six. He became a Grandmaster in 1990 at the age of 24. He held the title of World Champion for a year, winning the championship even though he was nowhere near being the world's highest-rated* player at the time. He now plays professional chess in Germany and runs a chess academy in St. Petersburg.

Viswanathan Anand (FIDE 2000–2001)

Viswanathan Anand was born in 1969 in India. He learned to play chess at the age of six, and became Indian National Champion at the age of 16. His highest rating is number two in the world (PCA and FIDE). Viswanathan Anand seems to collect nicknames, among them: "Vishy, the Tiger of Madras" and "The One-Man Indian Chess Revolution".

Vladimir Kramnik (unoffical 2000–present)

Vladimir Kramnik was born in 1975 in Russia, and by the time he was five was already attending professional chess clubs. He went to the Botvinnik Chess School, like Kasparov and Karpov before him. He claims that the secret to beating Kasparov lies in not being scared of playing him, and is famous for his calmness while under pressure.

Ruslan Ponomariov (FIDE 2001–2002)

The Ukrainian Ruslan Ponomariov was born in 1983. At 14, he became the youngest Grandmaster in the world at that time, and in January 2002, he became FIDE World Chess Champion at the age of only 18, making him the youngest person ever to claim the title of World Champion.

Future electronic champions?

Computer programmers know their software cannot often beat the very best human chess players. Even though computers don't have "off days", their powers of analysis, however fast, are still only as good as the brains that designed them. One of the latest chess "supercomputers" is called *Deep Fritz*. World champion Vladimir Kramnik faced *Deep Fritz* for a showdown in 2002, and the match ended in a draw.

Internet link
For a link to a Web site where you can read a fascinating article about the 1972 Fischer-Spassky World Championship game, go to **www.usborne-quicklinks.com**

*For more about the ratings system, see page 78.

Champions of the future

Until recently, chess has been a very male-dominated sport. Lots of rising stars are now women. Computers also keep improving, and may one day rule the chess world.

Judit Polgar

Judit Polgar, born in 1976 in Hungary, is the world's highest-ranked woman chess player ever. She became the only woman ever to have beaten Garry Kasparov in a chess match in 2002. She has never taken the title of women's World Chess Champion, preferring to set her sights on the men's World Championship title.

Judit Polgar has two sisters who are also successful competitive chess players. One runs a chess academy in New York. Their parents encouraged all three sisters to excel at chess from a young age, preferring the sport over mathematics.

At 15, Judit Polgar became the youngest player ever to be awarded the title of Grandmaster, beating Bobby Fischer's previous record. (Her record was subsequently broken by Ruslan Ponomariov, when he was 14.)

Judit Polgar is renowned for her fierce, attacking style of chess playing.

Zhu Chen

The 2001–2002 women's World Chess Champion was Zhu Chen of China. Born in 1976, she started to play Chinese chess when she was five and learned chess at age seven. She is currently at a university in China, and is married to a chess Grandmaster from Qatar.

Zhu Chen becomes women's World Chess Champion in Moscow, 2002.

Alexandra Kosteniuk

The Russian player Alexandra Kosteniuk became 2001–2002 women's World Chess Vice-Champion at the age of 17, after being beaten by Zhu Chen in the final. She had already achieved the title Woman Grandmaster at the age of 14, and had also already achieved the title of International Master among men.

She was born in Russia in 1984, and was taught by her father to play chess. To help her succeed, he made her memorize the names and colors of all the squares on a chess board, and tested her until she knew the chess board inside-out.

Alexandra Kosteniuk, dressed to promote chess.

Internet link
For a link to a Web site where you can find out all about Judit Polgar with links to biographical information, interviews, articles, games and photographs, go to
www.usborne-quicklinks.com

The first chess machine

The first chess-playing machine was designed by Hungarian Wolfgang von Kempelen in 1770. It looked like a man dressed in oriental costume, sat at a chess board. The machine was nicknamed "the Turk". People believed that the machine could play chess by itself, even though now we know that it must have been operated by a human.

This picture shows a chess-playing automaton similar to the Turk. The mechanical workings may have concealed a human operator.

Champion chips

Modern chess computers actually do have the ability to evaluate billions of different positions themselves and "decide" on the best move to make. It is this calculating ability that may one day give chess computers the potential to beat even the very best humans all the time.

Deep Blue was the fastest chess computer in the world when it beat Kasparov in 1997. (The faster the computer, the more calculations it makes, and the more positions it compares.) *Deep Blue* didn't even have to calculate every single position – it could discount irrelevant searches to save time.

The chip from *Deep Blue's* processor. It is small enough to fit in the palm of your hand.

How a chess computer works

All chess computer programs work in a similar way. Their software has an "evaluation function" that uses mathematical formulas to compare possible board positions.

For example, *Deep Blue's* software allowed it to evaluate four factors: material, position, King safety and tempo. Each possible position was then given a score. A positive score meant a good position for White; a negative score was a good position for Black.

A screenshot from a home computer program called Chessmaster.

Mind-blowing possibilities

At the start of a game, White has 20 possible moves. Black has 20 possible responses to each of White's possible moves, making a total of 400 possibilities, just for the first two moves. By the end of White's second move, there are 8,000 different possible positions.

Within ten moves, there are trillions of positions for the computer to evaluate. This is why chess-playing computers need extremely powerful processors.

Internet link
For a link to a Web site where you can find out all about how chess computers make their calculations, go to **www.usborne-quicklinks.com**

Chess words

algebraic notation The standard method of recording chess games. It uses letters and numbers to identify squares on the board, and letter codes for the pieces. An example of algebraic notation would read as follows:
1. e4 e5
2. Nf3 Nf6.
This describes a typical sequence of two opening moves – each player advances a Pawn to the center of the board, then develops a Knight to support the Pawn.

anchorage Support provided from behind by Pawns for pieces that may be unable to escape from long-range attacks quickly, like Knights.

back rank mate A type of checkmate where the King is trapped on the back rank by its own pieces (often the same pieces that were intended to defend it) and is unable to move away from an attack.

backward Pawn A Pawn that has been left behind by the adjacent Pawns. It is vulnerable to attack as it cannot rely on the support of other Pawns.

bad Bishop A Bishop that its trapped behind its own pieces. An example of this would be a black-squared Bishop surrounded by Pawns that occupy black squares.

castling A special move for a King and Rook. The King moves two spaces toward the Rook, and the Rook jumps over the King to the space next to it. This protects the King and brings the Rook closer to the middle of its rank where it can effectively attack open files.

check An attack on the King.

checkmate An attack on the King that cannot be defended. This is the end of the game and the checkmated player loses.

checking piece A piece that attacks the King.

chess clock A special clock with two faces that records the time each player spends on moves in a chess game. If a player runs out of time in a tournament game, they lose.

chess variant A game based on standard chess that has vital differences, for example different rules or a different board. Some famous examples of chess variants include Suicide Chess, Fischerandom Chess, Scotch Chess, Hexagonal Chess and 3-D Chess.

closed diagonal A diagonal that is blocked by pieces.

closed game A strategy that keeps the attacking pieces behind a strong Pawn structure until the game is in progress. This results in a board that is crowded with pieces and sometimes the position can become blocked, where neither player is able to make effective attacks or advances.

counter-attack A way of responding to an attack by posing a new attack.

dangerous/non-dangerous corner The corner square on which a King is exposed to/safe from the opposing Bishop.

development Moving pieces from their starting positions during the opening stage to positions where they will be useful in the next stage of the game.

diagonal A line of diagonal squares.

discovered attack A piece moves to reveal an attack from a different piece.

discovered check A piece moves to reveal an attack on the enemy King from a different piece.

double check A piece moves to give check, revealing another checking piece at the same time. The result is two different checks on the King at once.

doubled Rooks Two Rooks of the same color on next-door squares. These form an extremely powerful attacking force – if one attacks and is taken, the other Rook can immediately attack the same square.

double Pawns Two Pawns of the same color on the same file. This is a weak position for two Pawns as they cannot defend each other and block each other's movements.

draw A game that ends with no winner.

en passant The rule that allows a Pawn to capture another that has moved forward two squares, and in doing so, bypassed the threat of capture. The attacking Pawn moves to the square it would have captured the other Pawn on had it only moved one square.

exchange Trading a piece for an opposing piece of the same type or that has the same value.

exchange advantage The player with pieces of greater combined value following an exchange has the advantage.

fair exchange Pieces of a similar value are exchanged and neither side loses out.

fianchetto An opening move that places a Bishop on the longest diagonal where it can threaten many squares. The Bishop moves to the square that was originally occupied by either the b-Pawn or the g-Pawn.

fifty-move rule If either player has made fifty consecutive moves without there being a capture or a Pawn move, they may claim a draw.

file A line of squares that runs from the top to the bottom of the board.

flank One of the edges of the board.

fork A sneaky move – a piece moves to a square from where it can threaten two or more opposing pieces at once. Only one piece can escape the attack – the other will be captured on the next turn.

gambit A move made during the opening stage of the game, that offers a Pawn or a minor piece to the opponent, in return for better positions for the pieces on the board.

good Bishop – a Bishop that is not trapped by its own pieces. For example, a black-squared Bishop that is surrounded by its own Pawns that occupy black squares will be unable to move freely.

hypermodern A movement in chess that started in the 1920s, where a player ignores the most usual method of developing pieces and Pawns to the central squares early on in the game. Instead, the hypermodern player tries to control the center using pieces placed at a distance.

initiative Had by the player who is directing the course of the game.

insufficient mating material Too few pieces on the board for checkmate to be possible.

Kingside The four files on the two Kings' side of the board.

losing a tempo Losing time – usually a bad thing, especially in the opening stage of the game, when the race is on to develop your pieces. However, you may choose to lose a tempo, for example if you are trying to gain the opposition when advancing your King during the endgame.

material The pieces that are left on the board.

material advantage/disadvantage Having pieces of a greater/lesser combined value than the enemy's.

mating net Pieces placed in such a way that wherever the enemy King moves, it will be trapped.

mobility The ability of pieces to move freely.

open file A file that is not blocked by Pawns.

open game A strategy that develops the pieces quickly, positioning them in front of the Pawns. This type of game often leads to lots of attacks and exchanges early on, opening up lines on the board.

opening The stage between the first moves of the game and the completion of piece development.

open lines Ranks, files or diagonals that are clear of pieces.

opposition When a square separates two advancing Kings, the player that moved last is said to have the opposition. The opposing King cannot move closer or it would be in check, and so must move aside or move away.

outpost A square that cannot be attacked by opposing Pawns.

overloaded piece A piece that has more than one defensive job to do, leaving the pieces it is defending open to attack.

overprotection Defense of a square by more than one piece.

passed Pawn A Pawn that has left the opposing Pawns on adjacent files behind, and so has a good chance of promoting (as it is less likely to be captured).

Pawn chain Two or more Pawns on adjacent files arranged along a diagonal. Each Pawn is protected by the one behind. The enemy can only safely attack the base of the chain.

Pawn island A group of Pawns cut off from the others. They are vulnerable to attack.

Pawn structure The way your Pawns are arranged.

perpetual check A player is put in check repeatedly but cannot be checkmated. The result is a draw. Typically the checked King will jump between two squares, as it is checked, escapes, and is checked again.

pin An attack on a piece that is shielding one of greater value.

pinned piece A piece that must stay still to protect another piece of greater value.

plan A series of moves designed to achieve a particular goal, for example to promote a Pawn, castle the King or checkmate the opponent. It is important to have a plan for every stage of the game.

position A measure of the amount of attacking control that you have over the squares on the board.

promotion When a Pawn reaches the other end of the board and can be traded for a more powerful piece, usually a Queen.

queening square The square on the far side of the board that a Pawn needs to reach to gain promotion (usually to a Queen, but it may be any other piece).

Queenside The four files on the Queens' side of the board.

rank A line of squares that runs from the left to the right of the board.

sacrifice The deliberate loss of a piece as part of a strategy.

skewer An attack that forces a valuable piece to move, exposing one of less value to attack.

smothered mate The King is completely surrounded by its own pieces and so cannot move out of checkmate.

stalemate The player whose turn it is cannot move legally, but is not in checkmate. The result is a draw.

tempo (pl. tempi) A unit of time in chess – equivalent to a single move.

triple Pawns Three Pawns of the same color on the same file. They are vulnerable as they cannot protect each other and block each other's movement.

variation In an opening strategy, a variation is a unique combination of moves that develop from a particular type of opening.

zugzwang This is a German word that means "forced to move". If a player must make a move that leads to a worse position or even checkmate, they are in a *zugzwang* position.

Puzzle solutions

King puzzles 15

King puzzle 1 1. Kd5 (White forks two Knights).

King puzzle 2 1. Ke2++.

King puzzle 3 1... Kc7++.

King puzzle 4 1. Kf4 g3, 2. hxg2++.

Knight puzzles 23

Knight puzzle 1. Nxg4 (Knight also now forks black King and Rook).

Piece puzzles 30–31

Pawn puzzle 1 1. gxh3 is the best white move – otherwise Black will promote its Pawn.

Pawn puzzle 2 The g-Pawn – 1. h6 gxh6, 2. g7 (Black cannot now stop the Pawn from promoting), 3. g8 (Q).

Knight puzzle 1. Nb6+ Qxb6, 2. cxb6.

Bishop puzzle 1 1. Bh3+ or 1. Bd3+. Bh3+ is better as it skewers the Black Queen, instead of the Rook. White can then take the Queen on its next turn.

Bishop puzzle 2 1. Bb2++.

Rook puzzle 1... Rb4+. Black forks the White King and Knight, so will be able to take the Knight next turn after the King has moved out of check.

Queen puzzle 1 Five ways to check with the Queen: 1. Qf2+ wins Rook on g1; 2. Qd4+ wins Rook on a7; 1. Qd6+ wins Knight on b8; 1. Qc3+ wins Bishop on c8; 1. Qb2+ wins Pawn on b5.

Queen puzzle 2 1... Qb8++. White's a-Pawn cannot capture the Queen as it is pinned to the King by the Black Rook on a1.

King puzzle 1 1... Kc7++.

King puzzle 2 1. 0-0++. An example of late castling.

The Indian problem (in Did you know? box) 1. Kb1 b4, 2. Bc1 b5, 3. Rd2 Kf4, 4. Rd4++.

Middlegame puzzles 48–49

The right move 1. Bd8++.

Nowhere to run 1. Ne6++.

Well-placed piece 1. Bxf6++. The white Bishop moves to reveal a double check on the Black King from which it cannot escape.

Two-move mate 1. Rh5+ gxh5, 2. Qxh5++.

Defending the King 1 1. Re5++.

Defending the King 2 1. Bf4++ or 1. Ba5++. The white Bishop moves to reveal a further discovered check from one of its Rooks.

Defending the King 3 1. Rd6++. The Rook cannot be taken by either of the Pawns as they are pinned to the King by White's Bishop and Queen.

Square overload White can make use of a barrage of attacks on the same square to crush Black's defense here – 1. Qh8+ Rxh8, 2. Rh8++.

Noble sacrifice 1. Qxh7+, Kxh7, 2. Rh5++. The Black King cannot escape – the squares are cut off by White's Knight on e7.

Deadly initiative 1... Bd3++. The White King is caught in a web of attacks from the black Bishop, Rook and Queen and Pawn.

Tactical tricks puzzles 52–53

Slice the defense 1. e5+ Kxe5, 2. Bg7+ Kd5/Kf5 (Black King has to move, leaving skewered Rook exposed), 3. Bxa1.

Don't get pinned down 1... Qxb4+, 2. Kxb4, Ra4+. Black has skewered the White Queen.

Lethal weapon 1... Ne3, 2. fxe3 (White must take the Knight to avoid immediately losing its Queen) Qh4+, 3. g3 Qxg3++.

Cutlery crusade 1. Bc5+ Qxc5 (White's Bishop forks the Black Queen and Knight, but is captured), 2. Ne6+ (White forks again, forcing the King to move), 3. Nxc5 (the white Knight takes the Black Queen).

Protected Pawn 1... Be6+, 2. Kxe6. The White King shields Black's Pawn from White's Rook.

Rook revenge 1. Rh8 Rxa7, 2. Rh7+. White skewers the black King to win the Rook.

Battle of the Bishops 1. Qxc6 Bxc6, 2. Bxc6++. A Bishop pin followed by a Queen sacrifice.

Forked lightning 1. Rf8+ Ke5, 2. Nc6+. A Knight fork means that White will capture Black's Rook next.

Widen the gap 1. Be8+ Kxe8, 2. Nd6+. Once Black loses the Queen it cannot hope to win this game.

Inevitable capture 1. Qd5+. Queen fork by White.

Combination puzzles 56–57

Checkmate surprise 1. Ng1 Bc7, 2. Nf3++ **or** 1. Ng1 g4, 2. g3++.

Push for victory 1. Qxf7+ Rxf7, 2. Re8++.

Weak spot 1. Qxh5+ Rxh5, 2. Bg6++.

Wrongfooted Rooks 1. Qxh6 Bxh6, 2. Rxh6++.

Tragedy for the King 1. Qxd7+ Kd7, 2. Bf5+ Ke8,

3. Bd7+ Kf8, 4. Bxe7++ **or** 1. Qxd7+ Kd7, 2. Bf5+ Kc6, 3. Bd7++.

Spoiled for choice 1. Qf4+ Kxc5, 2. Qd4++ **or** 1. Qf4+ Kd5, 2. Qd4++.

Early mate 1. Qh6 Bxh6, 2. Ne7++ **or** 1. Qh6 Bxf6, 2. Nxf6+ Kh8, 3. Qxh7++ **or** 1. Qh6 Bxf6, 2. Nxf6+ Qxf6, 3. exf6 (whatever Black does now, White's next move is inevitable), 4. Qg7++.

Inevitable defeat 1... Bg1+, 2. Kxg1 Qxe1+, 3. Qf1 Qxf1+, 4. Kh2 Qh1++ **or** 1... Bg1+, 2. Rgxg1 Nf1+ (double check), 3. Kg2/Kh1 Qh2++ **or** 1... Bg1+, 2. Rexg1 Nf1+ (double check), 3. Kh1 Rxh3+, 4. Rh2 Rxh2++.

Humble mate 1. Qe1 Rxe1 (releasing White Pawn from pin), 2. g2++.

Long-term goal 1. Rg4+ fxg4, 2. Qg5+ Kh8, 3. Qh6, Qd8/Raa8, 4. Qxh7++ **or** 1. Rg4+ fxg4, 2. Qg5+ Kh8, 3. Qh6 f5/Bxd3, 4. Qxf8++.

Sacrifice puzzles 60–61

Bury the King 1. Qg7+ Nxg7, 2. Nf6++.

Sacrificial barrage 1... Qxb2+, 2. Kxb2 Rgb8++.

Building a wall 1. Rd8+ Rxd8 (White's Queen is now released from the pin), 2. Qxa7++.

King-baiting 1... Bb4+, 2. Kxb4 Qa5++.

Coming from behind 1. Nb6+ axb6, 2. Ra4++.

Brave monarch 1. Qg8+ Rxg8 (White sacrifices its Queen in order to trap the Black King in a web of its own pieces), 2. Nf7++.

Danger all around 1. Qxg6+ hxg6, 2. Rh8++.

Piledriver 1. Qxa7+ Kxa7 (White sacrifices the Queen as part of a mating combination), Ra2+ Qa4, 3. Rxa4++.

Wriggling free 1... Qg3+, 2. Kxg3 e1(Q)+, 3. Kh3 Re3+, 4.Kh2 Qg3++ **or** 1... Qg3+, 2. Kxg3 e1(Q)+, 3. Kh2 Qxh4+, 4. Kg1 Re1++.

Closing in 1. Qxf7+ Bxf7, 2. Rxc8+ Be8, 3. Rxe8++.

Endgame puzzles 64–65

Mate surprise 1. Be5 Qe8 (Black defends against a White underpromotion) 2. f8(N)++ , 2. Bf5++.

Sticky end 1. Rc2 Bd2, 2. Raxb2++ **or** 1. Rc2 Kxc2/Kxa2, 2. Na3++ **or** 1. Rc2 Kxa2/Nxc2/bxc2, 2. Nc3++/Na3++.

Cavalry charge 1. Ba4 d6, 2. Nbc7++ **or** 1. Ba4 e4, 2. Qxe4++ **or** 1. Ba4 f6, 2. Ndc7++ **or** 1. Ba4 f5, 2. Qg8++.

King pressure 1. Kg8 Qxg5+, 2. Bg7++ **or** 1. Kg8 Rxf6+, 2. Qxf6++ **or** 1. Kg8 Qb1, 2. Nf7++.

Forced to move 1. Qd1 Kd3, 2. Rxd5++ **or** 1. Qd1

Kc5, 2. Qg1++ **or** 1. Qd1, Kxe5, 2. d4++.

Defensive collapse 1. Qxg7+ Rxg7, 2. Rxg7++.

Impending doom 1. Qxd4++.

Best move 1. Nd7+. This move puts the Black King in check, forcing it to move, so the Queen cannot take White's passed Pawn on f7. At the same time, the black Knight protects the Pawn's queening square (f8) so the Pawn can safely promote on White's next turn.

Good clean fun 1. Kg6 Kg8, 2. Rc8++ **or** 1. Kf7 Kg8, 2. Rc8++.

Cornered King 1. Qxf6 gxf6, 2. Rg1+ Kh8, 3. Bxf6++.

Checkmate puzzles 70–71

Walled-in King 1. Qh6++.

Discovered doom 1. Be7++.

Surrounded! 1. Qh8++.

Humble attacker 1. Rb7++.

Repeated blows 1. Rf7+ Kg8, 2. Rxe8++.

Buried alive 1. Qg7+ Nxg7, 2. Nh6++.

Sealed fate 1. Rh6+ gxh6, 2. Qg8++.

King in the bag 1. Qd6+ Kf6, 2. e5++.

Against the wall 1. Qg6+ Kh8, 2. Rf8++.

Double death threat 1. Ra8+ Kxa8, 2. Qa7++.

Drawn game puzzles 74–75

Playing to draw 1. Ra2 Rxa2. Stalemate.

Material loss 1. Rb5+ Kxb5. Stalemate.

Treacherous mate 1. Ke5 e6, 2. d6 cxd6, 3. Kxd6 e5, 4. c7++.

Hidden King The King should be placed on the h1 square to be in a stalemate position.

Bouncing King 1. Qxf8+ Nxf8, 2. Nf7+ Kg8, 3. Nh6+ Kh8. The Black King is in perpetual check – stalemate.

Give it up 1. Rg8+ Kxg8. Stalemate.

Futile promotion 1... Kg6/Kh6, 2. a5 Kh5, 3. a6 Kh4, 4. a7 h5, 5. a8 (Q). Black has no legal moves left, so it is stalemate.

Last-ditch attempt 1. e8(N) – by underpromoting, White manages to stay in the game long enough to play for a draw.

Missing royal The King should be placed on the g1 square to be in a stalemate position.

Fighting chance 1. Kd6 is the best move for White to play for a win. The Black King will have to move aside, allowing the White Pawn to promote – white then stands a chance of winning the game. (1. Ke6 would force stalemate and this would be a draw – better for Black.)

Index

A

Alekhine, Alexander 62, 80, 81
algebraic notation 10, 11, 86
Anand, Viswanathan (Vishy) 72, 83
anchorage 23, 26, 86
attacking 26, 27, 32, 33, 36, 37, 40, 44,
    46, 58, 59, 62
    in the middlegame 48
    pieces 16, 20, 23, 27, 35, 58, 62, 63, 87
    squares 54
    the King 66–67
    with Bishops 20
    with Knights 23
    with Pawns 24–25
    with Rooks 19
    with the King 12, 14
    using tactical tricks 50, 51

B

back rank, the 9, 14, 40, 55, 63, 68, 69, 77
    mate 14, 15, 63, 86
Bishops 20–21, 29, 37, 69, 72
    bad, 21, 27, 62, 86
    fianchettoed, 43, 87
    good, 21, 62, 87
    moves 11
    puzzles 30
    value 28
board
    diagrams 10, 11
    edges 22, 23, 68, 69
    positions 45, 48, 85
    set-up 9
Bolsheviks 79
Botvinnik, Mikhail 79, 81
    chess school 79, 82, 83
Burmese chess, see *Sittuyin*

C

Caissa (patron goddess of chess) 70
Capablanca, José Raúl 80
Caro-Kann, the (opening) 34, 40
Carroll, Lewis 35
castling 12, 13, 15, 18, 33, 34, 36, 55, 56, 86
    Kingside 13, 34, 26, 42
    notation 10
    Queenside 13, 42

center of the board 20, 22, 24, 25, 26, 29,
    33, 34, 40, 42, 62
Charlemagne 76
check 12, 13, 14, 19, 29, 37, 51, 56, 66–67, 72, 86, 88
    announcing, 52
    notation 10
checking pieces 12, 13, 66, 67, 86, 87
checkmate 12, 13, 14, 18, 19, 21, 29, 37, 43, 52, 54,
    56, 60, 64, 66, 67, 68–69, 70, 72, 73, 86
    early, 48, 62
    in four (see also Scholar's Mate) 59
    notation, 10
    puzzles 70–71
    quickest, 47
chess
    books 37
    clocks 45, 86
    clubs 54
    computers 32, 83, 85
    history of, 76–77
    in movies and novels 35
    matches 32
    on the Internet 6–7, 73, 82
    organizations 73, 78
    pieces 23, 24, 30, 35
    politics 78–79
    theory 34, 35, 37
    variants 76, 87
Chess Player's Chronicle, The 31
Chinese chess, see *Xiang Qi*
closed games 35, 41, 46, 81, 87
Cold War, the 82
combinations (of moves) 34, 41, 56
combined force (of pieces) 68, 72
Communist Party, the 79
controlling
    center of the board, the 33, 34, 35, 37, 38, 39
    game, the 41
    diagonals 21
    space 46, 55
    squares 19, 20, 32, 37, 55
corners 20, 69, 87
counter-attacking 37, 43, 87
Crusades, the 76

D

damage limitation 58, 59
Dame, die 16
dame, la 16
Deep Blue 32, 85
Deep Fritz 83
defending 27, 37, 44, 59
    against pins and skewers 50
    more than one piece 47
    space 46
    with Pawns 24, 25, 26, 55

Korchnoi, Viktor 79
Kosteniuk, Alexandra 84
Kramnik, Vladimir 44, 79, 82, 83

L

Lasker, Emanuel 50, 80
Lenin 79
losing a tempo 14, 15, 54, 87

M

material 47, 60, 64, 72, 85, 88
  advantage 46, 47, 88
  disadvantage 47, 88
  gain 28, 29
mating net 64, 68, 69, 88
middlegame, the 8, 17, 25, 26, 33, 44–47, 48, 62
Mohenjo-daro 76

N

Nimzowitsch, Aron 34, 44, 59, 81

O

open
  games 35, 36, 41, 46, 88
  lines 35, 62, 63, 88
openings 21, 34
  for Black 40, 41, 42, 43
  for White 36, 37, 38, 39
opening, the 8, 15, 22, 25, 32–35, 59, 62, 88
  variations 34, 41
opposition, the 14, 15, 68, 88
outposts 23, 88
overloaded pieces 47, 88
overprotection 59, 88

P

patzer 26
Pawn
  chains 26, 27, 40, 88
  islands 27, 88
  promotion 10, 14, 18, 19, 25, 26, 28, 29, 54, 55, 62, 63, 88, 89
  structures 26, 27, 33, 35, 40, 46, 47, 54, 87, 88
  support 23, 24, 26, 27, 42, 46

Pawns 24–27, 21, 29, 33, 36, 37, 39, 40, 42
  backward, 27, 86
  central, 25, 43, 55
  doubled, 27, 37, 47, 55
  in the endgame 62, 63
  isolated, 27, 55
  locked 42, 46, 63, 72
  moves 11
  passed, 26, 27, 55, 62, 63, 88
  sacrificing, 38
  triple, 27
  value 28
PCA, the 82, 83
perpetual check (draw) 67, 72, 88
Petrosian, Tigran 81
piece
  codes 10, 86
  development 15, 17, 20, 21, 32, 33, 34, 35, 38, 40, 54, 87
  mobility 46, 47, 62, 88
  moves 11, 12, 16, 18, 20, 22, 24, 25, 34, 38, 41
  values 12, 16, 18, 20, 22, 24, 28–29, 46, 47, 50, 51
pieces 39, 44, 46
  major, 9, 40
  minor, 9, 33, 36, 38, 69
  pinned, 37, 50, 51, 58, 89
pins 37, 50, 51, 52, 58, 59, 89
plans 8, 29, 32, 33, 38, 39, 41, 44, 45, 54–55, 67, 89
Polgar, Judit 84
politics of chess 78–79
Ponomariov, Ruslan 83, 84
position 72, 85, 89
  assessing, 54, 55
  improving your, 29
  strong, 46
  weak, 47
positional advantage 54, 55
Professional Chess Association, see PCA
puzzles 15, 23, 30–31, 48–49, 52–53, 56–57, 60–61, 64–65, 70–71, 74–75

Q

queening squares 25, 54, 55, 63, 89
Queen puzzles 31
Queens 16–17, 33, 39
  checkmating with, 68, 69
  history of, 16
  moves, 11
  promoting Pawns to, 25, 62, 63
  value 28
Queen's Gambit, the (opening) 38
Queenside 9, 38, 89
quiet game, the, see *Giuoco Piano*

Acknowledgments

Every effort has been made to trace the copyright holders of the material in this book. If any rights have been omitted, the publishers offer to rectify this in any future edition, following notification. The publishers are grateful to the following organizations and individuals for their contribution and permission to reproduce material.

Photography credits (t = top, m = middle, b = bottom, l = left, r = right)

Cover ©Michael Neveux/CORBIS;
p1 ©George B. Diebold/corbisstockmarket.com;
p2 ©Wartenberg/Picture Press/CORBIS;
p4 ©Lawrence Lawley/PhotoDisc;
p8 (bl) ©Hulton-Deutsch Collection/CORBIS;
p13 (tl) ©Burstein Collection/CORBIS; (m) ©Archivo Iconografico, S.A./CORBIS;
p23 (r) ©Archivo Iconografico S.A./CORBIS;
p26 (bl) ©Dover Publications;
p29 (br) ©Hulton-Deutsch Collection/CORBIS;
p32 (br) ©Najlah Feanny/CORBIS SABA;
p34 (br) courtesy of the Edward Winter Collection;
p35 (r) courtesy of Warner Bros.
HARRY POTTER, characters, names and related indicia are trademarks of and © Warner Bros.
(s02)
Harry Potter Publishing Rights © J.K. Rowling;
p37 (l) courtesy of the State Library of Victoria, Melbourne, Victoria, Australia;
p41 (tr) ©Bettmann/CORBIS;
p44 (br) courtesy of the Edward Winter Collection; **p45** (tr) Image 100/Royalty-Free/CORBIS;
p50 (tr) courtesy of the Edward Winter Collection;
p62 (tr) courtesy of the Edward Winter Collection;
p66 (l), **p67** (bl) ©Walter Hodges/CORBIS;
p72 (tr) ©Despotovic Dusko/CORBIS SYGMA; **p73** (b) ©Touhig Sion/CORBIS SYGMA;
p76 (tl) ©CORBIS; (bl) ©Richard Bickel/CORBIS; (br) ©The British Museum; **p77** (br) ©Bettmann/CORBIS;
p78 (tl) courtesy of FIDE; (tr) ©Bettmann/CORBIS; **p79** ©Barry Lewis/CORBIS;
p80 (l) all courtesy of the Edward Winter Collection; **p81** (l) all courtesy of the Edward Winter Collection;
p82 (tl) ©Bettmann/CORBIS; (l) courtesy of the Edward Winter Collection;
(l) ©Hulton-Deutsch Collection/CORBIS; (bl) ©Richard Schulman/CORBIS;
p83 (tl) courtesy of the Chesspawn Web site; (l) ©Despotovic Dusko/CORBIS;
(l) ©Ruet Stephane/CORBIS; (bl) permission granted by Chess-Sector Web site;
p84 (bl) Copes Van Hasselt Johan/CORBIS SYGMA; (tr) ©Photo ITAR-TASS;
(br) courtesy of courtesy of the Kosteniuk Web site;
p85 (tl) Laurence Kesterson/CORBIS SYGMA; (bl) courtesy of Chessmaster;
(br) Bettmann/CORBIS;
p86–89 (b) ©Malcolm Piers/Image Bank.

All additional photography by Adam Constantine.

Chess pieces and boards for in-house photography provided by The London Chess Centre.

First published in 2002 by Usborne Publishing Ltd,
Usborne House, 83–85 Saffron Hill, London EC1N 8RT, England.
www.usborne.com

Printed in Italy.

American editor: Carrie A. Seay